Caroline Hulse lives in Manchester with her husband and a small controlling dog. Her books have been published in fourteen languages and optioned for television.

All the Fun of the Fair is her third novel.

By Caroline Hulse

The Adults
Like A House On Fire
All the Fun of the Fair

All the Fun of the Fair

Caroline Hulse

ORION

First published in Great Britain in 2021 by Orion Fiction,
an imprint of The Orion Publishing Group Ltd.,
Carmelite House, 50 Victoria Embankment
London EC4Y 0DZ

An Hachette UK Company

1 3 5 7 9 10 8 6 4 2

A CIP catalogue record for this book is
available from the British Library.

ISBN (Hardback) 978 1 4091 9723 2
ISBN (Export Trade Paperback) 978 1 4091 9724 9
ISBN (eBook) 978 1 4091 9726 3

Typeset by Input Data Services Ltd, Somerset

Printed and bound in Great Britain by Clays Ltd, Elcograf S.p.A.

www.orionbooks.co.uk

All the Fun of the Fair

PROLOGUE

Every year at primary school, the teachers held a special lesson when the fair came to town.

When I was six, we drew the fair.

Hunched over my section of the art table, I scratched out stick figures and shapes, mashing the coloured pencils across my sugar paper with a hard fist. I zigzagged across the page, showing the blur of a busy crowd.

'Great work!' Mrs Finnegan said. 'Now get your names on your pictures so we can put them on the wall.'

Mrs Finnegan must have taught little kids for so long, she'd forgotten what good pictures looked like.

Six-year-olds' drawings. On the *wall*.

When I was seven, we painted it.

I outlined a smash of candyfloss and people and lights. I circled my brush through purples and yellows in a whirling merry-go-round, stopping before the colours turned brown. I painted shapes round the edges, filling the paper.

I felt I was doing OK – until Martha leaned over the art table. 'Is that a *chicken?*'

I dropped my paintbrush. I shot my arms straight by my sides, hands pointing down like a soldier's. 'No.'

'It's got a beak, though.'

Green paint glooped from my brush onto the picture.

'You do know what the fair is, *Fi–on–a*? You're not getting confused with pets' corner?'

'I *did* paint a chicken, I remember now.' I gripped my seat with both hands. 'One of the farmers brought his best chicken to the fair with him. As a treat.'

Martha looked round the table at the others and held her mouth open in a silent laugh. A string of spit hung between her top and bottom sets of teeth.

I knocked my paintbrush onto my skirt, making a green splat, which worked because Mrs Leyland came over and made a fuss. But then I went home and Mum made that revving noise in her throat, and went on about *being careful* and *is that washable? Please tell me it's washable,* and *Jonathan, have a look at this mess,* and *you're lucky we won't make you go to school in your pants tomorrow, Fiona.*

Which I knew wasn't true, even then.

And now I'm eleven, I *know* it's not true. (Because of paedos.)

Still, I was in trouble.

When I was eight, school had just broken up for the summer when the fair came to town.

That was a good year.

When I was nine, we wrote haikus.

The fair is so loud
The rides spin and people scream
And so do my ears.

I knew how the fair sounded. I'd hung out of my bedroom window like Rapunzel – except a crap Rapunzel who has nothing to dangle out, whose hair only reaches her shoulders because her mum says it's easier to manage that way.

I leaned out of the window and I heard the screams and the fast, fuzzy music. I watched the glow of the dancing lights, bouncing back from the metal shutters of the garage over the road.

The rides are so fun
That the people inside feel
The joy of a king.

When I was ten, Mum had a word with my teacher, and there wasn't a special lesson.

But kids brought their winning toys in anyway, a fluffy turquoise army of stuffed owls, all propped up fatly up at the side of the room against their owners' lunchboxes. *This is what you could have had.*

'Where's your owl, Fiona?' Martha asked, though she knew the answer.

'Didn't get one.' I held my voice light. 'Don't like owls.'

That evening, I stopped with Mum and Grandma at a service station, and spotted a claw machine magically full of the same stuffed owls, all wedged inside, edge-to-edge, in a turquoise, big-eyed sea.

When Mum and Grandma went into the toilet cubicles, I nipped back out to the machine with the pound coins Grandma had just given me.

I put the first pound in the slot and concentrated on the buttons.

Steer steer steer stop. Steer steer steer stop. Drop.

A wing! Yesss, hold on tight! It's going up but what's that, don't slip, no no no, please don't, please don't – no!

I put the next pound in.

3

I hooked an eye. The pincer looked firmly lodged behind the plastic and lifted the owl confidently, straight up, with only the tiniest sway, but – *hang on, what are you doing? You were gripping! KEEP GRIPPING, please don't – no!*

I put the coins in, one after another, pushing desperately at the buttons. Watching the claw pinch my chosen owl and lift it for a few magical seconds. Watching in slow motion as the claw dropped the owl, sending it rotating slowly through the air, bumping back into the fluffy turquoise sea.

Mum and Grandma found me there, in tears.

'You spent it all?' Grandma's T-shirt said *Don't Worry, Be Happy.* 'But why, darling?'

Mum made a line with her lips. 'You just snuck out of the toilets without asking? And thought it was OK?'

'All the kids have owls. They got them at the fair.'

Grandma turned to Mum. 'Gail,' she said softly.

Mum made hard eyes at Grandma. 'What were you think-ing of, Mum, giving a kid ten pounds for no reason?'

'Hey now.' Grandma stood up straighter. 'I can give my granddaughter treats when I can afford it.'

Mum shook her head. 'If you'd asked me, I'd have told you she wouldn't spend it on anything useful.' Mum made a jerky gesture at me. 'And now she's all upset.'

I cried some more. 'Can you give me more money, Grandma?'

Grandma glanced at Mum and gave me a flat smile of *no.* And it wasn't mentioned again, though Grandma did post me a stuffed owl toy when she was back in Glasgow at the weekend. I said *thank you,* like I meant it, and didn't tell her the owl was the wrong size and colour, with long skinny woven legs rather than a ball of fluff. I didn't tell her it was the wrong owl, and a week too late.

*

Mr Lincoln might not have mentioned the fair in class that year – the year I went double digits, not as life-changing as I was expecting – but it was all anyone talked about in the playground.

'If you're a group of girls, you get pushed by the fit boy on the Waltzers.' Martha cradled her owl like a baby, supporting its head. 'How old do you think the boy is, Fiona?'

I swallowed a crisp. It spiked my throat from the inside. 'Eighteen?'

'Hmm.' Martha looked at Amy and back. 'Did anyone see Fiona at the fair?'

The other girls shook their heads with their whole bodies, the action reflecting sunlight from the big owl eyes they all had sticking out of the tops of their rucksacks.

I swallowed hard but the crisp stayed lodged. 'Probably no one saw me because I went at night. On Thursday.' I put my hands to my throat. 'At eleven o'clock. My parents say I'm mature so I'm fine to stay up.'

Martha nodded. 'What was your favourite ride?'

I thumped my throat with my fists to make the crisp move. 'Ghost Train.'

Martha looked at the others and back. 'The Ghost Train was out of order on Thursday.' She spoke in a voice that was so kind, it did a whole circle back to not being kind at all.

'It *was* out of order.' I didn't notice the stuck crisp anymore. 'But my dad fixed it.'

Martha looked at the others and back at me.

'He used to fix things,' I said. 'He was an engineer before he was a postman. That's actually true.'

I know now that if you say *that's actually true*, it doesn't help.

Martha shook her head at me. 'The Ghost Train wasn't broken on Thursday. It was a test.'

I pretended to see something fascinating in the nature area.

'You failed the test,' Martha said.

I narrowed my eyes at the imaginary thing. 'Hang on, is that . . .'

I moved across the playground, as if pulled by the beam of a UFO. Past Mr Crane, who was shouting, 'Stop bunching!' at the footballing boys moving in one zigzagging clump.

I stood by the nature area, studying a bit of soil. I pretended I didn't notice what the girls were saying behind me. Even though the words were being said specially for me.

That might have been the same day I cut off Martha's plait.

In fact – I'm pretty sure it was.

But because school scissors are rubbish, I didn't get the whole way through. I was still sawing at the plait when Mr Lincoln ran over and grabbed me. Still, I was happy with all the hair on the floor by the time he managed to pull me away.

Turns out kids like me are the reason they give you blunt scissors in primary school.

That night, alone in my bedroom *to think about what I had done*, I sat with my book of lists.

Next Year

1) I'll be eleven
2) It'll be 1996
3) I'll have started high school
4) I'll finally be in the same school as Lewis Harris from swimming club

5) I'll have other friends too – proper ones. Girls, even.
   Definitely not Martha.
6) I won't do weird stuff anymore
7) I'll be <u>normal</u>

Normal. No more of the bad stuff, the *Fiona* stuff – like the plait-cutting, or that thing with the monkey bars. The kind of stuff I didn't know why it happened, except it just did because I was STUPID STUPID FIONA.

Not next year. If anyone asked about me next year, people would say, *Fiona Larson? Oh, she's the normal one. Really normal.*

I added the most important line.

8) I'll GO TO THE FAIR

I snapped my book shut.
Next year. It was happening.
Next year.

I

One year later

A good spy stays alert to changes in his surroundings.
The Junior Spy's Secret Handbook™

Thirty-nine days to the fair
I found the secret bag on the way to school, on the first day back after half-term.

I'd been walking through the park, looking up at the blackening sky, wondering when summer would feel, well, *summery*, like in the adverts, when I spotted a white shape between the leaves of the park's second-biggest bush.

I dropped my rucksack on the grass, hitched up my skirt, and crawled into the bush's open den-space. I pulled the white shape – a plastic bag – from the leaves, my heart beating fast. I took a breath and opened the bag.

Magazines. Nine magazines – all with girls on the front.
So many girls.

Girls in underwear, girls in bikinis. Naked girls with their arms covering their bits.

It's a long time since I've believed in hidden treasure, but still.

I flicked through the first magazine.

Inside – girls, *everywhere*. Naked girls, *without* arms over

9

their bits. Girls in the shower, lying-down girls. Girls on all fours, sleepy girls, confused-looking girls. Girls with no clothes on, but still in shoes. Girls who looked both old and young at the same time, who didn't look anything like the girls I knew. Or the mums. I didn't think even Selina Baker and the sixth-formers would look like *this* naked.

After looking at so many pages, my brain was swimming with bellybuttons and legs and boobs, so I took a break by reading an article: *My Favourite Things, by Kelly, 18, 36–24–36, from Winchester.*

Turned out Kelly liked spending cosy evenings in with a nice fella, watching the soaps, and taking long rosy-cheeked walks with her dog in the New Forest.

I turned the page and Kelly and her friends were gone, replaced by new, shiny girls in underwear. I closed the magazine and looked up at the trees.

All in all, it was a lot to take in. I wasn't sure I actually liked the magazines, though they were clearly treasure, so the best thing that had ever happened to me.

But I couldn't be late for registration or I'd get done, so I slotted Kelly from Winchester back in with the others and pushed the bag back between the branches.

I crawled out of the bush and hurried into school.

I'm not meant to walk into school on my own, even though I'm nearly twelve. The hours either side of the school day are the best hours – *my* time. I don't have to hurry home from school or tell my parents what I'm doing, not as long as I'm with a friend.

I was only on my own on the way in that day because, for some reason, Lewis wasn't there to meet me at the lamppost, and you can't always rely on Sean.

It's fair enough that Sean doesn't always want to walk in with us. He might have been good friends with Lewis back when they were both at Beech Avenue Primary, but there are two hundred kids in our year at high school. There are a lot more kids for Sean to choose from now.

Lewis is my best friend – has been since I lent him 10p for a cup of Ribena in the leisure centre café after swimming club, when we were seven. But Lewis isn't as good as other boys, and it's not his fault, exactly. It's just Lewis doesn't like football. And he doesn't have a good coat and rucksack, and everyone knows, if you go to his house, the glasses taste of dishwasher. But Sean *does* have a good coat and rucksack, and he *does* like football, so Sean can make friends with better boys – maybe not the lads from the blue estate, not all the time, but better boys than Lewis. And *actual* boys, so better than me.

These are the facts of our school so, once you get your head round them, you can't mind.

I was desperate to tell Lewis about the secret, but he's not in my registration class.

Dr Sharma, who is my form tutor as well as my science teacher, watched me hurry into the room just as the bell was ringing. She sat at her high lab bench with the locked fridge behind her, the fridge that kids say holds bleeding animal hearts.

Dr Sharma marked me off in her book. 'Fiona. I was just asking who needs the day off for the farm show tomorrow, but I don't need to ask you, do I?'

I tried to hold Dr Sharma's gaze. I ended up looking at the bleeding-heart fridge.

'The *day off for the farm show* rule only applies to farming families, as you well know,' Dr Sharma said. 'Are you saying you're from a farming family now?'

I gave a tiny nod.

'Fiona, your mum's car is always outside school and it says *Gail Larson, Driving Instructor* right there on the side.'

That got a laugh from the other kids. And a round of *'(cough)-Gail!*'s.

Mum's job causes me loads of problems. If you wanted to design a job to make your kid look stupid, it would be one where you wait outside the school gates in a car with your kid's surname on it. Mum doesn't understand why *'(cough)-Gail!'* is a problem. But she also doesn't understand Lewis's parents shouldn't have taken him to France at Easter – that no one had thought how easy to chant *'Lewis Harris went to Paris'* would be.

Dr Sharma was still talking.

'And I know your dad's a postman, Fiona, because he delivers to my house. We talk about the seasonal visitors at my bird table.'

I shuffled to an empty lab bench and pulled out a stool.

Dr Sharma gave me a long look. 'So I don't appreciate being treated like I was born yesterday.'

I sat down. 'I'm not asking for a day off for the farm show.'

Dr Sharma moved on to taking the register while I unpacked my pencil case.

The bell rang and I stayed where I was for science. Some kids left the room and others came in. The high lab tables were all made for two stools, and every table except mine had two people on it, but that was fine. It meant I had a spare stool for my bag and I could get my books out without leaning down. On experiment days, I even got the Bunsen burner to myself, and didn't have to take turns with another kid.

It was better this way. I would have chosen it this way.

Today was a day to work on our summer projects. There was clattering and unzipping all around, and I watched the other kids get their project books out. Most of their projects had pictures of leaves and trees on the front – probably because we'd just been taught photosynthesis. And because kids could fill lots of pages by gluing in leaves.

I pulled my own project book from my bag. *Blood, by Fiona Larson, 7E.* I'd written the title in postbox-red bubble letters and drawn the letters dripping down the cover, into a pool of blood at the bottom.

I've always liked blood. I've even said to Lewis we should swap blood, prick our fingers and mash them together to show we're proper friends. But he didn't like that idea.

I smoothed down the next blank page and started copying sentences from the textbook.

Blood is a bodily fluid. It has four main parts. They are plasma, red blood cells, white blood cells and platelets.

I kept copying for a bit longer until I remembered the secret bag, and then the excitement and daydreaming took over.

When the bell rang for break, I thought I'd finally get to tell Lewis about my secret, but I couldn't find him anywhere. And he wasn't in my English class, either. So there was nothing to do but listen to Mr Kellett bang on, while I imagined Lewis's face when I told him what I'd found.

This would *blow his mind.*

Sean *was* in my English class, but when I turned around to look at him, he didn't say *hi*, so I just turned back. It's fine, Sean's still my friend – it's not his fault he can't talk to me with other kids there. He's not the one who made the rules of school.

Mr Kellett was late, of course. He hurried in, his tie skew-whiff. As well as teaching English, he teaches PE. And when he moves from one type of class to the other, he has to get changed.

He turned to write *paradox* on the board. 'A paradox is a seemingly absurd or contradictory statement that, on reflection, may prove to make sense after all.'

Mr Kellett talked some more and I sort-of listened.

He didn't used to get changed between lessons. He used to do our English classes in his PE kit, his whistle round his neck, the hair on his legs just there, like a coat of fur. But that changed when our school got the New Head. These days, instead of a whistle round Mr Kellett's neck, there's a tie.

'So how can something,' he asked, 'mean two things at once?'

Things I Know About the New Head

1) She's called Mrs Shackleton
2) She makes Mr Kellett change out of his PE kit to teach English
3) She always wears an animal badge on her blouse
4) She likes things Just So – *Dr Sharma**
5) She makes it so you can't do anything right – *Miss Jarvis, RE**
6) She's an iron fist in a velvet glove – *Mr Carter, IT**
7) She's got gumption, I'll say that about her – *Mr Kellett**
8) She just doesn't understand about the relevance of RE, that it's about so much more than just organised religion, it's about society – *Miss Jarvis, again**

9) She's as bad as bloody Thatcher – *still Miss Jarvis**

10) She wants to get rid of us all and bring in her own teachers, and then where will we all be? – *Miss Jarvis talks a lot**

*I use spying techniques from The Junior Spy's Secret Handbook™ *to listen in on people. Grandma got me the handbook as a Christmas present. Mum wishes she hadn't.***

** Grandma also taught me about asterisks

Mr Kellett went on a bit longer. He talked about what's true and what's not, and different perceptions, and two things being true at once, and it was all a bit complicated for someone whose mind was on important bag-related things.

He cleared his throat. 'Now write a paradox of your own.'

After finding those magazines, I didn't even have to think. I picked up my pen straight away.

The best secrets can be hidden in plain sight.

Mr Kellett leaned over my pad. 'Perfect. And also intriguing, Miss Larson!'

I held my breath because he was so close, though his smell wasn't as bad as some teachers'. Mr Kellett did loads of sport, but his smell was wet towel mixed with broken twigs, whereas Mr Matheson in Music did *no* sport and smelled of *actual* BO. He was always lifting up his arms to conduct us on our triangles and recorders, shaking the smell up and wafting it over.

Mr Kellett smiled at me. 'And what are the best secrets, I wonder?'

I gave my head a tiny shake and took a gulpy breath. *Wet towel broken twigs.*

From the back of the room, Liam leaned back in his chair.

15

'Sir, how about people saying Leeds United are a quality football team – is that one?' Which I don't think counted, and Liam only said it because Mr Kellett supports Leeds. But everyone burst into laughter and Mr Kellett smiled. And Sean caught my eye while he was laughing and then looked quickly away.

I found Lewis in the computer room that lunchtime.

'You should have walked in with me.' I threw my rucksack down onto the floor and dropped into the chair next to him. The chair rolled backwards on its wheels. 'You'll wish you had.'

Lewis kept tapping the keyboard, like I wasn't there. His rhino on the screen leapt up platforms.

I got my sandwich box from my rucksack. 'I found a bag. Of secrets.'

Lewis paused his tapping. A baddie walked into his rhino and the screen flashed red, black and white. *Game Over.*

He wanted to ask, I know he did. But he was being stubborn.

I opened my sandwich box. 'Why didn't you meet me at the lamppost? And where were you at break?'

He inched his chair round, finally looking at me. 'You wouldn't let me show you my magic trick at the weekend.'

'But we were outside the newsagent's. There were *people* around.'

Yes, I'd stopped Lewis doing a magic trick. But he knew the rules.

How to be Normal

1) Don't eat any weird food for packed lunches. And no eggs.
2) Don't talk to yourself when you're on your own
3) Push your socks down
4) Have a school jumper exactly the right shade of green. <u>Don't let your mum buy one from the market.</u>
5) If you're wearing sports clothes, make sure they always have exactly three stripes
6) Don't get angry if you're being picked on, just pretend you don't notice
7) Don't do any old-Fiona stuff, like the thing with the monkey bars
8) <u>Definitely</u> no magic tricks where anyone can see you (LEWIS)
9) Be allowed to go to the fair

This list is not exhaustive. That's what it said at the bottom of the new school rules Mrs Shackleton brought in.

Anyway, number eight, right there, in ballpoint pen. *No magic tricks.*

Even though Lewis is the only person allowed to look in my book of lists, he doesn't always seem pleased.

'Anyway,' Lewis couldn't wait any longer, 'tell me about this bag of secrets.'

After lunch, we had drama. It was the only class I had with Lewis and we sat together in the circle of kids in the school hall.

He'd forgiven me, of course. How could he not? I had a *secret bag*.

'All right, everyone.' Mrs Vernal clapped her hands and the circle of kids went quiet. 'What does drama mean to you? Really?'

Mrs Vernal was new. The old drama teacher left to have a baby and this one took up just as much space as the pregnant teacher in the corridors. Mrs Vernal was made up of lots of layers, and always had a bit of scarf flapping about her.

'Drama's about acting,' Katie Russell said.

'Not *just* acting,' Mrs Vernal said. 'It's bigger than that.'

Mrs Vernal made eye contact wth me, but there was no way I was answering. Nothing good ever comes from answering questions at school.

'Drama' – Mrs Vernal made sure we all felt her looking into our eyes, one by one – 'is about self-development. It's about *life*.' Pause. 'It's about getting to the *emotional truth* within.'

We all nodded.

'Do you all understand what I mean by *emotional truth*?'

We all nodded again. Nodded just hard enough for her not to say it again. Not so hard that she asked us to explain.

No, I don't answer questions in class. There was a kid once, about ten years ago, who said 'orgasm' in science when he meant to say 'organism'. Simon Rutherson, that was his name. He's a scaffolder now. Whenever kids in Monkford see scaffolding, we stand underneath and shout up *'Orgasm!'* – just in case he's there.

Mrs Vernal clapped. 'Everyone get up!'

We dotted ourselves around the school hall. I stood in front of a long curtain, looking at the layer of dust across it like a lace sheet. Hundreds of dust speckles. Millions.

Numbers too big make me feel weird and dizzy, so I made myself stop thinking.

Mrs Vernal weaved between us, her heels like tap shoes on the polished floor, the noise echoing up to the hall's high ceiling.

'I don't want you to act. I want you to *feel*.' *Tap, tap, tap.* 'I want you to think about a time you were really excited.' *Tap, tap, tap.* 'How does it feel in your toes? In your fingertips?' Mrs Vernal tapped over to the other side of the hall. 'I want you to hear what you heard and smell what you smelled. *Go!*'

I heard thumping sounds behind. Flashes of movement reflected in the windows as kids fist-thrusted the air and jumped up and down.

I closed my eyes and remembered how it felt to wait for the special sundae in the American diner on my last birthday. But it was hard to get *that* worked up, ten months later.

Mrs Vernal circled the room. Making little comments, adjusting people. *Tap, tap, tap.*

I noticed a lot of kids were showing excitement by scoring goals. England had drawn with Switzerland the week before in their first game of Euro '96, which meant there was even more football talk at school than usual.

It also meant Nino – the shy Year Eight Swiss kid whose dad came over here to work at the medical plant – wasn't having a brilliant time of it.

'Now,' Mrs Vernal said, 'let that feeling go. Shake yourselves.'

I stared at the dust on the curtain, listening to the rustling and jangling of bracelets against watches. The sound of thirty kids flapping limp arms round their bodies.

I've always tried to like football. It's a boy thing, so a good thing, and liking it would be really useful. I mean to keep trying it till I like it. You have to put the effort in with a lot of the best things − cigarettes too, I hear. You can't stop trying just because they're awful at first, or you'll *never* learn to smoke.

'Let's do a different emotion.' *Tap, tap, tap.* 'Think about a time you were sad.'

I felt a hand on my shoulder.

'Don't do the sad exercise, Fiona. Join in for the next one.' Mrs Vernal patted me twice and was gone.

Twenty minutes later, we were doing *thoughtful* (lots of frowning and fingers on lips) when the bell rang.

'That's it.' Mrs Vernal clapped her hands. 'Enjoy your evenings.'

I turned to get my rucksack.

'Fiona.' She caught my arm. 'Stay with me.'

I waved Lewis to go on ahead.

Mrs Vernal waited until the last kid had left. 'I just wanted you to know, I'll look out for you in this class, Fiona. Drama can be a purpose, a saviour − but also a risk.'

I felt my forehead bunch.

'It might get hard for you, the more we zero in on the emotional truth within.'

I nodded.

'Fiona?' Mrs Vernal made her voice a special soft. 'I heard that your sister died.'

I felt my forehead unbunch. *Ah.*

'You will have more powerful feelings than most kids your age. You're in control of those feelings and it's up to you whether you use them. This class should be a safe place for you.'

'OK,' I said.

'If things ever get too much, I'm always here.'

'Right.'

Mrs Vernal seemed to be waiting for something. 'Always here. For you to talk to.'

'OK,' I said. 'Thanks. Bye.'

I hurried out of the school hall. Lewis was waiting with our coats.

He handed mine over. 'What did you do?'

'Nothing.' I took the coat and put it on. 'She wanted to talk about Danielle.'

Lewis shook his head. *People.*

2

The best secrets can be hidden in plain sight.
(paradox)

Thirty-nine days to the fair
Lewis and I headed straight for the park after school, down pavements damp and black from the recent rain shower. Water droplets glistened on bushes as we passed, and that smoky just-rained smell filled the air.

Despite the rain, when we got to our bush, the den-space inside was dry.

The two of us sat cross-legged inside, pulling magazines out of the plastic bag and sliding them back in.

'It *is*. I didn't believe it could happen, but it *is*.' Lewis looked up from leafing. 'It's hidden treasure.'

'I don't know how Finders Keepers works in a park situation.' I picked up a magazine. 'Are these ours now?'

I held the magazine up to look at the cover.

This girl stood in a bra and tiny shorts. She pulled her shorts down at one side so you could see how flat her tummy was. Her body was wet but her face was thick with make-up, like she'd had a shower but kept her face out of the water. She looked sleepy.

'Do you like her?' I asked.

Lewis kept looking at the girl. 'She's fit.'

He glanced at me.

'Fit,' he said again. He looked away.

I nodded and pretended it didn't sound wrong coming from Lewis. We've all got to practise this stuff, and it's better to do it in front of friends.

He turned the page. *My Favourite Things, by Kelly, 18, 36–24–36, from Winchester.*

'I know she's scowling in the picture,' I said. 'But she's friendly in the article. See, she's given out her phone number.'

'She can't want loads of calls though – she's only given the short number.' Lewis tapped *36–24–36*. 'You'd have to look up the area code if you weren't local.'

He closed the magazine and handed it back.

I slid it back into the plastic bag. 'I don't like leaving these here. It's not safe.'

'Who do you think they belong to?' Lewis had to ruin it.

We both went quiet.

I pictured a huge, scary man, shaking with anger – a massive snarling face on a wall of man-rock. Arm muscles veiny and bulging like Popeye's.

'Let's leave them here for now, and make a decision tomorrow,' I said.

'Let's not tell anyone. Or they'll all want a look.'

'Does this mean you've forgiven me?'

'Almost,' Lewis said.

I pushed the bag between the branches. 'Sweet.'

On the way home, I saw our next-door neighbour, Mrs Carpenter, across the street, walking her Papillon. She was wearing a baseball cap, even though she was nearly as old as Grandma.

We waved.

I like Mrs Carpenter, even though I'd preferred Mr Carpenter when he was around. He always offered me Polos and, if we had shopping bags, he'd make a point of coming over and asking if we'd bought tomatoes or courgettes and how much we'd paid for them, because *the supermarkets see you coming* and it's *so much cheaper to grow them yourself*!

He'd tell us this every time, even though we'd heard it before. Even the times we hadn't bought any tomatoes or courgettes.

But he moved out last year and moved in with his brother's wife, and I'm not meant to ask about him.

His brother's wife was *welcome to him*. I found that out from Mrs Carpenter, in one of those spying missions that left me understanding less, not more.

The bad side of finding things out by spying is that you can't ask people to explain.

Later, I sat with Mum and Dad on the stools round the peninsula, eating Dad's homemade pizza.

That's what we call the bit of kitchen surface that sticks out: *the peninsula*. It sticks out of the wall under the diagonal bit where the stairs are, and I sit in the stool that fits under the stairs. It's fine, I just have to remember not to jerk my head around while I eat.

'I'm just wondering. If you found some special things in a public place'– I picked a piece of sweetcorn off my pizza – 'would it be stealing to sell the things?'

Dad looked at Mum. He'd finished work for the day, but was still wearing his postman's uniform.

'What valuable things have you found?' Dad asked.

'I haven't found anything, I'm just wondering how Finders Keepers works, exactly.'

He stared at me and I looked down.

Dad is too good at reading faces. He was born *significantly hearing-impaired*, but he says *deaf*. I forget most of the time, until something happens, like Dad needs me to make a phone call. He usually asks Mum to make his calls, but he always asks me if he wants to phone a premium rate line for a TV quiz show because *it's just less hassle this way, darling*.

Dad being deaf doesn't affect things much, except that he can't use the phone, and sometimes he needs something he's missed explaining. The good bit about it is he's always able to lipread what a footballer on telly is swearing. The bad bit is that our overhead lights flash when someone rings the door-bell. I've asked Mum and Dad if we can stop that, because it's embarrassing when kids come over, but Mum's face went hard and she said I *need to think about my priorities*.

So I just don't invite people over now. I love Dad – I wouldn't swap him. I wouldn't even swap Mum, most of the time. It's just sensible not to hand kids bullets about how your family's different from other people's.

Mum peered across the peninsula at me, eyes made into slits. 'Why are you asking about valuable things and Finders Keepers? Is this about the car boot sale?'

'It's nothing to do with the car boot sale.'

She wiped her fingers and adjusted the clip in her hair. She wore clips like two claws, that bounced back when stretched too far open. 'You wouldn't lie to me, Fiona? I really hope not.'

'Mrs Vernal mentioned Danielle today, out of nowhere,' I said quickly. 'Mrs Vernal. She's the new drama teacher.'

Mum reached for a slice of pizza. Pieces of her grey-blonde hair fell out of the clip again. She glanced at Dad and back to me. 'What did she say?'

'She just really, *really* wanted to talk about Danielle.'

Mum put the pizza slice down. 'What did she say *specifically?*'

'She said that I could use having a dead sister to get better at drama. She talked about *emotional truth*. She held me back at the end of class and told me she was *here for me.*'

Mum looked at Dad. '*Mrs Vernal*, you say?'

Dad put his pizza slice down. He put his hand on Mum's leg.

'Some people,' Mum adjusted her hair clip jerkily, not even wiping her fingers this time, 'like to insert themselves into other people's business.'

She pushed her plate across the peninsula, even though she hadn't finished her food, and the force of the push made hair fall out of her clip again. But my catalyst had worked because there was no more talk of Finders Keepers and the car boot sale.

Dr Sharma taught us about catalysts in science. I use Danielle as a catalyst to change conversations.

Thing is, when you're not quite twelve in a town that's thirty miles from the nearest city – where there's meant to be a retail park coming, with a cinema and megabowl but they've *still* not been built – where the most exciting events are kids putting bangers in cow pats, or farm boys riding into school on tractors on their sixteenth birthdays, and by *riding* I mean *trundling in slowly*, it sounds better than it is – well. Being a kid and being able to change a conversation is like a superpower.

My big sister died.

Some people head-tilt and go quiet. Some people ask questions.

Mrs Vernal is one of those who tell me how sad I am. She *wants* me to be sad, though she either doesn't know the full story or she hasn't thought it through. Because you don't get sad about someone you never met. Except if you're told there was this girl who used to live in your house, who *still* has a better bedroom than you, who laid the table without being asked and was a *good eater*.

So maybe I *am* sad. Maybe I'm sad I can't go back fourteen years and grab Danielle's arm and say *fine, you're going to die and I'm sorry, but could you say you don't like eggs? In fourteen years' time I'm going to have to eat sweetcorn because of you.*

Sometimes, when Mum talks about Danielle, it's like she forgets we were never all here at the same time. She talks like our family once had the right number for Hungry Hippos. Like we were once a family who once needed the fourth peninsula stool, rather than keeping it in the cupboard under the stairs.

And sometimes I wonder whether I should stop pointing out that I'm the replacement. Whether I should forget what the truth is, and try to believe Mum's instead.

Mum especially forgets me and Danielle weren't around at the same time when it comes to summer holidays.

She was looking at Cornwall hotels in the kitchen with Dad later that night, while I worked on a jigsaw in the lounge. I could hear what she was doing without needing to spy at all.

'SHIT THE BED!' There was a furious tapping – Mum

27

stabbing at a brochure with an angry finger. 'Jonathan, look at the single supplement for this one!'

Things That Make My Mum Angry

1) Single supplements
2) Me *not thinking about my priorities*
3) Me, generally
4) People cutting her up at roundabouts, especially if they're driving BMWs
5) People who walk *too* slowly in front of her, on the street or in a supermarket
6) Me telling another adult that she wanted to know how much money they had*
7) People who say they knew Danielle really well when they didn't
8) Snails on the step that don't move out of the way because *it's their fault if they go and get stepped on* and *they can't come crying to me*
9) Grandma buying unsuitable presents
10) The women from work who treated Danielle's funeral like an outing because they stopped at M&S on the way back
11) The timing sheets system at Parents' Evening
12) Me asking to go to the fair
13) Mrs Vernal (new)

I only did this once.
This list is definitely – definitely – not exhaustive.

Mum was still with Dad in the kitchen – 'LOOK! JONATHAN! What are the single beds made of, actual diamonds?' – when I heard a thud at the lounge window.

I pushed my jigsaw away. I ran to the window and looked out.

A sparrow lay on the paving stone below the window, its legs sticking into the air, cartoon-upright.

I let myself out of the front door. I picked the bird up carefully and rested it on my hand.

It was warm. I felt a flutter of movement inside it.

I rested the sparrow on top of the hedge so the estate cats couldn't get it. I looked back at the window, at the round greasy mark, whirling like a massive fingerprint.

When I checked the bird a few minutes later, it had gone. But the bird-head-fingerprint mark was still there. Below the mark was the back of a photo frame.

I sniffed. I bet I knew why that bird got distracted and flew into the glass. I knew what it was thinking.

Another one, I can't believe it. Another *photo of that dead kid on a windowsill.*

3

If you tell a kid not to do something, you might give them
the idea in the first place.
(paradox)

Thirty-eight days to the fair

I met Lewis at our lamppost on George Street the next
morning. He walked towards me, his anorak hood up, even
though it was hardly raining.

We nodded at each other and fell into step, crossing the
road when we reached the postbox.

'Wait for me!' Sean hurried to catch us.

I looked at Sean's feet. 'You're only allowed to wear black
socks with the uniform, You're going to get done.'

Sean pushed his hand through his hair. 'So, I get done, so
what?'

That's when I knew we were meant to notice his white
socks, but he was pretending we weren't.

These things might sound complicated if you're not at
our school, but they make sense once you've been there a
while.

*

The three of us walked through the park and Lewis and I glanced at each other. We knew what the other was thinking. We wanted to check the bag of magazines was still there, but we didn't want to tell Sean.

Sean's not as good at keeping secrets as us.

Or not as good with *our* secrets anyway. Sean told everyone Lewis was rubbish at the high jump after we held an Olympics in Lewis's back garden. Sean told everyone I was trying on a new accent – and really, there was nothing wrong with that, loads of people who only ever lived on cul-de-sacs in Monkford talk like the brothers from Oasis.

So I got nervous as we approached the second-biggest bush because Lewis is a panicker. Causes me loads of problems.

I thought quickly. 'You know when I turn twelve in August, I'll overtake Danielle. She was eleven when she died.'

Sean and Lewis both looked away.

'Our second-biggest bedroom is still kept for Danielle. But *I'll* be the oldest when I turn twelve.' I could make out a hint of white plastic through the branches. '*And* I'm alive. Do you think Mum and Dad will give me the second bedroom on my birthday?'

'No.' Lewis was looking at gravel path in front of him. 'And I definitely don't think you should ask your mum.'

Lewis is scared of my mum, more than any other adult. He's not used to a shouty mum because his is the quiet type.

Anyway, my catalyst worked, because we were now past the second-biggest bush and nearly at the playground.

Lewis and I glanced at each other. I gave a small nod.

A day, that bag of magazines had been there now. A whole day – at least. And no one had come to collect it yet.

*

After registration, we had a year-group assembly in the sports hall. We sat cross-legged on gym mats, low-level conversation all around as we waited for the assembly to start.

It was meant to be one of those *talent* assemblies, with kids with hobbies showing off, all hoping to wow the crowd. Kids who'd been told skills impressed people and won friends.

Kids who hadn't thought through what would happen when they left the sports hall. Who'd spend all lunchtime begging bigger kids for their juggling balls back.

Mrs Vernal stood at the front of the sports hall, waiting. Something felt different today. Dr Sharma and the other Year Seven form teachers looked more serious than usual.

I felt the waft of the door opening and shutting behind me. At the back of the room, the chattering stopped. The kids at the side of the hall, the ones with their jazz shoes and flutes, stood straighter. Even *the teachers* stood straighter.

I felt her before I saw her. The New Head.

Across the aisle, Liam hadn't noticed the air change. 'And his stereo has got two CD players and—'

The New Head padded up to him. She waited, looking at the floor, doing an impression of someone shy. The eyes of a cheetah brooch glinted out from her neat turquoise jumper.

Finally, Liam glanced up.

He shrank – instantly. *Liam.* One of the best kids in our year.

The New Head stood there a moment longer, letting Liam's fear properly soak in.

She walked to the front of the room and turned to face us. 'I've been contacted by the head at Radcliffe High School.'

Just the sound of her voice made my stomach squish. It was so calm and quiet, in the room that was otherwise silent.

'A group of his Year Tens were playing *chicken* on the railway track, and a child has been seriously injured by an oncoming train. He is in hospital. He will never be the same again.'

Not a whisper.

'I wanted you all to hear me say, personally, that playing *chicken* is the stupidest thing a child can do. And if any of you – *any of you*' – she looked into as many eyes as possible – 'risk the safety of yourselves or your fellow children in that way, you will feel the full force of my wrath.'

The New Head nodded to Mrs Vernal and walked out of the room. The only sound was the brush of the door as it came to a close, behind her.

Mrs Vernal took a step forward. 'That must be such upsetting news for you all.' Her eyes were shiny, but not crying-shiny. 'Awful.'

No one said anything.

'You need to take this as a learning opportunity. You're going to learn how not to follow the herd. You're going to learn about real life at this school – especially in drama.'

Did Dr Sharma exchange a look with Miss Jarvis?

'Resilience, not just the syllabus. You're going to *grow*.' Mrs Vernal pulled at her scarf like it was too tight. 'Does anyone have anything they want to share with the group?'

Everyone looked at the floor.

'These can be difficult years.' Mrs Vernal paced in front of the sports ladders at the front of the room. 'Remember – you are the star of your own life. You flower for yourselves, not for anyone else.' She turned and paced in the other direction. 'Being a teenager is hard.'

Teenager. *If only.* I wasn't even twelve till after the school year ended.

If I could change one thing in my life, I'd have been born in September, not August.

And being allowed to go to the fair, obviously.

And Danielle not being such a good eater.

And Mum realising dead people don't need bedrooms.

Still – *chicken*. And a *train*. There was a kid in hospital right now, who would never be the same again.

Maybe, today, being Fiona Larson right now wasn't completely awful, after all.

Lewis and I hurried straight to the park after school.

We passed a bunch of kids gathered around the big wasps' nest, taking turns to go up close, practically touching the nest, before jerking away again, and indicating to the next kid to do the same. Playing *chicken*.

I shook my head. 'The assembly must have given them the idea.'

Lewis shuddered – at the wasps, or the thought of disobeying the New Head, or both.

We checked the kids weren't watching us and walked up to the second-biggest bush, as though it was any other bush in the park. We climbed into the den space and – *sweet!* The magazines were still there!

We spread them out and went through them again.

We learned how to keep a girl happy in bed (*foreplay* and the *clitoris*). We learned about *premature ejaculation* and how to *keep the wolf from the door* by thinking about snooker and *Gardeners' World*. We learned to always flick past *Readers' Wives*, which raised more questions than answers and made Lewis, especially, feel like he needed a little break.

One of the magazines was different from all the others, and only showed the girls in underwear, not naked. It broke up all the girl pictures with other things – an interview with an actor, a page giving star ratings to different shaving foams, and a small section on films. We wouldn't get as much money for this magazine, but it was our favourite.

I stared at the picture from a film's car chase scene. 'When I'm a spy, I'm going to be the clever one who gets to drive, not the girl one who's the passenger.' I turned a page. 'And there's no way I'd let myself get kidnapped.'

With all our attention, some of the magazine pages were starting to look a bit ruffled. The cover with the sleepy wet/dry girl had got creased where Lewis had accidentally sat on it.

'The owner will be able to tell we've read his magazines.' I pushed the cover with my fist, straightening it. 'He's going to be furious now whatever, so I might as well take them. Finders Keepers rules says two days is fine.' And before I could think too much about it, I slid the magazines into the plastic bag and into my rucksack. I hurried out of the bush before I could think about what I'd done.

Lewis rushed after me, trying to put a rucksack on at the same time. 'I can't believe you did that!'

'We can sit on the swings and watch the bush. *Surveillance,* my spy book calls it. If the owner comes back, we can give him the magazines and say it was a joke.'

We sat on the swings. Out of the corner of my eye, I saw Lewis inch a pack of cards out of his pocket.

'Lewis! Not now!'

He pushed his cards back in.

I started swinging, even though I never swing anymore, not even when no one can see, on the swing in our garden. Only little kids swing. I just swung that day because we were there, doing surveillance.

I swung high enough for the chains to jolt, pointing my legs upwards, and made sure not to look at the sky. It's something about how big and empty space is – how the planets are just floating there and nothing's strapped in and there's so much *nothing*. It makes me dizzy.

Looking down, from this height, I could see the whole park. And there was no angry man going into the second-biggest bush to look for his treasure.

I'd done it. I'd taken the magazines and it was Finders Keepers, fair and square.

I was safe.

But I didn't have long to celebrate.

I'd said goodbye to Lewis and was heading back home, thinking how pleasingly full my rucksack felt, when I saw it.

I stopped and stared. I wrapped my arms around my body.

Opposite the petrol station, where there had been an advert for cat food that morning, there was now a new billboard.

Monkford Fair. Festival Field. Fri 19–Mon 22 July.

A clown face loomed out of the picture, the clown's smile so wide it looked mean. A cartoon picture of a Waltzer car whirled so fast that the people inside were just a blur.

I kept staring.

It's time.

My heart got fuller. My breath tighter.

I had to get this right this year. I had to *think*.

I had thirty-eight days to work out how to get to the fair.

4

In some families, the well-behaved kid is the bad one.
(paradox)

Thirty-eight days to the fair

Mum was in the kitchen when I got home, putting her home-made cover over the sewing machine. Next to the machine, a pair of curtains with horrible big flowers lay flopped over the peninsula. I could tell she'd finished making the curtains because she'd wrapped them in clear plastic.

Mum makes curtains for people around the village. She says she likes it, and it makes her extra money. It's really annoying.

'Hi.' I decided to work my way up to the billboard. 'Some kids from Radcliffe High were playing chicken on the railway and a kid got hit by a train.'

'What?' Mum stopped moving. 'Is the kid OK?'

I shrugged.

'How old was the child?'

I shrugged again.

Mum's eyebrows hunched up in the middle. 'That's really upsetting.'

With her face all screwed up with sadness, Mum looked old. Of course, she *was* old – fifty-two – she and Dad were so much older than other kids' parents. But she looked older still when she was upset.

'Mrs Vernal gave the assembly,' I said. 'She said being a teenager is hard.'

Mum shook her head. She started packing up the sewing machine again.

'She said kids should be the stars of their own lives.'

Mum slid the heavy machine under the peninsula. 'What does that *even mean?*'

I took a breath. 'I sometimes feel like I'm not the star of my own life.' I bunched up my hands. 'Mrs Vernal said I need to be my own flower and grow for myself. Or something.'

Mum gave me a look. 'I'm thinking I might need a little chat with this *Mrs Vernal.*' She looked younger again now she'd found a reason to be annoyed rather than sad.

I watched Mum reach for the plastic-covered curtains. She started folding them carefully, like she was handling a baby.

Don't say it.

But the words came out anyway. 'Mum, I've seen a billboard.'

Mum's movements slowed. 'No.' Her voice was calm.

'Everyone else gets to go.' My voice wasn't calm. It went wavy and uphill.

'When you're an adult, living an adult life, you can choose to go to the fair yourself.'

'But everyone else gets to go!'

Mum stared at the curtains, not folding anymore. 'You know why we don't want you to go? *You know why,* Fiona!'

'Just because Danielle died there doesn't mean I'll die!'

'Of course you're not going to die, that's not the point of the—'

'And I don't care about Danielle!' I screamed.

38

*

It's not my fault I do things like that. Every family has a good one and a bad one – fact. It just isn't always obvious because sometimes it's complicated.

Take Lewis's family.

Lewis *should* be the good one. He does his homework and picks up crisp packets in the street. But his dad likes Lewis's brother better, even though his brother doesn't pick up crisp packets and sometimes blocks us with his massive body when we try to get on the bus.

But it's simpler with my family. Danielle did loads of stuff that made my parents happy. She helped Dad put the toppings on his pizzas. She laid the table without asking and always cleaned her plate. She had a dance routine with Mum to songs on the radio and they danced round the kitchen together.

It's fair enough that I'm the bad one.

I'm the odd one out in my family. I'm the only one who's left-handed. You can tell we're related because I have the same small nose and big chin as Danielle, but my parents are tall and fair and so was Danielle – the *tallest girl in her class*, Mum never gets bored of saying, like Danielle managed it on purpose. I'm one of the shortest, and my hair's dark and heavy and stays where it is. It never falls out of a clip like Mum's.

If my family were *The Lion King* family, they would all be Simbas and I'd be Scar.

I don't want to be the Scar. But when you're the Scar, you don't get to choose.

Bad Scar Things I've Done – Countdown

6. Cut Off Martha's Plait

Everyone else thinks this was bad, but this was the least bad. Because Martha deserved it.

5. Put Grandma's Money in the Claw Machine

This wasn't really bad either. But it made Grandma sad and disappointed, and nothing feels worse than that. So it's on the list.

4. Scratched My Special Shape Everywhere. The Shape Made from *F for Fiona-s*

This one definitely wasn't my fault. And now I know what a swastika is, I don't want it to be my special shape anymore.

3. Asked Candy's Mum How Much Money They Had

Candy lived in the big house at the end of the road last summer, because her mum was working at the medical plant *on secondment*, which means you live somewhere new where you have no friends.

And, I admit, I got this one wrong. But Mum kept asking me questions – *'they went on a skiing holiday in January and now they're going to Rome?'* and *'a taxi to take her from school to the dentist, how much would that even cost?'* – and I honestly thought she wanted to know.

2. Stole Candy's Pencil Topper

I wanted Candy's Easter egg collection, all lined up on the shelf, even though Easter was *ages* ago. I even wanted Candy's mum instead of mine sometimes, like when she made us pancakes even though it wasn't pancake day.

But most of all, I wanted Candy's pencil topper. It was a perfect pale purple and shaped like a house, with a little fence and a cat in the garden.

Even though I'm not into stationery, I wanted it so much, it burned inside me. On one visit, I took that pencil topper and put it in my cardigan pocket.

When I went home, I put the pencil topper in my bottom drawer and said to Mum, 'I don't want to play with Candy anymore.'

And Mum looked really upset and said *you have to be open if you're going to have friends* and *not everyone's perfect* and she got angry then and said *beggars can't be choosers.* And then got upset again, and started apologising, even though it was fine – she wasn't lying.

I don't like to think about Candy.

I was happy when she moved away.

1. The Monkey Bars

This is the worst one. And everyone knows about it.

In the last year of primary school, the year I turned double-digits, we went to church services with the vicar once a month. And Mum got sad there because it was where they held Danielle's funeral.

One time, the vicar put his hand on Mum's shoulder and said, 'God takes the best of us and keeps them to himself.' And I thought and thought about that. About how God took Danielle, but let my parents keep me.

The next day at school, I hung upside down from the playground's monkey bars so my skirt flipped over my chest, showing my pants. Everyone pointed and shouted. Even when teachers shouted '*COME DOWN NOW!*' – even when the headteacher came out – I stayed on.

Two teachers had to pull me off the monkey bars, bruising my legs. I clung to that metal pole till it hurt. Then there were letters and doctors and people asking questions quietly, and I had to say that I'd bruised my own legs. That it was all my fault.

Which I had. And it was.

Proving I was the bad one. Proving it, once and for all. Just in case people weren't sure.

<u>To Go to the Fair I Need:</u>

1) Money for the rides
2) Girl friends, so the boy from the Waltzers will push my car
3) Mum and Dad to let me go

Sometimes the shortest lists can be the longest ones. Paradox.

5

Thirty-seven days to the fair

The next morning, I waited with Lewis as we watched Sean
slow-walk towards our lamppost, kicking puddles as he went.
White socks – again – peeked out from between his trousers
and his shoes.

The New Head was going to kill him if she saw those
socks. Sean was *playing with fire*, but I guessed that was the
point. Still, after seeing the New Head's face in the chicken
assembly, how she shut down Liam with just a look, I would
have shivered pulling those socks on that morning.

Sean arrived at the lamppost. 'All right.'

We walked for a moment. Lewis turned to cross the road
towards school.

I followed Lewis, but Sean just watched us. 'Why do you
two always cross the road at this postbox?'

Lewis stopped in the road. I stopped so I didn't walk into
the back of him.

'Every day,' Sean said, 'you always cross exactly here.'

Lewis and I looked at each other.

We shuffled back onto the pavement, facing Sean.

'We just do,' Lewis said. 'Habit.'

'And on the way home, you two always cross *there*. At the big tree.'

I turned to Lewis and we blinked at each other. Sean was right.

It was funny he knew stuff about us that we didn't.

Lewis turned to me. 'I cross here because you do.'

I frowned. 'I thought I crossed here because *you* do.'

'Maybe it just feels like the best place,' Lewis said.

I thought about this. 'Maybe it *is* me. Mum always crosses here too.'

Sean pointed at a house. 'It means, in both directions, you never walk in front of that one.'

I looked at the house. 'Huh.'

His point made, Sean finally set off walking, talking about the weekend's England game. I took one last look back at the house, then Lewis and I followed.

In the park, Lewis turned to me. 'Shall we go into the bush then?'

I made big eyes at him. *Shush.*

'Oh,' Lewis gave a little laugh. 'I forgot you'd taken them already.'

I made my eyes bigger still.

That's when Lewis started to panic. He staggered to the left. 'I – I –'

Sean looked from one to the other. 'Taken what?'

I glared at Lewis.

I don't know exactly what it looks like when an eleven-year-old has a heart attack, but I bet it was something like this.

I looked back at Sean. 'Don't tell anyone. But I found some magazines, and they're mine now.'

Sean looked at the bush and back. 'What kind of magazines?'

I looked at Lewis and back. 'You promise you won't tell?'

'On my dog's life.' Sean made round eyes. 'And you know how much I love Alfie.'

I nodded. I looked at Lewis and took a breath. 'They were sexy magazines. With girls in.'

'Not only *girls*,' Lewis said. 'Old ladies. Remember *Readers' Wiv*—'

'*I told you to stop talking about* Readers' Wives*!' My mum* is a wife. *Lewis's mum* is a wife. *Mrs Vernal.*

I turned back to Sean. 'I took the magazines home because Finders Keepers. I'm going to sell them at the car boot sale to make money for the fair. For when I get to go. Because I *will* get to go.'

Lewis shook his head and kicked a stone in his path.

'Of course you will.' Sean nodded like I was the wisest person in the world. 'Can I, erm, see these magazines?'

'No.'

Sean leaned over when I was in English later. *Spoke to me,* in front of other people.

'How many magazines? And how much do you want for them?'

'Why do you want to know?'

'People are asking.'

'How do people know about the magazines?' I glanced round but Mr Kellett was on the other side of the room. '*Have you told people about them, Sean?*'

He shook his head.

*

Things were going topsy-turvy.

Sean was speaking to me in English and yet Richard Plant, the popular kid who moved here from Edinburgh and trains for Stoke City's youth team, walked through corridors alone. Everyone stuck their legs out extra-long to trip him in corridors now. Nino the Swiss kid was off the hook because England played Scotland in three days.

Now, when Richard Plant walked down the corridor, people wrinkled their noses and said, 'Can you smell Haggis?' or put their hands to their ears – 'Is that bagpipes?' Or, from the kids who couldn't be bothered with the effort of thinking, he got a shove in the back and 'Your team's shit, *aaah!*'

When Lewis and I walked out of the school gates that afternoon, Mum was waiting at the roundabout, leaning against the *Gail Larson, Driving Instructor* car.

I felt someone lean closer to my ear. A pretend cough. *'Gail!'*

I wished my mum wasn't a driving instructor. I wished that it wasn't seventeen-year-olds who learned to drive. I wished our school didn't have a sixth form.

That's a lot of wishes – but just one of those things would make my life better.

I usually pretend I haven't seen Mum. It's not great to admit to having a mum at the best of times, and it's worse when your mum's so much older than everyone else's.

But Selina Baker, the best girl in sixth form, was the one hurrying up to Mum's car today, so I decided to own my mum, for once.

I wandered over but Lewis hung back. Like I said, he's terrified of my mum.

'Hi.' Mum smiled at me, like she couldn't remember me screaming at her the night before. She was always happy to own me as her daughter – even though, in our school, that wasn't a good look for her. 'Selina, do you know my daughter, Fiona?'

'Hi, Fiona!' Selina was *beautiful,* close up. As beautiful as Kelly from Winchester. 'Nice to meet you. I love your mum. I've been *so* nervous about learning to drive since I got my provisional licence, but Gail is so patient!'

I looked at Mum. She kept smiling.

'My parents can't teach me at all,' Selina said, 'they get really frustrated. But your mum is so calm and so nice, and she never even raises her voice.'

Mum caught my eye. She kept smiling.

On the other side of the road, Lewis frowned.

I couldn't believe this. 'What about people who cut her up at roundabouts? People in BMWs? Does she not even shout at *them?*'

Mum's smile cracked. 'I'm very patient in a professional capacity.'

'We all love your mum,' Selina said. 'And she's funny. You're so lucky, Fiona.'

'Right.' I felt dazed. 'Bye.'

I headed over to Lewis.

'That conversation just got weirder and weirder,' he said.

I nodded.

I could hear Selina talking as we walked away. 'Oh. I can do the appointment next Saturday after all, Gail, if you've still got it? Shopping with my boyfriend's cancelled because all the lads from school want to go to some lame car boot sale all of a sudden.'

*

That made up my mind. I was never going to get a chance to get money for the fair like this again. This was my one shot. So on the way home, for research, I made Lewis go with me into Paper Rack, the newsagent's in the precinct.

When I say *precinct* I mean the bad, British kind – the square shopping area off the high street lined with shops. It has an off-licence, a Chinese takeaway and a tiny Co-op where everyone buys the things they forgot at the big shop. I don't mean *precinct*, like in an American cop show. No one here *ever* rolls over car bonnets with guns, shouting *freeze, punk!*, not here, outside our Co-op. We don't get that kind of good stuff in Monkford.

I walked past the pile of kids' bikes, piled up outside Paper Rack, and pushed open the door, Lewis following.

A bell rang above my head. I strode up to the counter and queued behind a bigger kid – one who'd taken off his jumper and tie, but was still, clearly, in school uniform. 'Two singles and a pack of Euro '96 please.'

The bald man in the stretched polo shirt didn't say anything. He reached behind the counter and got two cigarettes out of an open pack. He handed them over with a pack of stickers, and the kid pushed a fiver at him and hurried out of the shop.

I glanced at the magazines on the top shelf. They were all tucked behind each other, so you could only see a little bit of the title, a *Fi-* or *Ra-*. No boobs, just a tiny sliver of thigh or arm.

'They're so high,' I whispered, but Lewis wasn't looking. He was making serious faces, holding up two Euro '96 annuals, like he was deciding between them.

The bald man behind the counter peered at me. 'Yes?'

I panicked. 'I'll have' – I picked up a local paper – 'this, please.'

The man folded over a paper and gave it to me. I handed him the last of my change, furious with myself for panicking like Lewis. I was doing this research because I needed *more* money, not *less.*

'Something else?'

'I'm just looking.'

The man followed my gaze to the shelf with the magazines. He looked back at me.

'At my gentlemen's recreational magazines?'

'No. Though, now you mention them, what age' – I trailed my hand along the counter – 'do you have to be to buy those magazines?'

He stared at me. 'Eighteen.'

'And anyone can buy them? Boys and girls?'

'Yes,' he said finally.

'Great!' I gave a beaming smile. 'Thanks.' I waved my newspaper in goodbye and trotted out of the shop, Lewis slotting his annuals back hurriedly in the rack.

On the way out, he knocked a pack of crisps off the shelf with his rucksack. He put the pack back with hands as slippery as a squid in a bath.

Lewis and I stayed in the park for a while. When I got home, Mum was already back from her driving lesson. She was at the peninsula with the sewing machine out, making *another* pair of curtains.

'Good day?' Mum asked through the pins in her mouth.

I threw the newspaper I'd bought down next to her. 'Sweet.'

'Sweet?' Mum took the pins out of her mouth. 'Is that a new school saying?'

'No, I've always said it.' I felt my face going red. *Sweet* was a new school saying.

She looked at the paper. 'Was that put through the door?'

'No, I bought it.'

Mum gave me a funny look. She watched me as I got five digestives from the biscuit barrel *to keep the wolf from the door.*

'It's fine. I'm not on a diet yet,' I said, leaving the room.

After a moment, Mum shouted, 'Yet?'

I was nearly at the top of the stairs, so I didn't reply. I didn't know how to, anyway. I wasn't sure of the rules when girls have to go on diets – whether it's something you get to decide yourself or if you get instructions at school. Or a letter through the post. *Skimmed milk. It's time.*

I sat on my bed, eating, realising I was making crumbs. I was about to shake the duvet off but I got distracted. By a brilliant idea.

Yesterday, Mum said *When you're an adult, living an adult life, you can choose to go to the fair yourself.*

And today, when I threw that accidentally bought newspaper down, she looked at me like I'd confused her. Like she saw me in a different light.

So maybe there *was* something I could do to change Mum's mind about the fair, after all?

At the idea, the tips of my fingers and toes went light and fizzy. I put the last biscuit in my mouth in one go, and reached for my book of lists.

<u>Things I Can Do to Make Mum and Dad Think I'm More Grown Up</u>

1. Let them see me reading the newspaper
2. Put my dirty clothes in the washing basket every time

3. Use more long words
4. Get new friends. Better friends, older ones.
5. Take drugs
6. Get some condoms and leave them round my room
7. Get flashed at
8. Ask to listen to the news in the car
9. Change a lightbulb without being asked
10. Wear my glasses all the time, not just for distance stuff
11. Ask to watch a foreign film, with subtitles
12. Get a new name
13. Get pregnant
14. Get a job. Not a paper round. A grown-up job, like a police person or nurse
15. Act interested in *Gardeners' World* – and snooker

6

**A good spy always carries a notebook, in case he needs
to pass on a secret message.**
The Junior Spy's Secret Handbook™

Thirty-six days till the fair
School news!

Mademoiselle Brun, the student language teacher that all
the lads fancy – her real name's Miss Brown – brought in a
special French meal for her Year Ten class. Baguettes, smelly
cheese, tablecloths. And there was a massive food fight!

Massive. Brie in hair and shredded baguettes down jumpers. Quiche on the walls! By the end, the carpet was covered
in bits, like the bottom of a hamster cage.

Mrs Parton, the stern old lady French teacher, came in to
see what the trouble was, and Mademoiselle Brun told her
in a wavy voice that she had the situation all under control.
Behind her, a clump of pâté fell down a 3D display of the
Eiffel Tower.

Mrs Parton shouted at everyone and dragged three cheese-
covered kids to the New Head. Then the bell rang and all
the kids ran out, leaving Mademoiselle Brun to clean up the
mess.

And when someone saw Mademoiselle Brun in the corridor later, she'd been *crying*.

And there was more school news! School news about *me*!

Kids stopped and whispered now as I walked down the corridors. Normally, I jumped over the feet of the bigger kids who lined the benches at the side of the corridors and tried to trip people. But no one stuck their legs out as I walked past. Not that breaktime.

One older boy with an undercut stopped me. 'Fiona Larson?'

'Yes?' I said carefully.

'I'll give you a fiver for the lot.'

'If you want them, be at the car boot sale.' I might have tossed my hair. 'A week on Saturday, Festival field, two p.m. Look for the blue car that says *Gail Larson, Driving Instructor*. You know the one.'

And I walked away.

I'll be honest – I hadn't wanted to tell Sean about the magazines. But now I had, it felt pretty good.

I was feeling so good that I didn't even tell Sean off for blabbing when he sat with us in the computer room that lunchtime.

We sat in a line in front of the computers, playing Ninja Combat (Sean), Rhino Rampage (Lewis) and Park Ranger (me), but I wasn't concentrating.

'I've decided.' I spun my chair round to face the boys. 'I need Mum and Dad to think I'm more grown up. Then they'll let me go to the fair.'

Lewis pushed his chair away from his game. He pulled a can of drink out of his bag. 'Your parents know how old you are though.'

He opened the ring pull and drink splattered on him.

Sean and I both laughed. Lewis shook his shirt out, sending drips onto the floor.

'Jizzed on yourself,' Sean said.

'So childish. And it's called *premature ejaculation*.' I took my book of lists to the other side of the computer room and opened the book to look at my list from the night before.

'What are you doing? Homework?'

'No, Sean!'

He ripped the book off me anyway.

Lewis let his rhino die and peered over Sean's shoulder, both reading.

I felt my face flush. 'Not all the ideas are good ones. It's an early list.'

'Get new friends,' Lewis said. 'You mean rather than us?'

'Not *rather* than you,' I said. '*As well* as you.'

'Get pregnant?' Sean said. 'Who's going to want to get you pregnant?'

I snatched my book back. 'I knew I shouldn't let you see this. I knew you weren't mature enough.'

'Your parents are never going to think you're older,' Lewis said quietly. 'Whether you're wearing your glasses or not.'

I scratched the back of my neck and looked at my list again.

I underlined *14. Get a job. Not a paper round. A grown-up job, like a police person or nurse.* Then I underlined *12. Get a new name.*

I turned to Lewis and Sean. 'From now on, you have to call me *Fi*.' I paused. 'That's what other people call me. People from other schools.'

I waited for them to catch me out, but Lewis just shrugged. Sean said, 'OK.'

Lewis was watching me.

'What?'

'Are you going to put your glasses on now or later?'

After school, Mum made me go to the Co-op but, for once, I didn't mind. The Co-op had a pinboard for lost cats and step classes – and adverts for grown-up jobs.

I walked with Mum and her big shopping bag down the road.

'You've got your inhaler?' Mum asked.

'Yep. I should really have stayed at home. All this is going to change when I'm twelve.' I waved my arms to show *all this*. 'When you're twelve, you're allowed to be home alone.'

'We'll talk about it then.'

We reached the precinct. I got a trolley from the nest and pushed it through the Co-op doorway. I waited till Mum was in the fresh food aisle, choosing vegetables, then snuck over to the pinboard.

I glanced past the cards for coffee mornings and lost cats.

Babysitting Opportunity. *Two evenings per week. Two well-behaved primary-age children and one small dog. Requires . . .*

Kid's job.

Paper Rounds *available for motivated, responsible teenagers. Enquire at Paper Rack. Applicants need to be early risers, reliable . . .*

Kid's job. And with the Paper Rack man? *No way.*

I looked up, to check I was safe. Mum was heading over to a kid in a Co-op uniform, stacking baskets of oranges. I recognised the kid from school.

'Excuse me,' Mum said.

I glanced at the next advert.

Hairdressing Assistant required. *Must be presentable with good customer service skills and . . .*

A girls' job, but it couldn't be helped.

I got out my spy notebook and wrote down the details. I hurried back to Mum and grabbed the trolley handle again, like I'd never been gone.

'Like I said, we do *usually* have cherries.' The kid stacking oranges noticed me and blinked. 'Are you Fiona Larson from Year Seven?' He glanced at Mum and back. 'Have you got a sec?'

I gave the boy *not now* eyes. I turned hurriedly to Mum. 'Shall I tell you about my day? Do you know blood makes up seven per cent of the weight of the human body?'

But, out of nowhere, Mum jammed her hands on the trolley and swerved into the fridge aisle.

I skittered along after her, still holding the trolley. *Surely she couldn't have worked out about the magazines from . . .*

Mum leaned down. She kept her face there, too close to mine. 'So what did you learn at school today?'

'I was just telling you. Seven per cent of the human body weight is blood.'

'Seven per cent? Wow! So heavy! And what's in blood, is it plasma? Tell me about—'

'Hi, Gail.'

Mum raised herself to an upright position.

A man with a ponytail stood in her path, a half-smile on his face.

'Hi.' Mum got her house keys out of her bag. 'We're in a bit of a hurry, I'm afraid.'

The man's basket held a four-pack of lager and some chewing gum. 'It's been a long time.'

She gave a tiny nod. 'I thought you'd moved to Bristol.'

'My mother died a couple of weeks ago.'

The hard line of Mum's mouth didn't change.

'I'm not back properly, just living in the house while I sell it.'

'Right.' Mum put her hand on my shoulder. 'We need to go. I think I've left the iron on.'

A piece of hair fell out of her clip and into her mouth. She pulled the hair away roughly as she turned to me. 'Just leave the trolley.'

We hurried out of the shop.

'You were rude to that ponytail man, Mum,' I said. 'You didn't say you were sorry his mother died.'

'I just didn't feel like talking.'

I looked behind me. The man was outside the shop now, smoking a cigarette. He smoked quickly, barely finishing one puff before starting the next.

'Don't you like him?'

Mum adjusted her clip. 'Not really.'

I looked behind again, but the man had gone. 'Why, what's he done?'

'Nothing.' She took a deep breath. 'He's strange. That's all. Now, tell me again – what was that you were saying about blood?'

Mum asked about my blood project all the way home.

And it turned out she hadn't left the iron on – it was still in the cupboard! When I pointed that out, she hit herself on the forehead and said, 'Aren't I the prize numpty?' and we both laughed at her silliness.

Adult Sayings

1) Keep the wolf from the door
2) SHIT THE BED!
3) Nobody expects the Spanish Inquisition
4) Single supplements
5) A preposition shows relation, like on the bridge or at the station*

*I saw this saying on a wall at school, but no kid would ever say this, so I'm calling it an adult saying.

Adult Words

1) Paradox
2) Catalyst
3) Provisional
4) Antidisestablishmentarianism
5) Secondment
6) Foreplay
7) Clitoris
8) Premature
9) Ejaculation
10) Asterisk

7

The Scottish kids should hope England beat Scotland tomorrow.
(paradox)

Thirty-five days till the fair
I waved to Lewis and Sean as I walked towards the lamp-post, bouncing a little as I walked. It was getting warmer so I didn't have a coat with me, which made everything feel lighter. I actually had a plan to get to the fair now, a sweet, *sweet* plan – and now the sky had decided to cheer up too and stop raining.

We all turned to walk towards school. Lewis stepped to cross the road and—

'See, you're doing it again!' Sean's face was bright, like he'd caught us out. 'Crossing in the same place! Like robots!'

I looked at Lewis. We gave each other little *oops* smiles.

'And look,' Sean said, pointing. 'There's a man in the house you never walk past.'

I turned towards the house, 56 George Street. There was usually an old lady behind the net curtains, sitting on the sofa at all times of day, but she wasn't there now. Instead, there was a shape right behind the netting. A man, looking out.

'Do you think he's looking at us?' I asked.

'Definitely,' Sean said.

'Maybe because we're staring at his house?' Lewis said.

The man hadn't moved from the window. It was like a Mexican stand-off, but with no guns.

I felt a shiver of something both good and bad up my spine. 'Do you think he's a flasher?'

Lewis snorted. 'You and your flashers.'

'And you have your mercenaries. We all have our things, Lewis.'

It's not that I *want* to be flashed, exactly – it's just something that happens to the older girls. It happened to Selina Baker in the cut-through down the side of the newsagent's. Selina had to cancel her driving lesson so she could look at photos of flashers at the police station, on what sounded like the best day ever.

'I wonder if it's *him* back?' Sean spoke thoughtfully, like he was holding a conversation with himself, but I knew it was an act. His words were definitely for us. 'I know why your mum doesn't walk in front of that house, Fi – I remembered. My dad told me once what happened at number fifty-six.'

Lewis and I glanced at each other. We both knew something big was coming.

Sean put his hands on his hips. 'That's the axeman's house. A man went mad there and cut all his brothers' heads off once. On Halloween.'

My neck went colder. 'That can't be true.'

'You wouldn't have only just remembered that now,' Lewis said.

'The man must be due out of prison around now. He'll be back to get revenge on the village for grassing him up.'

I stared at the man in the window. 'Shut up.'

'How many brothers' heads?' Lewis asked.

'After the man cut off their heads, he cut up their bodies in the shed. He buried bits of his brothers all around the village.'

'That's not true,' I said.

'My uncle Neil found a foot in the fresh food aisle at the Co-op.'

'Now that's *definitely* not true,' I said.

'The foot was in with the bananas,' Sean said. 'Still wearing a flipflop.'

The three of us stood there, staring.

'Shall we go and ring the doorbell?' Sean said.

'NO!' Lewis had never sounded surer. 'You're so stupid, Sean!'

Lewis started walking towards school, his arms pumping. After taking one last look at the house, Sean and I followed.

Thing is, you can know something isn't true and still be a little bit scared.

I was starting to wish we met at a different lamppost.

I forgot about Sean's axeman story as the day went on. The school corridors were buzzing with football talk, and things were getting worse for the Scottish kids. Even Lewis, who usually piped up 'I'm one-eighth Scottish' whenever he could, was very quiet now about his great-granddad from Aberdeen.

It made me worry about my grandma up in Glasgow. An English person, all alone.

Grandma moved to Glasgow before I was born, to live with Kenneth, her old boyfriend from school. She hadn't seen him in forty years, but he sent her a letter after Grandpa John died. And now she's married to Kenneth. And that's fine because the first time Grandma was with Kenneth, she hadn't met Granddad John. And the second time, Grandad John was dead.

So no one minded. It was all fine.

I just hoped Grandma was OK in Glasgow.

The next day was Saturday and I spent the morning on my bed, working on my letter.

Dear British Hairways,
   I am Fiona Larson and I would like the job of Hairdressing Assistant you advertised. Please. I am young and quite small but mature for my age. I am. . .

I looked at my scribbled notes.

presentable with good customer service skills. I—

'*Gail!*' Dad shouted from the lounge. 'There's been a bomb! In Manchester!'

'Oh my God!' Mum's footsteps thundered down the stairs.

I grabbed my glasses and hurried after her.

On the TV, a reporter with a microphone stood in front of a row of police vans, lights flashing. Mum, Dad and I sat in a line on the sofa and stared.

'*The nearest estimates are several hundred injured. The number of dead and seriously injured yet to be confirmed, but sources expect it to be in double figures.*'

Behind the reporter, I could see an empty city street with blackened buildings. Police tape shivered in the wind. Dad had the teletext subtitles on.

'Are the bombers still around?' I asked.

'They will have left quick-smart,' Mum said quickly.

'The device was believed to be in a lorry parked on Corporation Street, outside Marks and Spencer's.'

Mum clucked her tongue against her teeth. 'Marks and Spencer's.'

'A warning with an IRA code word was phoned in to Granada Studios ninety minutes before. A hundred thousand were evacuated.'

'Why send a warning?' I asked. 'If they wanted to hurt people?'

Mum did a flapping thing, like a pigeon about to take off. 'Please.' She dropped her hands into her lap. 'I can't believe it's happened. *Here*. I want to cry.'

I looked at the clock. It was only two hours till England versus Scotland.

I shook Dad's arm so he was looking at me. 'Is the football going to be cancelled?'

At first, neither of my parents reacted.

Mum sat up straighter. 'Is it?'

Dad grabbed the remote.

Mum hunched forward to the front of the sofa. 'I mean, they don't think anyone's been *killed*.'

Dad booted up Teletext and jabbed numbers into the remote.

Mum flapped her hands at Dad, all pigeon again. 'Hurry up!'

'Page four of seven, Gail, *page four of seven!*'

Mum tried to grab the remote but Dad lurched his hand away.

'And we've just received notification from the FA that the match at three p.m. is still going ahead. I'll repeat that,

England versus Scotland at Wembley is still going ahead.'

The subtitles on the screen flashed up, *'ENGLAND SCOTLAND FOOTBALL STILL ON'.*

Mum sat back. 'I mean, it would have been fine if they'd cancelled it, of course.'

Dad nodded. 'Of course.'

We watched some more news. We even ate our lunch in front of the telly, listening to the presenter in the studio.

'And England v Scotland is still on. I will say that again for anyone who missed it: the football is still on.'

I adjusted my glasses. It was strange to be able to see this well. 'When will the police solve the mystery? They'll catch the criminals, right?'

'Oh.' Mum looked at Dad. 'Probably soon, Fiona. Don't be scared. As soon as we know what's happened and the bad people are caught, it will all be OK.'

We watched the news until the football came on. The news never changed, it was just the same reporters in front of the same wrecked black buildings and wind-rippled police tape; the same reporters saying the same thing, again and again.

I'd shown I was interested in the news, but it was wasted. It didn't make me look grown up at all. Every kid, everywhere, would be watching the news that day.

And the whole time, neither of my parents said anything about my glasses.

An hour later, still on the sofa, I watched the footballers run and spit.

I fidgeted. Who knew a day of telly could be this long?

The commentator kept his voice at all one level. *'Gary*

Neville there, protecting his keeper with a run from right-back position.'

'Position.' I sat up straighter. 'Like *preposition.'*

Mum glanced over and back at the telly.

I took a deep breath. 'A preposition shows relation, like on the bridge or at the station.'

'Nice block,' Dad said.

Mum nodded.

'Neville jogging back there, he knows he's done his job and done it well.'

I made my voice louder. 'A preposition shows relation, like on the bridge or at the station.'

Mum turned slowly to face me.

'What did she say?' Dad asked.

There was a pause.

'I'm not exactly sure.'

On screen, a whistle blew.

Mum yanked her head to look.

I pushed my lips together and glanced at the screen. A Scotland player jerked his hands angrily, shouting at one of the England players.

Mum and I both turned to look at Dad. Waiting.

Dad made a big drama of rolling his eyes. 'He said *you're an effing diving effing cheating mother-effer.'*

But even *that* didn't cheer me up. 'I'm going upstairs.'

Mum bounced forward on the sofa. 'Have fun.'

I walked upstairs slowly, trailing my hand along the wall. I bumped it over each door frame, one by one.

I stopped at the closed door where there used to be a tile sign with a yellow flower under the words *Danielle's room.* Dad chiselled the sign off when I was in primary school.

I stared at the closed door for a second. I hurried back to my own room and sat on the bed.

The shouts from downstairs were getting louder. There was a muffled banging of hands on sofa arms.

'YES, SHEARER, YES!' Mum.

'GET IN, MY SON!' Dad.

I was thinking hard.

Mum had said, *as soon as we know what's happened and the bad people are caught, it will all be OK.*

She wasn't talking about the fair, of course. She was talking about the bomb. But still . . .

I took my glasses off and folded in the arms.

The idea was *perfect.*

As well as showing my parents I was grown up enough to be trusted, I could prove that what happened to Danielle at the fair would never happen to me.

And that meant – *solving the mystery!*

I looked at my bookshelf, past Grandma's long-legged wrong owl.

I tapped *The Junior Spy's Secret Handbook*™ gently, like I was saying *good girl* to a pet, then reached past it to my book of lists.

How to Investigate How Danielle Died

1) Ask the police
2) Ask *Crimewatch*
3) Ask the local paper
4) Ask Mum and Dad*
5) Ask someone else to ask Mum and Dad**
6) Ask Grandma
7) Ask Mrs Carpenter next door
8) Ask anyone and everyone else
9) Eavesdrop on people
10) Look for clues in Danielle's bedroom.

*carefully
**better

8

Dead people still have bedrooms.
(paradox)

Thirty-three days to the fair
The next morning, I wrote a letter.

> Dear Monkford and District Advertiser,
>   Please can you send me a copy of your newspaper that
> covers the night of 24 July 1982.
>   I can pay.
>   If you can't send me a newspaper, can you tell me the
> name and address of the reporter who covered news and
> fairs in 1982.
>   Thank you,
>   Fiona Larson

I'd only been to Danielle's grave once, before Mum and
Dad decided *it wasn't helpful*. But I remembered her death
day, because it was carved in gold on the sticking-up
stone. Right above *God takes the best of us and keeps them to
himself.*
    I took two envelopes and stamps from the Cupboard of

69

Office Things. I enveloped up the letter, along with the letter I'd written to British Hairways.

And I ran to the postbox, as fast as I could. I pushed the letters into the slot and felt a fizzle up my spine.

No going back now.

My investigations had started.

And now I knew I'd *definitely* need money for the fair, I decided the next thing to do was to start planning for the car boot sale. I ripped out a page from a plain notebook and wrote in my best handwriting:

Available Magazines

Mayfair, *June 1996*
Razzle, *May 1996*
Fiesta, *June 1996...*

I didn't put any prices on. I didn't know what to write.

I wrote the same list out nine more times in my best handwriting, ready to hand out to customers at the car boot sale. When I'd finished writing, I put my leaflets and magazines in a cardboard box, and dug out old ponies and bears from my wardrobe. I threw them on top of the magazines, as decoys.

In the back of my wardrobe, I saw Sprinkles. I paused. She was my old favourite pony – from back when I thought it was OK to have a favourite pony.

I picked her up and turned her over in my hand. Remembering how I used to make her canter over the lawn while I whispered what a good horse she was. How Dad peeled carrots for me to leave for her on the bedside table.

How weird I felt about that now. How the thought made me want to kick Sprinkles down the stairs.

I shoved Sprinkles in the box, under the other toys, so I couldn't see her anymore.

Later, I read the Sunday paper at the peninsula. Mum sat next to me, sewing curtains on her machine. Across the kitchen, Dad chopped vegetables for tea.

I turned the pages as loudly as I could.

It took ages. Turns out there's *a lot* of news in a newspaper. And it takes even longer to read if you're making notes.

Grown-up Topics

1. The Manchester bomb
2. The IRA
3. How Paul Gascoigne is a mercurial player
4. The new constitution in Ukraine
5. The elections in Turkey
6. The situation in Bosnia
7. Bin collections
8. The chancellor Kenneth Clarke's upcoming Rolls Royce budget and the predicted economic growth of 2.5 per cent in 1996

Look Up

1. Tremble Trigger
2. Ammonium Nitrate
3. Criminal Injuries Compensation Authority
4. Republican
5. Masonry

6. Callous
7. Mercurial
8. Constitution
9. Chancellor

After what felt like *hours*, I closed my list book and turned the newspaper back to the front page.

People read that *every week*? Every *day*?

'The bomb's a lot to take in.' Dad glanced at Mum and back. 'Maybe best not to look in so much detail?'

Maybe I'd have better luck with Danielle's bedroom. 'I'm going upstairs.'

But then Dad came upstairs too and stood sorting out washing, so it wasn't safe to look. Then Mum said she wanted us all to have a nice tea and watch an old film that she thought I'd like. She wanted us to spend the evening together, as Dad was staying at Uncle Jim's the next night, for *a pool and pub and talking the hind legs off a donkey* session.

So I didn't get to sneak into Danielle's room that night. But the film was called *Caddyshack* and it turned out Mum was right. It had a dancing gopher in it, and it was actually pretty funny.

On Monday morning, I was up early before school. *Perfect.* I woke up at the sound of the door banging, as Dad went to do the post.

I went 0–60, just like that. Sleep. *Bam.* Wide awake.

Before I could get scared or think too much about what I was doing, I slipped into Danielle's room.

They've never said I'm not allowed to go in there. It's just I've never wanted to.

*

I put my arms around myself in a safety hug.

Danielle's room was so much bigger than mine. And so *pink*. As pink as a stationery set for girls.

Big, pink – and *cold*. And not because Danielle's ghost was haunting it. Mum had been really clear after I went in that one time – that the room was always cold because the radiator hadn't been switched on for fourteen years. Nothing to do with ghosts.

The room was faded. Even Danielle's few colour posters had the brightness sucked out, so they looked like posters from another century.

I felt a slow shiver trickle up my back.

Ghost or no ghost, it was like going into a cold pink time machine.

I'd better touch something soon, or I'd be too scared to do it, so I stepped across the room and made myself put my hands flat on Danielle's dressing table.

The table had old nail varnishes on it, the bottles dried up. Faded photos of Danielle and her friends lined the mirror, with thin scarves hanging down, scarves that – I knew from photographs – Danielle used to tie in her hair.

I caught my reflection in the mirror. I looked scared.

I shouldn't be in here.

On the shelf next to Danielle's bed sat a record player, a stack of records propped up against it. I leafed through the records.

Turned out Danielle *really* loved ABBA.

I opened Danielle's wardrobe and pulled out a *thing* on a hanger. An all in one shirt-thing, the trousers connected to the top.

73

No wonder Mum liked Danielle so much. That kid was so nice she even let Mum *make her clothes*.

I held the *thing* up against me, and the bottom of the legs draped on the floor.

I pushed it back into the wardrobe roughly. A bunch of unused hangers fell to the floor – a clattering of metal on wood.

NO!

There was a noise from across the landing. A rush of feet, and Mum burst into the room.

She stopped in the doorway, hand still on the door knob. She shut her eyes. 'Fiona.'

'I'm sorry.'

Mum put her thumb and first finger on her eyelids.

'I'm sorry,' I said again.

'Love.' Mum let her hand drop and opened her eyes. 'What are you doing in here?'

I thought I saw a dog run in.

I wanted to borrow a pen.

'I wanted to see if there was anything to sell for the car boot sale. I'm sorry, Mum. Don't be cross.'

Mum sank slowly onto the bed next to me. 'I'm not cross.'

'You are,' I mumbled.

'Danielle's stuff is really important to me.'

'I'll go, I'm sorry. I don't need anything to sell.'

Mum gave a big sigh. 'I know I'm being silly. It's just a room. Just – stuff.'

She patted the space next to her. I didn't want to, but I sat down on the heart-covered duvet. The bed creaked. *Dead girl's bed.*

'I'll have a think. Whether there's any of this stuff we don't need. I know your dad thinks . . .' She stopped talking and pushed hair out of her eyes. 'I'll look out for some stuff for you today.'

'You don't need to.'

'No.' Mum stared at the fluffy rug. 'I'll look today.'

And I didn't want to leave her there, but she made a shooing gesture. 'Close the door after you.'

9

The good spy practises to improve his craft, as the gifted musician practises with his instrument.
The Junior Spy's Secret Handbook™

Thirty-two days to the fair
I tried to distract myself from my new levels of Scar badness by telling Lewis my plans at the lamppost, and showing him *The Junior Spy's Secret Handbook™*.

Lewis took the handbook from me and I followed his gaze to the cover – to the picture of a man in a hat and long coat, peering at fingerprints through a magnifying glass.

'The book only has pictures of men and always says "he",' I said, 'but it doesn't say anywhere that I definitely *can't* be a spy. I promise I won't get kidnapped.'

'I'll do the practising bit.' Lewis handed the book back. 'I'll make invisible ink out of lemons and practise crawls with you, that's fine. I'll even sew a secret pocket. But spying on your parents or investigating how Danielle died? No *way*.'

I put *The Junior Spy's Secret Handbook™* away. 'But the whole point of practising is so you can be better at the *actual spying*!'

He made that stubborn face he does when I know he's going to ruin everything.

'OK,' I lied. 'We'll just do the spy practising.' I decided not to show him my latest list, after all.

How Did Danielle Die?

1) Fell off the big wheel
2) Fell out of a chair swing
3) Choked on candyfloss
4) Had a heart attack on the Waltzers
5) Got hit on the head with a whack-a-mole hammer – accidentally
6) Got hit on the head with a whack-a-mole hammer – deliberately
7) Fell through a funhouse mirror
8) Took a drug overdose
9) Got killed by a flasher
10) Got killed by a paedo
11) Got killed by a zombie
12) Got killed by someone who wasn't a flasher, a paedo, or a zombie

I know about paedos. They're the adults who tell you to sit on their knees when it's your birthday. They offer to tie your shoelaces and act interested in your day when – let's face it – adults have cars and go to nightclubs and can buy whatever they want – they're not *really* interested in kids' days. The only people who are really interested in kids' days are your mum and dad or grandma, the people who *have* to be interested – it's their *job*.

I put *drug overdose* on my list just to make Danielle seem

more interesting, but it definitely wouldn't be that. And I was pretty sure she wasn't killed by a zombie, either.

If there'd ever been a zombie at Monkford Fair, I'd have definitely heard.

Sean came round the corner and I rushed to zip up *The Junior Spy's Secret Handbook™* safely in my bag.

He bumped his shoulder into Lewis's in a friendly hello. He looked from me to Lewis. 'Did you see McAllister's face when he missed that penalty?' Sean put a hand to his forehead and made the *tosser* sign. 'Wanker!'

Me and Lewis both nodded hard.

'*What* a wanker,' Lewis said.

'Complete wanker,' I agreed. 'His face!'

I wondered whether to add *Gascoigne is such a mercurial player*, but thought – *not now*.

Sean had been hanging around us a lot more since everyone had heard about the magazines. At breaktime in the main corridor, a crush of kids came up to me and he made himself into a barrier. 'Come on, people.' He held his hands up like a lollipop lady. 'Let the girl through.'

And the crowd parted like I was ... well, like I was Kelly from Winchester herself.

There was no real school news that day, probably because there was so much news from outside of school. Liam said his dad knew the policeman who stopped the bomb (not true – the bomb *went off*) and Sean said his dad was one of the people who scooped up the arms, legs and heads and put them all in a big paramedic bucket (and because I'm a good friend to Sean, I didn't say his dad drives an ambulance in Stoke, not Manchester. Or point out – *heads? Nobody died*).

I don't think anyone talked about anything but the magazines, the bomb and football all day. Not even the teachers.

Though the teachers didn't talk about the magazines, of course. Which was a good thing.

Oh – and Richard Plant, the kid from Edinburgh, was off sick. Bad tummy, his mum said.

I don't think anyone, kids or teachers, was surprised.

Mr Kellett was late for our English lesson, of course.

'Quiet!' He ran in, his face a little red, his tie skew-whiff. 'Today, we've got a very important lesson. Settle down.'

He started writing on the board. As his shirt stretched, you could see a line of sweat down his back.

There were some mutterings from the class, bored already.

Mr Kellett made his face into a rock. 'I said *settle down.*'

He turned to write more. His back's big, with lots of muscles, because Mr Kellett does lots of boxing and used to be a semi-pro footballer and played for Altrincham Town. He's the one in our school who everyone knows would win if there was a teacher fight.

Dr Sharma would win if it was girls-only. Mr Kellett would win the overall.

'OK.' Mr Kellett stopped writing. 'Get your exercise books out. Today we're going to talk about. . .'

He stepped back and pointed at the board.

Gascoigne's genius volley, Seaman saving that penalty, and how England are DEFINITELY DEFINITELY GOING TO WIN EURO '96!

The class went wild. *Wild.* Kids jumped up, banged their desks, hooted like weird monkeys – and Mr Kellett just smiled.

It's things like this, why everyone likes him so much. Things like this, and how good he is at sports and fighting.

Sean ran across the room – 'He leaps like a salmon and ...' He did an impression of a footballer heading the ball, and Mr Kellett didn't even stop *that*.

Even I was enjoying the class a little bit.

At least, I was enjoying it until Mr Kellett said, '*And* are we going to annihilate the Netherlands tomorrow night?'

Everyone roared and Mr Kellett said, 'Now, who can tell me the meaning of *annihilate*?'

Kids started shouting words – '*destroy*', '*take down*', '*murder*', '*crush*'.

But not me.

Tomorrow night? Again?

I supposed it was good for Richard Plant, at least. And I didn't think we had any kids from the Netherlands in our school – though if we did, I'd soon find out.

And I supposed it gave me more time for spying round the house. It was useful to know one time I could be pretty sure that my upstairs-downstairs, jack-in-the-box parents wouldn't be getting up from the sofa.

The bell rang and everyone rushed out.

I went up to Mr Kellett with my book of lists, a finger wedged inside to mark the right page. 'Mr Kellett?'

'Fiona.' He beamed. 'Not your kind of lesson, eh?'

'No, I love football,' I said quickly. 'Did you see McAllister's face when he missed that penalty?'

'Ouch.' Mr Kellett smiled. 'Poor man. Must have smarted.'

'I was wondering, as you're good at words' – I opened my book to show him – 'if you could tell me about these?'

He looked at my list.

He glanced up. 'Mercurial?'

'Gascoigne,' I said.

'Constitution?'

'Of Ukraine.'

He seemed to be waiting, so I added, 'I've been reading the paper this weekend.'

Mr Kellett laughed like I'd said *I went on a spaceship.*

'OK' – he pulled up the chair next to me – 'well, far be it from me to discourage *that*. Let's concentrate on *mercurial* and *constitution* for now, and maybe leave *ammonium nitrate* and *tremble triggers* for another time.'

Mrs Vernal didn't want to talk about football, of course. *Two hundred hurt* was more her kind of thing.

'Shocking. And less than thirty miles from here!' Mrs Vernal put her hand on the scarf at her neck. 'You kids. I don't know how you can even take something like this in at your age. The *futility*.'

It's things like this that make me want to like football. I feel I'd fit better on Mr Kellett's team than Mrs Vernal's.

She shook her head slowly. There was a long pause. Around our drama circle, kids shifted in their seats.

'Should we talk about the footy instead?' Greeney asked.

'Hard as it is,' Mrs Vernal said, 'we need to acknowledge these things. In my classes, what matters is authenticity. Real life. And all the horrors that come with it. Because that is how we flower and grow.' Mrs Vernal looked around the circle of chairs. 'Does anyone have anything they want to share with the group?'

No one answered.

'Surely some of you have some feelings about what has happened?'

The room was quiet. Even the *hands-up, me-me-me-miss* kids weren't going to talk about a bomb. However much Mrs Vernal wanted us to.

Mrs Vernal could try to make us talk about it till she'd run out of voice ... but even the smart-arse kids couldn't know where to start with knowing what the right answer was about *a bomb*, could they?

School distracted me from thinking about Mum and how Scar-bad I'd been, going in Danielle's room that morning.

After school, I was in a good mood in the park, as Lewis and I practised different spy crawls from the handbook.

I watched Lewis attempt feline crawl, using the broken bit of fence round the tennis courts for cover.

'The book says don't drag your feet,' I said. 'And it's important you keep your head low. Stop bobbing.'

'I'm not bobbing.'

'You're bobbing *all the time*. It's like you've got a chicken's head.'

He got up and dusted his hands off. 'You try.'

I threw the handbook down. 'Seal crawl.' I made sure my whole body was on the ground and just moved my arms.

Pretty quickly, I got out of puff. 'It's all very well for the book to say *pull with your arms and use your toes and push down to move forward*,' I said, my hot breath coming back from the grass in my face, 'but they don't have skinny arms like me, do they? *And* my toes hurt.'

'I think you're doing fine,' Lewis said. 'You've moved a few metres now.'

I stretched over to grab *The Junior Spy's Secret Handbook™*, which still felt closer to me than it should. 'I'm going to practise flat feline crawl instead. You try too.' I looked at the handbook and threw it on the ground. 'You have to stay down, and crawl with one leg straight. *Always.*'

And Lewis and I stopped talking and concentrated on pulling one dead foot behind us, like soldiers in a war film.

Crawling a distance in a proper, professional crawl is harder than it looks. Like doing doggy paddle, but without water. Lewis and I were so busy trying to stop our heads bobbing, we nearly flat-feline-crawled right into each other.

'Ow!' When Lewis lifted his head, he had light in his eyes. 'Look at us! It's like Spy versus Spy!'

We burst into giggles and rolled over onto our backs. We laughed into the sun. My laugh was still a bit breathy from being puffed out.

'You got your inhaler?' Lewis asked.

'Always.' I rolled back over onto my front to get my breath back. 'But I'm fine.'

'This is enough fun, just practising,' Lewis said. 'We don't need to investigate Danielle. See?'

I nodded. It *was* fun. Maybe Lewis was right. I didn't need to do any actual spying.

I thought how sad Mum had looked when she found me in Danielle's room that morning.

'OK,' I said. 'We'll just practise.'

'You mean it?'

I got down on the ground and made front crawl arms. I lifted my head. 'I mean it.' I tried to seal crawl again, the bumpy grass pressing against my tummy. 'And I'm not even lying this time.'

*

When I let myself in through the back door afterwards, the house was silent.

Nearly silent. I could hear the soft sound of music upstairs.

I remembered Dad saying he was staying at Uncle Jim's tonight. 'Mum?'

No answer.

The music got louder as I moved through the kitchen into the lounge. A woman sang in a high, sad voice about a winner who was taking it all. And a loser who was somewhere, standing small.

I dropped my rucksack. I moved to the bottom of the stairs and leaned against the wall.

Invisible creepy crawlies marched across my neck.

The song faded out.

I was about to walk up the stairs when the piano started up again. *The same song.*

I stood there, uncertain, as the sad woman sang. About victory and destiny. About gods throwing dice and people playing aces and building fences. The woman's voice was pretty, but strange. She sang *loo-serr* rather than *loser.*

I looked down at my feet, the creepy crawlies back on my neck again.

Suddenly, I felt hot. Boiling, *boiling* hot.

I stamped upstairs. 'MUM!'

I burst into Danielle's bedroom.

Mum sat on the floor next to the record player, her legs tucked to the side. The room was a mess – books off shelves, records out of sleeves. There were clothes all over the bed. Mum even had one of Danielle's scarves tied in a bow on top of her head.

The sad woman was reaching the long bit of the chorus.

'the winner takes it a-ll-ll-ll'

Mum slowly raised her head to look at me. Lots of hair had fallen out of the scarf, into her face. She didn't even try to adjust it.

We stared at each other.

I looked at the glass next to Mum. At the big bottle that said Bells on it, next to the glass.

The room smelt of pub. 'Have you been here all day?'

Mum looked at the bottle and glass, like she'd only just noticed they were there. She looked back up at me, her eyes filling with tears. 'Fiona, I'm so sorry.'

I folded my arms. 'Are you drunk?'

The song finished again.

Mum lifted the lid of the record player. She moved the arm so that it was back on the start of the record.

She dropped the lid and the piano music started up. The sad woman sang about how she didn't want to talk.

I just stood there. Frozen. Shivery.

Mum jerked her head up. 'I'm sorry. I'm sorry, I'm sorry, I'm sorry. Don't tell your dad, Fiona. I'm so sorry.'

I couldn't look at her screwed-up, pleading eyes.

I looked away. 'Did you find anything for me, then?' My voice sounded tighter, stretched like an elastic band.

'Any what, darling?'

'You were in here to look for stuff for me. For the car boot sale.'

Mum reached up and out with her arms, like a baby wanting a hug.

I ran out of the room.

I stood in the hallway as the song finished. The piano of the song started up again.

I stood there for a second, wavering. Then I made a decision, hard.

Never mind what I'd decided earlier. I'd changed my mind – I would investigate Danielle's death after all. I'd go to the police station, first thing tomorrow.

And with Mum out of the way, there was something else I could do.

I took a pair of scissors to the peninsula and cut a slice from Mum's curtain fabric. I took the slice upstairs with a needle and thread, and went to work on my coat, making a secret pocket.

If Mum ever left Danielle's room, I was going to steal that record and sell it at the fair.

So Mum could never *ever* play it again.

10

People always say Monkford is a great place for kids to
grow up – but it's only ever adults who say it.
(paradox)

Thirty-one days to the fair
I didn't see Mum the next morning.

I didn't even try to speak to her when I got up. I just
got in my school uniform and went straight to the police
station.

I threw my rucksack on the floor and put my hands on the
counter. 'I'd like some information, please.'

The man in glasses behind the counter blinked.

When he didn't ask, I said, 'About a murder in 1982.' I
looked at my feet. 'Well. *Maybe* a murder, it's not clear. I'm
not sure how she died. That's part of the problem.'

The man looked at his colleague and back to me. 'How old
are you, darling?'

'Nearly twelve.'

He leaned forward and put his elbows on the counter.
'We're quite busy catching adult criminals here. Probably
best you head into school, eh, love?'

I shifted my weight from one foot to the other. I swallowed.

'You've not left yet, little one?' The man looked at his colleague again and back at me. 'There something else?'

I made myself say it. 'Have you got any jobs?'

When he just started laughing, I picked up my rucksack and hurried to school.

I wouldn't be correcting anyone if they called police *the filth* later.

And I wouldn't want a job with *the filth* anyway.

School news!

Turns out we do have a kid from the Netherlands; we just didn't realise for a while because her name's Zoe Peters and that doesn't sound very Dutch. But all the kids did loads of looking until we found one.

So that's good.

Except maybe for Zoe Peters.

And those people who say Monkford is a great place for kids to grow up? They've never been in the girls' toilets at our high school.

It was my mistake. I shouldn't have bought that can of Sprite at the shop next to the police station. And I shouldn't have sung to myself in the toilets, especially not the song the Little Mermaid sings as she brushes her hair with a fork. I don't even watch kids' films anymore – haven't for ages. I must have heard someone else singing that song, and if I knew who that was, I'd be *furious*.

Bang bang bang on my toilet door. 'Who's that singing?'

I stayed completely still.

'If you don't come out, we'll batter you.'

I peeked through the slit at the side of the cubicle. Three older girls stood around, all arms and boobs and hair. Bigger than me in every way. If I was the Little Mermaid, they were all Ursula the Sea Witch.

I unlocked the door. I burst through the cubicle door as quickly as I could, a tough cowboy in a saloon bar.

'I was singing by accident.' I put my hands on my hips and stared the tallest one in the eyes. 'No big deal.'

'You're the girl who has the magazines.'

I looked up at her without blinking. 'Yep.'

She stared back. 'And you're also the kid who shows her pants.'

'I'm *the kid with the magazines*,' I said.

'Ew, monkey bars. That's so dirty,' another sea witch said.

You do something *once,* for a reason you don't even re-member, and it stays with you for ever, like it's been written on all your school jumpers in permanent marker.

I made my voice strong. 'That was ages ago. In primary school.'

'Once a pants girl, always a pants girl.'

I strode towards the door. The three sea witches blocked me.

I folded my arms. 'Like I said, now I'm the girl with the magazines. Do you want me to tell my friends in Year Ten that you're picking on me? Do you want me to tell *Craig Parsons?*'

Craig Parsons was probably tall enough to buy his own magazines but, at the mention of the hardest kid in Year Eleven, the sea witches looked at each other.

I took that second to rush between them and out into the corridor.

'And they just let me go!' I said triumphantly to Lewis. 'I didn't get a Chinese burn or my head flushed or anything.'

We sat on the grass after school outside the second-biggest bush in the park, hunched over, concentrating. We were making spy kits out of matchboxes, our foreheads going sweaty in the sun.

'Everything's changed now.' I unfolded my matchbox's end sections. 'We're popular! If there was a school trip now, we could probably sit near the back of the bus. Three rows from the back, even.' I wrote *code flap* on each of the unfolded end sections in tiny writing. 'This is a bit fiddly.'

'At least you're not the one about to cut your fingers off.' Lewis sawed wobbily at two pushed-together pencils with his penknife. His job was making a short pencil for each of our spy boxes.

He stopped sawing and looked up, sunlight in his eyes. 'Did you see the section in the spy manual on teamwork? We can learn secret codes and write each other letters that only we would understand? In case they get intercepted.'

That was hope in his eyes, not sunlight. 'No way. That sounds more like mnemonics than spying to me.' I picked up a tiny piece of paper and wound it round a matchstick. 'So, are you going to help me sell the magazines at the car boot?'

'I'm not sure.' Lewis's penknife skittered off the pencils. He glanced up. 'Is . . . is your mum going to be there?'

I sniffed with laughter. But then I thought of my mum, on the floor, drunk and listening to that song, reaching up to me like a baby. I stopped sniffing.

I watched Lewis saw at the pencils. I picked up a piece of paper to wind round my matchstick. It seemed to make the paper take up *more* space, not less – but I supposed the people at *The Junior Spy's Secret Handbook*™ knew what they were doing. 'I know they say matchboxes are great because they're a common household item.' I wound the paper some more. 'But I still think there are going to be questions asked if people see kids carrying round matchboxes.'

'We'll keep them in our secret pockets though,' Lewis said. 'So it'll be OK.'

'And the problem with the secret pockets,' I said, 'is it's only been a day, and already five people have said, "*Aren't you hot in that coat, Fiona?*"'

Lewis didn't answer.

I looked up. 'What's wrong?'

'It's the football tonight.' Lewis sawed at the pencils. 'I just can't wait for this stupid championship to be over.'

I made *sad fish mouth* at Lewis. Lewis's dad would be getting him to watch the football, trying to make him like it. And Lewis would keep having to jump up and celebrate and say stuff like *Did you see McAllister's face when he missed that penalty? Aaah,* or his dad would give him little punches on the arm and say *Buck up, son, don't be such a girl.*

Lewis concentrated. 'I think ... nearly there ...'

There was a crunching as the pencils broke. We whooped. Lewis's penknife skidded into his leg, but it was fine, it stopped at his trousers.

Lewis helped me with winding paper onto matchsticks, and I thought some more about Lewis's dad.

There are some days I'd prefer other kids' parents. Like Sean's mum, who lets him stay up to watch *Crimewatch*. Or Candy's parents, who let her have a telly in her bedroom and have pancakes when it wasn't pancake day. Or even Greeney's parents, who – I hear – let you eat sweets right before your tea *and* have a ride-on lawn mower.

And Lewis's mum is OK, though she only buys brown bread and won't buy biscuits with chocolate on. But I *definitely* wouldn't want Lewis's dad. My parents might have flashing doorbell lights, drive a car with our name down the side and keep our house's second-biggest bedroom for a dead girl – but they never *made* me watch the football or punched me on the arm all day and called it a joke and said I acted *like a little girl.*

I picked up *The Junior Spy's Secret Handbook™*. 'We need to find hollow twigs next. For putting secret messages in.'

Lewis waved at someone. I looked up.

Sean wandered towards us, his hands in his pockets, kicking every stone he could see as he walked.

He stood over us and looked at our equipment, all laid out. 'What are you doing?'

'Making spy kits,' I said. 'To keep in our secret pockets.'

Sean bumped down onto the grass and stuck his legs out. 'Secret pockets?'

I flapped open my coat to show him.

Sean looked at Lewis. 'Show me yours.'

'I haven't made mine yet,' Lewis said.

'It's a great idea, though.' Sean lay down and folded one foot over the other. 'Hey, Fi, you can keep all your money from the car boot sale in that pocket, can't you? You're going to be loaded.'

I watched Sean jiggle his body on the grass, making himself comfortable, and smiled. Never mind Mum. Life was *good.*

Sean blew his fringe out of his eyes and closed them. 'So this is where you two go when I'm not around, hey? It's a good spot.'

I glanced at Lewis nervously. We hadn't told anyone where we'd found the magazines. We thought it was safer that way. In case the owner with his angry face and veiny Popeye arms came back.

'Now.' I stood up and dusted my skirt off. 'There have to be hollow twigs round here somewhere.'

I came back from school to find Mum at the kettle.

I threw my rucksack down. 'Hi.'

Mum gave me a big smile. 'Do you want a cup of tea?'

I shook my head. I never want a cup of tea, and she knows that.

'Your father's back from seeing Uncle Jim.' She turned back to the kettle. Her movements were jerky as she stirred the teabag. 'They had a good time drinking and whatnot. Dad has a sore head today. He's out at the shops now.'

I didn't say anything.

She put the spoon on the counter with a *ching*. 'I'm sorry about yesterday. I wasn't myself.' She made her voice lighter. 'But don't tell your father, hey? We don't want to ruin the nice night he had with Uncle Jim. Or ruin the match. He's really looking forward to watching England on telly tonight.'

I still didn't say anything.

She kept her back to me, still facing the kettle. 'I'm really sorry, Fiona.' So quiet, I could hardly hear. 'It won't happen again.'

She put her hands flat on the countertop and waited.

'OK.' I slid off the stool. 'I'm going upstairs.'

I walked into the lounge, trying to work out if this was a good kind of secret to have or the bad kind. Either way, if Dad was out and Mum was in the kitchen, it was a good time to steal another stamp and envelope from the Cupboard of Office Things.

So I peeled off the last stamp in the book and carried it upstairs carefully on my finger. I sat on my bed and wrote a letter to the police asking about Danielle, making sure I used my best grown-up writing.

And hoping – really hoping – that if it was the man with the glasses who opened the post at the police station, he wouldn't be able to tell that the letter was from me.

II

While you're shadowing your quarry, remember –
enemy spies might be shadowing you too! A good
spy stays vigilant, and has tricks up their sleeve
to shake off a tail.

The Junior Spy's Secret Handbook™

Twenty-seven days to the fair

Summer was starting to feel like proper summer now. It was shiny-pavement hot. Ice-lollies-not-just-as-a-pudding hot. No one was wearing their jumpers to school anymore, and some kids even wore short-sleeved shirts. Not the good kids though, I don't know why – but I noticed, so I made sure I didn't wear short sleeves either.

England beat the Netherlands 4–1, so there was no decent school news because that was all anyone talked about. England had made the quarter finals and the next game was on Saturday, against Spain.

Another game.

I really hoped England started losing soon.

Speaking of losing – Richard Plant came back in, three days after the England–Scotland game. I saw him walking round the playing fields at lunchtime on his own, so things weren't back to normal for him yet.

And not for me, either. I walked through the corridors, my head held higher than it had ever been, and older kids spoke to me.

'All right, Fiona.'

'Great to see you, Fi.'

'Nice coat. Good toggles.'

And I'd answer with a smile.

'Hi!'

'Thank you.'

'Looking good yourself.'

It wasn't quite so good for Lewis, as no one knew his name. But, still, he got to walk next to me, so no one tried to trip him up in the corridors all week.

It was official. The magazines had changed my life – for ever.

Finally, the day was here.

Dad parked up on Festival Field, the place alive with cars and boxes, and the buzz of conversations and laughter. Camping tables were piled high with cooking dishes and ashtrays, alarm clocks and electric whisks. There were people *everywhere*.

I must have been really distracted because when Dad reached for two folding camping tables in the boot, he said. 'You're thoughtful today.'

I unfolded the legs of the other table.

'Aren't you hot in that coat?'

'I'm fine.'

Neither me nor Mum had told him about Mum playing records in Danielle's room when he was at Uncle Jim's. But then, Dad had asked me to phone a premium rate number to apply for a quiz show earlier that week. And neither of us told Mum.

I think that's just how families work.

I placed my cardboard box on the camping table and opened it. Under the toys, I could just make out a bit of blonde hair and the *e* of *Razzle*.

My heart beat loud in my ears. I was really going to do this.

I started pulling out the ponies and bears from my box, sitting the bears upright. I made their bodies lean forward and their feet stick out, like fat babies.

Dad opened his box to reveal plates and napkins from my other dead grandma's old house. I spotted our old kitchen lampshade. Mum's sewing patterns.

'You can have that other table for your stuff,' Dad said.

'Good,' I said.

'Let me know if you need any help with pricing. Or closing a deal.'

I nodded and laid my things out. The ponies. The bears. I felt my face going red that I'd ever played with this kids' stuff. I reached for Sprinkles and held her for a second, before making myself put her on the table with the others.

I pulled out the leaflets I'd made, listing all the magazines. I tucked the lists under a bear and left the magazines in the box. I folded the box's flaps in and slid it under my table.

'I'm gonna teach you to sell, Fiona. Watch and learn.' Dad puffed himself up as he looked out over the field. 'We don't put the price on the items in writing, so we can start high and adjust with the market.' He waved his hand over his table. 'We don't want to let the good stuff go too soon, too cheap. We listen to offers, and we set a good price.'

A woman came over. 'How much for the knitting patterns?'

Dad looked at her for a moment. 'Fifty pence each, or three for one pound twenty.'

The woman looked through the patterns and bought three.

Dad put the coins into his bumbag and zipped it up. He winked at me. 'How good's your dad at selling?'

'You are.'

'A proper barrow boy!'

I didn't know what that meant, except that Dad was proud of himself.

I thought I saw Dr Sharma walking down between the cars on the next aisle.

'Dr Sharma!' I did a big wave, windmilling both my arms. '*Dr Sharma!*'

But it couldn't have been Dr Sharma because the woman turned straight round and walked in the other direction.

Dad started chatting to the man at the table next to him. The man was dusting off a beige electric fan that was so old, it must have been from the war or something.

A woman pointed at my bears. She had a young kid trailing off her arm. 'How much for these?'

I leaned on my homemade leaflets, covering them with my hand. 'Fifty pence each,' I said. 'Or three for a pound.'

I looked up to share a secret smile, but Dad was still chatting to the beige fan man, his hands shoved in his jeans pockets like he was Del Boy, his thumbs fluttering against the denim.

The woman scooped up two bears – *and Sprinkles.*

I didn't have time to think about kids' stuff now, not with magazines to sell. So I let her drop the pound coin into my hand and put it carefully into my secret pocket. I watched the woman walked away. Trying not to feel anything.

It was fine. It was all fine.

Dad took a few steps away from our camping table, still talking to the fan man. 'What kind of auction?'

'*General household goods auctions*, they're called.' The man folded his arms. 'Dead people's stuff. I guarantee, you get the best gardening tools at dead house auctions.'

'Really?' Dad picked up a pair of secateurs and started squeezing them, testing the spring.

Now.

I grabbed my magazines from the box. I put them at the end of my table, furthest from Dad's. I arranged bears and ponies and jigsaws over them hurriedly.

Dad put the secateurs down. 'Well, I've learned something today.' He turned away from the fan man, smiling.

I looked around. Some boys from school were starting to gather at nearby stalls, looking carefully at plates and coat hangers.

A Year Ten kid came up to my table, his centre-parted hair sticking in two directions like a washing-up brush. 'Hi, Fi.'

I checked Dad was looking in the other direction. I snuck him a leaflet.

Dean Prince, who plays for Port Vale under sixteens, trailed his finger across my camping table. 'All right, Fi-oh.'

He swiped a leaflet and was gone.

One kid with baggy skater clothes picked up a pony and turned it over, like he was studying the quality. 'How are you doing, Fi?'

Dad looked over at that point. I waited until he was looking the other way, before nodding to the boy to take a leaflet.

'You need to share those leaflets,' I said, so all the boys could hear. 'I'm selling each *pony or jigsaw* at 1 p.m. Though I will listen to offers before then.'

99

The boys at the table melted back into groups, huddled and muttering. The boy with the washing-up hair had his arms round some other boys, talking and focused, like they were a sports team before a big match.

'I didn't think you knew so many people!' Dad turned to me. 'But Fi, don't get your hopes up. I know I said we should aim high, and listen to offers, but I don't think you should expect to get too much for your ponies.'

I nodded. I kept my gaze on the buzzing crowd.

Dad tapped me on the back. 'Mind the stall while I check out the competition.'

He walked up the aisle, looking at other people's tables as he went.

Dean Prince rushed up to the table. 'Fifteen quid for *Mayfair*.'

'Twenty-five and it's yours right now.'

Dean nodded. In seconds, we'd swapped the magazine for the money.

I rearranged my bears and ponies over the remaining mags and slipped the money into my secret pocket.

The skater kid came up. 'A tenner for *Fiesta*.'

I shook my head.

The kid looked like he was going to say something else, but I jerked my head. Dad was coming.

'Some advice.' Dad joined me at the table. 'Don't be buying anything from the last two stalls on the left.' He spoke to both me and the skater kid, who was now closely studying sewing patterns. 'A lot of things there off the back of a lorry.'

The kid picked a package of shiny fabric off Dad's table. He looked at it closely. 'Right you are.'

'That's an ironing board cover,' Dad said.

'OK.'

Another baggily dressed kid came up. He took the ironing board cover off Skater Kid thoughtfully, like they were
a team, considering buying it together. 'There's more where
that came from,' Dad said. 'My wife makes them. Fit all
standard sizes.'

I saw a familiar bobbing walk in the distance. 'LEWIS!'

He waved. His mum waved, too.

I shouted, 'Aren't you coming over?'

He jiggled up and down like he needed a wee. 'Is your
mum there?'

I narrowed my eyes. 'No.'

Lewis came scurrying up, his mum following.

'Hi, Mrs Harris,' I said.

'Hi, Fiona. Aren't you hot in that coat?'

'I'm fine.'

'I hear you're coming to visit after tea tonight.' She gave
me a big smile. 'What lovely ponies. I—'

'Don't touch them!' I barked.

Mrs Harris stopped reaching for a pony.

'Sorry,' I said. 'I mean, I've laid them out carefully. In the
best selling positions. Sorry.'

Dad leaned towards Mrs Harris. 'Fiona is taking her selling very seriously today.'

Mrs Harris nodded. 'Right you are.' Dad and Mrs Harris
chatted to each other, something about the bomb – 'so awful',
'so pointless' – but I stopped listening.

A lad with bright chin rash stepped up. He stood so close,
I could smell Skittle breath. 'Twenty-five quid for *Razzle*.'

Lewis's eyes went wide. He glanced at his mum, but she
was still talking to Dad.

'Sold. But' – I glanced at Dad and back – 'You can pick it
up when the coast is clear.'

Chin Rash Skittle Breath nodded and handed me two notes.

Dad looked at the money. He looked at the boy.

Chin Rash Skittle Breath picked up a bear and walked on. Dad watched after him, looking dazed.

I dropped the money into my secret pocket. I moved my fingers around in there so I could touch all the notes and coins at once. Fifty-one pounds already. And I still had seven magazines to go.

I could feel the fair now. It was getting closer. I could practically *smell* the candyfloss.

I was going to be so popular at school after this.

To Go to the Fair I Need:

1) ~~Money for the rides~~ √
2) Girl friends, so the boy from the Waltzers will push my car
3) Mum and Dad to let me go

Sometimes, I'd prefer it if people didn't listen to me.
(paradox)

Twenty-seven days to the fair
I didn't get twenty-five quid for *all* the magazines. I only got the cover price for the film magazine, and only a fiver for *Readers' Wives*. I reckon if the boy who'd bought it had been able to see inside, I wouldn't have got that.

But – one hundred and twelve pounds. That was more money than I'd ever had in my life. That was fifty-six goes on the Waltzers.

Fifty-two goes, if you threw in popcorn and candyfloss. Which I definitely would, thank you very much. When I finally got to the fair, I would be doing it *in style*.

While Mum and Dad watched the England–Spain game downstairs, I opened the jewellery box where I keep my hair bobbles. The ballerina turned, the plink-plonk music played, and I tucked my money in the pouch at the back. I shut the box with a snap.

I ignored all Mum and Dad's shouts to come downstairs, even Mum's, 'Penalties! Fi, *surely* you want to come down for the penalties?'

There were roars from downstairs and I could guess the result, even before Dad shouted up, 'Semi-finals, Fi! We're in the *semi-finals!*'

I came downstairs to find out who'd scored what, and Dad and Mum had their arms round each other. They danced around the lounge to 'We Are the Champions' like they were dancing round Blackpool Tower ballroom, and I knew school was going to be *awful* all week, again.

While our teatime baked potatoes were in the oven, Mum and Dad decided to *use the time usefully*, so their good moods were over pretty quickly.

I eavesdropped on my *quarry* at the garage door. Just practising really. I didn't expect to hear anything good.

And I didn't.

Mum and Dad had been meaning to paint the hallway for as long as I can remember. *This* was as far as they got – occasionally checking if the paint in the garage has gone hard. And, for some reason, because they hate painting so much, that means they *both* had do it, which doesn't make sense, but that's my mum and dad for you.

'What, really?' Mum's voice went high. 'Fiona *made more money* than you?'

'Don't start, Gail.'

'I'm not starting. I just knew I should have gone. Did you sell *any* ironing board covers?'

'She seemed really popular with the older boys, Gail.' I heard the sound of shuffling feet and clanging tins. 'We don't need to be worried, do we?'

The clanging stopped.

'Of course not,' Mum said eventually. 'She's eleven, Jonathan. We're not *there* yet.'

I wondered where *there* was.

Didn't matter. I wanted to go *now*.

More shuffling and clanging.

'Do you think that one's OK?' Mum said. 'Poke it. No, harder. Break the crust.'

There was a crispy noise, like slicing through burnt toast.

'I reckon it'll do,' Dad said. 'So long as we give it a good stir.'

I heard the sound of the lid going back on the tin.

'OK, so that's paint sorted.' Mum said it like she'd run a marathon. 'Now, where on God's earth did we put the Polyfilla?'

Half an hour later, the three of us sat eating jacket potatoes at the peninsula.

Dad sliced into his potato. 'I've been hearing you get good stuff to sell on at dead people's auctions. So maybe I'll do that for the next car boot sale.'

'Sounds like you need to.'

'Don't start, Gail.'

'I'm not *starting*, just *saying*.'

I watched Dad chase a baked bean round his plate sadly. I was almost pleased it was the football the next day.

It didn't help that when he finished eating before us, he went to the Cupboard of Office Things.

'Bloody hell, Gail, why are we always, *always*, out of stamps?'

And then Mum and Dad had a big back-and-forth about why each other would have taken the last stamp without saying something, and I cut a big piece of potato and shoved it in my mouth and made myself eat it, even though it was way too hot.

*

After tea, Mum and I were in the car, on the way to the big out-of-town shopping centre to get new school shoes. So I was surprised when she pulled up at the precinct.

'Why are we here?' I asked.

'While I remember. To shut your father up.'

I followed her till I saw where we were going – Paper Rack – and slowed. 'I'll wait outside.'

'Don't be silly. And you can dawdle on your own time, Fiona.'

I zigzagged across the car park after her. 'Dawdle on your own time, *Fi*,' I muttered.

I passed some older kids gathered round a car with its doors open, rave music pumping. Two of the kids were swapping tapes, but I wasn't as impressed by older kids these days – not since I realised some of them *couldn't even get their own porn.*

And – *tapes.* Not even CDs.

Being older was wasted on some of these kids.

I followed Mum into Paper Rack and she went right up to the bald man at the counter.

'One book of six first and one of six second-class stamps, please. And I'll pay the paper bill while I'm here.'

The newsagent looked down at me.

I shuffled a little under his gaze.

'Larson, fourteen Archer's Way,' Mum added.

The newsagent jerked his head at me. 'This one yours?'

'For my sins.'

The man looked at me for a bit longer.

I stood up straight and did my best smile.

Mum looked at me and back at the man, her smile bright.

'That'll be twenty pounds forty,' he said finally.

Mum did a giggly laugh, being friendly enough for two.

'Now, my purse.' She started getting things out of her hand-bag and clanging them onto the counter – hairbrush, car keys, spotty umbrella. 'Hang on – sorry.' Mum always made up for strangers' rudeness by being overly, fussily nice. Unless she gets angry and decides to eyeball them back – you never quite know what you're getting with my mum. That's why she's so hard to live with.

When we hurried out of the shop, Mum put the stamps in her purse. 'I'm not sure I like that man.'

I walked quickly past the car with rave tunes. 'I don't think I do, either.'

We got back in the car and set off for the shopping centre.

'Can I listen to the news?' I said. 'I want to find out the latest in Bosnia.'

'Too depressing.' Mum flicked an indicator. 'So, Fi, you sold more than your father at the car boot today.'

I nodded.

'Your father's too nice, that's his problem. How much did you make?'

'Eighteen pounds,' I lied quickly. 'But I'm saving it.'

'Wow!' Mum looked genuinely proud. I felt a stab of something, knowing I'd have to write this on another Scar list someday.

Sometimes I really wish I didn't have such a good memory for the bad stuff I've done.

Mum shoved the middle of the steering wheel. The horn screeched.

'Oh, COME ON!' Mum threw her hand up. 'Yes, you *may well* wave. *Apology not accepted.*'

Mum sighed. She moved her head from one side to an-other, like she was stretching her neck, and kept driving.

*

We pulled up at the big out-of-town shopping centre and Mum bought my new shoes. She let me carry the bag and I banged it against my leg as we walked back to the car.

I saw a man who looked familiar, in the walkway by one of those stalls with a big awning. Those stalls that sell soft cookies and ice cream. The good stalls.

Was that Mr Kellett?

But the man stepped to the side and I realised it couldn't be Mr Kellett after all because he was holding hands with another man.

But then the Mr Kellett man dropped the other man's hand and turned so he was fully facing me – and it was *definitely* Mr Kellett. And he'd been smiling and chatting to the other man before, but now he wasn't. He was staring at me, and standing completely still.

The other man turned around with two cookies, and he handed one to Mr Kellett.

Mr Kellett took it without saying *thank you*.

And then I smiled, realising what I'd seen. The men weren't *holding hands*. What I'd seen was Mr Kellett giving the other man money to buy him a cookie.

I waved.

After a second, Mr Kellett waved back. His friend looked from him to me, then turned to look at something in a shop window.

'Dawdling again, my little sales pro?' Mum said.

'Just thinking.' I tugged on the sleeve of Mum's coat. 'Can I have one of those big cookies?'

'No.'

I followed Mum towards the exit. And I was so busy thinking about how much I wanted one of those cookies, and how big and soft and melty they looked, I forgot to even mention I'd seen Mr Kellett.

'How about next time?' I said in the car, nearly home.

'We'll see next time,' Mum said.

'It's just they're really soft.'

'I don't want to talk about cookies anymore, Fiona.'

We took a left down George Street. I pointed out of the window. 'That's our lamppost. Where I meet Lewis and Sean to walk to school.'

Mum didn't say anything.

I pointed at the postbox. 'We always cross the street *here*. And on the way back, we cross *there*.' I looked at the house in between. 'Did an axeman live at that house, Mum?' I pointed. 'The one back there. Fifty-six George Street.'

Mum didn't answer for a few moments. 'An axeman? What do you mean?'

'A man with an axe. Sean said a man lived there who cut off his brothers' heads and arms and legs and . . .' I stopped before saying *and they found a foot with a flipflop in with the bananas at the Co-op.*

Mum stared straight ahead. 'What a ridiculous thing to say.'

'If there was an axeman there, you would have heard, wouldn't you?'

She looked at me, finally. '*Of course* we would have heard.'

'But we don't walk in front of that house, we always cross the street before it. I think I don't because you don't and—'

'But I do walk in front of that house.'

I blinked. 'You don't.'

'I walk in front of it *exactly* as much as any other house. You kids! Making up stories, based on silly little things like where people cross the road! With your imaginations, you could drive people crazy, you know?' Mum shook her head and turned to face me. '*Of course* it won't be true about the man with an axe. You think something like that could have happened, here, in Monkford, and the only person who knows about it is a twelve-year-old kid called Sean?'

She gave me a tight smile and turned back to face the road.

We reached our road and Mum parked up in the drive. I thought the conversation was over, but she said, 'There's been no axe killings in Monkford and I don't give any of this a second thought. We don't want you having nightmares.'

She patted me on the shoulder and got out of the car.

I unclipped my seatbelt and got out of the car slowly. I followed Mum into the house, questions popping like fireworks.

Because Mum *didn't* walk in front of that house. And how was I meant to forget *that*?

I know Mum wants me to be like her. She doesn't notice things if she doesn't want to notice. If she gets a scab, she puts a plaster over it straight away.

But if I get a scab, I pick it off and roll it up and wait for the skin to scab up again. Then I pick it again, and pick deeper.

Even if the area keeps bleeding. Even if my skin hurts.

13

When I try to make myself look older, it does the opposite.
(paradox)

Twenty-seven days to the fair

'I don't want to talk about it anymore.' Lewis gave himself a hug. 'I don't want to think about the axeman. It's not true, and it's horrible. So let's talk about something else. About how we're going to be so popular now you've sold all those magazines. The best kids in school.'

I smiled at him. I'd never dared even *dream* of us being the best kids at school. But that was before. Before the car boot sale.

The two of us sat on his bed that evening, the Scrabble board between us. Scrabble wasn't my first choice for a Saturday night, particularly a Saturday night when I'd made *a hundred and twelve pounds* – but I'd left *The Junior Spy's Secret Handbook™* at home, and I *really* didn't want Lewis to get out his book of magic tricks.

I looked at my tiles. *XJYAPCB.* 'Have you made your secret spy pocket yet?'

He moved one tile to a different place on the rack. He shook his head.

I put X down on a triple letter score in front of the letter I. Lewis stared at me.

'Xi's a word.' I pronounced it 'chee' like Grandma did.

'Xi?'

'Xi.'

'It's not a word.'

'It is! Go and get your Scrabble dictionary, I'll prove it.'

'We don't have a Scrabble dictionary.'

'I promise, I've seen it in the Scrabble dictionary with my own eyes.'

'What does it mean then?'

I jumped up. 'Let's ask your parents.'

I ran down the stairs, Lewis following. Lewis's parents were sitting, one on each sofa, watching telly.

'Mrs Harris, will you tell Lewis *xi* is a real word for Scrabble?'

'Chi? Short for cheese? I don't know.' She gave a little laugh. 'You kids know more than me.'

'Your mother's rubbish with word things,' Lewis's dad said, reaching for the remote control. 'No point asking her.'

Lewis's mum laughed again, like she always did when he was being mean about her. Sometimes she didn't even need Lewis's dad to be mean, she did it to herself. *What a mess I look today! Oh, this old thing? Oh, I'm sorry it's a little overdone, I'm a hopeless cook.*

I turned to Lewis's dad. 'Do you know *xi* then? If you're better at words?'

'It's not a real word. And you need to be careful with that cheek.' He turned back to the telly.

'Can we phone my grandma, then? She'll tell you.'

'Give it up, little girl.' Lewis's dad switched the volume up. 'Quit when you're behind.'

I looked at Lewis. He begged me with his eyes not to say any more, so I walked upstairs.

'Leave that bedroom door open,' Lewis's mum said.

'No harm if the boy's feeling red-blooded, Lisa.'

I shut the door and sat on the bed again.

Lewis looked at the letters on his rack. 'You shouldn't be cheeky to him.'

'Your dad doesn't know *anything*, so I don't know why he always calls your mum stupid. I would never let anyone call me stupid like that.'

I left a gap. Lewis was always letting his dad say that about him.

'I don't believe *xi*'s a word,' Lewis said quietly. 'Dad says it isn't.'

'I *promise* it's in the Scrabble dictionary. I'll bring it in to school with me on Monday.'

I counted up the score in both directions, including the triple letter score, and wrote *38* on the score sheet.

I picked out a new letter from the bag. *T.*

I shook my head at how unlucky I was and put it on my letter rack. 'Why does your mum want us to keep the door open? She thinks we're going to be kissing? Or having sex? She's crazy.'

Lewis punched me lightly on the arm. 'I don't want to kiss you.'

'I know.' I shook my head. 'Maybe your dad's right after all.' I moved my letters around. 'Maybe your mum *is* stupid.'

The next day was Sunday and Mum and Dad were both around, so I used the time first thing in the morning to write letters. And the good thing was, we had stamps again.

I applied for a job at the dog rescue centre, one at the

laundrette and one at the chicken farm, though I almost hoped I didn't get that one. The advert said you needed a *strong stomach*, and I thought I did – but I really didn't want to have to find out.

Later, I helped Mum and Dad do the gardening. Dad was trimming the bushes with his big clippers while Mum weeded the flower beds.

My job was deadheading the roses. I quite liked it, as jobs went. Walk along the flowerbed, check out each flower. If it's dead – *snip*. Head tumbles like Anne Boleyn's. Pick up the head and put it in my basket.

Maybe I should be an executioner when I grow up. 'I've been thinking of watching *Gardeners' World.*'

They both kept weeding. Even though Mum, at least, would *definitely* have heard.

I snipped the head off another rose. 'You won't believe this. Lewis's parents don't have a Scrabble dictionary.'

'That's not an *actual* crime,' Mum said.

Dad stopped clipping to watch the conversation.

'And they don't know *xi* is a word.'

Mum dug her trowel into the soil. 'I think that's fair enough, Fiona.'

I snipped the dead head off another rose and looked at the next rose along. It wasn't properly dead.

They all would be soon though. *Snip.* 'Lewis's mum says we shouldn't shut the bedroom door after us. Though his dad says it's fine if Lewis is feeling red-blooded.'

Dad snorted.

I picked the deadish head off the grass and put it in my executioner's basket. 'What?'

Mum lifted her knees and adjusted the position of her knee protector. She twisted and gave Dad a look.

I stared at Dad. 'What?'

'Nothing.'

'Shall I ask Lewis's dad?'

Mum gave Dad another look. She kneeled down again and put her trowel on the grass. 'Geoff wants Lewis to be normal. People find it easier for their kids to be normal.'

'Lewis *is* normal.' Even as I said it, I knew it wasn't true. He was Lewis-y, and being Lewis-y was something you carried about with you. Kids can smell these things from the other end of the playground.

'*Of course* he's normal,' Mum said. 'Your dad means that we want our kids to take the easy path in life. That's what Geoff will be thinking with this red-blooded stuff.' She hunched her eyebrows. 'Don't ever – *ever* – tell Geoff I said this.'

'But *normal*. Mum, what—'

Mum moved round on her knees so she was looking at Dad. 'Jonathan, you started this conversation.' She dug at the soil with her trowel. 'You can have the pleasure of finishing it.'

Dad put his clippers on the grass and sat down at the bench. He patted the seat.

I placed my secateurs and basket on the ground and sat next to him.

'Lewis is a sensitive boy.' Dad smiled. 'Sometimes sensitive boys can take different paths from the herd. Not necessarily. But sometimes.'

I folded my arms at this. 'Can girls take different paths too? Or is it another thing that's just for boys?'

Mum put down her trowel. She and Dad looked at each other.

'Do you think that you're on a different path?' Dad asked.

They were both looking at me closely.

Mum shook her head at Dad. 'We're confusing her.'

'But if—'

Mum cut me off. 'Another time.'

Frustrated, I snipped off two not-completely-dead heads and tipped the content of the basket onto the compost heap.

And maybe it's because I was frustrated. Maybe that's why I chose that day to ask.

I'd got money for the fair now, but I was still no closer to getting Mum and Dad to let me go. I needed to do some *concrete investigating*.

And that meant asking about Danielle.

I wasn't stupid. I knew, by asking, my parents probably wouldn't tell me about her death. But they probably wouldn't be able to help giving me something, would they? Give me some clues to work with?

And while Lewis had said it would be a bad idea to ask Mum and Dad how Danielle died, he didn't know how much chattier my parents got when they were talking about England winning the football and besides – as had been proven many times – Lewis Harris didn't know everything.

I waited till we were all eating Dad's spaghetti bolognese that night.

'Thing is,' Mum said twirling spaghetti on her fork, 'we've had penalty practice now. So that stands us in good stead.'

I ate a mouthful and swallowed. 'Can I ask something about Danielle?'

Mum stopped chewing for a second. 'This had better not be about bedrooms.'

'You know when Danielle died . . .'

I said it casually, but it didn't matter.

Dad put his knife and fork down on the peninsula, so quietly they didn't make a noise.

Mum stopped chewing, properly now.

I looked down at my plate. I made swirls with my fork, leaving parallel tracks on the plate, like four ice skaters had made trails through the sauce.

'I hope it was quick,' I said. 'For her sake.'

Mum took a deep breath. She looked at Dad again. 'Fiona.'

'I like Fi now.'

'Fi.' Still looking at Dad. 'We talk about how your sister lived. Not how she died.'

I crunched my toes up in my shoes.

'People want to talk about how she died all the time,' Mum said. 'And she was so much more than a tragic story. She was a wonderful, wonderful little girl. And I will tell you *anything* you want to know about her. I will talk about her all day, if you want. And I will talk about anything, except how she . . .'

When Mum tailed off, Dad squeezed her arm.

I swung one foot out and kicked the metal leg of the peninsula. *Clang.*

Hurt charged through my toes.

Frustration bubbled up in my chest.

I took a deep breath. 'OK.' A different angle. 'Was she fun? What did she do for fun?'

Mum looked at her plate. 'She was *so* much fun.'

And Mum looked up and told me the story about the routine they had when they danced round the kitchen to a song about a highwayman. I didn't listen. The whole point of these stories is they never actually changed. They were as dead as my sister.

Though I will say, I feel embarrassed for Danielle when Mum tells these stories to Danielle's mates, when they come to see Mum and Dad on her birthday. Dead or not, Danielle wouldn't want her mates hearing that, would she?

Not unless high school was a really different place in 1982.

'She was our miracle baby, you know. We didn't think we could have children, and then she came along.' Mum looked at Dad softly. 'Everyone said she was special.'

'Special,' I kicked the peninsula leg again. *Clang.* Toe-pain. *Don't say it.*

'She lit up a room,' Mum said. 'She was just one of those people. So special.'

'Special.' I kicked it again. *Clang.*

Don't say it.

'The world wasn't made for people that special,' Mum said.

Don't say it. No, don't –

'Special?' The words just rushed out on their own. 'Like the kids at St Joseph's?'

Mum dropped her knife and fork.

'GO TO YOUR ROOM! NOW!'

Her voice was the shakiest I've ever heard.

And Dad spent ages in my bedroom that night, explaining that Mum just needed some time, and that I probably didn't understand what I was saying – that I was being mean to both Danielle *and* to the kids from St Joseph's, and those kids don't find life as easy as I do. And I can't have meant it, because making fun of both Danielle and those kids was the worst thing I could ever do – and *surely* I wasn't the kind of kid who meant to say things like that?

I listened. Thinking I didn't know how in seven words I'd managed to deeply offend both Danielle and the kids in the special class, and that was quite *special* in itself.

But that was me. Scar-bad again.

The Bad Scar Things I've Done
1996 Summer Term Update

1) Called Danielle special, which made fun of her and the kids from St Joseph's
2) Cut up Mum's curtain fabric to make a secret pocket
3) Tried to sell stuff from Danielle's room
4) Sold jazz mags to underage boys

I haven't put these in order because I don't know what order they're in.
And I don't want to think about it anymore.

14

Tiny arteries and veins serve the individual muscles and skin on your head, so it can bleed a lot if you get a head injury. For example, if you were hit on the head with a whack-a-mole hammer.

Fiona Larson, 7E's Blood Project

Twenty-five days to the fair

On Monday morning, in Dr Sharma's lesson, everyone was meant to be working on their science projects on their own. But kids were really talking about the game and how they'd step over the ball to fool the keeper when *they* were taking penalties for England.

Dr Sharma must have known she wouldn't get people to stop talking because she pretended not to notice.

She saw me with my hand up. 'This had better not be about penalty kicks.'

She sat at the stool next to me.

'I've got a question. Two questions.'

Dr Sharma raised her eyebrow. 'And?'

I looked down at my lap uncertainly. 'Do you know I had a sister? Danielle?'

Dr Sharma straightened her blouse around her waist. 'I do.'

'Did you teach her?'

Dr Sharma kept straightening. 'What has this got to do with your project?'

'I was just wondering what you knew about her.'

'Very little, I'm afraid. And Fiona, this is no place for soap operas. Science questions only.'

I stared at the edge of the table. I should have known she wouldn't help.

I noticed the outline of the special shape I'd drawn there earlier that year. Before I'd learned the word *swastika*. Before I'd learned it wasn't *my* special shape, after all.

I moved in front of the shape so Dr Sharma didn't see.

'Was that both questions?'

'No. Just one.'

She sighed. 'Is your second question about your project, at least?'

I nodded. 'What does it mean if you say someone's *red-blooded*?'

'Nope. Not science either, Fiona.' She got up from the stool. 'It's a metaphor.'

'That's what I thought.' And now I had to look up the word *metaphor*.

'When someone says *red-blooded*,' Dr Sharma said, 'they're talking about a person being full of life. They eat a lot, that kind of thing.'

I wouldn't exactly call Lewis *full of life*, but he did eat a lot of raspberry laces.

If red-blooded wasn't a science thing, that made it an English thing. A *metaphor* would be something like a *paradox*, something to make conversations more confusing and take longer.

I arrived in the classroom for English later than some of the other kids. Sean nodded at me, but didn't say hello, just looked away again.

What?

I sat down and got out my pencil tin. I rearranged my pens in confusion.

But aren't I the best girl in school now?

Surprisingly, Mr Kellett hardly spoke about the football. He just stood at the front, banging on about the play we were reading.

Finally, he looked up from his book. 'Any questions?'

Loads of hands went up.

'Were you any good at penalties when you played for Alty Town, sir?'

'Are we going to beat Germany five-nil?'

'Questions about Katherine or Petruchio? Or Shakespeare? Even Italy?' Mr Kellett looked round the room. 'Anything related to *The Taming of the Shrew* at all?'

All the hands went down.

I put my hand up. 'Can I ask about something else?'

Mr Kellett closed the book in his hands slowly. He hugged the book to his chest. 'Everyone discuss the play, in your pairs.'

He came over to me.

I put my hand down. 'It's another word question. Something I've been wondering since the weekend.'

Mr Kellett slowly crouched next to me. One of his knees made a crunching sound, like a rustled-up crisp packet. 'Go on.'

'I just wanted to know. What does red-blooded mean?'

He stared at me.

'Mr Kellett?'

The bell rang. And kept ringing.

Mr Kellett sprang up despite his crisp-packet knee. *'Fire drill!'* He grabbed his yellow vest-thing from the back of his chair, the one the colour of a highlighter pen.

And all us kids hurried after him onto the school field, hoping and hoping – some crossing fingers and everything – that it was a real fire this time.

Even better than a fire! *School news, school news, school news!*

It was a bomb threat. *Someone threatened to bomb our school!*

Well, not *exactly* bomb our school. They threatened to bomb the train station nearby, and our school's really close to the track. Someone had called the police and used an IRA codeword – that turned out not to be an IRA codeword after all. Or an old one. Or something.

There were so many rumours.

It wasn't the IRA after all, but angry ex-pupils trying to get their own back. It was that kid who got his face blown off in a science experiment. It was Simon Rutherson, losing it after twenty years of kids shouting *orgasm* up scaffolding.

Either way, there was no bomb.

But you should have seen the teachers! Mrs Vernal kept muttering with the New Head about whether we should regroup in the car park instead, even though that wasn't the instruction when there was a fire drill. Miss Jarvis rushed back and forth like a mad rabbit, telling us to *step back from the railway line, no, further back, please kids, listen to me, kids, it's important this time – PLEASE!* Her face was so red and strained, Dr Sharma put her hand on Miss Jarvis's arm and said *calm down, Carrie. Nothing good comes of getting agitated.*

Carrie. The day of the bomb was getting better and better. *Carrie!*

It wasn't all good though. At one point, the New Head looked up and I met her dark gaze. It was like I was looking at Medusa and her head of hissing snakes. A coldness spread across my neck and my back and it stayed there, tingling and spreading, long after the New Head had turned away.

Mr Kellett wasn't happy either. He stood in his highlighter vest, directing kids, looking more serious than I'd ever seen him. I caught his eye once and he stopped directing kids and looked *really* worried.

But the most worried faces of all were on the poor Year Nine girls who'd been doing gymnastics when the bell rang. Now they were on the field with no skirts on, all standing in just Aertex T-shirts and gym pants – *all* of the class. The fat ones, the skinny ones, the ones whose boobs had grown too quickly, the ones whose hadn't grown quickly enough – all trying to cover themselves up, with only their arms to do it. All the while, everyone – *everyone, the whole school* – made comments on how thick their legs were, or how much their boobs had grown, or not grown, like we were presenters on a nature show, or observing penguins in their pool at the zoo.

At teatime, I sat at the peninsula and practised reading the newspaper.

I turned over pages of the business section, waiting for Mum to notice.

On the next page was a cartoon. A man in a suit with a big red face held a bottle labelled *The Economy*. He was trying to protect the bottle from a hunched-over devil, who was trying to take the stopper out of the bottle.

I stared at the cartoon, waiting for it to be funny.

I turned another page.

'Fiona?' Mum said.

I put the paper down flat on the table.

'Fiona, while you're not doing anything, do you want to help me with laying the table?'

'I *was* doing something. I was reading the business section.' I got down off the stool and opened the cutlery drawer. I put the cutlery on the table in a heap. 'Should I put my paper away?'

Mum looked at the paper open on the peninsula. *City jitters expected to stabilise after chancellor's statement.*

She looked at me for a long minute.

I folded the paper up neatly and started arranging the knives and forks in our places.

Mum eventually went back to stirring her sauce. 'Oh.' She jerked her head at the sideboard. 'You've got some post. What's it about?'

'Could be anything. I get letters all the time.'

I took the letter up to my room to open it.

Dear Miss Larson,

Thank you for your recent application for the position of hairdressing assistant.

We have been overwhelmed with applications and have received an abundance of CVs for the role. After careful consideration, we have decided to go in a different direction. I'm sorry to tell you we won't be offering you an interview at this time.

We will keep your application on file in case any positions come up in the future, so there is no need to reapply.

We wish you the best of luck with your continued job search.

Kind regards,
Katie Guest
Salon Manager

I was getting a bit bored of words now, to be honest. So I wouldn't be looking up *abundance*.

I never wanted to be a hairdresser anyway.

15

Calling someone 'red-blooded' has nothing to do with actual blood.
It's a red herring.
Which has nothing to do with actual herrings.

Fiona Larson, 7E's Blood Project

Twenty-four days to the fair

The next day, I waited for Lewis by the lamppost. I still had my glasses on, after wearing them with my parents all through breakfast.

I watched Lewis walk towards me, his edges much sharper than usual. I was about to take the glasses off when I glanced at 56 George Street.

The house had sharper edges too. As did the man inside.

After a moment, the man raised a hand in a wave.

My stomach swished with cold water.

The man Mum had met at the supermarket – the one she called *strange* – was the man in the window of 56 George Street.

'Lewis,' I grabbed his arm, 'run.'

*

'Why are we running?'

I slowed as we reached the park. 'You know the man in the axeman's house?'

'It's not an axeman's house.' Lewis saw my face. 'Go on.'

'I know who he is and Mum says' – I left a pause – 'he's a strange man. Coincidence?'

Lewis opened his eyes wider. 'Of course it's a coincidence.' But his voice was wobbly at the edges. 'I asked Mum about the axeman and she said Sean's having us on and they'd never found a foot in a flipflop in with the bananas at the Co-op. *Never!*'

'My mum said the same,' I admitted.

'And think about it, Fi. Flipflops slide off easily.' Lewis folded his arms in a big message. 'And there's no way a whole family got killed like that and we don't know. You *can't* believe the axeman story.' He saw my face. 'Surely?'

'Fine, he's not the axeman.'

'Great.'

'He's just a normal man, so we can investigate him for spy practice anyway. Find out *why* he's strange.'

'But he might not like it.'

'He won't find out though.'

'He might be dangerous.'

'*Of course* he might be dangerous, Lewis, that's what *strange* means!'

Lewis looked at his shoes.

I gave a little shiver. 'We have to find something to practise spying on eventually. We could either investigate this strange man, or Danielle's death. Your choice.' I was planning to do both, obviously, but it's always best to ease Lewis into things.

He still wouldn't look at me, so I deliberately crossed his path and stood in front of him.

'We talked about this before.' He looked up. 'And you promised me you wouldn't investigate Danielle.'

I put my hands on my hips. 'It's OK for you. You get to go to the fair.'

Lewis just looked at me.

'What?'

He started hurrying towards school, arms still folded, making sure I knew he was still angry with me. In that position, his body leaned forward and he couldn't pump his arms, making rushing away harder.

I watched him for a moment, hitching my rucksack further onto my shoulder. With a sigh, I ran to catch him up, but he must have heard me. He unfolded his arms and hurried quicker now.

I slowed, deciding not to chase him anymore.

With Lewis, it's often best to give him a chance to calm down before I come at him with my good ideas for another round of trying.

School news!

Liam's sister heard the New Head telling off Mr Carter, the IT teacher, when they thought no one was around.

Turns out Mr Carter's getting the computer room rewired and he signed the form with some builders without checking the cost or dates with the New Head, who says the wiring's *non-essential* and *an extravagance* and *she'd only agreed to it in principle, she hadn't signed off the details.*

And now the rewiring is taking longer than expected and the computer room's going to be closed for building work before the end of this term, not just over summer, as Mr Carter had said.

Which isn't great for me and Lewis, obviously, but that's not important right now.

The rumour is the New Head said Mr Carter *forgot himself*. That she'd been clear she needed to be asked about every money decision in the school, *down to the last paperclip*.

Then the rumour is that the New Head punched him to the floor, and kept kicking Mr Carter as he was curled up in a ball – and that's the one bit everyone talked most about as the day went on, but that's the one bit of the story I don't believe.

Apart from that, in school, there was a lot of talk of sausages. People smelling them everywhere, talking about them a lot. Something to do with England playing Germany soon in the semi-final. I pretended to understand, and laughed when other people did.

And, in rubbish school news, all the girls are into fortune tellers – those folded bits of paper where someone picks a number and the paper tells them what to do, or gives them a prediction.

You have to . . . run round the tennis courts.

The number of kids you'll have is . . . two. Twins. One nice, one evil.

The man you marry will have . . . black hair and a wooden leg.

Being at school comes with all kinds of homework. Now, on top of learning who scored what in the football, if I was ever going to make any new friends, I needed to find out how to fold a stupid fortune teller.

And I *definitely* needed new friends. It wasn't just about getting girl friends for the Waltzers. Lewis had walked off from me that morning, and Sean hadn't been at the lamppost this week. He wouldn't look at me in English, even when we thought the building was on fire. And when I'd tried to talk to him in the playground, he'd walked right past me, like I was invisible.

I tried with Lewis, though. I really did.

I saw him in the corridor between lessons and grabbed his coat as kids pushed past us. 'Why are you cross, Lewis?'

'I can't believe you said you want to investigate Danielle's death again. After I asked you not to.'

'Think about it. We need to investigate because what if she's haunting the fair?' I got bumped to the side by a massive rucksack. 'Do you *want* to go to a haunted fair?'

Lewis hitched his own bag higher onto his shoulder. '*Please* never say anything to Gail and Jonathan about Danielle haunting the fair.'

Gail and Jonathan. Who did he think he was? *A mum?* 'You're being selfish. You get to go to the fair, so you don't care about me!'

A group of Year Eight boys charged down the corridor, chanting. '*Eng-er-land!*'

Lewis moved out of their way. 'I'm not taking any part in this.'

'*Eng-er-land! Eng-er-land!*'

'You won't help me?' I said. 'When you know how much I want to go?'

'I think it will get you into trouble. And investigating the strange man isn't safe either. Let's find another secret. A better one. A safer secret.'

I made a *pah* sound.

'Or we could do something fun.' Lewis stepped to the side for Miss Gold and her pile of textbooks. 'I could teach you how I do my card tricks and we could practise mnemonics? We could get a tray out and put household objects on them and take turns to—'

I shook my head.

'Or we could make some badges to pin on our school bags? We could give them to people and make it a style thing? Like you're one of a good crowd if you have one of the badges?'

I couldn't believe this. 'LEWIS! Card tricks is bad enough, but you're *twelve*! You don't go around making badges like a little kid at *twelve*!'

His mouth twitched.

'You're so scared about investigating things,' I said. 'Your dad's right, you're not red-blooded. I've never met anyone *less* red-blooded in – my – life.'

The bell rang.

'If I was a boy, I'd be so much better at it than you,' I added. 'Better at making friends, better at football, better at fighting – everything.'

And Lewis walked off.

I couldn't find Lewis all lunchtime. I hurried around school looking for him, jumping over the feet of the bigger kids who lined the benches at the side of the main corridor. But he wasn't sitting in a corridor.

He wasn't in the computer room, either. And Mr Carter, who's normally so nice, looked annoyed when I went there and told me to *please leave, Fiona, the room's off-limits today, I've got stuff to do.*

I sat in the playground, leaning against the science block wall, and ate my lunch. When I finished, I flattened my empty crisp packet. I folded the rectangle, again and again. I tucked in the final edge until the packet was a tiny triangle, no bigger than a 50p.

Forty-five minutes is too long for a school lunchtime. Especially if everywhere you can think of to go is just a whole list of places you don't want to be.

The Worst Things Lewis Harris Has Ever Done

1) Put his name down to do magic tricks in the *Monkford High 'Year Seven Search for A Star!'* assembly
2) Learned about mnemonics and bought a special tea tray to use for memory games
3) Asked for a clarinet for his birthday
4) Let his parents take him to France on holiday (Lewis Harris went to Paris)
5) Kept showing how he could make his nostrils flare
6) Brought in sandwiches made with dinosaur cutters
7) Couldn't sleep for a week after dreaming swans lived under his bed

If that kid doesn't want to be friends with me anymore, that's sweet by me.

16

Friends can be the worst people to tell secrets to.
(paradox)

Twenty-three days to the fair

It had been nearly a whole day since I shouted at Lewis and told him he wasn't red-blooded, and he *still* wasn't waiting for me at the lamppost.

I waited there anyway, looking at the newspaper I'd picked up from the bus shelter bench. The whole of the front page was taken up with a picture of two England players roaring in army helmets. *ACHTUNG! SURRENDER! For you, Fritz, ze Euro '96 Championship is over.*

I folded up the paper and tucked it under my arm. I looked towards 56 George Street.

The red Astra in the driveway had a dent in the back bumper and a *Baby on Board* sticker.

The house had a new *For Sale* sign in the flowerbed. The sign called the house a *desirable three-bedroom property*, with *early viewing recommended*. I waited a bit longer before heading into school.

*

In registration, Kirsty and her friends huddled round their fortune tellers, moving their fingers and thumbs, taking turns to pick a number.

'Number eight,' Olive said.

Kirsty peeled back the paper. 'You will get tonsillitis.'

I watched the girls pick numbers and pull back the paper. It was all about the folds, I decided.

Olive saw me looking and whispered something to the other girls. I heard the words *magazines* and *dirty*.

I shuffled in my seat.

'She's disgusting.'

I shuffled some more.

The girls went back to playing fortune tellers, Kirsty holding out the paper to Olive to choose.

'Number seven.'

Kirsty peeled back the paper again. 'You will go to the fair.'

I sat up straighter.

I zoomed in on Kirsty's piece of paper, my gaze an invisible laser.

When the bell rang, Kirsty hurried out with her friends, leaving the crumpled fortune teller on the desk behind her.

I picked up the fortune teller and put it carefully in my secret pocket.

I took it to maths. I spent the lesson pretending to listen to Mr Adams, but kept my hands under the desk, making the paper move.

I picked number seven, again and again. I opened the paper. I traced Kirsty's words with my thumb. Again and again.

You will go to the fair.

*

At break, I rushed towards the canteen because I knew Lewis would be wanting a snack. A rice crispy cake, to be exact.

I spotted him on the main corridor, right on time. 'Lewis!'

He pretended he hadn't heard.

I chased him.

He ran away.

I puffed after him. He had one part of his shirt spilling out of his trousers, one shoelace undone. He ran lopsidedly because of his schoolbag on one shoulder.

I heard giggling from some of the girls sitting on the benches. 'Look at the *state*.'

And I *still* didn't stop chasing him. 'Lewis!'

Still, undone shoelace and everything, he got away.

School news. And not good, this time.

My time of being magazine queen was *definitely* over.

I was on my own in the main corridor at lunchtime when Sean came up with a bunch of lads from the blue estate, and Liam and Greeney too.

I didn't even care how Sean had managed to get back in with them. I didn't want to know.

'Got any magazines, Fiona?' Liam said. People were still saying it, but in a different way now. Like . . . like it wasn't a good thing anymore.

I shook my head.

'You like porn?'

'I like boys' things.'

Liam narrowed his eyes. 'Like football?'

'Love it.'

There was a sudden hush. I turned to see the New Head walking down the corridor, a silver lizard badge on her pale blue cardigan today. In her path, kids picked up rucksacks and scurried out of the way.

The crowd kept parting in front of her, quiet spreading all around. Even *the three sea witches* grabbed their bags and scattered.

After a few seconds delay, when the New Head was out of sight, the chattering in the corridor started up again.

'You love football.' Liam turned to me again. 'Did you watch the Spain game, then?'

'Of course.' I swallowed. 'Did you see McAllister's face when he missed that penalty? *Aaah.*'

Liam and everyone straightened. Eyes flicked into focus. Lions all spotting the same old limping wildebeest.

'That was the Scotland game, of course,' I stammered. 'I meant, how good was Seaman in the Spain game? Those *saves.*'

The others crowded in. Sean stood at the back of the group, hands in pockets. He stared at the floor.

'Aren't you hot in that coat?' Liam flicked a flap. 'Why's the front all bumpy?'

I took a step back. *No.*

Liam threw the flap of my coat open, showing the secret pocket.

He took the spybox out of my coat. 'Matches?' He opened it up. 'Not matches.'

Liam threw the box to Sean. 'What's this?'

Sean licked his lips. 'It's a spying kit. They keep them in their secret pockets. Her and Harris.'

I stared at Sean. *Eight days ago*, I'd told him that. When we were lying on the grass in the park, being friends. *Eight days.*

Sean must have remembered too because he looked at the floor again.

'Girls can spy too,' I muttered. 'There's no rule against it.'

'There's the other one!' someone shouted.

'Hey!' Lewis's voice.

Across the corridor, kids jostled Lewis, opening his coat to get his spy kit out.

I looked away. Watching it happen to Lewis felt so much worse than it happening to me.

Greeney threw my spy box on the floor. 'Spying kits? This is *high* school. Grow up.'

And he kicked my spybox to Liam. Who kicked it back.

And the boys started laughing as they all joined in, trampling over my spybox.

Sean didn't join in. But he didn't move away either.

The bell rang for the next lesson and Greeney gave my box one last kick. Everyone scattered.

In the empty corridor, still ringing with the sound of kids' footsteps, I picked up my broken pieces of spybox from the floor. Carefully, I collected the torn code flaps. I picked up the hollow twigs, now snapped and scattered at the edges of the corridor. I reached for my matchstick-wound pieces of paper, stamped flat.

I looked up to see Lewis, but he looked away. And he didn't get down on the floor to put his spybox back together.

He just turned and walked away, leaving his spybox destroyed and on the floor, in pieces.

17

People often say 'in the blood' when they mean 'in the family'. Blood itself does not hold all the information people think it does.

Fiona Larson, 7E's Blood Project

Twenty-one days to the fair
The next couple of days at school could have been worse.

England lost to Germany that night, which meant I wouldn't have to do football homework for a very long time. It meant everyone at school was miserable too, which was good for me. Being sad is tougher when everyone else is happy.

It was still sunny. And I still had Kirsty's fortune teller. I kept moving the paper flaps and picking number seven. Letting it tell me again and again *you will go to the fair*, like my papery fairy godmother.

And I still had my hundred and twelve pounds. And Lewis would forgive me soon – he always did. I could make a new spybox. You could get paper and matches anywhere.

It wasn't over.

*

And the school news on Friday was particularly good.

A Year Seven kid phoned Childline!

His dad wouldn't let him have a Magnum before tea and Stu Meaker, this kid, had had enough. He actually *called*! He'd threatened and threatened, and this time – well. His dad had pushed him too far.

No one knew what was going to happen. No one had ever *phoned* before. There was so much excitement down the corridors.

'Do they have dogs, and vans? How does it work?'

'He'll go to prison. For life.'

'I just came back from his house and there were police there.'

And Stu Meaker just shrugged. 'Look, I love him, but he deserved it.' And he tried not to look too scared. But he definitely rushed off somewhere, hurrying out of school at the end of the day.

Best of all, when I got home on Friday afternoon, there was an envelope addressed to me on the hallway table.

I took the letter out to the back garden and sat on my old swing to read it.

Dear Ms Larson,

Thank you for your letter, and for your interest in our newspaper.

I'm afraid we can't send old copies of the newspaper to individuals, or disclose the personal details of our staff. However, all copies of the newspaper are archived and can be accessed using the microfiche in the library.

But we thank you for your continued interest in the activities of our newspaper. We are always looking for

new supporters and you can join our team of enthusi-
astic fundraisers by . . .

I read it again. The important bit, not the fundraising bit.

. . . all copies of the newspaper are archived and can be
accessed using the microfiche at the library.

I didn't have a clue what that meant.
But I'd find out.

The day got worse, of course. With *Fiona Larson* luck, things
always do.

I helped myself to some macaroni at the peninsula. 'What
shall we do tonight? Can we rent a film?'

I splatted the spoonful of macaroni onto my plate. Mum
and Dad looked at each other.

Mum adjusted her hairclip. 'Didn't we tell you?'

'We've got our group coming round tonight.' Dad leaned
forward. 'It's our turn to host. Sorry, Fi.'

Our group.

The *Dead Kids Group.*

'Can I come?' I *really* don't know why I said that. Sometimes I just say things I don't mean.

'You can stay in your room or go to Mrs Carpenter's?'
Mum said. 'I'm sure she won't mind.'

'You want me out of the way, so I don't remind them,' I said.
'A live kid like me, making people with dead kids jealous.'

'That's not it.' Mum frowned. 'Not at all. Don't say things
like that, Fi.' She paused. 'And it's not just a group about
people losing children, some people got widowed young.'

'It's not that we don't want you there; it's just adult time.'
Dad leaned forward so I had to look into his eyes. 'Like Date

Night. So do you want to stay in your room or go to Mrs Carpenter's? Or I could call Lewis's mum?'

'I'll stay in my room,' I said, knowing I sounded sulky, but not quite able to stop.

I sat cross-legged on my bed, listening to the music and chatting of the Dead Kids Group downstairs. Way too much laughter and fun when you realise these people became friends only because the vicar got them together after *their kids died.*

Or husbands or wives died – whatever. Either way, someone died young to make them sad. And now it's like, they've known each other so long, they have parties.

I wonder what the dead kids would think, looking down/up from heaven/hell.

I once said something like that to Mum. That the parties sounded like people were having too much fun.

'It's such a relief,' Mum said, 'to be with people who *get it.* Something so big changes your relationship with your friends because they can't understand. It was a lonely time.'

'It doesn't sound lonely now,' I'd said.

With the sound of chatting and laughter downstairs, I sat on my bed with some drawing paper. I cut it carefully into a square, and then folded it, copying the way Kirsty's paper was folded.

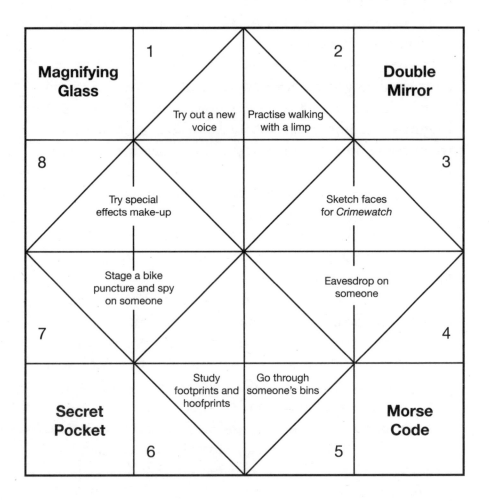

I slotted my fingers and thumbs into my new spy fortune teller. 'What should I do tonight?'

I moved the paper with my fingers and made my choices. *Morse Code. 4. Eavesdrop on someone.*

I sighed. I folded the fortune teller into its resting position and placed it onto my bedroom table.

I sat on the landing, tucked behind the top of the stairs so I was invisible. Hoping no one needed to come upstairs to the toilet.

'She was well out of order, saying that,' a man said. '*Well out of order.*'

'And what did you say to that?' a woman in a green skirt said.

'I told her, that's not how I operate.'

'Fair enough,' Green Skirt said. 'I don't like having a female boss myself. They're *so* much harder to work for. Women can be so bitchy.'

'Exactly. And you know me, I'm the kind of person who says things straight.'

I heard footsteps at the base of the staircase. I jumped up and hurried to my room.

When the toilet had flushed, I waited a minute and came out again.

'But she shouldn't have been so bossy. And you know me,' the man was saying, 'I'm the kind of person who hates unfairness.'

There was a pause.

'Shame about the football,' Green Skirt said.

'Yes.'

There was a pause.

'How's Fiona doing now?' Green Skirt said.

I wondered why she was asking the man – *you know me, I'm the kind of man who knows about other people's kids* – but it made more sense when Mum's voice replied, 'Oh. You know.'

I licked my lips.

'A proper handful,' Mum added.

I wondered whether to get angry, but thought – *fair enough.*

'She's started watching *Gardeners' World* and reading the newspaper every day, and I'm not sure what I feel about that. And glasses must be in fashion at school because she wears hers all the time now.'

I pushed my glasses back up my nose.

'She wanders round the house in those glasses like a little skinny owl,' Mum continued. 'Quiet for ages, then piping up with a fact about the constitution of Ukraine.'

I thought about this. Yep. Sounded like me.

I was pleased Mum had noticed.

'Is she still . . . you know?' – Green Skirt had put on a sad voice – *don't put on your sad voice for me, Green Skirt* – 'The stuff at school?'

'She's OK.' Mum sighed. 'Still a bit of a loner. Though she does have one good friend and he's worth his weight in gold. So nice and patient.'

I thought of the last time I'd seen Lewis, running away from me in the corridor. I looked at my feet.

'I worry about her a lot,' Mum said. 'How she drives nice kids away.'

Sometimes, when I'm not around, I want my parents to be thinking about me. And then I find out they *were* thinking about me and I think – *oh.*

'She pushes all the boundaries. She acts out' – *don't tell them about the monkey bars don't tell them about the monkey bars don't tell them about the monkey bars* – 'and she wants to know everything. Always listening at doorways. She never misses a trick.'

Never misses a trick. I felt my chest swell. *Yes.*

'It's not uncommon,' Green Skirt said. 'Dr Ali told me kids who've had traumatic childhoods are often very astute when it comes to—'

'*What?*'

At the tone of Mum's voice, the whole room went quiet.

I leaned back against the wall. *Whoa.*

'Gail, I—'

'She hasn't had a traumatic childhood.' Mum's voice was *cold.*

I felt sorry for Green Skirt.

'She wasn't even *here.*' Mum's words were pointier than usual. 'She's had a very happy childhood. We dealt with everything long before she was born.'

'I just meant, it would be hard, having parents who, with the best will in the world, would find having another kid—'

'Are you saying I've messed up my child?'

'Gail. *No.*'

She was, though. Green Skirt was.

'You know I didn't mean anything, Gail, I was just making conversation.'

At the sound of footsteps on the stairs, I scurried back to my room and threw myself onto the bed.

I didn't want to think about what Mum had said, so I picked up my fortune teller and slotted in my fingers and thumbs.

Double Mirror. 2. Practise walking with a limp.

I nodded firmly and stood up. I made my left leg heavy and dragged it after me, deciding maybe I wouldn't eavesdrop again for a while.

*

But I didn't have to try to eavesdrop later. Not when I went to the toilet in the middle of the night.

Downstairs, there was the sound of clinking glasses and fluffing cushions.

'Did you hear *the nerve* of Andrea?'

Mum's voice was so spiky, I paused on the landing.

'It was all I could do not to scream *get out of my house!*'

'Don't sweat it, Gail.'

'Of course I'm not sweating it. It's ridiculous, that's all.'

'Andrea's just one of *those*. She likes to poke and prod till she gets drama.'

'If she does it again, I'm going to poke and prod her right under a moving car.'

I went into the toilet, shutting the door after me. And wondered if maybe Mum didn't have that much fun at the Dead Kids Group after all.

Except – this time it was my fault.

Another one to add to the list.

18

Interesting things can happen in libraries.
(paradox)

Twenty days to the fair
By Saturday morning, I'd done enough spy practising. You couldn't just practise for ever, not unless you wanted to be Lewis.

I ate my cereal opposite my parents at the peninsula. 'Can I go to the library this morning? There's a book I want to borrow.'

Weekends are different from after school – it's not my own free time, and my parents expect to know where I am. I'm not exactly sure why the rules work differently, but they do.

'We can't take you. Your dad's doing the big shop,' Mum said. 'And I'm taking the car to get the oil changed.'

'Can I go on my own?'

Mum and Dad looked at each other.

I mean, the *library*. What kind of trouble did they think I'd get into? The *whole point* of a library is there's nothing to do.

'I'm meeting Lewis. We said we'd meet at ten.'

Mum blinked at me. 'You've already arranged to meet Lewis, but you're just asking me now?'

'It was provisional,' I said. 'We made a provisional appointment.'

Mum and Dad looked at each other. Both laughed.

'You and Lewis. Making *provisional appointments*,' Mum said.

My long words weren't meant to be funny, but it was OK, for once. I was pretty sure that meant I was allowed to go to the library.

And I knew for definite when Dad stood up and said, 'Just make sure you take your inhaler.'

On the way there, I walked past the precinct. Past the boys on skateboards, jumping up, trying to ollie but not doing it very well. Liam was one of the boys, but he didn't look happy. Despite his efforts, he wheels stayed firmly on the ground. He was pretending he couldn't hear the older girls who were standing outside the Co-op, smoking and watching and taking the piss.

I looked at the pile of bikes, to check if Lewis's bike was piled up with all the others. But it wasn't. Of course it wasn't. Mine and Lewis's never were.

I wondered what Lewis was doing this weekend. Whether he was missing me.

I wasn't missing him, of course. Not with my investigations to do.

If anything, I was too busy to think of him at all.

I strode straight up to the friendliest lady on the counter – the white-haired lady wearing the glasses with green sparkly bits.

I put my rucksack onto the counter. 'I want to' – I looked at my letter and read – '*access an old newspaper using the microfiche.*'

I said it like *micro-fitch*.

'Do you now? The micro-*fish*?'

'Yes. I want to *access* the *Monkford and District Advertiser* for July 1982. Please.'

The woman smiled. 'Why?'

Sometimes people think that, because they're an adult and you're a kid, everything's their business. But *a good spy prepares*. 'My mum was in a play once. She said there was a photo of it in the paper.'

The woman smiled. 'How lovely!'

I smiled back.

'Come with me.'

I followed the woman to the back of the library, past the kids' section, with the caterpillar made of letters on the wall. Past the tiny chairs on the open patch of carpet, the boxes of brightly coloured toys. The smell of that area wafted up to me, like it was yesterday.

I flushed.

Thing is, I spent a lot of time on that carpet once, singing rhymes and woofing to stories. The fact I ever did makes me squeeze all my muscles really tight. But when I'm trying to forget something, my head doesn't always do what it's told and—

> *'Lar-ry the pup-py goes*
> *Woof woof woof*
> *Woof woof woof*
> *Woof woof—'*

STOP IT! I screamed at my singing brain. *STOP IT STOP IT STOP IT!*

The woman stopped at a desk in front of a machine. She patted the chair and I sat down.

'What date was it again, darling?'

'July 1982.'

She got a box from a filing cabinet and placed a reel on the machine. She slid the film into a clip and pressed a button.

The reel shot forward and a heading appeared on the screen. *Monkford and District Advertiser.*

I sat up straighter.

The woman peered at the screen, turning a knob. 'What date do you want to start with?'

'The one after the twenty-fourth of July.'

The woman moved the lever. 'You just have to keep scrolling till you find what you need.' The writing on the screen moved down. 'If you want a copy, printing's ten pence a page.'

'Thanks.'

'You move it side to side with this handle.'

'OK.'

'And you can rotate it with this. Do you want me to stay and help?'

'I'll be fine.'

She smiled like I was cute. 'Come and find me if you get stuck. It might be difficult to get the hang of it.'

I smiled and watched the woman walk away, her soft shoes sinking a little into the carpet. I turned to look at the screen.

Monkford and District Advertiser, Friday 30 July, 1982.

Monkford Girls' and Edge Street High schools to merge

I scrolled on to:

Precinct development on track to be completed in Autumn 1984

There was a drawing of our precinct, except it had loads of extra trees and looked really clean. And the names on the shop signs weren't right.

I felt a prickle up my back for no reason. I scrolled further.

Census – Small Area Statistics

Pedestrians Urged Not to Drop Litter as Pigeons in Park Declared Nuisance

I kept scrolling, past pictures of people in roll neck jumpers and thick glasses.

Family Pay Tribute to 'Perfect' Daughter After Fair Tragedy

I took a sudden breath.

A woman browsing nearby shelves looked at me. 'You OK, hon?'

I nodded. 'Fine.'

The woman turned back to the shelves and I looked at the article. Next to it was Danielle's last school picture. The one Mum has on top of the mantelpiece.

FAMILY PAY TRIBUTE TO 'PERFECT' DAUGHTER AFTER FAIR TRAGEDY

By Adrian Sykes

Monkford is mourning local girl, Danielle Larson, who died on Saturday, whilst attending Monkford Fair. The incident is being investigated but her death is not believed to be suspicious.

Father Jonathan Larson said, 'Danielle was the perfect daughter and words cannot express how we feel. She was taken from us too soon and leaves a gap in our lives that will never be filled. She will always be our perfect angel.'

Emergency services were called to Festival Field just after eight p.m. on Saturday 24 July, but Danielle was dead when paramedics arrived.

A memorial service will be held at Dean Road Crematorium on Wednesday 11 August. The family have asked for any donations to be made to the RSPB, of which Danielle was an active member.

'Have you found what you're looking for?'

The woman in the green-speckled glasses stood over me.

I forced myself to smile. 'No. Not yet.'

I watched her walk away. I got my pad and pen from my rucksack and copied out the article, even though it didn't really tell me anything. Except that Danielle was perfect, which I already knew.

I scrolled through the next week's paper, and the one after that, looking for more information. But I couldn't find anything else.

I re-read the article I'd copied out. And realised there was something helpful, after all.

I circled the words.

By Adrian Sykes.

19

If someone's blood type is A positive, they can joke they're a positive influence. If they don't mind their jokes not being funny.

Fiona Larson, 7E's Blood Project

Nineteen days to the fair

On Sunday morning, I knew I should be trying to find out who Adrian Sykes was.

What was stopping me was, I kept imagining him. I pictured a man bigger than Mr Kellett – a man made of too much ham, with a neck wider than Dad's head, and a furious expression.

It was the same face I pictured when I imagined who I'd stolen the magazines from.

So I didn't feel like looking for Adrian Sykes. At least, I did, just not right then. Instead, I got out my fortune teller so I could do some safer spying.

Lewis's words came into my head – a *safer secret* – and I scowled as I slid my fingers and thumbs into the paper.

Lewis Harris didn't know what he was talking about.

I moved the paper with my fingers and mouthed my choices. *Double Mirror. 3.* I opened the tab. *Sketch faces for* Crimewatch.

I folded up the fortune teller and tucked it back in my pocket.

Problem was, I didn't have a suspect for Danielle's death right now. Though there *was* the strange man, I supposed. The strange man, walking the streets with his ponytail, going in supermarkets and standing in windows – being suspicious.

I grabbed a pad and paper and drew him.

I sat back and looked at what I'd done. It wasn't brilliant. If it wasn't for the ponytail, the picture could have been of anyone. He could even have been a girl, till I drew the beard on him.

And – problem was – the supermarket man hadn't had a beard.

I was just thinking this when the doorbell rang and the lights flashed. I heard a girl's voice downstairs – *Selina Baker!*

I threw open my bedroom door. I rushed across the hallway and down the stairs.

Knowing Selina was there, watching me, made walking down the stairs harder. 'Hi, Selina.' I felt like a baby calf, stumbling around on new hooves.

'Hi, Fiona.' Selina looked from Mum to me, making her long ponytail fly horizontally. Her fringe stuck a little way off her forehead, in gelled lines, and she gave me the kindest, nicest smile I'd ever seen.

I'd been wrong when I thought she was as beautiful as Kelly from Winchester. Selina was *even more* beautiful.

'Hi.' I'd already said that. *Stupid mouth.*

Mum picked up her car keys from the side. 'Fiona, look after Selina for a second while I just have a word with your father.'

I nodded. I turned to Selina and smiled.

She smiled back.

I screamed at myself – *say something!* She was too pretty, that was the problem. 'I need to get a job, Selina. A proper one – a grown-up one. Do you have a job?'

'I do! I work at the stables. I muck out the horses. Best job ever – I love it.'

I tried not to wrinkle my nose. 'Sweet.' I knew what *muck out* meant. And horses' muck must be *massive*.

'They don't pay me for it, but this way I get to spend time with the horses and ride them for free.'

I frowned. *FOR FREE?* 'Sweet,' I said again.

Mum came back then, and that was probably best because I really didn't know what to say to Selina after that.

Girls and horses. I'll never get it.

While Mum was out with Selina, I sat at the peninsula, working on my blood project. I could hear Dad moving beneath me as he cleared out the cellar. He shuffled, he grunted. He muttered an occasional *bollocks* or *arse*.

Dad isn't normally grumpy. But there's something about weekend tasks – the kind of tasks that need cellars and big boxes and tools – that brings out the *moody* in both my parents.

When Mum let herself back in after the lesson, she tossed a newspaper onto the peninsula. 'For you. The business section's at the back.'

She was making a joke but I said, 'Thanks,' like she meant it. I opened the paper up to a random page.

Mum put the kettle on.

I gave a fake sigh. 'Looks like Radovan Karadžić's up to something again. But then, there's talk of him' – I practised the word in my head – '*relinquishing* power.'

'Who?'

'Radovan Karadžić. You know, leader of the Bosnian Serbs.' I closed the paper. 'But I'll look later. I don't like to read too much at once. I like to give the news a chance to sink in.'

I pulled my exercise book towards me and drew a table, concentrating on keeping my ruler straight.

Mum re-clipped her hair back. 'What are you doing now?'

'My blood project.'

'It always makes me shudder when you say it.' Mum pulled up a stool. 'I take it you chose that topic yourself, my little vampire?'

I nodded. I wrote the headings in the first row of boxes: *Me, Mother, Father, Sibling One.* Under *Me,* I wrote *O positive.* 'But I'm writing *about* blood, not *making* blood.' I pushed my ruler to the side. 'What's your blood type?'

'AB, I think.' She tipped her head slightly to the side. 'AB positive.'

Under *Mother* in my table, I wrote *AB positive.*

'What about Dad?'

Mum sat back in her chair. 'I don't remember, darling. You'll have to ask him. Is he still in the cellar? I hope so.'

'How come you don't just *know?*'

'Fi. How is it I disappoint you so often, and in so many ways?' Mum kicked off her shoes and let them fall beneath her stool. 'Most people don't just go around knowing each other's blood types.'

I looked at my chart. 'Can you give blood to me, an O positive?'

'God knows!' Mum went to the sink and filled a glass of water. 'Though I can promise you if any of us need emergency blood, Fiona, there will be doctors to take charge. They won't be looking to us to decide what to do with the needle.' Mum gulped her water and refilled the glass. 'So you're interested in Bosnia now?'

'I've always been interested in Bosnia. Can you go and ask Dad his blood type?'

'Can't you ask him?'

I looked down at the floor. 'He's in the *cellar*,' I said quietly. I never went down there; it was a rule I had. I didn't like not knowing where a spider would spring from and scuttle across the floor.

Mum smiled like I was cute. She pushed herself off the stool. 'I'll go.'

I should point out: I'm not scared of spiders. Being scared of spiders is a girl thing. I just don't like being taken by surprise, that's all.

I heard some conversation beneath me and, a minute later, Mum came back upstairs. 'Dad's A positive. He said to tell you he's *A positive influence.*'

I wasn't sure if that was meant to be a joke, so I let it pass. I wrote *A positive* in the box under *Father*.

I looked at the next box. *Sibling One.* 'And Danielle? What was her blood type?'

Mum's smile stayed there for a second, all relaxed.

And then everything was different. Mum's face. The air of the room.

I realised my mistake. I stared at my exercise book.

'I—' Mum said. 'I—'

I kept staring.

Her words had a waver in them. 'I don't remember.'

I smoothed my page with my hand. 'I don't really need to know. It's not a problem.'

'I'll ask your dad.' She ran down to the cellar again. I could hear Mum's voice now, through the floor, going high-pitched as she fired questions at Dad. 'But how could we *just forget?*'

She ran back up the stairs. 'Your dad doesn't remember either.' She tried to smile, but when she picked up her glass again, her hand was shaking.

'It doesn't matter, it's—'

Mum slammed her glass down. 'NHS records. But where did I put them?' She jabbed both hands into her hair.

'I don't need to fill in anything for Sibling One. I can say I haven't got any siblings, it's fine. It's even true.'

'As long as your dad hasn't thrown the records out.'

Mum threw the cellar door open and ran down the steps. I heard the high up-and-down of voices as Mum took the fizzed-up air from the kitchen down there again.

I turned the page on my blood project and tried to focus on the next topic.

Mum hurried back up the stairs and into the room with a box in her arms. She dumped it onto the peninsula, next to me and my stuff.

I watched her pull files out of the box and scatter them on the table. The box shifted with the movement, scuffing the top page of my textbook.

'If they're not in here' – she pulled out a file marked *Boiler* and dumped it on the file called *Wills* – 'they'll be in the attic.'

I picked up my books. 'I'll finish this upstairs.'

I tucked the newspaper under my arm so she could see me taking it. But she didn't notice.

20

Sometimes, it's good to be a girl.
(paradox)

Eighteen days to the fair

Lewis *still* wasn't there when I got to the lamppost on Monday morning.

I stood and looked at 56 George Street for a while. The front lawn was the size of my bedroom and untidy, grass and higgledy-piggledy bushes all crossed over each other. The wooden boards on the top half of the house were different shades of brown, where the paint had faded in patches.

I looked at the *For Sale* sign – *desirable property*, with *early viewing recommended* – and looked back at the house.

The net curtain in the front window had gone, so I could see inside the room. I could just make out an old wood-coloured telly and high-backed sofa, an ugly shade between green, grey and brown.

When Lewis wasn't there by 8.30, I walked to school.

Tell the truth, I was getting sick of this.

But maybe it was a good thing Lewis was angry at me. If I was going to be normal, I needed normal friends. If I was going to be spun on the Waltzers, I needed different friends.

Friends who the boy on the Waltzers would want to push.
There was nothing for it. That meant—
Girls.

Thing is, boys are better than girls. They just are.
And I can say that because I am one. Though I'm not a *proper* girl – not really.

Why I'm Not a Proper Girl

1) I talk back
2) I get angry
3) I throw overarm
4) I'd make a good boss
5) I don't like cleaning or cooking
6) I don't care about stationery*
7) I like camping, not making jam**

*apart from Candy's pencil topper. That was a one-off.
**In Monkford, the scouts go camping and the guides make jam. And everybody else is fine with this.

The best things you can say to a girl end with *like a boy. You throw like a boy. You ride your bike like a boy. You fight like a boy.* If you're a girl, that's all you can hope for. You might still wear make-up and have long hair – you have to, if you want to be with boys when you're older – but you have to pretend that 'looking pretty' stuff just happened, without you doing anything about it.
And in the areas that really matter – like rounders and throwing and knowing the names of the third-division football stadiums – you can't let the boys beat you. Even if that

means practising throwing against a wall on your own in the garden, or learning names and places in football annuals in bed with a torch in the dark.

But you mustn't let people know you practise in the dark because then they'd know you cared. You have to make it all look easy and natural, like a boy would.

And if you do what boys do, as well as they do, and make it look easy and natural, then it's like you're not a girl anymore, but somewhere in between. A Girl Plus or a Boy Minus.

I looked round the playground. *How to choose my new friends?*

I hitched my bag on my shoulder and started walking.

The first group I walked past were the worst kind of girls. They sat on the school field, making daisy chains and friendship bracelets. Brushing each other's hair.

Never. Ever.

I passed the sea witches. They normally stood in three equal corners – an equilateral triangle – but the bigger two had just taken a book triumphantly from the third sea witch, who now stood to the side, uncertainly, while the other two flicked through her book. The equilateral triangle had gone isosceles – for now.

Anyway. *Too old, and too mean.* I couldn't risk a flushing.

I passed Martha, the evil one from primary school.

No way no way no way.

I wandered around the school's outside space in big loops, looking at groups to see which one would best fit me.

I noticed the best girls all had their school jumpers round their waists, tied around by the arms, in that way Mum says *stretches the wool*, so I took my jumper off and tied it round my waist.

As I passed one group of girls I heard giggling.

'What does she think she looks like?'

I looked down. I reached for the arms of my jumper. I lifted them up uncertainly and dropped them again.

There needed to be rules for this stuff, like how to wear jumpers round your waist. It needed to be *written down.*

When the bell rang for the end of lunch, I hurried to the maths room.

I had my exercise book out and my protractor set unpacked, and was copying triangles from the board before all the other kids had even arrived.

School news!

That day, Mrs Vernal was wearing a silky cream blouse with black dots. The blouse was so thin it was nearly see-through. You could tell her bra was lacy, because it made the surface of her blouse bobbly.

When Mrs Vernal stretched and the blouse sat close to her skin at the back, you could see everything. You could see her bra straps. You could see where the label hung down at the middle, next to the back fastening.

Everyone noticed. Mrs Vernal walked around our circle in the hall and there was a special energy in the air.

It's things like this, such basic mistakes, that make me wonder whether some teachers ever *went* to school.

Mrs Vernal clapped her hands. 'Get into pairs.'

I walked towards Lewis, but he turned and headed deliberately for Katie Russell.

Everyone was pairing up around me. I moved my weight from one foot to another, waiting.

Eventually, there was no one left alone but me and Jodie Mackintosh.

Jodie Mackintosh?

She had a decent bag and coat. She wasn't too clever or too dumb. She was from the red estate, she was pretty enough, and I'd never heard anyone saying she smelled of food or wet dog.

I took a nervous step towards her.

She smiled and stepped towards me. It wasn't a trap. Either that, or the bad *surprise!* part was coming later.

Mrs Vernal tapped her way round the hall, weaving between pairs. 'Face your partner. Look closely at each other.'

I glanced at Jodie and away again.

Looking at a stranger is harder than you think.

'Pick who's Person One in your pair.'

I pointed to Jodie. She nodded.

'Person One,' Mrs Vernal said. 'Walk around the room, or just go about some normal business. Person Two, watch your partner very carefully and see how they move. I want you to become that person.'

I *really* wished I was doing this with Lewis now. Even though becoming Lewis was pretty much the worst thing that could happen to a kid.

Jodie set off walking, her steps light. I tried to walk like her, bouncing on the balls of my feet, treading carefully. She had long black hair, so long it nearly reached her bum, and rippled as she walked.

I was Jodie for a bit longer, following what she did, sitting down and getting up again, running my hands through my hair, till Mrs Vernal shouted. 'Now swap!'

Nervous now, I crossed my arms over my front.

Jodie crossed her arms over her front.

I started to walk. Knowing Jodie was watching, I moved heavily, like I'd forgotten how my legs worked.

I glanced at her.

Jodie was pretending to be me, walking slowly, but the weird thing was, she didn't make an ugly face or stomp around or anything. She actually walked around pretty normally, like she could have been copying any kid in the room – a kid who was good or bad or anywhere in between.

At the end of class, Jodie and I headed out of the hall together.

Selina Baker was walking down the corridor towards us with a friend, both carrying long tubes of coloured paper. Selina was wearing a short top that showed an inch of skin above the waistband of her leggings.

She saw me and smiled. 'Hi, Fiona!'

'H-hi!' I said.

Selina turned back to her friend and they continued their conversation.

Jodie looked at me, eyes wide. 'You know *Selina Baker?*'

'Kind of.'

'Wow,' Jodie said.

I smiled at her. And wondered if maybe – just maybe – I might be able to make girl friends after all.

But Lewis couldn't avoid me for ever.

We both had swimming club at the leisure centre after school. And, while Lewis could run away in school, and he could swim away in the pool like I was a great white shark, loose in Monkford Baths, he couldn't avoid me in the café bit afterwards. Not if I waited by the vending machines.

Nothing makes Lewis hungry like swimming.

When I got out of the pool, I got dressed quickly without having a shower. I ran to the café bit without tying my shoelaces and made sure I was leaning against the wall when

Lewis got to the café. I rested my arm on top of the snack machine, like I owned it.

He paused when he saw me.

He walked over to the machine.

I knew this kid so well. 'Hi,' I said.

Lewis put coins in the machine. A packet of cheese biscuits uncoiled and fell into the chute. Lewis took the packet and moved to the next vending machine for a cup of blackcurrant squash.

I followed him to a table and sat down opposite. 'I'm sorry I said you weren't red-blooded.'

'Can you stop dripping your hair on my table please.'

I wiped the surface with my sleeve. 'I just wanted to investigate Danielle and I was angry you didn't want to. I didn't mean to be horrible.'

Lewis opened his cheese biscuits and placed the packet on the table – the packet open from the top, not torn down the side for sharing.

'Lewis? I said I'm sorry.'

He ate a biscuit with a room-filling crunch.

'It's just you're the one who's there for all my secrets.' I twisted my dripping hair with both hands, squeezing water onto the carpet. 'I don't tell anyone else my secrets or plans.'

He took another biscuit. 'Your *terrible* plans.'

'My terrible plans. They're not all terrible, some are quite good, but OK.'

Lewis nodded. He put the biscuit in his mouth.

'Can I have one?'

'No.'

I jiggled my knees up and down. 'Can you forgive me?'

'Maybe.' He softened his face. 'On one condition.'

He pulled a string of multicoloured fabric out of his pocket.

'Lewis!' I pushed his handkerchief hand down under the table. 'Not now! *Anyone* could come in.'

He looked at his hand. 'You said *not in school.*'

I glanced around. 'Not *anywhere,* not where anyone can see.' I shook my head. 'Kids from the blue estate might come in. Older kids.'

I glanced up at two women entering the café, wearing supermarket uniforms under their coats.

I gave Lewis a look. *You see?* 'And you don't know *who* they might tell. That could be Greeney and Liam's mums, for all you know.'

'They look way too young to be—'

'You know what I mean. Lewis, magic is for babies. I didn't make the rules. You can show me your tricks when we're in your bedroom, how's that?'

He took a slow sip of blackcurrant.

'This isn't just about me, Lewis. I'm doing this for both of us.'

'But you'll let me show you the trick in my bedroom.'

I rolled my eyes. 'Yes.'

'Can I wear the cape?'

'Do you really think that's a *red-blooded* thing to do?'

Lewis looked up at me. 'I don't know what *red-blooded* means.'

'I don't either.'

But we did, sort of. We both knew if you looked up *the opposite of red-blooded* in a dictionary, it would say *Lewis Harris in a cape doing magic tricks with handkerchiefs.*

Lewis crunched up his cup. 'If you had some hobbies you liked doing, I'd let you show me. You're much better at saying what you don't like doing.'

'That's not true! I like investigating, don't I?'

Lewis looked at the crunched-up cup in his hand.

I needed to get him spy-practising with me. So we could have some fun together, and he would remember we were friends. 'Let's investigate the strange man. Just as spy practice, I promise. We know he's not an axeman, don't we? So it's fine. Harmless.'

He got up to put the empty containers in the bin.

When he came back, I added, 'We'll be careful. And it'll be fun.'

I opened my coat and showed Lewis my secret pocket.

A minute later, he did the same.

We gave each other a secret smile and let our coat flaps fall back.

'We can start investigating him this afternoon.' I reached into my secret pocket and got out my spy fortune teller. 'And this will tell us what to do.'

'Just – only the strange man. Not Danielle's death.'

'OK,' I said. 'I'll listen to you. You're very sensible.'

He frowned.

'Honest.'

He stood up. 'I think I'll get another pack of biscuits, to celebrate.' And I watched him get up and put more money in the vending machine, grateful he'd saved me from having to lie to him too much – which would have been such a shame, when we'd only just made up.

What Might the Strange Man Have Done to Make Mum Call Him Strange?

1. Axeman stuff
2. Paedo stuff
3. Flashing

4. IRA terrorism – Manchester bomb
5. Drink-driving
6. Cut Mum up at a roundabout
7. Went to Danielle's funeral even though he didn't know her, or
8. Went to Danielle's funeral and stopped at M&S on the way back
9. Vandalised Monkford Precinct Christmas display with graffiti that time*
10. Killed Danielle

* 'Jesus is a bellend' and 'Mary and Joseph shagged ↓ these camels'

21

A good lookout stays cool, calm and collected – ideally,
he has nerves of steel.
The Junior Spy's Secret Handbook™

Eighteen days to the fair

I stayed crouched behind the parked car opposite 56 George
Street, my heart beating in my ears.

Now? I mouthed.

Lewis fidgeted, all alert, moving his weight from foot to
foot like he was fielding in a game of rounders. We'd agreed
our signals in the leisure centre café but now – an hour later,
now it was actually spy time – Lewis wasn't doing either of the
signals we agreed. He wasn't yawning *or* hooting like an owl.
Instead, he just jiggled by the lamppost, looking wide-eyed.

I strained my neck to make my eyes go as wide as his. *Do
something.*

'Now!' he barked.

Barked. Not *mouthed.* And he still didn't hoot.

Still, I ran.

I ran down the driveway of 56 George Street and towards
the house's black bin. My heart pumped hard as I grabbed
the twigs out of my pocket and arranged them in front of

the bin in a criss-cross shape. Too late, Lewis remembered to owl-hoot, *finally* – his owl sounded sad, more *unhappy pigeon* – and I took the lid off the bin, grabbed my prize, put the lid back on and ran.

Ten minutes later, we sat across from each other on Lewis's bed, the bin bag open between us.

Things in the Strange Man's Bin

1) Fourteen teabags, used
2) A microwave meal carton – chilli con carne, eaten
3) Three takeaway trays with scraps of sauce and noodles. Assume sweet and sour.
4) A bumper tin of value white emulsion paint, empty
5) A third of a bag of potatoes, sprouting
6) Three pairs of curtains with netting, old lady
7) An IKEA receipt for three pairs of curtains, six houseplants and a tap
8) A bottle of WeedBeGone! weedkiller, empty
9) A can of air-freshener in Outdoor Breeze, empty
10) Three family-size packets of Hot 'n' Fiery beef tortillas, empty
11) A two-pence coin, green on one side
12) A cigarette lighter, half full, broken spark
13) A box of twenty Silk Cut, empty

'He buys cigs in twenties.' Lewis nodded thoughtfully. 'That's odd.'

'A lot of adults do.' I tapped one of the packets of Hot 'n' Fiery beef tortillas. 'He got those from Paper Rack in the precinct. Eighty-nine pence.'

'Impressive!' Lewis said. 'How do you know?'

'Because that's where I always got mine. Not lately, though.'

Lewis pressed his lips together in pity – he knew I was avoiding the Paper Rack man.

I looked at our haul again. I moved the teabags so they were more central, to stop so much cold tea seeping onto Lewis's duvet. 'I was hoping to find something Irish. Is any of this stuff Irish?'

Lewis stared at our haul. 'I don't think so. He could still have done the IRA bomb though. He could be a mercenary.'

I shook my head. 'Things aren't always about mercenaries.'

Lewis poked at a carton. 'I suppose bombers eat food too.'

'Good point. And just because there's no bomb stuff here, it doesn't mean the man didn't build the bomb. Just that he didn't put any of the bomb wrappers in this bin.'

There were footsteps on the stairs. Lewis and I locked gazes in panic.

'Lewis?' Lewis's mum's voice was soft. 'Why's this door shut?'

'DON'T COME IN!' Lewis shouted.

I never heard Lewis shout. But I suppose if there's ever one person to make you feel like you're in charge, it's *this old thing, sorry, I'm so stupid* Lewis's mum.

'Why shouldn't I come in?'

'Mu-um!' Lewis made it have an extra syllable. 'I've *told* you!'

She threw the door open. 'And *I've* told *you* that the rules are you keep the door open when Fiona's here.'

'We're not having sex, Mrs Harris,' I said quickly. 'I promise.'

'I can see that, thanks, Fiona.' She sniffed. 'It's chlorine-y in here. You both definitely had showers?'

We both nodded, me furiously, hoping Lewis's mum wouldn't see how tangled my hair was. From not showering.

'Well, I know you kids wouldn't lie to me.'

I gave her a big smile. Mr Kellett would call it *irony* – that Lewis got the trusting mum, when he didn't even need one. When I was the kid who, last Christmas, had to go into school with a *real* temperature of 102, just because of that *one time* with the thermometer and the light bulb.

Mrs Harris looked at the bed. 'Is that a bin bag? What are you keeping in there?'

Lewis looked like he'd forgotten how to speak.

'A school project,' I said. 'It's fine.'

'Is that an *actual* bin bag *from an actual bin?*'

'No,' I said quickly.

'Is that paint? And teabags? On the *duvet?*'

The telly noises from downstairs stopped suddenly.

'Lisa?' Lewis's dad shouted up the stairs. 'What's the boy done now?'

Me and Lewis went still.

So did Mrs Harris. 'He's done nothing.' She lowered her voice. 'Get rid of that, *now.*' She gestured for Lewis to bundle up the stuff and put it under his bed.

Lewis gathered everything up, the paint tin and the air freshener clanking together.

I was about to shove the chilli con carne meal carton into the bin bag, when I saw something papery inside the carton. A shiny flyer, the size of a small envelope. The kind of flyer that comes through the door with the local paper.

And the picture on the flyer looked like—

There was no time to think. I pulled the flyer out of the meal carton and shoved the carton into the plastic bag. I pushed the flyer into my coat pocket, crumpling it in my rush.

Lewis was just pulling the duvet straight when his dad reached the top of the stairs.

He looked from me, to Lewis, to Lewis's mum. 'Everything all right?'

'Everything's fine,' Mrs Harris said.

'It smells like chlorine in here.'

'They've been swimming after school.'

'And paint. Chlorine and paint.'

I jumped up. 'I'd better go.'

I grabbed my bag and hurried out.

I waited until I was out of sight of Lewis's house to slow down and pull the flyer out of my pocket. I unfolded it.

Monkford Fair. Festival Field. Fri 19–Mon 22 July.

There was a smear of chilli sauce over the clown's face.

I turned the flyer over. On the plain side, someone had written messily, in biro:

registrar – death cert
will
account numbers

I stared and stared.

I didn't know the word *registrar*, but the next two words couldn't have stood out more. Not if they'd been written in neon highlighter.

Death cert.

I felt a splatter of rain on my shoulder. Then another on my head. Then another, and another – the droplets splatting down faster now.

I jammed the flyer into my pocket to keep it dry. I pulled up my hood and hurried towards home.

I'd been joking, investigating the strange man. Playing, practising. I'd been messing around when I wrote *killed Danielle* on the list of things the strange man might have done.

I'd been joking – till now.

Death cert.

Certain death.

Words written *on a flyer for the fair.*

I realised the splatters of rain had turned into a full-on shower without me noticing. Heavy rain drops exploded on my coat, like mini-bullets. I started to move, hurrying home.

I turned down George Street just as the shower was finishing. So I slowed at number 56.

The red car was in the drive, a light on inside the house. The criss-crossed twigs in front of the bin were how we left them, undisturbed.

I pulled the flaps of my coat tighter round me and ran the rest of the way home.

22

Sometimes a spy has no choice but to confront his quarry.
The Junior Spy's Secret Handbook™

Seventeen days to the fair
I didn't tell Lewis about the fair flyer on the way to school. We walked past 56 George Street that morning without a peep from me.

Lewis stared at the bins. 'The twigs haven't moved!'

I made myself smile and kept walking. 'Maybe there'll be another bin bag tomorrow.'

It was too nice having him as my friend again. I couldn't ruin it so soon.

School news! Greeney's had a shit haircut!

Really bad as well, like his mum's done it or something.

He swears she didn't. 'I had it done at the place on King Street, the one with the shampoos in the window – British Hairways. And by a barber, not a hairdresser. I can ask him to write a letter to prove it? I'll show you all the letter, that's fine. As if I'd let my mum cut my hair!'

But he would say that, wouldn't he?

His hair's longer on one side of his fringe than the other. Where he used to have two curtains, he now has exactly one curtain, one half-curtain. Which are called *tiers* when you're Mum, making fabric curtains.

I think Greeney should have cut the other side to match, but he obviously decided it was better to have half a shit haircut than a whole shit haircut.

Swings and roundabouts, Dad would say.

Anyway, now every time anyone passes Greeney in the corridor, any kid from any year, they shout *Haircut!* Our corridors get busy between lessons and you can hear when Greeney must be close by, because it's all, '*Haircut!*' '*Haircut!*', '*Haircut!*', '*Haircut!*', like a weird mating call across the school. Though no one would mate with Greeney, not when he looked *that* shit.

Greeney usually hangs around with the blue estate crowd, but I'm guessing he doesn't anymore.

Not for a while.

I didn't trust myself not to spill *death cert* and, besides, I needed time to think. So I told Lewis I didn't have time to hang out after school.

I sat cross-legged on my bed, the Scrabble dictionary and fair flyer on my lap. I stared at the hand-scribbled words.

registrar – death cert
will
account numbers

I looked up the words in the Scrabble dictionary.

Registrar – n – *keeper of official records*
Cert – n – *certainty*

Will – v – *used as an auxillary to form the future tense or to in-dicate intention, ability or expectation* – n – *strong determination*

I knew another meaning of *will*, from detective books – but Danielle wouldn't have had one. Kids don't have any money to leave.

And then ... *will* could also refer to a person? A person called *Will*?

The doorbell rang and lights flashed. I didn't move, not even when I heard a pretty laugh downstairs. Even Selina Baker couldn't tear me away from *death cert.*

I looked back at the flyer.

It could all be a code, of course. *Hide important information in lists,* that's what *The Junior Spy's Secret Handbook™* said.

But the whole point of codes was that they were impossible for people to break, without the key.

I pushed the flyer and Scrabble dictionary to one side in frustration.

One of my legs started jumping, on its own. Sending me a message.

Because – seventeen days to the fair. I had to do *something.*

I waited till Selina and Mum had gone out for their lesson and hurried downstairs. Dad was on the sofa, watching a quiz show.

'Fi!' He looked up. 'What do you know?' That was Dad's way of saying *How was your day?*

I pushed *death cert* out of my head and concentrated on what I'd memorised that morning. 'Well, Biljana Plavšić is in charge of the Bosnian Serbs now. Like we expected, Radovan Karadžić has relinquished power.'

Dad's smile faded.

'And Costas Simitis has been elected president of the Panhellenic Socialist Movement of Greece. *And* it's the Russian elections coming up, but I guess you knew that.'

Dad just stared up at me.

'Can I borrow the polaroid camera?'

He kept staring.

'Dad?'

Finally, he took in what I'd said. 'I know you like that camera but the film's so expensive, Fi. I've only just put in a new one. That camera's special occasions only.'

'Lewis has a new packet of film. We can replace yours with it.' Not true, but I could buy film with my money from the car boot sale.

'You promise you have film?'

I nodded.

'And you also have to promise you won't take the camera into school.' Dad got up from the sofa and got the camera from his high cupboard. 'I don't want you getting it confiscated and me having to beg for it back from Dr Sharma. If you break it, you'll have to give up your birthday present to get me another.'

He handed the camera over. Carefully, I cradled it. 'I'll only use it after school, I promise.'

'Oh. And there's one other condition.'

I waited.

'You make a call for me.' Dad smiled and jerked his head at the television. 'That number on the screen? Request an application form. And do me a favour – don't tell your mother.'

I made the call to the quiz show for Dad and gave our details for the application form.

Back upstairs, I sat on my bed, cross-legged, and took the polaroid camera out of its case. I turned the camera over, looking at the curves. I looked through the camera's window, imagining taking a photo.

I hate lying to Dad. But sometimes I have no choice.

This was crossing a line, I knew. Moving from kid's spying to adult spying. Taking secret photos was very different from sketching faces.

But that was fine. I was too old for kid's spying, anyway. No more hoofprints and practising limps. No more of the bits Lewis liked. I needed to focus. And, while I was focusing, I made another decision.

There was a smudge on the camera's window where my eye had been, so I wiped the glass with my sleeve.

No one had taken me seriously applying for any of the adult jobs. The news thing wasn't working, Dad's face downstairs told me that. My parents didn't think I was mature, just weird. *And* it was taking up too much time. It was bad enough having to learn about Bosnia and Greece but, with everything I had going on, I *really* didn't have time for the Russian elections right now.

I zipped the polaroid camera up in its case and placed it carefully into my rucksack.

It was time to get serious. No more kids' spying. No more trying to get my parents to think I was grown up. The key to going to the fair was finding out what happened to Danielle.

Death cert.

And the key to finding out what happened to Danielle was the strange man.

23

A good spy is clever, using red herrings and decoys to mask his true intentions.
The Junior Spy's Secret Handbook™

Sixteen days to the fair

Lewis took a lot of persuading to ring that doorbell at 8.30 that Wednesday morning.

'It's just a bit of fun, Lewis.' I tried to smile, trying not to look as scared as I felt. 'Just fun spying.'

'Of course, I'd help – normally.' Lewis looked at the pavement to avoid my eyes. 'If it wasn't the strange man's house, I wouldn't mind. But you haven't given me time to prepare. That house is the one place. . .'

'It's got to be right now.' I kept my arms folded. 'There are too many people around later, and the sound of that lawn mower will cover the noise of the camera. And it's got to be you. I can't do both jobs.'

Lewis gave a sad nod. He trailed after me.

I positioned myself down the side passage of 56 George Street. I jerked my head at him – *go on*.

Lewis rang the doorbell. We waited.

And waited.

'He's not in,' Lewis whispered, ventriloquist-style.

'Ring it again,' I whispered.

Lewis pressed the button again. Nothing.

He rang the doorbell a third time.

Lewis pulled his hand away and the door opened.

The strange man stood there in just a T-shirt and checked boxer shorts, his hair all messed up round his face.

Lewis went as still as one of those painted men who pretend to be statues in town centres.

The strange man looked down at Lewis. 'Hi.'

Lewis hurried the words out, extra squeaky and fast. '*Dyouneeanyjobsdoin?*'

'Sorry?'

Lewis took a breath and put more space between the words. 'Do you need any jobs doing?'

'Jobs?' The strange man ruffled his hair. He reached behind for a hairband and started tying his hair back. 'What are you on about, mate?'

'Like scouts do. Car washing. Cleaning up leaves.'

'Oh.' The strange man finished tying his hair back. 'OK, I get it. Now you come to mention it, maybe I wouldn't mind some help with a bit of gardening, maybe some—'

I leapt out and took two photos. I darted back into the side passage and let the two pictures spit from the camera into my hand.

'RUN!' Lewis shouted. To *himself.*

I shrank back in the side passage while Lewis legged it. He was up the road and around the corner, heels flying, as fast as I'd ever seen him move.

The man watched him go, reaching behind for a cigarette and lighter. He stood, facing out of the front door, smoking.

I waited until he had gone back in the house before I put the camera back in my bag and zipped it up.

Wafting the two polaroid photos, barely daring to look, I strolled out of the side passage, making my arms and legs extra loose, trying to look like I belonged down there.

At breaktime, Lewis and I stood at the far end of the school field, looking at the photos.

The strange man looked funny in his boxer shorts. In one of the photos, he had his mouth open. In the other, he was mid-blink, leaving his eyes looking drunk. He had curly hairs sprinkled unevenly across his chest and, though he was skinny, he had a rounded lump of tummy just above the waistband of his boxer shorts.

'He's a bit blurry,' Lewis said.

'The pictures are fine.' I snatched the photos back. 'Unless you want to do it again?'

'NO! You're right, they're great.' He scratched his chin furiously. 'Do you think he saw you?'

I felt a cold wind on the warm day.

'No.' I shook my head, hard. 'No, there's no way he could have seen me. I waited till he was back in the house.'

I thought some more.

'I'm positive. He definitely, *definitely* didn't see me.'

School news! It was a bad lunchtime for Craig Parsons, the hardest lad in fifth year.

He'd been on a bench at the side of the corridor, acting big in front of a crowd, showing how to snap a pencil using a karate chop.

Craig had his hand out, ready. 'You have to keep your wrist

straight, see?' He was so busy demonstrating, he didn't see the New Head coming, or the other kids stepping to the side to make room.

The New Head just waited. Craig looked up.

She didn't even have to put her hand out before Craig picked up the pencil and handed it straight over. She walked away, leaving Craig on the bench with nothing to chop, while everyone around, boys and girls, pointed and went *'Aaah!'* and *'Do your karate now, Bruce Lee!'*

Despite Lewis's panic, I'd got the photos I needed, so I worked on my letters in my bedroom that night. Dad was out at the pub and, outside my door, the attic ladder was down. Bumps and shuffling from above told me that Mum was up there, rummaging around.

Dear *Crimewatch*,

There is a strange man who lives in Monkford. I don't know his name but he lives at 56 George Street.

This is a photo of him. His mouth looks funny because he was talking. He didn't know he was having his photo taken.

I think he might be linked to the death of Danielle Larson at Monkford Fair in July 1982.

I thought you could compare the photo with the suspect's description in unsolved cases? Particularly any certain deaths at fairs.

I will keep investigating him and let you know if I find out more.

Thank you,

Fiona Larson

I wrote the same letter to the police, just changing the

section about his mouth to fit the other photo – *his eyes look weird because he's blinking*. I put both letters and photos in envelopes. I was just licking an envelope, thinking Mum and Dad were nearly out of stamps, *again,* when there was a shout from the attic.

'*YES!*'

There was a clanging of someone coming down a ladder too quickly. The floor shook as Mum jumped down.

I shoved my envelopes under my pillow just as she threw my bedroom door open.

'I found it!'

'Found what?'

She beamed at me. 'I *knew* I wouldn't have thrown the NHS records away!' She dusted her hands off. 'They were in the attic, with her old schoolbooks. Danielle was B. B positive.' Mum grinned like she'd found a lost pet.

It took me a minute to realise.

Mum stayed in the doorway, her smile fading a little. 'Go on, then! What are you waiting for?' She made shooing hands. 'Don't you want to write it in your book?'

I slipped off the bed quietly. I got my project book from the bookshelf and filled in *B positive* under *Sibling One* on my chart, next to the others.

Mum nodded. 'Told you I'd find it.'

When I looked up again, she'd gone.

I put my project book away. I got the two letters from under my pillow and put them in my rucksack, ready to post.

I reached for my paper fortune teller and slid my fingers and thumbs between the folds. I moved it, making deliberate choices. Knowing what my future would hold.

Secret Pocket. 7. Stage a bike puncture and spy on someone.

Lewis wouldn't like it. But Lewis had shown that he wasn't a reliable accomplice.

Maybe, this time, Lewis didn't need to know.

24

An effective spy finds a reason to linger near his quarry. He can wait for a bus, or repair a bicycle puncture.
The Junior Spy's Secret Handbook™

Fifteen days to the fair
The most amazing school news!

The teachers have moved the cross-country course this year. The course now does an extra loop round the school field and the back of the sports hall, rather than going down to the railway line and through the fields with long grass, as it used to.

That doesn't sound exciting?

There's a second bit. They've moved the cross-country course this year because of . . . *flashers*.

The rumour is that flashers know where us kids run, and there are men in suits and ties, dotted around in bushes, just waiting to flash any kid they can. According to the story, if we ran round the old course, we'd risk seeing some kind of old man, peckers-out, Mexican wave.

I'm not sure it's true. It can't be true. Some facts are too interesting to be true.

*

After managing to keep my plan secret from Lewis all day, I told Dad I was going out for a bike ride after school.

In the garden shed, I pocketed the puncture repair kit and stabbed my bike's back tyre with secateurs. I wheeled the bike to the lamppost on George Street.

I pulled the bike up onto the pavement and lay it down to 'examine' my flat tyre, my best sad face on.

Every so often, I looked up.

The strange man paced across his lounge. I could see him through the front window, talking into a phone.

I did some huffing and puffing. I blew up the tyre with my bike pump. I put my hands on my hips and watched the air hiss back out.

I sat cross-legged in front of my bike.

The strange man came out of the front door, still talking on the phone. He smoked a cigarette.

I tried not to look, but I could still hear his conversation.

'Thanks, Chris. Yep, I'll do that. Yep. I'm on it.'

'Of course. I'll double-check with logistics, but I think we're good to go.'

I looked up and the man looked quickly away. He jiggled the phone between his hands, like it was too hot to hold.

I tried to remember his conversation so I could add it to a future list of facts. I was just trying to memorise everything he said when I looked up – *right into his eyes.*

'Hi there.' The man stood over me, smiling. 'You got a puncture?'

I tried to breathe. I made myself nod.

He crouched down. 'Let's have a look.' He put his mobile phone on the pavement. I couldn't help staring at it.

He reached for the tyre and pressed it. 'It's a big puncture. Like you've ridden over a hedgehog or something.'

I was about to frown and say *but that would mean loads of tiny punctures, not a big one.*

Then I realised. It was meant to be a joke.

Adult jokes need to be funnier if they want kids to get them straight away. Either way, something about him making such a bad joke made me feel less scared.

He stood up. 'I wonder if there's somewhere round here we could get a puncture repair kit?'

I took the kit out of my pocket and handed it to him.

He smiled. 'Girl guide?'

'No. I don't like jam. I mean, I like eating it rather than making it.'

He opened the kit. He unfolded the instructions to read.

'It says start by *taking the wheel off.*' He waved his hands at the instructions. 'But it doesn't say *how* to take the wheel off.'

He kept reading. For ages.

I shifted the bike's chain to the small cog to make slack, and opened the brake. I pushed back the lever and took out the wheel.

The strange man gave a nervous laugh. 'Right.' He looked at the instructions. 'Point two says *unseat one side of the tyre.* Unseat. What does that even mean, *unseat?* What kind of word is *unseat?*'

He was so weird, in an awkward-rather-than-murdery-paedo way, I forgot to be scared. I used the lever to pull the inner tube out, like Dad had taught me. 'Are you any good at this stuff?'

'Not really. I'm useless. But I'm a grown-up, so probably better than you, right?' He adjusted his ponytail. 'Or not.'

I looked at his mobile phone again. The flip-out bit at the

bottom. The buttons. The yellow of the lettering, telling me the numbers would glow in the dark.

'You like my phone?'

'It's amazing. I've never seen one before.'

'It's really not that great. It's a work phone. If it rings, it means someone wants me to do some work.'

I kept staring at the phone.

'Do you want to hold it?'

I jerked my head up in a panic, but he was definitely just talking about the phone. His trousers were still zipped up.

I looked around. There were other people in the street. It was still daylight.

I took the phone quickly. 'Thanks.'

I felt the weight of it in my hand. I turned it over.

I opened the flip bit and held it to my ear. I said 'hello' into the silence.

'You can make a call,' the man said. 'If you're really quick.'

'No thanks.' I flipped the phone closed. 'My friend Lewis will be having a snack about now. Toast, probably. Peanut butter.'

The man put his phone in his pocket. 'Fair enough.'

He didn't seem to be looking to move, and the instructions were slack in his hand, so I reached down for the puncture repair kit.

'Is Lewis the kid you meet here in the mornings?'

I nodded. I unfolded the piece of sandpaper and started sanding the inner tube.

'Will you tell him to knock back on my door on the way past?' He folded the instructions back up. 'I think I spooked your Lewis, but I would be very interested to take him up on his offer about strimming.'

I nodded. I finished repairing the puncture on my own.

He watched me glue the patch on. 'Looks like I'm here as moral support.'

'Thanks anyway.'

'You're' – he made his voice light – 'Gail's daughter.'

'And you're the man from the supermarket who's come back because his mum died.'

'Yep.' Quickly, he looked at the instructions.

I screwed the lid back on the glue.

'*Seat*, again!' He held the instructions in one hand, batting the back of his other hand against the paper. '*Reseat* this time. What have they got about *seats*?' He turned the instructions over. 'We have to reseat the tyre bead. Any ideas?'

He watched me put the inner tube back in. 'Right. You're pretty good at this stuff, aren't you?'

I didn't tell him I was a girl plus/boy minus. I just smiled.

He helped me stand my bike up. 'I used to work in sales with your mum, a long time ago. Did she mention that?'

'No.'

'Does she still work at the brewery?'

'She's a driving instructor now.'

'Really?' He smiled. 'I can't imagine that.'

I thought about how angry Mum got at roundabouts. 'Nor can I.' I took a breath. 'Did you know my sister too? Danielle?'

'I just knew your mum a bit from work; I didn't know the family.' But he didn't react or look caught out.

I nodded.

He crouched down to pick his phone off the ground. 'My name's Carl.'

'I'm Fiona.' I watched him put his phone in his pocket. 'But everyone calls me Fi.'

'Fi.' He kicked the bike tyre. 'Looks good, that. You did a good job.'

I made myself ask. 'Carl, are you going to the fair this year?'

'Dodgems and donkey derbies?' He smiled. 'I'm forty-five, mate. A bit long in the tooth for hook-a-duck.' He handed me back the instructions. 'I should get back to work. Nice to meet you, Fi.'

He pushed his hands in his pockets roughly and walked away.

His walk reminded me a bit of Lewis when he knows he's being watched, his movements all awkward and spiky.

The Strange Man

1) He's called Carl
2) He has a mobile phone for his job
3) He does work for someone called Chris
4) He used to work with Mum in sales at the brewery
5) He says he didn't know Danielle
6) He wants to talk to Lewis about something called strimming
7) He doesn't know how to repair a bike puncture
8) He doesn't know how to follow basic written instructions
9) He wasn't that scary up close
10) He says he isn't going to the fair
11) If you didn't know he was a strange man, you'd think he was actually . . . quite nice

Maybe I should have included Lewis in the mission, after all.

If I'd included him, he might not have gone so *parent* about it. Because he stopped playing his computer game the moment I told him that Friday lunchtime. He let his rhino die and span his chair to face me.

'The strange man wants to talk to me about *what?*'

'Strimming.'

'Strimming! Strimming? What the hell is *strimming*? I can't *believe* you did that!'

'It's fine.' I waved a hand. 'Eat your sandwiches, Lewis. *Chill.*'

'A puncture. You really just got a puncture on George Street? And you needed to repair it, right outside his house?'

I nodded.

'Just like it says in *The Junior Spy's Secret Handbook*?'

I swallowed.

'Strimming!'

'I'm sure it's something fine.'

'What was the man like?' Lewis's voice was less squeaky now.

'He was nice, actually. He let me hold his mobile phone.'

'If he was nice to you, that means he's sneaky.'

'It was a really good phone. It had a flip bit at the bottom.'

'And if he's sneaky, we have to be even more careful. Your mum's not a liar. She wouldn't say he was strange if he wasn't.'

'She might not be lying; she might just be wrong.' I really needed to solve Danielle's death, but I wasn't convinced anymore that Carl was *definitely* the murderer. In fact – I was pretty sure now that I'd made a mistake. 'It wouldn't be the first time Mum got something wrong. Remember when she said it didn't matter what rucksack I got? That kids would make friends with me because of *my personality*?' I watched Lewis's rhino on the screen flash dead. '*And* she said everyone would soon forget about me showing my pants at primary school.'

I nudged Lewis's lunchbox towards him, hoping he'd get distracted by his box of raisins.

'He must have seen you taking his picture on Wednesday.'

Lewis left his raisins untouched. 'He suspects you. Otherwise why would he come out to help? Unless he was really good at punctures?'

He waited for an answer.

'He was useless,' I admitted.

'There then.' Lewis sat up straighter. 'He must either have seen you take a photo, or he's a paedo. Those are the only reasons he'd come outside. Which would you prefer?'

'He didn't touch his zip once.' I folded my arms. 'Or ask me to sit on his knee.'

'But paedos don't all act like paedos *all the time*, do they? They have to go to shops and stuff. They can't have their peckers out if they're paying for petrol or sitting in offices.'

'His name's Carl.' I nudged Lewis's box of raisins closer still. 'Carl's not a paedo name.'

Lewis started reaching. He paused. 'What's a paedo name?'

'I don't know. Bill?'

'*Bill?*'

I shrugged. 'Jack?'

Lewis stopped smiling. 'No, Jack's my grandpa. And – hang on, *the man told you his name?*'

'Stop flapping.'

'Did you tell him *your* name?'

I looked down at my lunch box. I put the lid carefully on the top and squeezed it till it clicked.

He gasped. 'Fi-on-a!'

'Fi.'

'Fi! You're *playing with fire*! Don't talk to him again. Promise me you won't.'

I looked down and pretended to brush a bit of dust off my skirt. 'I'm positive I won't talk to him again.'

'Not positive. Promise?'

I took breath. 'Promise.'

The thing is, if you're already really bad, there's not much lower you can go.

But Lewis had scared me. I pretended I needed to speak to Dr Sharma, and went to look at the encyclopaedias in the school library. I needed something better than a Scrabble dictionary to investigate what the writing on the flyer had been on about.

In the library, I got the R edition of the encyclopaedia from the shelf and carried it to one of the big tables in the middle of the room. I put it down with a thud and found the right page.

A **registrar** *is an official keeper of records made in a register. The term may refer to (see specific sections below):*

- *Education*
- *Government records*
- *Medicine . . .*

There were *loads* of sections.

Not all spying is fun.

After what felt like hours, something under *Government Records* caught my attention.

The General Register Office or General Registry Office is the name given to the government agency responsible for recording vital records such as marriages, births and deaths, and items related to property transactions. Marriage, birth and death certificates are issued . . .

I stared. *Death certificates.*

I pulled the crumpled fair flyer out of my pocket.

registrar – death cert
will
account numbers

*Registrar – death cert*IFICATE.

I shoved the encyclopaedia back onto the shelf and crumpled the flyer up in one hand.

I could see it now, as clear as anything. Carl had been on the phone to someone about paperwork. Stuff to do with *his mum* dying, not Danielle. And he jotted down notes on the nearest piece of paper – which happened to be a flyer that had come through the door – a fair flyer. Something that he thought was junk.

That list had nothing to do with certain death. Or the fair. Or Danielle.

Which meant *Carl* had nothing to do with Danielle's death. There was no reason to link them at all.

The bell rang and I picked up my rucksack. I pushed the crumpled flyer into the library bin.

If my investigations had been a game, I would have just bumped back down a long snake. I was nearly back where I'd started.

I had two weeks to go. *Two weeks*. And, now Carl had turned out to be a red herring, I only had one lead. The article on the microfiche at the library. The only clue I had left.

By Adrian Sykes.

25

Sometimes my parents say they've done something for my
benefit but it actually makes my life worse.
(paradox)

Thirteen days to the fair

The next morning, Saturday, I knew Mum was out on lessons. I stood on the stairs, planning to make a dash for the
phonebook while Dad wasn't looking.

Happily, Dad was distracted. His quiz show application
form had arrived, and he was filling it out at the peninsula.

Dad saw me on the stairs. 'Fi, look at this!' He waved me
over. 'What's the capital of Italy, *see*? Twenty grand top prize,
and *these* are the questions!'

I smiled and pulled the kitchen door closed between us. I
grabbed the phonebook and ran upstairs.

I knew I was born unlucky as well as bad. Get this.

There were *twenty-three* A Sykes in the local phonebook,
and *none* of them might be Adrian Sykes the reporter.

I called the first number and a woman answered. 'Five one
two eight three nine.'

I coughed. 'Can I speak to Adrian?'

'Who is this?' The woman sounded like she was eating crisps.

'Fiona Larson.' *I* wanted to be eating crisps.

'Fiona who?'

'Larson. L-A-R-S-O-N.'

Crisp crunch, crisp crunch. 'How old are you?'

'Twelve this month.'

'And you want to speak to *who?*'

'Adrian.' I drummed my pen on my bedside table. 'A-D-R-I-A-N.'

The woman chuckled. 'But there's no Adrian here, pet!' *Crisp crunch.*

I put the phone down and tried the next one.

An old lady answered. '*Hello?*'

'Can I speak to Adrian please?'

'Adrian who?'

How many Adrians did this woman have living with her? 'Adrian *Sykes.*'

'Wrong number. You've got me out of the garden for nothing!'

The dial tone told me she'd hung up, just like that. Rude for an old lady, I thought.

It went on like this. Eleven more wrong numbers. Eleven more people who couldn't hear me properly, or asked me to repeat myself, or talked down to me, like the man who said, in a slow careful voice, 'Can't your mum help you make calls so you get the right number?' – like he couldn't tell the difference between a little kid and someone who was *nearly twelve.*

The fourteenth call took ages.

'What number did you ring?' This woman sounded like she had a cold.

'It doesn't matter because it's not you, is it? Sorry for bothering you.'

'But what number did you ring?'

I checked the phonebook and said the number again.

'That's the right number, but there's no Adrian here.'

I raised my gaze to the ceiling.

It's like, the more time I spend dealing with adults, I'm not sure they're the geniuses we're always told.

'Thanks,' I said.

'Where did you get my number from? I'm wondering if someone's registered it incorrectly in a phonebook and I'm going to start getting lots of calls, or—'

I decided to act like the rude old lady earlier, and hung up. I never usually do that, but this woman *wouldn't stop*.

I dialled the fifteenth number. 'Can I speak to Adrian?'

'I'll just get him.' A friendly female voice. 'Who is it?'

I panicked. 'Fiona. Fiona Larson.'

'Hang on.' There was the clunk of the woman putting the phone down on something. 'Adrian!'

More muffled clunking as the phone was handed over.

'Hello?' A man's voice.

'Adrian Sykes?'

His voice sounded crinkly. 'Speaking.'

'You are a reporter on the *Monkford and District Advertiser*?'

A pause. 'It's been a while. Who is this?'

He didn't sound like a scary wall-of-ham man. 'Fiona Larson.'

'Right. And you are. . .?' He sounded quite nice, actually. Like a nice old grandpa.

'Someone looking for some information. You wrote an article about my sister in 1982 and I found the article on the microfiche at the library.'

'1982!' There was laughter in his voice. 'Well, now.'

I pressed the phone hard against my ear. 'She died. At the fair. And I want to know how she died. Danielle Larson in 1982. She was eleven. Can you tell me?'

When he didn't answer straight away, I added, 'Please?'

There was quiet for a minute.

'You're Fiona, you said?'

Fi. But, 'Yes.'

'How old are you, Fiona?'

'Twelve in August.'

'Do your parents know you're calling?'

'I don't want to bother them,' I said. 'They're busy.'

'Love. Some advice. If you want to know more about your sister's death – and I was very sorry to hear about it, by the way – your mum and dad are the ones to ask.'

'They won't talk about it.'

He didn't say anything.

'And seeing as you're on the phone now, Mr Sykes, and I've already got you up from whatever you were doing . . . it will only take a second. Could you tell me how she died? I definitely won't ask any more questions afterwards.'

The line was quiet. My ear ached where I pressed the phone against my head, and I moved it further away.

That was better.

'Fiona, I couldn't tell you if I wanted to. I wrote a lot of articles for that paper. Thousands. I was a news reporter. And it was a long time ago.'

'But she *died.* You'd remember a girl who died.'

'I'm sorry, love. When you work on a local paper – a lot of people die.'

'But she was *eleven.* People don't die at eleven. You'd remember *that.*'

He said nothing.

'You *said* she was perfect.' I realised I was pressing the phone hard into my head again. 'You *said* my parents were devastated. You said she was active in the RSPB, and she was dead when the paramedics arrived. Danielle Larson. Blonde hair. Smiley. Tall for an eleven-year-old. Pretty as a picture. You *must* remember! Surely no one else has ever died at the fair?'

He still didn't reply.

'Are you still there?'

'I don't know what to say to you, Fiona.'

'Is there any way you can find out?'

'I retired, love. Five years ago.'

'But do you still know some people at the paper? Do you have your own records or—'

'I'm sorry. I'm going now.'

I switched the phone off. I looked at the address of the number I'd dialled. *23 Chestnut Walk.*

I closed the phonebook and I sat there on my bed, for a very long time. I didn't even hear Dad come up the stairs, till he was in my doorway.

'Come to the shops with me, Fi. Let's go and get something interesting for dinner.'

It was a shame, I decided, that if you wanted to have your secret pocket, you needed to wear a coat.

Because today, the sun had fully *got his hat on*, as the song went – and now everyone was smiley and other people were all *hip hip hooray*-ing in their T-shirts and shorts.

But not me.

The first thing Dad said as we left the house was still, 'Have you got your inhaler?' But we weren't even out of the drive before he followed it with, 'Aren't you hot in that coat?'

Have you got your inhaler? and *Aren't you hot in that coat?* follow me around like *haircut* follows Greeney.

'You never know when you might need a coat,' I said. 'We might bump into some kid from school and they might ask me over for a barbecue. And it gets cold at night.'

We turned down George Street and I tried to imagine something less likely than me bumping into some kid from school and them inviting me over for a barbecue.

I trailed behind Dad when we reached 56 George Street, out of habit. Just to see what he did.

But Dad didn't cross at the postbox, just walked straight in front of Carl's house. He smiled at me as he walked.

I pointed at the postbox. 'I usually cross the road here with Lewis and Sean.'

Dad nodded. 'So I hear. Your mum said there's a story about an axeman killing his brothers and sisters in that house.' His voice was even.

'Just his brothers, I think. No sisters. Or maybe he didn't think to mention the sisters.'

'Do you believe the story?'

'I don't think so. Hardly at all.'

Dad smiled. 'Is your friend Sean the kind of kid who makes things up?'

I nodded. 'He has an awful lot of cousins. Drummers in bands. Racing car drivers.'

'Do you need me to tell you that story about the man with the axe isn't true?'

I shook my head.

Dad and I reached the park and passed the big wasps' nest. I watched the wasps buzz around it in a cloud, circling the nest like moons around a planet.

'You know you mentioned going to a kid's house later for a barbecue? Why do you never invite kids over to ours?'

I would never say it was because of the flashing lights when someone rang the door. 'It's just easier to go to Lewis's.' He looked sad, like he knew anyway, so I added quickly, 'And because I don't really have any friends.'

But then Dad looked sadder still, so I said, 'It's fine.' *Change the subject.* 'Now, I hear Mum used to work in a brewery?'

Dad nodded. 'She worked in sales there. Your mum was good at sales.' His smile faded. 'But it's really unfair for her to expect other people to be as good when they haven't had any formal training. And, as I tried to explain to your mother, not a lot of people *want* ironing board covers.'

It took me a second to realise what we were talking about.

'Anyway, Mum worked in sales at the brewery,' Dad said, 'but she changed jobs when she was pregnant with you. We both made the decision to change jobs at the same time. You know I used to be an aeroplane engineer?'

I frowned. 'It was my fault you stopped being an engineer?'

'No, silly!' He smiled. 'Me and your mum both worked long days and we didn't always see each other that much. My work was over an hour away, and your mum was always on the road, driving all over the country. And we wanted a different life. Something happening, something big, makes you rethink what you want. And when Danielle—'

I held up my hand. 'Right. That.' Always.

'We wanted to be better to each other, and we both wanted to be around more for you, Fi. To be better parents. We wanted to make the most of our time with you, and we don't regret it for a second.'

I looked at the park's second-biggest bush.

A bunch of boys and girls sat on picnic blankets, smoking

and drinking Coke, flicking through magazines. These kids were made differently from the kids from our school. They were shinier, with newer clothes, and the boys talked in a different kind of loud and, I knew – even though they weren't in uniform – they wore blazers and school uniform, even in sixth form.

Chester Road School kids.

I'd once asked Mum if I could go to Chester Road and she laughed like it was the funniest thing ever, and said, 'Yes, fine. And we can get a chauffeur and a butler, too.'

I saw what the kids were doing and my heart stopped.

These Chester Road kids were, right now, sitting in front of our bush – *reading magazines*.

Had I stolen the magazines from *these kids*? Would they look at me and just *know*? Chester Road kids weren't as hard as Monkford High kids – it was just a known fact – but still.

I moved onto the other side of Dad, trying to look casual and un-thief-like. But none of the kids said anything as I walked past. I'm not sure they even noticed me there, at all.

26

A spy cell is only as strong as its weakest member.
The Junior Spy's Secret Handbook™

Eleven days to the fair

The rest of the weekend passed without anything exciting going on. When I waited for Lewis at the lamppost on Monday morning, there was a big truck outside 56 George Street, and a dirty yellow skip in the driveway. Carl was outside in a T-shirt and shorts, talking to a man in grey overalls.

He saw me and waved. I waved back.

Lewis walked up and stared.

I shrugged. 'Just waving to Carl.'

'Hey, kid!' Carl waved both hands now, trying to get our attention. 'Lewis, is it?'

Lewis looked at me in panic. He set off in a rush.

'Come back!' Carl crinkled his face up in confusion. 'Why are you running? I won't bite. I just want to talk to you about some strimming!'

I hurried after Lewis and found him in the park.

'Strimming.' He looked like a wild animal was after him. 'Strimming! *What is strimming?*'

'I'm sure it's nothing bad. He wouldn't shout it in the street, would he?'

'We don't know what he's capable of, Fi! That's the whole point!'

'I've decided Carl might not be a strange man after all. I've got him all wrong. And think about it. If strimming is like flashing, he wouldn't be making a big deal of it. Flashers don't shout *I'm flashing*, do they? They just open their coats and do it.'

'I feel dizzy,' Lewis said. 'And I've got a tummy ache.'

'You've just got scared and ran too soon after breakfast.'

'Do I look right to you?'

I stopped and gave a big sigh. I turned to study him.

His skin was shiny with sweat. He had a fuzzy look in his eyes.

'You look fine,' I said kindly. I pulled on his arm. 'Come on.'

School news. But not good school news.

Turns out Lewis *was* ill.

He threw up in English, all over his copy of *The Taming of The Shrew*, and his mum had to come and pick him up. I'm not in that English class, but I heard Mr Kellett told all the kids to get back, while the rest of the class laughed and pointed and made Jaws music *ner-ner-ner-ner* and Robert Kitson shouted, *Harris is about to blow!*

Which – turned out – he was.

Everyone heard about it. Which meant I hoped Lewis was off ill for a few days, at least. For his own sake.

On the way home, I headed down George Street. It was fine – I felt *way* more relaxed walking past Carl's house now.

The van had gone but, next to the skip, there were boxes

and old household things. A broken lamp. A metal shelf. A frilly tissue box.

Carl came outside carrying a box. His T-shirt had a cartoon with *Duff Beer* on it, even though that's from *The Simpsons*, and *The Simpsons* is a show for kids.

He rested the box on the edge of the skip and started pulling things out.

I crossed the road. 'What are you doing?'

'Getting rid of Mum's stuff.' Carl got a lamp out of the box and placed it on the lid of the skip. 'We're exchanging contracts on the house in a couple of weeks. Hopefully.' He nudged the lamp with his foot. 'Keep or throw away? Would anyone want this?'

The lamp was one of those desk ones with a little hat, on a long bendy stem that folded in on itself. This lamp had a broken bit of stem which made the hat loll to one side, like a rose that needed dead-heading.

'*No one* would want that stuff.'

He looked down at the lamp. He picked it up and put it in the tip after all.

'Your mate, Lewis.' Carl leaned on the skip. 'I don't get that kid. He knocks on my door to offer to help me and then I say *great, thanks* and he just runs off? And now runs off whenever he sees me?'

I pressed my lips together. *What can you do?*

'Now, I've got something for you and I think you're going to like it.' He turned and opened his front door. 'Come in.'

I took a step to follow him, then stopped. A hand of fear squeezed my stomach.

'Sensible girl. Don't go into strangers' houses.' He nodded. 'Wait here.'

I watched him go inside.

He came out, holding his flip-bottomed mobile phone. He gave it to me to hold and I turned it over, admiring it.

Now he had his hands free, I waited for him to pull what he'd got for me out of his pocket.

He didn't move.

I looked up. We stared at each other.

I waited again.

'Aren't you going to say "thank you?"'

I frowned. 'Aren't you going to give me something?'

He nodded at the phone. 'What do you think *that* is?'

I looked at the phone and back at Carl. I still didn't get it.

Thing is, I'd been alive nearly twelve years now, and things like this just don't happen to me.

Carl sighed. 'My work have given me a new contract mobile with a new number, so I don't need this old pay-as-you-go anymore. I was going to throw it away, then I remembered the little girl who looked so interested in my phone while we fixed her puncture. And I thought – *why not make her day?*'

I looked at the phone again.

'It's yours. If you want it.'

I turned the phone over in my hand. I was misunderstanding. Hearing what I wanted to hear, like Mum said I did. Because it sounded a bit like—

'Fi.' Carl shoved his hands in his pockets. 'Don't make this weird. I didn't mean it to be weird.' He took out his hairband and retied his hair. 'I'm not weird, I promise. I'm not . . .' – he gave a high laugh – 'God, no, nothing like that. Oh Jesus, I really wish I hadn't started this. I'm just giving you this because I don't need it and you liked it. But I could just throw it in the skip with the other junk. And you don't owe me anything. It's not a big deal.'

I looked down at the phone.

'There's less than a fiver of time left on it.'

A *phone.*

A real, proper phone.

My phone.

'But if you don't want it—'

'No!' I gripped it tighter. 'Please can I have it?'

Carl nodded. 'That's more like it!'

'It's mine? Really mine?'

He laughed. 'No one else here, is there?'

I looked around, just in case. Like I said, things like this don't just happen to Fiona Larson every day. *Especially* not Fiona Larson.

'I'd suggest phoning your friend to test it out, but you probably don't want to waste your credit.'

I held the phone in both hands.

He scratched his top lip. 'Probably best not to tell your mum and dad it's from me.'

I looked up. 'Why?'

He left a long pause.

'I'm a stranger, aren't I? We don't really know each other. Your parents' – he took out his hairband, retying his hair *again* – 'well. Never mind.'

We stood there in his driveway, both looking at the ground.

'Thank you for the phone. Carl.'

He rolled back on his feet, his hands in his pockets. He rolled forward again. 'No problem, Fi.'

'Do I need to write you a thank-you letter?'

'Definitely not. Careful crossing the road, now. You seem in shock.'

'I am.' I shielded my eyes from the sun and looked up at him. 'Carl, people don't go around giving me presents every day.'

He raised his palms. 'Look, it's not *that* great a present. The screen's scratched and the three button sticks. Sometimes it freezes for no reason and you have to hold down the off button to get it going. Takes ages. Like I said, there's hardly any credit on it. I just thought, rather than throw it away, I'd give it to you.'

I nodded. 'Thank you.'

'Bye for now.'

'Bye.'

I slid the phone into my secret pocket and turned towards home. I tried not to run. I tried to walk like this was just any normal day. Just feeling the outline of my phone, jiggling against my chest as I walked.

I'd been so sad this weekend. And that seemed so long ago now.

Because this – *this* – changed EVERYTHING.

This phone was absolutely, positively, the best thing that had ever happened to me.

27

Lewis doesn't want good things to happen to us.
(paradox)

Eleven days to the fair

I rang Lewis after tea – from the house phone, of course. I wasn't going to waste the credit on my new mobile.

His mum answered. 'He can't come to the phone, lovey. It's nice you're concerned and I'll pass on your regards.'

'I need to talk to Lewis though. Urgently.'

'He's too ill to talk, the poor thing. No one will tease him about being sick, will they? The other kids will be kind?'

I picked up the mobile phone. I tested the weight of it in my hand. 'No, Mrs Harris.' I kept my voice level. '*No one* will tease him at all.'

'I'll tell him you called. I'll tell him you said to get well soon.'

I took the phone downstairs, to where Mum and Dad were on the sofa.

I put the phone back in the cradle. 'Mum. I've got a word question.'

Mum paused. 'A *word question*, hmm.' She turned to look at Dad, then gave me a small smile. 'What do you think, Jonathan? Hypothesis?'

Dad put his finger on his lip, like he was thinking. 'Provisional?'

'Or am I going to be asked again to explain'– she pronounced it carefully – 'an-ti-dis-est-ab-lish-ment-a-r-i-an-ism?'

'Not antidisestablishmentarianism.' I said it more easily than her, but then, adults don't say it as much as kids do. 'I'm sorry if this is a really bad thing to ask about, but I really, *really* need to know.'

Mum and Dad looked at each other.

'Oh God,' Mum said.

'Not *fellatio*, again?' Dad said. 'Please, Fi. Trust us when we said we'd explain that when—'

'Please don't get angry.' I took a breath. 'But what, exactly, is *strimming*?'

At lunchtime the next day, I stood in the playground, near the tennis courts, my mobile phone to my ear. When any kids walked past, I talked like I was having a conversation.

'He said *what*?'

and

'What did she do then?'

I took my phone away from my ear when I saw a teacher because you never know with Lost Property. There's a rumour Dr Sharma wears confiscated earrings to wine bars at the weekends.

I walked up in Sean's direction, but he mustn't have seen the phone because he turned and walked away.

It was fine. Besides, Sean was no good to me now – it was girl friends I needed for the Waltzers.

I walked around the school field and weaved between the groups of girls on the grass. Every so often, I said something into the phone.

'That's so funny!'

'He said he fancies me?'

'No! Things sound so much better at your school than mine!'

I kept this up for the whole of lunchtime.

That night, I took the house phone to my bedroom to ring Lewis again.

'It's so sweet of you to care so much, Fiona, it really is,' Mrs Harris said. 'His temperature's dropped and he's kept some toast down, so he might be back in before the weekend, if you're lucky.'

'Can I speak to him?'

'If you're quick, hon.'

I heard Lewis's mum's footsteps. There was a rustling and a clunk.

'Lewis? Is that you?'

'Hi, Fi.' He sounded so weak and ill. Tiny Tim in *The Muppet Christmas Carol*.

'*LewisI'vegotamobilephone!Lewisanactualmobilephone!*'

It took a while to explain because he didn't believe me. Which was fair, because I didn't believe me either. If you'd told me I'd made the whole thing up, that would have made *loads* more sense, actually.

To Lewis, too. 'He can't have *given* it to you!'

'He definitely did.'

'Is this like when Sean's uncle let him drive a Ferrari that day on the farm?'

'Nothing like that.'

'You haven't stolen it?' A softer voice now. 'Fi. I'll forgive you as long as you don't lie. Have you stolen it?'

'LEWIS!'

'OK, sorry.'

'I promise – he said straight out that it was mine. Quite a few times.'

'Promise or positive?'

'Promise. Actual *promise*.'

I picked up a pen and tapped it against the bedside table. I waited for him to catch up.

'Does the phone work?' Lewis asked.

'I think so, I haven't tried it. Either way, it's still a good thing.'

'I don't like this, Fi. I have a bad feeling.' It's like Lewis doesn't *want* good things to happen to us. 'First strimming, now this. He's *got to be* a paedo.'

'LEWIS! Strimming means he wants you to cut his lawn, because you knocked on his door and offered to do jobs for him, *you absolute fool*. And he's not a paedo, he's never tried to touch me, not even once. *Or* got his pecker out. Not even just the end.'

Lewis went quiet.

'Are you still there?'

'Your mum says he's strange, Fi.'

I shook my head. 'You're missing the point, as always. It doesn't matter that—'

'Why would your mum say he's strange if he wasn't?'

'She probably said *a strange-r*, I didn't tape-record the conversation. And you know what Mum's like, she gets stuff wrong. She blames me for everything, doesn't she? She blames the snails on the step for getting stepped on.'

He didn't answer.

'It's been fourteen years and she *still* mutters about those ladies from work who went to Danielle's funeral in one car and stopped at M and S.'

Lewis still didn't say anything. He was making his point the sneaky way, with silence.

'Look. Carl's a really good man. Really, *really* good. He gave me a mobile phone. That's proof. What more proof do you need?'

'Carl is either really, really kind,' Lewis spoke carefully, like an adult reading a story. 'Jesus-kind. *Or* he's really, really bad. Because no one—'

'That's enough.' Lewis's mum's voice in the background. 'You need your rest. Say goodbye to Fiona.'

'Bye, Fi.'

I put the phone down. I pulled back my pillow and touched the mobile phone. And tried really hard not to think about what Lewis had said.

28

Teachers get more upset about stuff happening to us kids
than we do.
(paradox)

Nine days to the fair

Dear Miss Larson,

Thank you for your letter to *Crimewatch*, dated 3
July 1996.

It is always encouraging to receive correspondence
from our younger viewers, especially those with such
a strong sense of justice.

I'm afraid we do tend to start our investigations
with specific crimes in mind, rather than with a sus-
picious-looking character. And we have no open cases
in our files from fairgrounds – about certain death, or
otherwise. But we revisit unsolved cases regularly and
we have made a note of the information you sent.

I'm sure you understand we can't update members
of the public on case progress, but we do appreciate
your help and encouragement.

Thanks again for writing in.

Yours sincerely,
Aimee Sweetman
Crimewatch Liaison Coordinator

School news! Mr Kellett is moving to Glasgow!

He smiled around as he told us at the end of class. 'You've not driven me away, I promise. And you've got me till the end of the year.'

There were lots of sad looks – more than you'd expect for a teacher. I think some of the boys wanted to cry.

Greeney looked like he'd lost his favourite dog. 'Who's going to teach us football?'

'They'll be getting a replacement. And there's always Mr Corbett in the meantime.'

Grumbles ripped through the room.

'He's a hundred.'

'He's shit.'

'He's never played for Alty Town.'

Mr Kellett stopped me as the class rushed out. 'Fiona. You're friends with Lewis Harris in my other Year Seven class?'

I nodded.

'His mum's asked for some homework to keep him busy while he's off.'

I frowned. The *unfairness* of Mrs Harris.

'But he doesn't have a copy of *The Taming of The Shrew* anymore.'

'He does,' I said, 'he's just got sick all over it.'

'Quite. Well, not *quite*, because I've binned that other one. So Mrs Harris says can you drop this in for him?'

I shook my head slowly.

'You can't drop it in?'

'It's fine, I can do it, I just think it's *really* unfair of Mrs Harris.'

He smiled. 'It's one of the better pieces of homework to do when you're ill, I would have thought? English? Reading a comedy?'

I was about to reply, but he confused me, so it took a second to remember what I meant to tell him. 'You know, if you want to know stuff about what to do in Glasgow, I can ask my grandma. She moved up there.'

'Thanks Fiona, that's very kind.'

'Are you leaving because of the New Head? Is it because she makes you change out of your PE kit?'

He laughed. 'No!' He stopped laughing. 'And she doesn't make me change out of my PE kit, that's not exactly it, she—'

'I just hear quite a lot about the New Head. Miss Jarvis said—'

'I don't know what you think you've heard, Fiona, but you must have got confused. Everyone here likes and respects Mrs Shackleton very much.' Was that a twinkle in his eye? 'All the teachers are very, very happy, and we thoroughly approve of the new way of doing things. We really appreciate having more structure in our lives. It helps us grow.'

I nodded.

'And definitely don't be telling people that's why I'm leaving. My partner has a new job in Glasgow, so that's why I'm leaving. Nothing to do with Mrs Shackleton.'

'What does she do, your partner?'

He scratched his mouth. 'My partner's a doctor.'

'Sweet.' I gave a nod. 'Can I ask you something else?'

'If you're quick.'

'Is it true the cross-country course got changed because of flashers?'

Mr Kellett reached behind him for the teacher's table. He sat back. 'Where did you hear that?'

I shrugged. 'Playground.'

'We don't want anyone to be scared.'

'I'm not scared. Just interested.'

Mr Kellett looked behind me, like he was hoping someone would come and disturb us. 'There are few – very, *very* few – people out there that might cause kids harm, Fiona. And it's our job as teachers to consider risk and do whatever we can to ensure—'

'It's true? It's *actually true*?'

'I thought you said you knew?'

'The course has been moved because of *all the flashers*?'

'Not exactly that, not *all* the flashers, it's more about lighting and the density of the foliage and proximity to—'

'Thanks, Mr Kellett.' I waved *The Taming of The Shrew*. 'I'll take this to Lewis tonight.'

'Fiona.' He leaned forward. 'This must be hard to take in. Do you want to talk about it?'

When Mr Kellett said *Do you want to talk about it?* he said it less hungrily than Mrs Vernal. More like he could take it or leave it. Less like he wanted to have our feelings as a snack.

I shook my head. 'Unless you can tell me any more about the flashers? How many there are? What they wear and stuff? Whether they work in teams or alone?'

He took a moment. He shook his head.

'Thanks, then. See you later.'

At lunchtime, I perched on the low wall near the tennis courts, deliberately close to Jodie Mackintosh, the girl from drama. She stood with her group of three friends, all eating crisps, while I talked into my phone.

When Jodie looked over, I waved.

She waved back.

I kept talking into my phone, glancing up at Jodie and her three friends.

'Bye then!' I put my phone back in my rucksack. I sat back on the wall and looked up at the sun.

I closed my eyes and felt the warmth on my face.

'*Fiona!*' Jodie waved me over, a friendship bracelet slipping down her arm.

I picked up my rucksack and walked to stand with the group, like this kind of thing happened all the time.

'Hi, Jodie.' I nodded at Jodie's friends, who were also all wearing matching friendship bracelets. 'Most people call me *Fi*, not *Fiona*. My friends at other schools, I mean.'

'Is that phone yours?' Jodie asked. 'Can I have a look?'

'Yep.' I got it out of my secret pocket and handed it to her. 'Be careful. It's valuable.'

Her friends crowded round to look at the phone.

'Wow,' Yasmin said. 'Who gave it to you? Your parents?'

I pushed my hair behind my ears. 'Just a friend.'

'Who do you call with it?' Alison Fisher asked.

'Oh, you know. Just people.'

I've never spoken to Alison Fisher, but she's the one whose mum works as a receptionist at the doctor's. Her mum wears her hair in a scrunchie and calls everyone *duck*.

'Do you call Selina Baker on it?' Jodie turned to the others. 'Fiona knows Selina Baker. I saw them talk in the corridor.'

'I don't call Selina. We're friends, but not phone friends.'

Dean Prince walked past, dribbling a football as he walked. 'All right, Fi.'

'All right, Dean.'

Jodie looked at him and back. 'You know Dean Prince?'

I nodded. Turns out older kids are really nice if you've sold them a porno mag.

'He plays for Port Vale!'

'Yep. Under sixteens.' I sold him *Mayfair*, if I remember right. Gave me twenty-five quid.

Alison narrowed her eyes at me. 'Who do you call on your phone, then? If it's not *your best friends* Selina Baker and Dean Prince?'

'Friends from other schools. My boyfriend.'

Jodie looked at the other girls and back. 'Is your boyfriend at another school, too?'

'I know who he is,' Naomi pulled at her plait. 'I've seen them together. It's Lewis Harris.'

And for some reason – well, actually because I hadn't planned for this conversation, and say what you like about Lewis, but he's actually *real* – for that reason, I nodded.

And the other girls nodded back. They didn't say *Ew, Lewis?* or *Lewis Harris went to Paris*, or anything about how glasses at his house tasted of dishwasher. They didn't even call him *The Sickboy of the Shrew* – probably because there had been a fight on Festival Field since then, *and* a boy had come into school with boiled egg all down his tie, so we'd all moved on.

Jodie handed the phone back.

Alison was still looking at me like I'd made a bad smell. 'Your mum's the one who makes everyone's curtains.'

'Definitely not. That's someone else's mum. Your mum's the one who works at the doctor's?'

She looked at her feet. 'No. Fisher's a common name.'

'Got to go.' My lies were twisting up in my tummy like hot cartoon vines. 'I said I'd call Lewis before maths.'

I put my phone to my ear and hurried into the school building.

I reached the computer room and shut the door behind me. I sat completely still. I didn't play a game. I didn't even switch on a computer.

Well.

Everything had changed. *Everything.*

I looked at my phone. I put it in my secret pocket and patted it gently.

Now. I just needed to break the girlfriend news to Lewis. And break it to him in the right way, and make him realise it was OK – before he ruined everything and made us *both* look stupid.

How to Make Friends (According to Mum)

1) Remember beggars can't be choosers
2) Let it happen naturally, don't force it
3) Don't try to impress people with objects
4) Ask people about themselves
5) Don't try to fit in
6) Don't show off
7) Don't draw attention to yourself
8) Just be yourself

Mum didn't have a clue.

29

Some friends aren't very friendly.
(paradox)

Nine days to the fair
Lewis called me that night. 'Mum says you're allowed to come round with my homework.'

'Are you still infectious?'

'No.'

'Then I'll be there in ten minutes.'

I grabbed the letter I'd got back from *Crimewatch* and headed off to Lewis's house.

Mrs Harris let me in. 'Aren't you hot in that coat?'

'No. I hope he's feeling better.' I passed the photo on the wall of Lewis with a wand and a cape. 'I should have brought him some grapes or something.'

Mrs Harris smiled. 'You don't need to do that.'

'I do because . . . well, Lewis is my boyfriend now.' I needed to practise saying it. 'Can you wait for him to tell you first, though, in case he minds that I've ruined the surprise?'

Mrs Harris stared at me. 'Boyfriend?'

Mr Harris looked up from his paper.

I beamed. 'It's official. From today.'

'Does he know that?' Mrs Harris asked.

'He will do in a minute, don't worry.'

'Good lad!' Mr Harris looked to Mrs Harris, smiling, and back at me. 'And with a temperature and everything!'

Mrs Harris frowned at him.

Mr Harris chuckled. 'A chip off the old block.'

'Geoff, stop it.' She turned to me. 'Leave that bedroom door open.'

Lewis's dad turned a page. 'Don't do anything I wouldn't do.'

I held up my bag of schoolbooks. 'We've got a lot to talk about.'

I scampered up the stairs to Lewis's room.

I knocked and walked into a waft of *ill*.

I wrinkled my nose and decided not to shut the door. 'It smells of Grandma's soup in here.'

Lewis didn't get out of bed. 'Hi.' He still had that Muppet Tiny Tim voice.

I stayed at the other side of the room. 'Have you been sick again?'

'I'm nearly better. I haven't been sick all day.' He waved at the washing-up bowl. 'That's just in case.'

His hair looked greasy and stuck to his forehead. He was wearing Spiderman pyjamas. A book called *The Twenty Greatest Magic Tricks* sat on his bedside table next to his favourite stuffed raccoon.

I know beggars can't be choosers. Mum's right about *some* stuff. But, just for a second, I thought maybe I should have picked a better boyfriend.

'It's true it was flashers, why they moved the cross-country course. Can you believe it?' I pushed the door wider open to let the smell of Grandma's soup out into the landing. 'Now, I've got something to tell you and you've got to promise not to get cross.'

He didn't say anything.

I sat on the end of his bed. 'Lewis? You promise?'

'I'm thinking.'

'You don't need to be thinking. Just go ahead and promise, so I can get on and tell you.'

He folded his arms. 'I'm thinking about the past. How things have turned out when you've said things like that.'

'This is different.' I shifted closer. 'At first, you might not understand how what I'm telling you is brilliant. You might need me to explain it so you get it properly. Just remember that.'

I waited.

He lifted his head.

I made my voice light. 'It's a funny story and definitely an accident' – I looked past him, out of the window – 'but people think you're my boyfriend.'

I took one look at his face and went back to looking out of the window.

'*Which* people?'

'Jodie and Naomi and Alison Fisher and Yasmin. You know, my group. My group of girls.' I looked around his eyes. Not actually at his eyes, that was too hard, just in the centre, at the top of his nose. 'And, thing is, now everyone else thinks you're my boyfriend, too.' I shook my head. 'I know gossip gets around quick, but *still*. People were staring at me.' I looked from his left temple to his right temple. 'In a good way. No one tried to trip me up when I walked past the benches in the corridors. They took their legs *in* when I walked past.'

'What did they say to you? Tell me exactly.'

I looked away. 'Nothing.'

Do you do tongues?

Has he touched your bra?

Have you spanked his monkey?

'People think we're too mature to make fun of now. Honestly, Lewis, it's brilliant. We should have thought of this ages ago.'

'What did people say?'

'Nothing. Nothing much. I just sat there smiling and said "that's my business" and "get your own boyfriend if you're so interested". And people *listened*. It's like I've got a superpower.' I glanced at him. 'Like *we've* got a superpower. Lewis!' I leaned forward. 'You might even become friends with the lads from the blue estate! Especially if I tell people I let you put your hand up my top. And everyone's forgotten all about you being sick in English.'

Lewis just sat there. 'No one said anything bad?'

'Of course not.' Lewis *would* have to ruin this. He wouldn't want to know Liam said *Harris must have got ill because you gave him crabs.*

'We can break up soon,' I said, 'but not straight away, or it'll look fake.'

Lewis adjusted his pillows so he was higher up the bed. 'And why are we doing this again?'

'So people think someone would want to go out with us.'

'Am I going to have to kiss you?'

'No. Just get our stories straight about what stuff we've done. I thought that might be good for both of us?'

'Or it'll make things worse.'

'We *deserve* to be more popular, Lewis. Think about it. Who made the rules that you and me are on the bottom rung? We're the *best ones.*'

I tried not to look at his magic book or stuffed raccoon.

'I'm not kissing you. You're like my sister.'

I turned to stare out of the window for a long time. 'I wish I *was* your real sister. *My* real sister's a ghost.'

I kept looking out of the window. I waited.

I glanced back. 'Why aren't you saying something?'

'I'm cross you're trying to catalyst me.'

My face went hot. 'I wouldn't have to catalyst you, if you could just be mature and accept you've got a girlfriend now.'

Lewis looked down at his duvet. He stroked it.

'And this is your first girlfriend present.' I took the fresh copy of *The Taming of The Shrew* out of my bag and put it on the bed. 'Though, get this, Kellett called it a *comedy*.'

Lewis furrowed his brow. 'A *comedy*?'

'And look.' I got the phone out of my secret pocket and laid it on the duvet.

He picked the phone up.

'Isn't it beautiful?'

He stared at it for a moment. 'It's *too* good, that's the problem. Things like this don't happen to you, Fi. You know in a cartoon, when someone finds treasure and it's actually cursed?'

I snatched the phone away. 'Why won't you just be happy for me?'

'If you're so happy, why do you look scared?'

I stared at him. Why did he have to say that? I *wasn't* scared, but – now, because he said the word and made me think about it – my chest was going all cold. 'I'm not scared.'

'This could be something really *bad*. This isn't funny.'

I tried to ignore the chill creeping further down my body.

'No one would give you a mobile for no reason. *No one*.'

I looked at the carpet.

'You are scared, aren't you?'

'No. I was for a little bit though. I did think for a while when I was investigating Danielle, maybe Carl was the one who killed her at the fair and that's why my mum doesn't like him, but—'

At Lewis's reddening face, I stopped. I started to panic. 'I mean—'

His face went redder still. 'YOU PROMISED!' No more Tiny Tim. 'You *promised* you were going to stop looking into Danielle dying. You *promised*. WHY WILL YOU NEVER LISTEN TO ME?'

I grabbed the phone from Lewis and put it in my rucksack. He'd never sounded less Muppet-y.

'Go away and leave me alone!'

'Lewis?' Mrs Harris's voice came up the stairs. 'Are you shouting?'

'Shouting?' I said. 'He's braying like a donkey.' I looked him up and down. 'A *sweaty* donkey. I'll leave you to calm down. Bye, Lewis.' I picked up my bag and ran down the stairs.

With all Lewis's *braying*, I'd forgotten to show him my letter from *Crimewatch*. I'd do it next time.

Fortunately, Lewis is too nice. He *is* like Muppet Tiny Tim. Because however bad I am, whatever I've done, he always, *always* forgives me in the end.

30

Sometimes, the police don't want to solve crimes.
(paradox)

Eight days to the fair

When I checked the doormat the next morning, there was a letter for me in the pile.

Mum came downstairs in her dressing gown as I was squirrelling it away. 'What's that?'

'Nothing.'

'You're getting a lot of post.' She tied the belt of her dressing gown tighter. 'Why?'

I dumped the letters for her and Dad on the side. 'Blood project stuff.' I ran upstairs before she could ask anymore.

In my room, I opened the letter. My polaroid photo of Carl fell out.

Dear Miss Larson,

We have received your letter dated Wednesday 3 July 1996. It is not clear whether you intended the letter to be a prank.

If you have real concerns, please raise them with your parent or guardian. Unless your concerns are about a parent or guardian, in which case please raise them with a trusted adult.

If your letter was intended as a prank, please note the police are very busy protecting lives. We will not follow up on this occasion, but you would be wise to remember there is a criminal offence called Wasting Police Time.

I enclose the photograph you sent, which we will not be keeping on file.

Stay safe,

Cheshire Police

I pulled the bin from under my dressing table and dropped in Carl's sent-back photo. I didn't need it anymore. Not now he wasn't a suspect.

As I pushed the bin back, I tried not to notice the special shape – the bad Nazi shape – that I'd carved into the leg of the dressing table. I looked away and glanced under my bed.

There was a lot of junk under there. I should have remembered to look there before the car boot sale. Along with the dust, there was an old keyring with a bear on it. I spotted a hairband I thought I'd lost, and an old duckling jigsaw.

And I remembered. That was where Mum kept Danielle's Box of Special Things. Under her bed.

I'd forgotten that box completely.

I didn't have time to look before school. But soon.

And now I finally had a new lead. One that didn't involve knocking on the door of the house belonging to Adrian Sykes.

*

School news!

All the Year Nine and above girls got a free parcel in a special one-off class.

Rape alarms!

Attack alarms the teachers call them, but we know what they're really called. Everyone was using them at break – boys trying to steal them from girls' bags, hoiking them out by the strap. Kids going up behind other kids and pulling the pin out right next to their ears. Some kids made it into a game, setting traps for each other like Grandmother's Footsteps, seeing who could get the closest before the alarm went off.

I asked Dr Sharma why we Year Sevens didn't get a parcel and she just looked at the ceiling. 'Year Nine and above, Fiona.'

'On the day of the Tampax, Year Sevens got the free parcel, too.'

'Attack alarms are not toys.'

'I know they're not toys, that's why I want one.'

Dr Sharma made a *pff* air-noise with her mouth. 'Even with this one, Fiona? *Even with this one*, you don't want to be left out?'

At lunchtime, I walked with my mobile phone through the playground, to find Jodie and Naomi and Yasmin and Alison Fisher. I mean – my friends.

I spotted them in their usual place by the tennis courts, and walked up to them quickly before I got unbrave. 'Hi.'

Jodie stepped to the side to make space in the circle. 'Hi!'

The others kept eating their crisps. They weren't as smiley, but they didn't tell me to go away or call me *pants girl* either. So that was something.

'Is Lewis still not back in school?' Jodie asked.

'No. But I went to see him last night and he's getting better.'

Alison swallowed her mouthful of crisps. 'Is it true you gave him crabs?'

'Ha ha. Of course not.'

'Everyone said you two shag in a bush in the park,' Jasmine said.

'That's not true,' I said quickly, 'and we've never been anywhere near that bush.'

'How was Lewis?' Naomi asked.

'OK.' I scratched my nose. 'He didn't look as fit as usual. But then, he was in pyjamas, with a washing-up bowl by his bed.'

Jodie laughed. 'What pyjamas?'

I paused. 'Tottenham ones. He's really into football and his cousins live near the ground, that's why he never goes to games up here.'

'Heads up!'

A football bounced past me.

Sean chased after it. He stopped when he saw me, letting one of the other boys get the ball instead. 'All right, Fi!'

I blinked. It was the first time he'd spoken to me for weeks. 'All right, Sean.'

'I hear you've got a mobile now?'

I got it out of my secret pocket. I showed it to him.

He whistled. 'Sweet. See you in the computer room later? One last game of Rhino Rampage? The room's closed for rewiring after today.'

I shrugged. 'OK.'

He nodded. He put a hand through his hair and ran back to join the game.

Jodie looked between Sean and me. 'You're friends with Sean Anderton?'

'A bit.' I didn't add *when he wants to be.*

The girls looked at each other and giggled.

'Alison likes him,' Jodie said.

I frowned. 'Really?' *Sean?* He wasn't even one of the good ones.

'I like him sometimes. Not always.' Alison was blushing. 'Is it true he's had trials for Stoke City?'

'Yep.' Obviously, not true. 'But he's a Port Vale fan so he's turned them down.' I'm a better friend to Sean than he is to me.

'Can I look at your phone again?' Alison said.

'Of course.' I gave it to her.

She turned it over in her hand. Not so sneery now.

I licked my lips. 'Alison, do they have records of dead people at the doctor's? About how they died?'

Bam. The sneer was back. 'Why are you asking me?'

'Because your mum works there.'

'I *told* you, *she doesn't,* there are lots of Fishers. A *whole page* of them in Monkford and they can't all be my mum, can they?'

'Fair enough.' Alison Fisher's mum *definitely* works at the doctor's.

Jodie folded her crisp packet in half and put it in her bag. 'Who do you normally stand with at lunchtimes, Fi?'

'I'm normally with Lewis. Sometimes Sean.'

'No girls?' This Alison was a pain. 'Groups are meant to be all boys or all girls.'

I shrugged. 'Thing is, my girl friends all go to Radcliffe High. Mum sent me to this school so we didn't get into too much trouble together.'

Alison dabbed in her packet for the last bits of crisp. 'That's one slutty school. I keep hearing how the fit girls from there are always having sex with boys from here.'

'My friends aren't, though,' I said. 'The only person they know from here is me. So there's no point asking any of the boys who my friends are. In case you were thinking of asking. They just won't know, so there's no point.'

I put my phone back in my secret pocket. I started inching out my fortune teller. 'Do you girls like spying?'

Alison was quick. 'No.'

I pushed the fortune teller back down. 'Me, neither.'

'Fi.' Jodie looked at Alison and the others. 'If you want, you can stand with us at lunchtimes now? We always meet at this spot.'

I hitched my rucksack further onto my shoulder. 'I probably will, then. There's quite a lot of space here.' I ran my hand along the top of the wall. 'It's a good bit of wall.'

'We always eat the same crisps as each other,' Jodie said. 'It's tomato ketchup flavour on a Thursday. It's ready salted tomorrow, then prawn cocktail on Monday. Salt and vinegar on Tuesday and pickled onion on Wednesday.'

'I can do that.'

I put my hands on my hips and looked around me, at the view from *my* spot in the playground. From here, I could see the tennis courts. The school building. The school field.

It was *perfect*.

'So that's agreed.' I kept my hands on my hips and looked at Alison. 'Now. Next time the ball comes in this direction, do you want me to say how great you are in front of Sean?'

<u>To Go to the Fair I Need:</u>

1) ~~Money for the rides~~ √
2) ~~Girl friends, so the famous boy will push me on the Waltzers~~ √
3) Mum and Dad to let me go

31

A spy knows when it's time to go off-duty.
The Junior Spy's Secret Handbook™

Eight days to the fair
After school, my group walked together out of the school gates, heading for Naomi's house.

Mum was there, leaning against her *Gail Larson Driving Instructor* car at the entrance roundabout, and *even that* didn't dent my day.

'Back in a sec.' I dropped my rucksack and hurried over. I nodded at the Year Twelve girl in the passenger seat, who was changing out of DMs into thin-soled Nan shoes.

I looked at Mum. 'Just going to Naomi's house. With my girl friends.'

'Girl friends?'

I pointed. 'Jodie and Yasmin and Naomi and Alison Fisher.'

'Really?' Mum's face brightened. 'Then – have fun!'

I ran back towards the girls. I passed Mr Kellett, getting into the passenger seat of a car. The driver had the visor pulled down. It was Mr Kellett's friend from the shopping centre.

I thought about this for a minute as I headed back to the girls.

'And *then* Kellett said *Taming of The Shrew* was a *comedy*.' Naomi turned to me. 'What did your mum say, Fi? You look like you're thinking.'

'Nothing important. But I *was* thinking.' I picked up my rucksack. 'I was thinking, our group should get cookies one time. You know, those big soft ones they sell in shopping centres. We should get a whole bag each and eat them together at break.'

They all nodded, so I was pleased I said it out loud. We all walked on to Naomi's house, chattering together about cookies the whole time, and I had a warm feeling in my belly that I'd made it happen.

Turns out Naomi's house was one of the massive ones on the hill out of town. One of the houses set back from the road, not joined with a group of others, like normal houses. Naomi's house was just there, alone, behind gates.

The four of us stood awkwardly in the tiny bathroom attached to Naomi's bedroom. We squeezed in tight, as we looked at the sink and the shower and the Little Madam Make-up Set.

'It's on sweet,' Naomi said.

'It *is* on sweet.' It made sense, like *on fire.* I pointed at the half-toilet thing next to the main toilet. 'What's that?'

'A beeday,' Naomi said.

I shrugged in a question.

'It's not mine,' Naomi said. 'It was here when we came.'

We all squeezed out of Naomi's personal bathroom, and I looked at the little white cabinets, all matching and lining the bedroom, with no gaps. It was like the cabinets were born with the house, rather than added later.

Mum would *definitely* want to know how often this family went on holiday.

Naomi showed us all her CDs and toys and board games – and I mean *all*, I had a real *Candy's house* feeling. At the sight of a perfect orange pencil-topper on Naomi's dressing table, my gaze locked on like a laser.

I shoved my hands in my skirt pockets, just in case.

It's only stationery, I told myself.

I don't even *like* stationery.

Don't steal it don't steal it don't steal it don't—

I didn't. Which was a massive relief.

When Naomi had finished showing us her room, she took us through to her sister's room, which was even better. Same cabinets, but with so many extra eyeshadows. And every *Now* CD set from number 7.

I whistled.

'She's Year Ten,' Naomi said.

I spotted a photo card for East Cheshire College on the side. I picked it up. 'Your sister has *fake ID*!'

Naomi nodded. 'She knows someone who gets them done for a fiver. There's a machine that makes the plastic right at his Saturday job at the warehouse.'

I looked at the date of birth – 14.12.79. Naomi's sister was sixteen. Fake-sixteen.

I studied the card. I wouldn't say they'd got the plastic *right*. You could see the girl in the picture had shoulder-length dark hair, but the picture was bad, and the licence was all bobbly where the plastic hadn't stuck perfectly. It was almost like—

I felt a surge of something. *Yes.*

'Let's go out.' I waved the card. 'With this.'

Alison Fisher frowned. 'Why?'

'Hi, ladies!' Naomi's mum came into the room, not looking like a *mum* mum. She wore high heels in her own house and had make-up all over, an extra layer on her face, like a TV presenter. Not quite Kelly from Winchester, but more like her than normal mums.

She stopped smiling. 'What are you doing in Elizabeth's room?'

'Nothing,' Naomi said.

'Do nothing in your own room.' And, just like that, she was a normal mum. 'And you girls need to be gone before supper. You know the rules, Naomi, we eat on the dot of seven thirty.'

'We eat tea at six,' I said.

'Then you'll need to be home by six.' She gave a smile that was suddenly too kind. 'Fiona, isn't it?'

'Yes.' I looked away so I didn't see the head-tilt. It's always weird how adults know my name.

Naomi's mum left the room and I turned to the others.

'I'm going to borrow this.' I held up the college ID. 'Just for tonight.' I turned to Naomi. 'Please tell your sister I'll definitely give it back tomorrow. And I'm going to have a surprise tomorrow. Just you wait.'

And Naomi didn't say *no* – she didn't say anything – just led us back to her room. For the rest of the afternoon we recorded our voices introducing songs on her fancy stereo, being DJs. The whole time, I held onto that ID, feeling something bubbling up from my belly – a laugh that really wanted to come out, like a burp after too much Coke. That feeling when you know it's coming, and it's coming soon, but you don't know when it's going to happen, or how loud it's going to be when it does.

*

Outside Paper Rack, I took off my jumper and tie. I put them on the grass next to the pile of bikes.

I walked into the newsagent's, concentrating. *Fourteenth of the twelfth, seventy-nine. Fourteenth of the twelfth, seventy-nine.*

I took a deep breath as the door chimed.

The bald man looked at me. 'You.'

I slapped twenty pence on the counter with a ping. *Fourteenth of the twelfth, seventy-nine.* 'One single please.'

'You're how old?'

'Sixteen, sir.' *Fourteenth of the twelfth, seventy-nine.*

'*You're* sixteen.'

I nodded. 'Fourteenth of the twelfth, seventy-nine.'

'You're what – four foot six?'

'I'm a hundred and thirty-five centimetres. I was born small.' I shrugged. 'My sister was loads taller, I got unlucky.' I got out the ID and placed it on the counter. 'Here.'

The man didn't reach down. He moved his eyes to look at the ID, *surveillance-style.*

'I know you sell singles,' I said, 'because I've seen you sell them to other kids.' I paused. 'And by *other kids*, I mean *other sixteen-year-olds.*'

The man didn't even look, just handed me a cigarette from the packet.

I know I said finding the magazines was the best day of my life. And then I said it was the day of the phone. Both times, I was wrong.

It was *this*. Because this time, I'd done it *myself*.

I'd got *served*.

Everything was going my way. And, that evening, I even got the opportunity to look at the Box of Special Things.

Mum had gone out for a driving lesson after tea. I'd made

a phone call for Dad, to get him another application form. I'd even answered the sifting question for him– *'A baby deer? It's a fawn.'* Dad read my lips and gave me a thumbs-up, while I wondered what kind of person this quiz show was screening out, exactly.

Everyone knows a baby deer is a fawn. *Everyone.*

And now Dad was downstairs washing up and I could hear the water sloshing round, telling me it was safe. I'd get a *one-minute* warning when I heard the chugging as Dad pulled the plug out.

So I got on my hands and knees and kneeled on the carpet in Mum and Dad's room.

I looked under the bed.

Ugh.

Balls of hair-and-something lay around in lumps, like fur sheared from an animal. I had to get past a piece of toenail, a sock, and a piece of exercise equipment that looked like a butterfly's wings.

It was fine. I knew by then, that whatever the films show, spying isn't all private planes and casinos, and girls in silky dresses who look beautiful dead.

I moved a box of tissues. I pushed past an open shoebox of dusty standing-up books, glancing at the spines. *Dealing with Grief. Losing a Child. The Fundamentals of Male Infertility. Learning to Trust Again. When the Second Baby is Difficult.*

I felt myself flush, though I realised I wasn't in a position to mind. After all, the second baby – me – *was* difficult. But when I pulled the book out, it turned out to be about getting pregnant.

The encyclopaedias and novels went on the shelves in the lounge, and these were the sad books, kept in the dark.

I reached for Mum's Box of Special Things and dragged

it out. I took off the lid, trying to ignore the feeling of tiny creepy crawlies marching up my neck. Because it felt like being in Danielle's bedroom again.

On the top of the box was *Baby's Special Book,* with a picture of baby's footprints.

I flicked through the book but stopped at a see-through envelope, holding a curl of hair. I realised what I was looking at. *The baby hair of a dead girl.*

I snapped that book shut.

I put the baby book and scrapbook to one side, and looked at objects in the box.

There was a thin silver necklace, still in its plastic packet. The faded writing on the packet said *Christening Gift.*

There was a smooth stone from a beach, swirled with layers of different blue-greys.

There was a hand-painted mug with *Dani* painted in massive, little kid letters – a mug that any self-respecting kid would have thrown away when she turned eight.

And that was all. That was what Mum thought *special* enough to keep for fourteen years.

I wondered what she'd keep for me.

I reached for Danielle's scrapbook and opened it to a random page.

In a cutting from a newspaper, a fat-cheeked Danielle stood round a patch of soil with some friends. Each kid held a too-big garden spade, with one foot on the metal bit. They all wore corduroy trousers that went wide at the bottom. *Local children dig garden for charity.*

And there were the creepy crawlies on my neck again. Marching faster. Marching too fast now.

I shut the book and put it back in the box with everything else. I shoved it under the bed.

I scrambled to my room and got the cigarette out of my secret pocket.

I laid the cigarette on the bed and stared at it, trying to make myself excited again. Trying to remember that I was having the best time ever. Trying to remember that – only a few hours ago, I'd got served.

Trying – trying *really hard* – to forget there had ever been another kid who lived in this house. Another kid, who dug gardens for charity, and who was easy to have around, and did things for other people, and who always did everything better than me.

32

Sometimes when you're at your nicest, people think you're
being mean.
(paradox)

Seven days to the fair
Next day, at the lamppost, Lewis was back.

He was quiet on the way to school, but I didn't realise at
first. I had *so much* to tell him.

'I've got the grill lighter to light it with.' I patted the side of
my bag. 'We'll smoke it in our bush. And whenever anyone
asks what age I started smoking, I can say *eleven*.' I put my
hand on his arm. 'Though twelve's *nearly* as good.'

I glanced at Lewis. He had his hands in his pockets.

'Do you want to see my letters from the police? And
Crimewatch? I got *an actual letter* from *Crimewatch*.'

He shook his head. A really small shake.

'People say we shag in the bush, you know. But they're
babies. If they had a boyfriend of their own, they won't have
time to be making up—'

'You are going to come to the computer room at lunch?'
Lewis asked suddenly. 'I need to talk to you.'

'The computer room's shut from today though. For

rewiring. Also, I have a group now, and you have to stand with your group during lunch. That's how it works.'

'And I just have to eat my sandwiches on my own?'

I held up my hands. 'I didn't make the rules, Lewis. What do you need to talk about? We can talk now?'

He shoved his hands further in his pocket so his shoulders hunched and walked ahead, into the building.

School news!

In RE, Greeney's brother called Miss Jarvis *Mum*.

Before this, Greeney's brother was one of the best lads in Year Nine, pretty high up in the blue estate boys. He won't be anymore.

In fact, he'll probably have to move schools, if he knows what's best for him.

Those kids who call a teacher *Mum* – well. Things are never the same again.

And it's not good for Greeney either, coming so soon after his bad haircut. The school holidays are due to start in two weeks, but I bet they can't come soon enough for Greeney.

I showed the girls my prize in the playground at lunchtime, holding the cigarette up in the middle of our circle. 'Next time I'll get us one each.'

No one looked as excited as I'd expected. They just carried on eating their crisps.

I looked around the playground uncertainly. In all the excitement, I'd got the days wrong. I'd packed salt and vinegar, not ready salted.

'Are you allowed to smoke with your asthma?' Alison Fisher asked.

I should really stop thinking of her as Alison *Fisher*, I decided. Now she's one of my best friends.

'Alison. *None* of us are *allowed* to smoke. Remember?'

I noticed Naomi glance at Alison and back. 'I heard Dr Sharma say to make sure you have your inhaler on the trip to the science museum.'

'I don't really need the inhaler.' I shrugged. 'I only carry it because my mum freaks about my health. The doctor says it's up to me whether to carry it – she can tell I'm mature enough to decide.'

'You only carry it because your mum freaks about your health. . .' Alison looked at Naomi. The two had stopped eating.

Attack. 'What does your mum say, Alison? She's the doctor's receptionist.'

'No, she's—'

I put my hand up, as if to shade my eyes. 'Is that Sean? Want me to see if I can get him to come over?'

'Let me get this straight.' Alison folded the top of her crisp packet over. 'You don't really need an inhaler, but the doctor gave you it anyway, just to please your mum.'

I nodded.

Alison looked at Naomi and back at me. 'And the doctor said you don't need to bother taking your inhaler if you don't *feel like it.*'

I pulled my rucksack further onto my shoulder. 'Thing is, the inhaler isn't about me.' I left a gap. 'My sister *died*, you know. My big sister.' I left a longer gap. 'And when that happens, your parents get extra careful. So I let them fuss because it makes them feel better. And the doctor feels sorry for Mum and Dad, so she gave me an inhaler.'

The girls left a pause after my catalyst.

'Do you get asthma a lot?' Jodie asked.

'Hardly ever.' I held up the cigarette one last time and put it back in my pocket. 'Anyway, I'm going to smoke it after school with Lewis.'

Jodie pointed. 'There's Lewis now.'

Lewis walked through the playground, his coat completely done up – top button and everything – on the twelfth of July.

I raised my hand to wave. He turned and walked the other way.

'Are you *definitely* going out with Lewis Harris?' Yasmin asked.

'Definitely.' I hurried after him. 'I'll just check he's OK.'

But when I reached the school building, he'd gone.

I made Lewis sit next to me in drama. I chased him round the room with my chair, and it was like musical chairs, trying to make sure I was in the right place next to him when Mrs Vernal quieted the class down.

It worked.

The first exercise was something about expressing inner rage, but I wasn't listening properly. I was watching Lewis, who looked far away. As Mrs Vernal said, 'In your pairs, begin!', I could see his eyes going all watery.

I turned my chair to face his. 'You OK?'

'Something awful's happened.'

I glanced around but it was safe. For now, Mrs Vernal was supervising other kids' inner rage. 'What?'

'Dad's moved out. For good, Mum says.'

I felt something fill my throat. *No.*

'After you went that night, they shouted at each other. Then Mum made him go.'

His eyes were getting wetter.

I pulled his arm, hard. 'Not here! Never here. Stop that *right now.*'

'Very good inner rage!' Mrs Vernal stood over us, looking at Lewis's face. 'Very internalised!'

She looked closer, at the wetness of Lewis's eyes. Her own eyes gleamed.

I pulled Lewis round so she couldn't see his face. 'He's a good actor.'

Mrs Vernal stood looking at us for a second. She walked away.

'We should find our inner rage.' Lewis was staring at his shoes. 'We haven't got long.'

I glanced around to check no one was looking. 'Do you mean it? You think your dad's gone for good?'

'He's never left the house before. Mum sat me and my brother down and gave us a long talk about how they weren't good for each other. And it was after you said I was your boyfriend. Mum hated how happy Dad was. So it's your fault.'

'Lewis, hang on.' I sat up straighter. 'It can't be *my* fault!'

'Back to the circle!' Mrs Vernal called out.

I sat down and Lewis hurried quickly to a chair on the other side of the room. I shook my head at him, though he wasn't looking. I edged my chair nearer to Jodie's.

'Now.' Mrs Vernal sat down, her legs wide in her floaty trousers, like a man on the train who doesn't want anyone to sit next to him. 'In twos, I want you to discuss what you want to be when you grow up.'

Jodie and I moved our chairs to face each other.

'This really isn't drama,' I whispered.

'She said it's self-development when I asked,' Jodie said. 'She said it's an important part of drama.'

'I don't know what that is but it definitely isn't drama.'

Jodie glanced up at Mrs Vernal, walking by. 'So, what *do* you want to be?'

I thought. 'A farmer maybe. But I wouldn't be good at the early starts. Postman?"

'Early starts again.'

'I could work in sales for the brewery, like Mum did. Or be an aeroplane engineer, like Dad was?'

'I thought your mum was a driving instructor. I thought it was *Gail Larson, Driving Instructor.*'

'She used to work in sales though.' I pictured Monkford main street. 'Hairdresser – no. Newsagent – no.' I thought some more. 'I could work at the fair? Be the person who takes the money and starts the rides?'

Behind me, I heard a little laugh.

I flinched.

'Fiona! Can't you think bigger?' Mrs Vernal talked in a voice loud enough for the room. 'Newsagent? Taking money on the fair? Whoever taught you kids to think so small?' She shook her head. 'Do none of you want to travel the world in an orchestra? Or cure cancer? Imagine that! We're talking about living *dreams*. You can do *anything*.'

Me and Jodie looked at each other.

'I want to cure cancer now,' Jodie said.

I looked up at Mrs Vernal. 'I did say aeroplane engineer earlier, Miss, but you didn't hear me.'

She smiled at me kindly. 'And *why* did you say aeroplane engineer?'

I looked down. 'My dad was one.'

Mrs Vernal gave another little laugh. She moved on.

'Lewis,' I heard her say, 'what about you? I bet you've got big dreams.'

There was something about Mrs Vernal asking Lewis in front of people that made me freeze. *No.*

'I could be a train driver.'

I relaxed a little bit.

'You *could.* What else?'

'I could be a driving instructor.'

'But a creative boy like you, Lewis, can't you think of something else? You could be a dancer or a singer? An artist? A dress designer?'

There were titters round the room.

'You didn't see the horse he drew in art last week, Miss.' I jumped up. 'Two massive back legs and two spindly ones at the front. That horse wouldn't be able to *walk*, let alone canter. *No way* Lewis is an artist.'

Mrs Vernal stopped smiling. 'Fiona. *Enough.*'

Lewis stared at me. He looked back up at Mrs Vernal. 'I want to be a *train driver.*'

Mrs Vernal sighed. 'Where are all the actors and astronauts?' She looked around the room. 'Does *nobody* want to be an astronaut?'

'How about being a teacher?' I asked. 'Is that the job you always wanted?'

Mrs Vernal licked her lips.

The room was silent.

'Fiona, I will be telling Dr Sharma you've been incredibly nasty. And I will tell your parents, at Parents' Evening.'

I slumped back in my chair. *Nasty? How?*

I looked at Lewis, who was staring into space.

I hoped he – *at least* – would realise I'd been trying to help.

*

At the end of the lesson, we all started picking up bags and coats. I hurried over, but Mrs Vernal got to Lewis first.

'Can you stay behind?' she said.

I squeezed his arm. 'I'll be outside.'

I left in the crush of thirty kids, all trying to get through the doorway in one bunch. I waited for Lewis at the round-about outside school, kids flooding past me, knocking my rucksack.

The flood slowed to a trickle. No rucksack-knocking anymore, the pavement different now it was quiet. It was like that bit in *The Lion King*, when the wildebeest stampede turned to nothing.

Dr Sharma walked past, sunglasses on. 'I thought you usu-ally couldn't get out of here fast enough, Fiona?'

'I'm waiting for Lewis. Mrs Vernal made him join her for one of her special chats.'

'Special chats?'

'The ones when she tells us why we should be sad.'

Dr Sharma laughed, then stopped instantly. 'Don't be rude about your teachers.'

'I wasn't being rude!'

But she'd gone.

I waited for ages, but Lewis didn't come out past the roundabout.

I realised he must have gone a different way out of school for once, so I sat waiting for him in the second-biggest bush in the park, cigarette and grill lighter laid out in front of me.

I waited for an hour. But Lewis never came.

33

Dead people can be more interesting than live ones.
(paradox)

Seven days to the fair

I still didn't want to go home so soon – not on the day before Danielle's birthday. I needed to make the home part of the day as short as possible.

And Danielle's birthday being tomorrow meant it was only a week to the fair.

I needed to focus on my spying. I'd got nowhere with the Box of Special Things and I had no leads anymore. Except Adrian Sykes' address, and I was still working myself up to go there because – well. The thought was terrifying.

Carl wasn't even a lead anymore. Still, I found myself slowing as I walked past his house, spying on him partly out of habit. Partly because I needed to kill time before going home.

Mainly, because he was all I had.

I stood at the lamppost and put up the hood of my anorak as a disguise. And I got lucky because it started raining.

I stared through the rain at the house and waited. Carl's car was there, with its *Baby on Board* sticker and the picture of the blue buggy on the back windscreen. There was a car I didn't recognise parked next to it on the drive.

The rain got louder on the hood of my anorak. I tugged it further up.

'You OK there, hon?' A lady walked past with an Alsatian on a metal lead. 'You lost something?'

'I'm waiting for someone.'

The front door opened. Carefully, trying not to move too much, I hunched my hood further up.

Carl showed a man and a woman out. 'Just come back any time. Any questions at all.'

They shook hands and the couple got in the car. Carl gave the roof a tap goodbye – 'Adios!' – and turned to walk back in.

He saw me. 'What are you doing there in the rain, Fiona?'

'It's not raining anymore!' I shouted back. 'Not much, anyway.'

He beckoned me with a finger and I walked over.

'Those were the *excellent* people who are buying this house. Hopefully. They're getting a builder round, so keep your fingers crossed we still exchange contracts next week. They've had a couple of surveys fall through already. They've got a lot of questions about damp and termites. I was well out of my depth, though I know this is a newish house so they shouldn't have issues with—'

I stared at him.

Carl rubbed the back of his head. 'But you don't care about all that.'

We stood there for a second, Carl rocking on his heels.

'Why do you have a "baby on board" sticker when you don't have a baby?'

Carl looked at the sticker. 'Ah, but I *do* have a baby. He lives with his mother. I suppose I still live there too, kind of.'

He reached up with both hands and adjusted his ponytail. 'I'm not sure. We both had busy jobs and it was fine till the baby came along. That's partly why I've done the house sale direct, give her some space so she has some time to see sense and—'

He stopped.

Carl had a lot more extra words for a kid than most people do. Most people don't think it's worth telling a kid anything except instructions.

He swallowed. 'Anyway, I don't live with her. Well, I do and I don't. Anyway, how's the phone?'

'It's perfect.'

He smiled. 'Have you called anyone yet?'

I shook my head.

'Brilliant.'

He was so smiley, it made me take a step back.

He peered at me. 'What's up?'

I looked at my shoes.

'Spit it out.' Carl smiled. 'Lies are always worse than the truth. At least – that's what my wife says. Ex-wife. No – wife. It's just complicated because—'

One week to the fair – I needed to hurry this up. 'My friend Lewis thinks you want to flash me.'

There was a splashing noise. A car drove through a puddle.

Carl didn't move out of the way. Some of the puddle splashed up his jeans.

He *still* didn't move. 'What?' He gave an awkward bark, like a laugh made of fear. '*Flash* you? NO! *God!* It would never cross my mind!' He paused. 'But I'm hearing myself, and the more I *say* I'm not going to flash you, the more that sounds like something someone *like that* would say, and I'd never, NEVER—'

He kept going a bit longer.

Thing was, I believed him. Flashers didn't talk about damp course, and termites, and excellent people, and girlfriends who might be ex-girlfriends and *it's complicated*. If flashers talked to you at all, it was about puppies. Usually they just stood, in silence, macs open, peckers out.

'You promise?' I said.

'The fact you'd even ask...' Carl crouched, so I was the taller one, looking down at him. 'Fiona, I'm a normal guy. I'm a parent. And I don't go around ... you know.' He bounced on the balls of his feet. 'I like kids, but in the right way. Why does Lewis think I might be ... one of *those*?'

'Well.' I scratched an itch on my cheek. 'At first, it was because you wanted him to do strimming.'

Carl wrinkled his forehead. 'But only because he knocked on my door and offered to—'

'And then you acted interested in what I had to say. When I'm a *kid*.'

'But I was just making conversation.'

'And *then* you gave me the phone.'

'Right.' He stood up again. 'OK.' He turned away. 'Shit.'

The rain was getting heavier. I pulled my hood further up.

'I think, maybe' – he ran his hand through his hair – 'giving you that phone was a mistake.'

I pulled my coat flaps tighter. *No.*

'I'd forgotten how small towns work. Which is why I moved away. Have you got the phone with you?'

I pulled my coat tighter still. 'No.'

'I should take it back. Please go and get it for me.'

'You can't give a present and then take it away! That's not how presents work!'

'But if it makes you think I'm a—' He shuddered. 'Jesus.'

'I don't think you're a flasher.' He flinched every time I said it. 'It was *Lewis* who said you were a flasher. Lewis is a worrier and he gets everything wrong. Causes me *all sorts* of problems.'

Carl rubbed the bit between his nose and his top lip.

'Come and sit on the step, out of the rain.' He indicated the front step, under the little porch.

I took a step towards the road. 'Here's fine.'

'I thought you said you knew I wasn't . . . *one of those.*'

He made his voice softer. 'Fi?'

'I've got to go.' I rushed down the drive.

'This isn't right. I've done nothing wrong. *Nothing.*' He raised his voice after me as I hurried away. 'I promise you, Fiona. You don't understand. I'm actually a *really* nice man!'

I had to go home in the end. Sometimes, you have no choice.

I tried my best to make conversation with Mum and Dad over our Friday takeaway, as we ate burgers at the peninsula.

I didn't make a great start. 'It's rainy for July.'

Neither responded.

'Do you want to know the science behind why people say blood is thicker than water?'

Dad nodded, like I'd said a fact, not a question.

I sighed. Time to bring out the big guns. 'Mrs Vernal called me nasty today. She's going to tell you at Parents' Evening.'

They both looked up.

'Nasty?' Mum focused her eyes. 'Nasty, how?'

'She made us discuss what we wanted to be when we grow up.' *Ha! I won. Kind of.* 'She said there are other jobs apart from the ones you can see. Asked why we talked about being driving instructors and farmers and why none of us wanted to be astronauts or actors. She said our dreams were small.'

Mum looked at Dad. 'Hmm.'

'And then I asked if she'd always wanted to be a teacher.'

'And?' Mum said.

'And that's it. Hand on heart. *Is that the job you always wanted?* And she called me *nasty* for that.'

Mum nodded. 'OK.' She stared at her burger. Like she wasn't sure how it had got there or what she was meant to do with it.

Dad looked out of the window. He didn't tell me off, either.

Which meant it had started.

I forced a long chip into my mouth, letting it break in the middle so I could get it all in.

It wasn't the actual day till tomorrow, but that didn't matter. The air in the house had changed.

Danielle's birthday had started.

34

Sometimes the kindest thing is not to try to be kind at all.
(paradox)

Six days to the fair
When I woke up the next morning, I remembered straight away. The air was heavy on my duvet. *Danielle's birthday.*

I shuffled down to the kitchen, where Mum sat at the peninsula, wearing her smart coat. The one made of a dark, thick fabric, with neat tucks and folds like a carefully wrapped present.

'Hi.' I reached past the bunch of wrapped flowers and got the cereal box out of the cupboard.

Gerberas, those ones are called. If flowers ever committed crimes, I could pick these out of a police line-up. *'Flower, flower, flower – GERBERA!'*

I'm not into flowers, obviously. I just know the name of this one.

Mum spoke, finally. 'Gerberas were Danielle's favourite flower.'

I didn't say *I know because you always tell me.* I got a spoon out of the drawer. 'Do you know what my favourite flower is?'

I wasn't sure Mum heard me, but she looked up. 'You don't have a favourite because you don't like flowers.'

'Correct. But if I did have a favourite flower, it would be a foxglove. Or deadly nightshade. Something to make poison with.'

Grandma once bought me *The Young Person's Guide to Flowers*. I read it to be polite.

Anyway, Mum nodded, like I'd said something really interesting. Just nothing interesting enough to need an answer.

Grandma's train from Glasgow didn't arrive till the afternoon, so she couldn't babysit while Mum and Dad were at the grave. I spent the morning with Mrs Carpenter, the old lady next door, which meant no spying time.

Well, hardly any spying time.

'Danielle?' Mrs Carpenter stretched her feet out. Her chair tipped back and a foot support appeared. 'Don't know anything about her, I'm afraid. There's only been you next door, while I've lived here.'

'Oh.'

'Only moved in ten years ago. You were just a baby yourself.' Mrs Carpenter patted her lap. Snowy, her Papillon, jumped up and settled down. 'I'd forgotten you ever had a sister, till your mum asked me to look after you today.'

I kind of liked her for that.

So that bit of the day wasn't too bad. Mrs Carpenter made a big fuss of me. She let me watch Saturday cartoons and I ate a whole pack of fig rolls. I stroked Snowy and took him round the garden on his lead, and I remembered not to ask about Mr Carpenter, or his brother's wife who was welcome to him.

So even though I didn't get any spying done, I actually had quite a nice morning.

I was reading a magazine in my bedroom after lunch when the doorbell rang and the lights flashed.

I rushed to the door and pulled it open with a grin. *Grandma!*

Not Grandma.

A man and a woman outside, the woman carrying something all wrapped up in blankets. A baby or a Yorkshire Terrier, maybe.

The woman with the baby/terrier waved at me. 'Hi, Fiona.'

Annette was once Danielle's school friend, and the man with the hairy hands was her husband, Mike.

'Hi.' I walked them into the lounge. 'I'll go and make the tea.'

If I make the tea, it moves it along, and then this whole thing is over quicker.

I took the mugs of tea on a tray into the lounge. Dad was tidying up the shed, so he could show Mike something. *Something so they don't all have to be in the same room with all this loud quiet*, I decided.

The other three sat round, looking like they were waiting for an ammonium nitrate bomb to go off.

Annette beamed. 'Now that *is* service. Fiona's a credit to you, Gail.'

Mum didn't say anything. I put sugar in my tea, just to see if she noticed, but she didn't.

Annette bounced her baby on her knee. 'Do you want a hold?'

Mum nodded and they both stood up.

I stirred my tea loudly, banging the spoon against the mug.

'Hello, little one.' Mum took the baby from Annette and smiled softly. 'Aren't you a princess?'

The baby gripped Mum's finger. Mum looked like she was about to cry.

I looked down at my cup of tea and stirred it again. *I knew it.*

Annette put her arms round Mum and the baby. 'I'm so sorry, Gail. I shouldn't have brought her.'

'She's lovely,' Mum put her hand over her mouth. 'It's just—'

'I know.' Annette rubbed Mum's back. 'I know.'

I took a sip of my tea, all thick with sugar, and put my cup down. *Ew.*

Mum handed the baby back to Annette. ''Scuse me a minute.' She ran upstairs and shut the bathroom door.

I stretched my arms in a fake yawn. 'So, Annette, that night when Danielle died. . .'

She looked so shocked, I stopped talking.

I cleared my throat. 'So, that night at the fair—'

The toilet flushed. Mum hurried down the stairs. 'That's better.'

Annette gave a quick glance at me.

Mum sat down like nothing had happened. 'Danielle wanted four babies. *Four.* Can you believe it?'

The others smiled.

Eleven-year-olds must have been different in 1982.

'She said she was having two girls and two boys, and she was going to call them Benny, Bjorn, Agnetta and Anna-Frid.'

I glared at Mum. Even *Danielle* wouldn't want her mates

knowing she'd said *that*. She *especially* wouldn't want her mates knowing that *now* – now her mates had cars and coffee breath and husbands with hairy hands.

'We *really* liked ABBA, didn't we?' Annette said, smiling.

Mum smiled. 'Do you still like ABBA?'

'Oh.' Annette glanced at Mike and back. 'Of course. I mean – I'm mainly into indie now. But everyone likes ABBA, right?'

Mum looked wobbly round the mouth.

Annette turned to me. 'And who's your favourite band, Fiona?'

I shrugged.

'She's more into world events.' Mum tried to smile at me. 'Bosnia and Serbia. The elections in Russia and Greece.'

'Right. Wow.' Annette gave a little cough. 'I wouldn't even know where to start!'

I took another sip of too-sweet tea.

Dad came back into the room. 'Want me to show you that box of tools, Mike? Let the girls chat?'

Mike left the room as quick as he could.

I stood up. 'I'm going to go and make a fortune teller.'

I headed into the kitchen to take up an eavesdropping position, while Annette's voice travelled through the hatch from the lounge. 'She's smart.'

'Smarter than me. And her father,' Mum said. 'I don't know where she gets it from. Russian elections!'

'She's got spirit, too.'

I was thinking maybe Annette wasn't *so* bad, but then she said:

'Like Danielle.'

A whole ten seconds.

I got a piece of paper out of my bag. I hadn't been lying

about making a fortune teller – the girls didn't like my spy one, so I needed to make another.

I cut the paper into a square with the kitchen scissors and put them back in the drawer.

'Mike doesn't get it when I want to talk about her,' Annette said. 'Says it was half my life ago and I should try to get over it.'

'You know what other people say if I talk about Danielle? They talk about *distractions*. They talk about *closure*.'

I copied the folds of my old fortune teller. Next to the clean white paper, the folds of the old spy paper looked loose and grey.

'Closure!' Mum put on a little girl voice. *'Is it better now? Has enough time passed? Have you forgotten and moved on?'*

'They're trying to help,' Annette said. 'People can't imagine it, even if they want to.'

It was easier to do the folding, second time round. I'd make a *superpower* fortune teller. Because even girls want superpowers, right?

Even girls. They *must* do.

'They even had *Jonathan* talking about closure sometimes,' Mum said. *'People grieve differently*, that's what the counsellor said. But then, Jonathan was the one who wouldn't stop sleeping in Danielle's bed. When I hated him. But that was so long ago. It doesn't seem real now. And I can't bear to even think about my own moment of madness.'

I unfolded my new fortune teller and pushed the paper straight with my fist. I'd heard it all before, so I didn't let it upset me like it used to. *Yeah, yeah* – being sad made Mum and Dad go crazy and they argued a lot, but they were fine now. They changed jobs and spent more time together and had their date nights. They hardly ever argued now. Except about whose turn it was to do the DIY – and about me, of course, sometimes. But that was *my* fault. That was nothing about them.

I looked at my fresh fortune teller. I started writing in the fortunes.

You will be bitten by a bat and able to hear through walls.

'Everyone knows the pressure you were under,' Annette said.

You will be bitten by a chameleon and be able to camouflage.

'Not much fun being the town gossip.' Mum's voice was faraway in my head. 'But those people who talked about distraction – they were right, in a way. It switched my brain off for a while, however unreal it all seems now. But I was just opting out. From real life.'.

You will be bitten by an eagle and be able to fly.

'You did what you had to. It was so long ago.'

You will be bitten by a cheetah and be able to run fast.

Mum sniffed. 'Over twelve years ago and I still feel guilty. And so I should.'

The word *guilty* made me stop writing. Had Mum killed Danielle *herself*? Not *murder*, of course – but an accident? Is that why they didn't want to tell me, so I didn't think Mum was a murderer? I'd heard Mum say before, on bad days, that Danielle's death was her fault – but I just thought she said it so others went, 'No, it's not your fault, not at all.' Like when we kids learned to say *My drawing is so rubbish, yours is so much better*, so other kids said back, *No, your picture is so much better than mine!*

'Beating yourself up doesn't change anything. And life takes strange turns. One good thing came out of it, didn't it?'

'Exactly! *The* best thing, for all of us! So we can't regret it for a second.'

This was why listening made no sense sometimes. Especially half listening. Because this definitely couldn't be about Danielle anymore.

I shook my head and focused on my fortune teller. It was *hard*, thinking of new animals. *You will be bitten by a dolphin and be able to walk on water.*

'I'm so pleased you get it,' Mum said. 'If you'd told me back then – *you know who you're going to talk to about the complex emotional side? Annette Desai. You know, Danielle's little friend with the side ponytail. The one who thinks she's going to marry Shakin' Stevens.*'

They both laughed.

I was running out of animals. *You will be bitten by a bat – a different bat – and be able to sleep upside down.*

'So, how's Mike?' Mum said in a new, sunny voice. 'How's the factory?'

I finished off my fortune teller – *you will be bitten by an ant and be able to fit in a matchbox* – and heard *way* too much about Mike and the factory. About collective bargaining and shift breaks. About union reps and ballots and shop stewards – stuff that wouldn't have made sense even if I'd *tried* to listen.

I folded up my fortune teller. I tested it with my fingers and thumbs, checking it worked. I slid it into my secret pocket.

Annette comes to the house on Danielle's birthday every year, even though she always makes Mum cry. And one day, when Mum's not there, I'm going to tell her it would be kinder to Mum if she didn't come at all.

'I hate it, Grandma,' I said into her neck.

We sat together on my bed that night while Grandma rubbed my back.

'I know, lovey.' Grandma pulled back. 'But your mum and dad need to do this. Every other day of the year is about you. This is just the one day about Danielle.'

'Wrong, Grandma. *Every* day is about Danielle.'

'Everything your parents do, they do for you.'

'I don't want to argue, Grandma, but you're not actually here.'

'No?' She gave a sad smile. 'I'm sorry to hear it feels like that. But what about me, then?' She gave me a big smile now so I could see her corner teeth, the ones that are a bit vampire-y. 'Don't you think, to me, everything's all about you?'

'But you live in Scotland!'

She stretched her feet out. I looked at the plastic jewels of her flipflops. Beneath her toenails' orange varnish, ridges stood up, like lines in a map. 'But don't you realise I'm thinking about you all the time when I'm in Scotland?' She showed her vampire teeth again, though *no one* is less vampire-y than Grandma. 'When I'm on the bus. When I'm raking the leaves. Who do you think I'm thinking about then, hey? The prime minister? Batman?'

She tickled me and I squirmed away.

'Didn't you like Danielle, then?'

She sniffed. 'I loved Danielle. But she's not here, and you are. And you're what matters now.'

I raised my head hopefully. 'Can I come and live with you?'

Grandma gave another sniff. 'You wouldn't want to, not really.'

'You could clear out your ironing room and put an airbed down.'

She gave a sad smile.

'You could still use the room for ironing. Just as long as

you knocked before you went in. And put the ironing board away after.'

'Ah, lovey.' Grandma shook her head. 'This is just one day, Danielle's birthday.'

I watched her, watching me, and I felt a bubbling up inside. I didn't know what to call it, this bubbling, it was just *there* on days like this. And then I thought about how unfair things were, and the feeling bubbled more.

And then the bubbling made me think bad things. Like – how if Danielle wasn't dead, I'd still want her to be dead because of how she ruins things.

And then I felt even more bubbling, for knowing that's a bad thought. And then I wanted to scream, as loud as I could, so I couldn't hear the thoughts in my head anymore.

I raised my head a little. 'Am I bad, Grandma?'

She laughed. 'No! No, you're perfect.'

I gripped the corner of the duvet and looked up. *How did Danielle die, Grandma?*

But she was smiling at me so softly, I just couldn't ask.

She stood up. 'I'm going to check on your mum.' She gave her friendly-vampire smile. 'You're all right now, darling?'

I smiled. 'I'm all right.'

I watched her walk out and stopped smiling. I pinched my leg, hard, until it hurt. I did it again, harder, and kept doing it, till the bubbling calmed down.

It was good I hadn't asked. I wasn't going to ask.

I couldn't let Grandma find out that, deep down, I was bad. Right the way through to my blood.

I couldn't show her that. Not when she was the only person who'd ever liked me too much to notice.

35

Even if people know you're the bad one, they still act
surprised when you prove it.
(paradox)

Five days to the fair
When I woke up the next day, I made a decision.

I *had* to ask Grandma.

I didn't want to, but I had to. I had no choice, if I was going
to get to the fair.

I got dressed as slowly as I could, trying to put it off. I
found Grandma in the kitchen, wearing Dad's apron, stirring
a big pot on the cooker. The room smelled like fields and
sludge.

'Morning, little one,' Grandma said without looking round.
'Your dad said I must ask what you think about the trial of
some war criminals?'

I pulled myself up onto a stool. 'Where're Mum and Dad?'

'They went to buy painting stuff. They're going to do some
decorating.'

'They won't do any decorating. They'll just buy more stuff
and leave it in the garage.'

'I'm making soup.' Grandma tapped the wooden spoon on

the side of the pan and put it back on the chopping board. 'Tell your mother she'll need to put some milk in when she reheats it. And some parsley from the garden. It always tastes better with a bit of parsley.'

'I don't think we have parsley.' I took a deep breath. 'Grandma. What happened the night Danielle died? No one's ever told me.'

Grandma didn't turn around. Had she even heard?

I swallowed. 'Were Mum and Dad with her? At the fair?'

Grandma bent over. She concentrated on the cooker's temperature dial. 'Why are you asking, darling?'

'I don't want to ask Mum and Dad. I just keep thinking about Danielle. About how it feels to die.'

Grandma put her wooden spoon down.

'And I don't want to think she was on her own when it happened.'

Grandma put one hand to her chest and rubbed herself softly.

I tried to look in her eyes, but couldn't. 'Was she on her own?' I whispered.

Grandma lowered herself onto a peninsula stool, more carefully than usual. 'She wasn't alone. She went to the fair with her friends.'

'With Annette?'

'And others. Annette's dad was there too. Danielle was very loved, don't you worry.' Grandma stared at her lap. 'It's hard for me to talk about. I don't want to talk about this.'

Don't ask any more. 'But when she died—'

'It's so thoughtful of you to care about other people.' Grandma brushed her hand across the surface, pushing crumbs into a neat pile at the side. 'You're a good girl, Fiona.

The most precious thing in the world.' She kept brushing. 'You know that?'

I started to cry. We both knew that wasn't true.

'Come here.'

I let her hug me, my eyes and nose burning with tears. So much feeling bubbled up – in my chest, my throat. I shrugged out of Grandma's hug and ran into the garden.

'Fiona!'

But I couldn't let her look at me.

I ran into the garden shed with the spiders and the earwigs. I slammed the door, and locked myself in with the key.

Half an hour later, Grandma was still trying to coax me out of the shed.

And now there was whispering outside. Mum and Dad were back from the shops.

I *definitely* wasn't coming out now.

'Fiona.' Grandma's voice was soft. 'What's all this commotion for, darling? My train goes at one – I can't stay an extra night because I'm on the till at the charity shop tomorrow. Surely you want to say goodbye?'

I hugged my legs tighter to my chest.

'Goodbye, then. I love you, darling.'

'FIONA LARSON, GET OUT HERE AND SAY GOODBYE TO YOUR GRANDMA! NOW!'

If I wasn't coming out for Grandma, there was *no way* I was coming out for Mum.

'Right, well. Your father's staying in the house,' Grandma said, 'while your mum drives me to the station. I hope you feel better soon. I'm sorry we didn't get to say goodbye. I love you so much, darling.'

*

It might be hard to understand for someone who's not bad themselves.

But when someone says they love you and you know you've been bad, it hurts. And you have to do something to make the hurt stop.

After I heard the car start up and leave, and I was sure Dad was back in the house, I got the big saw off the hook in the shed. I held the saw with both hands and looked at it, feeling its weight.

I headed out of the shed and towards the swing.

It took longer than you'd think.

The metal handle cut into my hands. I had to keep putting the saw down to take a rest. My arms burned everywhere – my elbows, my fingers, my underarms. I had to lean on the saw, pushing it down to get through the wood. My T-shirt stuck to my back in the sunshine. My fringe stuck to my face.

Eventually, the wood broke in two.

I put the saw back on its hook in the shed. I shut the door, but didn't lock it. I sat down, cross-legged, and waited.

I bit my thumbnail at the side. I bit too far down, so it bled.

I tensed at the sound of the car in the drive.

'Where is she?' Mum's voice. 'She'd better be out of that shed.'

I took a deep breath and stared at the door. At the padlock, hanging down and open, where I'd left it.

'What the—'

I bit my other thumbnail and tore a piece off with my teeth. Pain rushed in.

I looked at the blood pooling at the bottom of my nail,

overflowing the white half-moon at the base. White blood cells. Platelets. Plasma.

'FIONA LARSON!'

One big pool of O positive.

Mum threw the shed door open. She stood there, shaking.

I stayed cross-legged on the shed floor. I stared at a dusty rake.

'Please tell me you haven't destroyed the swing. *The swing.* And that you haven't been playing with *a saw.*'

I stared at the rake. The plastic was rubbing away at the handle, leaving green bits that bobbled and peeled.

She pulled on my arm. 'Get up!'

I tried to pull my arm back, but she was too strong. She lifted me to my feet and half dragged me outside, my feet skittering along.

Pieces of hair fell out of her clip and into her face.

'Look at it!'

We both looked at the swing. At the metal frame. At the seat, which hung in two pieces from the chains, the two chunks of wood turning slowly.

She shook my arm. 'Look what you've done!'

I looked down at the grass.

'Your grandma says I should try to understand that you find Danielle's birthday hard, but she didn't see *this*, did she?' Mum still hadn't clipped her hair back, so it all hung in her face. 'No other kids go around sawing up swings, do they? Who else does this? *No one.*'

I looked at my thumb. *O positive. Plasma. Platelets.*

'Look at it. How does that make you feel?'

She put her hand on my head and turned it. I looked at the two bits of wood dangling from the chains.

'Say something.'

'No.' I ran away and upstairs. I slammed my door and sat on the bed.

I waited for Mum to stomp after me, but she didn't. I heard raised voices downstairs. Even though Mum and Dad must be furious with me, they had room to be angry with each other.

I looked at the blood on my thumbnail.

I pulled the notepad by the bed closer. I tipped my thumb onto the pad, dripping blood onto the paper.

I put my first finger into the blood and pressed hard, making a bloody red fingerprint, like on the front of a detective book.

I stared at it. At my bad blood.

I took a magnifying glass and looked at the fingerprint. The lines whirled and circled.

I heard footsteps heading upstairs. Slow and heavy. Dad's.

He opened my bedroom door. 'Hi.'

'Hi.'

He stayed in the doorway. 'We're very upset down there.'

'Mum's angry, not upset.'

'No.' He sighed. 'No, she's not. It might sound like it, but she's not.'

'She said she was furious.'

'Only because she's very upset.'

I looked down at my bloody fingerprint. At the platelets and plasma. The O positive.

'I think you'd better avoid your mother for the rest of the night.' Dad looked at the piece of paper and back. 'Is that part of your blood project?'

I looked down at the fingerprint. 'Yes.'

'Is it your blood?'

I gave a small nod.

I felt the mattress move beneath me as he sat on the bed. 'Where did you get that blood from, Fiona?'

I turned my hand so he could see my thumb.

'Christ! Did you do that with the saw?'

'I did it with my teeth. On purpose.'

'Don't move.'

He hurried out of the room and came back with a box of plasters and cotton wool.

He sat next to me and wiped my thumb with wet cotton wool. I winced as it stung, but I deserved it.

Dad pressed a fresh piece of cotton wool against my thumb. He held it there. 'Why did you ask Grandma about how Danielle died? Why did you try to upset her?'

'I wasn't trying to upset her. No one ever tells me anything.'

He took the cotton wool away from my hand and peeled back a plaster. 'And you must never play with tools.'

I watched him stick the plaster round my thumb.

'I know that.'

'Do you?' He pressed the plaster hard into my skin. 'Because you picked up that saw happily enough.'

'But I didn't use the electric saw. Just the still one.'

'FIONA!' Dad let go of my hand. 'I don't want you to *ever* even *think* about the electric saw.' He rubbed his hands through his hair. Strands stood up like he'd been rubbing a balloon. 'I'm going to have to lock the shed and hide the key now, you know? Christ, Fiona, what do you do to us?'

I didn't say anything.

'Do your friends do things like this? Does Lewis torture his parents this way?'

I put my blood-printed finger in my mouth and sucked it. My finger tasted of an old penny.

Dad made his voice softer. 'Never do that again. Promise me now.'

'I'm positive I won't play with tools like that again.'

'Take your hand out of your mouth so I can see and say it again. *And promise* me. Promise me or I tell you, Fiona – you're never leaving this room for the rest of your life.'

In the end, I promised. I stayed in my room until after tea-time, when I heard the phone ring and the overhead light flashed.

Mum answered the phone. 'Hello?'

I opened the door so I could listen.

Mum spoke again. 'That's good, Mum. No delays?'

I crept onto the landing.

'Thanks for calling. Tell Kenneth I said hi.'

I scooped my skirt underneath me. I sat at the top of the stairs, just out of sight, my back to the wall.

'No, I didn't,' Mum said. 'I was going to speak to her about why she asked but then . . . something happened. You don't want to know. But I handled it badly, of course I did, and—'

Mum sighed. 'Not *awful* awful.'

I put the end of my thumb in my mouth.

'She sawed the swing in half.'

I sucked the plaster.

'*Sawed* it.'

'I don't know how else to put it. *Sawed* it. With an actual saw . . . No, the wooden seat, not the metal bit. Who do you think she is, world's strongest man? I don't know *how*, exactly. She's got arms like spaghetti.'

I wrapped my arms round my body.

'*Is* it, though?' Mum's voice went higher. 'I feel like *every* age is a difficult age. When do the difficult ages end? How did you manage with me? But I was so much easier.'

I hugged myself tighter.

'Mum.' My mum's voice hardened. 'That was *forty years ago* and you know I paid the ice-cream van man back.'

At that, I raised my head.

Mum sighed. 'I know the point you're making; I just don't know what I'm meant to do. I'm not as good at this as you. I try *so hard.*'

There was a long silence while Grandma talked. I imagined what she was saying. *It's not your fault. Fiona was just born bad.*

'I just think – I'm really bad at this,' Mum said finally.

I felt myself frown.

'Jonathan can stay calm but I just can't. Maybe I was never up to doing this again. Maybe I shouldn't have ever thought I could do this, after everything.'

I looked at the plaster round my thumbnail.

Sometimes, I wish I didn't have spy skills after all.

I tiptoed into the bedroom and shut the door quietly, so I didn't have to hear Mum say she wished she hadn't had me.

<u>Bad Scar Things I've Done</u>
<u>New 1996 Summer Term Update – Part 2</u>

1) Looked up Danielle's death in the library and phoned Adrian Sykes
2) Took the polaroid camera to school when Dad told me not to
3) Accepted a present from a stranger Mum told me to stay away from
4) Went through Carl's bins
5) Lied to everyone about having friends in another school
6) Lied to everyone about Lewis being my boyfriend
7) Used fake ID to buy a cigarette
8) Asked Annette how Danielle died
9) Asked Grandma how Danielle died. Even though she asked me not to
10) Sawed up the swing
11) Didn't say goodbye to Grandma

I told you I was the bad one.

36

Many great spies end up working alone.
The Junior Spy's Secret Handbook™

Four days till the fair
I didn't speak to anyone before school the next morning. As I reached the bottom of the stairs, Mum came out of the kitchen, rearranging the clip in her hair.

We both looked quickly away.

I don't think Mum knows what to say when things like this happen, either.

Mum crouched in front of the Cupboard of Office Things and opened it. 'It's sunny out there,' she said into the cupboard.

And before she could say any more to the cupboard about the weather, I picked up my rucksack and hurried out of the door.

Lewis wasn't at the lamppost.

I'd made Mum so cross she was pretending I was invisible and talking into cupboards. And I'd made Lewis so cross that he preferred to have *no* friends than be friends with me.

It was fine. It was all fine.

I had new friends now.

*

But at break, I couldn't find the other girls. I looked and looked, but knew it must be one of those games where I didn't understand the rules, and I'd ruin the game if I asked.

So I stood there in our normal spot anyway, watching the boys play football.

Lewis was playing. I watched him chase after the ball and kick it to Sean. He didn't do too badly, actually.

I tried to catch his eye, but he didn't look over. Even though the only reason he was allowed to play football with the good kids now – with his wrong coat and rucksack, when he wasn't very good – was because of me.

I finally found my girl group on the far side of the tennis courts.

I walked over. 'Hiya.' I got out my blood project. 'Check this out. Actual blood.'

I got to the right crispy page of my project book and held it open in front of me, like a flasher with his mac.

The girls all jerked their faces back.

I frowned. 'It's my blood so it's fine. No one died or anything.'

Yasmine shook her head while looking at Alison Fisher. 'Why aren't you doing photosynthesis, like everyone else?'

I shoved my project book into my rucksack. I thought desperately.

'I've also made a fortune teller.' I got it out of my secret pocket and slid my fingers and thumbs in.

The girls looked at the four labels.

'*Cape, Boots, Mask, Cuffs,*' Jodie read.

'It's about superpowers.' I looked at the paper. 'That's *cape* as in *a superhero's cape. Definitely* not a magician's cape.'

Naomi looked at the others. 'We don't like superpowers.'

'Don't like superpowers?' I dropped the fortune teller against my leg. 'How does that even *work*?'

But the bell rang for the next lesson, so no one even answered.

School news was the worst yet. The very worst.

In RE, the school secretary knocked on the door. 'Can Fiona Larson please come to Mrs Shackleton's office.'

There was a ripple of interest round the room.

What's she done?

Who's she shown her pants to now?

Miss Jarvis looked at the school secretary in a question.

With a tiny movement of her mouth, the school secretary made an *eek* face.

Miss Jarvis looked at me with *actual sadness*. 'Take care, Fiona.' She waved me off with a pitying smile, like she was sending me to the guillotine.

I packed up my pencil tin and books, and hurried down the corridor with the school secretary. My legs felt like they were dragging behind my body, and it wasn't as easy to walk as usual. Everything about me trembled.

We turned the corner into the staff corridor and I dropped my pencil tin. My stuff scattered everywhere.

I crouched down, picking up pens and pencils. The school secretary crouched to help.

I reached under a big metal radiator to get to my protractor. I had to reach through a trailing clump of ruched-up spiderweb to get it, letting the clump flap against my hands. I didn't even shiver. I barely noticed the webbing – not now. Not now I'd been called into the New Head's office.

I stood up, cradling my equipment in my arms. The school

secretary handed me some stuff she'd picked up – a pen, a rubber and a pencil sharpener. She looked at my hands and I could tell she noticed they were shaking. She was about to say something, but then didn't.

We kept walking. Down the staff corridor, where I wasn't normally allowed to go. The place where—

Too soon, we stopped outside the New Head's office.

'You can go in,' the secretary said.

I looked up at her, my legs trembling even more. *Please!*

But she just opened the door.

I stepped inside. I had no choice.

The New Head, Mrs Shackleton, looked up from behind the big headmaster's desk. She stared at me like I'd deliberately kicked her best cat.

She wasn't alone.

Dr Sharma was there, in the chair next to her. And Mrs Vernal, standing behind the desk.

Both looked at me with that same *cat-kicker!* expression.

And I still didn't know. I'm that stupid – *Fiona Larson is so, so stupid* – that I still didn't get it.

Until I saw it, finally, just *there*. On the New Head's desk. The ruffled-up copy of *Mayfair*.

37

If you're afraid, you say your 'blood runs cold'. It is the release of the body's 'fight or flight' hormones causing a chain reaction that leads to the vasoconstriction of arterioles that causes this unpleasant sensation.

Fiona Larson, 7E's Blood Project

Four days to the fair

'Sit,' the New Head said.

I don't know how I got my legs moving, but I got into that chair somehow.

The New Head looked from me to *Mayfair* and back. 'Look familiar?'

I shook my head.

'A boy in Year Nine told Mrs Vernal you sold it to him.'

'I've never seen it before. Look, whatever Dean Prince says—'

The three teachers twitched into focus. Birds of prey, spotting a mouse.

I added in a rush, 'Or any other Year Nine boy.'

The New Head stared. 'How do you know we got this magazine from Dean Prince?'

'It's just . . . he's said to me before . . .' I kicked the table leg.

'Because he was the kid who bought the *Mayfair* one.'

The teachers looked at each other.

'Bought the *Mayfair* one?' the New Head repeated.

Dr Sharma looked from the New Head to me. 'There were others?'

Damn it, Fiona! I nodded.

'Were all the magazines . . .' Dr Sharma closed her eyes and put her finger and thumb to her eyelids. '. . . well, I'll just say it.' Dr Sharma took her hand away. She opened her eyes. 'Porn?'

'One had films in it. Only the others were porn. And I didn't sell them here. I sold them at the car boot sale. I never brought them into school.'

Mrs Vernal folded her arms. 'This is utterly shocking.'

Dr Sharma held up a finger. She kept her gaze on me. 'Where did you get the magazines?'

'I found them.'

'Just shocking. As if—'

Dr Sharma interrupted Mrs Vernal. 'Did you find them in your *father's* things?' Dr Sharma's lip went up at the edge at *father's*.

'No. He wouldn't like these magazines.' I hoped it was true. I *hated* these magazines now. Kelly from Winchester and *everything*.

'You don't have to defend him,' Dr Sharma said. 'He's not a pupil here.'

I shook my head. 'I found them in the park.'

Mrs Vernal looked at the New Head. 'This is serious. You've been extremely clear with the rules, Mrs Shackleton, you've set your stall out about sanctions, and—'

'Let's discuss this without Fiona here.' Dr Sharma's voice was calm. 'There's a complicated history, from before your time.'

I lifted my head a tiny bit. Was Dr Sharma using my catalyst?

But I saw her face and put my head straight back down.

The lunchtime bell rang.

'We will talk now, alone, Fiona,' the New Head said. 'Sit on the bench outside and we will call you back in shortly.'

I took a seat outside the room. I crossed my feet and tucked them under the bench, trying to make myself as small as possible.

Sanctions.

Sanctions meant *suspended.* Or *expelled.*

I imagined Mum's face as she got the call from the school. Dad's face as she explained to him what I'd done.

I was so scared, I couldn't even cry.

Even if I wasn't expelled– *me! Expelled! What would I do? Where would I go?* – this was *it.* It was over.

There was no way I'd be allowed to go to the fair.

I waited a bit longer. Through the open window, in the playground, a kid shouted 'Haircut!' Then a chorus started. *Haircut! Haircut!*

It couldn't still be about Greeney. But I didn't even have the energy to wonder who'd got a haircut now.

I jiggled my legs.

The teachers had told me to stay on the bench, but there was no way I was staying outside that office. My jiggling legs were telling me something.

I got up. Still too scared to cry – but so scared that I couldn't just sit there either.

Trying not to think what I was doing, I grabbed my rucksack and rushed down the staff corridor.

*

I hurried round the playground, my fear making it hard to focus – still, looking everywhere. Finally, I found my girl group at the far end of the field.

I took a minute, trying to calm down, hoping my face wasn't too red. They wouldn't want to hear what had happened. Alison had called my magazines *disgusting*.

I ran up to the group. 'Hi! I couldn't find you, you were miles away.' I pulled out the cigarette again. 'Da da!' I tried to make myself breathe normally. 'Me and Lewis didn't smoke it in the end. Let's go to the park and have it together now.'

The girls looked at each other.

'It's lunchtime,' Naomi said.

'But we could go anyway! The gates aren't locked.' I patted my rucksack. '*And* I remembered the grill lighter.'

The group widened their eyes at each other, like what I was saying was incredible.

I licked my lips. 'Jodie?'

She twizzled her friendship bracelet round her arm. She looked at her feet.

I grabbed my empty wrist. I'd forgotten to make a bracelet, *and* I'd forgotten my crisps.

'I'll tell her.' Alison turned to me. 'We've got some sad news. We've realised we're not the right size anymore. We're too big.'

'Are we going on diets? If we have to. I thought we'd wait till at least Year Eight, but . . .'

Jodie stayed looking at the ground.

'Bless,' Alison said. 'We've realised *this group's* too big now.'

A thud in my chest. This must be how it felt to get shot, for the second time. *Bang.* Falling to the floor. Just getting up again then – *bang.*

'Four is a good number. Five just feels too many.' Alison shrugged. *Can't be helped.*

She nodded at Naomi. *Continue.*

'We're starting a new group from scratch,' Naomi said. 'Me and Alison.'

I should have just walked away and pretended I didn't understand. But my heart was going too fast to think properly. And sometimes I can be *really really fucking stupid fucking stupid Fiona.*

I made a show of checking my fingernails. 'Who's in the new group?'

'It was just me and Alison originally. But then some others asked to join.'

I looked at Yasmin. I looked at Jodie.

Both looked at the grass.

I took my mobile out of my secret pocket with shaking hands.

Alison looked at it. 'Your mobile phone isn't going to get you back in the group.'

I swallowed. 'I'm going to phone a friend.'

'Selina Baker? Dean Prince?'

Even then, I narrowed my eyes. 'Definitely not Dean Prince.'

'One of the other sixth-formers? The kid who's definitely your boyfriend, *Lewis Harris went to Paris?*'

I took a shaky breath. 'I'm going to talk to one of my friends from Radcliffe High. Unless,' I turned to Yasmin and Jodie. 'You could be in two groups? Three's enough for a group, isn't it?'

'My mum says three's a crowd,' Yasmin said into her feet.

'We could start a new group. Get some other people. Better people. Maybe some boys?'

Naomi and Alison snorted.

'It doesn't work like that. I'm really sorry.' Jodie turned to me. 'You can't have boys in a group.'

I nodded. I did know that, really, but I was desperate.

'It's this sort of thing' – I knew Jodie was trying to be nice – 'that made Alison and Naomi start a new group. They say you don't understand.'

I took a deep breath. I put my phone to my ear.

Alison glanced at Yasmin. 'Don't you need to actually make a call first?'

I turned to leave. I hated Alison. *No – not Alison. Alison Fisher.*

'Sorry,' Jodie and Yasmin said, at the same time.

'We can still be friends in drama,' Jodie added. 'And in non-group situations.'

'OK.' I strode away.

I ran up to where Lewis was playing football. I tugged his sleeve.

'Lewis.' I tried not to cry. 'Shall we do some spying practice? Do you want to see my letter from *Crimewatch*?'

'What?' He shook me off and turned his back on me. 'Leave me alone.'

'Or the police?' I started crying now as I reached for him again. 'Because I also got a letter from—'

'Fiona. Get away from me. You're not a spy.' He shrugged me off again. 'This isn't real. No one cares whether you can do a seal crawl, or a feline crawl, or a flat feline crawl. No one cares if you can read hoofprints, or if you've got a secret pocket.' He was using his dad's meanest voice. 'Give it up.' He even had a look of his dad now. 'And leave me alone. I'm not messing. Just leave me alone – for ever.'

*

I hurried out of the school field and towards the park.

I just sat there, in the second-biggest bush, until it was time for the bell for afternoon classes.

I rested my head on my knees and cried.

Eventually, I lifted my head. The bell would definitely have gone by now.

The New Head would have found I wasn't outside the office anymore. And afternoon lessons would have long started.

I'd been scared of being expelled, half an hour ago. It had been a possibility. And now – just by being *Fiona* – I'd made things so much worse.

Now I'd *definitely* be expelled.

I had cried so much I was shaking again. I felt cold, despite the patches of sunshine, dappling through the branches and leaves above.

My brain was full. Full of words, all shouting how stupid I was. About how much trouble I was in.

I wouldn't be allowed to go to the fair.

I *had* to go to the fair.

I looked at the wasps' nest. From this distance, the wasps circled round it like specks. I remembered the kids playing *chicken* with the wasps – putting their hands near the nest, and pulling them away.

I imagined doing that for a second, how it would make everything change.

I had to do something. Something to get me to the fair. Something, anything, that could make all this OK.

I pushed myself up from the grass. I brushed the twigs off my skirt.

*

I hurried to Chestnut Walk and stood outside number 23. I made myself knock.

An old woman answered. She had an apron on, the curly writing saying, *Kiss the cook and bring her wine.*

'Is Adrian in?' I made myself taller. 'Adrian Sykes.'

The woman frowned. 'Yes.'

'Can you go and get him please?'

'Shouldn't you be in school?'

'I just want to speak to Adrian,' I said, and – *don't do it don't do it* – started crying again.

Ten minutes later I sat, shaking, with a glass of orange juice, on a squishy old sofa draped in blankets, inside 23 Chestnut Walk.

I took a sip. The glass tasted of orange juice and dishwasher, like in Lewis's house.

At the thought of Lewis, I sobbed more.

The two strangers sat facing me.

The man – Adrian – looked at the woman and back. 'Please tell me your parents' names. We need to call them.'

He was a lot smaller than I was expecting. Nothing like the man in my head. Not scary at all. Which made me cry even more.

'They'll be worried.' He glanced at his wife. 'They might already know you're not in school.'

I shook my head. 'I need to know about my sister.' My words came with extra burbles at their edges. 'The one who died at the fair. The one you wrote about in the paper.'

Adrian looked helplessly at his wife.

His wife took her apron off. 'What's your sister's name?'

Adrian frowned. 'Christine, I don't think . . .'

The woman shook her head at him. She folded her apron

and placed it on the sideboard. She looked back at me.

'Her name's Danielle. Danielle Larson.' I turned to Adrian. 'The girl from the fair in 1982. Active in the RSPB, dead when the paramedics arrived. Blonde hair. Smiley. Tall for an eleven-year-old. Pretty as a picture. Dug gardens for charity.' I glanced up at Adrian. 'You might not know that though. I found that out from the Box of Special Things.'

'And what was her address?' the lady – Christine Sykes – said gently.

'Fourteen Archer's Way, Monkford.'

'Is that where you live, too?'

I nodded.

The two glanced at each other. Mrs Sykes got up. 'I'm just going to refill the kettle.'

She went to a drawer behind the sofa.

I turned back to Adrian. 'Do I call you Adrian? Or Mr Sykes?'

I glanced at Mrs Sykes, who left the room with something in her arms. I heard an electrical chirrup and the sound of the backdoor opening and closing.

'Adrian is fine.' He stretched out his feet. 'You know – I've lived round here a long time. Sixty years. Can you believe that? It's changed a lot.'

I took a sip of dishwasher orange juice. 'The precinct must have got built since you moved here. There were just fields there before.'

He smiled. 'I'd forgotten there was a time before the precinct. Well, now.'

'And the schools merged. There used to be three schools around Monkford, and now there's two.'

'Wow! You know a lot for a little one.'

'I got it from your paper. From the microfiche.'

His smile faded.

'Did you know my sister?'

'Ah. I'm pretty sure I didn't know her. I'm just trying to think. 1982, you say?'

'July 1982. Happened on the twenty-fourth of July. The newspaper was on the thirtieth of July.'

There was another electronic chirrup from the kitchen. Mrs Sykes came back in. 'Do you want more orange juice, Fiona?'

'I'm fine.'

'Grand. I'll just finish off the tea.' She looked at Mr Sykes and the two had a mini-conversation with their eyes.

'Adrian, my sister—'

'I'm just thinking,' he said. 'Leave it with me.'

Mrs Sykes came back into the room with two mugs. She placed one in front of Mr Sykes and sat down. 'What did you do in school today, love? Before you came here to find us?'

I shuddered.

'OK, you don't want to talk about that,' she said quickly. 'That's fine.'

Adrian got up. 'While I'm thinking – it takes me a long time to think these days – I'm halfway through a jigsaw.' He showed me the big board on the dining-room table, on it a half-finished jigsaw of spaniel puppies in a basket. 'I could do with some keen young eyes. Want to help me, while I can try to think what I remember about your sister?'

I sat with Adrian at the dining-room table for a while, doing the jigsaw while he tried to remember. I put in at least fifteen pieces while Adrian congratulated me, because – Adrian was right – I *did* have keen young eyes.

And the jigsaw even helped a little with the churning feeling in my stomach.

The doorbell rang. Adrian and Mrs Sykes looked at each other.

Mrs Sykes got up. 'That must be the postman.'

I froze for a second, hoping it wasn't my dad. But no – he couldn't know I was here. And then I heard voices and relaxed, thinking it must be a lady postman and – *no!*

Mum burst into the room, the fabric belt of her dress undone and flying behind her.

38

A good spy knows when he's been cornered.
The Junior Spy's Secret Handbook™

Four days to the fair
Mum rushed straight to me. 'What's this all about, darling?'

I just cried, my shoulders heaving.

'Thank you *so* much,' Mum said to Adrian. She threw her keys on the carpet and crouched next to me. 'Fi, you can't just leave school in the day. However upset you are.' She looked up at Adrian. 'I'm so, so sorry. She looked down at me. 'What's happened?'

Mrs Sykes made a nice smile. 'She's had a falling out with some friends, I think.'

The worry flew off Mum's face. I watched it harden. 'That's *not* a reason to leave school.' She closed her eyes and pressed her thumb and forefinger to her eyes, like Dr Sharma had an hour before. This is what I did to adults now. Made them press on their eyes and make this face. 'You can't just leave when you want. You can't just *do* these things.'

I put my arm over my face and pushed my eyes into my sleeve.

'I'm so sorry – Christine, you said?' Mum said.

'Yes.' Mrs Sykes patted Mum's arm. 'It's been no bother. We had little ones once.'

Mum stood up from her crouching position. 'But I'm sure you're busy enough, Christine. Thank you for calling me. And for looking after her.' She picked her keys up from the table. 'Come on, Fiona. We're going home.'

We drove home in silence. Nearly silence, anyway. I was gulping and snuffling.

'Do you want this?' Mum's voice was soft as she held out my old Eeyore blanket.

I shook my head. That blanket should have been thrown out – *ages* ago. Why she kept it in the boot of the car, I didn't know.

Mum put the blanket on the back seat.

And that was it for our conversation on the journey.

At home, Mum pulled a stool out from the peninsula and waited for me to sit on it.

I sat down, my legs shivery.

'I've spoken to the school. We're to go in and see Dr Sharma together, after registration in the morning.' She pulled out another stool. She got on the stool and shuffled it forward, so our knees were touching. She nudged me with her knee. 'What's going on, hey?'

I looked down at the grey of my school skirt and the blobs of tears on it. 'I want to wait for Dad.'

'Dad's working. Why did you leave school? Why did you think it was OK to go to that house?'

I looked up. 'Didn't they tell you?'

I could tell she was trying to keep her face soft. It made her look weird.

'I want to hear it from you.'

'I thought if I found out what happened to Danielle at the fair, I could prove the same thing wouldn't happen to me.'

Mum closed her eyes. 'This is about the fair. This is all about the fair.'

'I thought I could prove I'd learned Danielle's lesson, then you'd have to let me go.' My voice was so small and wet-sounding, like a baby's. 'So I did some spying.'

'*That bloody spying book!* And I begged you not to ask what happened at the fair!'

After all the soft talking, Mum's sudden shouting made me tense.

'Sorry.' She looked down at my school skirt and stroked it straight. 'Fi, there's nothing you could find out that would make it OK to go to the fair. Nothing. Your sister died there. Don't you understand what that means?'

I shook my head.

She took a deep, noisy breath through her nose. 'I can't think about this now. I can't think about you spying about your sister's death. It makes me too angry.'

I flinched.

'We will talk about this properly another time.' She was trying her best to sound calm. 'But explain to me the other bits. Why today? Why did you decide it was all right to leave school and go there today?'

I looked down. Even if she did really want to know, where could I even start? It was like one of those puzzles where there are lots of different threads, all tangled up, and you have to follow the right thread through the mess and not get distracted to get free.

And I was pretty sure, this time, there was no right thread to get free.

'Lewis doesn't want to be my friend, no matter how much I make him.'

Mum stroked my knee. 'He puts up with a lot.'

'He thinks I'm the reason his dad's left home.'

'Well, that's just ridiculous.' She paused. 'Geoff's left home?'

'Lewis says his mum and dad rowed because I said Lewis was my boyfriend.'

Mum stopped stroking.

'It's not even true, I just made it up. But Lewis's dad was happy, though he's never liked me *and* he calls me *girlie*. And Lewis's mum was upset he was happy. So, Lewis blames me.' I took a breath. 'And my other friends have started a new group.'

'Is Geoff coming back?'

'I don't know, Mum.'

Mum nodded. 'OK. So, there's a new group.' Mum straightened my skirt pleats again. 'Can you join this new group?'

I scratched one fingernail with another so I didn't have to look in her eyes. 'The whole point of the new group is it's the same as the old group.' My voice was so quiet now. 'Just without me in it.'

'Oh.' Mum smoothed the pleats some more. 'I remember how hard this stuff can be.'

'I've got nowhere to go at lunchtime. And they said I can't be in the group even though I've got a ph—'

I stopped myself. *Not that thread.*

I had no friends, no fair, I was going to get expelled from school.

That phone was all I had.

'A ph—?' Mum prompted.

I licked my lips. 'A ph-riendship with Jodie.'

'Could Jodie start a new group with you?'

'She's got a group. You can't be in two groups at once, it doesn't work like that.'

'And if I spoke to Jodie's mum?'

'*NO!*' I jumped up. 'You said you remember being a kid and then you say things like *that*! You don't remember *at all*!'

'OK, OK,' Mum put her hands up, palms out. 'I'm just thinking aloud.'

'Speak to Jodie's mum!' I shook my head.

'It will get better.' Mum stroked my knee. 'But you still can't leave school in the daytime, however hard it gets. Can't you go to the computer room at lunchtime anyway? Even without Lewis?'

'The computer room's closed. They're putting extra wires in for something. It's going to be closed till the end of term.'

'But, still. Fiona, you can't just leave school in the daytime. It's a criminal offence.'

I waved a hand.

'Fiona. People go to prison for criminal offences.'

I finally stopped crying. 'I won't go to prison for missing school.'

Mum sighed. 'This was all so much easier when you were five.'

I shuffled forward so my knees were touching Mum's again.

Mum's voice was gentle. 'It's going to be OK, you know.'

I wiped my noise, sliming a trail up my shirt sleeve.

We sat there in silence, knees touching. With my feet bent beneath me, my knee looked hard, like a fist. A fist, with tiny hairs on top.

'Before we finish.' Mum took both my hands in hers. 'Have you told me everything about school?'

Mayfair.

I shook my head.

'I think it's best you tell me everything today. In one go. One day. And I won't get angry.'

I kept shaking my head. Though I'd need to find a way to tell her before the morning, I realised. Because – Dr Sharma. *The New Head.*

That thought made me cry again. *So hard.*

'Fiona?'

I stared at the carpet. 'I sold some – magazines. Porn mags. I found them in the park. I sold them to older boys at school. That's how I made so much money at the car boot sale.'

I risked looking up. I looked straight back down again.

'The teachers know. Dr Sharma. Mrs Vernal,' I whispered. 'The – *New Head.*'

Mum said nothing for ages.

'This is a lot to take in.'

I nodded.

'When I said I wouldn't get angry, I didn't realise that you'd be telling me something like this.'

We sat in silence for quite a bit longer.

Mum took another deep nose-breath. 'Now – can't believe I'm asking this – but is there anything else? Apart from the bunking school, the spying, the investigating your sister's death, the selling pornos from your father's car boot?' Mum squeezed my hand until I looked into her eyes. 'Because we need to get everything out, lady. If you tell me now, I'll forgive you anything. I think. I'll really try.'

I looked at my feet again.

'Fiona?'

'You won't get cross?'

'*Fiona?*'

I reached for my coat. I opened it up, and she saw my pocket.

She sat up straighter. 'Is that Eileen's curtain fabric? The one that ended up being too short and I had to buy again?'

I opened my secret pocket and got out the cigarette.

Mum's chest rose. 'What the—'

I put it on the table. 'I bought it using fake ID. Someone else's. Not mine.'

'BUT YOU'VE GOT ASTHMA!'

She'd said she wouldn't shout, but I couldn't blame her. Because she didn't know I was going to tell her *that*, did she? Mum's always been really funny about health stuff.

She pressed her lips together.

'Where are the rest?'

'I only bought a single.'

'But ...' She stopped. 'Not important. Why?'

'I thought my friends would like me if I helped them grow up.' I wiped one eye with my sleeve. 'But they don't.'

Mum's eyebrows moved a little towards each other. 'It's not grown up to smoke.'

I wiped my other eye. 'Course it is.'

'It isn't, and you can't just bring things to people to make them be your friends.'

I pressed my knees more tightly into hers.

'You weren't *really* going to smoke it?' She frowned. 'You couldn't have been, not with your asthma. You wouldn't be that *stupid*. Besides, you had nothing to light it with.'

I looked at her. At how she didn't look angry now, just tired.

I reached in my rucksack. I got out the grill lighter and placed it on the table.

'But *you promised*!' Mum's voice was uneven as she tried not to shout. 'You promised you wouldn't take risks with your health! You're our *only one*!'

'But that's not my fault, is it?' I leaned forward. 'You should have had extra kids if you were that worried.'

'WE COULDN'T HAVE MORE KIDS, FIONA. Don't you realise that? That's why Danielle was an only one in the first place. You were a miracle. A special, wonderful, unexpected' – she sounded *so* angry – 'miracle.'

You can say *miracle* like *bowl of shit*. In case you're wondering.

I saw my coat was open, showing my secret pocket. *No!*

I gripped my coat closed immediately. I edged it towards me.

Mum looked at the coat and back at my face.

'Fiona.' Her voice was hard. A warning. 'What else is in there, please?'

I hugged the coat.

'If there's anything – anything – you've not told me, and you don't tell me right now, while you've got the chance and I'm being so patient and nice, so help me, Fiona, I don't know what I'll—'

I unhugged the coat and opened the secret pocket.

I pulled out the mobile phone and placed it on the table.

Mum stared at it.

I rushed the words out. 'I didn't steal it.'

She raised her gaze. She looked so old.

'This time, it's true. Someone gave it to me.'

'Like the time Candy gave you her favourite pen topper?'

I looked down. 'No,' I whispered. 'Not like that.'

'But why would anyone give you a *mobile phone*? If you knew what was going through my head right now—'

'I didn't steal it! And I didn't ask for it, either! He just gave it to me.'

'*He?* Why do you do this?' Mum rubbed her eyes with her fists. 'All the *lying*! No one would ever give you—'

'*Carl* did!' I jumped off the stool. 'I didn't ask for the phone, Carl just gave it to me!'

Mum went still.

'*Carl!*' The room's air had gone weird but I was too angry to stop. 'You lie to me *all the time*. You said Carl's a strange man but he's not and this proves it. He's never flashed me, he's never got it out to show me – not even just the end – and he even helped me with my fake puncture. Carl's kind, and this proves it, because he gave me a *mobile phone!*'

I grabbed my phone and ran upstairs.

I slammed my bedroom door and sat behind it. I listened.

There was no sound of keys, no opening door sounds from downstairs. Just silence.

I got under my duvet and arranged it over me so no tiny bit of body was peeking out. Trying – trying as hard as I could – to make myself safe.

Half an hour later, I was still under the duvet cover, body completely covered, sweaty from my breath bouncing back onto my face. I heard the scratch and clink of Dad's key in the front door.

I heard him go into the kitchen. The up and down of voices.

Mum would tell him right away, of course. They had a *united front* when it came to me. Whatever the row was about, it always ended two against one. In our family isosceles triangle, it was always me on my own at the pointy end.

I pushed back the duvet. I sat up on my bed and waited.

The kitchen door opened.

'Going to the pub for a quick one, Fi!' Dad shouted up the stairs. 'Mum says not to disturb you doing your homework. See you when I'm back!'

I heard the front door go.

A minute later, Mum came into my bedroom, carrying a hammer and a hand towel.

I put the duvet over my head again.

She shut the door behind her. 'Give me the phone.'

No! I jumped out of the bed.

She held out her non-hammer hand. 'The phone.'

I widened my eyes. 'Mum! No!'

'Give me the phone *now.*'

I scrambled across the room till I was on top of my coat, protecting it with my body.

'Don't make me peel you off.' Mum's jaw was hard. 'You must never accept gifts from strangers. *Never.*'

'No! No please!' My voice went up to a squeak. 'I'm *sorry!* He helped me fix a puncture!'

'He's never fixed a puncture in his life. He's a *parasite.* And I can't let you keep that phone.'

'I'll never speak to strangers again. Just let me keep the phone. It's the only thing I have. It's the only way I can make friends. *Please!*'

Mum put the hammer and hand towel on the dressing table.

I pressed my back up against my coat. 'I won't even use the phone, I promise, I'll just hold it. I've never even used it anyway. Mum!'

She wrestled me away from the coat.

'I just hold it and pretend to talk to people! That's all I do!'

She opened the secret pocket, batting away my grasping hands. She took out the phone and placed it on the towel on my dressing table. She picked up the hammer.

She threw her non-hammer arm out in a barrier. 'Stand back.'

I screamed.

Mum lifted the hammer and smashed the screen. She did it again. And again.

The phone screen cracked. Bits of plastic flaked off, then keys and metal. Bits of green from inside the phone now.

I kept screaming. Mum kept swinging. The clip fell out of her hair and onto the carpet. Hair flew in front of her face as she hammered.

The phone skittered across the table, bouncing into the mirror. Mum mis-hit, dinging a yellow semicircle into the white wood of the dressing table.

Mum stopped hitting. She dropped her hammer against her thigh. She was panting. Bits of hair stuck to her red face.

I looked where she was looking. At the broken plastic and twisted metal on the towel.

She dropped the hammer onto the bed. She took a step back.

I ran over to the dressing table. I picked up the towel gently at the corners, holding the pieces of phone in a hammock.

Mum didn't stop me.

I carried the towel hammock back to my bed and placed it on my lap. I cradled it all.

Mum reached towards me. I cringed to the side, but she just reached past me and picked the hammer up off the bed.

She saw me flinch. 'Fi, don't. I'd never—'

She held the hammer against her thigh. She turned and left the room.

I lay folded over so I was covering my broken phone, protecting it too late.

I cried into my skirt, mouth open, my body folded over.

I stayed there for a long time.

39

**People talk about something being 'too rich for my blood',
but they are more often talking about taking some kind of
risk, rather than making a comment about a haematological
disorder.**

Fiona Larson, 7E's Blood Project

Four days to the fair
I lifted myself up. I'd left a dark mess on the pleats of my
skirt. A circle of snot and tears.

I'd been sad and scared.

But now, as I stared at the dark circle, I stopped crying.
Another feeling was building in me. I was crunching my jaws
so tightly together, I'd made my cheeks hurt.

How could she do this to me?

I jumped up.

It wasn't even my stuff she destroyed. It was Carl's.

She couldn't just *do* things like that to other adults, could
she? She wasn't allowed.

*Let him see me like this. Let him see what she's done. I'm going
to knock for him, then I'm going to show him my broken phone,
then. . .*

I folded my arms, imagining banging on that door.

Imagining Carl's face as I told him. *Your mum did what? That's terrible. Poor you, Fiona. Mums aren't meant to do things like that. I'll go round and give her a piece of my mind, right now.*

The thought of Mum getting told off calmed me down a little. Just enough so I could control my movements and be quieter.

With baby steps, I headed down the stairs and listened at the kitchen door. I heard Mum moving around. I stayed silent.

After a few minutes. I heard the back door open. The clink of bottles and cans – Mum taking the bin bag into the garden.

And I hurried out of the front door, out of there.

I didn't go straight to Carl's. I needed to be calmer, so I could explain properly. I needed to let off steam.

I walked loops of the park, trying to stop shaking. Past the second-biggest bush. Past the tennis courts. Past the wasps' nest. I walked like one of those old people who walk for exercise, arms pumping, my legs moving as fast as they would go.

But the shaking in my body wouldn't stop. It was like there were little explosions everywhere. *Pow, pow, pow.*

I sat on a bench and rubbed my hands up my arms, my skin pricking up in goose pimples. My thoughts were going too fast now. I was feeling *everything*.

And, suddenly, my anger turned off like a tap. A few drips left, then nothing.

Because I realised. This was nobody's fault but mine.

I'd done this. I'd done this to *myself*.

Lewis was right. I'd never been a good enough friend to him. He kept trying, and I let him down.

I was bad. *Really* bad. Everyone knew it. My family did. My teachers did. The girls did. Lewis did.

It was all my fault.

I deserved punishment.

I looked up. I imagined the satellites and planets, all held up by nothing, all hurtling towards me.

I looked over at the park's biggest bush. The one with the wasps' nest.

I walked over slowly, feeling empty, like I wasn't really there. Like I, the real Fiona, was somewhere at a distance, watching this Fiona walk.

I put my hand to the floor and lowered myself down onto my knees, a metre away from the moving sea of wasps. I watched the crawling lump of black and yellow bodies, antennae twitching.

Because I didn't deserve to feel OK.

I leaned closer.

The buzzing from the nest was soft, a radio that wasn't properly tuned in.

I watched the wasps crawl over the nest. Their tiny wings fluttered against their pointy bodies.

My head was full. Full of thoughts I didn't want. But if I pushed on this nest, right now, something would change.

I raised my finger.

I watched my finger to see what it did. I watched it move towards the nest.

I got into a high kneel and shuffled closer.

A wasp jumped off the nest and onto my finger. Another wasp jumped onto my shoulder.

One wasp landed on my cheek. I put my hand to my cheek and – *owowow!* – there was a flash, inside my head.

And my finger went on fire.

I pulled my hand away. I stumbled backwards.

And it worked.

Like I'd wanted – like I *think* I wanted – wasps followed.

I opened the back gate and ran dizzily through the garden. I staggered over the grass towards rockery.

Mum saw me through the kitchen window.

I made a shape as best I could with fat lips. 'Wasps.'

Mum put her hands to her mouth. A second later, she ran out with her car keys.

My skin hurt so much it buzzed. But the journey to the hospital was silent.

Mum had wrapped me in the Eeyore blanket. Everywhere the blanket touched, my skin sizzled.

I turned my head to look at Mum. She was driving, tears streaking the make-up on her cheeks.

I turned my head back to look ahead, so I didn't have to look at her face.

'Shit.' In the hospital car park, Mum fumbled in her purse. 'Shit, shit, shit.'

She shoved at the purse in her lap. Coins tinkled out, into the footwell.

Mum strained furiously against her seatbelt, like it had kidnapped her. She banged her hand on the steering wheel and closed her eyes.

After a minute, Mum opened the car door. 'They can ticket us. Let's go.'

Mum signed us in at A+E in her loudest voice. *'Of course I understand there's a triage process but just look at her! That's all the triage you need!'*

We sat in the waiting room, on hard chairs nailed to the floor. I felt Mum's thigh pressing into mine.

I stared straight ahead, my Eeyore blanket round my shoulders, while people moved around us with clipboards and walking sticks.

The pain wasn't a sheet covering my whole body anymore. I could focus on the different bits that hurt. My lip. My eyebrow. My cheek. My hands and arms.

I tried to test my lip by biting it, but it didn't feel like my lip anymore. It felt too big between my teeth, and numb. Like it wasn't part of me at all.

Mum didn't look at me. 'How are you feeling?'

'A bit better.'

'Do you need me to adjust your blanket?'

'No.'

A nurse came out. 'Mr Chapman.'

An elderly man got up and followed her to a room.

Mum watched. 'One sec.'

She strode over to the woman on the counter again. There were a few low urgent words, and Mum slumped back in the chair next to me.

I held myself as still as possible until, eventually, we were called in.

Mum had said earlier that I was *a miracle*.

I wondered whether I was *a miracle* now.

In the car on the way back, Mum was quiet.

'I'm feeling a bit better,' I said. 'So that's good.'

Mum flipped on the indicator.

'That doctor said it was fine,' I added.

'The doctor did *not* say it was fine. She said you had significant localised reactions.' She pulled into a junction jerkily, swerving to miss the kerb. 'Is there any way it could have been an accident?'

She glanced at me.

I shook my head.

She looked back at the road.

'You killed my phone,' I said.

'Christ!' Mum banged her hand on the steering wheel. 'I had to.'

'You wanted to.'

Mum gave a tight laugh. 'OK, I wanted to.' She gripped the wheel harder. 'You *don't understand.*'

I felt a stab of pain where my seat belt touched my arm. I changed position.

'That phone had to go.' If Mum kept flipping the indicator this hard, she'd break it. 'I believe you now, that the man gave it to you. But it still had to go.'

I pulled my Eeyore blanket further round me. I lowered my head till a bit of unstung face was touching it.

'Strange men don't give little girls presents for no reason.' Mum indicated again – *flick-flick, flick-flick*. 'Bad men like little girls, Fiona. I'm sorry, but it's true. I will never be angry if a man approaches you. But you have to tell me.'

She turned to face me.

'You do look *a little bit* angry.'

Mum flicked the indicator hard again. 'Well, I'm not.'

I let my chin rest on my arms. 'You're going to break that lever, you're so angry.'

'I'm angry *at the situation.*'

Mum pulled the car into the drive. She switched off the car.

She twisted round to face me. 'Your dad will be really upset about these wasp stings. Even more upset than I am, and I'm very upset' – she saw my face – 'yes, *upset*, not angry, *UPSET*.' She took a breath. 'Christ, Fiona! Your dad *must not find out* about that man and the phone. That will be hard for him to hear, and he's no need to know. You hear me? Nod your head.'

I nodded.

Mum nodded back. 'Good.'

In the kitchen, Dad jumped up from his stool. His voice was all breath. 'Fi-*ona*!'

He held both hands behind his head and stared, like a footballer who'd missed a penalty.

'Please don't hug me.'

'Your cheek! Your lip.'

Mum gave me a lying-eye smile. 'Don't worry, they're fine.' She glanced at Dad. 'She's been stung by wasps. I'll explain. We've been to hospital. Fiona's looking loads better already.'

'Not *Ff-iona*.' My fat lip made my *f*s longer and watery. 'Ff-i.'

Dad let his hands fall back by his sides. 'Yes.' He gave a big smile. 'You look fine, Fi. If your mum hadn't said you'd been stung by wasps, I could hardly tell.'

I lay in bed, with Mum and Dad taking turns to check on me every few minutes.

If I'd accepted every cup of tea and orange juice I'd been offered that evening, I reckon I could have drowned.

And I didn't hear *all* the conversations that were going on downstairs. I wasn't in the mood for spying. But some conversations were too loud to ignore.

'I just don't understand!' Dad's voice.

'What's not to understand?'

'Our eleven-year-old daughter was selling *porn*?'

I pulled my Eeyore blanket tighter.

'She found them, OK? She *found* them. She wasn't exactly selling porn.'

'How can you be OK about this? She was profiting from the sex industry.'

'Come on, Jonathan, you're not Victorian. She's not exactly Hugh bloody Hefner.'

'Are you trying to play this down? Saying it's OK?'

'Of *course* it's not OK! And how did you not notice? If she was selling them at the car boot sale, right under your eyes? *How did you not notice?*'

The door slammed shut. I pulled my Eeyore blanket tighter still.

Just before bedtime, Dad came into my room carrying a piece of paper. 'I'm very cross with you. But we're not going to talk about it today.'

'Ff-ank you.'

'Are you doing OK?'

I nodded.

'You feel sick?'

I shook my head.

'You look nearly mended. Just tiny bumps now.'

'I've got a mirror in here, Dad.'

He nodded. 'Right. Of course. Sorry.' He sat on my bed. 'Now, this might interest you. The Hague have issued arrest warrants for – hang on, I've written down the names' – he unfolded his piece of paper – 'Radovan Karadžić and Ratko Mladić.' He looked up. 'How about that, hey?'

I smiled as much as I could with my fat lip.

'I'll leave it here.' Dad went to put the paper on the dressing table. He stopped and frowned. 'What's happened here?'

He ran a hand across the table, where Mum had dinged it with the hammer. 'Why's the table damaged?'

Don't tell your father about the phone.

Dad looked up, still waiting for answer.

'I dropped a book or something.'

Dad kept examining the table. 'I'm not going to tell you off today, but you need to be more careful with your things.'

I nodded.

'You've carved the leg too – oh, *Fiona*!' Dad looked closer. 'Is that a swastika?'

'Not exactly.' *This day!* 'Let me explain.'

Half an hour later, Mum stormed into the room. 'This has been quite the day of developments, Fiona. First, you're peddling erotica.' She crouched to look at the dressing table. 'And swastikas now?'

'It wasn't a swastika, it was my special symbol I invented. Made of *F for Fiona*-s.' I paused. 'It's not my special symbol anymore.'

Mum stood up. 'The money you made. With the magazines. How much?'

I swallowed. 'A hundred and twelve pounds.'

Without her having to ask, I pulled off my Eeyore blanket and shuffled off the bed. I opened my jewellery box and the ballerina turned. The plink-plonk music played.

Maybe, if I was really good now. . .?

No. Just – no.

I handed Mum my fair money. I didn't even keep any back because I was being good now. It was too late, but still.

And Mum just took my fair money – all of it – and walked out of the room.

To Go to the Fair I Need:

1) ~~Money for the rides~~ √
2) ~~Girl friends, so the famous boy will push me on the Waltzers~~ √
3) Mum and Dad to let me go
4) Money for the rides (again)
5) Friends again. But any friends now. Any friends at all.

40

When you get what you wish for – you might wish you'd
never got it.
(paradox)

Two days to the fair

My parents kept me off school on Tuesday.

On Wednesday morning, I sat on a stool at Dr Sharma's high desk at the front of the lab.

Mum sat next to me, her legs crossed beneath her in a knee-length skirt. She looked smarter than usual and was wearing the jacket she wore for funerals, which wasn't a good sign, I decided.

The bell rang for the start of morning lessons. None of us moved.

Dr Sharma looked me over. Not rushing, just taking in every red, bumpy sting.

Out of the corner of my eye, I could see my own cheek.

Finally, Dr Sharma spoke. 'Proud of yourself?'

I shook my head.

She leaned forward. 'Are you sure?'

I inched closer to Mum, though knew I'd get no protection. Mum and me might be sitting on the same side of the table, but we were in another isosceles triangle with Dr Sharma – and I was *definitely* all alone at the pointy end.

Now I'd stopped hurting, I was feeling a bit stupid. I mean – *wasps?*

'I should make clear' – Dr Sharma made a show of putting a lid on her fountain pen – 'that if you break school rules, then deliberately injure yourself, that does not mean we will forget. I suppose what I'm saying, Fiona' – she put the pen down – 'is we were not born yesterday.'

I nodded.

'We grown-ups can think many things at once. We can feel sorry for you about your face – whilst also feeling irritated you did it deliberately – whilst *also* remembering that you were in a lot of trouble. Firstly, about the magazines.'

Dr Sharma's pen rolled slowly across the table. She gave it a light tap.

'And then by leaving school in the daytime. Without telling anyone.'

I shifted in my stool.

'*And* you brought cigarettes into school.'

I veered round to glare at Mum.

At the look on Mum's face, I shrank. *Pointy end, remember. You're always at the pointy end.*

'*One* cigarette,' I mumbled. 'And I only brought it in to show people. I wasn't going to smoke it in school.'

'Oh.' Dr Sharma gave a wave of her hand. 'That makes it OK.'

There was a shout outside. Something hit the lab window.

Dr Sharma glanced over. She lifted herself up and replaced herself in her seat. 'Now. What was I saying?'

'You were explaining to Fiona,' Mum said, in an echo of Dr Sharma's brisk voice, 'that children are not allowed cigarettes and porn. And that cigarettes and porn are not allowed at school.'

'Ah, yes.' Dr Sharma turned to me. 'Had those facts escaped you, Fiona?'

'No,' I whispered.

There was a long silence.

'Now,' Dr Sharma stared at me, 'the magazines.'

I looked at my feet.

'This is *school*. You may get exposed to that stuff at home—'

Mum sat up. 'Hey, now.'

'—and we teachers can't control what you see there,' Dr Sharma continued.

Mum sat up even straighter. 'You've misunderstood, Dr Sharma.'

Dr Sharma glanced over. 'Are you sure?'

'Of course.' Mum sat back. 'I mean, I'll ask Jonathan again, but—'

'I found them in the park!' I looked from one to the other. 'Honestly. It wasn't meant to be anything bad. It was just Finders Keepers.'

Dr Sharma linked her fingers. 'Mrs Vernal thinks it was no accident it was you who brought the porn into school. She thinks you're a troublemaker.'

Mum made a sound under her breath. A Mum-growl.

Dr Sharma turned to her.

'Sorry.' Mum waved a hand. 'It's just – that new drama teacher. She says Fiona should use her feelings about losing a sister to get better at drama. You know Mrs Vernal's trying to get them to want to be astronauts and actors rather farmers and driving instructors? The more I hear about that teacher, well' – Mum glanced at me – 'I'm just saying she seems confused. About how the world works.'

Dr Sharma gave a small cough. 'Mrs Vernal worked closely with the New Head at their old school. She is a valued new member of staff and very welcome. Her progressive and new-fangled suggestions are a breath of fresh air.'

'Of course.'

The two looked at each other for a long moment.

'Now,' Mum sat forward, 'are you going to suspend Fiona? You've got to do what you've got to do, of course, but I'm sure there's lots of paperwork. And it's difficult this end with work – I'm not begging exactly, though maybe I am a little bit, because—'

'I have put the case forward to Mrs Shackleton,' Dr Sharma said, 'that I don't think either suspension or exclusion are the right choices here.'

I tried to work out whether I was happy about that. I was, I supposed. But I couldn't trust myself to know what I felt about anything anymore. After all, I was the kid who, on Monday, *chose to get stung by wasps.*

But Mum was definitely happy. 'Oh!' She slumped back. 'Thank you.'

Dr Sharma stared at me. 'Your mum explained on the phone about your difficult day on Monday. She said you fell out with your friends.'

I felt myself flush.

'We all have bad days,' Dr Sharma said. 'I had one on Monday, too. That does not mean I ran away from school and into a bunch of wasps, in the hope everyone would see my swollen face and feel sorry for me.'

'I didn't want people to feel sorry for me.'

'Why, then?' Dr Sharma glanced at Mum and back. 'Did you want to hurt yourself?'

I shrugged. I was honestly the wrong person to ask about

all this – I didn't have a *clue* why I did the Fiona-y stuff.

'You've done three things.' Dr Sharma held three fingers up. 'You've sold porn and left school. You have also got yourself stung by wasps, which, I think you'd agree, is not a positive thing, and not to be recommended.'

She waited. I nodded.

'And the cigarette.' *Whose side was Mum on?*

But she hadn't mentioned the spying and Danielle. Mum wanted to keep the punishment for that all to herself.

And she hadn't mentioned the mobile phone, I noticed. That phone didn't exist.

'*Four* things. And those four things,' Dr Sharma said, 'are clearly bad. But you – Fiona Larson – are *not* bad. Bad *things*, not bad *person*. Can you see the difference?'

I shrugged again.

They glanced at each other.

Dr Sharma sighed.

'Fiona is far from forgiven.' Mum adjusted her jacket. 'But do you think you could speak to the friends?'

Dr Sharma looked at Mum for a moment, then to me. 'Fiona? Do you want me to speak to your friends?'

I shook my head.

'Thought not.'

'It's lunchtimes,' I whispered. 'They're the worst. The computer room's shut and there's nowhere I can go.'

Dr Sharma nodded. 'You can sit here in my lab, if you want. You can watch my fridge for me. Make sure no chancers come looking for my animal hearts.'

I nodded, though there was *no way* I was coming to Dr Sharma's lab at lunchtime.

'All the colours and shapes!' Dr Sharma peered at my face, like I was behind glass in a museum. 'Does it hurt?'

'A little bit.'

'You ever going to walk into a wasps' nest again?'

'No.'

'Then I think we've all learned a lesson here.' Dr Sharma stood up. 'Get to class, Fiona. I will tell Mrs Shackleton we've had a full discussion and say it's my recommendation that this is the end of the matter. And if Mr Kellett asks why you're late, tell him to speak to me.'

I slipped out of the room and left Mum with Dr Sharma.

I walked the empty corridors to my English class and knocked on the door.

'Sorry I'm late.' I walked to my table and sat down. 'Dr Sharma says it's her fault.'

Sean glanced at me and quickly away. It was like we'd never met.

Then, the whispering started.

'Oh my God. What is that?'

'She looks like a monster.'

'What's wrong with her lip?'

Mr Kellett stared at me. 'Quiet, everyone.'

'It was just wasps. Just normal, everyday, park wasps.' I got my books out of my bag. 'I'm fine. So, let's all please just get on with the lesson and please, *please,* no one look at me.'

School news!

Was about my face. Obviously.

I held my head high as I walked down the corridor at lunchtime, whispers following.

'It's the elephant man.'

'So ugly.'

'If I looked like that I'd top myself.'

I walked those corridors looking straight ahead. Trying not

to see kids at the side of me, reacting to my face. I pretended to myself the sides of my eyes didn't work, imagining I was in blinkers, like one of Selina Baker's horses.

In the distance, down the corridor, I saw the New Head in the distance, carrying a tray with frilly plates and a teapot and saucers.

I abandoned my blinkers plan and darted into the classroom to my left. I knelt behind the door, so no one could see me through the glass window. I only stood up again when one of my legs went dead, a few minutes later, and I was pretty sure the New Head must have gone.

I headed outside and went to find Lewis playing football because – well. It seemed wrong all the other kids had seen my face and Lewis hadn't.

Lewis looked so normal as he waited to be passed the ball, his hands on his hips. Not that it mattered if he was normal or not anymore. I'd take him as my friend any day. Cape, magic tricks – the lot.

I coughed. 'Lewis.'

He turned slowly. He looked at me.

I waited.

'Wasps?'

I nodded.

'The big bush in the park?'

I nodded again.

He shrugged.

'My finger. I pushed the nest with it.'

Lewis didn't react.

'Mum was furious I left school at lunchtime.'

'Why did you leave school?

'To find the newspaper man who wrote about Danielle's

death. And Mum destroyed my phone, Lewis! Can you believe that?'

'You're still investigating Danielle.' He didn't even sound angry – just tired. 'Even though I begged you not to. Even though you *promised* me.'

I looked at my feet. I could feel him looking at me, making his face all *disappointed parent*, and felt my cheeks going red. My skin started prickling, in waves. It was nothing to do with wasp stings, this time. I was going red and prickly, from the inside out.

The feeling of letting down Lewis was worse than the wasps.

I stood there, prickling. 'I'm going to listen to you from now on.' I spoke into my shoes. 'You know better than me. You know better than me about everything.'

'I would *certainly* never run into a wasps' nest.'

'Exactly. I should listen to you more. And I will, from now on.'

I waited. I looked up.

'You're too hard to be friends with, Fi.'

I nodded. I scuffed one of my shoes into the other.

'But you're not going to stop investigating, are you? So you really want to know about Danielle?'

I looked up. The prickling stopped. 'What?'

There was a long pause.

'What do you mean, Lewis?'

Lewis shoved his hands in his pockets. 'Asthma.'

I waited. 'Asthma?'

'Your sister died at the fair, but not because of the fair. She died of asthma.'

I stared at him.

'I've always known. Mum told me ages ago.' He looked

right in my eyes. 'Your parents didn't tell you because they don't want you scared you're gonna die.'

A tennis ball bounced off the wall next to me, but I didn't move.

Asthma.

Asthma, asthma, asthma. I said the word over and over in my head. So it made sense, and then it didn't. And then it did again.

You can die of asthma?

Despite the sun beating down, I pulled my coat flaps closer round me. 'I'm going to die.'

'You're not going to die.'

'But I've got asthma, Lewis.'

'Yours is nowhere near as bad. Danielle's was a really dangerous kind and it was a completely different situation, and I know that because Mum promised me. But I always made sure you had your inhaler with you.' He didn't even sound angry. 'And now you know everything, you don't need to investigate anymore, do you?' Lewis turned away. 'And you can finally leave me alone.'

I stumbled away and round the school field, through the corridors, bumping into people, half blind from my own thoughts.

Asthma.

I tried the computer-room door. Locked.

I turned towards the main block.

People don't die *of asthma. They just get a tight chest and use inhalers to get better.*

I reached the library, but it was shut. The sign said *Closed for Stocktake.*

I banged on the door anyway. 'I want to look up asthma!'

No answer.

I headed back outside.

You can die of asthma.

I *could die of asthma.*

And Lewis knew, all along.

I did another loop of the tennis courts. I saw my group of girls, back standing in their old place, eating their pickled onion crisps. Their new group looked so much like the old group – it was like I'd never been there at all.

Asthma.

I walked round daisy-chainers and football players. I walked round kids sitting on jumpers, kids with fortune tellers. I walked around kids bouncing tennis balls and kids standing in groups that were just the right size.

After I'd gone everywhere else in school a person could possibly go, there was only one place left.

I took a big breath and knocked on the door. I opened it.

Dr Sharma sat at her desk, hunched over a pile of exercise books, writing with a red pen. She wore Princess Leia headphones, the wire connected to something in her drawer.

She pulled one headphone speaker slightly away from her ear. 'Make sure you don't get crumbs on the desk.'

She let the headphone speaker spring back. She continued marking.

I headed for my usual stool. I sat there for a moment, listening to the kids screeching and laughing outside.

I slid my lunch box from my bag and opened it.

I set my pickled onion crisps to one side. I didn't even *like* pickled onion.

I took one last look at Dr Sharma, and picked up a sandwich and started to eat.

325

41

People don't always like being told they're in the right.
(paradox)

Two days to the fair

After school, I looked into the mirror in the lounge, arranging my scarf around my face. Trying to make it hang in a way that made me look OK.

Mum and Dad were both home. Both just sitting there, on the sofa. Both off work, on a weekday. Because of me.

I didn't want to think about that. 'Can I go and see Lewis?'

Dad was eating toast and jam. He swallowed as Mum said, 'Absolutely not.'

'Just to apologise? He hates me.'

'He doesn't hate you.'

'He definitely does.'

Dad put his half-eaten toast down. 'You know it can't possibly be your fault Geoff left home. Not everything's about you, sweetheart.'

'It is my fault. A little bit.'

I brought my pack of French playing cards out of my bag. Lewis had always loved them. 'I was going to take him these.

They say *D* for *Duchess* instead of *Q* for *Queen*.' I waited. 'Am I allowed to go to his house?'

Dad glanced at Mum. 'You're going straight there?'

I nodded.

'And straight back?'

I nodded.

'And definitely not visiting any wasps' nests on the way?'

'I won't be doing that again,' I said quietly.

I knocked at Lewis's door.

Mrs Harris opened it and blinked. 'Oh! I'd heard, but I never believed they'd be *that* bad.'

I pulled the scarf higher up my cheeks.

Mrs Harris stared. 'A scarf's not going to cut it, you need a balaclava to hide those, hon. And it's Geoff's afternoon. Lewis is off playing mini-golf with his dad.'

I held up the pack of cards. 'I brought him a present. They say *D* for *Duchess* instead of *Q* for *Queen*. They'd be good for,' I made my lips say it, 'magic tricks.'

'That's thoughtful.' Mrs Harris stepped back and held the door open. 'Why don't you come in?'

Mrs Harris eyed my face from the other side of the table.

She picked up her mug. 'How come the wasps didn't mind their own business?'

'I pushed on their nest. With my finger.'

'Ah.' She took a sip of tea. 'That'd do it.'

I wobbled my glass of blackcurrant accidentally. Some purple jumped out of the glass. 'Sorry.'

'No bother.' Mrs Harris tore off a piece of kitchen roll to dab the spill. She moved a pile of letters out of the way. The top one said *Mr Geoffrey Harris*.

'I meant to hand those to Lewis to give his father this afternoon. I forgot.' Mrs Harris started ripping the kitchen roll absentmindedly. 'You kids won't make fun of Lewis, will you? For his parents splitting up?'

I frowned. 'Never.'

'Are you sure?'

'Of course. It will make him better, if anything.'

'Better?' Mrs Harris was leaving paper confetti all over the table. She didn't seem to notice. 'Better, how?'

'A lot of the best kids don't live with both parents,' I said. 'And now he'll get a new rucksack and pencil case whenever he wants.'

'No, he won't.'

'That's what happens, though.'

Mrs Harris picked up her cup jerkily. 'That *definitely* won't be happening.'

'And Lewis will be pleased his dad moved out in the end. He didn't like the way Mr Harris spoke to you. The way he acted like you weren't as clever as him.'

Mrs Harris slammed her cup down on the table. She put both hands over her face.

'Mrs Harris?' I said carefully.

She gave a kind of yowl.

I looked at my lap uncertainly. 'I just don't think he is cleverer than you.'

'Oh God,' Mrs Harris moaned, her hands still over her face. 'I'm so humiliated.'

'You were *definitely* better at TV quizzes.' I wasn't sure what she wanted to hear. 'That time when he said a baby horse was a *pony*. When he said it was a *herd* of camels and you were wrong because *it can't be a caravan, caravans have wheels, Lisa.'* I shook my head. *'You* should have been the one telling *him* what to do.'

'No one should be telling anyone else what to do!' Mrs Harris pulled her hands away. 'Maybe Lewis would be your friend again if you didn't tell him what to do all the time. Have you thought about that?'

I looked down.

'Sorry,' she said.

'He told me, today, that my sister died of asthma.'

'Oh.' She was about to take a sip of her tea, but stopped. 'Then your mother's going to wring my neck.'

'It's good he told me. Because I thought she'd been got by a paedo. Or murdered. Or both.'

'Christ.' Mrs Harris shook her head at her cup. 'It was definitely asthma.'

'Lewis said Danielle's asthma was worse than mine. But was it? And how do I know without asking my parents?'

'Please don't ask your parents.'

'Am I going to die?'

'No.'

'Then how do they know her asthma was worse?'

There was a long silence.

'If your mother ever finds out I said this, please explain the circumstances.'

I nodded. It seemed *everyone* was afraid of my mum.

'I gather Danielle had lots of attacks before that one.' Mrs Harris put her drink down. 'Bad ones.'

'Am I going to—'

'No. And Lewis said you've barely needed your inhaler in all the time he's known you.'

I thought about this. It was true. I'd usually only take a puff to make a point, or for something to do.

'From what I've learned,' Mrs Harris said, 'because I've never actually asked your parents, *obviously* – your sister had a chest infection. It was a humid day. And something to do with pollen. All the bad stuff just came together for her.'

'I can ask my parents.'

'*Please* don't ask your parents.'

'So it wasn't the fair that killed her.' My voice was breathy.

'It *happened* at the fair. It's the *one place* that really upsets them,' Mrs Harris said. 'So why would they ever want to go?'

I thought about this.

'And you wouldn't want to upset your parents by asking again, I'm sure.'

I swallowed. Mrs Harris had a higher opinion of me than I did.

But maybe she was right. After all I'd done, there was no way I could ask about the fair again now.

Mrs Harris got up. 'I need to get on with making tea.'

I stood up too. 'Can you give Lewis the pack of cards and say he can show me magic tricks with them? As long as we're on our own. Tell him I'll be nicer from now.'

'It's hard to change.' Mrs Harris gave me a *look*. 'Personalities get set early on.'

'You think I can't be nicer?'

She picked up her mug and my glass and placed them in the sink. 'You can't just *say* you're going to change. Fine words butter no parsnips.'

'Parsnips?'

'But I don't think your personality's set,' she gave me another *look*. 'Not if you don't want it to be.'

*

While I walked home, I thought about what Mrs Harris had said about personalities setting.

Maybe that meant I wasn't completely bad. My personality couldn't be completely set. The old Fiona wouldn't have given Lewis my best pack of cards.

But then, old-me Fiona had never poked at a nest full of wasps for no reason. So if my personality was just setting, I hoped it didn't set *exactly* this week.

At bedtime, in my pyjamas, I sat on my bed reading the leaflet.

The phone rang and I heard the up-and-down of Mum talking to someone.

I kept on reading.

Do not use:
- *If you are allergic to salbutamol or the other ingredients of this medicine (listed in section 4)*
- *If you unexpectedly go into early labour or threatened abortion*

Warnings and precautions
Talk to your doctor, nurse or pharmacist before using if you have any of the following:
- *Any diseases affecting the heart or blood vessels*
- *Any infection in your lungs*
- *Overactivity of the thyroid gland*
- *Low levels of potassium in your blood*
- *Diabetes*

Dad stood in the doorway, a sheet of sandpaper in one hand. 'Can I come in?'

I put the leaflet down. 'Yes, please.'

Dad put the sandpaper down on the bed. 'You're reading your inhaler leaflet?'

I nodded.

He sighed. 'Mrs Harris has just phoned. We know she told you about Danielle's asthma.'

'Don't tell her off.'

'We won't tell her off.'

'At least I know Danielle wasn't murdered now.'

'Dear God.' There was a hiss of breath outside the room. '*Murdered.*'

Dad saw my face and frowned. 'What?'

'Mum's listening outside the door. And making snake sounds.'

'She is?' Dad turned to face the door. 'Didn't we agree you'd leave us to it, Gail?'

Through the gap at the side of the door, I saw a flash of blue. I heard Mum's footsteps go down the stairs and into the kitchen.

'Has she gone?'

I nodded.

'We didn't tell you because we didn't want you to worry. Are you worried?'

'Mrs Harris said my asthma's not as bad.'

'*Nowhere near* as bad.'

'How do you know, though?'

'Danielle had lots of other attacks. We had to go to hospital a lot. It was terrifying.' Dad stared at the worn knees of his jeans. 'But we didn't want to stop her doing fun things. We wanted her to have a normal life.'

I squeezed his hand.

'She was a kid. It felt like the right decision.' Dad kept

staring at his jeans. 'We didn't want you to be scared and we don't like talking about this.'

'Because you want to talk about Danielle's life, not her death.'

Dad smiled. 'You're a good girl, really.'

I wondered whether Danielle got *you're a good girl*, or *you're a good girl, really.*

I looked at the sandpaper on the bed. 'What's that for?'

'To get rid of the swastika,' Dad said. 'Your dad's about to do some DIY. Unless you *want* a Nazi symbol on your dressing table for ever?'

I shook my head.

He smiled. 'That's a relief.' He knelt down on the carpet and looked at the carving. 'What did you do this with anyway? Kitchen scissors?'

'Compass.'

He touched the carving. 'It's all blue.'

'I coloured it with a biro.'

'Course you did.'

Dad put the sandpaper to the dressing-table leg and started scratching. Dust puffed into the air.

After a minute or two, he sat back on his heels. Where he'd sanded, the wood was a lighter colour.

Dad looked up hopefully.

'It looks awful,' I said.

'We can stain it later.' Dad picked up the bin. 'Here, get this bin out of the way so your dad can get a better angle.'

He glanced in the bin as he passed it over. Suddenly, he stopped. He pulled the bin closer and reached inside.

I waited, but he didn't seem to be passing me the bin anymore.

I let my hand drop. 'I'm just going to read for a bit.' I got under the covers. 'I'll definitely clean my teeth before I switch the light out.'

I made myself comfy. I rearranged my pillows, punching them, getting them fluffed up right.

Dad was still there, on his knees, the bin in front of him. Not moving.

'Dad!' I waved my hand in his eyeline so he looked up. 'You don't need to do more sanding tonight. I can hardly see the bad *F*s now, anyway.'

He nodded and stood up. He had the bin in his hand – Dad always empties my bin for me, though not usually at night. I realised I'd thrown Carl's photo in there, but that was fine – I didn't need his picture anymore.

I reached for my book. 'Goodnight.'

I turned back to check he'd seen me speak, but Dad and the bin had gone. There was just the whoosh of wood across carpet and the click of the latch, as Dad shut my bedroom door behind him.

42

Bad blood isn't a real thing. Type B isn't good and type O isn't bad. You can't tell if someone's good and bad from their blood.

Fiona Larson, 7E's Blood Project

One day to the fair

The sandpaper was still on the floor when I got up the next morning. I shook my head. *Dad.* I couldn't even put it in the bin because Dad had forgotten to bring that back, too.

When I opened my bedroom door, Mum was on the phone. 'Just tonight after school, till just after seven.' Mum spoke quietly. 'I'd really appreciate it, Lisa. I've got to work till seven and Jonathan . . . Jonathan's away. For a few days.'

I frowned.

'Well – you get it. You of all people,' Mum said. 'I'm sure things will be fine, it's just complicated.'

She was talking so quietly that I was struggling to hear.

'I wouldn't ask if I wasn't super-stuck,' Mum whispered. 'I'll find a longer-term solution after tonight.' There was a pause. 'What, tonight? No, I'd completely forgotten, what with everything. Thanks so much, Lisa. I owe you.'

A moment later, Mum stood in my bedroom doorway.

'You're to go home with Lewis after school today.'

'Lewis is angry with me, though.'

Mum made a swatting motion, like there was a fly in front of her face. 'It's not up to Lewis, it's up to his mother. I'll pick you up from there before Parents' Evening tonight.'

Parents' Evening. How had I forgotten that?

But then – *fair-phone-Adrian-cigarette-porn-wasps-New Head*. That's how.

Either way, Mum hadn't remembered either. And she didn't sound happy about it.

'Why am I meant to go to Lewis's after school? Where's Dad?'

'He's gone to a conference.'

'He should have told me. When he was doing the swastika last night.'

'Yes.' Mum turned to go downstairs. 'Yes, he probably should.'

It was only mid-July, but our flash of summer was over already. The rain poured down that morning, drumming hard on my coat hood as I half ran into school.

I passed Carl, who was carrying several shirts on hangers. He hunched over to keep the shirts dry before putting them in his car.

'Carl!' I shouted.

He didn't hear me over the rain. He went straight back into his house, leaving his car boot up.

I kept walking. It was probably better to tell him about Mum and the phone some other time anyway. Some time when it wasn't raining so hard.

And I couldn't be late for school today. Not when I was in too much trouble already.

*

School news!

They found *a turd* in the corridor behind the science labs! A human turd!

It was definitely human because animals can't get in the school without people noticing. And the turd was *massive*. Like someone had been saving it up.

All day, kids who hadn't seen it had been trying to describe the size and shape. By the afternoon, it was the biggest, curliest turd that had ever been known.

The kids noticed before the teachers did so, all morning, kids kept appearing at classroom doorways, saying each other needed to be called out of lessons because *I've got an urgent message from his mum.*

Everyone says The New Head was furious because the turd was so big she thought it might be one of the teachers'. But she calmed down now she's been told this happened last year too.

I'd forgotten it happened last year. Sometimes, there are just too many school things to remember, and you can end up remembering the wrong ones.

Anyway, the turd was the talk of the school today. It was the new *Greeney's haircut*. It was the new *Fiona's wasp-face*.

I was pretty grateful to that turd actually.

'And it was *so* curly, Dr Sharma. Like a brown Mr Whippy.'

'I said you could sit here at lunchtime, Fiona.' Dr Sharma didn't even look up from her marking. 'I didn't say you could talk to me.'

Dr Sharma glanced at my face and sighed. She closed the exercise book. 'Come on, then. While you're here, show me this blood project you've been working on.'

'Dr Sharma! It's *lunchtime*!'

Dr Sharma patted the chair at her side.

I slid my blood project book out of my bag and walked up to her marking table.

Dr Sharma let the book fall open, at the page with all the bits of bloody paper.

'That's *my* blood.' I slid into the chair next to her. 'So it's fine.'

Dr Sharma hunched her eyebrows together. 'You cut yourself, Fiona? On purpose?'

'Who would cut themselves on purpose? No, I was showing you what O positive looked like. I took the opportunity when I made lots of blood with my teeth. But it was by accident.' I glanced at her. 'I didn't do it with the saw.'

Her eyebrows moved up now. 'The saw?'

'But I didn't do it with the saw,' I repeated patiently.

She just stared at the page for a moment. 'So much blood. So unnecessary.'

She turned the page, to my family blood chart.

'See?' I tapped my table. 'O positive. We've got all the different letters in my family. Mum's AB, Dad's A, Danielle was a B. But we're all positive. Dad said he's *A positive influence.*'

Dr Sharma kept looking at the page. She put her forefinger and thumb to her mouth. She pulled her bottom lip forward a millimetre.

'Exactly,' I said. 'I didn't think it was very funny either.'

There was a scream of excitement from the playground outside.

Dr Sharma took her hand away from her mouth. 'Right.' She snapped the book shut. 'I'm delighted to say you've done some good work on this project.' She held the book to her chest, arms folded over it. 'But I'm going to keep hold of this because it's actually unsanitary.'

'The blood won't spill, it's dry.'

Dr Sharma opened her top drawer and threw the book in. I saw confiscated earrings, a penknife, a Walkman. That drawer was a treasure chest. 'Dr Sharma—'

'That reminds me. You keep asking about your sister.' She slammed the drawer shut. 'What did you want to know? I taught her briefly.'

I blinked. 'You taught Danielle?'

She nodded.

'What was she like?'

'Oh, you know.' Dr Sharma leaned on her elbows. 'Like a kid.'

'What does that mean?'

'Fiona.' She gave a kind smile. 'I'm afraid none of you are that different. You all merge' – she wafted a hand – 'into one.'

'But you can't have forgotten *Danielle*. She was perfect and special.'

'I think I would have remembered if I'd ever taught a perfect kid, don't you?' Dr Sharma chuckled. 'Perfect kids. *Honestly*. What are you like?'

'But wasn't she as pretty as a picture?'

Dr Sharma raised her gaze. 'Fiona, I don't know what you think goes on in teachers' heads, but we just want to get through the day and get on with our lives. I do remember Danielle a little. Not because she was perfect, but because she died. She was polite and she did her work without a fuss.' She studied me. 'She wasn't a troublemaker. Making dramas didn't run in the family.'

'Please don't say that to Mum at Parents' Evening.'

'I think your mother knows. I got that sense when I called her in *just yesterday.*'

'Go on,' I said quickly. 'Tell me more about Danielle.'

'There's nothing else to say. She concentrated in class. She didn't cause trouble. But special?' Dr Sharma sniffed. 'She was no more or less special than any other kid I've ever taught.'

I slumped back in my chair.

'Why do you look so shocked?'

I licked my lips. 'Are you just saying that to make me happy?'

'Why *on earth* would I want to make you happy?'

There was a thud. A ball outside, hitting the wall of the lab.

'Dr Sharma, can you tell from the blood type who's good and who's bad? Is O blood the bad kind and—'

'*No!*' Dr Sharma's shout filled the room.

I stopped.

'You've just done a *whole project* on blood. I thought you'd actually learned something. Then you come out with this nonsense. Am I wasting my time? I am, aren't I?'

I wasn't sure if she wanted me to say *yes* or *no*.

She folded her arms. 'Blood just ferries oxygen round the body. That's all.'

'It fights diseases, too.'

She waved a hand. 'Yes, yes.'

'And carries oxygen and nutrients. It carries hormones—'

'Well done, Fiona.'

'And heat. It carries heat too.'

'Yes, enough, you know a lot about blood.'

'I only ask about blood types because . . . I'm wondering if I'm bad, right down. Down to my blood.'

'*Fiona!*' Dr Sharma shook her head like I was stupid. 'Blood doesn't tell you whether you're good or you're bad.

In fact – this will really blow your mind, get ready for this – *there's no such thing as good or bad.*'

'O isn't bad blood?'

'What would that even mean?'

'And B blood isn't good?'

'Stop talking. I don't ever want to hear you speak of blood types, ever again.'

I shuffled in my chair.

She walked over and opened the door. 'If I ever hear you talking about blood types like horoscopes, I will be furious. That reflects on me, you know? On my professional skills. On *my teaching.*'

I picked up my school bag and stood up. I looked at her drawer.

She looked where I was looking. 'Your project book's confiscated.'

'Will I get it back?'

'No.'

I did a few loops of the school field for the rest of lunchtime, and headed into my geography class.

Halfway through, the school secretary knocked on the door. 'Is Fiona Larson in here?'

She looked around the class and spotted me. The shaky-legged girl she'd help pick up pens and pencils in the corridor, two days ago. The one she'd taken to the slaughter.

Not *slaughter.* You get what I mean.

'Your mum rang. She says you're to go straight home today, after all.' The secretary glanced at her note. 'Your grandma will be there.'

I was so relieved it was only that, I barely noticed all the *ooh, grandma!* noises.

But the secretary kept looking at me. 'Also, Mrs Shackleton said to say, you must go to see her tonight. Introduce her to your parents. At Parents' Evening.'

The *ooh grandma!*s stopped.

The secretary smiled at me – like she hadn't just dropped a bomb in my lap – and left the room.

I tried my best to have a lovely time with Grandma after school. She said it was a *surprise holiday*, and that *surprise holidays are the best holidays*, and she made a big fuss of me and we baked a coconut cake while we waited for Mum to get home from work.

But, still. I couldn't forget.

The New Head.

Parents' Evening.

43

Parents' Evening is the one time kids don't comment – or
seem to notice – that you have parents.
(paradox)

One day to the fair
It's like a whole-school ceasefire. It's like when those World
War One soldiers stopped shooting and played football on
Christmas Day.

For most kids, anyway. As long as no one's mum wears
a top that's too low-cut, or calls their kid *Mr Tickles* or *my
special little man* or something. Then it's different rules again.
For that kid, the ceasefire's definitely off.

The tables in the school hall were laid out like a grim res-
taurant and I went up to table after table with Mum and
Grandma, while teachers talked about me like I wasn't even
there.

I'd got those appointments in a deliberate order, leaving
Mrs Vernal and Dr Sharma till last. Hoping the world would
end before we got there.

But the world didn't end. And, too quickly, it was time.
We sat in the waiting area in front of Mrs Vernal's desk –

and I *still* hadn't introduced Mum to the New Head.

This, I decided, was going to be worse than the wasps.

'That's the teacher?' Mum's gaze narrowed a millimetre at Mrs Vernal. 'The one who said you should use your feelings about Danielle to get better at drama?'

I tugged on her sleeve. 'Mum, please don't . . .'

Lewis walked past with his mum and dad.

'That Mr Kellett's got his head screwed on,' Mr Harris was talking to another parent, smiling, making conversation like he was playing World's Best Dad in a sitcom.

Mrs Harris saw us all. 'Hi, Larsons!'

On seeing my mum, Lewis quickly rushed round to the other side of Mr and Mrs Harris.

'Jonathan's still at a conference,' Mum said.

'Whereas Geoff's actually *here*.' Mrs Harris looked dazed. 'And asking loads of questions too. He never came to Parents' Evening when we were together. Though,' she scratched the side of her mouth, 'he *is* mainly asking about PE.' She nudged Lewis. 'It's polite to say hello, you know.'

Lewis stayed behind his mum. 'Hi.'

Mum sighed. 'Lewis, I know you told Fiona about the asthma.'

Silence.

'I'm not cross,' Mum added.

'OK,' Lewis said, still behind his mum. 'I just like standing here.'

'Fiona Larson!' Mrs Vernal beckoned us with a finger.

Mrs Vernal sat opposite Mum, me and Grandma, a brochure titled *Drama Brings Out Life!* on the table between us.

Mrs Vernal gave a smile that was polite on the surface, something else underneath. She left one of her special pauses.

Grandma smiled back – a proper smile, like the world was a sunny place and she had all day.

Mum folded her arms.

Mrs Vernal continued with her special pause.

Mum sighed. She shifted in her seat.

'I'm afraid to tell you, Fiona can be disruptive.'

Mum nodded. 'Tell me about it.'

'She doesn't always follow instructions.'

Mum picked up the brochure and started flicking through. 'You should have been there for primary school.'

'And the magazines—'

She kept flicking. 'We've spoken to Dr Sharma and it's been dealt with. My daughter's not exactly Hugh Hefner.' Mum turned another page of the booklet.

Mrs Vernal pressed her lips together. 'Fiona seems to have trouble integrating.'

'She does.' Mum kept flicking. 'Is that everything?'

'Well—'

'Now.' Mum threw her brochure down. 'I hear you've been telling them to become astronauts.'

Mrs Vernal gave a little laugh. 'I've just tried to help them lift their horizons.'

'You don't think they should work in farms and florists.'

'It's about opportunities. Don't we all want better for our children than we have for ourselves?'

'I just don't think it's *helpful* to be telling eleven-year-olds to expect to go into space. And please never, ever again tell my daughter to use her feelings about having a dead sister to get better at drama.' Mum stood up. 'Don't want to be late for Dr Sharma. Thank you very much for your time, Mrs Vernal.'

Grandma beamed, like Mrs Vernal had given her a present. Over-smiling, to make up for Mum.

We took a seat in Dr Sharma's waiting area. Mum stared straight ahead.

She smiled at another parent. 'Disruptive,' she muttered.

The points of the Isosceles triangle were moving quickly tonight.

I looked around for a catalyst.

'See that family, Mum?' I nodded at Naomi and her mum. 'They live in one of those massive houses on the hill. Naomi's room is massive and she has little cabinets that are stuck to the wall, like they came with the house. She has her own bathroom.'

Mum frowned. 'On sweet?'

'*Very* on sweet. It even has an extra half-toilet. And they call tea *supper* and they have it at half-seven. Sometimes eight.'

Mum looked at Naomi and her family with interest. 'I bet they do.'

'Fiona Larson!' Dr Sharma shouted.

I noticed Dr Sharma had got changed since school earlier – at least, she was wearing a special scarf. Like Mrs Vernal did.

Like Mum's funeral jacket, this felt like another bad sign.

But Mum was much nicer this time.

'Thing is, Dr Sharma,' Mum leaned forward on the table. 'She's not *exactly* Hugh Hefner.'

Dr Sharma held up a palm. 'I have no intention of discussing that tonight. I'm sure you've had a conversation with her father now.'

'They weren't his magazines.'

'I notice he's not here.'

'He's at a conference.' Mum sat up straighter. 'Nothing to

do with the magazines, don't read anything into him not—'

'The obvious aside, Fiona's done some good work for me.' Dr Sharma looked at me. 'She did a great blood project. The enthusiasm was dripping from the page.'

'I've heard her talk about that a lot,' Mum said. 'A little ghoulish, but whatever.' She turned to me. 'Can we see the final project?'

'The problem was, that book was a health hazard,' Dr Sharma said. 'It had so much human blood in it.'

Mum looked at me.

'The day with the saw,' I explained.

Grandma's smile wavered.

'And I don't think you would have felt it necessary to keep the project, Mrs Larson, if you'd seen it.' Dr Sharma crossed her arms. 'I can describe it to you, if you like. Along with all the pages of Fiona's actual blood, there was information about haemoglobin and clotting.' Dr Sharma looked across the room. 'A lot about how blood transports nutrients around the body. And a table of all the blood types in the family, which I had no interest in lingering on.' Dr Sharma smiled at someone walking past. 'But apart from all the good work, the main takeaway was that the book was full of actual human blood.' She looked back at Mum. 'I decided it was so unsanitary, I put the project in the incinerator.'

Mum looked down. 'Thank you.' She cleared her throat. 'I mean – thank you, Dr Sharma. I really appreciate it.'

Dr Sharma gave a brisk nod. 'Anytime. But, in case Fiona's forgotten, before you go ...'

Dr Sharma looked up and waved.

I looked up.

At the New Head, *who was heading over.*

I jumped up. 'Mum, Grandma, this is Mrs Shackleton.'

Mum stood up, looking faraway.

I tugged her sleeve. 'Mum.'

'Hi! Sorry.' Mum put her best smile on for the New Head. 'Thank you for your leniency with Fiona. I can assure you she is extremely sorry. She understands how severe her punishment will be if she does – well, anything. Expect perfect behaviour from now on.'

I looked at my feet. I shuffled them a little.

The New Head smiled back. *Smiled*, like a normal person. 'Dr Sharma says it's out of character. And said that she will keep a close eye on the situation.'

Mum coughed. 'Thank you.'

'Father's not here?'

'He's at a conference.'

'Ah.'

'No, not like that. He's really at a conference.'

The New Head smiled again. 'Well, it was nice to meet you anyway.'

And Mum smiled back.

And that was all. I was *free*.

I shook my head as we walked away. Mum was nice, the New Head was nicer. *That really wasn't how I thought it would go.*

Mum glanced backwards and I followed her gaze. The New Head had walked over to Mrs Vernal. The two were talking, and looking over.

Mum stopped smiling.

I put my hand on her arm. *Don't.*

Grandma put her hand on Mum's other arm.

'I really wish Dad was here,' I said.

'So do I,' Mum said. She got her car keys out of her bag, not taking her eyes off the New Head and Mrs Vernal. 'I've never wanted him to lipread more.'

44

Trying to forget something makes you remember it more.
(paradox)

Zero days to the fair

I wasn't quite as cross with Mum when I got up early and rang the doorbell for Carl the next morning.

After all, Mum had defended me to Mrs Vernal. She had got Grandma to come down for a surprise holiday. She hadn't said anything bad to the New Head, and even told her I would behave in future – which I had mixed feelings about, actually, because that wasn't always in my control, was it?

But Mum was trying. I could tell she was trying. She was being really quiet round the house, but that was OK. Quiet was better than shouting.

So I wasn't quite as angry anymore – but, still. I was planning to tell Carl what she'd done anyway, just so he knew. In case he heard I didn't have a phone anymore, and thought I had been careless and hadn't looked after it properly.

But when I rang Carl's doorbell, there was no answer. And his car wasn't in the drive.

He must be up and out already.

Even though he never really did look like an early riser.

*

I tried not to do it. But with all my free time before school, I went the long way, to look at Festival Field.

As I walked through the village, Monkford looked different. Barer. People were bringing in their hanging baskets and their gnomes, moving their window boxes inside. The fair was coming, bringing visitors from nearby towns. And Monkford people clearly believe visitors from nearby towns steal hanging baskets.

Eventually, I reached festival field and walked up to the fence. I held the metal in front of my face, my hands like claws.

The field was *full*.

Trucks with pictures of clowns were parked up all around, mud tracks behind them on the grass. People in woolly hats unpacked the rides – talking and laughing, unboxing and clipping sections into place, like the fair was a LEGO set.

A group of men stood around smoking, but none of these men could be the Waltzer boy. Too old. Too ugly.

A smoking man adjusted his beanie. 'Anyone tested the chemical toilets?'

I turned to listen to another conversation.

'Will you be there in Hull?' another smoking man said.

But I didn't hear the answer.

Slowly, I pushed myself away from the fence.

I wasn't going to the fair now. I'd accepted that. But even knowing it wasn't for me, knowing how much it hurt, to stand there and stare – I still couldn't quite pull myself away.

I stared at the field for a long time.

*

School news!

Stu Meakin, he of the Childline dad, heard Miss Jarvis call Mr Kellett *Kev* at Parents' Evening! Mr Kellett's got a first name, and we know it, and it's *Kev!*

Poor Mr Kellett. He can't move in school without someone shouting *Kev! Kev, Kev, Kev!*

And *Kevin Kellett* – were his parents *mad?*

Also, Sean heard Liam's dad say *she can teach me history anytime* about Miss Gold. And now all the boys have decided that Miss Gold is fit.

It's changed everything. The boys can barely speak in her classes now – they look away when she asks questions and go red when she's talking to them. There's lots of talk of boys with books over their laps in her class, but I don't know if that's true. Besides, I don't mean this nastily – I like Miss Gold – but she's no Kelly from Winchester.

Despite the good school news, the day was generally awful – as it's always going to be when people are getting excited about something amazing you can't do.

'As soon as I get off the dodgems I'm going to run round and get right back on.'

'I've heard our Year Nine are gonna have a fight with Radcliffe High Year Nine by the doughnut shed.'

'Dad says he'll pay for the rides so I've got enough in my money box for four hotdogs.'

It didn't matter that Mum and Grandma were extra nice to me when I got home. It didn't matter that Grandma had made fairy cakes and we had a takeaway. It didn't matter that my face was healing a little, with the bumps going down.

Just because you want to forget something, it doesn't mean you can actually make yourself forget.

And sometimes – even if you don't want to – the more you want to forget, the more you find you're making yourself remember.

And though I promised myself I wouldn't do the Rapunzel thing, when I went to bed that night, I found myself opening my bedroom window and leaning out anyway. Taking in the bright lights reflecting off the garages over the road. The screams and the fast music. The sharp onion smell.

I breathed it in. I breathed it all in.

The fair had started.

45

The people who love you most can keep the most secrets
from you.
(paradox)

Minus one days to the fair
I got the letter the next morning.

Dear Fi,

By the time you get this, your Parents' Evening will be over. I'm
sure you had good reports from all your teachers and I'm so sorry
I didn't get to hear them. I went to a conference, then Uncle Jim
had an emergency and he needed me to come over and help.

I'm sorry I left without talking to you. At the times we're not
dealing with his emergency, I'm having a lovely catch up with
Uncle Jim. We've been talking about the antics we got up to at
school when we were your age, and we've been lounging on sofas
in his attic, drinking beer. His children have left home now, so
Jim's converted Nick's bedroom into a space just for him and his
records. It's like a palace up there. You'd love it.

It's times like this I am really sad we can't talk on the phone.
See you soon.
Loads of love,
Dad x

I folded the letter and slid it back into the envelope.

Dad had never been gone for more than a couple of days before.

A conference, and he hadn't said goodbye.

A conference – then straight to Uncle Jim's for an emergency?

I traced Dad's writing on the envelope. Something wasn't right.

I felt something big, like a plum, in my throat.

Mum was working, so I found Grandma was on her knees at the rockery by the front door, weeding. She liked *making herself useful*. She always said *it doesn't suit me, being a guest.* Along with *it's dangerous to lean back on your chair* and *you need to leave that tea towel to air, darling, or it'll go musty.*

'Grandma. Has Dad left us?'

Grandma wiped her forehead with her hand. 'What's that, darling?'

'Has Dad moved out?'

She took her time. 'Of course not.'

'Where is he, then?'

Grandma gave a little laugh. 'Are you the Spanish Inquisition? Am I going to get the rack?'

I shook my head. I can tell when people are lying to me.

'Shall I ask Mum?'

'No! Honestly, darling, he's at a conference.'

Something was going on. And they weren't going to tell me.

I crept about the house all weekend, trying to listen to Mum and Grandma, putting the radio on in my bedroom to pretend I was in there.

On Sunday morning, Grandma came out of the spare room with an armful of washing. She stopped when she saw me on the landing carpet, peeking through the crack.

'Fiona!' She put a hand to her heart. 'You'll be the death of me, darling. You nearly gave me a heart attack.'

She chuckled to herself and walked on, still carrying the pile of clothes.

On Sunday night – *bingo*.

Mum and Grandma were washing up together while I crouched outside, underneath the window. I had my radio on in my bedroom as a decoy.

'Can we talk? Where are those little ears?' Grandma said.

'Upstairs,' Mum said. 'Be careful, though.'

'Have you heard from ... you know?' Grandma kept her voice low. 'Has he been in touch?'

He. Dad.

'No,' Mum said. 'I hope he got the message when I spoke to him. He acts like he's the good guy – but he can't exactly pretend to be the good guy with Fiona's best interests at heart anymore, can he?'

I moved from a crouch to a sit. But Dad *was* a good guy. Of course he had my best interests at heart.

'What was I *ever* thinking of, Mum?'

'That doesn't matter now. The important thing is, is he staying away?' Grandma asked.

I frowned. *Grandma!*

'I think so,' Mum said. 'I don't think he meant to start anything. He just – didn't think.'

Something was big in my throat. I couldn't breathe properly.

'But you're still not going to tell her.'

'Don't look at me like that,' Mum said. 'I am going to tell her one day. Just not yet.'

I looked at my shoes uncertainly.

'He's completely irresponsible,' Mum continued. 'A sob story about a marriage gone wrong and, what? He thinks he can come back and mess things up for everyone, walk back in, just walk into Fiona's life like there's been a *vacancy*, and—'

'Mum, please!' I jumped up and ran into the kitchen. 'Don't say your marriage has gone wrong. Of course Dad can come back!'

Mum stared at me, frozen in her washing-up gloves. The soap suds from the plate she was holding dripped into the sink.

Grandma looked afraid. Like it was a brown bear that had rushed through that back door.

'*Please* let Dad come back. He can't live somewhere else, he's not like Lewis's dad. This is where he belongs!'

The plate slipped from Mum's hand, into the washing-up water.

'I don't care what Dad's done.' I felt my eyes wetting. 'Just let him come back. *Please!*'

Grandma put her hand on Mum's arm.

'WHY ARE YOU LISTENING AT WINDOWS?' Mum screamed.

'BECAUSE YOU NEVER TELL ME ANYTHING!' I screamed back.

'Gail. It's OK.' Grandma squeezed Mum's arm. 'Calm down, Gail. Think about it.' Grandma rubbed Mum's arm in quick hard strokes. 'It's OK, don't say anymore. Just *think*, darling.'

Mum closed her eyes. Still in her washing-up gloves, she

put one thumb and forefinger on her closed eyelids.

Grandma took a step forward. 'Your dad is just taking a few days to himself. That's all.'

'Fiona.' Mum opened her eyes. 'Your dad and I have had a row. Married people argue all the time. Your dad will come back and everything will be OK.' She reached for my hand.

I squeezed her fingers through the wet rubber of the washing-up glove. 'You promise?'

'I promise, Fiona.' Mum squeezed my hand so hard it hurt. 'Dad will come back, then you'll stop listening at doorways to things you don't understand, and then I promise, *promise*, everything will be OK. And go and get me your spy book. *Now*. Because, Mum,' she turned sharply to Grandma, 'that's the final straw. She's left the radio on upstairs while she's listening, out there, and *where do you think she got that idea?* I'm binning that book. I still can't believe you actually bought it, for a *child – what were you thinking of?*'

46

I know more about the fair than people who actually went.
(paradox)

Minus three days to the fair
School news! Was about the fair. Obviously.
 I tried to avoid hearing about it.
 It was *everywhere* on Monday morning.

The Fair This Year

1) There aren't as many dodgem cars as last year
2) It's *actually impossible* to get a basketball through any of the oval hoops
3) No one knows where the ghost train has gone
4) The amazing boy still works on the Waltzers
5) The field is mushy and turning into mud soup
6) The hotdog buns are too warm and crispy
7) There are still a few turquoise owls, but it's mainly pink panthers. Though they're not properly pink, they're orangey. Pink(ish) panthers.
8) The rides aren't as much fun in the rain, the droplets hammer on your face like bullets

9) The fair finishes tonight

10) It sounds amazing

I was crossing the playground at lunchtime, trying to find somewhere to go, when I heard, 'Wait! Fi!'

I turned to see Sean running after me.

'There's a rumour going around that you've split up with Lewis.'

'Is there?' I shrugged. 'OK.'

Sean shoved his hands in his pockets. 'I didn't tell anyone it was never true in the first place.'

'You keep our secrets now? Makes a change.'

He licked his lips. 'It was good for Lewis. You can tell, the lads are letting him play football now. Even though he's shit.' He fell into step next to me. 'But I was just wondering.' He coughed. 'Seeing as Lewis isn't speaking to you and doesn't seem that grateful.'

I slowed.

'Would you mind being *my* pretend girlfriend instead?' Sean couldn't look me in the eye. 'And it would be *really* good' – a blush crept up his neck – 'if you'd let me tell the lads I've touched your bra.'

More school news!

In between all the *'(cough) Kev!'*-s, in Mr Kellett's class, we found out he's not the only teacher leaving school at the end of the year. The New Head is leaving, too!

Mr Kellett looked scared when he saw our surprised faces. 'Has no one told you?'

'*You* have now, sir!' Greeney said cheerfully.

'Oh, God.' Mr Kellett sat back on his desk. 'Maybe I'm not meant to have told you. I'm sure everyone knows.'

He ran a hand through his hair. 'They *must* do.'

'Is this why Miss Jarvis is saying *hello* and *what a lovely day it is* and smiling at us all in the corridors?' Greeney said.

'Of course not.' He paused. 'And I'm sure she isn't acting any different.'

'She definitely is,' someone said quietly.

'Has the New Head been sacked?' Katie Russell asked.

'No! She's very ambitious, this was only a stopgap for her. She's moving on up, to a school with better prospects.' Mr Kellett paused. 'Though this school has great prospects, of course. And, before you ask, I've not been sacked either. Like I said, my partner's got a new job in Glasgow.'

'No one would sack you, sir.'

Greeney realised what he'd said and went red. He did an extra loud cough and *'Kevin Kellett!'* to make up for it.

'Everyone's leaving,' Zara said. 'Mademoiselle Brun left too.'

'She was a student teacher, she just went to a different rotation.'

Mademoiselle Brun! I sat back. I hadn't thought about her in ages.

I wondered if she still wanted to be a teacher, after all. Or whether the food fight had put her off.

'So don't be losing any sleep this summer, kids.' Mr Kellett opened his copy of *The Taming of the Shrew*. 'I'm sure there will still be enough teachers left to educate you all.'

I waited till the other kids had gone before I went up to Mr Kellett.

'Fiona.' Mr Kellett sat on the edge of the teacher's desk. 'Good to see your face is healing.'

'Is Mrs Vernal leaving?' I asked hopefully. 'She's friends with the New Head.'

He smiled. 'No. No, it doesn't work like that.'

'Dr Sharma?'

He shook his head again. 'The rest of the teachers will still be here in September.'

I squidged my mouth to the side. 'Oh. OK.'

He smiled politely. 'Is there something else?'

'I wanted to ask you a word thing again, if that's OK? Seeing as you were so helpful last time.' I zipped *The Taming of The Shrew* into my rucksack and took a breath. 'Mr Kellett, who is *Hugh Hefner*?'

On the walk home, I thought about what Mr Kellett told me, imagining how it would feel to live in my dressing gown in a house with loads of girls like Kelly from Winchester.

I let myself in and stopped.

Dad was at the peninsula with Mum, mugs of tea in front of them.

I dropped my rucksack and rushed over to hug him. I pressed my cheek to his chest.

I felt his arms, tight around me, and his heart, beating quickly. He smelt of a different deodorant than usual – of washing-up liquid mixed with the sea.

I looked up so he could see my lips. 'Are you back?'

'I am.' He smiled. 'I'm so sorry I missed your Parents' Evening.'

'It's not like Lewis's dad?'

'It's not like that at all.'

'Your father and I have been talking.' Mum picked up her mug. 'Everything is OK now.'

Dad nodded. 'Promise.'

'Has Grandma gone?'

Mum gave a half-smile. 'Your grandma's gone to Keep Fit at the leisure centre. She's going to stay around tonight, so the two of you can say goodbye.'

'And,' Dad picked up a big book from the side, 'I bought you this.'

He handed the book to me. It was *heavy*.

A Comprehensive History of the Balkans by P.T.R. Cavendish. I stared at it. 'Thanks.'

'Come on.' Dad stood up. 'Let's go for a walk, Fi, just you and me.'

We walked through the park, past the second-biggest bush.

Dad slowed, looking at the tennis courts.

I tugged on his sleeve. 'You always stare at the tennis courts when we come to the park.'

'Do I?'

'That's where you taught Danielle to serve. She had a strong forehand, but you especially helped her with her backhand. And making sure she used the whole of the court.'

Dad looked at the ground. 'We talk about her too much.'

'Yes. But it's OK.' I don't know why I said that.

We walked through the park and the fields, then down by the brook.

Dad sat by a silver birch tree, legs sticking out. 'Sit with me.'

I did.

'Your face is looking better. You haven't disturbed any more wasps while I've been away?'

'No,' I said quietly.

'How about bees' nests? Lions? Sharks?'

I shook my head. I scratched a piece of the silver birch's skin and peeled it down. The strip narrowed to nothing and jumped into a spiral, like a ribbon curled with scissors.

'I had to go away.' I could feel Dad watching me. 'And it was nothing to do with you.'

I concentrated on my peeling. 'Did you really go to Uncle Jim's?'

'I did, for one night. But I spent most of the time at a hotel. I was cross with your mum.'

'What did she do?'

'She was worried about something and she didn't tell me.'

'Was it about me being given . . . a something?' I'd worked it out. It took me a while.

Dad nodded. 'She thought I'd be upset about a strange man giving you a phone, so she didn't tell me. Which really hurt me. Me and your mother shouldn't have secrets. We promised ourselves a long time ago that we'd never have secrets again.'

'Does the strange man know I don't have the phone anymore?'

Dad paused. 'Yes. I went to see him, to explain that he shouldn't be giving little girls presents. And he understood.'

'What's strange about Carl, Dad?'

'Nothing, he's just a stranger, that's all.' Dad made a funny half-smile. 'That's the whole point – he's absolutely no one.'

I picked up all the peelings from the ground and rested them on one palm. 'Who was in the wrong, then? You or Mum?'

'I said we're OK now, Fiona.'

I made my voice quieter. 'Mum told everyone you were at a conference.'

'Sometimes you don't have to tell people everything.'

'Like you and Mum didn't tell me about Danielle's asthma.'

Dad sighed. 'We're your parents, Fi. It's our job to work out what to tell you when.'

I shook my head and kept peeling.

'Did you want to know Father Christmas didn't exist when you were three?'

I stopped peeling instantly and clenched *everything*. The fact I *ever* believed those icing sugar footsteps were made by a herd of reindeer trotting through our lounge made me want to run, just *run*, as fast as I could – just to get away from the thought of *stupid young stupid STUPID Fiona*.

'But you've told me everything now,' I said. 'And you won't ever lie to me again.'

Dad looked across the field. 'Something's hovering. Is it a kestrel?'

I nearly looked. 'Promise me, Dad.'

Dad crossed one leg over the other. 'Are you a grown-up, Fiona? Do you pay for your own food and clothes? Do you drive a car and vote for a government and go to work and earn money?'

'You know I don't.' My voice was tiny.

'Do you remember when you wanted to stay up and watch that film about the clown? And we said you wouldn't like it, so you pretended to go to bed, but watched it in our bedroom instead?'

I flushed. I concentrated on peeling. 'No.'

'Do you remember you had to sleep in our bed for weeks? That you kept picturing that scary clown and the blood in the bathroom?'

I stopped peeling for a second. 'Please never tell anyone from school.'

'We made the decision long ago, that we would tell you about Danielle's asthma when you were thirteen, and not before.'

I looked down at the peelings in the lap of my school skirt. 'But I'm nearly twelve and I'm fine. You were wrong.'

Dad leaned further back on his hands, not taking his eyes off me. 'We made a judgement.'

'What age will I know everything?'

Dad laughed. 'I'm fifty-two. I still don't know everything.'

'Dad.'

He looked at me and sighed. 'You know pretty much all there is to know. The *Comprehensive History of the Balkans* has got nothing on you. But eighteen's a good age, isn't it?'

Eighteen. Would I ever, *really*, be eighteen? That was older than even Selina Baker. That was Kelly from Winchester age.

I'd be so tall at eighteen. I'd have had a massive growth spurt and overtaken everyone. I'd wear a bra every day. I'd wear shoes with heels and no straps. I'd have long straight hair that I could flick behind my shoulders, like Kelly's. I'd drive everywhere – but in a car like a boy's, without stuffed toys in the hatchback. I'd drive past lads in the street, poking my cigarette out of the window to flick ash while they watched.

Dad was still talking.

'Say that again,' I said. 'I wasn't listening.'

'I said, if there was anything we were keeping from you, we'd tell you at eighteen. And that's a promise.'

I thought about this. 'But you aren't keeping any secrets from me now?'

Dad gave me a big smile. He pulled me in for a hug.

'You know I'm a good spy. I find out in the end,' I said. 'Always.'

I felt Dad go stiff for a second.

Then he went softer. 'Then it's a good thing,' he said into my shoulder, 'that we don't have any secrets. Isn't it?'

After our walk, Dad let us back into the house.

Mum came into the lounge straight away, smiling at me. 'What did she say?'

'I haven't told her yet.'

I looked from one to the other. 'Haven't told her what yet?'

'Two things.' Dad glanced at Mum and back. 'Your mum and I have been talking . . . a lot. And we think it might be a good time to move house. Get a new house.'

I tried to take this in.

'Still in Monkford,' Dad said.

I *still* tried to take this in. *A new house.*

The words didn't make sense.

'To live in.' Dad frowned. 'Fi?'

I got it. 'A *new* house?'

Dad nodded.

'No promises,' Mum said. 'We're just going to start looking. It's expensive to move, there's estate agent fees and stamp duty. And the prices removals companies charge' – she shook her head – 'are actually *criminal*.'

'Can I have the second-biggest bedroom?'

'We don't know what the house is, so we can't answer that question.' Mum rearranged the clip in her hair. 'Depends on the layout, where the light is, which room has the best view. And it isn't definitely happening yet.'

'But you won't have to save a bedroom for Danielle?'

Dad went to speak, but Mum interrupted him.

'No,' she said. 'We won't have to save a bedroom.'

'You can save her the third-biggest room, if you want.'

Mum was looking sad, so I tried to cheer her up. 'And if we're moving, that means you don't have to paint the hallway anymore, doesn't it?'

'No.' Mum sighed and leaned against the wall. 'I'm afraid, Fiona, this time, it means we *definitely* have to paint the hallway.'

She and Dad made eye contact.

'This weekend,' Mum said.

Dad nodded hard, like nodding would make it happen.

They turned back to me.

Dad coughed. 'So that was the first bit of good news.'

I nodded.

'And,' Dad made his voice bright. 'The other news is that we've taken in what you said. That you really *really* want to go to this fair.'

I held my breath. *No.*

I raised my head slowly to look at him. *It can't be.*

'We've spoken about it' – Dad looked at Mum – 'at length – and your mum and I don't think we can go.'

'But I could go on my own?' I said hopefully.

Mum gave a faint smile. 'Your grandma's going to take you. After tea, when she's back from Keep Fit.'

'*I'm going to the fair?*' I shrieked.

'Though please don't tell us about it afterwards. It has very bad memories for us.' Mum rubbed her upper arms. 'I'm sorry, love.'

'I won't tell you anything. However good it is. I'll just keep it quiet.'

Dad gave a little smile. 'I'm not sure you'll manage.'

'And I haven't got any money.'

'We'll sort that. As long as you promise not to come back with a goldfish,' Mum said. 'Tell your grandma I said that.

Remind her if you start hooking ducks and she gets one of her ideas. *Massive stuffed toys* – fine. *Living things* – not fine.' Mum took a breath. 'Tell her, Fiona, and I'll tell her too, because there's *no way*' – Mum folded her arms, furious with Grandma in advance – 'that I am going out at ten on a Monday night to buy a bloody fish tank.'

47

Sometimes I get so happy it makes me sad.
(paradox)

Minus three days to the fair
I always knew what I was going to wear if I ever got to go to the fair, so I didn't need time to decide. I ran upstairs and got straight into my best jeans and denim jacket.

I took my trainers into the bathroom and cleaned them with wet toilet roll.

I put the front of my hair into a knot and put my dolphin chain round my neck. I smeared raspberry lip balm on and pressed my lips together. I slipped the pot into my pocket.

I came back downstairs casually and sat in the lounge, where Mum, Dad and Grandma were watching the weather.

My family glanced at me and smiled at each other. And no one said anything.

It was still light when Grandma and I walked to the fair.

We passed a woman, hand-in-hand with a toddler. The toddler was carrying one of last year's turquoise owls rather than a pinkish panther, but I supposed the kid was too young to know any better.

'Do you want me to come onto the rides with you?' Grandma asked. 'Or would you prefer I just watch?'

'Maybe just watch? Sorry.' The boy wouldn't push my car on the Waltzers if that car had an old lady inside. Even if the old lady was as great as my grandma, it just wouldn't happen.

The whooping and music got louder as we got closer to festival field. The sweet and sour mix of bitter onions and candyfloss filled the air.

A man shouted through a tinny speaker. *Place your bets! Donkey derby is ready to go!*

Grandma grinned. 'You're holding your breath. Try to breathe, darling. It's more fun if you breathe.'

I concentrated. *In and out. In and out.* My chest felt wrong, like it had Lewis sitting on it.

We turned the corner, onto the main road. I reached for Grandma's hand.

Across the road, festival field – the place of slippy leaves and dog mess, the place I'd practised cartwheels, where older kids practised drinking – was *transformed.*

Hundreds of people moved around behind the barriers. A big wheel carried cars into the sky, its shape outlined in white lights. A hut called *Games Shack* glowed with lights, all zigzagging and changing colour.

I took a step forward.

Grandma squeezed my hand. 'Careful. The road.'

The music was so loud now, it made my heart throb. Underneath the song, 'Blooded Face' by Knives of Pain, there was a continuous whirr, like someone was hoovering the field with a giant vacuum cleaner.

We crossed the road and slipped between the barriers. The floating onion and candyfloss smell was stronger still.

Just – *magical.* It was all magical.

We walked through all the people, past the hook-a-duck tent and the shooting range. Selina Baker passed by, carrying a pinkish panther. It was so neon bright it was almost orange, with skinny arms that whipped and dangled.

And even though I'm too old for stuffed toys, she was *Selina Baker*. 'Can we get a pink panther, Grandma? Mum only mentioned not getting a goldfish, she didn't say anything about a panther.'

'Only if we can find one to buy,' Grandma said. 'The games are all rigged.'

'Grandma!'

I looked closer at one pinkish panther, hanging sadly next to its friends in the front of the 'test your strength' stall, in what looked like a mass panther crucifixion. On closer look, the kids at school were right. The panther was too orange to be *the* pink panther. And the snout was too long.

Still. There was no way I was leaving tonight without one.

In front of the stall, a huge dad, his arms criss-crossed with sticking-out veins like ropes, raised a hammer and smashed it down on the metal button.

The red marker on the thermometer went a third of the way up, past *featherlight* to *weedy*.

'See?' Grandma grinned at me. 'Rigged.'

I frowned. 'It can't be. Not *the fair*.'

Grandma waved in the direction of the claw machines. 'Ever seen anyone win on one of those?'

I blinked. 'No, Grandma. I've never been to the fair. Haven't you been listening? That's the point of me.'

I looked up at the cars of the big wheel. I stilled.

Grandma looked at me softly. 'Breathe, darling.'

That made me think of Danielle. Of Danielle, at the fair, not breathing.

I looked at Grandma. She couldn't have realised what she'd said, so I tried to smile.

But I looked around me, at all the people. Wondering.

When *Danielle* happened, did the Waltzers stop? Did the hot dog turning machine keep going, or did someone switch it off? Were people still going on rides all around Danielle, while she was on the grass? When the ambulance came?

I shivered a little.

You have a different kind of asthma.

There was a chant of kids behind me – *'fight, fight, fight'*. I turned to look, and—

Lewis.

Not fighting, obviously. Just watching. He stood with his hands in his pockets, hitching up the bottom of his fake leather jacket so you could see a skirt of yellow football shirt.

I swallowed and walked up to him. 'I like your Tottenham shirt.'

'My dad got it for me.'

'I guessed that.'

Lewis glanced at Grandma and back. 'You were allowed to come in the end, then.'

I nodded. I looked up at Lewis's mum. 'Hi, Mrs Harris.'

'Hi, Fiona.' Mrs Harris was eating candyfloss, though candyfloss is for kids. 'Why don't you two go on a ride? Me and Helen' – she waved a hand at Grandma – 'can go and buy a very expensive coffee.'

Lewis looked at his feet.

'Lewis.' I'd never heard Mrs Harris's voice so *harsh*. 'You don't want to keep going on rides with me. I'm your *mother*, for God's sake.'

'We'll still be able to see you, mind,' Grandma said, 'so don't be putting any of your parents' hard-earned cash in that claw machine, Fiona. I will negotiate a good price for a panther later.'

They walked away. A kid I knew from primary school walked past, mouth open wide as he jammed a hot dog in, but Lewis and I didn't say hello. This kid was the year below, still at primary school. *And* he had tomato ketchup and onion trails down his T-shirt.

I turned to Lewis. 'Shall we do the Waltzers? Maybe?'

'Waltzers sounds good.'

We walked past two Year Eight kids, kissing under the tree. They kissed hard, lots of bobbling head movement going on.

Twelve other kids, separated into boys and girls, stood nearby. Still, and silently watching.

'I know they're Year Eight and amazing,' I said. 'But I just think it would look better if the boys and girls stood together.'

'Other people aren't as good as we are.' Lewis smiled. 'I think the boys like me more now, you know.'

'I knew it! It's because of the girlfriend thing. Honestly, Lewis, I did you a favour.'

'It's not because of you. It's because of *me*. My mum says you should be yourself and then everyone will like you.'

I gave that the biggest eye roll. 'Lewis—'

'Don't say my mum's stupid again.'

'I don't want to, do I? I *like* your mum. But then she goes around saying stuff like that. Look!' I pointed. 'Sea witches!'

I pointed to the three girls who had been mean to me in the toilets that time. But now, they looked scared, the two smaller ones hanging back. The main sea witch was getting picked on by an *even bigger* sea witch. A Queen Ursula.

I shook my head. 'The circle of life.'

I looked down. At nearly twelve, I *really* needed to stop saying things from Disney cartoons.

We reached the Waltzers queue. The cars were spinning so fast you couldn't see the people's faces. A boy in a baseball cap skipped across the platforms, spinning the cars faster. *The boy with the money pouch* that I'd heard so much about.

He stood tall suddenly and looked out at the queue, feet apart, keeping his balance on the moving platform. A disco ball threw colours across his face, over his cheekbones and eyebrows. The way he stood over us, the colours bouncing off him – he was lit up like a hero.

And I got it.

I could barely look at him, he was so perfect.

We shuffled forward in the queue, 'Blooded Face' playing again.

> *The reaper will take you, take everyone you love*
> *And we are all alone at the last.*

It was now my favourite song, and it was going to be my favourite song for ever.

'I'm not saying you're my girlfriend anymore,' Lewis folded his arms. 'I don't want people thinking I'm a fake.'

'Fine.' I glanced at him. 'Except do you still say you support Tottenham?'

'That's different,' Lewis said quickly.

'I know, course it is,' I said, even faster.

'And *Spurs*,' he said. 'I have to call them *Spurs*.'

'Spurs,' I said. 'Right.'

'I'm so unlucky though.' He kicked out at the barrier. 'Spurs are playing Stoke away in a testimonial next week. Dad's made Mum change our Saturdays so we can go. The ticket's an early birthday present, and I've got to go and watch the game instead of going to my cousin's party. And it's a swimming party. *And* he's getting one of those big floating things.'

374

Lewis looked so sad, I couldn't help laughing.

And then he started laughing, too.

And we just stood there in the queue, pushing each other, our eyes watering, like it was the funniest thing we'd ever heard. I couldn't catch my breath, and nor could Lewis, because he started hiccupping – and then he looked like he was in actual hiccupping pain, and it got funnier still. And even *Lewis* found it funny as he went all Tiny Tim again, and his hiccup turned into a croak. And it wasn't even *that* funny. It was just that we were friends again.

Lewis made a sign for me to hit him on the back, eyes streaming. Still smiling.

'Hi, Fiona!' Selina Baker walked past, grinning. 'Enjoying the fair?'

Instantly, Lewis stopped croaking.

I beamed at her. 'It's amazing!' My smile faded a little. As well as the pinkish panther in her arms, she now had one of last year's turquoise owls with her. *Didn't she know?*

She waved her pinkish panther's paw at me. '*I'm so pweased you're enjoying the fwair, Fwi-ow-na.*' Selina moved the panther's mouth along with the words.

My smile faded completely now.

Lewis and I looked at each other.

'*My name's Mwister Pink,*' she continued. '*Like in the film.*'

She lifted her owl's wing. I realised it was about to be the owl's turn to speak.

I shook my head.

She lowered the toys.

If I was the best girl in school, I'd definitely be better at it than *this*.

'I've been meaning to say, Fiona. You were asking about

375

my job? There are some jobs going in the stables now, if you want me to put a word in?'

'No thanks. Selina, this is my friend, Lewis.'

She grinned. 'Hi, Lewis.'

When Lewis couldn't say anything, she smiled at him and walked away.

He hit my arm with the back of his hand. '*Selina Baker* said my name!' He paused. 'It would have been better if she hadn't done the panther baby talk, but still. What's that about a stables?'

'Girl's job. Cleaning up horse muck. *Unpaid*. At *seventeen*.'

Lewis shook his head.

We moved forward in the queue. I saw Jodie outside the Sweet Shack with her group of girls. Their sugar dummies glowed red under the lights.

Jodie saw me and handed her dummy to Naomi. She ran over.

'I *told* them you were friends with Selina Baker!' Jodie looked from me to Lewis. 'Are you two back together?'

Lewis found his voice. 'Definitely not.'

'We're just good friends,' I said.

She nodded. 'I didn't think you'd be cheating on Sean Anderton. Look,' Jodie glanced back, 'Alison's thinking we might need to make the group bigger again soon. She thinks it might be better for ice-skating and stuff. Though she fancies Sean, so it could be weird.'

'I'll dump him, then,' I said.

'Really?'

I shrugged. 'Why not?'

'Sweet.' Jodie scratched her cheek. 'Though Alison *was* thinking of fancying Clark now. He'll get his brother's paper round when his brother starts work at the petrol station.'

I nodded. 'I'll dump Sean anyway, though. Just in case.'

'You're getting much better at girl stuff.' Jodie looked at the queue. 'Is there room for me in your Waltzer car?'

We nodded. Jodie crouched under the barrier and got in the queue with us, just as the boy with the money pouch came over to lift the barrier.

We scrambled into the car and pulled the metal bar down over us.

We all handed the boy our pound coins. It went quiet, for a second. Then that song started again. 'Blooded Face'.

I felt the vibration start under my feet. I looked beyond to the big wheel and all the lights and the people.

And I knew, right then, that this was about to be the best time I would ever have.

I held my breath as I felt the car start to move. I sat up straighter, grabbed the metal bar, and waited for the boy to spin us.

He didn't spin us. Of *course* he didn't.

I could blame Lewis for being a boy. But it probably wasn't *all* Lewis's fault. The car the boy span instead had four girls in it – all sixth-formers, in black eye make-up and purplish lipstick. They were grown-up height, with long brown legs in cut-off denim shorts, and tops so low you could see the rise of their boobs under long necklaces.

And I didn't really have time to mind about the spinning. My head was too busy trying to stop jerking as it was.

As the ride slowed to a stop, the boy with the money pouch helped the older girls out of their car. Taking their hands, like they were old ladies or something.

'Maybe he'll push us next year,' Jodie said. 'We might have boobs by then.'

I looked at the older girls, smiling and chatting with him. And I knew I wasn't going to look like those girls next year. Or the year after that. Or even the year after *that*.

'Maybe.' I turned to Jodie. 'But we can definitely wear more make-up.'

It was late when I got home that night but, still, I dug through the songs I'd recorded off the radio till I found 'Blooded Face'. I played it in my bedroom, over and over.

> *We will all die, and decay into dust*
> *And no one will care about my blooded face.*

I sat in my pyjamas on my bed, my knees to my chest. I hugged my pinkish panther, breathing in the vinegary smell of the fur. I threw one skinny panther arm over my shoulder and cried and cried into its neck.

Mum came rushing into my room. 'What's wrong?'

I didn't answer. I couldn't.

Mum approached the bed. 'Shush, Fi.' She held me. 'It's OK. It's all OK.'

I kept sobbing, harder and harder.

Mum stroked my hair. 'I wouldn't have let you go to the fair if I'd known it would make you this upset.'

'It's not the fair's fault,' I said between shudders. 'And I'm not upset.'

Mum just kept stroking my hair.

Dad came in. 'Hey now, love.' He sat on the bed. 'This'll distract you. They've just said on the telly Radovan Karadžić's resigned. He's been indicted for war crimes.' Dad scratched his cheek. '*Indicted* means – well, I don't know exactly what *indicted* means. It's like arrested, I think. Bad, anyway.'

I pressed my face into the sodden fur and cried more.

It was over. The fair was all over.

The best thing in my life. *Over.*

I would never, *ever* be this happy again.

Mum and Dad didn't tell me to go to sleep. And Dad didn't talk any more about Radovan Karadžić. They just let me sob into the panther, letting all the tears stream out.

And I just cried and cried, not even knowing why I was crying. Just listening to 'Blooded Face' and smelling my panther and sobbing till it hurt. Sometimes gasping, sometimes spluttering. Knowing nothing I ever did – no moment in time – would ever be that perfect again.

48

Not all presents are good.
(paradox)

Three hundred and sixty-one days to the fair
'Fi!' Dad shouted up the stairs the next morning. 'It's nearly eight o'clock!'

Then Dad was in my room – I don't know how long later – pulling my duvet off me.

'You can't be late on your last day of term!' He dumped the duvet on the floor. 'Now where do you want this? You left it downstairs.'

He gestured with a book. A big book. *A Comprehensive History of the Balkans* by P.T.R. Cavendish.

I pointed to the spot on the bookshelf next to Grandma's long-legged owl, in what was becoming The Corner of Wrong Presents. 'There's fine.'

I really needed to start doing and saying stuff, I decided, that I actually liked. No more football. No more Balkans. Definitely no more wasps.

'And look!' Dad waved a letter at me. 'The best news! How clever is your old dad?'

Dear Mr Larson,

Thank you for your application for Quiz Bounce, the fastest finger first game with all the bells and whistles!

We are delighted to tell you that you have made it through our initial sift, and we would like to invite you to a live audition on 1 August at . . .

I licked my lips. 'That's great.' I tried to sound like I meant it. 'Well done.'

Dad nodded happily and folded his letter. 'I'm going to write and accept straight away. You can come to the audition, if you like.'

'Thanks.'

'And now, you have to say goodbye to your grandma because she's going home today.'

'I'm so tired.'

'Was it worth it, though?' Dad asked.

The Waltzers, the lights, the pinkish panther.

'It was worth it.'

Dad hurried out of the room, and I got dressed quickly in the same jeans and T-shirt as last night. My best clothes, for 'out of school uniform' day on the last day of term.

A moment later, I heard a drawer slam. 'Bloody hell, Gail, again! Where are all the effing stamps, *again*?'

I said goodbye to Grandma in the lounge.

'Thank you for taking me yesterday.' I glanced at Mum and Dad and lowered my voice. 'To . . . you know.'

Grandma kissed my cheek. 'It was a pleasure.'

'My spies tell me you and Lewis went on the Waltzers together,' Mum said.

I looked up at her. 'Do you think that means he's forgiven me?'

'I expect so.'

'Do you think that means he'll be waiting for me to walk to school?'

Mum made a wafting motion with her hands. 'Maybe go there and find out?'

I grabbed my bag and my pinkish panther and ran to the lamppost.

I checked my watch. 8.20. Still loads of time for Lewis to arrive.

I looked at the house over the road.

Carl's car wasn't there. The house was dark, all the curtains drawn. Now I thought about it, his car hadn't been on the drive for a while. A bit of white leaflet had been peeking out of the letterbox for a few days, from where the postman hadn't put it all the way through. The estate agent's sign on the front lawn had an extra red banner across it. *Sold.*

I waited some more. I checked my watch. 8.26.

A few doors down, a woman was putting her window boxes and hanging baskets back outside, now it was just Monkford people in Monkford again.

I stared down the road. Still no sign of Lewis.

I looked at my watch. 8.28.

I took one last look down the road.

At 8.30 I put my bag on my shoulder and, with heavy feet, turned towards school.

In that morning's lesson, Dr Sharma didn't put an end-of-term video on like the other teachers. She wanted to punish us with learning, right up to the end, so she made us give presentations about our science projects. All the while she was telling us, kids piped up.

'*Did you* scarf *down your breakfast, Dr Sharma?*'

'*Are you* shawl *you want us to read out our science projects?*'
Cough. '*Scarf!*'

Dr Sharma had been walking away for this last one. She turned slowly on the spot.

The *Cough*, '*Scarf!*'-er, Liam, gulped.

'Why are you saying *scarf* to me, Liam?'

Liam looked from left to right, desperate.

'I'm waiting.'

He swallowed again.

'Shall I help you out? Is it because I wore a scarf at Parents' Evening? When I don't normally wear one?'

He was perfectly still. Then he gave a little nod.

She nodded too. 'And that's funny . . . how?'

He found his voice. 'I can't explain.'

'But it's definitely funny?'

'I'm not sure . . . I don't think it is anymore.'

'No?' Dr Sharma said. 'Have I ruined it? Well, that's a shame.' She turned to the class. 'Next project presentation.' She looked at her register. 'Amy Barton. You're up.'

'She's not in. She's got a sick gran.'

'A sick gran?' Dr Sharma shook her head. 'Poor effort. I will make a note to ask Amy's parents in September what date they went on holiday.' She looked back at her register. 'Mark Cutter.'

Mark stood up and went to the front. He coughed. 'Now. What *is* photosynthesis?'

Other kids went up to the front of the class, one by one.

Turned out pretty much *all* the other kids had done their projects on photosynthesis.

Dr Sharma sat at the front, marking other classes' exercise books.

I tried not to think about Lewis because it made a lump come in my throat. I wrote a list instead.

Things at the Fair That Weren't Quite as Good as I Thought They'd Be

1) The donkeys on the donkey derby wobble
2) The hotdog buns *are too* warm and crispy
3) The sugar dummies cost two whole pounds
4) The toys are really bad. The stitching's going on my pink panther's shoulder. And it smells of vinegar. And if I hold it for too long it makes my skirt stick to my legs.
5) The dodgems hurt your neck when someone drives into you
6) If you go on the Waltzers three times in a row, you feel sick. And not *good* sick. *Bad* sick.
7) The Waltzer boy isn't *that* great, and he looks pretty old, close up
8) Under the onions and candyfloss, the field smells of toilet
9) The mud ruined my best trainers

I'm *definitely* still going next year.

I closed my book of lists as Andrew Lane walked back to his desk.

Dr Sharma looked up. 'Fiona Larson!'

I went to stand at the front. I placed my hands together, like the vicar did in church.

'I did my project on blood.' My arms felt weird, like I had too many. 'I did loads of good stuff, but you'll have to take my word for it. I can't show you my project book because Dr Sharma stole it.'

There was a ripple of interest round the lab.

'I *said*, the book was unsanitary.' Dr Sharma leaned onto her elbows. 'Fiona decided to make hers a practical project. She put a substantial amount of her own blood in there.'

Someone muttered, '*Freak.*'

I fidgeted. 'It wasn't what it sounds like. And I made the blood with my teeth, not the saw.'

'Not the saw.' Dr Sharma drew a tick with a flourish. 'Still not going to ask *why not the saw.*'

'There are lots of different types of blood,' I said to the class. 'And you have white blood cells and red blood cells. And plasma. But mainly, I've learned that blood doesn't matter that much.'

Dr Sharma looked up. 'Doesn't matter that much?'

'I mean, blood groups don't make much difference – unless you're having an operation, they don't matter. Blood just ferries oxygen round the body. There are no good and or bad blood groups.'

Dr Sharma nodded. 'No horoscopes.'

'No horoscopes. Blood groups only . . .' I stopped. Something made me stop, and I tried to work out what it was. The thought was fluttering round my brain now, like a moth, and before I could catch it—

'Yes, yes.' Dr Sharma looked up sharply. 'And what is plasma, Fiona?'

I sighed. I'd been having a science thought; she should have been happy. 'Plasma is a light-yellow liquid. It carries water, salt and enzymes. It—'

Dr Sharma kept nodding, and made me go on for ages. Even though she hadn't asked anyone else any questions.

'Great. Good project, well done. Sit down.' She looked at her book. 'Michael Green.'

Greeney got up and I walked back to my seat.

'Now.' Greeney rocked forward on his feet. 'What *is* chlorophyll?'

At lunchtime I headed onto the school field. I walked a big loop, feeling the sun on my face. Being on my own was OK.

I would make friends with a girl group next year. I'd do it properly. I could learn to be different these summer holidays – learn to be someone else. I'd get a denim jacket in exactly the right shade of blue. I'd get a new rucksack for my birthday. I'd start drinking my milk skimmed and stop eating lunch. I'd—

A shout from faraway. 'Fi!'

I looked round.

Lewis sat, legs crossed, in the middle of the field, on a spread-out blanket. The blanket was loaded with some kind of picnic. Plates of cake and sausage rolls. A cool box. Some lumpy bits covered with a tea towel.

He pointed at the empty plate on his blanket. 'For you!'

I ran over. 'What's going on?'

'I asked Mr Kellett if I could bring a picnic in for the last day of school, and he said it was fine as long as I gave money to charity. Mum drove me in.'

'That's why you weren't at the lamppost this morning? I thought you were still cross with me!'

'What?' Lewis laughed. 'We made up last night, didn't we? And I couldn't exactly carry all this stuff in on my own.'

My throat was full. Too much feeling.

'You're going to sit down?'

I nodded.

I took my seat on the picnic blanket, tucking my feet underneath me. I didn't even notice the other kids crowding round us at first. Then, when I did notice, I tried not to.

Lewis opened the cool box. 'Lilt?' He handed me a can.

'Thanks.'

I looked up, at the crowds gathering round us. Quickly, I stared down at my can.

'Help yourself to cake and stuff.' Lewis opened the cool box again and pulled out an ice-cream lolly. 'Mini-milk?'

I took it. 'Don't mind if I do.'

Lewis opened his can. He took a sip. 'Aaah!'

He put his can on the blanket beside him, and got his sunglasses out of his rucksack.

Sunglasses on, he laid his head back and closed his eyes. 'This is the life.'

I unwrapped my lolly and nodded.

'Hi, Lewis.'

There were murmurs in the crowd.

Lewis looked at me and back. *'Selina Baker!'* His voice was a squeak.

'This looks fun!' Selina nodded to my lolly. 'You got any more of those?'

Lewis coughed. 'Strawberry or chocolate?'

Selina smiled. 'Chocolate.'

'May I?' And then Selina sank down and *sat cross-legged on the picnic blanket.*

And then *her friend Rachel did the same.*

Lewis handed them both lollies, as the crowds gathered and whispered. Around Lewis Harris and his weird picnic.

'I told you Fi Larson was friends with Selina Baker.' Jodie's voice.

'I got a pinkish panther at the fair. Like yours, Selina.' I looked at the picnic blanket. 'Though this one definitely doesn't talk.'

She smiled and bit into her lolly. 'Cool! So, are you two a couple?'

We both *pah*-ed.

'Just good friends,' Lewis said.

'That's so great.' Selina stretched her legs out. 'It's nice you're so comfortable with the opposite sex in Year Seven. I definitely wasn't that mature at your age.'

Rachel caught her eye. 'I'm not sure some of the boys we know are that mature *now*.'

The crowd was getting bigger. It felt like *the whole school* was watching. And, for once, that was a good thing.

Lewis picked up a plate and offered Selina some chocolate cake.

'Thanks, Lewis.' Selina took a slice – I didn't ask why she wasn't on a diet. She turned to Rachel. 'This is lovely, isn't it?'

Rachel took a slice of cake. 'Heaven. Maybe you'll start a new school trend with this, Lewis? This can be a Monkford High last-day-of-term ritual now, and *you* started it!'

Lewis looked at me, mouth open with joy.

And maybe, because everything was a bit too perfect, I should have been on my guard. Because we were sitting there, with the best sixth-form girls, and everyone was looking at us, and Lewis was so pleased with himself that—

'Selina,' Lewis pulled some fabric out of the cool box, 'tell me, what do you think when you hear the word *mnemonic*?'

'Lewis!' I jumped up, eyes wide. 'NO!'

I was too late.

Lewis was standing up now. Face flushed with pride, he whipped the tea towel off the lumpy bits on the picnic blanket. Under the tea towel, a tray was loaded with items – a notepad, a candlestick, a thimble, and a hundred other awful Lewis-y guessing things.

ALL THE FUN OF THE FAIR

There was a ripple in the crowd.

I couldn't even look.

'Oh my God, is that a cape?'

My heart was – hurting.

'You know what?' Selina got up. 'I'd better. . .' She pointed into the distance. 'Rach?'

'Yeah.' Rachel got up too. 'Thanks for the food.'

I watched them walk away.

Jodie shrugged. She mouthed *see you soon,* and headed back to her group.

The noises of the crowd were different now.

'Who brings in a picnic blanket? To school?'

'Trust Magic man.'

Cough. *'Lewis Harris went to Paris.'*

Cough. *'Gail Larson, Driving Instructor.'*

The crowd started moving away.

Lewis turned to me, tea towel drooping from one hand. His cape drooped from the other.

'Well, you ruined that,' I said. 'I hope you're proud of yourself.'

He put the cape and tea towel slowly into the cool box.

He clipped it shut and started smiling again, just a little. He sat back on the blanket. I closed my eyes, feeling the warmth on my face.

'This is nice,' he said.

I nodded. As long as I kept my eyes closed, I couldn't see anyone looking at us.

'Can I show *you* my memory game, Fi?'

I opened one eye and looked at the tea tray. At the thermometer. The box of matches. The special roleplay-game dice.

I glanced at the kids on the field, some still glancing over.

I *really* hoped everyone would have forgotten this by September.

'OK.' I turned to face him. 'But you can't wear the cape. And *please*, Lewis,' I glanced around, 'please, *please* be quick.'

49

People say blood is thicker than water because blood is a non-Newtonian fluid. This means it has flow properties that depend on conditions. Blood becomes less viscous under pressure so it can flow in narrow capillaries.
So does ketchup.
And this is why filmmakers use ketchup for blood.

Fiona Larson, 7E's Blood Project

Still three hundred and sixty-one days to the fair
Afternoon school news!

Miss Gold joined Miss Jarvis's GCSE class for the last RE class of the year. The two teachers put out a special Jewish *Shabbat* meal.

They sang hymns and lit candles and had blessings over bread, then had stew and salads. No cake or anything. It was meant to be a treat for the kids, but it didn't sound *that* great.

But it wasn't like Mademoiselle Brun's pâté-falling-down-the-Eiffel-Tower food fight. This time, *loads* of teachers were there, and they made sure they got there ten minutes early.

When the kids arrived, there were teachers all standing around like bouncers, like the RE room was a prison cafeteria. The teachers all had arms folded and hard faces, glaring at the kids, and no one dared throw as much as a crumb of bread.

And the other bit of school news happened in the last class of the year.

Like Dr Sharma, Mr Kellett didn't put on an end-of-term video. Instead, he made us read out 'What I'm Doing This Summer', the kind of thing I'd really hoped we'd left behind when we left primary school.

The other kids talked about holidays to France, and caravan parks in the Lake District, and cousins who could drive. Naomi even talked about a trip to Disneyworld in Florida.

When it was my turn, I talked about the trip to the hotel in Wales, and going to the American diner for my birthday.

I saved the best for last. '*And* we're moving house. I'm going to get the second-biggest bedroom.'

There were nods of respect at that.

'Not definitely, but probably. Mum says it depends on the layout and the light and stuff. But we won't have to save a room for a dead girl anymore.' At the awkward faces, I waved a hand. 'Sorry. Didn't mean to use my catalyst.'

After I said my bit, a few more kids went up, talking about trips to Benidorm and Crete. About grandmas in Cornwall and caravans in the Peak District.

Mr Kellett sat on his teacher's desk, listening.

When everyone had finished, he said, 'That all sounds excellent.' He picked up his pad. 'Now, my turn. What I'm Doing This Summer.'

(Cough) 'Kev!'

(Cough) 'Kevin Kellett!'

He smiled and bent his head to read. 'This summer, I'm moving house, and will be setting up a new home in Glasgow.'

He paused. 'I'm really sad to leave this school, but my partner's got a job at a teaching hospital there. He's a consultant in cardiology. I'm excited about the move, though I'm sure the kids in my new school won't be as much fun as you lot. But I'm hoping I'll get less stick about Leeds United.'

He looked up and smiled.

No one smiled back.

We must have misheard.

'Your partner's a consultant?' Greeney said carefully.

Mr Kellett made eye contact with Greeney. 'Yes. David's a consultant in cardiology.'

A pause. A ripple round the room. *David!*

But only a few kids said it. The rest of us just stared.

'But you teach *football, sir.*' Liam explained Mr Kellett to himself. 'You support *Leeds.* You were semi-pro.'

'I'm well aware of that, Liam.' Mr Kellett's voice was clipped, but he smiled kindly.

And then Mr Kellett looked down at his pad and read some more about his summer, about how he was going to walk up a mountain in the Lake District, like the massive thing hadn't just happened.

There were no more *(cough) 'Kev!'*s after that.

I waited after class. 'Mr Kellett—'

'Fiona. It's that time again, is it? Who are you going to ask about now?' He gave a patient smile. 'Larry Flynt?'

'I just wanted to say, *well played*, sir.' I nodded in respect. 'You hid it well.'

'No.' He sat up straighter. 'No, Fiona, that's not what happened here. I didn't hide—'

There was a cough from the doorway.

'We meet again, Fiona.' The school secretary nodded at me.

No.

'Mrs Shackleton and Dr Sharma need to see you.'

No, no, no.

Behind the school secretary, Lewis's face appeared in the corridor, his eyes wide with panic.

'I'll wait for you,' he said.

My legs had gone wobbly. 'You don't have to.'

'I'll help Mum put the picnic stuff in the car and then I'll wait for you.'

'Hurry up, Fiona.' The school secretary stood back from the doorway to let me through. 'Term's over. No time for being Romeo and Juliet.'

I turned back to Mr Kellett. 'Bye, sir.'

'Bye, Fiona. I hope, whatever they want with you, it's not *too* bad.'

I left the room.

With one last, scared glance at Lewis, I followed the school secretary down the corridor. Past kids, screeching through the hallways, throwing pens. Swapping phone numbers. Tearing their shirts off, writing on each other's in biro.

The school secretary pretended not to notice. 'Fiona, I hope I won't be meeting you like this quite so much next year.'

'I hope so too,' I whispered.

She waved me straight into the New Head's office.

I knocked anyway to slow things down.

'Enter!'

I took a breath, and made myself go in.

On the other side of the big desk, the New Head and Dr Sharma were waiting.

But, this time, there was nowhere for me to sit. The chair opposite was full. As full as a chair could be – if the kid in it was trying to make himself really small.

A Year Nine kid. *Chin Rash Skittle Breath.*

On the table between them – *Razzle.*

I looked up at the New Head and Dr Sharma. 'I'm not exactly Hugh Hefner.'

The New Head indicated the magazine. 'Jordan said he bought this from you at the car boot sale.'

I swallowed.

'*Did* he get it from you?'

They looked serious, but the teachers weren't shouting, just asking. And it hit me.

I'd already been in trouble for this. I was *safe.*

I was about to say *I don't grass,* but Chin Rash Skittle Breath looked at me and shrugged.

I turned back to the teachers. 'He bought it from me at the car boot sale.'

'Thanks, Fiona.' The New Head didn't sound thankful. 'You can go.'

I hurried out of the room, my legs working better by the second.

Lewis rushed up to me. 'Was it OK?'

'They had *Razzle.* But it was Chin Rash Skittle Breath they wanted, not me.'

Lewis nodded.

'Thanks for waiting.'

'Of course.'

'Would you have waited for me if you'd had to go in?'

'No way.'

'Fair enough.'

We walked through the empty school corridors. The noise of kids outside sounded faint and far away now.

At the computer room, we stopped and read the sign on the door.

Reopens in autumn term, when the school will be freshly connected to the World Wide Web!

'That's what they're calling the new wiring,' Lewis said.

I shrugged. 'They try to make things sound more exciting than they are. Don't get your hopes up, Lewis.'

'*Wait!*' Sean scurried up to us. 'Some of the blue estate lads took my PE kit. Mum would have battered me, but I found it in the end. In the big bins outside the canteen. I washed the gunk off, it's good as new.'

His voice was so loud in the quiet corridor.

'It's like we've got the run of the place.' Sean looked around. 'We *will* run the place next year, of course. When we're Year Eight. Those little Year Sevens won't know what's hit them. And we'll be thirteen, finally. We'll have paper rounds and everything.'

I kicked a drinks can. *Thirteen!* The can skittered away and down the stairs.

I hadn't even caught up with twelve yet.

'Are you two coming out for my birthday in August?' I said.

Sean nodded. 'Your boyfriend has to come out for your birthday.'

'Oh Sean, I forgot. You're dumped.'

'Did I get to touch your bra first?'

'You did.'

'And I can still come out for your birthday?'

'Yep. And you can come to the house, too.' I paused. 'Though I should tell you, the lights flash when the doorbell goes because my dad's hearing-impaired. Deaf.' I folded my arms. 'He's too good at reading faces, so don't bother trying to lie to him, and he can lipread when everyone's swearing in the football – even in other languages. As long as it's German.'

'Really?' Sean's face was all bright. 'Why didn't you tell us *that* when Euro '96 was on?'

I shrugged.

'We'll be watching the Olympics round at yours, then, this summer, Fi?'

'No way.'

On the way home, I made the boys go the long way around, past festival field. The three of us walked slowly up to the metal fence. We stood in silence.

The field was empty.

Not *quite* empty. Abandoned drinks cans glinted in the sun. In the distance, a grey-haired woman threw a ball for an energetic border collie.

But there were no trucks. No crowds, no lights. No throbbing music. No big wheel or Waltzers, or men in beanie hats.

No fair.

I let all the air puff out of my body. 'But it was *just here!*'

In the centre of the field – where the rides and crowds had been busiest – there was no green to see, only mud. Round the edges, the grass had been flattened, or churned up with tyre tracks. Just a few green untouched patches remained, showing what the field had been like before.

Lewis gave me a small smile. 'The fair will be back.'

I felt something brush past my leg. A plastic popcorn wrapper. 'Not for ages though.'

I watched the wrapper flutter and spin, over the road, under a car. I looked back at the field.

'Come on.' Lewis pulled lightly at my rucksack strap. 'It won't come back any quicker just for staring.'

We turned to walk home. The sky was changing, I noticed. Darkening.

'My dad told me something that will cheer you up, Fi,' Sean said.

Lewis and I looked at each other.

'Go on,' I said carefully.

'My dad told me there's a place in the East, by the sea, where all the fairs from all of Europe all join up, every October.'

We turned the corner into George Street.

'One big fair in every direction, as far as the eye can see,' Sean said. 'Loads of dodgems, big wheels. Waltzers and popcorn stands everywhere you look.'

Lewis raised his eyebrow. 'A magical place. In the *East*. By the *sea*,' he repeated.

We shook heads at each other, smiling.

'No, not like that! I promise! This time it's *actually true*!'

Lewis leaned on the postbox. 'What's this magical place in the East by the sea called?'

Sean stood up straighter. 'It's *real* and it's called *Hull*!'

'Hull?' Lewis's voice was scornful. 'What kind of place—'

I put my hand on his sleeve. 'Hull.' I remembered the fair workers talking. *Will you be there in Hull?*

Hull. The place in the East, by the sea.

'Lewis.' I clung tightly onto his sleeve. 'We're going to Hull.'

'You can't listen to *Sean*, Fi. He talks rubbish! He said an axeman lived *there*, remember?' Lewis jerked his thumb. 'Flipflops, in with the bananas, ring a bell?'

I looked over at the house.

There were two new cars in the drive now, Carl's car nowhere to be seen. A tower of empty cardboard boxes sat next to the front door. There were lights on in several rooms, and two kids' bikes were propped up under the front-room window.

Sean looked at the house. 'The axeman thing was a joke though. Surely you can take a joke?'

I noticed the sky felt blacker still as we all crossed the road.

I shivered. I mouthed the word to myself. *Hull.*

A woman came out of the front door of Carl's house wearing slippers, a black bag in her hand. Through the open door, I heard the sound of a Hoover going.

It started to rain. One drip, on its own, then three. Then – all at once – *whoosh.*

Too late, Lewis, Sean and I all pulled up our anorak hoods.

The boys each held up a hand in *goodbye,* and rushed off in the direction of their houses.

I took one last look at 56 George Street, staring for a second, but my face got so splattered, I couldn't look for long.

I hitched my rucksack further up my shoulder and tugged my hood forward. Hard bullets of rain drummed the top of my head as I started to move, then jogged faster still, until I was sprinting around the corner of George Street with my arms and legs flying, running at full pelt towards the safety of home.

CREDITS

Caroline Hulse and Orion Fiction would like to thank everyone at Orion who worked on the publication of *All the Fun of the Fair* in the UK. Special thanks to Ava Fouracre Gildersleve.

Editorial
Emad Akhtar
Lucy Frederick
Celia Killen

Copy editor
Clare Wallis

Proof reader
Marian Reid

Contracts
Anne Goddard
Paul Bulos
Jake Alderson

Production
Ruth Sharvell

Design
Debbie Holmes
Joanna Ridley
Nick May

Editorial Management
Charlie Panayiotou
Jane Hughes
Alice Davis

Finance
Jasdip Nandra
Afeera Ahmed
Elizabeth Beaumont
Sue Baker

Marketing
Helena Fouracre

Audio
Paul Stark
Amber Bates

Publicity
Alex Layt

Rights
Susan Howe
Krystyna Kujawinska
Jessica Purdue
Richard King
Louise Henderson

Sales
Jen Wilson
Esther Waters
Victoria Laws
Rachael Hum
Ellie Kyrke-Smith
Frances Doyle
Georgina Cutler

Operations
Jo Jacobs
Sharon Willis
Lisa Pryde
Lucy Brem

If you loved *All the Fun Of The Fair*, don't miss Caroline Hulse's hilarious and heartwarming debut novel . . .

Two exes. Their daughter.

And their new partners.

What could possibly go wrong ...?

'Funny, dry and beautifully observed. Highly recommended for anyone whose perfect Christmases never quite go according to plan!'

Gill Sims, author of *Why Mummy Drinks*

Another achingly funny, uncomfortably relatable novel from Caroline Hulse . . .

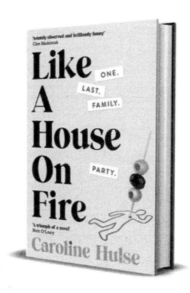

'acutely observed and brilliantly funny'
Clare Mackintosh

Like ONE.
LAST.
A FAMILY.
House
On PARTY.
Fire

'a triumph of a novel'
Beth O'Leary

Caroline Hulse

Stella and George are getting divorced.

But first, Stella's mum is throwing a murder mystery party.

All Stella and George have to do is make it through the day without their break-up being discovered – though it will soon turn out that having secrets runs in the family . . .

'Part Fleabag, part Agatha Christie, Like A House On Fire *is everything I love in a book . . . I was hooked from page one.'*

Josie Silver, bestselling author of
One Day in December

HISTORY OF CIVILISATION

The Celtic Realms

The
Celtic Realms

MYLES DILLON
Senior Professor, Dublin Institute for Advanced Studies

and

NORA K. CHADWICK
Honorary Fellow, Newnham College, Cambridge

WEIDENFELD AND NICOLSON
LONDON

First published 1967
Second edition 1972
Reprinted 1974

Weidenfeld and Nicolson
11 St John's Hill London SW11

ISBN 0 297 99580 5

Printed in Great Britain by
REDWOOD BURN LIMITED
Trowbridge & Esher

CONTENTS

The publishers deeply regret that, during preparations for the second edition of this book, Professor Myles Dillon died. They are grateful to Professor D. A. Binchy and Professor John Dillon for their assistance in completing these preparations and in reading final proofs.

PREFACE

THE Celts were one of the peoples in prehistoric Europe who helped to create the European civilisation of the past thousand years. Our purpose in this book is to trace their history from its remote beginning through the formation of the separate Celtic kingdoms in the British Isles, and down to the end of their independence. History is taken here in its widest sense, as the history of civilisation. We have included not only religion and institutions, but language, literature and art.

Celtic studies have advanced so greatly in recent years that we have felt bound to present in some detail the results of this research. There are pages that have been written for the student of Celtic as well as for the common reader. Those who have no special interest in language or literary history would do well to hasten through the early part of Chapter 9, but others may find it worthy of closer reading.

The story of the Celts begins in the prehistoric age, when archaeology and language are our only guides. It is in the early Iron Age, beginning about 800 BC with a culture known as Hallstatt, named from a site in Upper Austria, that we can first discern them fairly clearly. The late Iron Age, called La Tène after a site in Switzerland, is the great age of the Celts on the Continent, and La Tène art is theirs and is their great achievement, as Jacobsthal has so well shown. For the early period we are involved in a terminology and in kinds of evidence that will be unfamiliar to many readers. We hope that even though unfamiliar, they may prove not unwelcome.

The distribution of work has been as follows: Chapters 1, 5, 9, 10, 11 and the Epilogue are by M.D.; 2, 3, 4, 6, 7, 8, 12 are by N.C.

We have not always been in complete agreement, and we have simply given our opinions in matters of doubt. The common opinion now is that Medb and Fergus, Cú Chulainn and Cú Roí Mac Dáire, are not historical persons. N.C. prefers to regard Queen Medb as having reigned as queen at Cruachain. On the other hand, M.D. regards the druids as heirs to an ancient Indo-European priesthood, represented in India by the brahmins, whereas N.C. believes that they were not priests (chap. 7). These are the two chief points of difference between us, and they are matters for argument. However, the book is a collaboration. We have worked together on every chapter, and we are glad to accept joint responsibility. Once we reach Britain and Ireland we are on easier ground, although there is plenty of room for doubt and disagreement.

The attempt to present the Celts in history as one people, with a common tradition and a common character, is new, and in some degree, experimental. It seems to us to have been justified beyond our expectations, inasmuch as there does emerge in the history and institutions and religion, in the art and literature, perhaps even in the language, a quality that is distinctive and is common to the Celts of Gaul, of Britain and of Ireland. We hesitate to give it a name: it makes a contrast with Greek temperance, it is marked by extremes of luxury and asceticism, of exultation and despair, by lack of discipline and of the gift for organising secular affairs, by delight in natural beauty and in tales of mystery and imagination, by an artistic sense that prefers decoration and pattern to mere representation. Matthew Arnold called it natural magic.

In a field where the harvest is rich and the labourers have been so few, we have had to turn for help to other scholars, and it has been most generously given. Professor Binchy helped us with Chapter 5, even to the extent of placing his lecture-notes at our disposal. Chapters 9 and 11 could not have been completed without the constant advice and supervision of Proinsias Mac Cana. Our friends, Ludwig Bieler, Francis J. Byrne, Glyn Daniel, Michael Dolley, David Erlingsson, Christopher Hawkes, Ropary Hemon, Kenneth Jackson, Stuart Piggott, Terence Powell and Joseph Raftery have also been called upon. To these, and to those others who have been consulted on occasion, we wish to express our gratitude.

Our thanks are also due to the University of Chicago Press for permission to print passages from M. Dillon, *Early Irish Literature* (copyright University of Chicago 1947), to the Delegates of the Clarendon Press for permission to print two poems from G. Murphy, *Early Irish Lyrics* (Oxford, 1956) and several poems and extracts from T. Parry, *The Oxford Book of Welsh Verse*, and to the Council of the Royal Irish Academy and the author for permission to print translations from Professor Tierney's *Celtic Ethnography of Posidonius*.

We are most grateful to Miss Máire Bhreatnach for typing and retyping with endless patience, and to Máire, Bean Uí Chinnsealaigh who kindly undertook the tedious work of revising the index.

N. K. C.

M. D.

ILLUSTRATIONS

Between pages 164 and 165

ACKNOWLEDGEMENTS

The authors and publishers would like to thank the following for supplying photographs for use in this volume: Bibliothèque Nationale, Paris, Plates 11, iii and vii; British Museum, Plates 9, 23, 24, 29, 31, 32, 33; Bord Fáilte, Plates 54–6, 99; Cambridge Museum of Archaeology and Ethnology, Plate 27; Cambridge University Collection, Plates 15–17; Commissioners of Public Works in Ireland, Plates 34, 35, 44–6, 49, 53, 57–62, 98, 100, 101, 104; Fr. Foliot, Plates 4–8, 63, 64, 67, 68; Gloucester City Museum, Plate 21; The Green Studio, Dublin, Plates 36, 87–90, 97, 102; J. A. Hedley, Plate 42; Landesmuseum Trier, Plate 1; The Manx Museum, Plate 96; Ministry of Public Buildings and Works, Edinburgh, Plates 91–3, 95, 105; National Museum of Antiquities, Scotland, Plate 25; National Museum of Ireland, Plates 81–6; National Museum of Wales, Plates 22, 28, 30, 94; Walter Rinton, Plate 103; R. Rémy, Dijon, Plates 72–7; Jean Roubier, Plates 2, 3, 38–41, 65, 66, 69–71; H. Taylor, Plates, 47, 48, 50, 51; Walwin, Plate 26; The Warburg Institute, Plate 43.

MAPS

CHAPTER 1

DISCOVERING THE CELTS

AT the end of the sixth century BC the Celts were already known to Greek historians and ethnographers. Hecataeus of Miletus, writing at about that time, says that Narbonne is a Celtic town, and mentions Marseilles as being near Celtic territory. Herodotus, in the fifth century, twice mentions the Celts (the first occurrence of the name Keltoí), only to say that the Danube has its source – which he seems to suppose is in the Pyrenees – amongst the Celts, and that they dwell beyond the Pillars of Hercules and are the most westerly people in Europe except the Cynesians. But there is one written source even earlier than these, although it is preserved only in a later form. The *Ora Maritima* of Avienus (fourth century AD) has been shown to contain a description of the Mediterranean coast from Cadiz to Marseilles written in the early sixth century BC, and here too the Celts are said to dwell in Gaul and in south-western Spain.

We can go further back in time, and it appears that the original home of the Celts was east of the Rhine, in the country that is now Bavaria and Bohemia, and westwards as far as the Rhine itself. The evidence for this opinion is in a comparison of place-names with archaeology. In the Bronze Age, about the end of the fourteenth century BC, there appears in central Europe a culture marked by burial customs and by forms of decoration of weapons, ornaments, tools and pottery, that are hitherto unknown there and are found in association. The burials are in mounds (*tumuli*) of earth heaped over the grave, and some archaeologists identify this culture with the emergence of the Celts. Following on the *tumulus*-culture, there appears a new fashion of burial according to which the body was cremated, the ashes were placed in an urn, and the urns were deposited in cemeteries, known as 'urnfields'.

At the end of the Urnfield period iron tools and weapons appear, so that we speak of the Iron Age, and of this early phase as the Early Iron Age or Hallstatt culture (*c*. 800–450 BC). Hallstatt is a site in Austria where many such objects have been found. The late Iron Age is commonly called La Tène, from a site in Switzerland, and the period begins *c*. 450 BC and ends on the Continent with Caesar's campaigns.

Many archaeologists would identify the emergence of the Celts with the appearance of urnfields in south central Europe, as there seems to be a cultural continuum from the time when they appear, at the close of the Bronze Age, through the Hallstatt period and down to La Tène. But this is too late, in our opinion, for the separation of Celtic as a distinct dialect, and it is better to regard as already Celtic whatever can be dated to the beginning of the second millennium BC.[1]

Over all this area, Austria, Bohemia, southern and western Germany, and France, place-names occur which are compounded with elements such as: *briga* 'hill'; *dunum* 'fortress'; *magus* 'plain'; *nemeton* 'sacred place'; *ritum* 'ford'; *seno-* 'old', *uindo-* 'white'. And these words are familiar as Irish *brí* 'hill' (Welsh *bre*); *dún* 'fort' (*dinas*); *mag* 'plain' (*ma*); *nemed* 'sacred place'; W. *rhyd* 'ford'; *sen* 'old' (W. *hen*); *find* 'white' (W. *gwyn*). The Welsh place-name *Gwynfa* in Montgomeryshire, and Irish *Findmhagh* in County Antrim are exact translations of Gaulish Ὀυινδόμαγος (*Uindo-magos*) in Gallia Narbonensis, mentioned by Ptolemy 2, 10, 6. The name of the Rhine is Celtic, and all its eastern tributaries have Celtic names: Neckar, Main, Lahn, Ruhr and Lippe. The Isar, the Inn and the Tauber are also explained as Celtic.[2] It is a probable conclusion that these names, coinciding in their distribution with the early *tumulus*-culture, were given by the bearers of that culture; and the names are Celtic. The conclusion is supported by the fact that in France and Spain, the same coincidence of Celtic place-names and river-names occurs with the Urnfield culture; for archaeology shows the spread of material cultures westwards and northwards from that Central European area.

The name 'Celtic' has been explained as cognate with Old Norse *hildr* 'war', and this is possible.[3] It has no prior history, as has the name *Graeci*, once proper to a small community in the Peloponnesus, or the name *Rus* 'Russian' which was originally a Finnish name for the Swedes, and perhaps meant 'rower, seafarer'. But Strabo does say that it was formerly the name of the tribe of Narbonensis, and suggests that it may have come into Greek through Marseilles as a name for the whole people.[4] Caesar says that the Galli called themselves *Celtae*. The name came to be used as Strabo uses it, of a people distinguished from the Ligurians and Iberians in the west and from Illyrians and Scythians in the east. The Germans in their northern home were still unknown to the earliest Greek historians.

The Celts were distinguished in various ways, by social organization,

[1] See p. 205.
[2] A. Grenier, *Les Gaulois*, 82; see also H. Kuhn in *Völker zwischen Germanen u. Kelten* 110 f.
[3] See D'Arbois de Jubainville, *Les Celtes*, 171. For other suggestions see *G.P.N.*, 332.
[4] Strabo IV i 14. Cf. Diodorus Siculus V 32: 'It will be useful now to make a distinction which is unknown to most people. Those who live in the interior above Marseilles ... are called Celts, whereas those who are settled above Celtica in the area stretching towards the north ... are called Galatae.'

religion, dress, methods of warfare, for these are matters of which the early historians took account; but the main distinction then, as now, will have been that of language. Tacitus says of one tribe: 'Their Gaulish speech proves that the Cotini were not Germans' (*Germania* 43). Indeed this definition by language is the only useful one, for by reference to it one can speak meaningfully of Celtic archaeology or Celtic religion. But if we do not admit language as the criterion, these terms involve a circular argument. This does not mean that there was no confusion. Tribes speaking a Germanic dialect may have been taken for Celts on account of their dress and customs, or because they were subject to Celtic overlords. The observers of the time were not professional linguists, and could not have known without careful enquiry whether the dialect of a tribe in a border area was Celtic or not.[1]

Besides place-names, the names of Gaulish chiefs and peoples tell us something of the language of the ancient Celts. Many of them can be interpreted through Irish and Welsh: Dumnorix goes into Irish as *rí an domhain* 'king of the world'; Vercingetorix is made up of *uer* 'over', *cinget-* 'warrior' and *rīx* 'king'; Anextlomarus means 'Great Protector' (O.I. *aingid* 'protects'); Eporedorix 'king of horses' would be O.I. *rí echraide*; Bituriges, O.I. *ríg in betho* 'kings of the world'; Allobroges 'people from a foreign country'; Brigantes 'the exalted' (O.I. *Brigit*). Some words are mentioned by ancient writers as being the Gaulish names for things: χόρμα 'beer'; βάρδος 'poet'; δρυίδαι 'druids'; *reda* 'chariot'; μάρκα 'horse'. And the words occur in Irish as *coirm*, *bard*, *drui* 'druid', *riad* 'driving, riding', *marc*, with similar forms in Welsh. A more immediate source is provided by the Gaulish inscriptions that have been discovered in France and Italy. Some of the inscriptions of Cisalpine Gaul are in the Greek or the Etruscan alphabet, but the great majority of the inscriptions are in Roman letters. They are some sixty in number, apart from the graffiti on potsherds found at La Graufesenque, and the contents of the famous Calendar of Coligny (see p. 15). More will be said about language later (pp. 197 f.).

The Celts, then, are a people who appear in history in the sixth century BC. The early writers mention them only casually, as when Xenophon writes of Celts who fought as mercenaries against the Thebans in the Peloponnesus in 369 BC, and Plato includes them in a list of barbarian peoples who are given to drunkenness. Aristotle says: 'It is not bravery to withstand danger through recklessness, as when the Celts take up arms to attack the waves.'[2]

From their home in central Europe, the Celts spread westwards to the

[1] Many tribes east of the Rhine, referred to as Germanic, were Celts according to S. Feist, *Germanen und Kelten* 28 f.; and Celts were called Germans, *ib.* 9 f. See also R. Hachmann *et al.*, *Völker zwischen Germanen und Kelten* 43 f.
[2] *Nicomachean Ethics* iii 7 §7.

Atlantic coast and into Spain, northwards into the British Isles, and later south into Italy and east along the Danube, and as far as Galatia in Asia Minor. The early migrations were accomplished in prehistoric times and can be dated only by archaeological evidence. The evidence is incomplete insofar as swords, brooches and potsherds cannot tell us that the men who made them spoke a Celtic dialect. We cannot hope for more than a probable opinion. It is a fact that Hallstatt or early Iron Age culture spread into Spain; we have written testimony that the Celts were already established in south-western Spain by the sixth century, and there are Celtic place-names widely scattered in Spain, and as far as the mouth of the Tagus (*Arabriga*). It is a reasonable inference that the makers of these Hallstatt weapons and tools were Celts. But the earliest Celtic migrations date from the Bronze Age, for the urnfields, which appear in south Germany and eastern Gaul after the *tumulus*-culture and are recognized as Celtic, are found also in Catalonia and as far south as Valencia. There were later separate migrations of Celts in the Hallstatt period (*c.* 600 BC) and in the second phase of La Tène culture (third century BC); and some inscriptions testify to the presence of a strong Celtic element in the population. The Celtiberi, who resisted the Roman assault for so long, and so bravely, were a mixture of Celts and Iberians as their name implies.

The Celtic settlement of the British Isles is more difficult to trace. It seems now that we must choose between two extremes. About 2000 BC came Bell-Beaker people, whose burials are in single graves, with individual grave-goods. The remarkable Wessex Culture of the Bronze Age which appears about 1500 BC is thought to be based upon this tradition. The grave-goods there suggest the existence of a warrior aristocracy 'with a graded series of obligations of service ... through a military nobility down to the craftsmen and peasants',[1] as in the Homeric society. This is the sort of society which is described in the Irish sagas, and there is no reason why so early a date for the coming of the Celts should be impossible. We shall see that there are considerations of language and culture that tend rather to support it. From the middle of the sixth century BC the Early Iron Age people, builders of the hill-forts so characteristic of the insular Celtic world, begin to appear. From then until the Belgic invasion, to which Caesar refers as having occurred not long before his time, there were successive waves of Celtic immigration into Britain. But the common opinion among archaeologists seems now to be that there was no large-scale immigration into the British Isles between 2000 and 600 BC.

Archaeology has made great strides in recent years, and it is difficult for an outsider to form a personal judgement. It becomes a matter of

[1] Piggott, *Scotland before history*, p. 66.

choosing one's authority. Meanwhile important advances have been made in Celtic philology, and the great archaism of Irish tradition has been firmly established, as will appear from what follows. At present, in our opinion, either view is tenable, and we confess to preferring the early date. With the advance of research into prehistory, or perhaps even by some new discovery in linguistics,[1] a reasoned decision may be possible in the future. For the present we must be content to doubt.

With regard to the Celtic settlement of Ireland in particular, O'Rahilly in his 'Goidels and Their Predecessors', and again in his great book, *Early Irish History and Mythology*, put forward an entirely new theory. He distinguished four successive immigrations: the Cruthin some time before 500 BC; the Érainn (= Fir Bolg) perhaps in the fifth century; the Laigin (with Domnainn and Gálioin) in the third century; the Goídil who came *c.* 100 BC. The notion of a series of invasions is traditional, and is first recorded by Nennius who knew of three, those of Partholón, Nemed, and the Children of Míl.

In the Book of Invasions as we know it from the eleventh century recension there are five (or six): (Cesair), Partholón, Nemed, Fir Bolg, Tuatha Dé Danann, and the Children of Míl. But these legends are mere learned fiction, and have no value as history. Their interest is of another kind. The only bearing they have upon history is in so far as they betray a state of affairs which the literary men were trying to expound. What does appear from various references cited by O'Rahilly is the presence in Ireland of at least three ethnic groups: Cruthin (or Cruithni) who were mainly in the north-east and plainly akin to the Picts of Scotland (also called Cruthin);[2] Érainn, who were mainly in the south-west and in the south-east corner (Déisi); and Goídil (*Cland Míled*) who reigned over Tara, Cashel and Croghan and were the dominant people in the early historic period. Whether the Laigin were a distinct people or merely a Goidelic tribe is not clear to us.

O'Rahilly's most novel suggestion is that his first three groups spoke Brythonic dialects, that is that they were 'P-Celts', and that the Goídil were the only Goidelic speakers, the only 'Q-Celts'.[3] And he seeks to prove this from the evidence of Irish words that are not Goidelic in form and may be Brythonic. His demonstration is not convincing, and the notion that this more archaic language was brought latest, by a migration of the Quariates from south-east Gaul, is inherently improbable. We think it more likely that Goidelic was first established in Ireland, and that Brythonic tribes made settlements there, just as Irish settlements were made in Wales both north and south. In those early centuries, when there was constant intercourse across the Irish Sea, there

---

[1] Lexicostatistics do not provide a short-cut to the answer, see *Language* 39, 638 ff.
[2] *E.I.H.M.* 341 f.; see, however, Jackson in *The Problem of the Picts* 159.
[3] See p. 197.

was every chance of linguistic borrowing. Moreover, an unknown proportion of the Irish vocabulary may be non-Indo-European, an inheritance from pre-Celtic times. The Cruthin and the Érainn, being earlier immigrants than the Goídil, probably spoke Q-dialects. However, it is right to say that no certainty seems attainable in the matter. O'Rahilly's doctrine has been accepted by some scholars[1] and dismissed by others.[2]

Meanwhile the Celts had been spreading into Italy and along the Danube towards the Black Sea. Cisalpine Gaul was settled in the fourth century, and Celtic raiders penetrated as far as Rome in 390. The shrine of Delphi was plundered in 278, and the marauders then wandered through Thrace and Macedonia. The Scordisci founded the city of Singidunum (Belgrade), and other bands even made contact with the Scythians and formed a Celto-Scythian group. Finally an army of some twenty thousand crossed into Asia Minor, Tectosages, Tolistobogii and Trocmi, and founded in eastern Phrygia the three tetrarchies of Galatia. The Tectosages occupied the site of the modern Ankara. And like the Celts of Gaul at their shrine in the territory of the Carnutes,[3] like the Celts of Ireland at Uisnech and at Tailtiu,[4] these Galatians assembled from time to time at a sanctuary called *Drunemeton* 'the sacred oak-grove', faithful in this practice to their ancient tradition.[5]

At that time a territory stretching from Ireland to Galatia was in Celtic hands. 'For two centuries,' says Grenier, 'they (the Celts) were the greatest people in Europe ... About 300 BC the power of the Celts is at its height and seems inexhaustible in energy and in man-power.'[6]

This rapid expansion over an enormous area implies great fecundity and a great spirit of adventure. Moreover, like the Greeks in the Mediterranean, the Celts brought with them their civilization, and they imposed it upon the lands they occupied. And though they were 'barbarians' in the strict sense, theirs was no mean way of life. We have accounts of it from Polybius in the third century BC, from fragments of Posidonius who lived in the first century BC, and from Julius Caesar. Some of what Posidonius tells us is worth quoting at length, because it finds such extraordinary confirmation in later Irish sources.[7]

Polybius tells of the conquest of Cisalpine Gaul with a good deal of detail, and of the later struggle of the Romans with the Celtiberi in Spain, and the defeat of the Galatians in Asia Minor. He describes the weapons of the Celts, their preference for fighting naked, the habit of

---

[1] M. A. O'Brien in *Early Irish Society* 37. [2] Vendryes, *Études Celtiques* i 352 ff.
[3] Caesar, *De Bello Gallico* vi 14. [4] See D. A. Binchy, *Ériu* xviii 114 ff.
[5] Strabo xii, 5, 1. [6] A. Grenier, *Les Gaulois*, pp. 99–100.
[7] See J. J. Tierney, 'The Celtic Ethnography of Posidonius', PRIA LX C 5 (1960), whose translations are quoted.

taking the head of a slain enemy, and he mentions the splendid gold torques and bracelets worn by Celtic warriors. He also says that they attached great importance to clientship as the measure of a man's rank in society.[1]

The best known passage describing the Celts is that in the sixth book of Caesar's *Gallic War*, but Posidonius, who wrote a continuation of the Histories of Polybius, is the main source of information. His works are lost, but Diodorus Siculus and Strabo have preserved a good deal of what he said about the Celts. Here is Strabo's account of the Celts of Gaul:

> The whole race, which is now called Gallic or Galatic, is madly fond of war, high-spirited and quick to battle, but otherwise straightforward and not of evil character. And so when they are stirred up they assemble in their bands for battle, quite openly and without forethought, so that they are easily handled by those who desire to outwit them; for at any time or place and on whatever pretext you stir them up, you will have them ready to face danger, even if they have nothing on their side but their own strength and courage. On the other hand if won over by gentle persuasion they willingly devote their energies to useful pursuits and even take to a literary education. Their strength depends both on their mighty bodies, and on their numbers. And because of this frank and straightforward element in their character they assemble in large numbers on slight provocation, being ever ready to sympathize with the anger of a neighbour who thinks he has been wronged ...
>
> Among all the tribes, generally speaking, there are three classes of men held in special honour: the Bards, the Vates, and the Druids. The Bards are singers and poets; the Vates interpreters of sacrifice and natural philosophers; while the Druids, in addition to the science of nature, study also moral philosophy. They are believed to be the most just of men, and are therefore entrusted with the decision of cases affecting either individuals or the public; indeed in former times they arbitrated in war and brought to a standstill the opponents when about to draw up in line of battle; and murder cases have been mostly entrusted to their decision. When there are many such cases they believe that there will be a fruitful yield from their fields. These men, as well as other authorities, have pronounced that men's souls and the universe are indestructible, although at times fire or water may (temporarily) prevail.
>
> To the frankness and high-spiritedness of their temperament must be added the traits of childish boastfulness and love of decoration. They wear ornaments of gold, torques on their necks, and bracelets on their arms and wrists, while people of high rank wear dyed garments besprinkled with gold. It is this vanity which makes them unbearable in victory and so completely downcast in defeat. In addition to their witlessness they possess a trait of barbarous savagery which is especially peculiar to the northern

[1] For clientship in Irish society see p. 90.

7

peoples, for when they are leaving the battle-field they fasten to the necks of their horses the heads of their enemies, and on arriving home they nail up this spectacle at the entrances to their houses. Posidonius says that he saw this sight in many places, and was at first disgusted by it, but afterwards, becoming used to it, could bear it with equanimity. ...[1]

Diodorus describes the habits of the Celts of Gaul at a feast:

... the nobles shave the cheeks but let the moustache grow freely so that it covers the mouth. And so when they are eating the moustache becomes entangled in the food, and when they are drinking the drink passes, as it were, through a sort of strainer. When dining they all sit not on chairs, but on the earth, strewing beneath them the skins of wolves or dogs. At their meals they are served by their youngest grown-up children, both boys and girls. Beside them are hearths blazing with fire, with cauldrons and spits containing large pieces of meat. Brave warriors they honour with the finest portions of the meat, just as Homer introduces Ajax, honoured by the chieftains, when he conquered Hector in single combat: 'He honoured Ajax with the full-length chine'.[2]

Athenaeus, who names Posidonius as his authority, confirms the statement about the Hero's Portion:

'In former times', he says, 'when the hindquarters were served, the bravest hero took the thigh-piece, and if another man claimed it, they stood up and fought in single combat to the death.'[3]

This practice is vividly recorded in the Old Irish saga of Mac Da Thó's Pig (inf. p. 238), and it is the principal theme also of 'Bricriu's Feast'.

Another passage is of special interest from this point of view. It is the account by Diodorus of the Gauls in battle:

For their journeys and in battle they use two-horse chariots, the chariot carrying both charioteer and chieftain. When they meet with cavalry in the battle they cast their javelins at the enemy and then descending from the chariot join battle with their swords. Some of them so far despise death that they descend to do battle, unclothed except for a girdle. They bring into battle as their attendants freemen chosen from among the poorer classes, whom they use as charioteers and shield-bearers in battle. When the armies are drawn up in battle-array they are wont to advance before the battle-line and to challenge the bravest of their opponents to single combat, at the same time brandishing before them their arms so as to terrify their foe. And when some one accepts their challenge to battle, they loudly recite the deeds of valour of their ancestors and proclaim their own valorous quality, at the same time abusing and making little of their opponent and generally attempting to rob him beforehand of his fighting spirit. They cut off the

[1] Strabo IV iv 2, 4; J. J. Tierney, op. cit., pp. 267, 269.
[2] Diodorus V 28 (Tierney, op. cit., 249–50).   [3] Athenaeus IV 40 (Tierney, ib. 249).

heads of enemies slain in battle and attach them to the necks of their horses. The blood-stained spoils they hand over to their attendants and carry off as booty, while striking up a paean and singing a song of victory, and they nail up these first fruits upon their houses just as do those who lay low wild animals in certain kinds of hunting.[1]

Here again the Irish sources match closely the description of the Celts of Gaul. The warriors of the Ulster sagas go into battle in chariots, and the challenge to single combat is the central theme in the great prose epic *Táin Bó Cualnge*. Cú Chulainn, with Loeg his charioteer, in his two-horse chariot, armed with shield and spear and sword, is a Celtic warrior just such as Posidonius describes.

And here is a description of the Gauls by Diodorus, also based, it seems, on Posidonius:

Physically the Gauls are terrifying in appearance, with deep-sounding and very harsh voices. In conversation they use few words and speak in riddles, for the most part hinting at things and leaving a great deal to be understood. They frequently exaggerate with the aim of extolling themselves and diminishing the status of others. They are boasters and threateners and given to bombastic self-dramatization, and yet they are quick of mind and with good natural ability for learning. They have also lyric poets whom they call Bards. They sing to the accompaniment of instruments resembling lyres, sometimes a eulogy and sometimes a satire. They have also certain philosophers and theologians who are treated with special honour, whom they call Druids. They further make use of seers, thinking them worthy of high praise. These latter by their augural observances and by the sacrifice of sacrificial animals can foretell the future and they hold all the people subject to them. In particular when enquiring into matters of great import they have a strange and incredible custom; they devote to death a human being and stab him with a dagger in the region above the diaphragm, and when he has fallen they foretell the future from his fall, and from the convulsions of his limbs and, moreover, from the spurting of the blood, placing their trust in some ancient and long-continued observation of these practices. Their custom is that no one should offer sacrifice without a philosopher; for they say that thanks should be offered to the gods by those skilled in the divine nature, as though they were people who can speak their language, and through them also they hold that benefits should be asked. And it is not only in the needs of peace but in war also that they carefully obey these men and their song-loving poets, and this is true not only of their friends but also of their enemies. For oftentimes as armies approach each other in line of battle with their swords drawn and their spears raised for the charge these men come forth between them and stop the conflict, as though they had spell-bound some kind of wild animals. Thus even among the most savage barbarians anger yields to wisdom and Ares does homage to the Muses.[2]

[1] Diodorus V 29 (Tierney, *ib.* 250).   [2] Diodorus V 31 (Tierney, *ib.* 251).

9

The testimony of Julius Caesar, which is widely familiar, is the most valuable in some respects. He presents Gaulish society as divided into three classes, *druides*, *equites* and *plebs*, the three functions (priest, warrior and husbandman) of which Dumézil has made so much. And of the *equites* he says that the nobler and wealthier have numerous clients about them.

Caesar tells more about the druids than do the others, their twenty years of study, their oral tradition, and so on. And he says of the Gauls: *Natio est omnis Gallorum admodum dedita religionibus* 'The whole Gaulish people is much given to religion'. We are told that the druids taught the doctrine of transmigration of souls, that they were concerned with the worship of the gods, and that young men flocked to them for training.

> It is said that they commit to memory immense amounts of poetry, and so some of them continue their studies for twenty years. They consider it improper to commit their studies to writing, although they use the Greek alphabet for almost everything else.... They have also much knowledge of the stars and their motion, of the size of the world and of the earth, of natural philosophy, and of the powers and spheres of action of the immortal gods, which they discuss and hand down to their young students.[1]

This class of professional learned men, priests and scholars, seems to share a common Indo-European inheritance with the brahmins of India, for the later and fuller evidence of Irish sources shows a similar class, the *filid*, who, while shorn of their priestly office in a Christian society, have retained the scholarly functions of the druids as poets, genealogists, lawyers, and the practice of oral rather than written tradition. Both the form and content of their learning show astonishing similarity to brahminical tradition.

The archaism of this tradition can best be shown from the Irish evidence which is presented later (chap. 10), but two matters deserve mention here as requiring the assumption of a learned tradition inherited by the druids of Gaul and transmitted by them to the *filid* of Ireland.

The metres of the *Rigveda*, the earliest known forms of Indo-European verse, are based upon a line with a fixed number of syllables, of which the first half was free and the cadence was fixed in the form $\cup - \cup \cup$.[2] It was shown long ago by Meillet that the Greek metres have the same origin, and more recently Roman Jakobson has traced it in modern Slavonic verse. Calvert Watkins has now demonstrated, we think convincingly, that the Old Irish heptasyllabic line derives from this Indo-European form, and that other Irish metres are variants of it, thus confirming the antiquity of Celtic tradition, and the common heritage of the druid and the brahmin.[3]

[1] *De Bello Gallico* vi 14 (Tierney, *ib.* 202).
[2] With variants $- \cup - \cup$ and $\cup \cup - \cup$.
[3] 'Indo-European Metrics and Archaic Irish Verse', *Celtica* VI 194. We assume here that the Irish *fili* was heir to the poet's share of druidic learning.

The second matter of importance is that of legal tradition. The earliest passages in the Old Irish law-tracts date from the seventh, perhaps even from the sixth century. They are in verse, commonly a seven-syllable line ending in a dactyl (fixed cadence), showing their oral tradition; and their content belongs to a system of customary law for which close parallels can be found in the *Mānavadharmaśāstra*, the Hindu Laws of Manu.[1]

Binchy has drawn attention to the resemblances in certain points between the Irish and Indian law-books. In both countries the law consists of canonical texts, invested with a sacred origin, and interpreted exclusively by a privileged caste. There were law-schools in each case, with varying traditions of interpretation. The relations between pupil and teacher (Irish *felmac* and *fithithir*; Sanscrit *śiṣya* and *guru*) were similar, with eventual right of succession. The Hindu *sapiṇḍa*, a family group of four generations, descendants of a common great-grandfather, seems to have the same significance and functions as the Irish *derbfine* and the Welsh *gwely*.[2] The basic family unit was the same in both systems.

The law concerning the 'appointed daughter' is a feature of both Greek and Indian legal systems. In Greece the ἐπίκληρος was appointed by her father, if he had no sons, to bear him grandsons by a chosen husband, usually her nearest agnatic relative. These grandsons became his legal heirs, and succeeded to his estate. In India the appointed daughter is called *putrikā* 'the son-like one' (*putra* 'son'), and the parallel with the Irish system is even closer, for the custom of appointing a daughter lapsed, and if there were no sons a daughter was allowed to inherit. Later she inherited only for life, and the estate reverted on her death to her paternal kin.

This is the position of the Irish *ban-chomarba* 'female heir', but there appears to have been an earlier custom by which she married a kinsman and raised up heirs to her father. In India and in Ireland the development of the law was the same, presumably a coincidence, but the original status of *putrikā* and *banchomarba* is clearly a common Indo-European tradition.[3]

Even more impressive are the laws concerning marriage in Ireland and in India. In India there were eight forms of marriage, brāhma, daiva, ārṣa, prājāpatya, āsura, gāndharva, rākṣasa and paiśāca. In the first four the daughter is given by her father without purchase by the bridegroom. The fifth is marriage by purchase, the sixth is a voluntary union of maiden and lover, the seventh is forcible abduction (proper for

---

[1] See Thurneysen and others, *Studies in Early Irish Law* vi, 183, 223; D. A. Binchy, 'The Linguistic and Historical Value of the Irish Law Tracts', 23, 27, 30 (*Proc. Brit. Acad.* XXIX 1943)).

[2] See *W.P.*, 196, 222, 397.

[3] R. Thurneysen and others, *Studies in Early Irish Law* 183 f.

a warrior), the eighth is mere seduction by stealth, and is called a base and sinful rite (Manu III 20–34). In Ireland likewise there were various forms of marriage. Ten classes are recognized in the law-tract on marriage, of which only nine are explained. The first three are regular marriages, differing in the proportions of wealth brought by each party, equal proportions, wealth brought in by the man, wealth brought in by the woman. The others are temporary unions, and two of these agree exactly with two of the Indian forms, marriage by force (*lánamnas écne*) and seduction by stealth (*lánamnas tothla*). Indeed a third, 'union accepted on the man's invitation', may be equated with the *gāndharva*-marriage of the Hindus, the voluntary union of maiden and lover.

We can even claim agreement in the number of forms of marriage, for Binchy has suggested that two of the Irish 'unions' are a later development.[1]

In both systems succession to family property was in 'ideal' shares, without actual division of the property among the heirs; and in both there was a distinction, with important legal consequences, between inherited and self-acquired property.

In both systems there were various forms of suretyship, which were important for the enforcing of private obligations.

Of special interest is the custom of fasting by a plaintiff against a defendant, which is discussed later. It is recognized in both systems as a legal means of enforcing a claim.[2]

The Indo-European origin of Irish metres, and the striking similarities between the Hindu and Irish systems of law, which also point to Indo-European origin, go a long way towards proving that the Irish *filid*, and therefore the Celtic druids, were heirs to the same tradition as the brahmins.

Vendryes showed long ago that a group of words associated with religion and kingship has survived in Indo-Iranian on the one hand and in Italic and Celtic on the other, and he attributed their survival to the priestly caste represented in India by the brahmins and in Gaul by the druids.[3] We may now go further and say that druid and brahmin were heirs to a common tradition of learning and culture.

Irish society was based on the family-group of four generations (p. 92), and this may be assumed for the Celts. The wider unit was the tribe. In Caesar's time there were about fifty tribes in Gaul, of which only a few still recognized the institution of kingship. Most of them had adopted an oligarchical form of government. It is, therefore from Irish sources that we learn most about Celtic kingship.[4]

---

[1] *Studies in Early Irish Law*, p. vi.
[2] See p. 94. I am heavily indebted to Dr Binchy for advice about these similarities between Hindu and Irish law.
[3] MSL xx 275 (1920).   [4] p. 87.

About the religion of the Celts much has been written, but the picture remains obscure. Caesar tells us that the Gauls worshipped Mercury, Apollo, Mars, Jupiter and Minerva. But he is simply equating Gaulish deities with his own Roman gods. He does not give us a single Gaulish name. Other historians do give us names, and many names occur in dedications all over the vast area once dominated by the Celts, from Galatia in Asia Minor to Spain and Britain. We have more than 400 names in all, and more than 300 of them occur only once. Perhaps these are names of local deities, each tribe or group of tribes having a special cult.

One important name is that of *Lug*, Welsh *Lleu*. It occurs in dedications at Avenches in Switzerland and at Asma (Tarragona) in Spain as a plural, *Lugoues, Lugouibus*,[1] and once in the dative singular, *Luguei*, in the inscription of Peñalba de Villester.[2] It is common in the place-name Lugudunum, which is the name of Lyons, Loudon and Laon in France, of Leiden in Holland and Liegnitz in Silesia. *Lugus* must have been a great Celtic god, but we do not know what his special character was. In Ireland he was the god of *Lugnasad*, 1 August, which was evidently a harvest festival, and Lug may have been the god of fertility. At Lyons the feast of Augustus was celebrated on that day, apparently in substitution for the ancient feast of Lug. Máire MacNeill has shown that his feast was celebrated all over Ireland into our own times.[3] Lug's other name was Find, 'the Fairhaired One', and he survives on the Continent as *Vindonnus*, and in a few place-names: *Uindobona* (Vienna), *Vindonissa*, etc.[4]

The poet Lucan[5] says that Esus, Taranis and Teutates were the gods of the Celts, and two of these names are echoed in Welsh *taran* (Irish *torann*) 'thunder', and *tud* (Irish *tuath*) 'tribe'. The faintness of the echo suggests a long interval in time between the first Celtic settlement of the British Isles and the date of our Gaulish evidence. Esus may mean 'good' (Gr. εὐ-), cf. Vedic *ásura*, a name for Vedic gods. Ogmios, the god of eloquence, described by Lucian (p. 134), and Irish Ogma, who figures in the Battle of Moytura, are close in form, if not in function, although Thurneysen opposed the identification.[6]

The cult of the Mothers was certainly Celtic, i.e. Mother Earth as a source of fertility, worshipped in triple form under the title *matres* or *matronae*. The dedications that survive on monuments in Gaul are in Latin, and the figures are sometimes represented with baskets of fruit or

---

[1] RC vi 488 (Bromwich, *Trioedd* p. 177); Holder, *Altkeltischer Sprachschatz* 345; *CIL* II 2812; XIII 5078.
[2] A. Tovar, *The Ancient languages of Spain and Portugal* (N.Y. 1961), 86 and n. 45.
[3] *The Festival of Lughnasa*. O.U.P. 1962; see also M. Tierney, 'Lugh and Dionysus', *Éigse* x 265.
[4] *DF* III lxxxii.   [5] *Pharsalia* I 444–6.   [6] Beitr. zur Gesch. d. d. Spr. 61, 196.

horns of plenty, or with children in their laps. There is a Welsh place-name, *Moel Famau*, which preserves the tradition.

One of the gods most often represented is a three-headed god, of whom there are as many as thirty-two effigies. (In Ireland the Three Gods of Craftsmanship (*Trí Dé Dána*) are Goibniu, Luchta and Credne.[1] There are three Brigits[2] and three Finds.)[3] Sometimes the god has a female companion. Sucellos (the god with the hammer) and Nanto-suelta appear together on monuments, Luxovius and Brixia, Bormo and Damona. Madame Jonval, in her *Dieux et Héros des Celtes* suggests that the gods are national and protectors of the people, the goddesses local, rural spirits of fertility or of war. The marriage of the chieftain-god with the mother-goddess assured the people of protection and fertility.

Here again we are reminded of Hinduism, in which the god has a female companion, his *śakti* or source of power. Thus Indra has a spouse Sacī, Śiva has Umā, Viṣṇu has Śrī-Lakṣmī. Brahmā, Viṣṇu and Śiva form a trinity as Creator, Restorer and Destroyer, the Trimūrti ('in triple form'). The three-headed god is, however, found in many cultures.[4]

Another feature of Celtic religion that emerges clearly is that wells, rivers and sacred trees were objects of devotion and had patron gods or goddesses. Some rivers were themselves divine. There was a sanctuary of the Dea Sequana at the source of the river Seine, and one of the Dea Matrona near to the source of the Marne. In Ireland Bóinn (the Boyne) and Sinainn (the Shannon) were goddesses. Then there were animal gods: the bull, Taruos Trigaranus, who appears on the famous Paris monument in the Cluny museum [Plate 14]; the boar, Moccos; the goddess Epona, whose name suggests the cult of the horse; and the goddess Artio, perhaps a bear.[5] The horned god Cernunnos appears on the Gundestrup Cauldron with a stag [Plate 4], and the goddess Damona suggests a cult of the cow.

The priests who maintained the cult of these gods were the druids, and Caesar tells us a good deal about them. They conducted the private and public sacrifices. They taught that the soul was immortal and passed after death into another body, rather as the Hindus believed. They also thought that all men were descended from Dis, the god of the Underworld, and they were learned in astronomy and natural philosophy (*sup.* p. 10).[6]

[1] *EIHM* 316. Several effigies of the Three-Headed God have been found in Ireland. There are two in the National Museum in Dublin.

[2] *Sanas Cormaic* 150.

[3] *DF* III lxxviii n. 5. Cf. J. Vendryes, 'L'unité en trois personnes chez les Celtes', C.R. de l'Acad. des Inscr. 1935, pp. 324–41.

[4] See W. Kirfel, *Die dreiköpfige Gottheit*. 1948. But he is specially prominent in Gaul. Pettazzoni regards the Gaulish Tricephalus as a god of the sun, *The All-knowing God* 196 f.

[5] RC xxi 288. [6] *De Bello Gallico* vi 13, 16, 18.

After a victory, the captured animals were sacrificed to the god of war. Sometimes human victims were sacrificed, and Caesar says that criminals were preferred as being more pleasing to the gods, but that, failing them, others were chosen. This savage custom is mentioned by Lucan in a well-known passage where the gods Esus, Taranis and Teutates are said to be appeased by human sacrifice.[1] At a private ceremony or at the regular feasts of the year, there was probably a sacrificial offering, but we know little about Gaulish feasts or ritual, as the Gauls themselves have left no written records of them.

There is indeed one precious document that may be attributed to druidic learning, namely the Calendar of Coligny; for the order of the Calendar with its auspicious and inauspicious days was probably one of their duties. The Coligny Calendar is the longest single document in Gaulish so far discovered, and contains about sixty different words, some of which occur many times. It was found in 1897 in a vineyard at Coligny (Ain), and the discovery made an epoch in the study of Gaulish and of the culture of the Celts. It dates probably from the first century AD.

Many fragments of a bronze tablet were unearthed, and they proved to be a table of sixty-two consecutive months, approximately equal to five solar years. The months are of thirty or twenty-nine days, and are divided into two halves (15 + 15 or 15 + 14). The months of thirty days (except EQUOS) are marked as auspicious (MAT.) and those of twenty-nine days as inauspicious (ANM.). But certain days in an auspicious month are not lucky and certain days in an inauspicious month are lucky. The second half of the month has the heading ATENOUX ('returning night'?), so that the division was apparently into a bright half and a dark half; and MacNeill has shown that the seventh, eighth and ninth days of the month were days of the full moon.[2] The lunar year of twelve months was adapted to the solar year by intercalation of an extra month of thirty days in every third year. This year had thus thirteen months, twelve named months and one extra month of thirty days, each day of which was named from one of the twelve in serial order. The extra month had, as it were, no days of its own, and was intercalated so as to bring the lunar and solar cycles into approximate accord.

There was a carefully ordered system of transference, by which the notations proper to days in a given month were transferred to the corresponding dates of the preceding month, or interchanged between two consecutive months presumably for ritual purposes.[3] The details need not concern us, but the Calendar of Coligny is evidence of a considerable degree of competence in astronomy, and may reflect the

---

[1] Lucan, *Pharsalia* i 444.   [2] *Ériu* x 14.   [3] *ibid.* 7 ff.

learning of the druids. Moreover in the division of the month into a bright and a dark half, in the month of twenty-nine or thirty days with a three-year cycle, at the end of which an intercalary month was added, this Gaulish calendar resembles that of the Hindus.[1]

Learning seems then to have flourished in Gaul, though we know little directly of it.[2] Of Gaulish art we know more from the work in stone and metal that has survived. The art-form that is properly Celtic, as it seems to have been evolved by the Celts, is that of the late Iron Age, known as La Tène. Overshadowed by the prestige of Greek and Roman art and architecture, it has only gradually been recognized as a precious contribution to the culture of the West. In contrast to the realism and natural beauty of classical art, this Celtic art is imaginative, even wild, delighting in symbol and pattern, rather than in direct representation. And its affinity is with Scythian and Near Eastern forms, rather than with the Mediterranean. It derives in part, too, from abstract decorative motifs of the Bronze Age, even of palaeolithic time.[3]

> To the Greeks a spiral is a spiral and a face a face, and it is always clear where the one ends and the other begins, whereas the Celts 'see' the faces 'into' the spirals or tendrils: ambiguity is a characteristic of Celtic art ... It is the mechanism of dreams, where things have floating contours and pass into other things.[4]

A fine example of this delight in pattern is the sculptured pillar from Sankt Goar [Plate 63], on which the human head is merely one feature in the whole field of spirals and lozenges and ropes. Another is the little bronze terret from a chariot, where the head becomes actually part of the spiral motif (Jacobsthal, *Imagery*, pl. 66). It is, indeed, in metal-work that Celtic craftsmanship is seen at its best, and the famous Gundestrup Cauldron shows pattern and imagery combined. It is not, indeed, typically La Tène, and shows archaic Greek and Oriental influence, but it is generally accepted as the work of a Celtic craftsman [Plate 4]. A box-lid from Auvers-sur-Oise (Powell, *Prehistoric Art*, pl. 181) and the gilt helmet from Amfreville [Plate 8] are good examples of pure decoration. The British collar and torque [Plates 25, 32] illustrate the

---

[1] Zimmer, *Altindisches Leben* 364–71. Beside a five-year cycle, and other schemes, a three-year cycle (*idavatsara, samvatsara, parivatsara*) is mentioned, p. 370.
The most recent study of the Coligny Calendar is by Paul-Marie Duval, ÉC x and xi.
[2] Camille Jullian claims more than this: 'Toutes les formes de la littérature étaient représentées chez les Gaulois: la rhétorique, où excellaient tous leurs chefs de guerre; les épopées cosmogoniques, historiques ou éthiques, composées par les druides; les poésies lyriques ou les chants satiriques des bardes. Je vous assure qu'il y avait chez eux l'équivalent de l'*Iliade* ou de la *Genèse*, des *Atellanes* ou des odes de Pindare. Je vous assure que cette littérature était aussi riche, plus riche même, que celle de Rome avant Ennius. La langue gauloise rendait beaucoup à ceux qui s'en servaient.' (G. Dottin, *La Langue Gauloise* pp. ix–x.)
[3] See chap. 12.
[4] Jacobsthal, 'Imagery in Early Celtic Art', p. 10. Later he says: 'They did not decide for Greek humanity, for gay and friendly imagery: instead they chose the weird magic symbols of the east' (*ibid.* p. 19).

love of ornament that Polybius and Posidonius attribute to the Gauls.[1]

In their coinage, too, the Celts of Gaul, while they owed much to Greek and Roman models, showed their imaginative gift and originality. The coin of Vercingetorix [Plate 11, vii] is interesting chiefly for the name, but those of the charioteer and the galloping horses [i, v, and vi] and the two others that we have chosen, in which the heads melt into the ornament, are purely Celtic in temperament.

The Celts impressed the ancient historians as being impetuous and fearless in battle, easily roused and with a high sense of honour, arrogant in victory and desperate to the point of suicide in defeat, delighting in ornament, in feasting, in the recitation of poetry, *admodum dedita religionibus* 'much given to religion'. Aristotle, in the Nicomachean Ethics says: 'We have no word for the man who is excessively fearless; perhaps one may call such a man mad or bereft of feeling, who fears nothing, neither earthquakes nor waves, as they say of the Celts' (iii 7.7.). And Strabo quotes Ptolemy for the story that Celtic settlers on the Adriatic, when asked by Alexander the Great what they feared most, answered that it was lest the sky should fall. Cato the Elder says of the Celts of Cisalpine Gaul: *Pleraque Gallia duas res industriosissime persequitur, rem militarem et argute loqui* 'they have two great passions, to be brave in warfare and to speak well'.

The picture that we get is of a people brave and gay, physically powerful, and amazingly successful in the early period. From Galatia in Asia Minor northwest to Scotland, and south again to Andalusia, one could travel in the third century BC without leaving Celtic territory. And although there was no empire, it was one culture.

Jacobsthal says that Celtic art, in all its variety and even though spread over so wide a territory, is one culture.[2] And he adds:

> We are told that the Gauls were valiant, quarrelsome, cruel, superstitious and eloquent: their art also is full of contrasts. It is attractive and repellent; it is far from primitiveness and simplicity; it is refined in thought and technique, elaborate and clever, full of paradoxes, restless, puzzlingly ambiguous; rational and irrational; dark and uncanny – far from the lovable humanity and transparence of Greek art. Yet, it is a real style, the first great contribution by the barbarians to European art, the first great chapter in the everlasting contacts of southern, northern and eastern forces in the life of Europe.

Such were the ancestors of the peoples who emerge into history in the first centuries of the Christian era as Britanni and Hiberni, the Britons and the Irish.

---

[1] Strabo IV iv 5, see Tierney *op. cit.* 269; Diodorus Siculus V 27, see Tierney *ib.* 249.
[2] *E.C.A.,* i 160.

CHAPTER 2

THE HISTORY AND GEOGRAPHY OF THE BRITISH ISLES TO THE END OF THE ROMAN PERIOD

No written record of the occupation of the British Isles by Celtic tribes has come down to us, but we can form some idea of the period and distribution from their languages, from archaeology, and from the writings of Greek and Roman authors. The linguistic evidence has been briefly noted in Chapter 1. We have seen that in pre-historic times the Celtic-speaking peoples had entered the British Isles from somewhere in Central Europe, apparently in successive waves, at an uncertain period, but perhaps as early as the beginning of the second millennium BC. The oldest branch of these languages, referred to by modern scholars as Goidelic (or Q-Celtic), survives today in the Highlands and the Western Islands (Hebrides) of Scotland, and in Ireland and the Isle of Man; the later branch, commonly called Brythonic, to which Gaulish originally belonged, survives in Wales and Brittany. Brythonic was formerly spoken throughout south-eastern Britain also, and survives, widespread over our maps, in the names of mountains, rivers, and natural features such as forests. The survival of Brythonic in Brittany is explained as due to the colonization of Brittany from western Britain in the fifth and sixth centuries, to which we shall return later.

The oldest name under which Classical writers commonly refer to the British Isles is 'The Pretanic Islands'. They are thus referred to by Pytheas in the late fourth century BC, and by later writers – Polybius, Strabo, Avienus. The form implies for the name of the inhabitants *Pritani* or *Priteni*. The name is probably Celtic and of the Brythonic form – P-Celtic – probably Gaulish; the Gauls may have handed this name on to the Greeks. The older form continued in use in Welsh texts referring to the island as a whole, *Prydain*, 'Britain' from *Pritani*; and a variant from *Priteni* is used in the form *Prydyn* in early Welsh texts referring to the people north of the Antonine Wall, the 'Picts'.[1] In the Roman period the people of the Roman province called themselves *Brittones*, perhaps a corruption of *Pritani*.

The peoples who brought the Celtic languages into the British Isles first come before us as living inhabitants in the pages and atlas of

---

[1] K. Jackson, 'The Pictish Language' in *P.P.*, 134 f.; 159. Cf. also H. M. Chadwick, *E.S.*, 66 f.

Ptolemy,[1] a Greek geographer of Alexandria who flourished about the middle of the second century AD, and whose geography, including his account of Ireland, is based on the lost work of Marinus of Tyre,[2] who lived earlier in the same century, but O'Rahilly has suggested that the information which Ptolemy gives about Ireland is believed to be derived ultimately from the work of Pytheas, whose voyage took place *c.* 325 BC.[3] The information of Marinus is probably that of the first century AD and perhaps earlier; but various strata of information can be detected, including some later details. It may be added here that in addition to Ptolemy we have a valuable source for the geography of Celtic Britain in an anonymous work of the sixth century AD known as the *Ravenna Cosmography*,[4] which makes use of sources of Ptolemy's time, and of various other periods.

From the nature of Ptolemy's record we gather that, as in pre-Roman Gaul, the Celtic peoples in the British Isles were divided into a number of separate groups, of whom the fifth century geographer Marcian states that Ptolemy enumerates thirty-three in Britain,[5] seventeen of whom belong to southern Britain. Scotland[6] therefore probably had about sixteen.[7] Ptolemy gives the names of nine 'cities' (tribes or states) with their relative positions on the Irish coast,[8] but the latter are of uncertain authenticity, and are presumably derived from sailors' records. He names none away from the coast, and all the names which have been identified belong to the east and south coasts, while for the west coast too little information is given to supply us with even an impression of its occupants. The northern and west coast of Ireland is one of the stormiest in the world, and it was probably avoided as far as possible by sailors. The cities which Ptolemy names were probably places of assembly or royal raths – *oppida*, like Tara and Emain Macha, and two are referred to as *regia*.[9] None can be identified with any certainty, and other names suggest close relationship with corresponding tribal names in Britain. The Brigantes[10] in South Wexford can hardly be dissociated from the Brigantes who occupied most of north Britain in the Roman period. In general, the names in Ptolemy's account leave no doubt that Ireland was already Celtic-speaking when they were

[1] The latest edition for the section relating to the British Isles is that contained in C. Müller's edition of *Claudii Ptolemaei Geographia* (Paris, 1883) Vol. I, Lib. II, caps. ii Hibernia: iii Albion. References throughout are to this edition.
[2] For an account of the ancient geographers who have left records of the British Isles, see especially E. H. Bunbury, *History of Ancient Geography* (2nd ed. London, 1959) I, 591.
[3] E.I.H.M., 41.   [4] The British section has been published by I. A. Richmond and O. G. S. Crawford in *Archaeologia* XCIII (1949) 1–50, and separately by the Society of Antiquaries of London (Oxford, 1949).
[5] These are enumerated by Ptolemy *ed. cit.* in Cap II, p. 74 ff.
[6] A valuable study of Ptolemy's sources and methods with particular references to Scotland is given by I. A. Richmond in *R.N.N.B.*, 133 ff.
[7] See W. J. Watson, *C.P.S.*, 15.   [8] Ptolemy (*ed. cit.*), p. 74 ff.   [9] II, ii. 9.
[10] II, ii. 6; Cf. O'Rahilly, *E.I.H.M.* pp. 33, 34.

recorded. Very few of Ptolemy's tribal or 'city' names can be identified with names in Irish literary tradition, and therefore his Ireland is earlier than that of the Heroic Age (cf. p. 34 below). His Irish names have been derived directly or indirectly from some geographer considerably before Ptolemy's time, and Pytheas is the only competent candidate.

We have no records of any languages earlier than Pictish in these islands. All our evidence – linguistic, archaeological and historical – suggests that in pre- and proto-historic times the Picts were a great nation occupying the northern part of Scotland from the Firth of Forth to the Shetlands, whom Bede knew in the eighth century AD as the Northern and Southern Picts. Their proper names have been preserved on about two dozen stone inscriptions evenly distributed between the Northern Isles and the Tay, almost all written in a late form of the early Celtic alphabet known as *ogam* (cf. p. 198 below). Apart from the proper names the inscriptions have never been interpreted. The evidence of the proper names, and the few Pictish words which have survived, suggest that the Pictish language was nearer to Brythonic than to Goidelic, and nearer to Gaulish than to Welsh. This Pictish language may have been spoken as late as the ninth century, till the end of the Pictish hegemony (cf. p. 107 below).

It may be conjectured that in the British Isles, as in Gaul, some of the earlier Celtic kingdoms were large at first, and separated into detached groups either before or after establishing themselves here. This would explain the curiously wide distribution of some early names. Thus we find the Cornovii recorded by Ptolemy in the extreme north of Scotland, in the area of modern Sutherland or Caithness,[1] and the Cornovii on the north Welsh border with its *oppida* recorded by Ptolemy[2] as *Deva* (Chester) and *Viroconium* (Wroxeter). The first element *Corn-* appears in other places in western Britain, including of course Cornwall, as well as Cornouaille in Brittany. Another ancient name of wide distribution is that of the Dumnonii located by Ptolemy in the west of Scotland south of the Forth-Clyde line, but reaching into Stirlingshire.[3] He also assigns the whole of the south-western peninsula of England, however, including the modern Cornwall, Devon, and much of Somerset, to the Dumnonii.[4] In Ireland a people in the ancient kingdom of Connacht and part of Leinster were known as the *Fir* (Men) *Domnann*, evidently another group of Dumnonii.[5] Ptolemy marks three other tribes in southern Scotland, the Novantae[6] in Galloway, south of the Dumnonii; the Otadinoi[7] in Haddington and Berwickshire and south into Northumberland; and

[1] II. iii. 11; cf. W. J. Watson, *C.P.S.*, 16.   [2] II. iii. 19.
[3] II. iii. 9, where the name is spelt Δαμνόνιοι; cf. Watson, *C.P.S.*, p. 15.
[4] II. iii. 30, Δουμνόνιοι   [5] Watson, *C.P.S.*, p. 24.
[6] Ptolemy, II. iii. 7.   [7] II. iii. 10.

the Selgovae[1] between the two in the hill country forming the watershed between the Clyde and the Tweed.

Our knowledge of the tribal divisions in Wales before the Norman Conquest is incomplete. The principal tribes located by Ptolemy lie along the sea-coast, and no doubt include the mountain zones in the background which receive no separate names. From Ptolemy and other writers we learn that the south-east down to the Bristol Channel was occupied by the Silures.[2] Their tribal centre was evidently at Caerwent (*Venta Silurium*). Ptolemy refers to the Demetae[3] (later *Dyfed*) as in the extreme west. For north-western Wales our knowledge is not very precise. The whole of north Wales may lie within the territory of the Ordovices,[4] and Ptolemy's information for Anglesey[5] and Snowdonia is probably defective. To the north-east were the Decangi of Flintshire, referred to by Tacitus as dwelling not far from 'the sea which looks towards Ireland'.[6]

Apart from Ptolemy's map our principal guide to the settlement of the Celtic tribes in Britain in the Iron Age is the archaeological evidence of the Celtic fortifications and the course of the Roman Conquest, which we can follow from the contemporary records left by the Romans themselves. The fortifications have been classified in two main categories: first the great hill-top fortifications of Celtic Iron Age A; and second the Belgic-type fortresses of later pattern but sometimes in contemporary use with the first type. Of these the first, and in general the earliest in Britain, are the great *oppida*, or tribal 'hill-top cities', heavily and permanently defended, but believed to have been originally intended, not for permanent occupation, but to serve as a nucleus for the protection and concentration of the scattered surrounding population in time of national danger. In Brittany a type-example is the great Camp d'Artus at Huelgoat in Finistère, which would seem to have been formed as the rallying-point of the Osismi in the campaign of Caesar's invasion of 56 BC.[7] Such great *oppida* were undoubtedly the tribal centres of the 'city states'. Among the most impressive that have been fully investigated in Britain are the Stanwick fortifications,[8] undoubtedly the *oppidum* of the Brigantes[9] in the North; and the great hill-top city of Maiden Castle near Dorchester.

Briefly stated, the Celtic tribes of southern Britain during the Roman period consisted of old-established kingdoms found in strength chiefly inland. Of these the Cornovii[10] have already been mentioned. They

[1] II. iii. 8.   [2] II. iii. 24.   [3] II. iii. 23. Cf. further Pliny, *Nat. Hist.* IV, 102.
[4] Ptolemy, II. iii. 18.   [5] Cf. Tacitus, *Agricola*, cap. 18.
[6] *Annals*, XII, 32.   [7] Wheeler and Richardson, *Hill-forts* 23 f.
[8] Excavated by Sir Mortimer Wheeler in 1951–2. See his account in *Stanwick*.
[9] Ptolemy II. iii. 10.
[10] The most recent study of the *Cornovii* is that of Sir Ian A. Richmond, in Foster and Alcock, *C.E.*, 251 ff.

occupied[1] roughly speaking Cheshire and Shropshire. Their tribal capital in Roman times was *Viroconium Cornoviorum*, now known as Wroxeter, but unquestionably a later transference from the great hill-fort of the Wrekin, three and a half miles to the east, which stands like a great watch-tower, as a sentinel of the Welsh marches. Ptolemy also included within its boundaries *Deva*, the legionary fortress of Chester; and the kingdom of the Cornovii marched with the Coritani[2] of Lincolnshire and Leicestershire to the east, the great tribe of the Brigantes to the north-east, the Decangi[3] to the north-west, the Ordovices to the west, and the Dobunni to the south.

The Brigantes[4] occupied the valleys of the Pennines and the north-west of England as far as the Parisii in the east of what is now Yorkshire, and as far south as the Cornovii, and perhaps even reached up into south-western Scotland. They were a warlike people, and according to Tacitus numerically the largest in Britain. Their tribal capital, Stan-wick, in the North Riding of Yorkshire, extended over an area of 850 acres of lowland enclosed in more than six miles of rampart and ditch, and its widespread and diffuse character is comparable to the early Celtic tribal centres of Gaul, comparable also to Cruachain, the capital of Queen Medb in early Connacht (cf. p. 35 below).

To the east of the Brigantes were the Parisi, with their *oppidum* Petuaria.[5] They had come from the north-eastern plains of Gaul, probably in the third and second centuries BC, and their rich graves, reminiscent of the Marnian culture (cf. p. 290 below), have been identified by their chariot burials and rich horse-trappings, representing a warrior aristocracy. To such later groups of settlers from Gaul belong also the important kingdom of the Iceni[6] of Norfolk and Suffolk, and the Trinovantes[7] in Essex, and others. These tribes were ruled by kings[8] and aristocratic military families and all were centred in strong and wide-spreading hill-top citadels, and possessed some pretensions to wealth and culture. The Dumnonii were rich in minerals; the Belgic Dobunni[9] and the Iceni[10] and others minted their own coinage. Of the kingdoms of southern Britain the most advanced culturally were the Cantii, owing to their favourable position for trade with the Continent. Ptolemy refers to their *oppida* of *Londinium* (London) and *Rutupiae* (Richborough).[11]

In south-eastern and southern England the Celtic tribes of the closing

---

[1] Ptolemy, II. iii. 11.   [2] *Ibid.*   [3] See Richmond, *C.E.*, 252, n. 8.
[4] Ptolemy (II. iii. 10) notes as one of their oppida *Cataractorium*, believed to be identical with Catterick in Yorkshire (cf. p. 76 below).
[5] Ptolemy, II. iii. 10.   [6] Ptolemy, II. iii. 11.   [7] *Ibid.*
[8] Tacitus, *Agricola* XII. Cf. *Annals* XII, 36; *Histories* III, 45.
[9] See Chapter V by Derek Allen in E. M. Clifford, *Bagendon*.
[10] Richmond, *R.B.* (2nd ed., London, 1963), p. 15.   [11] Ptolemy II. iii. 12

centuries before the Christian era present a somewhat different pattern from the older and wider kingdoms of the earlier period. As in Gaul at the time of Caesar's invasion, political coherence was absent from the Celtic kingdoms already established in Britain. This disunity undoubtedly contributed to the penetration and supremacy of the Belgae, as it was to be the chief cause of the Roman Conquest later. When Caesar made his two expeditions to Britain in 55 and 54 BC he found that certain tribes of the Belgae had already migrated across the Channel from northern Gaul, and had gradually established an over-lordship over a large part of the earlier Celtic coastal tribes of southern Britain (see map 2, below). These movements from Gaul to Britain were more in the nature of an expansion than an invasion, and Caesar himself noted that within the memory of the Gauls of his own day some of the immigrants had come into Britain as tribal units, both as plunderers and colonists, and that their British communities continued to bear names identical with those which they had left behind in Gaul.

Among the most powerful of the new kingdoms which they established on this side of the Channel was that of the Catuvellauni in Hertfordshire, with their tribal centre[1] in the vicinity of what was to become St Albans (Roman *Verulamium*). The Catuvellauni extended an overlordship over the surrounding peoples, and completely absorbed the Trinovantes[2] in Essex, between the East Anglian heights and the sea, with their *oppidum* at Colchester. In addition to the powerful Catuvellauni and their subject kingdom of the Trinovantes, Belgic kingdoms rapidly established themselves in the south and west.

Caesar's initial expedition to Britain in 55 BC had as its object an appraisement of the situation. He himself tells us (Book IV, 20) he understood that in almost all the Gallic campaigns help had been forthcoming to the enemy from that quarter, and he believed that it would be of great advantage to him to have entered the island and observed the character of the natives, and the nature of the country which was little known to the Gauls. He tells us that as soon as the Britons observed his intention of landing they sent forward their cavalry and charioteers, whom 'it is their regular custom to employ in fights', and followed them up with the rest of their forces. The chariot fighting of the Britons evidently made a deep impression on Caesar, for after relating a difficult landing and a subsequent defeat of the British forces, he pauses in his narrative to give a somewhat detailed account of the method of their chariot tactics:

Their manner of fighting from chariots is as follows: First of all they

[1] Ptolemy II. iii. 11. '*Catuvellauni* in quibus oppida *Salinae, Urlanium (Verulamium)*,' Identified with Wheathampstead. See R. E. M. and T. V. Wheeler, *Verulamium*.
[2] Ptolemy II. iii. 11.

23

drive in all directions and hurl missiles, and so by the mere terror that the teams inspire and by the noise of the wheels they generally throw ranks into confusion. When they have worked their way in between the troops of cavalry, they leap down from the chariots and fight on foot. Meanwhile the charioteers retire gradually from the combat, and dispose the chariots in such fashion that, if the warriors are hard pressed by the host of the enemy, they may have a ready means of retirement to their own side. Thus they show in action the mobility of cavalry and the stability of infantry; and by daily use and practice they become so accomplished that they are ready to gallop their teams down the steepest of slopes without loss of control, to check and turn them in a moment, to run along the pole, stand on the yoke, and then, quick as lightning, to dart back into the chariot.[1]

Caesar had made a 'reconnaissance in force'[2] in his two expeditions to Britain in 55 and 54 BC. The actual conquest began under Claudius in AD 43, and spread northwards and westwards till the Celtic tribes of the English lowlands seem to have been over-run and subdued as far as the Severn and the Humber within three years. In 47 the Iceni were conquered, and for the most part the older established tribes, including the Iceni themselves, accepted the position of client kingdoms. In the north also Cartimandua, the queen of the Brigantes, entered into treaty relations with Rome, and accepted the position of a client state.

The ancient Celtic kingdoms beyond the periphery of Lower Britain, however, were in no sense reconciled to a conquest by the Romans. Resistance movements and rebellions broke out whenever and wherever opportunity seemed to offer any chance of success.[3] To follow the history of the Celtic kingdoms as the Roman conquest spread is particularly difficult as our only records are those of the conquerors, and we are in the position of seeking to trace an almost universal underground movement for which we have no continuous clues. We are thankful for such surface records as Roman historians have left us.

In Wales the most powerful resistance[4] came from the tribes of the Ordovices[5] in northern and central Wales, and the warlike Silures[6] of the south-east. Sir Ian Richmond's recent study of the Cornovii[7] has shown that Roman military arrangements for the control of this western border state were dictated by the need of active measures to counter unrest, and even raiding, by the native Celtic mountain tribes to the west (cf. p. 49 below). In South Wales Caratacus raised the warlike kingdom of the Silures[8] and marched northwards to join the Ordovices,

---

[1] *De Bello Gallico* iv 33 (transl. Edwards).   [2] Collingwood, *R.B.E.S.*, 22.
[3] Tacitus, *Agricola* XV.   [4] *Agricola* XV f.
[5] *Ibid.* XVIII.   [6] *Ibid.* XVII.
[7] 'The Cornovii', in Foster and Alcock, *C.E.*, 251 ff.
[8] Perhaps after an interval spent among the Belgic *Dobunni* in the Cotswolds. See Clifford, *Bagendon*, 160.

doubtless counting on an alliance with the Brigantes; but he was heavily defeated in a pitched battle in 51, and after taking refuge with the Brigantes, was handed over to the Romans in chains by Cartimandua their queen.

Cartimandua[1] is one of the outstanding women rulers of Celtic antiquity, comparable with her contemporary Queen Boudicca of the Iceni, and with the Heroic Age queen of Ireland, Queen Medb of Connacht. It is indeed impossible to have any true understanding of either Celtic history or Celtic literature without realizing the high status of Celtic women, and something of the nature of their place in society, in both Gaul and Britain. We hear from Polybius that they accompanied their husbands to battle, following them in wagons;[2] but Ammianus Marcellinus describes them as taking an energetic part in actual combat. Indeed he tells us that a whole troop would not be able to withstand one Gaul in battle if he summoned his wife to his assistance (cf. p. 146 below).

Cartimandua had been established by Claudius as queen of the Brigantes. She repudiated her husband Venutius, who apparently commanded wide territories to the north, and her only hope of survival lay in Roman protection. Her marriage with her husband's standard-bearer Vellocatus was doubtless a matter of policy, for Venutius, formerly loyal to Rome like herself, was now found to be disaffected and leading a resistance movement. It has been suggested with high probability that if the Brigantes could have been united as a strong buffer state, the cost to the Romans of occupying northern Britain might have been saved. This however was not to be. The conquest of the Brigantes was completed by Agricola, who established Chester, now a legionary fortress, as his base, and from there completed the conquest of Wales soon after his arrival in Britain in 77 or 78.

Already in AD 61, however, the Roman general Suetonius Paulinus had inflicted a severe local defeat on the Welsh tribes – perhaps the Ordovices – on the shore of the Menai Straits, and Tacitus has left us a vivid account of the encounter between the Roman soldiers and the druids of Anglesey in one of his most melodramatic passages:

> On the opposite shore stood the Britons, close embodied and prepared for action. Women were seen rushing through the ranks in wild disorder, their apparel funereal, their hair loose to the wind, in their hands flaming torches, and their whole appearance resembling the frantic rage of the Furies. The Druids were ranged in order, with hands uplifted, invoking the

---

[1] The story of Cartimandua is related by Tacitus, *Histories* III, 45: *Annals*, XII, 36, 40. See recent commentaries on the situation by Ian Richmond, 'Queen Cartimandua', J.R.S. XLIV (1954), 50 f.; also *ibid*. Appendix to Sir Mortimer Wheeler, *Stanwick*, 61 ff. See further Chadwick, S.G.S. VIII (1955), p. 60 ff.

[2] *Histories*, V, 78.

gods, and pouring forth horrible imprecations. The novelty of the sight struck the Romans with awe and terror. They stood in stupid amazement, as if their limbs were benumbed, riveted to one spot, a mark for the enemy. The exhortations of the general diffused new vigour through the ranks, and the men, by mutual reproaches, inflamed each other to deeds of valour. They felt the disgrace of yielding to a troop of women and a band of fanatic priests they advanced their standards, and rushed on to the attack with impetuous fury. The Britons perished in the flames which they themselves had kindled. The island fell, and a garrison was established to retain it in subjection. The religious groves, dedicated to superstition and barbarous rites, were levelled to the ground.[1]

Meanwhile Boudicca, the queen of the Iceni, led a powerful rebellion in East Anglia, in which the Trinovantes joined, and Suetonius was forced to return at speed, leaving the conquest of Wales to be completed by Agricola.[2] Under Boudicca's husband Prasutagus, and indeed probably before, the Iceni had of necessity become a client state, sacrificing their independence perforce for the protection of Rome, to whom their loyalty became due in consequence. As a client king Prasutagus could not appoint his successor in the kingdom, but he bequeathed half of his property to Rome and the remaining half to each of his two daughters. The royal family and the nobility were treated as a conquered kingdom, and the Romans did not appoint Boudicca to inherit the rule of the client kingdom. They further alienated the British nobility by treating the grants which had been made to them by Claudius as loans, and before absorbing the kingdom into the Roman province they proceeded to divide the legacy at the hands of the military and fiscal officials. No doubt some resistance was offered, but the brutality with which Boudicca and her daughters were treated involved the honour of the whole tribe, which rose in rebellion. The Trinovantes, who also had their own financial sources of grievance, joined the Iceni.

Dio Cassius has left us a portrait of Boudicca, which has been justly called 'the most dramatic picture of a Celtic heroine in classical literature':[3]

> She was huge of frame, terrifying of aspect, and with a harsh voice. A great mass of bright red hair fell to her knees: she wore a great twisted golden necklace, and a tunic of many colours, over which was a thick mantle, fastened by a brooch. Now she grasped a long spear, to strike fear into all who watched her ...[4]

To judge from Cartimandua and Boudicca the British women hardly

[1] *Annals* XIV. xxx (translation by A. Murphy); cf. *Agricola* XIV.
[2] Tacitus, *Agricola* XVI.
[3] G. R. Dudley and G. Webster, *The Rebellion of Boudicca* (London, 1962), 20.
[4] Dio Cassius, *Roman Histories, Epitome* of Book LXII, 3, 4.

fall short of their Gaulish sisters in force of personality and political and military prestige. Suetonius, by prompt action and skill in military tactics, succeeded in quelling the rebellion, but not without great difficulty, and the rebels were treated with such severity as might be expected. Suetonius was recalled shortly after, and Roman policy was able to concentrate on strengthening the defences of the frontiers.

Meanwhile the unrest of the Brigantes – the largest confederation of native tribes in Britain among the Roman client kingdoms – compelled Agricola, on his appointment as governor of Britain, to postpone the final subjugation of Wales – now virtually conquered by Suetonius – and turn his most concentrated efforts to the north. On his northward route he negotiated the difficult Lancashire country between the Pennines and the sea, founding his fort at Ribchester, guarding the entrance to the River Ribble, and so over the Pennines to his fort at Elslack en route for Ilkley and York, and also from his fort at Manchester leading to a network of Pennine routes into Yorkshire.[1] It was masterly strategy to impede both cross-country communications by the Brigantes, and Irish raiding from across Morecambe Bay against the Roman forts in Yorkshire.[2]

In AD 80 he began his famous campaign in southern Scotland, quickly reaching as far northward as the Tay, and establishing a line of temporary forts along the Forth-Clyde isthmus, encompassing the Celtic (British) kingdoms of the Selgovae and the Votadini in the south-west and south-east respectively, and penetrating and fortifying Galloway and Ayrshire. Reluctantly as he looked at the opposite coast of Ireland, clearly visible, he abandoned, or perhaps rather postponed, the dream of conquest yet further westward. As Tacitus tells us, 'He saw that Ireland . . . conveniently situated for the ports of Gaul, might prove a valuable acquisition', and Tacitus goes on to tell us that one of the Irish kings, who had been forced to flee owing to local political troubles, was received by the Roman general, and detained, under pretence of friendship, to be of use on some future occasion.[3]

'I have often heard Agricola declare', adds Tacitus, 'that a single legion, with a moderate band of auxiliaries, would be enough to complete the conquest of Ireland.'[4] But Agricola's dream was never fulfilled. Instead he took precautionary measures against Irish invasion of south-western Scotland.

The extent of the Roman occupation of Scotland is still a matter of enquiry, but north of the Highland Line the country of the Highland

[1] G. Simpson, *Britons and the Roman Army* (London, 1964), 18 f. See also her map of the Agricolan forts in the southern Pennines, fig. 4.
[2] Richmond, *R.N.N.B.*, p. 113 f.
[3] Tacitus, *Agricola*, XXIV.
[4] *Ibid.*, *loc. cit.*

clans was apparently never penetrated. In order to protect the Lowlands from raids or conquest from the north, Agricola penetrated into Perthshire and built the great legionary fortress of Inchtuthill ten miles from Perth, a strong position as a permanent base for winter quarters, but not for strategical purposes. Beyond this point his northern progress seems to have been chiefly through the great plain of Strathmore north of the lower Tay. Forts were built up the east coast as far as Kintore on the Don, and even further.[1] But progress northwards was checked by the powerful tribe of the Caledonians at the famous battle of Mons Graupius,[2] an unidentified place[3] apparently further north than the Perthshire Highlands, but almost certainly approached along the east coast. The Roman fort of Raedykes near Stonehaven has been shown to be the most likely site of the battle,[4] and the native tribes, the Caledonians assembled for the battle, would presumably therefore be Picts. In a preliminary engagement the Caledonians had made a night attack on the Roman camp where the ninth legion was unprepared. The attackers succeeded in penetrating into the very heart of the camp, and had not Agricola arrived for the timely relief of the legion the Caledonians would have been the victors. Tacitus tells us, however, that they were put to the rout, 'and if the woods and marshes had not served to protect them that single encounter would have been the end of the war'.[5]

The Caledonians were by no means dispirited, however, and to judge from their tactics they seem to have been more advanced in both their political and military methods than the Britons of the south. Tacitus, whose general account of the campaign is regrettably vague, leaves us nevertheless some significant details.[6] He tells us, for example, that the Caledonians sent their wives and children to a place of safety, which we have seen to be contrary to ancient Celtic tradition; and he stresses their newly acquired sense of the importance of unity:

> They listed the young men of their nation, and they held public conventions of the several states, and ... formed a league in the cause of liberty. ... Experience had taught them that the common cause required a vigorous exertion of their united strength. For this purpose, by treaties and alliance, and by deputations to the several cantons, they had drawn together the strength of their nation.

Tacitus adds that nearly thirty thousand men appeared in arms, and that their strength was increasing every day. Their chieftain, most renowned by birth and valour, was Calgacus, who harangued the

[1] For a discussion of the eastern advance and the forts, see O. G. S. Crawfor d, *T.R.S.* and the map in the binding. [2] Tacitus, *Agricola* XXIX.
[3] For a recent discussion, see Crawford, *T.R.S.*, p. 130.
[4] Crawford, *T.R.S.* 108 ff., and passim. [5] *Agricola*, XXVI.
[6] The campaign and battle are reported at length by Tacitus, *Agricola*, XXIX–XXXVIII.

assembled troops before the battle in a speech which Tacitus claims to have reported verbatim, and which we can hardly doubt reflects the well-known compelling characteristic Celtic eloquence:

> The extremity of the earth is ours, ... but this is the end of the habitable world ... The Romans are in the heart of our country ... No submission can satisfy their pride ... While the land has anything left it is the theatre of war ... They make a desert and call it peace.

Meanwhile Agricola selected his site in a close place between the hill and the sea, and stationed his troops, the infantry in the centre, numbering, according to Tacitus, about eight thousand men, the three thousand horse in the wings, the legions in the rear. The Caledonians were stationed on rising ground, with their charioteers lower down on the plain. 'The Britons', says Tacitus, 'wanted neither skill nor resolution. With their long swords and *cetrae* (small light shields), they managed to elude the heavy weapons of the Romans, and at the same time to discharge a thick volley of their own.' But the chariots seem to have obstructed the movements of the native soldiery in the narrow ground; the army on the heights at first descended slowly, hoping to take the Romans in the rear, then rushed down swiftly, but were forced to retire at speed:

> The vanquished Britons had their moments of returning courage, and gave proofs of virtue and of brave despair. They fled to the woods, and rallying their scattered numbers, surrounded such of the Romans as pursued with too much eagerness. ... It is a fact well authenticated that some laid violent hands upon their wives and children, determined with savage compassion to end their misery.

The battle of Mons Graupius, which took place in AD 84, ended the seventh and last campaign of Agricola in Scotland. It was the culmination of his effort to conquer the country, and he was recalled soon after. The result of the whole northern campaign was to leave the Romans in possession of all lowland Scotland; but the Highland tribes retained their freedom and were never penetrated by the Roman legions. Scotland has remained for ever an unconquered country.

Meanwhile the Highland tribes were by no means subdued, and as soon as the Roman power showed signs of weakening they were ready to take full advantage of the change by a series of acts of aggression and raids which culminated in the gradual withdrawal of the Roman defences southwards. The cause of the change was, of course, neither local nor British, but lay in the military crisis in the heart of the empire, necessitating the withdrawal of troops from the western frontiers. The change began in the Scottish lowlands soon after AD 100. The advanced garrisons were given up, and all the forts north of the Cheviot, and perhaps north of the Tyne-Solway gap, were evacuated. In 117 a powerful rising of the Celtic peoples in Scotland and northern England took place, serious enough to bring the Emperor Hadrian to England, and between 122 and 128 or 129 the great stone wall or, better, *vallum*, from Tyne to Solway was built in the hope of forming an impenetrable barrier.[1] An interesting inscription, apparently from the eastern end, seems to record the completion of the building of this great *vallum*, by Hadrian, as a *limes*, a 'barrier' erected as a 'necessity'.[2] In 139–42 a forward movement was again resumed, and a turf wall was built from Forth to Clyde under Hadrian's successor, Antoninus Pius. Nevertheless the second half of the second century saw the gathering of the Celtic forces in the Scottish Lowlands and the north of England. Revolts in 155–8 and 181 destroyed the walls and almost all the forts, and in 196 a large part of Britain was overrun. In 208 Septimius Severus arrived with his younger son Geta and subdued the 'Caledonii' and the Picts of Strathmore and Strathearn; but after the death of Severus in 211, Caracalla withdrew all Roman permanent garrisons to Hadrian's wall,[3] and further measures of defence were taken, chief of which were new advanced posts manned by irregular units or frontier patrols, the *exploratores*, e.g. at High Rochester, Risingham, Bewcastle and Netherby. The main burden of the northern defences was henceforth delegated to the Britons of the north, supported by Roman resources. The success of this measure can be gauged from the fact that during the third, and still more the fourth, centuries Roman Britain enjoyed her most prosperous period, when the villas flourished and town life developed.

The Roman occupation of Britain can best be likened to a great flood tide, and the close came, as the tide recedes, not by a sudden event, not even by a series of events, but by a gradual process, as the ebb-tide leaves the shore. It was in a sense part of a world crisis, the overthrow of a great civilization by the inroads of barbarians from the north. In 406 the barbarians crossed the Rhine and in 410 Rome, 'the mistress of the world', fell to the Goths. The same year the Anonymous Gaulish chronicler records a specially heavy raid on Britain.

During the third and fourth centuries the *pax Romana* had lulled southern Britain and Gaul alike into a sense of security. There can be no doubt that in Lower Britain the Celtic and the Roman peoples had to some extent settled during the centuries of the occupation into a community whose best hopes of continuing peace had lain in unity. Their

---

[1] For a recent brief recapitulation of the events leading to the building of the northern walls, see G. Simpson, *B.R.A.*, 34 ff.

[2] The inscription appears to be contemporary, and is of exceptional interest. See the study and interpretation by I. A. Richmond and R. P. Wright in *A.E.*, Ser. iv, vol. xxi (1943), 93–120, and Plate III.

[3] See Dio Cassius lxxviii. 1.

interests were by now combined, and their hope for the future lay in preventing raids from across the frontiers and permanent settlement by alien populations. To the Celtic peoples of the north and west however the situation presented a very different aspect. The weakening of the Roman hold on Britain, and the gradual withdrawal of the Roman forces, opened the way to hopes of conquest and occupation, not only to the Teutonic peoples of north-western Europe – the Angles and Saxons, the Jutes and the Frisians – but also to the unconquered Celtic kingdoms of northern Britain and Ireland.

The Barbarian invasions of the Continent, which brought Roman rule to an end, were not isolated from raids in Roman Britain. The history of the fleet is obscure at this period,[1] but a Roman admiral Carausius, who was in command of the English Channel, certainly reconditioned the fleet before he was murdered in 293 after setting himself up in Britain as emperor. His successor Constantius, who came to Britain in 296, constructed a new fleet, and before his death[2] in 306 either he or Carausius built and heavily defended some at least of the twelve forts along what is – perhaps ambiguously – called the 'Saxon Shore'[3] in south-eastern Britain, extending from Brancaster on the Wash to Portchester in Hampshire, while a corresponding series was built on the French coast.

Meanwhile the Picts of the far north, and the Irish, both of whom had been immune from the Roman conquest, were gaining in strength and boldness as the Roman strength weakened. Both possessed fleets more numerous and powerful than is commonly realized, and both were attacking British coasts throughout this period. Gildas recognized the heaviness of the Pictish attacks by sea 'de curucis' (from their 'curraghs', the Gaelic word for the native sea-craft), and the fourth-century writer Vegetius has left us an interesting section on the new British coastal patrols attached to the fleet, with their expertise in camouflage and maritime guerrilla tactics.[4]

During the fourth century, raids by the Picts of Scotland became more formidable, and in 367 occurred the greatest disaster which had yet befallen Roman Britain, in which a simultaneous attack was made on all three fronts at once – by the Irish from the west, the Picts from the

[1] For some accounts of the fleet, see D. Atkinson, 'Classis Britannica' in *Historical Essays in Honour of James Tait* edited by Edwards, Galbraith & Jacob (Manchester, 1933) p. 1 ff.; more recently C. G. Starr, *R.I.N.*

[2] According to the '*Origo Constantini imperatoris*', alternatively known as the *Anonymus-Valesianus*, Constantius died at York in 306, *Monumenta Germaniae Historica*, Vol. IX, *Chronica Minora* (Berlin, 1892), p. 7.

[3] The most recent study of the Saxon Shore is that of Donald A. White, *L.S.* Cf. also the important review by S. S. Frere in *Medieval Archaeology* V–VI (1962–3), p. 350 f.

[4] Flavius Vegetius Renatus, *Epitoma Rei Militaris* (Berlin, 1885), Book IV, cap. 37. It has been suggested that South Shields may have become a naval base under Constantius of a system of coastal defence in the north similar to that of the Saxon shore forts.

north and the Saxons from the east. Ammianus Marcellinus, a contemporary informant, describes it as a *conspiratio barbarica*.[1] The immediate effect of the attack was devastating though the damage has been exaggerated. The wall forts were repaired by Count Theodosius, but the outposts beyond were permanently abandoned, and the raids by sea continued. Signal stations were set up along the Yorkshire coast, probably by Theodosius also; but were destroyed by Saxon raiders in 390, and Stilicho's expedition of 395 brought defences still further south. The Gallo-Romans were still anxiously watching bulletins from Britain, now their chief defensive outpost against the barbarians, and in 399 or 400 the poet Claudian in his poem against Eutropius[2] declares that

> The Saxon is conquered and the seas are tranquil,
> The Pict is broken and Britain is safe.

The chief name which has come down to us in both history and tradition from this period of crisis in Britain is Magnus Maximus. The part which he actually played is matter for conjecture.[3] We cannot take any firm stand on the late and delightful Welsh medieval tradition of his marriage to a Welsh bride,[4] or his unsatisfactory pedigree.[5] On the other hand the brief entry in the almost contemporary *Anonymous Gaulish Chronicle*, s.a. 392 is weighty: 'Maximus strenuously overcame the Picts and Scots'.[6] His achievement was evidently outstanding as a check to the Celtic and Pictish attacks, for in 383 the army in Britain proclaimed him emperor and crossed with him to Gaul, where he set up his court in Trèves in 384 or 385. His troops were evidently the *Seguntienses*, 'the men from *Segontium*' (Caernarvon) who are named among the *auxilia palatina* (evidently his personal bodyguard) serving in Illyricum,[7] where he was killed (at Aquileia) in 388, and where an inscription undoubtedly records the event.[8]

In Britain the end came quickly. The governor Constantine was forced by the army in 407 to usurp the title of Emperor and apparently by friendly arrangement with the Emperor Honorius he crossed to Gaul, taking some British troops with him. This is our last farewell to a Roman governor. Procopius tells us that he was subsequently defeated in battle and slain together with his sons; and he adds: 'Notwithstanding

[1] XXVII. 8. 1. *Britannias indicabat barbarica conspiratione ad ultimam vexatas inopiam.*
[2] *In Eutropium* XXVIII. 3. 7.
[3] See the study by C. E. Stevens 'Magnus Maximus in British History', É.C. III. p. 86 ff.
[4] Related in 'The Dream of Maxen Wledig', translated by Lady Charlotte Guest in *The Mabinogion*, and by Ellis and Lloyd (Oxford, 1929), Vol. I, 135 ff.; also Gwyn Jones and Thomas Jones (London, 1949), 79 ff.   [5] Pedigree no. II in MS. Harl. 3859.
[6] '*Incursantes Pictos et Scottos Maximus strenue superavit.*' *Mon. Germ. Hist. Auctorum Antiquiss.*, IX, *Chronica Gallica*, p. 646.
[7] See *N.D.*, ed. O. Seeck ... *in partibus Occidentis*, V, 65 (p. 118); 213 (p. 124); VII 49 (p. 134).
[8] See C. E. Stevens, 'The British Sections of the *Notitia Dignitatum*', A.J. XCVII (1940), p. 134, and note 5.

this the Romans were never able to recover Britain which henceforth continued to be ruled by tyrants'.[1]

On the whole it would seem that this was virtually the end of at least the Roman military occupation.[2] Zosimus, a Greek writer who is believed to have obtained his information from Olympiodorus, a very reliable source, tells us that the Barbarians from beyond the Rhine:

> ...ravaging at will, forced the people of Britain and some of those of Gaul, to secede from the Roman Empire and act independently, no longer subject to the laws of the Romans. The Britons took up arms and defended themselves, and, struggling bravely, freed themselves and repelled barbarian attacks. The Armoricans, encouraged by the example of the insular Britons, had thrown off the Roman yoke. This British-Gallic secession occurred in the time of the Emperor Constantine.[3]

In 410 came the famous rescript of Honorius informing the 'cities' (πόλεις) ('city states') of Britain that they might look after themselves.[4] The correct interpretation of this probably is the formal withdrawal of the Roman prohibition of the natives from bearing arms. The precise year of the official evacuation is of small account. By the middle of the fifth century Britain had become an independent country, ruled over once more by Celtic princes, except for Kent and some regions further north, where Jutes and Saxons had established themselves.

In consequence of her seclusion and inviolability Ireland has preserved in miniature for future ages the economy and institutions of the ancient Celtic world of the Iron Age. She is the microcosm of the early Celtic race. The art of the La Tène style continued without a break to form an organic element in the Irish art of the Middle Ages. The intellectual classes of Gaul reappear in ancient Ireland to carry on the intellectual life and historical traditions by oral transmission till written records begin with the introduction of Christianity and Latin learning. In the absence of Roman penetration of Ireland her political geography changed only slowly, and we lack the external evidence of either contemporary Latin documents or early vernacular written records to help us to trace the early settlement and population groups.

On the other hand Ireland possessed a greater wealth of carefully preserved oral tradition from the earliest period of our era than any other people in Europe north of the Alps. Further, archaeologically speaking Ireland is a museum of the ancient world. The Industrial Revolution which changed the face of Britain left the Irish countryside inviolate, a paradise for the archaeologist and place-name specialist.

---

[1] *Vandal War* I. ii. Procopius was a Byzantine historian of the first half of the sixth century.
[2] See M. P. Charlesworth, *L.P.*, 35 f.
[3] Zosimus V. cap. 5, 6.   [4] *Ibid.*, cap. 10.

The absence of Roman disruption and of recent industrial development combine with the discipline of modern scholarship to enable us to reconstruct conjecturally something of the early settlement of Ireland before the days of written history. The process of reconstruction is under way, and it may well add centuries to the history of the periphery of western Europe.

When the Irish historical period begins early in the fifth century the dominant peoples were the Goidels, with strongholds at Tara in Meath, Croghan in Connacht, and Cashel in Munster. The chief Irish families claimed to be of 'Goidelic' origin, and to be related to one another closely through the parent stock. They were a group of leading families, 'over-kings', who held their lands free of rent or tribute, while themselves exacting tribute from the provincial subject kingdoms.

Our oldest genuine traditions, however, relate to a period which has been credibly shown to be that of Ireland during the previous period, and in fact to be, not learned speculation, but genuine oral tradition, embodying a reliable picture – within certain well-defined limits – of Ireland as she was before the introduction of writing, of European culture, and before the dominance of the dynasty of Meath over the north. The historical geography and political institutions of this traditional picture of Ireland offer a remarkable contrast, on the one hand to the construction of the late 'pseudo-historians', working in the interest of the historical dynasty of Tara, and an equally strong contrast on the other to the conditions known from genuine historical records to have prevailed from the fifth century onwards, as we shall see. This traditional picture is that of a heroic society in the late Iron Age, much like that of Gaul before the Roman conquest. It has been preserved for us intact by the exceptionally high quality of Irish oral tradition. This phase which immediately preceded the historical period merits our keen interest and attention. It offers us a picture of Celtic society which is unique in Europe.

Tradition claims to extend reliable Irish history back to the Heroic Age, and it can be shown to be appropriate to a period as early as the fourth century AD. Many traditions may even be authentic for the close of the third century, for example the person and some of the stories about Cormac mac Airt, supposed to have reigned as king of Tara from 227 to 266. Our fullest and most authentic picture of Ireland in the prehistoric period, however, is the great prose saga, *Táin Bó Cualnge*, 'The Cattle-Raid of Cooley', which has preserved for us an intimate record of a European society in the late Iron Age.[1] The story has come

---

[1] The historical basis of the *Táin* was first demonstrated by Sir William Ridgeway, 'The Date of the First shaping of the Cuchulainn Saga', P.B.A. II (1905–6). For a more recent and fuller study with corrections see K. H. Jackson, *O.I.T.* We are further indebted to Professor Jackson for an earlier personal loan of his notes on this subject.

to us through many centuries of oral transmission, and was the first written, probably in the early eighth century. The storyteller recognizes the period as belonging to the far past, but the allusions and traditions have been preserved with great fidelity, as can be seen from the consistency of the internal evidence, and from comparison with other Irish heroic stories.

In the *Táin* Ireland is divided into four kingdoms, but they are called 'fifths' (*cóiceda*). The fifth kingdom, known in historical times as *Mide*, 'the middle one', appears later with the establishment of the Uí Néill in central and northern Ireland in the fifth century. But the notion of a five-fold division, by the four quarters and the centre, may have been independent of actual boundaries, just as in the Vedas the earth is sometimes thought of as in five parts.[1] The central area was perhaps formed into a separate kingdom around the sacred site of Tara by Niall Noígiallach, from whom the Uí Néill are descended (p. 55). It included the country around the hill of Uisnech in Co Westmeath which was regarded as the centre of Ireland, and to which the name *Mide* seems first to have belonged.[2] At no time is there a clear division of the country into five kingdoms, for at the dawn of history in the fifth century the kingdom of the *Ulaid* in the north is already shattered into several lesser divisions; and by the ninth century, Ossory in the south is a separate kingdom not always subject to Cashel. The four provinces known to the *Táin* tradition were large kingdoms, like the oldest Celtic provinces of Gaul and Britain, and they bore the names *Ulaid*, *Connachta*, *Laigin* and *Mumu*. The names of the four-fold division have survived till the present day as Ulster, Connacht, Leinster and Munster. The province of the *Ulaid* ('people of Ulster') consisted in the *Táin* of the whole of northern Ireland, including Donegal in the far west and Dunseverick on the Antrim coast. It was a great monarchy with its chief *ráth* or 'court' at Emain Macha, two miles west of Armagh, and its king was Conchobar mac Nessa, a prince of the *Érainn*.

The second of the *Cóiceda* at this period was *Connachta* (modern Connaught), with its centre of power spreading widely over the hill of Cruachain (Map 8). In the *Táin Connachta* is ruled by a woman, Queen Medb, whose consort is Ailill, and the province of *Connachta* is the rival and enemy of the *Ulaid*. South of the *Ulaid* were the *Laigin* (modern Leinster). The *Cóiced* of *Mumu* (modern Munster) was ruled by small kings their chief being Cú Roí mac Dáiri, whose seat was in West Kerry, and who had close relations with the heroes of the Ulster Cycle. As yet the Eóganacht dynasty of the great rock citadel of Cashel had not arisen.

The tradition represented by the *Táin* and its framework of the four

---

[1] *E.I.H.M.* 172 ff.; *Celtica* I 387; A. and B. Rees, *Celtic Heritage* 118 f.; A. A. Macdonell, *Vedic Mythology*, p. 9.   [2] *E.I.H.M.* 166.

great provinces gives us our first introduction to Irish history, comparable to our picture of Britain at the time of the Roman conquest. Christianity is unknown. Tara plays no part. Everything in the *Táin* suggests that the political and religious conditions preserve an unbroken tradition from before the fourth century, a 'Heroic Age' civilization of the sub La Tène period. For these reasons the oral traditions preserved in the *Táin* may be said to represent the earliest period of Irish history, which dates from the fourth century while the Heroic Age was still a living memory.

Moreover, the sympathies implied in the *Táin* are all with the *Ulaid* and therefore with the *Érainn*, not with the later dynasty of Tara. The Ulster places and the Ulster heroes are more familiar to the narrator than those of Munster and Connaught. This suggests that the *Táin* is an Ulster composition, and as the monastery of Bangor, Co. Down, was a centre of historical studies in the seventh and eighth centuries, it is probable that the *Táin* may have been finally written down in this monastery. And the motive for the compilation of this great prose epic? Perhaps we may suggest that it is a proud assertion of the past greatness of the *Érainn*, the ancient Celtic rulers of Ireland, against the parvenu line of the Uí Néill of the Tara dynasty, and the northern Uí Néill, who had destroyed Emain Macha and reduced the *Ulaid* to a small territory in northern and eastern Antrim. It may be suggested that the final formulation of the story and its record on vellum was inspired by a political motive.

Subsequently to the period represented by the *Táin*, a new dynasty arose with its royal *ráth* at the prehistoric sanctuary of Tara in Meath. The founder of the new dynasty was Níall Noígiallach, and his descendants subsequently ruled all the centre and northern half of Ireland. The southern half, consisting of half Leinster and all Munster, was never subject to the Uí Néill ('descendants of Níall'), but was ruled by a branch of the Eóganachta, a Munster dynasty seated at Cashel. It is believed that the new dynasty of the Uí Néill and the province of Meath rose to prominence as the result of invasion, and that Tara had belonged to the Laigin.

The ancestry of the Uí Néill is traced in late pseudo-historical texts to a certain fictitious *Míl Espáine* who was supposed to have come from Spain. Hence the name *Milesians*, by which name the Goidelic conquerors are commonly referred to in modern histories. *Míl Espáine* is evidently a translation from Latin *miles Hispaniae* 'the soldier from Spain', and in the Book of Invasions he is given a fictitious pedigree going back to an eponymous ancestor, *Goídel Glas*. In fact the name *Goídel* is borrowed from Welsh *Gwyddel* 'Irishman'. It may be derived from Welsh *gwydd* 'wild'.

O'Rahilly says that the people of this last invasion of Ireland and the Goidelic form of the Celtic language were introduced simultaneously at a comparatively late date, and he uses the term Goidelic of both the people and their language (p. 5 above). He says: 'If anything is certain about the Goidels, it is that they reached Ireland direct from the Continent', and he held that they 'must have come to Ireland from Gaul', and suggested that their migration was from south-eastern Gaul, perhaps from Gallia Narbonensis, whence they passed to the western coast not later than 120 BC, and migrated to Ireland towards 50 BC.[1] The late date and the course of events suggested by O'Rahilly are difficult to accept in view of the silence of Roman historians on so long and important a migration at this late date. The question must be regarded as at present unsettled. A more acceptable theory would be that the Milesians (Goidels) did come from Spain, as the Book of Invasions says. The discovery of Q-Celtic inscriptions in Spain by Tovar shows that in that lateral area the older forms had survived.[2]

If, however, we accept the provisional date suggested in Chapter I (p. 4 f.), that is to say some time early in the second millennium BC, for the spread of the Celtic peoples to the British Isles, it becomes reasonable also to accept the conclusion that the differentiation of the Celtic languages into two principal groups, known as Goidelic (commonly called Q-Celtic) and Brythonic (commonly called P-Celtic, cf. p. 197) originally took place after the settlement of the British Isles at some period between c. 2000 and 600 BC. Very possibly these changes may have been taking place throughout the whole Celtic world, and the Quariates may have preserved a backward mountain dialect. The origin of the Uí Néill and how they came to possess the sanctuary of Tara are problems still unsolved. In the search for a solution the following facts are important:

1. Although only four provinces are known in the earliest Irish traditions of the Heroic Age, we are told in the earliest written sources of the *cóic cóiceda*, 'the five provinces'. Therefore one has been added in the earliest historical period.

2. The political institutions of the earliest historical period imply a dominant dynasty in Meath, with military off-shoots in the north and west. Therefore Meath was probably the 'fifth' province of the *cóiceda*, with its centre at Tara.

3. Whether by external invasion, or by internal stimulus, the dynasty of Tara became predominant in the northern half of Ireland, as the dynasty of the rock of Cashel did in the south. Tara was an ancient

[1] *E.I.H.M.*, 207–8. He mentions the Quariates, a tribe of south-east Gaul.
[2] See Mac White, ZCP xxv 16.

heathen sanctuary. The subsequent Christian history of Cashel suggests that sanctity doubtless gave prestige to Cashel as to Tara.

4. Consistent tradition suggests that the ruling dynasty of northern and central Ireland obtained their power by military conquest, in the late fourth and early fifth century A.D. Meath, with its rich soil and an ancient sanctuary, would have been a tempting prize, and it may be that the Connachta of Cruachain drove the Lagin from their stronghold, and so established the lasting enmity between the Uí Néill and the Lagin that is reflected in the legend of the Bórama (p. 60).

During the fifth century and earlier the weakening power of the Roman Empire gave a great impetus to the movements and expansion of the Insular Celtic peoples, always seeking to extend their territory. The Irish in particular took advantage of the military weakness of the Roman defences of western Britain to penetrate the western promontories of Britain. We have seen from the statement of Ammianus Marcellinus that already during the fourth century Irish raids were no less formidable than those of the Picts and Saxons from the north and east. The Irish Sea had always been, and continued to be, a purely Celtic area, both politically and culturally. Here the Romans had no part, and there was no unified Celtic power to preclude the free transit and transport of the individual Celtic communities to and fro.

Among the most significant of these Irish expansions was the occupation of south-western Wales, the area of a wider Pembrokeshire, later known as the kingdom of Dyfed. This area was occupied by a dynasty from Leinster, who led a migration and settled in sufficient numbers to render the population bilingual in the fifth century, and to form what was virtually a little Irish kingdom. The pedigree and the story of its foundation are exceptionally well preserved, and these and other traditions enable us to trace also Irish settlements from the same quarter all the way along the south coast of Wales and the Bristol Channel, and even into the little mountain kingdom of Brecknock in the interior. At the same period Irish penetration of the Caernarvonshire peninsula has left abundant traces in place-names, and in the archaeological evidence of Roman defences. We have already traced some of these late Roman defensive measures in the preceding pages.

The peninsula where this Irish influence is strongest is Dyfed. It would seem indeed that Dyfed, and perhaps the peninsula of Lleyn in Caernarvonshire also, were bilingual at this period, and certainly in Dyfed, the ruling class were Irish-speaking. Inscriptions in the *ogam* alphabet, which is characteristically Irish, are more numerous here than anywhere else in Wales. Their number suggests a strong Irish aristocracy on the spot, which extended to the neighbouring area of Carmarthen-shire, the county which has the largest number of Ogams after Dyfed.

Moreover the Irish settlers seem to have been well established and continuous in Dyfed. A unique family group of three generations is commemorated by four inscribed stones in the area. A stone in Llandeilo churchyard commemorates in both Latin and Ogam letters a certain Andagellus, son of Cavetus.[1] Another pillar-stone in the same churchyard commemorates in Latin, Coimagnus, son of Cavetus;[2] another at Maenchlochog commemorates Curcagnus, son of Andagellus.[3]

Interesting confirmation, both of the intensive settlement of the Irish in south-west Wales at this time, and of the Roman appointment of barbarian princes to protect the outlying provinces, is afforded by a stone inscription on a round-headed tombstone believed to date from *c.* 550.[4] It is now in the Carmarthenshire Museum, but formerly stood in the entrance to Castell Dwyran graveyard. The inscription in Latin lettering is in three horizontal lines and runs:

Memoria

Voteporigis

Protictoris.

The round head of the stone is original and not due to weathering, for on the left arc at the top an Ogam inscription is cut which translates the Brythonic (British-Welsh) name into Goidelic (Irish) and reads:

Votecorigas.

It will be remembered that the Irish language has *c* corresponding to Welsh *p*.

Voteporigis of the inscription is believed to be the *Vorteporius* whom Gildas attacks in the first half of the sixth century as the *tyrannus* ('tyrant') of the Demetae ('the men of *Dyfed*' or Pembrokeshire).

These memorial stones are especially common in the districts known to have been occupied by the Irish in historical times, and it is therefore interesting that *Voteporix* (gen. *voteporigis*) is of Irish descent and in a Déisi (i.e. Irish) district, and that the Irish form *Votecorigas* is also given and in Ogam writing. The implication is that both Welshmen with a knowledge of Latin, and also Irish speakers, are expected to be equally interested in this early ruler, the 'Protector'. For our immediate purpose, that of watching the change from Roman to native Celtic rule in Britain, and the measures taken by the Romans in the latter part of

[1] Nash-Williams, *E.C.I.W.*, no. 313. [2] *Ibid.*, no. 314.
[3] *Ibid.*, no. 345. [4] Jackson, *L.H.E.B.*, 139.

their rule in Britain to train and make use of their native Celtic elements, the important thing about the inscription is the word *protictor*, 'protector'. This is not a grateful adjective, or a laudatory epithet, but a Roman title. It is the title given by the Romans to the barbarian princes honoured with the status of *foederati*, i.e. 'protectors' of the frontiers on behalf of the Romans. *Voteporix* in the sixth century doubtless bore it hereditarily. No one would be so well qualified to keep the Irish out of Dyfed as an Irish dynasty with Irish subjects.[1]

The peninsula of Caernarvonshire, and also Anglesey and West Merioneth, were settled by Irish about the same time as Dyfed, and the Irish language was spoken all over the area, perhaps in remote parts down to the Norman Conquest,[2] and is deeply embedded in place-names. At the head of Afon Lledr in Caernarvonshire is *Llyn Iwerddon*, 'Lake of Ireland'. Lower down, near the falls of the Conway River is a hill or place called *Iwerddon*, 'Ireland', and half-way between is *Dol-wyddelan*, 'Gwyddelan's meadow', Gwyddelan being derived from *Gwyddel*, 'a Gael', an Irishman.[3] Even as late as the fourteenth century one Welsh poet could say of another that his Welsh was *diseisnig* and *diwyddelig*, 'uncontaminated by English and Irish'. The old view that the Irish element in west Wales is a relic of the ancient Goidelic population is now completely discredited. The Irish of Caernarvonshire, however, came apparently from further north than those of Dyfed, for the northern peninsula was known, and is still known today, by the name of *Lleyn*, from Irish *Laigin*, 'the Leinstermen', while the little village on Nevin Bay still bears the name *Porth Dinllaen*, 'the harbour of the fort of the Leinstermen'.[4] The choice of Aberffraw on the west coast of Anglesey as the capital of North Wales at a later date was probably dictated by fear of an *adventus Scotorum* (an 'Irish occupation'). The gravity of this fear lies behind the tradition of Cunedda and his sons.

According to late Welsh tradition, preserved in what is believed to be the oldest part of the *Historia Brittonum*, and dating perhaps from the seventh century though finally compiled by Nennius in the early ninth century, a certain Cunedda came to North Wales with his eight sons and grandsons from Gododdin, the ancient territory of the Votadini, to the south of the Firth of Forth, and 'they drove out the Irish with immense slaughter from those regions, who never returned again to inhabit them'. The passage is our sole authority for the expedition. The tradition – if it can be trusted – implies a military movement, presumably along the thirty-seven miles of the Antonine Wall and then by ship from Dumbarton to Anglesey. It is not true that the Irish were in fact driven out of Wales, but these British chiefs from the north presumably

---

[1] See *P.E.W.*, 220.   [2] W. J. Gruffydd, *Math*, 342 f.   [3] W. J. Watson, *C.P.S.*, 228.
[4] W. J. Gruffydd, *Math*, 343, n. 90.

came with the intention of settling, and later traditions have been at pains to specify the kingdoms which they were believed to have founded in northern and western Wales. The establishment of these kingdoms came to form an important element in the early history of Wales.

By far the most important of the Irish expansions of the fifth century was that from north-eastern Ireland to the islands and coast of the south and south-west of Scotland. The coast of either country is clearly visible from the other, and we have seen (p. 27 above) in Tacitus how the Roman general Agricola had looked across from the Ayrshire coast and speculated on the ease with which Ireland could be conquered. On the other hand as we trace the Irish settlements up the west coast of Britain, and the defensive measures adopted by the Romans against Irish penetration, the expansion of the Irish from the Antrim coast into western Scotland in the fifth century becomes a natural sequel. Irish consolidation on a wide scale in western Britain was only possible beyond the Roman frontier of the Antonine Wall. Here a permanent Irish kingdom was founded in the fifth century, but whether by military or peaceful penetration is uncertain, though no tradition of military conquest has come down to us. The expansion and consolidation of this Irish settlement and Irish dynasty as the kingdom of Dál Riata will be traced in the following chapters.

In south-western Britain the most important movement and expansion was that of the Britons of the Devon-Cornwall peninsula and the Severn Sea into Armorica, the most westerly peninsula of Gaul. Prior to its conquest by Caesar in 56 BC the powerful sea-faring tribe of the Veneti in the south-east had had close transmarine relations with western Britain. We have seen that according to Zosimus the weakening power of the Roman Empire had stimulated the people of Armorica to follow the example of the Insular Britons and throw off the Roman yoke. During this period, probably already in the fourth century or earlier, the colonization of western Armorica from the south-west of Britain began to take place, and continued without apparent opposition from the Romans till the British language superseded that of the original Gallo-Roman peoples of Armorica. The British emigration has commonly been attributed, on the testimony of the sixth century British historian Gildas, to the settlement and establishment of the West Saxons in eastern England. A closer study of the pressure and penetration of the Irish on the western peninsulas of Britain, however, leaves one the impression that the British emigration was yet another result of the Irish pressure on western Britain at this period. In a later chapter we shall trace the development of this British immigration in the rise of the kingdom of Brittany.

CHAPTER 3

THE CELTIC REVIVAL

WHEN the Roman legions were withdrawn, the problem for the British princes was to maintain themselves against the encroachment of peoples from outside – the Teutonic peoples from the east, the Picts and Dalriadic Scots (Irish) from the north, and the Irish from the west. With the withdrawal of Roman organization and protection, the island of Britain stood like a great pharos off the Atlantic coast of Europe, and like the Celtic peoples of Gaul faced a struggle for existence against the shock and breakers of barbarian advancing tides. This problem of the Celtic independent princes was the principal fact in the history of Britain in the fifth century. Our first concern is to examine the situation among the Celtic kingdoms within Britain, and to enquire what measures they took to consolidate their political integrity and to meet their frontier difficulties. Our next concern is to survey the history of the Celtic peoples on the outer periphery of Celtic Britain.

For the British it was on the whole a close fought rearguard movement on three fronts. They stretched in an unbroken line from the Firth of Forth to Land's End, with no central organization or coordination. They had to defend themselves against Saxon penetration from the east, Pictish from the north, Irish from the west. In the present chapter we shall attempt to show what steps they took to maintain their new-found independence, and how far they were successful. It may perhaps be said here in anticipation that they ultimately succeeded in preventing large-scale occupation by the Irish in the west, south of the Highland Line, even while founding a new colony overseas in Armorica. On their eastern front they were able to offer a stubborn resistance, and even to take the initiative in attacking the Saxon invaders, at least in the north; but the absence of centralization and unity among the Celtic peoples, combined with geographical difficulties of communication in hill country, eventually brought it about that the whole of Lowland Britain fell into Saxon hands.

The first task of the British princes was to establish some form of stable government and central organization with the aim of defending the Borders. In this they were apparently successful, for no hint of anarchy following upon the Roman withdrawal has come down to us in our traditions of the period.

One of the most marked developments in the recent attitude to the Roman occupation of Britain is a fuller realization of the continuity which persisted throughout the period between the earlier Celtic tribal life and that which emerged when the last Roman military convoy left the Island. On the whole the country had probably not greatly changed. It would seem that Roman civilization had hardly affected Britain in depth beyond the part of central and south-eastern England, generally included in the term 'Lower Britain'. This was the principal area of the villas and the towns – London, Canterbury, the country towns such as Silchester, Verulamium, Bath, Cirencester, Gloucester, Caerwent. In general the traditional Celtic life seems to have been little disrupted or even transformed. The Romans appear to have interfered little with the religious, domestic, and civil life of the native Celtic peoples. The ancient Celtic kingdoms seem to have continued as *civitates*, political 'cantons' for administration, carried on by an *ordo*, a permanent executive 'council', which functioned in the cantonal capital, consisting of *decurions* or ex-magistrates who had been elected by the city. The native religion lived on apparently without interference side by side with Roman cults, and native temples and shrines continued to be built. Most significant of all, Latin never gained wide currency in Britain, although there are many Latin loan-words in Welsh which were borrowed in the period of the Roman occupation.[1] Much has been made of *graffiti*[2] scratched on small objects, such as the word '*satis*' scratched on a single tile at Silchester, and attributed to a weary brick-maker by Haverfield,[3] and charmingly translated by M. P. Charlesworth as 'Time to knock off'; but this slender trace of workman's Latin is more probably the 'exeat' of a satisfied Roman foreman.

In regard to the civil government of Britain in a wider sense after the departure of the Romans, we are largely dependent on conjecture. In a treatise which claims to be contemporary, and which bears the title *De Excidio Britanniae*, and is generally regarded as the work of an early sixth century ecclesiastic, Gildas, we are told (cap. 23) of a powerful British ruler, a *superbus tyrannus*, who is made responsible for the introduction of the Saxons into Britain. Gildas himself tells us, however, that while the Britons were being harried by the Picts *de curucis* ('in their sea-going craft') all the councillors, together with the supreme dictator (*omnes conciliarii cum superbo tyranno*) invited the warlike (*ferocissimi*) Saxons into the country. The responsibility for the invitation is clearly

[1] *L.H.E.B.*, 76–80; 97–106. About eight hundred words were borrowed into British.
[2] Evidence for *graffiti* is collected by A. Burn, *The Romans in Britain* (Oxford, 1932). See also *R.R.B.* 28 ff.; cf. *L.P.*, 67.
[3] *R.R.B.*, 30.

stated to lie with the *conciliarii* – by whom we are probably to understand the *civitates* – with the *tyrannus* at their head. The invitation was an official one and the Saxons were first invited in to act as mercenaries against Pictish raids, receiving their keep in fixed monthly supplies (*annonas*, *epimenia*). The procedure as depicted by Gildas was perfectly regular, and in accordance with continental Roman practice in relation to the Franks and other barbarian peoples. Gildas's account suggests that the ravages of the Saxons only began when their payment failed or proved inadequate to their demands. Moreover it implies a stable government, anything but anarchy. The native British ruler in charge of the defences, acting with the authority of all his councillors, presumably members of the *ordo*, was taking constitutional measures for dealing with a crisis inherited from the preceding period. Bede in his *Historia Ecclesiastica* calls him *Vurtigernus*, which means 'overlord' and may have prompted Gildas to call him *superbus tyrannus*.[1]

Few certain facts are known about Vortigern; but he seems to have been the leading Celtic figure in Britain *c.* 425, and it is very possible that he formed a buffer state on the Welsh Border – possibly at a time when the outlying peninsulas had already passed largely into Irish hands (cf. pp. 38–41 above). It seems reasonably certain that he had authority to strengthen the native military defences of his own country with Saxon *foederati*. He became the subject of a large number of unfavourable legends, among others a fantastic story of his encounters with St Germanus;[2] but what stands out with some clarity is his position as a powerful Romano-British prince who played an official part in cooperation with the governors of the provinces in hiring Saxon mercenaries to protect Britain against barbarian inroads from the north after the removal of the Roman army of occupation. There is no suggestion anywhere that his Celtic sympathies imply anti-Roman politics, and he seems to have acted as though he were a Roman official.

The picture so far presented by archaeology is that the Saxons came in the first place, not as invading armies, but in a series of civil settlements, beginning before the end of the second century and under Roman auspices. How far there may also have been independent private or trading settlements is at present *sub judice*; but Roman employment of the Saxons as *foederati*, 'mercenaries', is beyond question, and is, of course, fully in accordance with the Roman practice on the continent. Roman military use of the Saxons as *foederati* had taken place between 390 and 400, and it has been pointed out that east of a line between York and Bedford there is scarcely a Roman walled town apart from

[1] On the significance of the title, see N. K. Chadwick 'Bretwalda, Gwledig, Vortigern', B.B.C.S. XIX (1961), 225 ff.; also 'Note on the name Vortigern', *S.E.B.H.*, by H. M. Chadwick and others, 34 ff.; *P.E.W.*, 220.

[2] *Historia Brittonum*, caps. 39, 41, 48.

the Saxon shore forts and similar sites in the Lincolnshire Wolds, without an accompanying Anglo-Saxon cemetery, while pottery of fourth century date in Roman technique and Saxon decoration points to close association of Roman and Saxon in both the neighbourhood of the 'Saxon Shore' forts and the East Riding near to York. We have reason to believe that by the end of the third century the 'Saxon Shore' had already been partially settled, or that the forts themselves were partly manned, by Saxons, or were the focal points of more or less organized trade relations with the Teutonic tribes across the North Sea.[1] There is no evidence of a general massacre of the native population, and the possibility may be dismissed as most improbable on practical grounds. After the departure of the Romans, however, the encroachments became military. Here, as in Gaul, what apparently began as numerous relatively small-scale Teutonic enterprises and settlements, developed, as Roman power weakened, into military conquest, and the creation of an alien barbarian kingdom displacing Roman and Celtic dominion alike.

After a lurid description of the depredations of the Saxons, Gildas tells us (cap. 25 f.) that a remnant of the Britons took up arms and challenged their victors to battle under a certain Ambrosius Aurelianus, whom he praises as 'the last of the Romans', and to these men came a victory.

Ambrosius seems to have represented the rearguard of the withdrawing Roman army, and he is described by Gildas as a *vir modestus* and a *dux*. Nothing more is known of him from early sources, but he is very probably the *Emreis Gwledic* whom Nennius in the *Historia Brittonum* relates to have been victorious in a series of hostilities against Vortigern, in the course of which Vortigern was driven to take refuge in Snowdonia. These legends are in the nature of folk-tale, and doubtless arose when mounting hatred against the Saxons was heaping obloquy on Vortigern.

In recent years a growing body of opinion tends to regard King Arthur as historical,[2] and some would identify him with Ambrosius Aurelianus, though the questions are in reality quite distinct. We have no satisfactory evidence for a historical Arthur. Nevertheless cumulatively the amount of legendary evidence is arresting, and there may have

---

[1] We are chiefly indebted to Dr J. N. L. Myres for the conclusions briefly stated above. Supplementary matter has also been added by K. Dauncey and the late R. R. Clarke; cf. also P. Hunter Blair, *Roman Britain and Early England* (Edinburgh, 1963), 162 f. The principal references to all these preliminary studies are entered by N. K. Chadwick in 'The British or Celtic Part in the Population of England', in *A.B.*, 138 ff.

[2] Sir John Rhŷs, *Celtic Britain*, 238. See Sir F. Stenton, *A.S.E.*, 3; Sir J. E. Lloyd, *H.W.* I, 125 f. Collingwood, *R.B.E.S.*, 321 f. The most recent and authoritative studies are those of K. H. Jackson, 'The Arthur of History', and 'Arthur in Early Welsh Verse', in R. S. Loomis (editor), *A.L.M.A.*

been a British commander in the late fifth or the sixth century who bore the Roman name Arthur (*Artorius*).

Turning now from the Saxon penetration of the east to the northern frontiers, it has been suggested above that the chief defences against Pictish incursions from the north were the British tribes of southern Scotland, who had apparently been entrusted already in the Roman period with the defences of the northern border, and had probably been to some extent trained and equipped for this purpose by Roman military methods. For the British of southern Scotland[1] we are largely dependent in the last instance on Celtic tradition, as we shall see. We have, however, in addition one all-important contemporary Latin document which is our safe conduct – so far as we can interpret it – through the change-over from Roman to Celtic rule in southern Britain, and which is especially significant in its negative evidence in regard to the border defences in the north and west. This is the *Notitia Dignitatum*,[2] a document believed to have been drawn up in the chancellery of the Eastern Roman Empire in the late fourth or early fifth century, giving under each province of the Empire the lists of returns furnished from time to time by local officials throughout the Empire. The document is therefore not a survey representing the civil and military conditions of the Roman Empire at any given moment, but something resembling a card index kept over a period of time. It is a dynamic register, and for the closing phase of Roman rule in Britain it is our most illuminating document. Its bare entries can be supplemented from Celtic traditions by the genealogies of the princes of the frontier kingdoms on the northern border. These genealogies show significant changes in the names during the fourth and fifth centuries, from those of Pictish appearance, to names suggesting Romanized Britons, and these again give way to names of Celtic princes in the fifth century. The *Notitia Dignitatum* shows no entry for the *dux*, an old office of the Roman military leader of the northern defences. If his duty had been delegated to the north British *foederati* it is natural that no returns would have been sent in for him, and his place would have been taken by some British leader. Perhaps after Stilicho had finally withdrawn the chief Roman supply base in the north to York some powerful British chief may have succeeded him as *dux*. With the help of the Latin document of the *Notitia* and the Celtic genealogies the course of history on the northern border is reasonably clear.

[1] For the Britons of Southern Scotland at this period the best accounts are those of K. H. Jackson, 'The Britons in Southern Scotland', *Antiquity* XXIV (1955), 77 ff.; and more recently 'Angles and Britons in Northumbria and Cumbria', in *A.B.*, 60 ff. See further Salway, *F.P.R.B.*, 198 f.

[2] Edited by Otto Seeck (Berlin 1876). For valuable studies see C. E. Stevens, A.J. XCVII (1940); E. Birley, T.C.W.A.S. XXXIX (1939), No. XIV, 190 ff.; more recent research by A. H. M. Jones, *L.R.E.* III, Appendix II, p. 347 ff.

During the closing years of the Roman occupation of Britain, and especially in consequence of the great raid of 367, the Romans had sought to ensure that the unconquered northern tribes were contained beyond the range of the impoverished Roman power, and they followed here the policy already inaugurated on the Continent[1] of training and incorporating native troops to police their northern frontier, probably furnishing them to some extent with Roman equipment and perhaps bestowing on them Roman insignia. We have here no direct contemporary authority, but this at least would seem to be the position as suggested by the *Historia Brittonum*[2] of Nennius and by the Welsh genealogies. Although these texts are not earlier than the beginning of the ninth century, Nennius has made use of records going back to the seventh century or even earlier, while the genealogies are derived from conservative and carefully preserved oral tradition.

A study of these records suggests that the Romans either established, or at least supported, a native dynasty to guard each end of the northern (Antonine) wall, – a distance of only thirty-seven miles. The genealogies of these dynasties have fortunately been preserved.[3] On the whole the best authenticated and the most stabilized of these dynasties is that of Strathclyde, with its stronghold at Dumbarton. The most eminent name in the Dumbarton dynasty at the close of the Roman period is that of a certain *Ceredig Gwledig*, generally identified with the *Coroticus* whose soldiers were accused by St Patrick in his famous letter of having carried off newly baptized members of his flock from Ireland, doubtless as slaves. Dumbarton was still described by Bede in the early eighth century as a *munissima urbs*, 'a very strongly fortified place'. The branches of this dynasty can be identified as far away as Galloway. The genealogy has probably been preserved with care, for its genuineness can be checked from external historical sources. The most famous king among them, Rhydderch Hen, figures in later traditions of both St Kentigern and the prophet Myrddin (later *Merlin*), as well as in Adamnán's *Life of St Columba*. The slave raiding of Coroticus in Ireland in the fifth century might be construed as providing the practical resources of these princes when Roman financial resources failed. This at least is Gildas's explanation of the Saxon raiding on Britain when the *epimenia* due to them as Roman *foederati*, were no longer forthcoming.

---

[1] For the system here suggested see P. Hunter Blair, *O.N.*; M. P. Charlesworth, *L.P.*; H. M. Chadwick, *E.S.*

[2] The chief edition is that of Mommsen, *MHG, Auctores antiquissimi*, t. XIII, (Berlin, 1898), 112 ff. A more recent edition is that of F. Lot, *Nennius et L'Historia Brittonum* (Paris, 1934). A useful English translation by A. W. Wade-Evans, *Nennius and the History of the Britons* (London, 1938) contains also the *Annales Cambriae* and the Genealogies of the British (Welsh) princes. These texts, published in English by Wade-Evans, constitute the compendium of texts contained in the British Museum MS. Harleian 3859, and are an important historical document in their own right.

[3] Cf. p. 74, n. 1.

Indeed, the British princes of Dumbarton to the north would be no more eager to be overrun by the powerful Picts than were the Romano-Britons further south.

At the eastern end of the Antonine Wall was the old kingdom of the Votadini, the name which survived later as Gododdin, the original home of Cunedda (cf. p. 40 above). According to the Welsh genealogies Cunedda's name, like that of Ceredig, is preceded by three Roman names, *Ætern* (L. *Eternus*), *Patern* (L. *Paternus*, to which is added the epithet *pesrut*, 'of the red tunic'), and the third Tacit[us]. Before these come a series of two pairs of names which resemble the curious lists of pairs of names on the pedigrees of the Pictish kings.[1] The territory of the Votadini stretched from south of the Firth of Forth to Berwickshire while to the north of the Firth was the kingdom of the powerful Southern Picts.

It is tempting to hazard a guess that the important fifth century treasure from Traprain Law in Haddingtonshire[2] is pirate's loot, and that the Roman *foederati* of this great stronghold, like their fellow princes of Dumbarton, had taken to piracy when Roman subsidies failed at this time. The epithet *pesrut* has been thought with great probability to refer to the red tunic of a Roman army officer.[3] It seems probable that both Ceredig and Cunedda were Romanized Britons guarding each end of the Antonine Wall. Following the three generations of Roman names on these pedigrees the names are of British form. These succeeding lists would on a normal computation carry us back to the fourth century, and the evidence leads us to surmise that as a result of Pictish raids, and especially the great Pictish raid of 367, the Romans had 'authorized' native princes to guard the northern defences on behalf of the Empire as *foederati*. Then in the fifth century, during the so-called 'national revival', native British names succeeded the Roman.

What was the general position in the west, where the Celtic peoples had never been fully Romanized? Here again the *Notitia Dignitatum* fails us, for no returns of any kind were sent in from the Welsh marches, or indeed from western Britain at all. This is the more remarkable since we know that Caernarvon (*Segontium*) was occupied till as late as 383 when Magnus Maximus departed with his Seguntienses; and Manchester and Ribchester show coins till the same date. Chester had been occupied by the Twentieth Legion and Caerleon by the Second, and only a part of the latter had been removed to Richborough at an earlier date. How then can we account for the total silence of the *Notitia* in the fifth century with regard to Roman officials on the western border?

Part of the explanation perhaps lies in the fact that when Magnus Maximus removed some of the troops to Gaul he left the entire western

---

[1] See *E.S.*, 3.   [2] *T.T.*   [3] *L.P.*, 28.

defences in the hands of the native troops. This period corresponds roughly with the devolution, the change to the *foederati* on the northern border, and there is some corroborative evidence that by a similar devolution the Romans transferred a part of the responsibility in the west to native princes, more especially on the western sea-board.

Just as the peril to the northern frontiers came from two distinct peoples, the Picts and the Irish, so on the western frontier the peril came independently from two distinct peoples, the Welsh and the Irish. It has recently been convincingly demonstrated by Sir Ian Richmond[1] that the Cornovii, the chief ancient tribe of the western border provinces, were in a position of great insecurity, owing to the disaffection and mountain raids of the Ordovices immediately to the west. Consequently they already held exceptional responsibility and exceptional privileges under the Romans. They were the only British tribe that gave its own name to the unit of Imperial auxiliary troops; and this unit, also contrary to custom, continued to serve in its own province.

The chief peril to southern Britain came, however, from the Irish, and thus a major consideration of the defences, first by the Romans, and later by the independent British princes, was always the defence of the western shores. Several Irish settlements on the western peninsulas of Wales were already taking place during the Roman period. The evidence of an early inscription in Dyfed (Pembrokeshire) records the title of *Protector* as having been held by a native prince (p. 39), and this is an official Roman title bestowed on *foederati* responsible for defending the frontiers. The later genealogies attach the same title to Magnus Maximus and his son and grandson.

The Romans had long been alive to the Irish menace, and from the third century onwards the Romans and the Britons of Wales faced a common enemy. In south-eastern Wales the chief defences were no longer at Caerleon and Caerwent, to act as defences against the Welsh, but at Cardiff, where a late large fort was built in the third century against the Irish on the site of a second century one. In Caernarvonshire the early fort of Segontium built on the hill above Caernarvon was abandoned and a new one built at the mouth of the river by the shore to protect the valuable Roman trade of the Anglesey copper mines from Irish raiders,[2] while the late small fort at Holyhead was probably built at this period against the Irish.[3] Further the line of defence of the Saxon Shore forts of the east and these Welsh ones on the west was continued in the north – in Lancashire, on Morecambe Bay, and even east of the Pennines.

An early tradition of Irish kingdoms on the coasts of the Severn Sea in

---

[1] 'The Cornovii', in Foster and Alcock, *C.E.*, 251 ff.   [2] Richmond, *R.B.*, 155.
[3] *Ibid.*, *R.N.N.B.*, 113, and fuller references in n. 5.

Wales and south-western Britain is preserved in an Irish text known as *Sanas Cormaic*[1] ('Cormac's Glossary'), a kind of encyclopedia and glossary believed to date from the ninth century. Here it is claimed that from the time of St Patrick the Irish had had divided kingdoms, the more important halves being in Britain, and that they had held that power long after the coming of Patrick:

> The power of the Irish over the Britons was great, and they divided Britain between them into estates ... and the Irish lived as much east of the sea as they did in Ireland, and their dwellings and their royal fortresses were made there. Hence *Dind Tradui* ... that is, the triple rampart of Crimthann Mór,[2] son of Fidach, king of Ireland and Britain as far as the English Channel ... From this division originated the fort of the sons of Liathán in the lands of the Britons of Cornwall ... And they were in that control for a long time, even after the coming of St Patrick to Ireland.[3]

The source of Cormac's information is not known, but although the tradition is referred by him to several centuries before his time, the statement that the situation which he describes survived to a time 'long after the coming of Patrick', suggests that his information is fairly recent and it is certainly consistent with such other evidence as we have. Cormac's reference suggests that *Dind map Lethain* is on or near the northern shore of the Dumnonian Peninsula. The tribe is probably to be identified with the Irish Uí Liatháin of Munster, and Cormac is evidently using a Welsh source which he feels under the necessity of translating for his Irish readers: 'Dún maic Liatháin – for *mac* is the same as *map* in British'.

Nennius, writing about the same time, is probably relying on the same Welsh source when he tells us (*Hist. Brit.* cap. 14) that 'the sons of Liathán occupied the region of Dyfed, Gower and Kidwely'.

Traditionally, then, all the South Welsh seaboard was occupied in the fifth century by a Munster tribe[4] which Cormac locates on the opposite shore of the Severn Sea, and this tribe, or certain Irish kingdoms, command all the approaches to the south-west of Britain – south and south-western Wales, the Bristol Channel and the Dumnonian Peninsula.

It is against five British princes of these troubled western maritime kingdoms that Gildas (cap. 28) hurls reproaches early in the sixth century. They appear to be his older contemporaries, rulers of wide territories on the western sea-board, and he addresses them by name,

---

[1] Edited by K. Meyer, *S.C.*, No. 883, s.v. *mug-eme*, p. 75 f. Cf. also W. Stokes, *T.I.G.*, p. 62 The passage is translated on p. xiviii.

[2] His traditional dates are 366–379.

[3] I have followed the translation of K. Jackson in *The Celts* (edited by J. Raftery, Dublin, 1964), 75.

[4] See the valuable map of the various 'tribes' of Ireland by Liam Price in *L.C.*

apparently in geographical order, beginning with Constantine, 'tyrant' of Dumnonia (the Devon-Cornwall peninsula) and continuing round the Welsh coast till he reaches the 'island dragon', Maglocunus. The three western princes can all be identified in the Welsh genealogies, Maglocunus being the great Maelgwn Gwynedd, great-grandson of Cunedda, and ruler of North Wales and Anglesey. Gildas has named the wide British kingdoms from Devon to Lancashire which must have been the bulwarks against Irish penetration in depth. Archaeology and tradition alike reflect the danger of an *adventus Scotorum*.

It was precisely at the period of the departure of the Romans from Britain, the assumption by the Celtic princes of the rule of Britain, and the mounting threat of Saxon, Pict and Irish to British independence, that the colonization of Britanny from western Britain was taking place in force.[1] It had doubtless already begun not later than the fourth century, and proceeded with impetus throughout the fifth century, reaching its climax in the sixth. Linguistic evidence indicates that the language of the immigrants was most closely allied to that of Cornwall, but a large proportion of the colonists are believed to have gone from Devon, because the extent to which Devonshire acquired English place-names suggests that this Celtic area was only thinly populated by Britons when the English arrived there; and indeed the Irish settlements on the Severn Sea would make British emigration from Devon more than likely. The late Breton hagiographical traditions, however, associate the princely leaders of the movement and the ecclesiastics with east central, central, and even western Wales.

It is commonly assumed that the cause of the migration was the pressure of the Saxon invasions, and this is the impression conveyed by Gildas. The *De Excidio*, attributed to him, is our earliest native authority for the evacuation from Britain. In cap. 25 he refers to 'part of the population' emigrating sorrowfully across the sea, chanting 'beneath the swelling sails' a passage of lamentations from the Psalms instead of sailors' shanties. He does not actually state that they were sailing to Armorica, but the historical evidence for this is overwhelming. In the light of what has been said above of the Irish penetration, however (cf. pp. 38 f. above), the imminent fear of an *adventus Scotorum* must have been even greater to the inhabitants of Cornwall, Devon and Wales, and especially to all living on the Severn Sea, than fear of Gildas's *adventus Saxonum*. These people were in a pincer movement, but the Saxon threat as yet touched them only remotely.

The kingdom of Wessex was founded early in the fifth century, and it was the advance of the Saxons westwards, culminating in the Battle

---

[1] The most authoritative account of the colonization of Armorica is that of J. Loth, *E.B.*

of Durham, in 577, that cut off the Britons of Devon and Cornwall from the Britons of Wales.[1] By then, indeed, Saxon pressure must have been a powerful factor in the migration, as Gildas implies. Only slightly later than Gildas we have a statement by Procopius of Caesarea[2] that large numbers of independent Britons and others, ruled by their own kings, were sent annually to the land of the Franks, who planted them as colonists in the thinly populated areas. Procopius clearly obtained his information from Frankish envoys at the court of Constantinople, where he held office in the first half of the sixth century, exactly the time when the colonization of Brittany was at its height. The serious Saxon raids in Gaul would naturally make the Frankish kings view friendly immigrants favourably. Moreover, it has been pointed out[3] that if we can trust the statement of Procopius, and the statement of Gildas (cap. 26) about the long peace that followed the Siege of Mons Badonicus (cap. 26), the Saxons cannot have extended their frontier far to the west during this period, and we cannot assume that the threat to the Britons was as yet crucial. The Frankish chroniclers, it is true, attributed the British immigration to Saxon raids, notably Eginhard, friend and biographer of Charlemagne, and Ermold le Noir, who had accompanied Louis on an expedition to Brittany in 824; but the literary nature and the late date of these statements rob them of their value as evidence. They may derive ultimately from Gildas himself, for he was well known and widely read in Brittany in the ninth century.

Meanwhile the nearest refuge of the Britons was western Brittany. Yet during the fifth century the Romans in Brittany were suffering from Saxon attacks no less than Britain, and to meet the emergency the Roman administration introduced changes in their defensive system, seeking to concentrate the defences as near as possible to the eastern border, and also to protect the coastal areas and the estuaries of the rivers.[4] The *Notitia Dignitatum* (cf. p. 46 above) shows extensive changes, the military command having now been removed from the interior to the coast, the defence of the whole coast being reorganized to oppose Saxon landings. No measures seem to have been taken to protect the west, and this must have facilitated small-scale landings and settlements by the incoming Celtic population. The Saxons never succeeded in making a permanent kingdom here as they did in Britain, but they succeeded in destroying much of the Roman civilization, especially round the coasts.

[1] The founding and progress of the English settlements is well summarized by Jackson, *L.H.E.B.*, 200-19.
[2] *De Bello Gothico* IV, 19.   [3] F. M. Stenton, *A.S.H.* (2nd ed., Oxford, 1950), 6.
[4] For the Roman city states and the changes in the Roman defence system in Armorica, see R. Couffon, 'Limites des cités gallo-romains et Fondations des évêchés dans la péninsule armoricaine', *S.É.C.*, Tome LXXII (1942); F. Merlet, 'La Formation des Diocèses et des Paroisses en Bretagne', *M.S.H.A.B.*, Tome XXX (1950), Tome XXXI (1951)

Yet the fact that the Saxons had not succeeded in displacing the Breton immigrants suggests that some kind of internal organization still existed. We have no clue as to the nature of this organization. In the absence of any shred of evidence, and with the course of events in Britain before us, one is tempted to guess. Can the Gallo-Romans have acted as the *superbus tyrannus* and his *conciliarii* are said to have done in Britain, and encouraged the British immigrants to enter as *foederati* to help against the common foe? We have seen evidence that the British chiefs of the Welsh Marches lacked neither experience nor valour in such warfare. And this is precisely the area which, according to Breton tradition, furnished the leaders of the immigrant Bretons.

The Romans were fast losing their hold on Armorica. Already in 409 Armorica had revolted, and Zosimus tells us that 'encouraged by the example of the insular Britons, they had thrown off the Roman yoke' (cf. p. 33 above). From this it would seem that there was close political intercourse between Britain and Armorica already before the beginning of the fifth century, apparently of an organized kind. This is doubtless the underlying motive of St Germanus's visit to Britain in 429, for we are told by his biographer Constantius[1] that before he was made bishop of Auxerre he held the office of *dux tractus Armoricani*, and we know from the evidence of the *Notitia Dignitatum* that as such he would be responsible for the *litus tractus Armoricani*,[2] and the Saxon devastations in Armorica would be his main concern. We know that the Gallo-Romans of Armorica were in a state of rebellion, not only in 409 and 429, but throughout the fifth century,[3] and Constantius refers to them as 'a fickle and undisciplined people', led by a certain Tibatto whom the anonymous *Gaulish Chronicle* twice mentions, first s.a. 435, where he is referred to as the leader of an independence movement on the part of 'Gallia Ulterior' (i.e. Armorica), and again in 437 among those captured and slain when the rebellion was put down. The movement seems to have been at its height following Germanus's visit to Britain in 429.

At the same time that the Gallo-Roman centres of Armorica moved eastwards, the new Celtic population entered Armorica by sea, concentrating on the coast-lands and occupying large tracts of the interior of the country, especially in the west. The chief Roman centres of Nantes,

[1] The life of St Germanus by Constantius has come down to us in two versions. The shorter and better, which is believed to be the older, is edited by W. Levison, *Mon. Germ. Hist.: Script. Rer. Merov.* VII (1920), 225 ff.

[2] The offices attributed by Constantius to St Germanus present a difficult problem, and are not wholly free from suspicion. See Gaudemet, 'La Carrière Civile de St Germanus' in the volume of studies issued at Auxerre by G. Le Bras and E. Gilson, *St Germain d'Auxerre et son temps* (Auxerre, 1950), p. 111 ff. For a brief discussion of the question as it relates to the defence of Armorica, reference may be made to N. K. Chadwick, *P.L.*, p. 263 f.

[3] For an account of the rebellions of the Armoricans, see W. Levison, *Neues Archiv* XXIX, 139 ff.

Vannes and Rennes, i.e. the eastern border states, had adopted Roman defence measures and remained Roman in character and institutions, and enclosed themselves in defensive walls owing to the Saxon scare;[1] but all the rest of the peninsula gradually changed its character and its language from Gallo-Roman to a form of Celtic closely related to Cornish and Welsh, Cornish more particularly. The country changed from Armorica, a peripheral Gallo-Roman province, a shabby outpost of the Empire, facing east, to a country with its back to Gaul, and its contacts, its culture, its political sympathies, its social relations, its Church and its population closely united with those of Celtic Britain, especially western Britain. It became once more a Celtic country.

Passing from the Ireland of the late Iron Age, and at the dawn of history, to the opening of the historical period, is a dramatic experience. It is the change from a country developing in isolation on its own traditional lines to a country open to the influences of an outside and higher civilization. It has already been emphasized that the high development and professional devotion of the intellectual classes of ancient Ireland have preserved for us their oral records of a native civilization on the periphery of the ancient world till their traditions passed into the crucible of Latin letters. This revolution in culture came about by the opening up of contacts with more advanced civilization to the east. In Ireland some isolated hoards from Roman Britain, such as the silver hoard from Balline, give concrete evidence of direct contact across the Irish Sea in the fourth or fifth century.[2] This is a different and much more immediate contact than Ireland's earlier foreign contact with the outside world by way of the longer Mediterranean sea-routes in the Bronze Age, or that of the earlier centuries of our era, perhaps as early as the third century, when Gaulish warriors, probably exiles, crossed to southern Ireland and entered the service of Irish kings,[3] or that of cultural contact directly stimulated by the barbarian invasions of Gaul.

With the fifth century we enter a new phase of history, and leave the Ireland of the ancient world behind. The prestige of written records claims to displace oral tradition, and though we now know that our written annals and many records of institutions of the early millennium are themselves based on oral tradition, the fact of their subsequent written form when incorporated into the annalistic histories gives them

[1] On the erection of defensive walls around the Gaulish open towns of this period, see Jullian, *Bordeaux*, 34, 43 ff.; *La Gaule* IV, 594, n. 4, and references. Cf. also the brief but valuable account of O. Brogan, *Roman Gaul* (London, 1953), 221 ff.

[2] See S. P. Ó Ríordáin, 'Roman Material in Ireland', P.R.I.A., LI, Section C, No. 3 (1947), p. 39 f.

[3] For evidence and references see Kuno Meyer, *Ériu* IV (1910), 208; and cf. *Learning in Ireland in the Fifth Century* (Dublin, 1913), 7 f., and notes 15-17.

a place for the first time in the historiography of Europe. How far these records are to be depended on is a very difficult question and one which is at the moment much debated.

This change from what we may call the Iron Age form of recording history, the traditional oral saga, to the chronicle style which reached Ireland through Latin channels under ecclesiastical influence, is startling to the student of Irish historical records. Events are henceforth recorded in chronological order in the form of annals on foreign models. The entries are brief and laconic, and are generally in Latin, though sometimes interspersed with entries in Irish, as in the *Annals of Tigernach*. History is now the work of clerics educated in the Latin tradition, trained in a Continental type of education, and in chronology – the root of historiography.[1]

But the clerics, like their predecessors the *filid*, could only do their work under patronage, whether monastic or more directly princely. In either case their work was invariably written for a direct purpose, under direct political influence. Propaganda is never absent, even though unavowed. This principle underlies all our early Irish annals and has coloured the record of our early historical period. The same influence has virtually ignored the province of Munster and flood-lit the family of Níall Noígiallach and their rise to power in Ulster. This does not mean that genuine history is absent from the annals. It means that it is difficult to assess correctly.[2]

The early traditions of the family of Níall Noígiallach form a bridge between the oral records of prehistoric Ireland and the later written records, and it is with the rise of Níall and his family to the chief power in central and northern Ireland that Irish history really begins. The traditional dates[3] of Níall are given as 379 to 405, or more probably 428. The pedigree[4] of Níall and his family is unreliable; but Irish tradition, derived from early Munster poems, especially elegies, fragments of which have survived,[5] claim that he was the son of Eochu Mugmedón and of 'Cairenn, the curly black-haired daughter of Sachell Balb of the Saxons' (cf. below). This is apparently the only occurrence of the name *Cairenn*, an Irish transformation of L. *Carina*. The term *balb*,

---

[1] On this subject see the illuminating study of Cennfaelad by E. MacNeill, 'A Pioneer of Nations', *Studies* XI (1922).

[2] As J. V. Kelleher has pointed out, 'Early Irish History and Pseudo-History', S.H., no. 3 (1963), 113 ff.

[3] His dates are a matter of considerable uncertainty. He is believed to be the father of Loegaire, whose accession in AD 427 or possibly 428, and whose death in 462 or 463 are believed to be our first secure dates of an Irish king. See O'Rahilly, *E.I.H.M.*, 209. But the chronology of the fifth century is very uncertain. See O'Rahilly, *loc. cit.*, and for an important discussion see J. Carney, *S.I.L.H.*, 330 ff.; cf. also H.M. Chadwick, *E.S.*, 133 ff.

[4] This is given by O'Rahilly, *E.I.H.M.*, p. 221.

[5] For the texts see K. Meyer, *Otia Merseiana* II (1899), p. 88 ff.; 'Totenklage für König Níall Noígiallach' in *F.W.S.*, p. 1 ff.; *ÄID* I, p. 14 ff.; II, p. 21 f.

'stammerer' is used elsewhere of people of foreign tongue. Presumably Níall's father obtained his wife from Roman Britain. It was widely believed that Níall met his death abroad,[1] and that he met it while raiding in Britain is by no means improbable. Traditions of activities and death abroad are also attributed to Dathí,[2] a prince of Connacht, Níall's nephew and immediate successor as 'king of Ireland', according to the later genealogists. Foreign contacts were a marked feature of the family in later generations also. In the *Additamenta* by the scribe Ferdomnach in the *Book of Armagh*, Níall's own grandson Fedelmid has married the daughter of a British king, and she and her son are able to converse in the British tongue with St Patrick's British nephew Lomman. We shall see the first fruits of this contact overseas in the migration of St Columba, a member of the family of the northern Uí Néill, to Scottish Dál Riata, in the following century.

Our earliest traditions of Níall associate him closely with contemporary poets. An eighth or ninth century poem, purporting to be an elegy, claims that Níall was the foster-son of the famous Munster poet Torna Éices, 'Torna the learned'. The poet refers to Níall's father Eochu Mugmedón and his grandfather Muiredach, and claims that, now Níall is dead, the enemies of Ireland (i.e. the Saxons) will prosper. The opening verse recalls his mother's British name and stresses Níalls' fair hair. Tuirn son of Torna laments:

> When we used to go to the gathering with Eochu's son,
> Yellow as a bright primrose was the hair on the head of Cairenn's son.[3]

A saga[4] on the death of Níall adds the comment:

> Cairenn, the curly black-haired daughter of Sachell Balb[5] of the Saxons was the mother of Níall.

In the same saga his own official poet is said to have been the well-known early Munster poet Ladchenn mac Bairchedo, whose surviving genealogical poem is ascribed by Kuno Meyer to the seventh century.[6] These poems and poets and their relations with Níall illustrate very well the importance of early Irish poetry for the reconstruction of early Irish history. It is significant that this famous head of the Goidelic dynasty was remembered in after times as a heroic warrior, with his heroic poets to celebrate him and his ancestors; and it is doubtless to these poets and their close association with Níall and his family that we

---

[1] On the variant traditions of his death cf. O'Rahilly, *E.I.H.M.*, p. 217 f.
[2] O'Rahilly dates the death of Dathi or Nathí in AD 445, *E.I.H.M.*, p. 215.
[3] K. Meyer, *A.I.P.*, p. 69.
[4] Edited and translated by Kuno Meyer in *Otia Merseiana* II, p. 84 ff.
[5] See *E.I.H.M.* 216 n. 3.　　　　　　　　　　　　[6] *ÄID* I, p. 15 f.

may attribute the exalted and indeed even exaggerated prestige of the Uí Néill in the later annals. This in itself would account for the support of the cause of the poets by Columba (cf. p. 175 below), himself a member of the northern Uí Néill. There can be no doubt, however, that Níall and his family owe their importance to a fundamental change which came about in the political divisions of Ireland in their time, and for which they are mainly responsible – the disappearance of the political divisions of Ireland represented by the *cóiceda* (cf. p. 35 f.).

The chief change in the development from the age-old political geography which took place during the early historical period was the destruction and partitioning, about the middle of the fifth century, of the ancient *cóiced* of the Ulaid, which had included the whole of northern Ireland from Donegal to Antrim. Tradition claims that this process had begun at least as early as the time of Cormac mac Airt;[1] but as a broad fact, according to our so-called historical records, the change was brought about by the northward and eastward expansion of the family of Níall, with their allies from Connacht. The result was the dismemberment and finally the conquest of the Érainn in the north, in all probability by the three sons of Níall himself, Eogan, Conall and Enda, and at Níall's instigation.[2]

An early stage in this dismemberment was the conquest of a group of peoples between the eastern and the western Ulaid known as the Airgialla ('Oriel', 'subject peoples'),[3] ultimately by the Uí Néill and their Connacht allies. Their territory consisted of the modern counties of Armagh, Monaghan, Tyrone, and most of Fermanagh and Derry. Its possession by the Uí Néill carried with it Emain Macha (two miles from Armagh), the ancient capital of the Ulaid. The conquest of Oriel had placed most of Ulster under the Uí Néill. Of the old independent Ulaid there now remained unconquered by the new 'Tara dynasty' only Donegal and the north-eastern coastal strip from Antrim to Dundalk – in the north and north-east were the little kingdoms of Dál Riata and Dál Fiatach; to the east of Lough Neagh, the kingdom of Dál nAraidi.[4]

A further step in this dismemberment of ancient Ulster was the conquest *c.* 428 of Donegal, the country which still remained independent to the west of Oriel, and the formation on the spot of the new kingdom of Ailech or Fochla (lit. 'north'), by two of Níall's sons, Eogan (d. 465) and Conall. The new province later formed the nucleus of the kingdom of the northern Uí Néill. These two sons of Níall now occupied territories known later respectively as *Tír Conaill* in the Donegal mountains to the west; and Tyrone (*Tír Eógain*) to the east. Their capital was

[1] MacNeill, *Phases*, 124 f.
[2] O'Rahilly, *E.I.H.M.*, 223, 227 f.; Binchy, S.H., no. 2 (1962), p. 150.
[3] On the subject of the establishment of Oriel see O'Rahilly, *E.I.H.M.*, 225.
[4] O'Rahilly, *E.I.H.M.*, 234.

Ailech [Plates 18, 20].[1] In 563 they gave a crushing defeat to the Dál nAraidi, whose country seems to have become the possession of Eogan's line, as we understand *A.U.* 562 (recte 563).

From the fifth century onwards the ruling dynasty of northern and central Ireland were the Uí Néill,[2] the descendants of Níall Noígiallach. The next in succession to Níall at Tara was his son Loegaire who was reigning at Tara in St Patrick's time,[3] and who is the first Irish king whose dates are regarded as approximately established (cf. p 55, n. 3). According to the traditional history[4] the succession as head of the dynasty from 506 to 734 alternated between the descendants of his two sons Eogan and Conall, jointly known as the northern Uí Néill, who had founded the kingdom of Ailech in the north, and the descendants of a third son, Crimthann, known as the southern Uí Néill, who claimed their capital at Tara.[5] The two dynasties of the kingdom of Ailech are represented as having held together in unity, alternating in their turn with the southern Uí Néill, till the Cenél Eógain overcame the Cenél Conaill in battle in 734. From 734 to 1036 the succession is represented as alternating between the Cenél Eógain and the southern Uí Néill of Meath. In the rivalry between the Cenél Conaill and the Cenél Eógain the former had the advantage of the natural fastnesses of the Donegal mountains, while the Cenél Eógain could expand eastwards and southwards till the power of Oriel, their eastern neighbours, was broken in 827 by Níall Caille, king of Ailech, and Oriel became subject to the kings of Cenél Eógain, known later as the kings of Tyrone. It was possibly an earlier phase of this eastward expansion of the Uí Néill of Ailech which prompted the movement of members of the dynasty of Dál Riata on the Antrim coast overseas to Scottish Argyll (cf. p. 64 below).

The chief kingdoms which had formed constituent but independent kingdoms in the wider over-kingdom of Ulaid consisted of (1) the small kingdom of Dál Riata in the extreme northern coastal strip of Co. Antrim, who had their dynastic stronghold on the rocky promontory of Dunseverick, at the terminus of the *Slige Midluachra*, the ancient royal route north from north Leinster and Meath.[6] Their ruling dynasty, it will be remembered, claimed to be of Érainn stock; (2) the Dál Fiatach on the eastern sea-board of Co. Down, also Érainn and perhaps the true Ulaid of the Heroic Age tradition, though this is disputed; (3) the Dál

---

[1] The splendid fortress known today as the Grianán Ailigh, just inside the eastern border of Donegal.

[2] The *Uí Néill* are the descendants of Níall Noígiallach. The term is to be sharply distinguished from *Ó Néill*, which is proper only to the descendants of Níall Glúndubh, who fell in battle against the Norsemen on the Liffey in 919. See MacNeill, *C.I.*, 90.

[3] As we learn from Muirchu's *Life of St Patrick*.

[4] For the biassed nature of the sources of this tradition see Kelleher, S.H., no. 3, 120 ff.

[5] On this claim see Kelleher, S.H., no. 3, 123.

[6] See Colm Ó Lochlainn, 'Roadways in Ancient Ireland' in *E.S.E.M.*, 465 ff., and map *ad fin.*

nAraidi, remains of the ancient Cruithni, between the Dál Riata and the Dál Fiatach, occupying a wide area around Lough Neagh. They were the largest and most powerful people in these parts. In the sixth century their most important king was Mongán (d. 624), who is widely celebrated in the very considerable corpus of sagas and poems relating to him. His residence was at Moylinny, practically the modern town of Antrim on the eastern shore of Lough Neagh. The capital of the ancient Ulaid, Emain Macha, which manifestly gave birth to Armagh, only two miles away, came into the possession of the Uí Néill,[1] on the conquest of the Ulaid.

The destruction of the old *Cóiced* of Ulster and the annexation of its centre of power by the dynasty of the Uí Néill, is the most important fact in early Irish history. Henceforth the chief power is in central Ireland, where the southern branch of Níall's descendants claimed to occupy the prehistoric sanctuary of Tara, and are commonly referred to as the 'Tara dynasty'. By their annexation of the ancient Ulaid capital of Emain Macha about the middle of the fifth century they had gained a stronghold close to St Patrick's sanctuary of Armagh, and with it the patronage of the chief saint of the defeated Ulaid. Moreover, as this is claimed as the centre of the earliest learning and of the introduction of the art of writing and Latin culture into Ireland, its possession may have given to the Uí Néill the control of spiritual and intellectual, no less than of political, prestige, and of the teaching and writing of history.

Our literary texts recognize two great divisions of Ireland, known as 'Conn's Half', comprising northern Ireland, and 'Mug's Half', comprising Munster and Leinster. The names originate in a fictitious story claiming that Conn Cétchathach ('of the hundred battles'), ancestor of the Uí Néill (*Connachta*) and Mug Nuadat ('slave of Nuadu') whose proper name was Eógan (ancestor of the Eóganacht) had divided Ireland between them. This conception was undoubtedly the creation of the historiographers. It appears in annals and genealogies, but not in the Book of Invasions.[2]

The literary tradition undoubtedly reflects a historical division between the territory dominated by the Uí Néill and that which developed from the old *cóiceda* of Munster and Leinster from the fourth to the tenth centuries. Our traditions for this 'southern half' ('Mug's Half') are on the whole less full than those of the north; but we can trace in the annals and genealogies of Munster a class of historiographers attached to the interests of the dominant line of the Eóganacht of

[1] See Binchy, 'Patrick and his Biographers', *S.H.*, no. 2 (1962), p. 150. On the early relationship of these three independent kingdoms to the over-kingdom of *Ulaid* see E. MacNeill, *Phases*, 185; *ibid.*, *C.I.*, 185; O'Rahilly, *E.I.H.M.*, 222 f.
[2] *E.I.H.M.* 191–2.

Cashel comparable to those working in the interests of the Uí Néill in the north. Literary evidence suggests on the whole, however, that from the fifth century onwards Munster was developing intellectually perhaps even more than by military and territorial expansion, and that her outlook was continental rather than insular. It may well be that in fact during the early historical period Munster was the most civilized part of Ireland.

Whereas in the Heroic Age the seat of the chief king, Cú Roí mac Dáiri, was in west Munster, we find that in the early historical period the chief dynasty of 'Mug's Half' was the Eóganacht with their chief seat at Cashel near the borders of Leinster. The Munster dynasty of the Eóganacht formed a consolidated realm, generally peaceable and flourishing, and probably, as suggested above, always in touch with the continent. The culture of both Munster and Leinster was high. It is claimed that writing in the vernacular had already begun in Munster by 600, and that panegyric poetry from Munster has been preserved in written form from the second half of the sixth century,[1] and contact between south-eastern Ireland and Gaul had evidently had an unbroken sequence from at least as early as the third century, and was actively stimulated between Aquitaine and southern Ireland during the barbarian invasions of Gaul.[2]

The rise of the Eóganacht had been rapid. In the earliest period they are never heard of. By St Patrick's time their chief branch are already ruling on the great rock of Cashel though other branches of importance are located in the west in Cork and Limerick. The growth of their strength in east Munster is in some measure at the expense of the old kingdom of Leinster, which had been greatly reduced by the expansion of the power of Meath.[3] The conquest of north Leinster by the dynasty of Tara had been accompanied by the imposition of a heavy annual tribute, which according to a continuous tradition[4] was resisted in a series of battles lasting for centuries. According to tradition King Loegaire of Tara, son of Níall Noígiallach, met his death in 462 or 463 in seeking to exact it, and the last heroic saga, that of the Battle of Allen,[5] fought c. 722, records the death of Fergal, son of Mael Dúin, king of 'Conn's Half', who had invaded Leinster and perished seeking the tribute.

The tribal histories and genealogies enable us to trace the means by

---

[1] R. Flower, I.T., 18.

[2] See the brief but impressive studies of this subject with fuller evidence and references by Kuno Meyer, L.I.F.C., p. 7 f.; 'Gauls in Ireland', Ériu IV (1910), p. 208.

[3] The stages by which Tara traditionally extended its sway over Leinster are outlined by E. MacNeill, Phases, p. 120 ff., and more especially p. 187 ff.

[4] See 'The Boromean Tribute', text and translation by Standish H. O'Grady, S.G., no. XXVIII.

[5] Text and translation by Whitley Stokes, R.C. XXIV (1903), p. 41 ff.

which the eastern Eóganacht gained control, by the fifth century, over the provincial kingship of Munster at the expense of the Érainn of West Munster, who had hitherto been the overlords. This growth of power the Eóganacht appear to have achieved by enlisting various tribes, including both Lagin and some sections of the Érainn themselves, as allies in conquering the dominant sections of the Érainn and in consolidating their own position against them.[1] The principle was analogous to the Roman establishment of *foederati* on their frontiers. Of these federate allies of the Eóganacht the most interesting are the Déisi.[2]

The Eóganacht of Cashel employed the Déisi to expel the Osraige from Mag Femin, and settled them in the conquered territory. While part of the Déisi migrated to Pembrokeshire, under their leader Eochaid Allmuir ('from overseas'), the rest settled in south Tipperary and Waterford, where their name survives in that of the baronies of Decies.[3] The grand-daughter of their chief married the king of Cashel, Oengus mac Nadfroích,[4] who is in fact the first king of Cashel mentioned in the annals. The intermarriage of these ruling families and the position of the frontier troops ensured peace, and this eastward extension and consolidation of Munster power was of importance for the subsequent history of Ireland. It is claimed in the *Tripartite Life of St Patrick* that Oengus mac Nadfroích was baptized with his sons by the saint at Cashel, and that Patrick prophesied that none of his descendants should ever die of a wound, which was tantamount to declaring them clerics, and the same source adds that no one is king of Cashel until Patrick's successor instals him and confers ecclesiastical rank upon him.[5]

Ancient tradition ascribes the initial rise of the Eóganacht, not to Oengus mac Nadfroích but to the legendary ancestor of the Eóganacht, Conall Corc, son of Lugaid, who was fostered by Crimthann Mór mac Fidaig, and succeeded him as king of Munster. According to this tradition, Conall Corc, having been treacherously banished by his uncle Crimthann, eventually reached the palace of the Pictish king Feradach Findfechtnach, king of Cruithentuath, and married his daughter Mongfind. Eventually Corc returned to Munster, taking her and their sons, and succeeded to the throne. The story occurs in several variant forms, and it is interesting to note that Corc's uncle is the Crimthann Mór mac Fidaig to whom Cormac's Glossary refers (p. 50). The story of Corc cannot be regarded as historical, but it has interesting traditional elements.[6] The kingship of Cashel alternated between two septs of the Eóganachta, that of Cashel proper and that of Glennamain

[1] Ó Buachalla, C.H.A.J. LVII (1952), p. 113.   [2] *Ibid.*, p. 116.   [3] *E.I.H.M.*, 64.
[4] Slain in 490 according to the *Annals of Inisfallen*, s.a. 492.   [5] *Tripartite Life* I, 194 f.
[6] The text of the story in saga-form is incomplete. For references to the sources and a discussion of the bias and historical elements in these Eóganacht traditions see Ó Buachalla, *op. cit.*, 67 ff. Cf. also Dillon, *C.K.*, p. 34 ff.

(Glenworth), with occasional intrusions from the other septs, from the fifth to the ninth century.[1]

The most powerful of the pre-Norse kings of Cashel was Cathal mac Finguini (*c.* 721–42) to whom the *Annals of Inisfallen* (s.a. 721) claim that Fergal, son of Mael Dúin, King of Tara, made submission. Indeed these annals, which are, of course, of Munster provenance, claim in his *obit* s.a. 742 that he was 'king of Ireland', whereas the *Annals of Ulster*, which are of northern provenance, refer to him only as *rex Caisil* ('king of Cashel'). The Battle of Allen took place in the time of Cathal mac Finguini. It violated a truce previously made between Cathal and Fergal.[2] Accordingly, as in honour bound, Cathal returned the head of Fergal, which had been cut off in the battle, to the Uí Néill, in compensation for the breach of the truce that had been made between them.

It has been claimed, nevertheless, that during the early Christian centuries, Munster was on the whole perhaps the most consolidated realm in western Europe.[3] Political changes, migrations and dynastic strife are of relatively limited intensity, and the fact that only two or three of the score or so of kings who ruled Munster at that period died violent deaths demonstrates her relatively peaceful condition.[4] This quiet political history of Munster is to be interpreted in direct connection with the history of culture and the church. It is in Munster that we find the thickest concentration of ogam inscriptions – a sure sign of a cultured and wealthy aristocracy; our earliest records of writing; our earliest cultured monastic contacts, as demonstrated by the 'Irish Augustine' at the monastery of Lismore on the Blackwater (cf. p. 168 below); and finally the ecclesiastical associations of the kings of Cashel, who, during the historical period, were sometimes bishops. Tradition claims that this unique combination of the status of king and bishop dates back to the time of the consecration of Oengus mac Nadfroích by St Patrick. The tradition is late, but this close association of the kingship and bishopric of Cashel is undoubtedly the key to the history of Munster throughout the early historical period.

[1] Ó Buachalla, *op. cit.*, 73–6.   [2] *Annals of Inisfallen*, s.a. 721.
[3] MacNeill, *Phases*, 12.   [4] Ó Buachalla, C.H.A.J., LVI (1951), 87.

CHAPTER 4

THE FORMATION OF THE
HISTORICAL CELTIC KINGDOMS

In the preceding chapter we have traced the emergence of organized Celtic realms on the western periphery of Europe following on the decline and withdrawal of Roman power. Native Celtic dynasties now carried on the internal administration of the country, and defended the borders, which were beset on all sides by neighbouring peoples, Teutonic, Pictish, and Irish, all seeking expansion and permanent settlement in Britain after the withdrawal of Roman defences. During the sixth and following centuries the earlier political fragmentation of the Celtic peoples developed into more extended and unified communities. The Celtic peoples on the borders of southern Scotland and throughout southern Britain had already established native dynasties ruling wide kingdoms; and these kingdoms spoke a single Brittonic language, throughout all Scotland south of the Forth-Clyde line, and north-western England, Wales, Cornwall and now on to Brittany.

Beyond the area which had been under Roman rule lay two great Celtic realms which the Romans had never conquered. These were the powerful Picts of the Highlands and islands of Scotland, protected by their mountains; and the Celtic peoples of Ireland, immune in their isolation across the Irish Sea. The conquests of the Goidels during the fifth century had welded the kingdoms of Ireland into two great dynasties – northern Ireland under the control of the descendants of Níall Noígiallach, southern Ireland under the Eóganacht of Cashel. In the present chapter we shall trace the development of the Picts during the sixth and seventh centuries into the two powerful divisions, referred to by Bede as the 'Northern and Southern Picts, separated by steep and rugged mountains.' We shall also trace the development of the last and greatest of the Irish settlements in western Britain, which succeeded in establishing an important kingdom in the west of Scotland to the north of the Roman defensive line of the Antonine Wall. The relations of these Pictish and Irish settlements with one another and with the Britons to the south of them, and later with the Angles settled to the south and east of them, are the beginnings of modern Scotland, while the British dynasties of southern Scotland combined with those of north-western and western Britain to develop later into the much smaller but more consolidated kingdom of Wales.

After the conquests of the Uí Néill in northern Ireland three small independent kingdoms which had formed a part of the ancient *cóiced* of the Ulaid (pp. 58–9) remained independent and developed a future importance for the countries across the Irish Sea far in excess of their rôle in insular Irish history. Both claimed to be of Érainn or pre-Goidelic stock. The first of these is the little kingdom of Dál Riata, whose dynasty claimed to be of the 'seed of Conaire Mór', their pre-historic king. This remnant of the Ulaid now had their chief seat at Dunseverick on the small strip still left to them on the north coast of Co. Antrim. We know little of the dynasty till St Patrick's day, but in the ninth-century text of the *Tripartite Life of St Patrick* the kingdom is governed by Erc and his sons, Loarn and Fergus, the latter of whom is blessed by the saint, and Patrick prophesies to him that one of his descendants shall occupy the throne of Dál Riata and Fortrenn for ever. Fortrenn is the name of one of the kingdoms of the Southern Picts in historical times, but seems to be used here for Scotland as a whole. We also hear of the expansion of the kingdom of Dál Riata under the sons of Erc in the *Annals of Tigernach;* 'Fergus mór mac Erca (*sic*) with the people of Dál Riata held part of Britain and died there.'[1] Here the event corresponds to one which in the *Annals of Ulster* is recorded s.a. 502. It probably took place about the middle of the fifth century or possibly a little later. Meanwhile the kingdom of Dál Riata in Ireland from which they had come still continued; but little is heard of it after the Battle of Mag Rath (Moira) in or about 634, when they fought in alliance with the Dál Riata of Scotland in an unsuccessful encounter against Domnall, son of Aed, king of Tara. Henceforth the history of Dál Riata and the 'seed of Conaire Mór', as they called themselves, belongs to Scotland, where the term continued to be used in relation to the dynasty of Scottish Dál Riata as late as the twelfth century.[2]

The second surviving kingdom was Dál Fiatach, traditionally related to Dál Riata, and claiming descent from the same stock. Having lost their ancient citadel of Emain Macha, they occupied the sea-board of Co. Down and part of Co. Antrim. The dynastic name, *Dál Fiatach*, is derived from their legendary ancestor, Fiatach Find.[3] Their ruling dynasty lasted down to the Norman Conquest, but it plays comparatively little part in the Irish annals, and, like Dál Riata, its more notable historical associations lay eastwards and overseas. Their most out-standing king was Baetán mac Cairill (d. 581), who is said to have compelled Aedán mac Gabráin, the contemporary king of Scottish

[1] RC xvii 124. [2] Cf. H. M. Chadwick, *E.S.*, 35, n. 2.
[3] *C. G. H.*, 136a 46.

Dál Riata, to submit to him at Rosnaree on Belfast Lough, and to have subdued Manu (the Isle of Man).[1] (Cf. p. 72 below.)

The third was Dál nAraide, the most important of the surviving groups of Cruithni, or Cruthin, who were akin to the Picts of Scotland, also called Cruthin.[2] They were probably earlier subject to Dál Fiatach, but later emerge as an independent kingdom.

In tracing briefly the relations recorded from the early historical period of the small kingdoms in north-eastern Ireland which survived from the prehistoric fragmented Ulaid we are in reality entering on a new area, this time a maritime one. Its geographical centre was an island, the Isle of Man, which we have not yet brought into the picture because no early records have been preserved, and it is only from the evidence of the later historical period that we are able to trace something of the early history of the island. The key to this lost history is contained partly in the language, partly in the local stone inscriptions and archaeological remains, but most of all in the history of the surrounding countries – Ireland, Scotland, north England and Wales – with all of which the Isle of Man was in close communication. Before passing to a fuller consideration of northern and southern Britain in the sixth and seventh centuries therefore, we will pause to take a brief survey of the Isle of Man, Ellan Vannin, to give it its Manx name.

In prehistoric and early historical times, when the sea offered a quicker and easier means of transport than land routes, the Isle of Man occupied a key position. In these times of the rapid backward and forward voyages between Ireland, Scotland, and Wales, the Irish Sea and the waterways to the north of it were busy intersections of sea-routes, the northern extension of the Atlantic coastal route of pre-historic times, and the Celtic peoples were no mean seafarers. Throughout the historical period the narrow and stormy straits between Ireland and the Hebrides and south-western Scotland were traversed readily, and the Irish Sea afforded a lively communication, sometimes friendly, sometimes hostile, between all the lands in its coastal areas.

In view of this position, and perhaps even more owing to its genial climate and fertility, the Isle of Man has had colonists from both Ireland and Wales from pre-historic times.[3] We have no early vernacular records,[4] but much can be deduced as to its early history from the annals of the Celtic countries in its orbit, for it undoubtedly played a part of very considerable importance in the struggle among the fragments of the Ulaid, that is to say the new Irish kingdom of Dál Riata in western Scotland, the relatively large and important kingdom

---

[1] For references see O'Rahilly, *E.I.H.M.*, 504.
[2] *E.I.H.M.*, 341–6.
[3] For a brief account of the prehistoric evidence see R. H. Kinvig, *H.I.M.*
[4] The earliest written Manx is the translation of the Prayer Book *c.* 1625.

of Dál nAraidi around Lough Neagh, and the small but by no means inconsiderable kingdom of Dál Fiatach on the north-eastern coast of Ireland. Something of its history and its relationship with all the surrounding countries is also reflected in the language, or rather languages, which we can trace on the stone inscriptions, of which the island possesses a considerable wealth in the Ogam and runic alphabets as well as in Latin.

It is suggested that there may have been some colonization from Ireland in the fourth and fifth centuries, about the time when the Irish immigration into Scottish Dál Riata was at its height, and this is very probable. The island seems to have been British-speaking at an earlier time, but there were Irish speakers there at least by the fifth century.[1] The language spoken in the island until recently is not of the Brythonic Group, but Goidelic. We know that Gaelic was spoken in Man at least as early as the fifth century AD, because several Ogam inscriptions of this period are found there, and the language was probably brought to Man in the fourth century, just as it was probably brought at this time to the Highlands and islands of Scotland and the western peninsulas of Wales (cf. p. 38). There are signs, however, that British (Welsh) was also spoken in Man in the period of the Ogam inscriptions and both languages were probably spoken there in the Dark Ages.[2]

The Gaelic of Man is not an independent survival from the original parent Goidelic stock, however, but is closely linked to medieval Irish and Scottish Gaelic, nearer to Scottish Gaelic than to Irish. From the Viking period till the late thirteenth century the Isle of Man had close political relations with western Scotland. Scottish Gaelic was spoken in Galloway, less than twenty miles from the Isle of Man, as late as the seventeenth century, and both historical and linguistic indications point to close communications between Man and Galloway from at least the early ninth century onwards. The close relationship which still subsists between the Manx language and the Scottish Gaelic of today reflects the time when the Gaelic of Galloway provided a connecting link between the two.[3]

We shall see that Welsh historical records suggest incursions into North Wales from Galloway across Morecambe Bay (cf. p. 109 below), and in the early ninth century a dynasty perhaps from Galloway established itself in the Isle of Man before founding a new dynasty in Gwynedd.

Before the occupation of Argyll by an Irish dynasty in the fifth century the whole of Scotland north of the Antonine Wall, including the

---

[1] For the evidence given below see K. H. Jackson, P.B.A., XXXVII (1951), 77 f.
[2] K. H. Jackson, in E.C., 209 f.; E.I.H.M., 504, n. 4.
[3] T. F. O'Rahilly, I.D.P.P., 117.

northern and western islands, had been ruled by the powerful dynasties of the Picts, and they continued to be the rulers of several eastern kingdoms till as late as the ninth century. In the earliest period of which we have record, groups or tribes known as the Cornovii and the Dumnonii – names also familiar to us from south-western Britain – occupied the north-western and the south midland areas of Scotland respectively, and these were not Picts but Britons.

The word Pict is a somewhat general term which covers a number of peoples in Scotland, known to Latin writers both on the Continent and in this country as *Picti*,[1] and in our earliest vernacular sources as *Cruthin*. But some of the peoples of Scotland are referred to by classical writers under more specific names. In Roman times two of the important tribes who were certainly 'Picts' were the *Verturiones* concentrated on the upper Forth and the river Earn, known later as the 'Men of Fortrenn' (cf. p. 64 above), and the Caledonii in the valley of the Upper Tay.

We know little about the organization of the Picts in the early centuries of their history. Bede, writing in the early eighth century, evidently visualized the Picts as divided into two main bodies whom he distinguished as the Northern and the Southern Picts, for he mentions that 'the provinces of the former are separated from those of the latter by steep and rugged mountains'; and he tells us further that St Columba arrived in Britain in the ninth year of the reign of Brideus son of Meilochon,[2] the *rex potentissimus* of the northern Picts, and that he converted them to Christianity. The Southern Picts, who live 'on this side of the mountains' (*qui intra eosdem montes habent sedes*), adds Bede, had been converted long before by the preaching of St. Ninian. The mountains which separated the Northern from the Southern Picts were the Grampians. Bede's division was probably a political reality. Land communication between the Northern and the Southern Picts must always have been very difficult and hazardous, especially after the establishment of the kingdom of Dál Riata.

Direct statements of relations between the northern and the southern Picts are rare in the early annals. Through the whole of the historical period the southern Picts appear in our records as divided into four separate provinces or kingdoms, all of them enclosing the valley of the Tay.

1. *Atholl*, roughly the Perthshire Highlands and the carse of Gowrie, the old kingdom of the Caledonii, with its capital at Dunkeld, dominated by Schiehallion, which was possibly their sanctuary. This kingdom

---

[1] N. K. Chadwick: 'The name Pict', S.G.S. VIII (1958).
[2] The name is basically identical with that of Maelgwn, the ruler of North Wales (cf. p. 51 above).

controlled the valley of the upper Tay and during the Pictish historical period its capital was at Scone.

2. *Circenn*, i.e. Forfar, now Angus, and Kincardine or the Mearns, i.e.
Strathmore, the northern territory of the Lower Tay Valley and
the eastern seaboard to the watershed of the river Dee.

3. *Fortrenn*, the genitive case of *Fortrinn* (pl.), later used as a nomina-
tive,[1] situated to the south-west of the Tay, and including the upper
waters of the Earn and the Forth, with its confluents.

4. *Fib* (Fife), the rich corn-growing country between the Tay and the
Forth. Traditions of fifth century saints and of early kings with their
seat at St Andrews point to its seaboard concentration. The earliest
name of St Andrews was *Kilrymont*.

This aggregate of Pictish kingdoms was known in later Latin medieval
records as *Pictavia*; in native speech and records as *Cruthentuath*, 'the
people of the Cruthin'.

Both the Picts of Atholl and those of Fortrenn were on through routes
to the Irish kingdom of Dál Riata in the west, and for this reason play a
larger part in Irish records than the Picts of Fife or Circenn. Yet the rich
agricultural kingdom of Circenn (Angus) was probably always the most
important centre. The finest and most advanced of the famous Pictish
sculptured stones are scattered throughout this area; and as one stands
on the great Iron Age hill fort of Castle Law above Abernethy on the
south bank of the Tay and surveys the line of hill forts along the north,
the whole Firth of Tay comes into view as a nucleated area, surely
always the heart of Pictavia.

We are in the dark as to the precise political relations between the
Northern and the Southern Picts at the time of which Bede speaks. It is
just possible that in the sixth century the centre of Pictish power was in
the neighbourhood of Inverness under Bride mac Maelchon, Brude
mac Maelchon as he is generally called in later records, Bede's *rex
potentissimus*. He had a fleet, and certainly controlled the northern isles
and the Hebrides. Adamnán, in his biography of St Columba, speaks of
the saint meeting a *subregulus* of the Orkneys at his court, and it is
inconceivable, in view of Columba's relations with him, that the saint
could have established his sanctuary on Iona had not the control of the
Hebrides been with Brude.

But the situation does not suggest that even in the late sixth century
the Northern Picts held any ascendancy over the Southern Picts. A
century later, when Ecgfrith of Northumbria sought to destroy the

[1] *E.I.H.M.* 26.

Pictish power in 685, he was slain at Dünnichen in Circenn, though his opponent, Brude mac Bile, is called king of Fortrenn in the annals. Perhaps the two kingdoms of Fortrenn and Circenn were united already at this time; but clearly Circenn, as Ecgfrith's objective, was the heart of Pictavia.

The kingdoms known collectively as *Cruthentuath* were the earliest native power in Scotland, a strong and, in some ways at least, a highly developed civilization into whose western seaboard the kingdom of Dál Riata had penetrated, growing into a powerful kingdom itself, even waging aggressive warfare in *Cruthentuath*. From the sixth century onwards the struggle for supremacy between the Picts of both north and south on the one hand, and the Irish kingdom of Dál Riata, later called Argyll, on the other, forms the most important theme of the history of Scotland till the union of the two peoples in the middle of the ninth century, and with the union, the beginning of what we mean today by the country of Scotland. A subordinate but important theme during the whole period, is the relations, now friendly, now hostile, between the Irish kingdom of Dál Riata and the Britons of southern Scotland. Meanwhile the Anglian dynasty of the Bernicians of Northumbria were gradually extending themselves northwards, and making heavy inroads into the British territory of south-eastern Scotland.

Although all indications confirm our traditions of the Picts as a powerful nation we are very much in the dark as to their internal history. About two dozen Pictish inscriptions exist, and their distribution covers the north and east of Scotland and corresponds closely with that of Pictish art represented on the 'symbol stones' to be described later. With two or three exceptions, in which the inscriptions are written in Latin letters, the Pictish inscriptions are written in a late form of the Ogam alphabet, and they have not been interpreted.

It is uncertain at what precise period the Picts as a whole became literate in the common use of the term. We have occasional references to 'the ancient documents of the Picts',[1] but this is thought probably to have reference to brief notices in calendars kept in the Pictish churches. A number of versions of what is commonly called a 'Pictish Chronicle' have come down to us,[2] but these contain for the most part little more

---

[1] Reference may be made to a suspicious document claiming to be an ancient record of the foundation of St Andrews, which assures us that the scribe has copied the contents as they are found *in veteribus Pictorum libris*. See Chadwick, *E.S.*, 28. Cf. M. O. Anderson, *S.H.R.* XXIX (1950), 17.

[2] Most of the texts of the early *Chronicles* were published by W. F. Skene, *P. and S.*, and discussed by him in *C.S.*, Vol. I. For detailed extracts, translated into English, see A. O. Anderson, *E.S.S.H.*, I, *pass.*, and cf. especially the Bibliographical Notes, p. xiv ff. For a general study of the subject see H. M. Chadwick, *E.S.*, *pass.* A more recent and quite indispensable study is that of M. O. Anderson in three contributions to S.H.R. XXVIII. 1 and 2 (1949), XXIX (1950). The best version of the Pictish king lists is that of Skene, *P. and S.*, p. 4 ff.

than lists of early kings, sometimes with brief notes attached. From
c. 550 these lists appear to be fairly trustworthy, for we can check them
by the frequent references to the same kings in trustworthy Irish, Welsh,
and English records. Before 550, however, the Pictish king lists cannot
be regarded as historical.

We are in a stronger position with regard to the history of the
Scottish kingdom of Dál Riata. In the first place our sources from
neighbouring peoples are much fuller. The Irish annals throughout our
period and down to c. 750 serve as a useful check on Scottish events,
especially the events of Dál Riata. Moreover, the Scottish kingdom of
Dál Riata, Irish in origin, had kept a short Chronicle,[1] probably on the
Island of Iona, from the seventh century at latest.

All our authorities, with the exception of Bede (H.F. I, v) are
in agreement that the kingdom was founded by Fergus mac Eirc ('Son
of Erc'), at a period believed to be towards the close of the fifth century.
An interesting document, containing a survey or inventory of the
'houses' and general muster for sea and land, attributed to Dál Riata,
has survived (cf. p. 72 below). The inventory is preceded by a brief
narrative giving some details of the invasions and the landing, and the
document may well be based on some institution of later times – perhaps
a basis for taxation or personal (?maritime) service – and so probably
preserves echoes of earlier tradition. The fleet is said to have carried a
hundred and fifty men, led by three brothers – Fergus Mór, Loarn and
Oengus Mór. Little is known of Loarn himself, but his family, known as
Cinél Loairn, occupied the northern part of Argyll, with their chief
seat on the rocky promontory now occupied by the ruin of Dunolly
Castle at Oban. The site was well placed for ready communications with
Ireland, and the external relations of the Cinél Loairn are chiefly with
Ireland. The rivalry of the Cinél Loairn and the Cinél Gabráin formed
the chief internal incidents of Dalriadic history.

Of Oengus Mór little is known, save that his family occupied Islay.
Fergus's grandson Gabrán, who had Kintyre and Knapdale, with his
chief stronghold on the rock of Dunadd in the midst of Crinan Moss
[Plate 37], was killed in 557 in a serious clash with the Picts under Brude
mac Maelchon, and was succeeded by his cousin Conall. It was during
Conall's reign that St Columba settled on Iona and as a result of a
visit to Brude's court, which we may interpret as a diplomatic mission,
is said to have converted the Picts to Christianity.

The eventual rise of the Cinél Gabráin to pre-eminence in Dál Riata
is doubtless to be ascribed to the political sagacity of St Columba. He
was undoubtedly the great man in the expansion of Dál Riata during
the sixth century. His biographer Adamnán would have us picture him

[1] On this subject see M. O. Anderson, S.H.R. XXIX (1950), 18.

as a recluse saint; but his relations with the Picts must have secured the tenure of the new colony of Dál Riata. His monastic settlement on Iona may have been dictated by the contemporary religious habit of the monks of the Celtic Church of making their sanctuaries on solitary islands; but one cannot fail to be struck by its excellent strategic position for communications with the northern and perhaps also the eastern Picts and all parts of Dál Riata, both Irish and Scottish. Despite late Irish traditions to the contrary, Columba more than once returned to Ireland on political missions on behalf of the new Scottish kingdom of Dál Riata. Of these the most famous was to the Convention of Druim Cett (575) which was held under the Irish king, Aed son of Ainmire, and on this occasion Columba was accompanied by the king of Dál Riata, Aedán mac Gabráin.

The kingdom in Argyll grew in area and importance, even penetrating further eastwards into the ancient area of the Caledonii in the Perthshire Highlands. The true founder of this expanding Irish kingdom was Aedán mac Gabráin himself. He remained Columba's firm friend to the end of his life and there can be little doubt that it was their joint statesmanship which guided the destiny of the little Irish-speaking kingdom of Argyll till, partly by conquest, and probably still more by alliances, gradually under Aedán's descendants it amalgamated ultimately with the kingdom of the Picts to form the united kingdom of Scotland.

His own personal record is largely maritime. In 575 he and St Columba jointly attended the Convention of Druim Cett in northern Ireland and Aedán evidently possessed, or had some control of, an allied fleet, for according to the *Annals of Ulster* s.a. 579 (recte 580) he made an expedition to the Orkneys, which at this time were apparently in the control of the king of the Northern Picts. In 578[1] the Irish annals record a battle in Manu in which Aedán was victorious, and the battle was evidently widely known since it is mentioned in the Irish annals. Aedán's maritime activities are puzzling. He certainly had access to the sea from his seat on Dunadd by way of the Crinan River; but his position was hardly an ideal one for a sea-going fleet. On the other hand our records tell us almost nothing of Oengus mac Eirc after his settlement on the island of Islay. Here, however, a fleet would have been a necessity to him, and it is just possible that he and Aedán made joint maritime expeditions, and that the Dalriadic panegyrists, whose poems must have formed the basis of all the later Scottish annals of this period, would credit the expeditions solely to Aedán. The question of Aedán's seafaring activities are particularly interesting for their bearing on his warlike relations with Baetán mac Cairill (d. 581 or 582, cf.

[1] Cf. *E.I.H.M.* 237, n. 3; 504, and cf. F. J. Byrne, S.H., no. 4 (1964), 58.

pp. 64–5 above) including their rivalry for the Isle of Man. At this period Baetán was the most considerable of the kings of Dál Fiatach (p. 69). The Isle of Man now begins to figure in the authentic history of the Irish Sea and the surrounding countries, and to appear under her own name *Manau* in the Irish and Scottish annals, and in the *Annales Cambriae*, and even in the Northumbrian history recorded by Bede. The whole record is obscure owing to variant readings both in the tribal histories and in the annals, but it seems probable that Baetán first compelled Aedán to submit to him. He then conquered the Isle of Man, which Aedán re-took two years after Baetán's death, i.e. in 582 or 583. The dates are not wholly reliable and are undergoing drastic revision at the moment.[1]

Apparently a struggle was in progress between Scottish Dál Riata and the king of Dál Fiatach first on the shores of Belfast Lough, then in the Isle of Man – doubtless a struggle between these two branches of the same Érainn stock for supremacy in north-eastern Ireland, perhaps resistance to the Uí Néill. In these obscure but important relations of the kings of Dál Riata and Dál Fiatach at this period it is probable that Dál nAraidi around Lough Neagh played a part. An interesting Irish saga relates that Aedán received military help from their king Mongán (d. *c.* 624). The Isle of Man would have formed an important base for both Aedán and Baetán, and indeed Aedán's maritime power must have been considerable. This is doubtless true of all Dál Riata, and is, in fact, indicated by the Irish document referred to above which enumerates the units forming the fleet.[2]

Aedán's most permanent achievements, however, were his activities against the Picts, especially in the east of his dominions, and though he suffered some heavy reverses he seems to have gained control of some Pictish territory.

Aedán has left his impression on history as Dál Riata's greatest king. Already in 628 the *Annals of Ulster* refer to his successor, Eochaid Buide, as *rex Pictorum*. Meanwhile the growing power of the Bernician kings, and the advance of Aethelfrith of Northumbria northwards, prompted Aedán to march south against him with a large army, doubtless in alliance with his southern neighbours, the Britons; but he was severely defeated by Aethelfrith at a place which Bede (*H.E.* I. 34) calls *Degsastán* in 603; and, adds Bede, 'from that day until the present no king of the Scots in Britain has dared to make war on the English'.

The outline of the early history of Scotland is a particularly difficult one to trace owing to the fact that at the dawn of the period of our

---

[1] There can, I think, be no doubt that O'Rahilly's interpretation of the Irish annals is correct as against those of some earlier scholars. See O'Rahilly, *E.I.H.M.* p. 504.
[2] Ed. J. Bannerman, *Celtica* VII 142; see also *P. and S.*, p. 308 ff.

contemporary written records, from at least as far back as the early seventh century, Scotland was divided among four nations, differing widely from one another in origin, and all speaking different languages. Of these the Picts of the north and east are the most archaic, both in language and institutions, while the kingdom of Dál Riata (Argyll) in the west is comparatively new. The Britons occupied the whole of the south between the two walls at least from Roman times and probably earlier. By the middle of the sixth century a new Teutonic dynasty had superimposed itself in the north-eastern territory of Roman Britain, founding the Anglian kingdom of Bernicia, and this new political element rapidly extended its authority up south-eastern Scotland, annexing the British area of Gododdin, the whole of the old territory of the *Votadini*.

The British kingdoms that the Bernicians superseded had emerged as a result of the withdrawal of the Romans from the northern defences. But when they enter history in the sixth and following centuries under independent native princes the territory of these British-speaking peoples seems to have corresponded in some measure with that of the Roman territorial units whom they superseded and probably preceded. In all probability they developed with no great change of territory, or of range of influence or change of dynasties into the group of independent kingdoms known to later Welsh records as *Gwŷr y Gogledd*, 'The Men of the North'.

These Britons of southern Scotland developed into a number of independent kingdoms of varying size and importance, each governed by its own native dynasty, but capable of forming temporary alliances. Those in the east were known as the *Gododdin*, keeping their old name, derived from the *Votadini*, and it is from this area that Cunedda and his sons are said to have migrated (cf. p. 40 above), though Cunedda is nowhere referred to as a king, or even a *dux*. The kingdoms in the west stretched from the Clyde probably to the borders of Mercia. The most important of these western British kingdoms were those of Strathclyde ('the valley of the Clyde'), and Cumbria immediately to the south of it, Cumbria reaching from the Clyde right down north-western England till it joined the Welsh of Wales on the Welsh border. It is probable that these independent western dynasties were originally members of large and important British families, whose genealogies are derived in Welsh records from a certain Coel Hen to the south, and Dyfnwal Hen, further north.

Perhaps we should speak of both Strathclyde and the British countries to the south of it under the single term of *Cumbria*, and their language as *Cumbric*, for Latin writers speak of them as *Cumbri* and *Cumbrenses*, which is a Latinization of the native word *Cymry*, the meaning of which is

73

'fellow-countrymen', and which both they and the Welsh of today use of themselves. But however the two areas were divided, they were quite distinct from one another, as references in Early Welsh poetry make clear. Of the Welsh kingdoms which composed the confederation of Cumbria probably the most important during the sixth and seventh centuries was that known in early Welsh sources as *Rheged*. Its precise extent and boundaries are unknown, but its capital was almost certainly Carlisle, and its sphere the coast-lands of the Solway Firth and More-cambe Bay, and it seems to have extended a wider political influence to the borders of Strathclyde in the north, Galloway in the west, Gododdin in the east, and Lancashire and perhaps north-west Yorkshire in the south. Its wide influence and what we know of its area and history would suggest that it constituted a kind of 'over-kingdom', like the Irish *cóiced*, perhaps a continuation of the ancient Celtic wide kingdoms of Western Britain like Dumnonia, and again like those of pre-Roman Gaul.

These North British communities have left no written records, but at some period annals relating to the sixth and seventh centuries seem to have been kept in a North British scriptorium and have been incor-porated into our Welsh annals, and into the *Historia Brittonum* by Nennius early in the ninth century,[1] and also into an eighth century document incorporated in Symeon of Durham's *Historia Regum*;[2] but no wholly independent records have survived, even from the Church, though later traditions and the clear evidence of inscriptions on their tombstones prove these 'Men of the North' to have been Christians. In addition to these early written records incorporated into later Latin works, we have a great wealth of vernacular traditions composed in the form of oral poetry, largely panegyric and elegiac. These North British poems have not survived in the North[3] but were preserved and trans-mitted orally by a highly trained class of official court bards, such as are referred to in this period in the *Historia Brittonum* (ch. 62) where we are told:

> Then Talhaern Tataguen ('father of inspiration') gained renown in poetry, and Neirin and Taliesin and the Blwchfardd and Cian, 'the wheat of song', gained renown together at the same time in British poetry.

These bards, or their successors at a later date, probably after the Anglian annexation of Cumbria, sang their songs afresh in the courts of their southern neighbours, and in Wales the poems were written down

[1] See K. H. Jackson in Chadwick, N. K. (Editor), *Celt and Saxon*, p. 20 ff. Cf. 27 ff., 53 f.
[2] See P. Hunter Blair, in *S.E.H.B.*, p. 86 ff.
[3] See I. Williams, *Early Welsh Poetry*, 22. Three stanzas of Old Welsh poetry were, however, written down in the first half of the ninth century on the upper margin of a folio in the Juvencus MS. of the metrical version of the Psalms, preserved in the Cambridge University Library. See Williams, *E.W.P.*, 28, 72.

at a still later date in manuscripts of which four have survived to our own time.[1]

The picture thus transmitted to us by a highly cultivated and jealously guarded conservative tradition[2] enables us to know at first hand many of the ruling families[3] of the North and their history, and gives us the entrée into these little courts, though it is not always easy to locate them precisely. Our general impression is that of a confederation of small local princes, and a society living in conditions which characterize heroic society everywhere. There was no central government or organized state. Accordingly there was no developed trade or coinage, no architecture except in wood or earth and rough stone forts. Society was based on a military aristocracy, with its emphasis on *noblesse oblige*. The prestige of birth and heredity was great, but was equalled by the spirit of individualism which pervaded society, and the heroic honour which stimulated effort, and was inseparable from the princely standard. A prince and his followers constituted a *teulu* ('warband'). In time of peace they lived in close proximity to one another, sharing the evening feast and its accompaniment of music and song. In time of war they moved as one man, led by the chief unquestioningly to victory or to death. Of policy, of any conception of a state, we hear nothing. The most famous of their battles, recorded in the Welsh annals, and widely celebrated in poetry, was fought, not against external enemies, nor against their powerful neighbours, the Irish of Dál Riata or the Picts to the North, or the encroaching Anglians of the east and south, but among the Britons themselves. This was the battle of Arthuret, recorded in the *Annales Cambriae* s.a. 573 as *Bellum Armterid*. From Welsh traditions we gather that it was fought between one of these British princes, Gwenddoleu and his cousins Gwrgi and Peredur, and that Gwenddoleu was killed. The site must have been near the modern village of Arthuret on the outskirts of Longtown not far from the Roman *Castra Exploratorum* and if the local place-name Carwinley represents an earlier *Caer Gwenddoleu*, as seems probable, we may associate Gwenddoleu with the Roman fort. For most of us the battle has the more romantic interest that it is claimed in Welsh poems that the prophet Myrddin (Merlin) fought and won a gold torque in the battle of Arthuret, in which his lord Gwenddoleu was slain, and that as a result of the battle he lost his wits and afterwards lived the life of a wild man in the forest of Celyddon in

---

[1] A valuable brief account of the process outlined above is given by R. Bromwich, 'The Character of the Early Welsh Tradition' in *S.E.B.H.*, Ch.V.

[2] See H. M. and N. K. Chadwick, *G.L.*, I, 163 f.; H. M. Chadwick, *E.S.*, 143.

[3] A number of the genealogies are recorded in Harl. 3859; also Jesus College (Oxford), MS. XX; and Peniarth 45. They are published by W. F. Skene, *F.A.B.W.* II p. 454. Cf. further H. M. and N. K. Chadwick, *G.L.* I, 149. See now P. C. Bartrum, *Early Welsh Genealogies* (Cardiff, 1966), 77 ff.

Scotland (p. 261). There are some grounds for regarding Merlin as the domestic bard of Gwenddoleu.

The North British princes were nevertheless able to form temporary alliances among themselves, and under these circumstances they were still strong enough to take the offensive against the Angles of Bernicia. In Ch. 63 of the *Historia Brittonum*, which is evidently based on seventh century written material recorded in some northern scriptorium, possibly at Carlisle itself, Nennius tells us that Urien of Rheged and his son fought against Theodric, son of Ida, king of Bernicia (572–9). He also tells us that Urien with three other British princes – Riderch (i.e. Rhydderch) *Hen* ('the old') and a certain Guallauc, and Morcant – fought Hussa, Ida's son, king of Bernicia (585–92), and besieged him in the Island of Metcaud (i.e. Lindisfarne) for three days and nights; but Urien was betrayed by Morcant out of jealousy (*invidia*) and killed, because he was the greatest war leader of them all. And so in their first brilliant encounter with the Angles, the Britons were in a position to take the initiative and wage aggressive warfare against them; but they were never able to combine permanently. We possess a splendid collection of poetry known as the *Gododdin* (cf. p. 208 below), commemorating a disastrous expedition of the men of Gododdin into Northumbria and the battle of Catraeth, probably near Catterick or Richmond in Yorkshire, in which they were annihilated almost to a man. This is the last forward movement of the North Britons against the Angles. If they could have formed a united British kingdom in the North, and combined with the Picts, no Anglian dynasty could have stood against them.

From now onwards the history of the North Britons is that of a rearguard movement. The new Anglian kingdom of Bernicia had been founded in the middle of the sixth century. Probably the name itself, and certainly the population, were British, but the dynasty, of unknown origin, appears to have been Anglian. The first ruler of whom we hear was Ida (*c.* 547–59), and the capital was at Bamburgh. After the murder of Urien of Rheged, and the breakdown of the British offensive under the four princes, the British princes of Gododdin were over-run by the Angles of Bernicia, and in the seventh century the Angles of Bernicia were already in possession of the whole country between the Tees and the Forth. Bede tells us (I, 34) that their king Athelfrith 'conquered more territories from the British than any other king, either making them tributary or expelling the inhabitants and planting Angles in their places'. The Anglian expansion westwards with the gradual elimination of the British kingdoms south of the Highland Line was more tardy. Indeed the expansion into Rheged may have been a peaceful one, the result of a royal marriage between King Oswy of Northumbria (642–71) and Riemmelth, perhaps, a grand-daughter of

Urien,[1] prince of Rheged. The British kingdoms were by this time reduced to Strathclyde, which nevertheless retained its independence till early in the eleventh century. The northward extension of the Angles was checked a generation later at Forfar in 685 when Oswy's son Ecgfrith met his death in his northward thrust against the Southern Picts in the Battle of Dunnichen Mere, and the English Border had to fall back on the line of the Forth. Nevertheless it was the gradual extension northwards and westwards of the Anglian territory and the Anglian speech which ultimately created the Scottish Lowlands and the gradual encroachment of the Anglo-Saxon language.

Owing to sparsity of records for North-western England we have little direct evidence in the early period for communication between the Britons of the North and those of Wales, but a sense of unity would seem to be implied by the two Welsh terms *Deheubarth* (literally 'the right hand' or 'southern part') commonly used to denote south Wales, and *Gwŷr y Gogledd* (literally the 'men of the left', or 'north'), denoting the North British, or, as we may interpret the term, 'our northern half'. A glance at the map of the kingdoms of Wales in the earliest traditions, and the dynastic genealogies of which we have record, shows a large number of small kingdoms, each independent and ruled by a royal house claiming inheritance from father to son. The pattern looks very similar to that which prevailed in Cumbria and Strathclyde and also earlier in Gaul – in fact a common Celtic type resulting from the fragmentation of the wider pre-Roman kingdoms. As we trace the separate history of these small kingdoms to the gradual unification of Wales under the house of Merfyn Frych and his son Rhodri Mawr in the ninth century, and finally in the person of Hywel Dda in the tenth, we shall be surprised at the length of the history of most of these little kingdoms, and the long period during which they were able to maintain their identity. Some of their ruling lines had a life of more than 500 years. This is strong evidence that the Welsh were not originally and inherently a warlike people till forced to defend their land against foreign invasion.

The districts which modern historians believe to owe their origin to the sons and grandsons of Cunedda (cf. p. 40 above) are those which still bear their names in the late lists which are recorded; but the names have probably been created as eponyms of the little Welsh kingdoms of northern and western Wales – Rhufon from Rhufoniog, i.e. southern Conway; Dunod (L. *Donatus*) from Dunoding, round Harlech (where the line persisted till 900); Ceredig from Ceredigion; Edern (L. *Aeternus*) from Edernion; Meirion (L. *Marianus*) from Meirionydd etc. During

---

[1] See the *Historia Brittonum*, ch. 57. Although it is not specifically stated, the *Rum* (*Run*), father of Riemmelth here mentioned, is probably Run, son of Urien.

the ninth century, native historians in all the Celtic countries created eponymous ancestors in the fifth century where the genuine traditional pedigrees ceased. We may compare the pedigrees of the ruling family of Argyll (Loarn, Gabrán etc.) and also the eponymous *Cruithne* and his sons, and certain surveys of the Picts which are wholly antiquarian in character and origin. The Welsh list is of later authority than the original notice of Cunedda[1] and may be based on a mnemonic like the list purporting to record Arthur's battles.

Moreover the statement of the total and final expulsion of the Irish (cf. p. 40 above) credited in the original notice to Cunedda and his sons cannot be accepted at its face value, for we know that the Irish formed a prominent element in the population of north Wales long after the fifth century. Indeed it may be added that the districts in which the sons of Cunedda are supposed to have settled are not in all cases areas where the Irish are likely to have settled in concentration. The orthodox view is, however, that the sons of Cunedda formed the earliest ruling dynasties of the principal kingdoms of the northern and western seaboard of Wales, and that they established themselves there shortly after the middle of the fifth century.

We can trace the history of many of the Welsh dynasties and their descendants, and thus follow in some measure the political history of Wales, from the sixth century – the period of Gildas's princes and the early phase of the establishment of the Saxon dynasties in Britain – till the South Welsh prince Hywel Dda ('the Good') submitted to Edward the Elder in the tenth century. Of these Welsh dynasties by far the most outstanding is the line of *Maglocunus* who, we are told in the *Historia Brittonum*, ruled over the Britons in the region of Gwynedd (*apud Brittones regnabat, id est in regione Guinedotae*) and of whom Cunedda is here stated to have been his *atavus*. The founder of the dynasty, Einion Yrth (*Girt*) had his seat at Rhos, where he seems to have been succeeded by one of his sons, the father of Cynlas, identified with *Cuneglasus*, one of the 'wicked' princes singled out for censure by Gildas. Einion's other son, Cadwallon Llaw Hir ('Cadwallon of the long hand'), the father of Maelgwn (Gildas's *Maglocunus*), ruled in Môn (the modern Anglesey). This line, with its seat at Aberffraw, had a history of 800 years from the fifth century to 1282, and under Maelgwn the dynasty was destined to become the most influential in Wales.

The Maglocunus of Gildas is a typical heroic prince surrounded by his court bards. The whole dynasty were zealous Christians, for the little church of Llangadwaladr, two miles from Aberffraw, the royal church of this little capital of the dynasty, still preserves a Latin inscription in memory of King Cadfan to which we shall refer later. The monument

[1] Cf. J. E. Lloyd, *H.W.* I, p. 118.

to Cadfan, with its ambitious rhetorical phraseology, is witness to an interesting continuous history of the family on the spot, suggesting that Aberffraw had already become the chief seat of the dynasty. It was Cadfan's son, Cadwallon II, who in 633, in alliance with King Penda of Mercia, overthrew and slew Edwin of Northumbria, the first English king to invade Wales. For a time it seemed as if the Welsh might destroy the Northumbrian kingdom; but in the course of a determined march to the North with this end in view Cadwallon was slain in 634.

Some of the Welsh kingdoms did not claim origin from the sons of Cunedda but developed quite independently. The most important is Powys, the 'Paradise of Wales', as the Llywarch Hen poet describes it (p. 212 below), which is believed to have grown out of the ancient kingdom of the *Cornovii*, and which in early historical times comprised the valleys of the Severn and the Dee. In the early Middle Ages the southern portion of Powys included Builth and Gwrthrynion on the upper Wye. The royal line of Builth had an undisputed claim to be descended from Vortigern. It had its own royal line, and a king of this line, Fernmail, was still ruling when Nennius was writing *c.* 830. The romantic little kingdom of Brecknock in south Central Wales was never conquered and retained its independence from the fifth to the tenth century. Its royal pedigree[1] claims to be derived from a native princess Marchell (L. *Marcella*) who married an Irishman. Their son Brychan[2] is evidently an eponym. Other Irish names occur in the pedigree.[3]

In addition to Powys, Builth and Brecknock, the whole of South Wales continued to be ruled by independent kings down to the time of Hywel Dda. The kingdom of Dyfed, as we have seen (p. 38 above), was ruled by a line of princes whose origin was almost certainly Irish, and the dynasty lasted from the fifth to the tenth century. Three genealogies are extant.[4]

South-eastern Wales was always independent and formed the distinct kingdom of Morgannwg. This was the most romanized part of Wales, with a good climate and fertile land, and included Cardiff, Caerleon and Caerwent, and also the early Christian monastic centres of Llanilltud, Llancarfan and Llandaff. The history of this kingdom is chiefly interesting from its early and important ecclesiastical influence. It remained under its own princes till the eve of the Norman Conquest.

Wales is essentially a sea-board country. The great mountain masses inland made communication between north and south difficult, and

---

[1] In Jesus College (Oxford) MS. XX, viii, the genealogy is confused with that of Dyfed, which is not surprising in view of the Irish elements in the tradition. See further *Y Cymmrodor* VIII, 85.
[2] For legends about Brychan and his son Rhain, see *H.W.* I, p. 270 f.
[3] See Wade-Evans in the *De Situ Brecheniauc*, *V.S.B.G.*, p. 313.
[4] See K. Meyer, 'The Expulsion of the Déisi', *Ériu* III 135 f.; *Y Cymmrodor*, XIV 101 f.

from the earliest times a political division between north and south makes itself increasingly a force in the historical life of the country. The communications and sympathies of the north Welsh linked them with the British of Cumbria and Galloway, a link reflected in the term *Gwŷr y Gogledd*, which implies 'our northern neighbour'. The link with the north was strengthened rather than weakened when the power of the kingdom of Northumbria qualified them to be valuable allies against a threatened Viking conquest of north Wales. On the other hand the relations of Deheubarth had always been closer with southern England, and during the Viking Period the South Welsh kingdoms gradually came to a realization that safety lay in alliance with their stronger eastern neighbours. We shall trace the gradual union of the small Welsh kingdoms into a constructive political unity in chapter 6.

In concluding this outline of the formation of the Celtic kingdoms in the historical period a word may be added on the nature of the Breton settlements and the formation of the independent Breton kingdoms. We have seen that the settlers brought with them their native British language, having its nearest affinities with that of Cornwall, a poor country whence the majority of the colonists must have been drawn. On the other hand, for what Breton traditions are worth – and in this case they are in general consistent and in no way inherently improbable – the leaders of the migrations, both aristocratic and ecclesiastical, were chiefly drawn from eastern and southern Wales.

Whatever the object of St Germanus in his journey to Britain (cf. p. 53 above), if he had any political hope of cutting off her intercourse with Armorica he had no success, for the colonists continued to pour into Brittany throughout the fifth and sixth centuries, and by the sixth they had established British kingdoms round the entire coast of Armorica, which ceased to be called by its old name *Armorica* ('along the coast'), and became known as *Brittany*, a name which first occurs in a letter of Sidonius Apollinaris. In Britain it is known as *Britannia Minor*, 'Little Britain', in Latin writers, and also as *Letau*, *Letavia* – probably the native name.

The names of two of the three great British kingdoms in Armorica contain echoes of their British connexion. In the north the wide kingdom of *Domnonia* covered almost all northern Brittany, including, after 530, the province of Léon in the north-west, which was at first independent. In the earliest of the Breton saints' *Lives*, that of St Samson of Dol, Domnonia is referred to as *Prettonaland* (i.e. 'Brittany') – a tribute to its early importance. The country was traditionally founded by a king Riwal of the royal stock of Gwent, in south-eastern Wales. No early account of the settlement of Cornouaille in the south is historical before the ninth century, and our legends are chiefly contained in the *Lives* of the local saints, Guénolé, Corentin, and Ronan, and in the forged charters of the great abbey of Landévennec. Legend claims early communication between Cornouaille and western Wales.

The third of the great kingdoms is *Bro Waroch* ('the land of Waroch'), which comprised the whole of the rest of southern Brittany, including the western part of Vannes. East of this limit the area was still Roman and long known as *Romania*. This is the wealthiest part of Brittany, the old kingdom of the *Veneti*, conquered by Caesar, and having an early connexion with Britain, on whom they were said to have been accustomed to draw for their naval supplies. Most of our traditions point to Wales as the region whence the leading settlers came. A particularly striking example is that of St Gurthiern, whose name and story, despite his Breton sanctity, correspond to those of the British 'tyrant' Vortigern.

No contemporary records of the conditions of the settlement have come down to us; but Breton scholars have come to realize that the 'saints', i.e. the non-militant educated elements, were the true organizers of the expeditions and settlements. 'The Immigrants organized themselves, and in this essential task everything conspires to give us the impression that the spiritual leaders enjoyed the principal rôle.'[1] Indeed traditions of the migration point to close association throughout our period of the princely leaders and clerics, who were often members of the same family, and went to Brittany together, prince and cleric forming the hard core of the migration movement.

We may be assured that the Gallo-Romans would not have allowed the Britons to occupy their land and eat them out of house and home if they had not a fair return from the immigrants. Late traditions, preserved in Latin medieval saints' *Lives*, such as those of St Leonorus and St Méen, relate how the Britons cleared the land, which even to this present day shows evidence of having been in earlier days largely covered by forest and heath. These traditions reflect their forestry methods, especially the *Life of St Méen*, a saint from Archenfield, in south-eastern Wales, who had perhaps learnt his forestry in the mysterious Forest of Dean, and who established a great monastery in the Forest of Brocéliande in eastern Brittany. He was of the royal family of Archenfield and throughout his life kept his close relationship with the king Judicaël of *Domnonia*, a descendant of the legendary King Riwal. Judicaël eventually retired to end his life in Méen's monastery in the Forest of Brocéliande, not very far from the spring where tradition tells us that Vivien enchanted Merlin. The real importance of the monastery – the greatest of many early, small forest monasteries in Brittany – lay in the fact that it was remote from the attacks of the barbarians. And

[1] Waquet, *H.B.*, 20.

this immunity continued down to Viking times, for it is on record that a bishop of Dol retired there for safety.

These *vitae* borrow freely from one another, and in the *Life of St Malo*, we learn that in the process of clearing, St Leonorus had found a golden ram, doubtless of Roman workmanship, thrown up by the moles, and this he took to Paris while on a diplomatic mission to King Childebert (d. 558), asking for the exact value of the ram in land, and also security of tenure. He argued that the land had been a wilderness till they had cleared and tilled it, and that it was only fair that they should occupy it without hindrance – a request which the king granted. The interest of this tradition lies in the picture of the cleric as diplomat and lawyer on behalf of the settlers; in the nature of the relations implied with the Frankish king; in the steps taken to ensure permanent legal tenure; in the fact that Leonorus in effect bought the land, asking only the exact value of the ram. Another interesting point in these stories is that not only in the original home in Wales, but also after the migration, the narratives suggest that prince and cleric – often relatives – continued to work together in Brittany. All this suggests close organization. The emigrations were not haphazard; and the stories imply that these royal and clerical combinations were not confined to the earliest generations.

The importance of Brittany to the Celtic Church in our own islands must have been especially high at this time as affording communication with the Continental Church, and as avoiding the necessity of the more dangerous crossing of the Straits of Dover. This Breton route was, of course, the route taken by St Columbanus (cf. p. 180 below). We have also to bear in mind that in general the sea was a great unifying factor. It joined rather than divided. It is said in Cormac's Glossary that at this period certain Irish kingdoms extended on both sides of the Irish Sea (pp. 49–50). In traditions of the settlement of Brittany we again come upon traditions of such double kingdoms. Tradition claims that King Riwal, the legendary founder of the kingdom of Domnonia, came with a great fleet in the time of the Frankish king Lothair 1 from his kingdom in eastern Wales and 'continued to rule as *dux Brittonum* on both sides of the sea till his death'.[1] We are led by a certain amount of evidence to think that a tyrant of Domnonia, Cunomorus, Count of Poher and of Carhaix, the great Roman centre in Western Armorica, may also have ruled simultaneously in British Domnonia.

All that we learn from Breton traditions shows it as an expansion of western Britain. Communication was kept up between the royal families who migrated and the old stock. The so-called 'missionaries' were the educated men who negotiated the settlements and organized the colonists, attending to their spiritual and legal needs. The Frankish court

[1] See Baring-Gould and Fisher, *L.B.S.*, III, 343, n. 2.

encouraged them, and in general the intellectual life of the colonists must have been relatively high, possibly owing to contacts with the Gallo-Roman population. We possess a number of saints' Lives, written in Latin and dating from the ninth century, whereas the earliest Welsh Life – that of St David – dates from the late eleventh century.

Our picture is not that of a fleeing host of emigrants under a highly spiritual leader, but a political expansion of peoples, organized from leading Welsh princely families, whose political rights and privileges and spiritual integrity are in the charge of literate clerics. As our principal sources are monastic and late, it is not surprising that some of the early princes have been transformed into saints. The most striking case is that of Vortigern who, as already mentioned, appeared in the records of Quimperlé as St Gurthiern.[1]

Meanwhile in Brittany, as in our own islands, the sixth and seventh centuries were the period which saw the rise of the historical kingdoms. It is a matter of regret that the contemporary narrative of Gregory of Tours does not concern itself to any serious extent with the two Breton states of Domnonia and Cornouaille, for the history of which we are largely dependent on records of ecclesiastical institutions and the less reliable narratives of saints' Lives. In the earliest of the latter, the *Life of St Samson* of Dol, Domnonia (*Prettonaland*) is not referred to as a kingdom, but a realm, a duchy or county, and in Frankish sources it was ruled by a 'royal count', though these seem to have inherited from father to son. In this Life we have a vivid account of the relations of the Domnonian princes with both the Frankish king Childebert, and also with the regent Cunomorus, who is said to usurp the kingdom during the minority of the young prince Judual who died *c.* 580. St Samson conducts us to the sixth century Frankish court to solicit the help of Childebert for young Judual, and we witness the triumph of the rightful heir – so we are assured – and the downfall of the usurper.[2]

Cunomorus is the most interesting figure in early Breton history, which may be said to begin with his relations with the Frankish kings. By origin he was one of the small ruling Breton chiefs, having his stronghold in Pou-Castel, today Carhaix, and his 'county', or little city state, was the surrounding country, now Poher. His traditional dates, first as regent, then as usurper of Domnonia, are calculated as approximately 540–54. He seems to have been a Christian in early days, but having incurred the enmity of the Church he has come down to us in tradition as a usurper, a murderous tyrant, and even a Bluebeard. By his usurpation of Domnonia, and as master of Poher and Léon, he already

---

[1] For St Gurthiern see the note in Chadwick and others, *S.E.B.H.*, 39 ff.
[2] For a discussion of the historicity of the narrative see Durtelle de Saint-Sauveur, *H.B.* I, p. 52 f.

possessed half Brittany, and was evidently aiming at the supremacy of an independent principality. However, on the triumph of Judual, Domnonia rose against the 'tyrant', who was defeated and slain in his native Poher, whither he had retired in the hope of finding refuge and reinforcements.

While the Bretons were occupying the peninsula, the Franks had been gradually extending over Gaul, and under Clovis (c. 481–511) the Gallo-Roman cities of Armorica formally recognized the Frankish authority. The Franks regarded themselves as the true successors of the Roman rulers, and refused to recognize Breton independence in the rest of the peninsula, while the Bretons on their part refused to accept the Frankish claim, and on the contrary sought to extend their own independence eastwards.[1] According to the contemporary Gregory of Tours[2] the successors of Clovis deprived the Breton rulers of the title of king, substituting that of 'Count', the title borne by the Frankish officials responsible for administering the various city-states on behalf of the Frankish kings. Nevertheless, under the title of counts, the Breton chiefs continued to defy the authority of the Merovingian kings. This was the period in which the Gallo-Roman state of Vannes was in process of becoming *Bro Waroch*, 'Territory of Waroch', from the name of a Breton chief Waroch II (577–94), under whom the town became Breton in 579. Waroch was, in fact, a particularly formidable adversary of the Franks, and the pages of Gregory are lively reading as he traces the sensational military career of this redoubtable prince and his political relations with the Frankish rulers. In 587 he invaded Nantes and in the following year Rennes and again Nantes; and although in 590 a powerful Frankish army invaded Vannes, the event proved a disaster to the Franks, whose army was defeated and partly destroyed by Waroch's son Canao.[3] It is in no way surprising under these circumstances that the picture presented to us by Gregory of Tours is that of violent rulers, Breton and Frankish alike, constantly at war with one another, the Franks seeking to enforce control, the Bretons of Bro Waroch laying waste the Gallo-Roman border city-states of Rennes, Nantes and eastern Vannes.[4]

The struggle between Bro Waroch and the Frankish kings lasted for centuries. Sometimes the armies of the Frankish kings suffered disaster at Breton hands; but the Breton chiefs were unable to consolidate their gains. Charlemagne ordered no less than three expeditions into Brittany, and Louis the Pious came in person twice. Finally Louis the Pious appointed Nominoe, a native Breton, first as count, later duke;

---

[1] See Durtelle de Saint-Sauveur, *G.B.* I, P. 46 f. and references.
[2] *Hist. Franc.* IV, 4. [3] *Ibid.*, X, ix.
[4] *Ibid.*, IX. 17; X. 9; cf. de la Borderie, *H.B.*, I, p. 442 ff.

but in 846 Nominoe himself forced Charles the Bald to recognize the independence of Brittany. Charles was indeed glad of the help of the Bretons as allies no less than as subjects, for he now had to face the far more serious problem of the Viking invasions. In 849 Nominoe openly rebelled, but he died in 851 in a campaign near Chartres.[1] His son and successor Erispoe was assassinated in 857 by order of the famous Salomon, who succeeded him. From 863 Salomon recognized the Frankish hegemony and promised to pay homage to Charles the Bald, though he soon withheld both his tribute and his loyalty, and paid for his crimes and treachery with his life in 874. With Salomon Brittany had entered upon the feudalism of the Middle Ages.

[1] For a brief account of Nominoe, see A. Rebillon, *H.B.*

CHAPTER 5

SECULAR INSTITUTIONS:
EARLY IRISH SOCIETY

THE sources of information about the secular institutions of Ireland are plentiful, but they have not yet been fully explored. Much can be learned from the sagas, and a great deal more from annals, genealogies and, above all, the ancient law-tracts. The Irish law-tracts are probably the most important documents of their kind in the whole tradition of western Europe, by reason of their mere extent, and of the archaism of the tradition they preserve. Their roots are not in Roman Law, but in ancient Indo-European custom (p. 199).

The basic unit of territory and administration in Ireland was the *tuath*, and it seems sometimes to correspond in area to the modern barony.[1] The word means 'tribe, people', and is used also for the territory they inhabit. Many names of baronies are ancient *tuath*-names; but the Book of Rights, in the eleventh century, lists only ninety-seven *tuatha* as against the two hundred and seventy-three baronies of today.

It would be a mistake to suppose any close connexion between *tuath* and barony. The barony was a Norman tenure, and when Strongbow or De Lacy granted estates in barony they may have taken advantage of existing territorial divisions as rent-bearing units, so that a barony might consist of one or of several *tuatha*. But in the areas which were shired later, the barony was probably a newly delimited area with no tradition behind it.

A larger unit was the *trícha cét* 'thirty hundreds' which was originally a military term for a force of three thousand men. MacNeill suggested that it may preserve a very old tradition and have a common origin with the Roman legion, also three thousand in its earliest form.[2] The term is later used in a territorial sense and we have the names of twenty-nine *trícha cét* from various sources.[3] But it never occurs in the text of the Laws, and is equated by the glossators with *tuath*, which shows that by their time the term was obsolete.[4]

---

[1] See Binchy, *Críth Gablach* p. 109; MacNeill IPG 88 f.   [2] IPG 104.

[3] See Hogan, 'The Trícha Cét and Related Land-Measures' pp. 191 ff. (PRIA xxxviii C 1929).

[4] Giraldus Cambrensis has been credited with the statement that there were a hundred and seventy-six *trícha cét* in Ireland in his day. But this is an error. He does not mention the *trícha cét*, and his reckoning of 'cantreds' in Ireland is fanciful. See Top. Hib. III v (ed. Dimock p. 145).

Each *tuath* was ruled by a king (*rí*), 'originally a sacred personage, tracing his descent from one or other of the ancestral deities and mystically invested with sovereignty by means of immemorial inauguration rites'.[1] The inauguration of the king was a symbolic marriage with Sovereignty, a fertility rite for which the technical term was *banais rígi* 'royal wedding'.

Sovereignty was imagined as a goddess whom the king must wed, presumably to ensure the welfare of his kingdom. We are reminded of the Hindu *śakti* (p. 14), and of the female companions of some of the Gaulish gods. The notion is perhaps a development from the primitive idea of a marriage of the tribal god and a goddess of the earth, or of water, as the source of fertility. The Greek cult of Poseidon and Demeter is akin to it.

There are many Irish tales in which this idea is expressed, and it persisted into modern times. Probably the earliest is *Baile in Scáil* 'The Phantom's Frenzy', in which Conn, king of Ireland, finds himself in a fairy dwelling where a phantom prophesies the future kings of Ireland, and a woman seated on a crystal throne pours out a cup of ale for each king that is named (p. 148). In others an old hag is transformed into a beautiful girl by the embrace of the future king. This story is told of Niall of the Nine Hostages, and also of Lugaid Laígde, father of Lugaid Mac Con.[2] In the *Dindshenchas* version the maiden says to Lugaid:

Atbér-sa fritt, a meic mín,	I will tell you, gentle boy,
limsa foït na hairdríg:	With me the high-kings sleep;
is mé ind ingen seta seng,	I am the graceful, slender girl,
flaithius Alban is Hérenn.	the Sovereignty of Scotland and Ireland.[3]

The legendary queen Medb, whose name means 'intoxication', was originally a personification of sovereignty, for we are told that she was the wife of nine kings of Ireland, and elsewhere that only one who mated with her could be king. Of king Cormac it was said: *nocor fai Medb lasin mac/níba rí Érenn Cormac*, 'until Medb slept with the lad, Cormac was not king of Ireland'.[4] The lesser kings too were wedded to their kingdoms. As late as 1310 the Annals record the espousal of Fedlimid Ó Conchobhair (Felim O'Connor) to the province of Connacht. In the seventeenth century Ó Bruadair refers to a king as 'the spouse of Cashel'. Even in the eighteenth century the poets called Ireland the spouse of her lawful kings.

Giraldus Cambrensis describes a ritual, reported to him as still

[1] D. A. Binchy in *Early Irish Society*, p. 56.   [2] *CK* 38 f.   [3] *MD* iv 142. 125.
[4] ZCP xvii 139. See also O'Rahilly, *Ériu* xiv 14 ff., where other reff. are given; and J. Weisweiler, *Heimat u. Herrschaft*. The most recent discussion is by Professor Mac Cana, 'Aspects of the Theme of King and Goddess in Irish Literature', ÉC vii 76 ff.; 356 ff.; viii 59 ff.

practised in one of the northern kingdoms, which involved the sacrifice of a mare. The king-elect went through a symbolic union with the victim, which was then slaughtered, and he bathed in the broth of its flesh and drank thereof.[1] This account has been discredited by some scholars, but there is little doubt that it is well founded. It resembles closely the Hindu rite of *aśvamedha* in which the queen goes through a symbolic union with the slaughtered stallion, plainly a fertility rite. In this northern Irish kingdom it was the king who sought fertility for himself and his tribe by means of the ancient ritual. The cult of the goddess Epona of the Gaulish pantheon seems here to have survived in Ireland in the twelfth century. But the ordinary form of inauguration of a king was by giving him a white rod in token of sovereignty. The rod was given to a high king by his principal vassal king, to a vassal king by the high king.[2]

In early times the king was hedged about by taboos (pp. 101–2). No man who was physically blemished was eligible for kingship. The king was bound too by the magic power of Truth (*fír flatha*); and if he was guilty of injustice, disaster might overtake his people, just as the sins of Oedipus were visited upon Thebes. It is told of the famous king Cormac, when he was in fosterage at Tara, that king Lugaid Mac Con gave judgement against a man whose sheep had grazed the woad-garden of the queen. Lugaid adjudged the sheep as forfeit. The side of the house in which he sat fell down the slope. 'No,' said Cormac, 'the shearing of the sheep is enough in compensation for the grazing of the woad, for both will grow again.' The house then stayed and fell no further. 'That is the true judgement,' said all, 'and it is the son of the true prince who has given it.' For a year afterwards Lugaid remained king of Tara, and no grass came out of the ground, nor leaves on the trees nor grain in the corn. Then the men of Ireland expelled him from the kingship, for he was a false prince; and Cormac became king.

Two points are here worth noting, first that the land became waste from the king's falsehood, and second that the house began to fall and was then stayed by the true judgement. This notion of the magic power of Truth appears in other Irish tales, and forms another curious link with Hindu tradition. Lüders showed in a famous article the Hindu belief that the mere utterance of a true statement could work wonders, and there are clear traces of the same belief in Ireland.[3]

[1] *Top. Hib.* III xxv.

[2] J. O'Donovan, *Tribes and Customs of Hy Fiachrach* 425; *Medieval Studies presented to Aubrey Gwynn S. J.* (Dublin 1961), 197; cf. the rod of Agamemnon, *Il.* ii 101, see G. L. Huxley *Achaeans and Hittites*, 45–6. J. Carney has shown that the Feast of Tara was the inauguration ceremony of the king of Tara, SILH 334 ff. See also Binchy, *Ériu* xviii 134.

[3] 'Die magische Kraft der Wahrheit im alten Indien', ZDMG xcviii (1944), 1; 'The Hindu Act of Truth in Celtic Tradition', *Modern Philology* xliv (1947), 137; Maartje Draak, 'Some Aspects of Kingship in Pagan Ireland', *The Sacral Kingship* 651–63 (Leiden, 1959).

The king was ruler of his people in times of peace and military leader in war. He presided over the annual assembly (*oenach*) which was held at a sacred burial-ground, but he was not above the law. He had a special judge (*brithem ríg*) whose duty it was to decide cases in which the king's rights were involved. This judge might also act in disputes between different kindreds within the *tuath*, but recourse to him was not compulsory: the parties were free to choose any qualified judge.

The king (*rí*) of the *tuath* was bound by personal allegiance to a superior king (*ruiri*) who in turn was similarly bound to a 'king of superior kings' (*rí ruirech*), the king of a province, the highest king known to the Laws. The notion of a King of Ireland to whom the provincial kings owed allegiance was a later development, perhaps not earlier than the tenth century. The inferior king gave hostages to his overlord, and received from him a stipend in token of his dependence. He was bound to certain services, notably tribute and 'hosting' (help in war), and the suzerain was, presumably, obliged to help him in his own quarrels. But the bond between them was solely one of personal fealty: in theory, at least, the over-king had no authority over the territory and people of his subordinate. We have, in the eleventh century Book of Rights, detailed lists of the tributes paid by the kings and the stipends they received, but they are probably mere invention, an antiquary's attempt to present traditional customs, the practice of which had been partly forgotten. Later sources mention tributes of food, sometimes commuted into ounces of gold or silver. The form of the stipend is uncertain.[1]

As with the three degrees of kingship, there were three kinds of *oenach*:

> A fair convened by an overking, to whom the rulers of several *tuatha* owed allegiance, might be attended by tribesmen from these petty kingdoms also. Such for example was *Oenach Raigne* for the tribes of Ossory. Most important of all was the provincial fair held in the neighbourhood of the chief stronghold and attended by all the tribes of the province; it lasted for several days, and there was an elaborate program of public business and entertainments.[2]

Such were Oenach Tailten in the great kingdom of Uí Néill, Oenach Emna in the kingdom of the Ulaid, Oenach Carman in the kingdom of the Lagin, Oenach Téite (Nenagh) in Mumu (Cashel), and Oenach Cruachan in Connacht.

After the king came the nobles (*flaithi*), who were the warrior-class and patrons of the 'men of art' (*oes dána*), poets, historians, lawyers, leeches and craftsmen. The third estate was the *grád féne*, the ordinary free-men who tilled the soil and paid a tax of food-rent to the king. The free-man was normally a *céle*, bound by clientship (*célsine*) to a nobleman 'who in return for a fixed render of provisions and a certain amount of

[1] See *LC* p. xvii.　　　[2] Binchy, *Ériu* xviii 125.

unpaid labour gave him stock to graze his land and guaranteed him a limited protection against the violence of powerful neighbours.'[1]

Clientship seems to have been the basis of a nobleman's prosperity and of his social standing. The law-tracts distinguish two sorts of clientship, according to the terms of the contract, 'free' clientship and 'base' clientship. The relationship between lord and client consisted of the granting of a fief (*rath*) of cattle by the lord in return for a fixed rent, in kind and in service, from the client. The rent was calculated as an annual payment for seven years equal to one third of the value of the fief. In 'base' clientship, which is more commonly mentioned, the client received, in addition to the *rath*, a payment equal to the lord's honour-price, and the lord thus acquired additional rights in his regard – for instance, he was entitled to a third share of the penalty if the client were killed. But the 'base' client, like the 'free', remained a free man. The relationship was a contract, and could be repudiated by either party on certain conditions.

Much of the tract on 'base' clientship is devoted to details of fief and rent. The annual rent for six cows is a calf of the value of three sacks of wheat, a salted pig, three sacks of malt, half a sack of wheat and a handful of rush candles. For twenty-four cows the rent is a fat cow, a salted pig, eight sacks of malt, a sack of wheat, and three handfuls of rush candles. The prominence given to clientship in the Irish law-tracts reminds us of what Polybius and Caesar tell us of the Gauls (pp. 7, 10). We need not doubt that it was an old Celtic institution; but the Welsh law-books do not mention it.

There were slaves (*mug* m., *cumal* f.), perhaps mostly captives of war, but they do not appear to have been a large element in the population.

The word *aire* means 'free-man' and is an inclusive term for both *flaith* and *aithech* or *grád féne*.[2]

In Ireland there was a special class, which may be regarded as a sub-class of nobles, the *oes dána*, whose art ennobled them. The *oes dána*, or learned class, included the judge, the leech, the joiner, the metal-worker, and, most important of all, the poet (*fili*), who seems to have inherited much of the prestige of the druid of pagan times. His duty was first of all to praise his patron, but also to preserve his genealogy, to be learned in history and literature, and to be a master of the craft of poetry. There are tracts prescribing the metres he must learn, the number of tales he must know, and the other learned works he must

---

[1] Binchy, *EIS* 58. For much of the material in this chapter we are indebted to unpublished notes lent us by Dr Binchy. A Welsh text says: 'There are three kinds of persons, a king, a brëyr and a bondman', Melville Richards, *Laws of Hywel Dda* 26.

[2] It is hardly to be doubted that the word is akin to Sanskrit *arya-*, although Thurneysen suggested an alternative explanation, ZCP xx 353. Binchy has pointed out to us that the genitive *airech* is to be explained by analogy with *ruire* 'over-king', gen. *ruirech*, The *aithech* was a freeman who was not noble, and was normally a céle.

study, during a course of twelve years. He demanded rich rewards for his service, and he was likely to satirize a thrifty prince or nobleman. The *fili* was honoured and feared, like the brahmin in India. He was no longer a priest in this Christian society, but he had means of divination akin to magic. Or at any rate, he had had them in the pagan past, and the tradition of his magical power survived.[1]

At no point is the kinship of tradition between India and Ireland more marked than in the status and conduct of the *oes dána*. Just as in Gaul the druids avoided the use of writing (p. 10), so in Ireland the *oes dána* preserved their old oral tradition into the Christian period and left writing to the monks. The evidence for this rests in the fact that the earliest texts we have are archaic legal tracts in a form of Irish that may be as early as the sixth century and was clearly unintelligible not only to the scribes who copied the manuscripts that have come down to us (p. 199), but even to the ninth century commentators who sought to explain it. These texts are composed in verse for the purpose of memorization, and must have been handed down for centuries by word of mouth. The same was true of the brahmins. Winternitz discusses the use of writing and argues that while writing was probably known and practised from about 800 BC, it was not used for the transmission of literature, but only for commercial and official purposes. There is no mention of writing in the sacred books of Buddhism, and 'old works on phonetics and grammar, even the Mahābhāsya of Patañjali in the second century BC take no notice whatever of writing'.[2] And he concludes that it was in the interest of the priests that the sacred texts which they taught should not be committed to writing. He who wished to learn had to come to them and pay their price. Moreover, the transmission of the text through the mouth of the teacher was an old established method of preserving it. Writing came only after they already had a rich oral literature. (The Chinese pilgrim I-tsing says that the Vedas were still preserved only orally in his time, in the seventh century.) The parallel with druidism is close.

Closer still is the parallel in the matter of court poetry. Both in Ireland and in India there were professional poets, whose duty it was to praise the king and his family and to preserve and recite his genealogy. In India the *suta* is a member of the king's household and ranks next to the king's brother. He is one of those who assist at the consecration of the king (*rājakrtah*).[3] By singing the praises of the king and his ancestors, these bards strengthened him to perform his royal duties and brought him prosperity, and their services were richly rewarded in cattle and

---

[1] For references see O'Rahilly, *EIHM* 340.
[2] *Hist. of Indian Lit.*, I 30.
[3] P. Horsch, *Die vedische Gatha- und Ślokaliteratur* (Bern, 1968) 422; J. Gonda, *Ancient Indian Kingship* 46–7.

land. We have examples of *dānastuti* ('praise for giving') and *nārāśaṃsī* ('praise of men') in the Rigveda and the Śatapatha-brāhmaṇa respectively, and this kind of eulogy may well be the earliest form of poetry in the Indo-European tradition. Verses of this praise-poetry were sung by the *sūta* as part of the ceremony at the consecration of the king in the Vedic period, and the tradition has lasted down to the present day. Even now in Rājasthan, there is a caste of bhats who are professional poets. At an initiation ceremony or a wedding, one of them will come to sing the praise of the family and recite the genealogy. And I have been told that this custom is also preserved in the Punjab.

In Ireland too the earliest poems we have are fragments of eulogy of famous men, sometimes of legendary heroes (pp. 217–21). The *file* belonged to a privileged class, divided into several grades of dignity, of which the highest (*ollam*) was equal to the king before the law. These Irish poets were notorious for their extravagant demands, and there is a well known satire upon them in Middle Irish, *Tromdām Guaire* 'Guaire's Burdensome Guests'.[1] They are even supposed to have been threatened with banishment at the Assembly of Druim Cett in 575 (p. 175). When Vendryes discussed the bardic poetry of Ireland and Wales at the Académie des Inscriptions et Belles-Lettres in Paris in 1932, his account of the poets evoked from Sylvain Lévi the comment that it was 'almost a chapter of the history of India under another name'.[2]

This is the tripartite society of priest (*fili*, *druí*), warrior (*flaith*) and husbandman (*aithech*) that Dumézil has traced so successfully in many areas of the Indo-European world. In Gaul *druides*, *equites* and *plebs* are the classes recognized by Caesar, so that early Irish society maintained the old Celtic, and apparently the Indo-European pattern.

The only officer of state whose name we know was the *rechtaire*, who controlled the king's revenues.

Within the *tuath* the important unit was the family, not the individual, and for most legal purposes the family of four generations (*derbfine*), descendants of a common great-grandfather; and this group was originally the unit in Welsh law too.[3] Land was owned jointly by the group, and in matters of inheritance and of liability all members of the *derbfine* had a share. And this was also true of succession to the kingship. An uncle or a grand-nephew could succeed as well as son or grandson, so that in theory there was a good field from which to choose the best man. In practice there were often several unscrupulous rivals seeking to maim or kill each other in order to secure the kingship for themselves.

Beyond the *tuath* lay the wider provincial kingdom, governed by a *rí*

[1] C.K., 90 f.
[2] *R.C.L.* (1933) 77.
[3] See Binchy, P.B.A. xxix 223.

92

ruirech or *cóicedach*. In prehistoric times there had been five such provinces, Ulaid, Lagin, Mumu, Connachta and Mide,[1] roughly corresponding to Ulster, Leinster, Munster and Connaught of modern times, but with Meath and Westmeath as a separate central kingdom, having the sanctuary of Tara as its capital. This division into five kingdoms has given us the word *cóiced* 'fifth' for 'province', but it was already a thing of the past when history begins in the fifth century. By that time there were three kingdoms in the north, Ailech, Airgialla and Ulaid; and in the south-east Osraige (Ossory) was a powerful kingdom, sometimes owing allegiance to Caisel (Mumu), sometimes to Lagin, but always with a will of its own. Later on, in the eighth century, the central kingdom of Mide fell apart, and a separate kingdom of Brega, corresponding to the present County Meath, south Louth and north Dublin, was established. The Brega dynasty seems to have come to an end by the eleventh century, and Brega was joined again to Mide.[2]

This is the political state of Ireland, as it appears from the old law-tracts, some of which date from the seventh century. But from the ninth century onwards, there were attempts by several powerful kings to establish themselves as masters of the whole country by taking hostages from the other provincial kings. This ambition was finally realized by Brian Boru in 1002, and from then until the Norman invasion, the Kingship of Ireland, at least as an idea, may be said to have prevailed.

In such a society commerce consisted of barter, an exchange of goods and probably personal service, not unlike the practice that may still be observed among Irish farmers. The great occasion for this trade was the annual *oenach*, but private bargains can be made at any time. The unit of value was the *sét*, half the value of a milch cow, and upon it were based these commercial transactions, and the various tariffs prescribed by the law as fines, honour-price or compensation.[3]

As there were no towns, and society was entirely rural, and since there was no public enforcement of law, and no use of money, the duties of the state were few and simple. The main source of wealth was in cattle, for there was no individual ownership of land, the land being joint property of the *derbfine*.

When a dispute arose between members of the *tuath*, the aggrieved party had various procedures open to him, but the affair was conducted privately between plaintiff and defendant. Normally they would agree to go before a judge, whose business it was to arbitrate, and he took a fee for his service. The law-tracts prescribe procedure for distraining the property of the defendant, the notice that must be given, the witnesses

---

[1] O'Rahilly points out that the name *Mide* is late. The old name of the central province is uncertain, *EIHM* 166, 174 n. 4. For the Five Provinces see p. 37 sup.

[2] *EIHM* 166.

[3] Binchy, *Proc. International Congress of Celtic Studies* (Dublin, 1962) 121.

that must be present and so on; and there was an elaborate system of suretyship, enabling the wronged party to enforce a contract, if the other party should fail to perform his part. Even in a case of homicide, the crime was treated as a private wrong.

In Ireland distraint played a large part in legal affairs, for it was the normal way of compelling one's neighbour to submit to arbitration. When arbitration was agreed, the case was heard in the judge's house. Both parties employed lawyers to do the pleading. The judge's fee was one twelfth of the amount involved.

A tract entitled 'The Five Paths of Judgement' distinguishes five forms of pleadings called *Fír* ('Truth'), *Dliged* ('Obligation'), *Cert* ('Right'), *Téchta* ('Propriety'), and *Cóir nAthchomairc* ('Right Enquiry'). The distinction is based on the matter in dispute. In questions of slander, inheritance, acceptance of a lord, or a claim to headship of the family, Truth is prescribed; Obligation is prescribed in contracts; Right in matters of quantity and value (e.g. if the Vendor has admitted defects in something sold); Propriety in questions of prescriptive rights (to a tenancy or a status or to exemption from a liability); Right Enquiry for all matters which do not fall under one of the other headings. The 'path' may have been simply the formulation of pleadings, but different kinds of surety or pledge are prescribed for each of the five.

The law-tracts also expound the capacity of witnesses, and the law of evidence and of proof. Finally, both parties had to find sureties for their abiding by the judge's decision.

Where the enforcement of law was not a function of the state, the institution of suretyship was of great importance. There were three kinds of surety, *naidm*, *aitire* and *ráth*. The *naidm* undertook only to join the creditor in enforcing payment, pledging his honour. The *aitire* pledged his own person and freedom in case the debtor should default. The *ráth* undertook to compel a debtor to pay his debt, and failing that, to pay the debt himself. In some cases all three kinds of surety were required.[1]

A point of special interest in legal procedure is the use of fasting as a means of securing redress. In certain cases where a defendant was of privileged rank (*nemed*), a plaintiff was obliged to fast in front of the defendant's house before making distraint, and this placed a grave obligation on the defendant to give pledges that he would submit to arbitration. The plaintiff came at sunset, and fasted until sunrise. The defendant was bound to fast too, and if he broke his fast he became liable for double the amount claimed. If he wished to take food, he was obliged first to offer food to the plaintiff, and to give a pledge that he would pay or that he would submit to arbitration. If he did neither of

---

[1] See Thurneysen, *Die Bürgschaft im irischen Recht*, 35 ff. (APAW 1928, Phil.-Hist. Kl. 2); Binchy *EIS* 63.

these things within three days, he could be distrained upon like a commoner.

Such a defendant, if he simply disregarded the fast and refused to pay, lost his honour; he could not enforce any claim of his own: 'He who does not give a pledge to fasting is an evader of all. He who disregards all things is paid by neither God nor man' (*AL* i 113).

This usage is closely parallelled in Hindu law, where the procedure is called *prāyopaveśana*. A creditor may sit fasting at the door of the debtor, until the debtor, lest he be liable for the death of the other, yields compliance.[1]

Compensation for a wrong was estimated according to the damage suffered and also according to the rank of the injured party. The fine (*díre*) was measured according to the honour-price (*lóg n-enech, eneclann*) of the victim.[2]

Besides the tracts dealing with clientship, distraint, suretyship, and the 'Five Paths of Judgement', there are tracts on marriage, on water-rights and on the ownership of bees, on 'sick-maintenance' (the liability of one who has inflicted corporal injury upon another to have his victim nursed back to health at his charges),[3] and on many other matters.

The law of marriage in early Ireland is of special interest, as it shows in great measure the persistence of ancient custom in spite of Christian teaching. Divorce is freely allowed. Indeed there is a trace of annual marriage. A marriage may always be ended by common consent. This freedom would explain the career of the famous Gormlaith, who was first the wife of Olaf Cuarán, Norse king of Dublin, then of Malachy, king of Meath, then of Brian Boru, and was later offered in marriage to Sigurd, Earl of Orkney.[4] As late as 1339 the Annals of Ulster record that Turlogh O'Conor, king of Connacht, took to himself the wife of an Ulster nobleman, and put away his own wife, a daughter of O'Donnell.

More remarkable is the fact that concubinage, as we would call it, is legally recognized: a man may take and maintain a second wife in the life-time of his 'principal wife'. The purpose of this was presumably to obtain sons, if the first wife were barren, but even this is not stated in the law-tracts. The law regulates the relationship of the secondary wife to the principal wife, and the compensation payable to the husband for a wrong done to her. But no such compensation was payable by the principal wife who was moved by lawful jealousy of her, even to the shedding of blood. This was one of the seven bleedings that did not

[1] Thurneysen, 'Das Fasten beim Pfändungsverfahren', ZCP xv 260 ff.; Jolly, *Grundriss der indo-arischen Philologie* II 8, 148; L. Renou, 'Le jeûne du créancier dans l'Inde ancienne', JA 1943–5, pp. 117 ff.
[2] See Binchy, *CG* 84 f.   [3] See Binchy, *Ériu* xii 1 ff., and *inf.* 97.
[4] She is the Kormlöd of whom the Saga of Burnt Njal says: 'she was endowed with great beauty and all those attributes which were outside her own control, but it is said that in all the qualities for which she herself was responsible, she was utterly wicked.'

cause liability. Moreover, she was known by the ugly name, *adaltrach* 'the adulteress'. The tract recognizes ten kinds of union, ranging from permanent marriage to temporary sexual relations. (Of these, two seem to be late, so that we are brought close to the eight forms of marriage in Manu, see p. 12.) How far these provisions represent actual practice in the Christian period may remain doubtful. But there is evidence for divorce, and the frequent mention of the secondary wife in the commentaries can only mean that she was of common occurrence.[1]

The practice of placing one's children in the care of foster-parents was a normal feature of Irish society, and it was not confined to the noble class. Sometimes children were fostered for love, but usually a fosterage-fee was paid, and it varied, according to an early text, from three *séts*[2] for the son of a freeman of lower rank to thirty *séts* for the son of a king. The commentary says that boys were taught riding, swimming, the use of the sling, and the playing of board-games; the girls learned sewing and embroidery. Or for children of lesser rank, it was herding and farm-work for the boys; the quern, the kneading-board and the sieve for girls. But it may be that here the commentator is indulging his fancy, as those commentators loved to do. He knew that there was an exact program of training for a boy who should enter the household of a *fili*, and he wished perhaps to imitate it. In practice, of course, the children in fosterage would pick up these accomplishments anyway. The time of fosterage ended for boys at seventeen, for girls at fourteen, and they returned home. But the tie of fosterage remained close: there was an obligation on the part of the children to support their foster-parents in old age, and those who had been fostered together were bound in close companionship. This relationship with one's *comaltae* is a recurring motif in the sagas. The tragic climax of *Táin Bó Cualnge* is Cú Chulainn's fight with his foster-brother, Fer Diad. In 'The Destruction of Da Derga's Hostel', the tragedy is the greater because the death of Conaire is at the hands of his own foster-brothers.

In Wales the practice of fosterage existed, and it is referred to in the laws several times incidentally, but there is no separate chapter devoted to it. The normal event was for a nobleman to send his son to fosterage with a *taeog* or serf, and the law says that the foster-son shares the inheritance of the serf like one of his own sons.[3] The word *cyfaillt*, which came to mean 'friend', is identical with Irish *comaltae*.

One other chapter of Irish law is of special interest, as it preserves very old tradition, namely the obligations of maintenance of the sick. There are two tracts on the subject, which were discovered in a fifteenth

---

[1] Thurneysen and others, *Studies in Early Irish Law*, p. 16 ff., 240ff. Here again we owe much to unpublished notes of Dr Binchy.

[2] The *sét* was a unit of value equal to half the value of a milch cow.

[3] See Melville Richards, *Laws of Hywel Dda* 77; *W.T.L.*, I 385.

century manuscript from the Phillipps Collection, acquired by the National Library in 1930, and both are very old, not later than the eighth century. One is entitled 'Judgements in Blood-Lyings' and the other 'The Judgements of Dian Cécht'. In many legal systems there was a rule that one who injured his neighbour physically was obliged to pay not merely the appointed penalty but also the cost of healing his victim, the leech-fee of the Anglo-Saxons. In early Ireland the offender was obliged himself to provide for the cure of his victim. Nine days after the wound is inflicted, a leech pronounces his verdict. If he says that the patient will recover, the defendant must take him into his house, or to the house of a kinsman, and provide for him till he recovers. The diet and the treatment of the patient are set forth in detail. Diet varies with his social standing. Besides a basic ration of two loaves a day and an unspecified quantity of fresh meat, to which every patient is entitled, a member of the 'noble grades' receives honey, garlic and especially celery, for its peculiar virtue as a remedy, salt meat every day from New Year's Eve till Lent, and twice a week from Easter to the end of summer. A member of the 'freemen grades' gets salt meat only on Sundays until Lent, and not at all after Easter. Celery is prescribed for all.

The prescriptions as to lodging are quite exacting. Fools, lunatics and enemies are not to be admitted. No games are played. Children are not to be beaten, nor may there be any fighting. There is to be no barking of dogs nor grunting of pigs. The patient is not to be awakened suddenly, and people may not talk across him as he lies in bed. There must be no shouting or screaming. But all this is only a part of the defendant's liability, for he must also entertain the retinue of his patient throughout the period of his sickness. Every freeman had the right to a company of followers according to his rank on certain occasions, and sick mainten-ance was one of them. Retinues of four and more, to as many as eight persons, are mentioned. And finally the defendant must find a substitute to do the patient's work during his absence.

Dian Cécht was the Irish god of healing, and the second tract is piously attributed to him. It deals largely with the amount that is to be paid to the leech, and this varies with the gravity of the wound, or, according to another doctrine, with the amount of the wergild, that is to say, with the status of the victim. One point of interest is the manner of measuring wounds by grains of corn. And there is a curious catalogue of twelve doors of the soul, parts of the body where wounds are specially grave.

This tract, 'The Judgements of Dian Cécht', is one of the very early ones and contains passages of verse that are probably as early as the sixth century. It has recently been edited by Professor Binchy.[1] The

---

[1] *Ériu* xx 1 f.

archaic custom of sick maintenance was already obsolete by the eighth century, for *Críth Gablach*, which cannot be later, declares that there is no such practice now, and goes on to describe the old procedure as we find it in *Bretha Crólige* ('Judgements in Bloodlyings').[1]

In Wales the picture is very different, and it is only with the aid of the Irish evidence that one can see traces of the old Celtic system showing through the Welsh texts as we have them. For there is a Welsh law-book, declared to have been compiled and published in the tenth century under Hywel Dda, whereas in Ireland there is merely a record of ancient custom, going back in part to the sixth or seventh century, with gloss and commentary to explain it. The Welsh tales, which also tell us something about institutions, are not earlier than the twelfth century.

The earliest manuscripts of the Welsh law-book were written *c.* 1200, long after Norman interference had begun, and the prestige of Norman institutions must be allowed for when we compare them with the Irish tracts.[2] In the time of Hywel, there was close contact between the great Welsh king and the royal house of Wessex. He often attended the Witenagemote; and Asser, the biographer of King Alfred, who was a Welshman, used to divide his time between the court of Wessex and his home in Dyfed. There was therefore a strong Anglo-Saxon influence at work even before Hywel's day, and this too will have left its mark upon the laws.

The Welsh legal manuscripts fall into three main 'families' or recensions, all of them presumably based on the original law-book issued under Hywel's authority, but containing much additional material supplied by later jurists, which affords interesting evidence of the subsequent development of Welsh law, including its adoption of Anglo-Norman institutions. These recensions are known as the Book of Iorwerth, the Book of Blegywryd[3] and the Book of Cyfnerth; none of the extant Welsh manuscripts is older than the thirteenth century, and the information they supply as to earlier conditions is not always reliable. Thus the account which all three of them give of the circumstances in which the 'Laws of Hywel' were drafted and promulgated is full of anachronisms. The earliest surviving manuscript (late twelfth century) is in Latin, but this would seem to have been translated from a still earlier Welsh text.[4]

The many small kingdoms that we find in post-Roman Wales of the

[1] *Críth Gablach*, ed. Binchy, 11. 47 ff.; *Ériu* xii 82 f.
[2] The late date of the manuscripts is not the decisive point, for the Irish manuscripts are, with one exception, very much later. In Ireland the native tradition proved stronger at first than Norman influence, and, as is well known, the Normans soon took to Irish ways.
[3] Translated by Melville Richards, *The Laws of Hywel Dda* (Liverpool, 1954).
[4] Hywel D. Emanuel 'The Latin Texts of the Welsh Laws' in the *Welsh History Review* 1963 pp. 25–32.

fifth and sixth centuries, presenting the same state of affairs as in Ireland, were gradually brought under the rule of a single dynasty descended from Cunedda, and in the ninth century Rhodri Mawr was king of approximately all of Wales that was to remain Welsh during the Norman period. On his death in 877, his kingdom was shared among his three sons, Mervyn, Anarawd and Cadell. From Anarawd the line of Gwynedd in the north is descended; and from Howel the Good, son of Cadell, came the lines of Powys and Deheubarth. This division into three kingdoms is the state of Wales reflected in the Laws.

Lloyd says at the beginning of his discussion of early Welsh institutions, that four institutions supply the framework, *cenedl*, *tref*, *cantref* and *brenin*, kindred, hamlet, tribe and chief (king). The corresponding terms in Irish are *fine*, *baile*, *tuath*, *rí*. But while the first two may fairly be equated, the Welsh *cantref* (or *gwlad*, which is the older name) had come to differ widely from the Irish *tuath*. The king in Wales maintained a Court with a whole body of courtiers whose duties and rights were laid down; and he administered a system of public law, and derived revenue from it in fines. The *cantref* itself, and the commotes (W. *cymwd*) into which it was divided, seem to have been late administrative divisions, which arose after the old *gwlad* had ceased to be a separate kingdom. Lloyd says that 'the larger *gwlads*, such as Môn, Ceredigion, Brycheiniog, Ystrad Tywi, were divided into *cantrefs*, the smaller, such as Meirionydd, Dyffrin Clwyd, Buellt, became *cantrefs* themselves, and thus the *cantref* everywhere took the place of the tribe as the means of enforcing justice and as the link between people and crown.'[1] This situation probably arose after the establishment of the three kingdoms.

Each *cantref* had its law-court, and in the south this was the old assembly of free-men. This assembly could even pass judgement on the king's conduct, and, by *dedfryd gwlad* or 'judgement of the people', declare him to have acted oppressively. It also retained the ordinary judicial powers of the court. But in Gwynedd and Powys there was a professional judge in each commote who did the work, and the free-men who sat on either side of the king as assessors of the court were a mere survival and had no judicial function. There seems to have been no fixed place of meeting, and the court could thus meet wherever it was most convenient.

While the old customary law, based on the blood-feud, is traceable in the law of *galanas* or compensation for homicide, the notion of delicts as offences against the state is fully developed in Wales. For serious crimes the normal penalty was a fine of twelve cows, the term for which was *dirwy* (Ir. *díre*): for lesser offences the fine was three cows. These fines were paid to the king, not to an injured party. Evidence consisted

[1] *HW* i 302.

mainly, as in Ireland, of oaths sworn on either side in accusation and denial, the accused person having to produce compurgators who swore in support of his testimony. Beside the court of the commote or of the *cantref*, there was a higher court in which matters concerning the king and his household were decided. And inferior courts were also held by the *maer*, or steward, and by the *canghellor*. Moreover, the bishop and the abbot had their separate courts. Law and procedure were the same for all these courts.

Three chapters of the Book of Iorwerth are devoted to homicide, arson and theft respectively, and these preserve some features of the old customary law. The penalty for homicide, called *galanas*, varied with the status of the victim, and was paid to the kin (of both father and mother). Honour-price (*wynebwerth*) was also payable, and if the amounts were not paid in full, the slayer might be slain with impunity. Something of the old blood-feud here survives. The payment of honour-price in addition to the fine is a point of agreement with Irish custom and must be of common origin with it. The distinctions of degrees of responsibility in cases of theft or arson show affinity with Irish law, but these matters are beyond our competence and must be left to experts in legal history.

Kingship survived in Wales until the end of Welsh independence. By the tenth century there were three kingdoms, Gwynedd in the north, with the royal dwelling at Aberffraw in Anglesey, Deheubarth in the south with its capital at Dinefwr, and Powys in the east with its capital at Mathrafael.[1] The king had an elaborate court, according to the law-books, and numerous officials. He appointed the judges and justice was administered in his name. But all of this seems to have been borrowed from Anglo-Saxon England. In the *Mabinogion*, and from some technical terms in the law-books, one can recognize traces of the old Celtic system. For example, the word *alltud* 'foreigner' (lit. 'from another tribe') shows that the *tud* (Ir. *tuath*) was the original unit of population, as in Ireland, before the three kingdoms were established.[2] The family of four generations, and family-ownership of land were as in Ireland. Also the custom of fosterage, and the system of suretyship were probably in origin the same.

One illustration, which is of special interest, may be given to show how ancient custom lies almost hidden in the Welsh texts. The Irish law of distraint has been discussed already, and distraint was normally of chattels, that is to say of livestock. Land could not be seized, as it belonged to the family-group. But if a man had a claim upon land – if he had been wrongfully deprived of his share – then he could make formal entry on the land by means of an archaic procedure (*tellach*).

[1] See *Wales through the Ages*, p. 107; *H.D.*, 122.   [2] *H.D.*, 129.

There were three 'entries' with fixed intervals: on each successive occasion the claimant brought with him an increased number of witnesses and a larger amount of stock. At the third entry they remained on the land overnight, and the claimant kindled fire. Then if the occupier of the land still refused to submit to arbitration, ownership was vested in the claimant.[1]

An action of title to land in Welsh law presents a complete contrast. The claimant comes before the Court which fixes a date for hearing. The occupant is notified. Both parties are represented by counsel, and there is a regular court procedure. Here we have a comparatively modern process of law, whereas the Irish form is a conventionalized method of forcible seizure.

But the Welsh texts record another legal means of vindicating title to land, namely by uncovering the fire on the ancestral hearth (*dadannudd*). It was apparently obsolete, for the jurists themselves did not clearly understand it; but it remains as evidence of the former practice of old Celtic customary law.[2]

The Irish sagas tell us more about the life of the people than do the tales of the *Mabinogion* for Wales. Among the free classes honour was a man's most jealously guarded possession, more precious than life.

In the saga of the 'Exile of the Sons of Uisliu', Derdriu puts Uisliu on his honour, and he cannot refuse to take her away. His brothers try to dissuade him, but when they learn that it is an affair of honour, they promise to join him. So too in 'The Feast of Dún na nGéd' it was the insult offered to Congal at the feast that led to the Battle of Moira. 'The most important element in the legal status of every freeman is his "honour-price",'[3] and upon it depended the amount that was due to him in compensation for a wrong.

The honour of a nobleman, even of a king, was threatened by the satire (*aer*) of a poet, and this was greatly feared. Refusal of a poet's request or failure to reward him adequately for a poem, might bring a satire upon one, and in the sagas a poet's satire might even disfigure a man. The demands of the poets, and the willingness of others to accede to them, whatever the cost, are a recurring theme.

The term for the formal request of a poet is *ailges* (*ail* 'reproach', *ges* 'request'). The word *ges*, *geis* (pl. *gessa*) alone has acquired the special meaning of 'taboo, prohibition', and expresses an idea that is familiar to us all in the simple form of superstitious avoidance of certain acts or circumstances. But in early Irish society *geis* was of great importance, and yet it is hard to define. It could attach to rank, as to a king, or to a place or thing: it was *geis* for anyone to turn the left side of his chariot

[1] See *A.L.*, iv 18. [2] See *W.T.L.*, I 259; *H.D.*, 75; *A.L.I.*, I 539, II 739.
[3] Binchy, *Críth Gablach* 85.

towards Emain Macha; *gessa* may be peculiar to a spear or a sword.[1]
But commonly they were restrictions on an individual. It was *geis* for
Fothad Canainne to drink ale without having the heads of the slain in
his presence. It was *geis* for Cú Chulainn ('The Hound of Culann') to
eat dog's flesh, and for Conaire, whose father was a bird, to hunt birds;
but Conaire was subject to many other *gessa*, and he perished by trans-
gressing them.[2] An old tract on the *gessa* of the kings of Ireland contains
some curious provisions. It is *geis* for the king of Tara to be still in bed
at sunrise in the plain of Tara, or to break a journey on Wednesday
in Mag Breg, or to travel over Mag Cuilinn after sunset. The king of
Leinster may not stay for nine days on Mag Cualann, nor travel over
Belach Duiblinne on a Monday, nor sleep between Dublin and the
Dodder River with his head to one side. The king of Connacht may
not make a circuit of Cruachain on the feast of Samain. The king
of Ulster may not eat the flesh of the bull of Dáire mac Dáire: he may
not drink the water of the river Bó Nemid between dawn and nightfall.
These are only some of the *gessa*, for there are seven for the king of Tara
and five for each of the other kings.[3]

Kings and nobles dwelt in fortified enclosures of earthwork (*dún* or
ráith), within which were several wooden buildings. Beside the enclosure
was a lawn (*faithche*), which was probably the home pasture.

Many of the sagas describe the feasting habits of the Irish, 'The
Story of Mac Da Thó's Pig', 'Bricriu's Feast', 'The Feast of Dún na
nGéd'; and we have in the Book of Leinster a description, and even a
plan, of the banquet-hall at Tara, in which the places assigned to the
guests, and the portions allotted to them, are set down. While these
sources are not historical in the simple sense, they do tell what was
accepted as traditional by a medieval Irish audience.

Bread and porridge were the normal diet, but beef and pork were
served at feasts, and beer (*coirm*) was drunk. Mead (*mid*) was also
drunk, and wine was served on great occasions. The principal meal was
taken in the evening. In a royal dining-hall the fire was in the centre,
and the cauldron. The drinking-horns were filled from a vat of beer.
The guests reclined on couches (*imdae*) arranged in rows from the wall
to the fire. Places of honour near the king were assigned according to
rank.

In *Fled Dúin na nGéd* (eleventh century?) we are told that when a king
of the southern Uí Néill was High King the king of Connacht was on
his right hand, and when a king of the northern Uí Néill was High
King, the king of Ulster was on his right and the king of Connacht on

---

[1] See J. R. Reinhard, *The Survival of Geis in Medieval Romance*, 56 f.   [2] *EIL* 27 f.
[3] See 'The Taboos of the Kings of Ireland', PRIA liv C pp. 1 ff. Also J. R. Reinhard,
op. cit., 106 f.

his left. In 'The Battle of Mag Rath', which is somewhat earlier, there is a conflicting and more detailed account: the High King sits in the middle of the hall, with the king of Munster on his right in the south end, the king of Ulster on his left in the north end, the king of Connacht behind him to the west and the king of Leinster before him to the east. Here the kings occupy places corresponding to their geographical order, but we may doubt whether such an assembly of guests ever took place.

The garments worn by men and women were the *léine*, a linen shirt worn next the skin, the *inar*, a short tunic, and over them a square woollen cloak (*brat*), fastened with a brooch (*delg*), which was sometimes a precious ornament. Rings, bracelets and torcs were of gold, silver and electrum (*findruine*).

Warriors were armed with shield (*sciath*), sword (*claideb*) and spear (*gae*, *sleg*); and other weapons mentioned are *bir*, *foga*, smaller spears, and *mánais*, a heavier weapon, which O'Curry says was for thrusting.

As regards warfare, the sagas of the Ulster Cycle preserve a tradition that corresponds closely to the descriptions of Gaulish custom given by ancient writers. The warriors drove into battle in chariots. The challenge to single combat and the taking of heads of the slain are frequently mentioned. Raiding for cattle was then, as later, the commonest occasion of fighting.

In historic times, while the old heroic customs will have become obsolete, the weapons and armour may have remained much the same until the Norse invasions presented a new challenge and introduced new fashions. But no comprehensive study of the matter has been made since the days of O'Curry and Joyce.

Hunting and cattle-raiding were the chief employment of the nobles. At home they listened to the poems of the *filid* and the bards, and to the tales of the storytellers. Board-games were a common pastime. The game most frequently mentioned is *fidchell* (Welsh *gwyddbwyll*) 'wood-sense', and other such games were *brandub* 'raven-black' and *buanfach* 'long striking'. Of *fidchell* we know only that the game was played for a stake, and that there were two sets of figures on a board divided into black and white squares.

The boys played a ball-game, sometimes called *áin phuill* 'driving a hole'. In one early account in *Táin Bó Cualnge*, each player has a ball, and one side attacks and the other defends the goal alternately.

The year was divided into two periods of six months by the feasts of *Beltine* or *Cétsamain* (May 1) and *Samain* (November 1), and each of these periods was equally divided by the feasts of *Lugnasad* (August 1) and *Oimelc* or *Imbolg* (February 1). The first name contains the word for 'fire' (*tene*, i.e. 'Bel's Fire'?), and there is a tradition that on that day the druids drove cattle between two fires, as a protection against disease.[1] The second feast, Samain, was the great feast of the year, probably a harvest festival. The word may mean 'end of summer', but this is not certain.[2] *Lugnasad* means 'feast of Lug', and *oímelc* seems to mean 'sheep's milk', which would be a name for the lambing season.

The dominant feature of society in both Wales and Ireland is its rural character. There were no towns, nor even villages in the English sense. Urban civilization remained foreign to the insular Celts until it was imposed upon them by conquerors. After the Roman legions were withdrawn from Britain, the British abandoned the cities and camps, and resumed their rural way of life. In Ireland, even after the Norman invasion, the towns were Norman strongholds from which the native Irish were excluded. The old cities, Dublin, Waterford and Limerick, were built by the Norse invaders; later ones such as Trim, Kilkenny and Clonmel, by the Normans. The town, with its market-place for commerce, with its corporate rights and duties, was foreign to Celtic society. The earliest Irish coins were struck for Sihtric III of Dublin about the end of the tenth century. Hywel Dda was the first king to strike coins in Wales. There was no native Irish coinage before the Norman invasion. Trading was by barter, with values reckoned in cattle, and the chief place of trade was the popular assembly, in Ireland the *oenach* which has given its name to the modern Irish cattle-fair. The Welsh laws do assess penalties in money, for they are late, but the memory of an older practice survives. The law says: *ar warthec y telyt pob tal gynt*, 'every payment was formerly made in cattle'.[3] In Ireland, even late commentators continued to reckon in cattle long after the Norman Invasion, when coinage must have been in use. But, indeed, the Irish may not have taken readily to coinage, for commutations are sometimes made not into currency, but by ounces of gold and silver, even in the sixteenth century.[4]

This conservative character of insular Celtic society gives it a special interest, and something of it is still with us. The countryside of Wales or of Ireland with its scattered homesteads, and the close pattern of fields, reflects even today the old rural pattern, when the kin-groups were owners of the land. Evans in his *Irish Heritage* and Arensberg in *The Irish Countryman* have shown, for Ireland at least, how slowly change comes in this environment.

[1] Binchy, *Ériu* XVIII 129. The mythical king Beli of Welsh tradition may preserve the name, but no Irish god Bel is known.
[2] See Vendryes, 'La Religion des Celtes' 313 (*Mana. Introduction à l'histoire des religions* 2, Paris, 1948).
[3] *ALI* II xxi 10.   [4] See *Studia Celtica* i 1 ff.

CHAPTER 6

THE EARLY HISTORY OF
THE CELTIC KINGDOMS

THE entente between the ruling houses of Dumbarton and Dál Riata (p. 72 above) must have broken down after Aedán's death. In 642 his grandson, Domnall Brecc, undertook a disastrous expedition against the Britons in the upper valley of the Carron under their king, Owen of Dumbarton, a collateral descendant of Rhydderch Hen (cf. p. 47 above), and the triumphant British bards sang how 'the ravens devoured the head of Domnall Brecc'[1] – an interesting hint of a British panegyric poem on the victorious British leader. After this we hear no more of Dalriadic aggression for the time being. For about a century the history of Dál Riata is largely a record of internal struggles for supremacy between the Cinél Loairn, and the Cinél Gabráin.

But the penetration of the Scots eastward into Pictish territory continued gradually. As early as 628 the *Annals of Ulster* speak of Aedán's son, Eochaid Buide, as *rex Pictorum*, so it is possible that the Dalriadic dynasty had been enforcing its influence, if not its actual conquests, eastwards among the Picts for several generations. The name *Atholl*, derived from *Ath-Fótla*, 'second Ireland', or 'New Ireland',[2] must have been given to this district by the Scots themselves already by the beginning of the eighth century.[3] It was originally one of the kingdoms of the Southern Picts with its capital at Scone.

Towards the middle of the eighth century Dál Riata came to a clash with Oengus mac Forgusa, the most powerful of all the kings of the Southern Picts. His precise origin is unknown, but he seems to represent a new line. During the century which preceded the union of the Picts and Scots (see below) the four kingdoms of the Southern Picts (cf. pp. 67–68 above) had been struggling for supremacy among themselves with varying success, but the outcome resulted in the establishment of Oengus mac Forgusa,[4] whose chief seat seems to have been traditionally at Forteviot in Fortrenn, but with whom the Picts of Fife and their capital at Kilrymont or St Andrews, were evidently associated. It is indeed

---

[1] The reference occurs in a stanza of a Welsh poem in the *Gododdin* (cf. p. 208) and is believed to be a later interpolation.

[2] The derivation appears to be *ath* – with the sense of Latin *re*, denoting repetition – and *Fótla*, one of the names of Ireland. See Watson, *C.P.S.*, 228 f.

[3] For the evidence see O'Rahilly, *E.I.H.M.*, 371.   [4] Skene, *C.S.* I, 305 f.

possible that at this period the term Fortrenn also included the modern county of Angus as well as Fife, and that the Pictish kingdom of Angus, with its capital at Forfar, has preserved his name. Already between 706 and 717 its king, Nechtan IV, had been able to negotiate independently with Albert Ceolfrith of Jarrow in Northumbria in what must have been fundamentally a political entente.

In 741 the Irish annals record a *percussio Dál Riatai* (a 'devastating attack') by Oengus on Dál Riata. In this year, nevertheless, began the long and brilliant reign of Aed Finn in Dál Riata, and in 749 we hear of the 'ebbing' of the power of Oengus, and in 768 of an invasion of Fortrenn by Aed of Dál Riata whom Flann Mainistrech[1] calls 'Aed the Plunderer', and the *Duan Albanach*[2] ('The Scottish Poem') calls *Aed ard-flaith*, 'Aed the high sovereign'. A serious aggression against the Picts is therefore being conducted from Dál Riata, and it seems likely that this is the period when the Scots of Dál Riata penetrated deeply into Atholl and Fife.

The period between 765 and 973 is very obscure because the Irish annals, hitherto our chief guide to Dalriadic history, now fail us. The period, however, must have been a momentous one, for we are on the eve of the union of the Picts and Scots; but the Picts have left few reliable records even at this late date. The union must indeed have come about as a gradual process, largely through intermarriage, and some time after 781 the royal lines of Dál Riata and the Picts seem to have become in some measure united, for after the death of Fergus, successor of Aed Finn, four of the nine kings of Dál Riata between him and Kenneth mac Alpin (see below) have Pictish names, and this cannot be the result of conquest because these Pictish names do not begin till after 781 (the year of the death of Fergus), when there is no hint in the annals of a conquest to account for it. Moreover all the Pictish kings known to have been ruling in Dál Riata have Dalriadic names except Constantine (d. 820). There can be no doubt that the Pictish law of inheritance through the female, together with patrilinear succession by tanistry among the royal family of Dál Riata, must have greatly facilitated a union of the two peoples by intermarriage. The actual union of the Picts and Scots, which gave us our modern 'Scotland', seems to have taken place somewhere about the middle of the ninth century under Kenneth mac Alpin (d. 858), perhaps as a gradual process; but the Vikings' attacks were now in full swing. The twelfth century English chronicler, Henry of Huntingdon, who probably derived material from documents of the reign of David I, evidently attributes Kenneth's initial success over the Picts to his having attacked them immediately

---

[1] An eleventh century Irish scholar, a synchronist and historian.
[2] Edited and translated by K. Jackson, S.H.R., XXXVI (1957), 125 ff.

after they had suffered a heavy slaughter at the hands of Danish pirates.

Little is known of the rise to power of Kenneth's family. Alpin's father belonged to the royal line of Gabrán, but his name indicates a Pictish mother. He had reigned in Dál Riata during the first half of the ninth century, but his home and origin are unknown. Henry of Huntingdon states that in 834 'Alpin, king of the Scots' had fought successfully against the Picts and many of the nobles of the Picts were slain; but that three months later he was killed in another battle, 'being elated with success', and the Picts cut off his head.[1]

Kenneth is said by Henry of Huntingdon to have attacked the Picts and secured the monarchy of Alba in 834, and to have fought successfully against the Picts 'seven times in one day'. It is clear that both Alpin and his son Kenneth were celebrated in elegiac poetry which has left its echoes in our records. This is what we should expect from an Irish kingdom like Dál Riata, and due caution must be exercised accordingly. The Chronicle of the united Picts and Scots, which dates from the tenth century, states that Kenneth ruled the Picts happily for sixteen years, after he had wiped them out (delevit); and other texts also speak of a destructio of the Picts. It is remarkable that no hint of such a conquest is given by records of Irish, British or English provenance. The Annals of Ulster call Kenneth king of the Picts in recording his death in 857 (recte 858), and the title remained in use by the Irish and even the Welsh annalists till the time of his grandson. But the actual subjects of Kenneth himself and of his successors are referred to as 'Scots', and the Picts soon came to be thought of as a people of the past.

The Irish kingdom of Argyll also gradually imposed its language over the north and west of Scotland. Did the widespread superimposition of Gaelic take place between the fifth and the ninth centuries? It is not impossible; but one is tempted to suggest that the new Irish influence had perhaps begun earlier than the immigration of the sons of Erc in the fifth century AD. In fact we may even suggest that the Irish had crossed the narrow seas at an earlier period, and that the coming of the sons of Erc is in reality not the beginning of an immigration, but the last stage, and the coming of a new dynasty.

However and whenever the Irish came, the Scottish 'Irish' element, though numerically far inferior to the Pictish, now becomes dominant over the whole of Scotland, and Dál Riata itself becomes unimportant. From the ninth century the western sea-board kingdom of Dál Riata plays little part in history. The centre of power shifts from the west to the east, and the Scottish element in the aristocracy of Scotland

---

[1] For the text see Skene, P. and S., 209, cf. ibid., C.S., I, 306.

seems to prevail though their numbers may have been small. The ecclesiastical capital was already at Dunkeld in the shadow of Mount Shiehallion on the bank of the Tay a few miles north of Perth, whither it had been transferred by Constantine, king of the Picts (d. 820).[1] The Dalriadic kings now live and rule in the old Pictish kingdoms. Flann of Monasterboice says that Kenneth mac Alpin 'was the first king of the Gaedhil (i.e. the Irish), who possessed the kingdom of Scone (i.e. Atholl)', which was already virtually Irish. It would seem, however, that, like the Bernician kings, the royal family was not entirely stationary, for we find them also at Abernethy, Forteviot, and Rose-markie, and apparently the various members were not always together in one place. Kenneth himself died in his palace at Forteviot in Fortrenn. Henceforth however the chief royal seat is at Scone, near the Roman camp of Grassy Walls in Scone Park in Atholl on the lovely bank of the Tay a short walk above Perth. The mound in the grounds immediately behind Scone palace still marks the old site of the traditional dwelling of the Pictish kings – the kings of Cruithentuath.

We now pass to one of the most interesting phases of Welsh history, leading up to the control of North Wales by Rhodri Mawr (d. 878), whose grandson Hywel Dda (d. 950) was the first to submit to an English king. In this phase of Welsh history the most important features are, first the gradual process by which the unification of the various Welsh kingdoms was effected within a few generations by a series of royal marriage alliances; secondly the defeat of the Danish army and the death of their king Gormr at the hands of Rhodri Mawr (p. 112); and thirdly, the end of Welsh isolation, and the begin-ning of her intellectual development and entry into relations with Wessex and the wider continental sphere. Of great importance also is the part played by the House of Wessex in Welsh politics, especially by Alfred the Great. The importance of the Celtic sympathies and the influence of Alfred in Welsh politics is one of the most important un-written chapters in the early history of our country. We shall not find Alfred's Celtic political concerns fully recognized in the Anglo-Saxon Chronicle, for the annalist had quite other interests; but we shall find them set forth in Asser's *Life of King Alfred*, a prime authority on this question, more especially as it affected South Wales.

Early in the ninth century, either in 816 or 828,[2] something of a change took place in the patrilinear succession of Gwynedd.[3] Merfyn

---

[1] See Skene, *C.S.* I, 302; cf. Chadwick, *E.S.*, 10 and *passim*.
[2] On the date of Merfyn's accession see J. E. Lloyd, *H.W.* I, 231; cf. also *ibid.*, 224, n. 145.
[3] Lloyd believed that with the accession of Merfyn Vrych in 825 'a stranger possessed

Frych (d. 844), was the son of Guriad. His mother, Ethyllt, was descended from the 'Island Dragon' Maelgwn, and the Catamanus from the famous Anglesey inscription (cf. p. 78 above), and also of the great Cadwallon, slayer of Edwin of Northumbria. His mother's was the most distinguished line in Wales. His father's line is not well authenticated in Welsh historical records, but Welsh poetry and genealogies suggest that he belonged to the 'Men of the North' and was a descendant both of the famous line of Coel Hen and of that of Dyfnwal Hen of Dumbarton, whose dynasties had given effective protection to our northern frontiers during the late Roman period. The family traced its ancestry to Llywarch Hen, a cousin of the great Urien of Rheged, and to others whose names occur in Merfyn's immediate family, but are not common elsewhere in Wales, though they occur among the 'Men of the North'. Probably the Northumbrian expansion westward had displaced branches of the old dynasties, especially from Galloway, causing them to expand across the narrow seas to Ireland and the Isle of Man.[1] The Irish *Annals of Ulster* s.a. 657 (*recte* 658) record the death of '*Guret (Gwriad)*,[2] king of Alcluathe' (Dumbarton), while the famous Manx Cross, inscribed Crux Guriat,[3] of approximately Merfyn's date, suggests that the family may have come to Gwynedd more immediately from the Isle of Man. The name is also that of Merfyn's father *Guriat* and that of his son or grandson.[4] It seems clear that Merfyn's own ancestors were among various chieftains of the 'Men of the North', and that the names of their immediate family in Wales were among the ancestral names of his father's line. Whatever his immediate place of origin, Merfyn established himself in Gwynedd, and allied himself to the royal house of Powys by marrying Nest, the sister of Cyngen (d. 854), the last king of the old line of Powys. After this the kingdom of Powys apparently passed to the line of Merfyn Frych, and on his death to his son Rhodri Mawr.

Merfyn was an outstanding king. We possess from a manuscript preserved at Bamberg in Bavaria, based on a ninth century original, the opening sentence of a letter – perhaps the earliest Welsh letter in existence – from Merfyn of Gwynedd to Cyngen, king of Powys, his brother-in-law: *Mermin rex Conchen salutem*, 'Merfyn the king salutes Conchen.'

---

himself of the throne of Gwynedd and of the royal seat of Aberffraw'. See however N. K. Chadwick in *S.E.B.C.*, 74 ff.

[1] Cf. Chadwick, *E.S.*, 146.

[2] Whitley Stokes equated the name of Merfyn's father *Gureat* (recorded in the *Hanes Gruffydd ap Cynan*) with L. *Vireatus*; cf. further Jackson, *L.H.E.B.*, 345. Skene identified the name with the Pictish Ferat (*F.A.B.W.I.*, p. 94).

[3] See J. Rhŷs, 'A Welsh Inscription in the Isle of Man', ZCP, I (1897), p. 48 f., with plate of *Crux Guriat*.

[4] The reading of the MS makes the precise relationship here uncertain.

The letter contains a learned cryptogram,[1] and in the letter itself Merfyn addresses the neighbouring king of Powys in polished terms, and it is clear that his court (referred to as *arx*) is a cultivated one, where a degree of education was established – some Latin, possibly a modicum of Greek, and at least two Celtic languages were spoken. The *arx* of Merfyn is evidently on a regular through route from Ireland to the Continent, for it is assumed in the letter that other travellers will follow. This is, in fact, the period of the early activity of Irish scholars in the scriptoria of the continental libraries, and we know that there were recognized hostels for Irish and also for British *peregrini* en route. When therefore we learn that Cyngen, to whom this letter is addressed, died at Rome in 855, we know that he is only one of a long series of pilgrims from Britain and Ireland at this time. Alfred the Great from Wessex made the journey to Rome twice.

Intellectually the reign of Merfyn[2] seems to have been of the highest importance. This is the period when the *Annales Cambriae* appear to have been drawn up in their present form,[3] and also the most important text of the *Historia Brittonum*. The genealogies of the North British princes seem to have been originally drawn up at the same period and in the same milieu.[4] Taken as a whole the evidence suggests that in Wales a school of antiquarian activity flourished in Gwynedd about the beginning of the ninth century and was fostered throughout that century at the courts of Merfyn and his son Rhodri, and from the beginning of the ninth century Wales evidently had something of a continental public, or at least audience.

This is also the period to which we owe our knowledge of the earliest Welsh poetry. The great collection of the earliest Welsh poetry claims in its title to be the work of Aneirin himself. One other extant collection of poems claims to be the work of Taliesin, but they can hardly date from this period (cf. p. 209 below). We do not know where these poems were first written down, but on linguistic grounds it was most probably somewhere in Wales in the ninth century. We do not even know where our extant manuscripts were written, but again it was almost certainly in Wales or, less probably, Cumbria. The contents of the poems must have been well known to the literary circle in Gwynedd, and in all probability the first written records of the poems from oral tradition were made in the same milieu as that which recorded the traditions and the annals and the pedigrees of the northern princes, i.e. in North Wales in the ninth century. As in Ireland, Latin learning was brought

---

[1] For a fuller notice of the letter and cryptogram, and references, see N. K. Chadwick, *S.E.B.C.*, 94 ff.

[2] For a fuller study of the intellectual level and contacts of the court of Gwynedd at this period, with full references, see N. K. Chadwick, *S.E.B.C.*, p. 29 ff.

[3] Chadwick, *G.L.* I, 146 ff. [4] N. K. Chadwick, *S.E.B.C.*, 46 ff.

into requisition to record in writing the oral traditions of the past, probably in the interests of the reigning dynasties. Gwynedd was a centre of culture and of native oral tradition, and the court, first of Merfyn, and later of his son Rhodri Mawr, was evidently largely responsible for having the records made. Here more than anywhere else the importance of exalting the northern ancestry, the splendid northern traditions and history, and the oral literature of the early members of the line of Merfyn's ancestors becomes obvious. They would be invaluable assets to the prestige of the new dynasty claiming descent from Llywarch Hen from the north.

The great intellectual achievement of the reign of Merfyn and his son Rhodri was perhaps the recording in written form of the ancient traditions of the north, the North British Heroic Age. In so far as their dynasty was partially a new one in North Wales, and also in support of their anti-English policy, the traditions of their heroic past in the north must have been invaluable in gaining them the support of their immediate followers and of the wider population of the country of their adoption.

The important part played by the court of North Wales at this period has hardly been fully appreciated. First Merfyn, then his son Rhodri, brought Wales from her isolation into the intellectual life of Europe. In politics no less than in literature Merfyn and Rhodri made a permanent contribution to the future history of Wales, working deliberately for the unification of the country, not by violence but by policy, in a series of diplomatic marriages. We have seen that Merfyn came to the throne by the marriage of his father Gwriad to Ethyllt, the daughter of Cynan, the last king of the island line of Gwynedd, and that Merfyn married Nest,[1] sister of the last king of the old line of Powys.

The son of this union was Rhodri Mawr, 'Rhodri the Great'. On his mother's side, therefore, he was heir to Powys, as Merfyn had inherited Gwynedd through Ethyllt, and on the death of Cyngen in Rome in 855[2] Rhodri acquired Powys,[3] in addition to Gwynedd. Soon after 872 Rhodri himself married Angharad, sister of Gwgon, king of Ceredigion and thus seems to have found himself in possession of the large kingdom of Seisyllwg, which had been formed more than a century earlier by the addition of Ceredigion to Ystrad Tywi, cutting off the little 'Irish' kingdom of Dyfed (cf. p. 38 above) from the rest of Wales. Dyfed had nothing to look forward to but slow strangulation at the hands of the sons of Rhodri. She was in a pincer movement. However, Rhodri's grandson, Hywel Dda, son of Cadell, son of Rhodri and Angharad,

---

[1] See the MS in Jesus College, Oxford, XX, Pedigree 20. This account, harmonizing with MS Harleian 3859 in the British Museum, is to be preferred to the one which reverses matters and makes Nest the mother of Merfyn, and Ethyllt his wife.
[2] *H.W.* I, 325, n. 17.　　　　　　　　　　　　　[3] *H.W.* I, 325.

relieved the apprehensions of Hyfaidd (*Hemeid*), king of Dyfed, and turned an enemy into a friend by marrying his grand-daughter Elen, so that on the death of Hyfaidd's son, Llywarch, in 892[1] Hywel added Dyfed to Seisyllwg, now part of his own domain, and ultimately, in succession to the sons of Rhodri Mawr, he also annexed Powys.

The dynasty is indeed a remarkable one. By a series of diplomatic marriages, and apparently without striking a blow, they had made themselves masters of most of Wales in four generations. Already by the middle of the ninth century Rhodri was the greatest man in Wales and the founder of a great family. But Merfyn had already set the stage for him. His marriage with Nest of Powys must have taken place just at the moment when both Powys and Gwynedd were suffering devastating attacks from the Mercians; and Mercia was getting help from Wessex. It was doubtless with the object of presenting a united front against English aggression that Merfyn had allied himself with his neighbour in this, the richest and most vulnerable part of Wales. This history of the gradual unification of Wales, no less than the long life of many of the early Welsh dynasties, demonstrates the fallacy of regarding the Celtic peoples as inherently war-like.

Yet Rhodri's military achievements are hardly less important than his policy of consolidation. In 855 (recte 856) the *Annals of Ulster* record the death of 'Horm' (Norse *Gormr*), leader of the Danes, at the hands of *Ruadri*, son of Meirmenn, 'king of the Britons'. This outstanding achievement probably reached the ears of the court of Charles the Bald at Liège, who about this time was gravely intimidated by the Vikings, for Sedulius Scottus ('the Irishman'), a member of Charles's court (cf. p. 183 below), composed an ode on a victory over the Danes.[2] In 876 the *Annales Cambriae* record the 'Sunday battle' in Anglesey, fought no doubt against the Danes, and this is doubtless the explanation of annal 876 (recte 877) in the *Annals of Ulster*, which record how *Ruaidri*, son of Muirmenn, king of the Britons, came to Ireland, fleeing before the Black Foreigners (i.e. the Danes); and the following year the death of Rhodri, and also his son[3] Gwriad, at the hands of the Saxons is recorded in the *Annales Cambriae*. His realm was inherited by his sons severally, Anarawd, probably the eldest, taking Gwynedd and Anglesey, Cadell probably having Seissyllwg, where his descendants ruled for many generations. The shares which may have fallen to the four remaining sons are unknown.[4]

---

[1] *V.S.B.G.* genealogy I.

[2] On the bearing of Rhodri's victory on events at Liège, and on the odes, see N. K. Chadwick, *S.E.B.C.*, 83 f.

[3] So MS A.; but MS B has *frater*, so also the *Brut y Tywysogyon*, MSS. *Peniarth* 20; and *Red Book of Hergest*. See the editions by Thomas Jones, Cardiff, 1952 and 1955 respectively.

[4] *H.W.* I, 326 and n. 27.

Rhodri, like the Men of the North, had been forced to fight on two fronts. His death was the heaviest blow that the Welsh could have suffered at this time. On the west the Danes were still a rising power; on the east the English in both Mercia and Wessex had been, and still were, an ever increasing menace. By Rhodri's inheritance of Powys he had fallen heir to the richest part of Wales, but also to the age-old feud along its borders, to which Offa's Dyke, built during the closing years of the eighth century, bears witness. Early in this century, in the life-time of Elisedd, the king of Powys (commemorated on the cross near Llangollen commonly known as Eliseg's pillar), the Welsh had been strong enough to gain some ground; but in 822 the *Annales Cambriae* record the destruction of Degannwy by the Saxons, who 'took the region of Powys into their own power' (*in sua potestate*). In the year 828 the *Anglo-Saxon Chronicle* reports Ecgbriht, the West-Saxon king con-quering Mercia and reducing the Welsh to submission, thus bringing Wessex into direct conflict with the Welsh for the first time.

A generation later in 853 the *Anglo-Saxon Chronicle* tells of the Mercians under their king Burgred obtaining the help of Aethelwulf, father of Alfred the Great, and making an expedition into Wales and reducing the country to subjection. It is this period of the subjugation of Powys by Burgred of Mercia, with help from Wessex, that Sir Ifor Williams has suggested as the background of the sad poems purporting to be the work of Llywarch Hen (cf. p. 212 below). There can hardly be any doubt that this moment of great political intensity and poignancy was the occasion of Cyngen's pilgrimage to Rome.

Rhodri's death at the hands of the Saxons brings to an end the long struggle for power, not only between Powys and Mercia, but also in its later stages between Gwynedd and Wessex. Asser fully appreciated the contribution of the dynasty of Gwynedd towards the creation of a unified Wales, in that the dynasty had brought a congeries of little states into a closely-knit realm. The annexation of Powys by Hywel Dda, Rhodri's grandson, was only the final stage. Asser says pointedly that after Rhodri's death, his sons worked together in unison against the other southern states, and it is the Wales of Rhodri's sons, Gwynedd in the north and Deheubarth (cf. p. 77 above) in the south, that Asser has in mind more particularly when he refers to Wales by the grandiose epithet *Britannia*. In the reigns of Merfyn and Rhodri the old glory of the 'Men of the North' was destined to flower again and to find its fullest expression, both politically and intellectually. It is in the earliest genealogy of this family[1] that we first meet with Rhodri's epithet *Mawr*. The *Historia Brittonum*, compiled in this

---

[1] This pedigree was published from Jesus College (Oxford) MS 20 by E. Phillimore, *Y Cymmrodor*, Vol. VIII (1887).

century, lays great emphasis on the traditions of the Romans preserved in Wales. In the reign of Alfred, Asser of St David's emphasizes the persistent effort of Rhodri's son and heir Anarawd to make a compact with the Northumbrians. There can be no doubt that in all this Rhodri and his sons were aiming at a united British nation and an ultimate conquest of the Saxons, as their ancestor Cadwallon had done. It is partly in the light of these ideals, and bearing in mind the common bond of race and language, that we must view the prominence given to the traditions and the poetry of Cumbria and the northern Britons in the Gwynedd of the ninth century. All the memories of the heroic past were called on to serve this great end, which even after Rhodri's death sent its fiery cross throughout all the Celtic lands in the last great Welsh heroic poem, the *Armes Prydein*[1] ('The Prophecy of Britain'), composed not before *c*. 900 or later than 930 (cf. p. 215 below).

It would be interesting to know how Asser first came into contact with Alfred. His own words suggest that he came as a refugee, for he speaks of his own king Hyfaidd of Dyfed, who often plundered the monastery of St David's and expelled the inmates; and he speaks of his own relative, bishop Nobis, and of himself also, as having been expelled.[2] Yet it is striking that both Alfred and William the Conqueror should have found it imperative to establish permanent relations with Dyfed and the church of St David's. Was it the Irish menace? We must surely associate Alfred's interest in St David's – a church and monastery wholly Irish in character – with his contributions to the Irish Church, of which we hear from Asser, (ch. 39) and also with other indications which Asser gives us (chs. 76, 91) of Alfred's interest in Ireland. In addition we have the unique record of the visit of three Irishmen to his court, and the notice of the death of the Irish scribe Swifneh (of Clonmacnoise), both related in annal 891 in the Parker Text of the *Anglo-Saxon Chronicle*.[3] Living on the Welsh border, Alfred could not fail to realize that Wessex and Mercia could never hope to remain secure from invasion from the west with a permanent and implacable enemy on their rear.

Hywel Dda began his career as joint heir of Seisyllwg with his brother Clydog, but probably ruled alone there after his brother's death, which took place two years after their submission to Edward the Elder. Hywel doubtless acquired Dyfed by his marriage with Elen, grand-daughter of Hyfaidd Hen (see pp. 111–12 above.) Early in life he visited Rome, and after his return he was closely associated throughout his life with the English court. In the *Anglo-Saxon Chronicle*, MS. D., s.a.

---

[1] Edited by Sir Ifor Williams (Cardiff, 1955).
[2] See Asser's *Life of King Alfred*, cap. 79, edited by W. H. Stevenson, new impression with article on recent work by D. Whitelock (Oxford, 1959).
[3] On this annal, and the identity of Swifneh, see Plummer's note *ad loc. T.S.C.* II, p. 105.

926, we read that Hywel of the 'West Welsh',[1] and Owen of Gwent, in fact the whole of South Wales, submitted to Athelstan. When, some ten years later, the tributary princes leagued themselves against Wessex, only the South Welsh seem to have stood aside, doubtless due to Hywel's influence.

Hywel had no claim on North Wales for most of his life, for the evidence of charters makes it clear that he and his cousin, Idwal Foel ab Anarawd, ruled North and South Wales separately under Athelstan. But in 942 Idwal and his brother, or possibly his son, Elisedd, were slain in battle against the Saxons. At this point Hywel seems to have annexed Gwynedd and doubtless Powys also, thus gradually by inheritance and marriage becoming the sole ruler of Wales under Athelstan.

Hywel's English sympathies are fully attested both in the part which he took in English legal procedure and in the English influence on his own Welsh institutions (cf. p. 98 above). Athelstan often summoned the *subreguli* to meetings of the *witan* when they were approving grants of land, and the names of Welsh princes appear from time to time among the witnesses; and from 928–49 Hywel's name appears on every charter containing Welsh signatories, and always the first in order. One of these grants made at Luton in 931 bears the testimony:

† *Ego Howael subregulus consensi et subscripsi.*

The cross doubtless represents Hywel's mark, doing duty for his signature. This English influence on his institutions is seen again in the silver penny now in the British Museum, the first pre-Conquest example of a silver penny struck by a Welsh king, which bears on the obverse the legend *Howael Rex.*

It is interesting to speculate as to what the history of Wales might have been if Rhodri had not been killed in warfare against the Saxons. He had failed to win Dyfed though he had succeeded in hemming it in; and it was from this corner of Wales that Alfred managed, with Asser's help, to inaugurate a pro-English policy among the South Welsh princes, a policy which was to bear fruit in the alliance between Rhodri's grandson, Hywel Dda, and Alfred's grandson, Athelstan in the following century. When Alfred obtained the services of Asser, and the homage of the South Welsh princes in opposition to the ambitions of the Sons of Rhodri, the battle between opposing policies of the North and South Welsh princes – between Celtic political separatism and hopes of freedom from the Saxons on the one hand, and on the other union with England in face of the common danger from the Danes – was virtually

---

[1] Plummer understands this to refer in general to the Cornishmen. See *T.S.C.* II, p. 452 s.v. *West Wealas.* This interpretation seems to me improbable in this context however; cf. further Plummer's note, p. 135 f.

over. The annexation of Powys by Hywel Dda, his submission to Alfred's son, Edward the Elder in 918, and his later submission to Athelstan are only the final stages.

There is a similarity in the aims and achievements of Rhodri Mawr and Alfred the Great. As a result of Viking pressure both had succeeded in developing from a group of small units into relatively consolidated states, each struggling for survival while threatened by foreign enemies. Each was the first in the history of his country to win the epithet 'great', probably after the example of the great western Emperor Charlemagne. Indeed each had some knowledge of continental affairs. The death of Rhodri, while Alfred was rapidly rising in power, undoubtedly facilitated the task of uniting under Alfred and Athelstan, first the South Welsh princes, and ultimately the whole of Wales, under an English king. In traditions of North and South Wales at this period we have passed from the heroic ideals of the north to the realistic political vision of the south. But we have also stepped out of the Old World into a new era.

We have seen how, at the close of the Classical Period, and after the Barbarian invasions had transformed the Roman Empire, two peoples of north-western Europe had continued to develop on their own traditional lines with comparatively little upheaval. The Teutonic peoples of Scandinavian lands and the Celtic peoples of the British Isles, though never wholly isolated from the Continent and the new conditions resulting from the downfall of the Roman Empire, were not at first directly affected politically. They continued to progress on their own lines in relative isolation. Here the growth of power of the kingship developed from within rather than by external agency, leaving the integrity of the Celtic lands unaffected except for the outer fringes.

During the eighth century a new Barbarian irruption took place from Northern Europe sweeping east over Russia and west over the British Isles and the peripheral countries of Western Europe. The wide scope and devastating impact of this movement can be inferred from the fact that it is universally known to historians as the 'Viking Age'. The eastern or Swedish activities of the Scandinavian Vikings concentrated chiefly on Finland and, more especially, Russia, where the great river systems of the Dniepr, the Don and the Volga served them as highroads to the richer lands of the south and east, for expansion, colonization, and the formation of city-states. The western Vikings in the early period set sail for the most part from Norway, and their nucleus may be gauged from the names by which they were commonly known in the Irish records of the period – *Lochlannaig*, people of *Lochlann* (Rogaland), the country round the Stavanger Fjord in south-western Norway; and perhaps *Hiruath*, the people of Hörthaland, immediately to the north of Rogaland.[1]

The cause of the Viking Age, as of all such barbarian irruptions, was food shortage. Norway in particular, with its long narrow axis consisting of a great mountain spine, and a narrow coastal strip, could not support a vigorous growing population. Emigration in some form was inevitable. The more precise dating has been attributed to various causes, one of which, it has been suggested, was the invention of the keel *c.* 600,[2] which must have had a far-reaching effect on ocean-going ships in the west. Scandinavian tradition emphasizes the effect of the policy of King Harold the Fair-haired (died *c.* 945)[3] who from his original kingdom of Vestfold in the south-east of Norway aimed at uniting the whole country under his rule. Many independent rulers emigrated to win for themselves land elsewhere, especially in Iceland, the Faroes and the Northern Isles of Britain.

The Celts themselves must have been intrepid seafarers for, as we shall see (p. 182 below) the Irish monk and scholar Dícuill, who wrote the treatise *De Mensura Orbis Terrae* about the year 825, probably in Iona, speaks of islands, probably the Faroes, in the ocean to the north of Britain, which had been inhabited by Irish anchorites for about a century, but had become deserted owing to Viking raids. He also refers to the island of *Thile* (evidently *Thule*, Iceland)[4] which had been described to him about thirty years earlier by priests who had spent some months there. Later, when the Norsemen settled in Iceland in the late ninth century, they found certain Irish hermits still living there whom the Norsemen called *papar* (literally 'priests').[5]

In all probability the ultimate causes of the avalanche from the north on the British Isles were external. Of these the first was the disappearance of the Pictish fleet from northern waters. Gildas spoke of the attacks of the Picts on southern Britain in Roman times (cf. p. 31 above). We know from Adamnán that in the sixth century the Orkneys were ruled by a *subregulus* under Brude, the powerful king of the Northern Picts, who evidently held supreme power throughout the Hebrides – a hegemony which can only have rested on his fleet. In the west this may have been threatened by new Celtic fleets, for already by the fifth century seafarers had established the kingdom of Dál Riata in western Scotland from

---

[1] C. J. S. Marstrander, *Bidrag til det norske sprogs historie i Irland* (Christiania, 1915), p. 56 ff. cf. also A. Bugge, *Contributions to the History of the Norsemen in Ireland* (Christiania, 1900), 4.

[2] A. Brøgger and H. Shetelig, *The Viking Ships* (Oslo, 1951), 52 ff.

[3] On Harold's dates see G. Turville-Petre, *The Heroic Age of Scandinavia* (London, 1951), 116.

[4] For two important articles on Dícuill and his work see M. Esposito in *D.R.*, Vol. 137 (1905), 327 ff.; *Studies*, Vol. III (1914), 651 ff.

[5] The account is given in the Icelandic Preface to the *Íslands Landnámabók* ('The Book of the Settlement of Iceland'), part of which dates from the twelfth century, and is on the whole accepted as a source of high authenticity.

their home in northern Ireland, and we have traced the importance of their fleet after the establishment of the kingdom in Scotland. The *Annals of Ulster* record an expedition (*fecht*) to the Orkneys by Aedán mac Gabráin *c*. 580 from Scottish Argyll. The Pictish power in the west was now challenged. In the east the seas were policed in the seventh and eighth centuries by the Frisians, who doubtless restricted the Picts to northern waters, and thereby curtailed their power. It may be taken as certain that the destruction of the power of the Frisians by Charles Martel in 734, and their final subjugation by Charlemagne, gave the freedom of the seas to the Vikings in southern waters.

The settlement of the Scottish Islands had taken place on a wide scale, partly it would seem by peaceful penetration.[1] The family of Rögnvaldr, Earl of Möre, a large province in western Norway, south of Trondheim, settled in the *Northreyjar*, 'the Northern Isles', i.e. Orkney and Shetland, probably as early as *c*. 860, and the Earldom of Orkney and the *Northreyjar* became their hereditary possession.[2] From there the kingdom spread over the whole of northern Scotland, and the power and wealth of its court is attested by the number of *skalds* or 'poets' who thronged to the court, and whose panegyric and elegiac poems have formed the basis of the historical sagas of the Orkney jarls – the *jarlasaga*, incorporated into the *Orkneyinga Saga*.[3] This great earldom was the key to the Viking world in the west, and it was only a matter of time before dreams of expansion and permanent rule led them to hopes of Ireland. Nothing less than such a dream accounts for the sagas and poems, and for the whole picture of the Battle of Clontarf[4] as the death of Viking hopes in Ireland. But this is to reach the Celtic winning post before we have made the start. A long and bitter agony was to intervene.

The earliest of the Norwegian kingdoms in the British Isles probably dates from still earlier times. It consisted of a kingdom comprising the Hebrides, known as the *Suthreyjar*, the 'Southern Isles' (later *Sodor*) to distinguish them from the *Northreyjar*, and it included also the Isle of Man. The precise date and origin of the Hebridean kingdom are unknown,[5] but from the number of Norse place-names it seems likely that already in early times a gradual Norse infiltration had penetrated

[1] On the early dating of the settlements in the Northern Isles see A. Bugge, *Vesterlandenes Indflydelse i Vikingtiden* (Christiania, 1905); A. W. Brøgger, *Ancient Emigrants* (Oxford, 1929); T. D. Kendrick, *History of the Vikings* (London, 1930); H. Marwick, *Orkney* (London, 1951), 36.

[2] See H. Shetelig, *V.A.G.B.I.*, Part I (Oslo, 1946), 22 ff. Cf. H. Koht, *Inhogg og Utsyn i Norsk Historie* (Kristiania, 1921), 34.

[3] See *The Orkneyinga Saga* edited by S. Nordal (Copenhagen, 1916); translation and study of the saga by A. B. Taylor (Edinburgh, 1938); translation and a valuable introductory study by Vígfússon in the Rolls Series, Vol. I, 1887; Vol. II, 1894.

[4] For a general account of the battle see 'The Battle of Clontarf' by the Rev. John Ryan, J.R.S.A.I., Vol. VIII, 7th Series (1938), 1 ff.

[5] For a general account see E. MacNeill 'The Norse Kingdom of the Hebrides'. S.R. XXXIX (1916) 254 ff.

into a basic Celtic population.[1] The Celtic people and the Norsemen had lived side by side in the Hebrides for many centuries. The Gaelic dialects of the northern Outer Hebrides had Norse elements from about 800 AD,[2] and the people of the Hebrides were recognized during the Viking Age as a distinct people with the name *Gall-Ghaedhil* (literally 'Foreign-Irish') to distinguish them from the original Gaelic population.

We know that this did not prevent the churches – Iona, and probably Eigg[3] and the Faroes[4] – from being among the victims of the earliest Viking raids; and in the ninth century our internal history of the Hebridean kingdom is limited to families who migrated to Iceland.[5] From the intervening position of the Inner Hebrides, between the Earldom of Orkney and Ireland, we may suppose that the kingdom of the Hebrides was probably in some measure dependent on the Earls of Orkney. This would account for the sparsity of Hebridean records and for the apparent absence of a central court with a body of panegyric poets. On the other hand no Hebridean contingent is recorded among the followers of Earl Sigurðr of Orkney at the Battle of Clontarf in 1014, while a Hebridean kingdom, centred in the Isle of Lewis, was operating in western Ireland in the thick of the Viking onslaught. The Isle of Lewis was more Norse than any other part of the Hebrides or of Gaelic Scotland elsewhere, and the density of Norse place-names is greater in Lewis than in any other part of Celtic speaking Scotland.[6]

The fiercest impact of the Viking attacks on Celtic lands was on Ireland. In the early ninth century it had brought the age of the Saints to an end, first by destroying the island sanctuaries on a wide scale, notably Inishmurray off the Sligo Coast, and Skellig Michael off the Kerry Coast, and the islands at the mouth of Wexford Harbour, and also the monastic coastal settlements and headlands, such as the famous Monastery of St Comgall at Bangor, Co. Down. By a swift crescendo in the same century these sudden and devastating plundering raids were followed by penetrating incursions into the interior, where bases were established for raiding inland.

In this early period the Norwegians were the leading Viking power in the attacks: the front door into Ireland was Limerick, and the Shannon the chief waterway leading to the north and east. Fleets were stationed on Lough Derg and Lough Ree, whence the great religious centre of

---

[1] See R. L. Brenner, *Saga-Book of the Viking Club* III (1902–4), 373.
[2] M. Oftedal, 'Norse Place-names in Celtic Scotland', *I.C.C.S.*, 48.
[3] See A. Sommerfelt, *De Norsk-irske Bystaters Undergang* 1169–71 (*Avhandlinger utgitt av det Norske Videnskaps-Akademi i Oslo* II. Hist. Filos. Klasse 1957, No. 4), 5.
[4] See p. 117 above. Dícuill reports these islands as deserted in his day (the early ninth century) owing to Viking raids (*causa latronum nortmannorum*).
[5] See Shetelig, *V.A.G.B.I.*, 31.
[6] M. Oftedal, *op. cit.*, 44 f.

Armagh was annexed and desecrated, and the western monasteries of Clonmacnoise, Clonfert and Terryglas, were burnt. It was from the west that the chief raids first penetrated to Leinster and the east coast, and it seems that the kingdom of the Hebrides, more specifically the kingdom of Lewis, may have been the immediate basis for this thrust into the heart of Ireland in the first half of the ninth century. In the latter half of the tenth century, when the Limerick Vikings were expanding into a realm wholly independent of Dublin, and concentrating their activities on forming their own colonies in Munster, their immediate connexion with the Outer Hebrides is demonstrated, at least in Irish tradition, by reference to a certain Morann, son of 'the sea-king of Lewis', who is said to have been killed in Limerick in battle against the Irish, while the recurrence of the names *Manus* (Old Norse *Magnus*), and *Somarlid* (O.N. *Sumarliði*) in both royal families suggests close connexion, possibly intermarriage, between Lewis and Limerick.

Throughout the ninth and tenth centuries Norse colonization continued on a wide scale, and proceeded to spread along the east and south coasts. Dublin had been fortified in 841, and Norse sea-port towns were founded in Wicklow, Wexford, Waterford, and Cork. In the tenth century each had its own independent king and was prepared to make independent alliances, whether by marriage or for plundering raids, with their own people or with the Irish chieftains indifferently. No central government existed, whether of the Irish or the Norsemen; but about the middle of the ninth century a resistance movement led to a series of Irish victories and the Norwegian supremacy crumbled. Simultaneously a great Danish fleet arrived in the east, probably from England, and captured Dublin, while their leader defeated the Norwegians in a great battle following their landing at Carlingford Lough. In the third phase of the Viking occupation which followed, the basis of operations was in the east and the attacks came from the Irish Sea.

The course of events which follows suggests that the main objective of the Danes was the destruction of the Norwegian power in Ireland, and it has even been suggested that they were hired by the Irish as mercenaries with this end in view. It is not easy to see a sound economic basis for such a supposition, but undoubtedly Leinster combined forces with the Danes now and with the Norse later at Clontarf, in pursuance of their ancient enmity against Meath. The Danes evidently had a formidable fleet, but in 852 (*recte* 853) the *Annals of Ulster* record the arrival of Amlaim (Norse *Ólafr*), the son of the king of Lochlann[1] (possibly *Ólafr* 'the White'), who regained possession of Dublin. Again s.a. 870 (*recte* 871) the same annals record how Ólafr and Ivarr came

---

[1] 'Lochlann' by that time meant Norway.

again to Dublin from 'Alba'. These two Norwegian leaders together made Dublin the chief Viking centre in Ireland, and the base for their fleet, operating against the coasts of the surrounding countries. The arrival of Ólafr from Lochlann close on the Danish victory in 854, is only one of a number of indications that the Norwegian settlements in Ireland were a part of a deliberate policy of expansion and colonization from south-western Norway.

The arrival of Ólafr and Ívarr and the establishment of their base about the middle of the ninth century again shifted the balance of power, and for some forty years Ireland seems to have been free from further invasions, though the two Norse leaders plundered the grave-mounds and sanctuaries, sometimes with the help of the Irish local rulers. The help may have been given under duress, and the Norwegian rulers must have been forced to find gold to pay their followers, if they were to maintain their newly-won lands in the British Isles. It was during the closing years of the ninth century and the opening years of the tenth that the Danes were establishing their kingdom in Northumbria and East Anglia. The danger to the Norwegian kingdom of Dublin from the east was a very real one.

Ólafr sought to meet it by attacks from Scotland. In 866 he invaded Fortrenn and pillaged this, the most southerly of the Pictish provinces. The *Annals of Ulster* tell us that in 869 (recte 870), the two kings of the Norsemen (*duo reges Normannorum*), i.e. the two rulers of Dublin, overcame the great rock citadel of Dumbarton, which gave them control of the entrance to the Clyde and to Strathclyde and Cumbria to the south. The destruction of Dumbarton is also recorded in the *Annales Cambriae* s.a. 870. This may have been merely a precautionary measure, for it does not appear that the monastery of Hoddom in Dumfriesshire was desecrated, while in 875 both Strathclyde and Galloway were harried from the Tyne.

In general the poverty of Wales and her mountainous interior gave her some immunity from any permanent occupation by the Vikings, though small Scandinavian colonies existed in South Wales.[1] It was inevitable, nevertheless, that Anglesey, the 'granary of Wales', should be devastated by the 'Black Gentiles', as the *Annales Cambriae* tell us, s.a. 853 (recte 855), doubtless under their leader Gormr, who is believed to have led the great Danish fleet to victory against the Norse forces in Ireland at Carlingford Lough, and probably the Danish force which had sacked Paris and held Charles the Bald and his Frankish realm in terror. In the year following the devastation of Anglesey, however, Gormr was slain, and the relief to the tension is echoed, not only in

[1] For Viking activities in Wales see B. G. Charles, *Old Norse Relations with Wales* (Cardiff, 1934). See further Melville Richards, 'Norse Place-names in Wales', *I.C.C.S.*, 51 ff.

the Irish Annals, but, it would seem, on the Continent, to judge from eulogies on a certain *Roricus* – in all probability Rhodri Mawr – composed at the court of Charles the Bald himself (p. 112).

The Isle of Man is exceptionally rich in Viking remains, including a wealth of runic inscriptions, and it is just about the period of Norse supremacy in Ireland – the middle of the ninth century – that the first permanent Norse settlements seem to have been established. It is believed that the starting point was Dublin, especially after the expulsion of a large number of Norsemen recorded by *A.U.* s.a. 901 (*recte* 902); but the Hebrides and Galloway probably contributed, for again the strong hand of the Orkney earldom shows itself when the Isle of Man was eventually conquered by Sigurðr the Stout, Earl of Orkney, the romantic owner of the famous raven banner, who perished at the Battle of Clontarf in 1014. The conquest of Man was undoubtedly a factor in his ambitious project of a southern kingdom, a western parallel to Normandy. Manx history may be said to begin with the Viking conquest. In later times the island came into the possession of Godred Crovan, a Hebridean, and his successors were known as kings of 'Man and the Isles' till the cession of the island in 1266. But although under Norse rule, and with a heavy Norse intake of immigrants, it remained, like Ireland, a Celtic country and a Celtic-speaking island to the end – even to our own life-time. It was, in fact, the last Viking kingdom to survive in our islands with a Celtic-speaking population.

In 902 Dublin was retrieved by the Irish and many of the *gennti* (foreigners, Vikings) were expelled. It may have been as a result of this resistance movement that about this period, and perhaps under these conditions, an unchronicled major settlement of Cumberland[1] and Lancashire[2] took place on a scale amounting to an invasion, though no records of conflict entered our annals. Our evidence comes chiefly from place-names, which suggest a Norwegian population with a strong Celtic element in their language. They practised agriculture on an intensive system, and have left many Norse-names along the Lancashire coast, between the sea and the foot-hills of the Pennines from the Dee northwards. The villages seem to be the homes of squatters, draining and cultivating small patches of unwanted land which has become in consequence jet black and richly fertile, and these villages are so close to one another that a day's walk, even today, will cover an area of villages with purely Norse names without a single intervening Saxon

---

[1] See B. Dickins, *The Place-names of Cumberland*, Vol. III (Cambridge, 1952), p. xiii.
[2] See an important paper by F. T. Wainwright, 'The Scandinavians in Lancashire', T.L.C.A.S. LVIII (1945–6), p. 71 ff., and the references there cited. Cf. also Ekwall, 'The Scandinavians and Celts in the North-West of England' (London, 1918); *Place-names of Lancashire* (Manchester, 1922).

name – Ainsdale, Birkdale, Meols Cop, Blowick, Scarisbrick, Bescar, Ormskirk, Burscough, Hoscar, Skelmersdale. The Saxons seem to have occupied the river banks and, still more, the higher and drier land between the Viking squatters and the hills, and here the names again reveal the settlement plan – Preston, Rufford, Whalley, Churchtown, Croston, Eccleston, Wrightington, Worthington, Shevington, Parbold, Appley Bridge. And the Saxon dairy farms have left traces of their summer pastures and transhumance in the hill country on the sunny, western slopes of the Pennine foot-hills. The absence of a written record in chronicle or annals is probably due to the fact that no wealthy monasteries with scriptoria had been established in north-west England. Burscough Priory near Ormskirk was not founded until *c.* 1190 and was an inconsiderable foundation.

The silence of our records on the extensive Norse settlements on the east of the Irish Sea helps us to realize that the picture of the Viking Age in Ireland is an exclusively monastic record. The monasteries, by their concentration and wealth, were the agonized victims of armed raiders. The record which they have left is unfortunately only too true. In the early stages of the invasions it may indeed be the whole of the truth. In Brittany we know that the monastery of St Méen in the Forest of Brocéliande was especially favoured and developed to serve as a refuge for the bishops of Dol from Viking attacks.

In 919 Dublin was recaptured, and Niall Glúndub, with twelve other kings and those who formed the core of the resistance movement, lost their lives, though the northern Uí Néill continued to put up a brave resistance. It was in the period immediately following that the Vikings developed the sea-port towns. Dublin grew in importance and was strengthened by closer intercourse with the Danish kingdom of York. Limerick, hostile and governed independently, probably by its original dynasty, consolidated its colonies in Munster. But towards the close of the century a certain Cellachán (d. 954), a ruler of the Eóganacht dynasty of Cashel, put new life into the Irish resistance, while in western Munster Dál Cais on the borders of Co. Clare was able to enlist the help of Connacht against the Limerick Vikings. By the middle of the tenth century the supremacy had passed from the Eóganacht dynasty of Cashel to Cennétig, the ruler of Dál Cais, and his two sons Mathgamain and Brian Bórama were strong enough to lead the offensive against the Vikings which culminated in the great Battle of Clontarf in 1014 and the end of the Viking supremacy in Ireland.

The importance of the Battle of Clontarf is sometimes disputed. The issue was by no means clear cut between the Irish and the Norse. Sihtric, the Norse king of Dublin, took no part in the conflict. In pursuit of their traditional jealousy of Meath, Leinster supported the Dublin Vikings, and the Limerick Vikings, always hostile to the Dublin dynasty, seem to have been on Brian's side. Even the Irish victory was marred by the death of Brian; and although the battle concluded as an undoubted Irish victory the break was not sudden and complete. The Norse settlements lived on under their own institutions, and even carried on trade with the English ports on the Bristol Channel. Moreover two centuries of adjustment in a small country had tended to bring the two peoples closer together. Frequent intermarriage and the conversion of many of the leading Norsemen in Dublin to Christianity, including Ólafr Cuarán and his son Sihtric 'Silken-beard', indicate the sympathy which had been growing between them. Brian had married Sihtric's mother, and perhaps gave his own daughter to Sihtric in exchange. The leading bards of the Irish and Norse courts were fraternizing. The true fundamental significance of Clontarf lay in the death of Sigurðr the Stout, the great Orkney Jarl, bearing with him into the battle 'his own devil' – the ill-omened raven banner; for the death of the Orkney Earl put an end to the supreme effort of the Norwegians to annex and exploit Ireland as another Normandy.

It was this ultimate spiritual, rather than the immediate political, effect of the battle which gave it unparalleled importance at the time. In communities where the spoken word rather than written propaganda is widely influential, the contemporary bards and saga tellers are the most trustworthy witnesses for the impact of contemporary events on the people living at the time. For scholars sifting evidence a thousand years later the emotion and the significance have become clouded. The Battle of Clontarf inspired in Irish and Norse alike both poetry and saga. To the Norse poets and saga-tellers particularly, the battle was fought not only by the Irish and the Norsemen, but between super-natural powers of the air. The old saga convention of the *Battle of Allen*, where the issue is fought out between St Bridget and Columcille, here reappears. Men throughout the Celtic world saw dreams and portents, while a man in Caithness beheld the ghastly vision of super-natural women weaving the great web of battle on a loom of slaughter, where men's heads were the weights, men's entrails the warp and woof.[1] In Ireland the prose narrative 'The War of the Irish and the Foreigners'[2] is imbued with emotion and picturesque quality equalled elsewhere only in the saga of the *Battle of Allen*, and with a rhetoric even more hectic in its excited flow.

There could be no going back. The Viking régime had brought

---

[1] This forms the subject of the Norse skaldic poem, the *Darratharljóth*, edited and translated by N. K. Chadwick in *Anglo-Saxon and Norse Poems* (Cambridge, 1922), 111 ff.
[2] *C.G.G.*, edited and translated by J. H. Todd (London, 1867).

changes in the economic life and institutions of the country which were fundamental. They had dreamed of settling in a pastoral country with a rich internal food-producing economy, self-supporting, and free from external commitments, and with an ancient, unquestioned system of inheritance and government more practical and dependable than any theoretical legislative system which could be readily devised. The Norse tenure had proved precarious, their dreams fallacious. The dispersed and elementary and conservative life of the ancient Celtic Iron Age, which was still the economic basis of life in Ireland, defeated the centralizing methods of the new-comers whose only chance of survival in a new land was in concentration.

Ireland had had no towns as we understand the term. Her royal raths – Tara, Cruachain, Emain – were more like permanent camps than royal cities and centres of bureaucratic government. She had no sea-ports. The Vikings gave her her coast-line, with development of harbours and town life, especially in the cities of Limerick, Dublin, Waterford, Wexford and Cork. It is a matter of common knowledge that the Irish terminology of ship-building and trade, and of their accompanying weights and measures, consists largely of Scandinavian borrowings. The first coinage struck in Ireland was that of the Viking kingdom of Dublin. It was no fault of the Vikings that Ireland did not become a commercial nation. They at least brought her into the orbit of the commercial world which they knew. And there they left her.

The influence of the Viking régime on the internal economy of Ireland is more subtle and more difficult to assess owing to the extreme conservatism of the Irish tradition embodied in the surviving written texts. This conservatism is especially remarkable in the Irish law-texts which were treated by the jurists as inviolable, and preserved with so great a fidelity that it is possible to trace, not only the original medium of oral tradition from which the written texts are derived, but even, in places, the oral poetical form in which they had been transmitted through centuries (cf. p. 199 below). Unlike the Welsh laws, which received certain modifications owing to the influence of their Anglo-Saxon neighbours, the Irish laws had never been subjected to serious modification from neighbouring peoples. Clearly changes were inevitable under the impact of a foreign occupation, and as early as the tenth century, radical changes had come about. Indeed the challenge which the Norse occupation offered to the traditional order of Irish society has been described as 'a watershed in the history of Irish institutions'.

Thus, indirectly, the Vikings brought it about that the Irish kings entered into the fellowship of those whose genius entitled them, each after each, to gather their people into a nation – Charlemagne in 800;

Rhodri Mawr *c.* 850; Kenneth mac Alpin about the middle of the ninth century; Alfred the Great shortly before 900; and last of all, Brian. Thus tardily and under Viking pressure the little off-shore island was brought into the political development of the western continental world.

The damage done to the artistic and intellectual life of Ireland was great. Both had been dependent on the monastic centres which had fostered them and inspired and stimulated them. Many of the monasteries had been burnt and pillaged and their treasures scattered, and many of the scriptoria with all their inherited traditions and techniques, all their mastery of the art of superb manuscript illumination, had been destroyed. The loss was incalculable and much of it irrecoverable. High creative art, like high intellectual achievement, can only flourish in an atmosphere of security. The monasteries were always dependent on the support of the governing chiefs. The chiefs themselves, however, were less liable to be pillaged than the wealthy monastic foundations. They were in a large measure necessary to the very subsistence of the invaders, who were themselves non-productive and depended on the traditional native Irish pastoral economy and the organized food-producing powers exercised by the native chiefs. They and their heirs survived, and so eventually the great monasteries revived and lived again. It is a remarkable fact that the period immediately following on the Viking occupation was so productive of artistic works, especially in metal, that it has been claimed as something of a Renaissance.[1] Here also the Viking influence contributed something, not only stimulating and revivifying, but even bringing in new artistic motifs.

The ravaging of the monasteries drove many of the monks overseas, and the lasting gain to European scholarship which resulted from their inclusion in continental monasteries[2] and their influence on European scholarship is widely recognized.[3] This movement of Irish, and indeed of Welsh scholars also,[4] to the Continent is no new thing. It was probably known to Notker Balbulus in the time of Charlemagne. The *Gesta Caroli Magni* tell of the arrival of extremely learned Irish monks who had come with some 'British merchants' to Gaul, and who were welcomed by Charlemagne and entrusted with the education of the young nobility. One of these scholars remained in Gaul, the other resided in the monastery of St Augustine in Pavia in Italy.[5] The *Anglo-Saxon Chronicle* records (s.a. 891) the arrival in a curragh on the coast of

[1] Cf. F. Henry, 'The Effects of the Viking Invasions on Irish Art', in *I.C.C.S.*, p. 61 ff.
[2] See Zimmer, *Keltische Beiträge*, III, 108.
[3] For an excellent general account of Irish scholars on the Continent from the eighth to the tenth centuries, and their sojourn and work in Continental monasteries, see L. Bieler, *Ireland*, 65 ff. See further J. M. Clark, *A.S.G.*, 18–54, especially p. 33. Cf. further for St Gall, J. F. Kenney, *Sources*, 594.
[4] See Clark, *A.S.G.*, 30; cf. also Chadwick, *S.C.B.C.*, 94 ff.
[5] See Clark, *loc. cit.*

Cornwall of three Irish monks who at once went to King Alfred's Court. Aethelweard adds[1] that they then went to Rome, intending to go to Jerusalem. The entry in the *Anglo-Saxon Chronicle* does not state that they were scholars, but a later addition to the text adds that Swifneh, 'the greatest scholar in Ireland died'. He has been identified[2] with Suibne mac Maíle Humai, anchorite and scribe of the Abbey of Clonmacnoise on the Shannon, whose obit appears in this same year in the *Annals of Ulster* s.a. 890 (recte 891). His tombstone, now lost,[3] was still extant at Clonmacnoise in Petrie's time,[4] and the spelling of his name in the *Anglo-Saxon Chronicle* makes it clear that the chronicler received the name in an oral form. The notice of Suibne's death was almost certainly brought by the three pilgrims.

It is surely an error to suppose, as is commonly done, that the Irish monks took their books with them when fleeing from Ireland during the Viking raids. This was undoubtedly done in some cases, but circumstances of travel at that time would certainly preclude the removal of monastic libraries to the continent on a large scale. The great gift of the monks to the continental centres, as innumerable references make clear, is their intellectual capital, which they had acquired in Irish monastic centres, of which Clonmacnoise was the most notable example in the west, as Bangor in Co. Down was in the east. The wanton destruction of the monastic libraries, especially through fire and exposure to weather, must have been enormous; but effective efforts to save them must have been chiefly made by hiding them near at hand. It is in no way surprising to find little topical occasional poems inspired by the Viking Terror, like the one expressive of the comfort to be derived from stormy weather which would prevent a Viking raid from the sea:

> Bitter is the wind tonight,
> It tosses the ocean's white hair:
> Tonight I fear not the fierce warriors of Norway
> Coming over the smooth sea.

[1] See D. Whitelock, *A-S.C.*, p. 53.
[2] C. Plummer, *T.S.C.*, Vol. II, p. 105.
[3] See Pádraig Leonard, 'Early Irish Grave-Slabs', P.R.I.A. Vol. 61, Section C, No. 5 (1961), 161.
[4] See Petrie, *The Round Towers of Ireland*, p. 328 where a wood-cut of the tomb-stone with Suibne's name occurs.

CHAPTER 7

CELTIC RELIGION AND MYTHOLOGY

THE Celtic world is exceptionally rich in memories of religion, mythology and the supernatural. In Gaul religious life was evidently very intense (cf. p. 13 above). Ireland has preserved the richest store of mythological traditions of any country north of the Alps, not even excepting Iceland. Yet the evidence for the supernatural conceptions for these two Celtic realms is somewhat paradoxical, and disparate. Gaul has much to tell us of the religion of the Celts. Memories of the ancient Gaulish gods and spirits have survived in innumerable dedications at local sanctuaries of rivers and springs, sacred lakes and forests (p. 14). Many records have survived in the writings of Classical authors, in place-names, and in material remains in metal-work, in coins and inscriptions. Native Celtic temples of the late Classical period have been excavated, and statuary in both wood and stone now witnesses to a native Gaulish conception of the gods in human form at least from early in our era. Our knowledge of religion in Gaul as a living belief and practice is therefore considerable.

On the other hand in Gaul, as in ancient Greece and the Teutonic world, there is no close connexion between religion and mythology, as the mythology has come to us in later and more fully developed stages. Mythology is always to some extent an artificial creation, an artistic expression of religious emotions or beliefs which are in the nature of things formless. Mythology is, in fact, an attempt to define the infinite and the indefinable, and what it offers is not a definition but a symbol. The mythology of the Gauls, the artistic symbolism of their religion, has not survived, owing to the fact that no Gaulish literature has survived. Their oral traditions, including their mythology, were never written down. As a result of the Roman conquest Gaul rapidly adopted Roman culture, including the art of writing, and the oral traditions died quickly.

In contrast to this, the oral literature of ancient Ireland, including the mythological traditions, survived, as we have seen, till a much later period. Ireland, virtually untouched by Roman culture till nearly half a millennium later than Gaul, preserved its oral traditions intact, including its mythological traditions, till the art and fashion of writing had become general in the Christian monastic *scriptoria*, from the sixth century AD onwards. The heathen religion was by this time a thing of the far past, and the Christian monasteries had no will to record it. For Gaul we have a wealth of evidence for Celtic religion but no developed system of mythology. For Ireland we have a wealth of mythological tradition in a highly developed literary form, but practically no evidence directly bearing on heathen religion.

Yet the hiatus is more apparent than real. Celtic Britain forms a bridge between the two Celtic realms of Gaul and Ireland. In material remains she has much in common with Gaul from which she has been directly influenced; in mythological traditions she has retained fragments which can be shown to be identical in origin with those of Ireland. Owing to the Roman conquest of Britain both material remains and mythological traditions are relatively sparse; but they are both relevant and valid, and we shall refer to them briefly here, to demonstrate the essential unity of Celtic paganism.

In tracing the unity between the continental religion and mythology of Gaul and their remains in the insular Celtic countries to the west we find links in the traditions of sacred islands off the Atlantic coast of Britain and Ireland – links which also remind us of earlier Greek stories of the 'Islands of the Blest' west of the Pillars of Hercules, and the magic island of Circe in the western seas. These sacred islands have a continuous history from the time of Homer to the Age of the Saints, when they were used as sanctuaries for Christian anchorites. Strabo (IV. iv. 6), writing in the first century BC, reports on the authority of Posidonius that a community of women occupied a small island off the mouth of the Loire, from which men were excluded, though the women crossed the sea to join their husbands from time to time and then returned. Once a year it was their custom to remove the roof of the temple of their god and to cover it again the same day. Should one of them let fall the materials she was carrying she was at once torn to pieces by her companions. The Irish *immrama* (cf. p. 188 below), some of which describe islands occupied solely by women, are hardly more remarkable than this ancient Gaulish tradition.

In the first century AD the Roman geographer, Pomponius Mela, speaks of nine priestesses called *Gallizenae*[1] under a vow of perpetual virginity on the island of Sena (the modern Île de Sein) within sight of the south-western tip of Brittany. They possessed magical powers, could raise storms, change at will into animal forms, cure the sick, and foretell the future to sailors who came to consult them. We shall find a meteorological station similarly credited in Irish mythological tradition to the god Manannán mac Lir in the Isle of Man. Again Plutarch, writing *c.* 83 AD, speaks of a certain Demetrius who had reported that among the islands lying near Britain many were isolated and had few or no

[1] *Chorographia III*, vi, 8. For variant readings of the word see Dottin, *Manuel*, p. 383, n. 5.

inhabitants, and some bore the names of gods or heroes. He had voyaged to the nearest of these which had only a few inhabitants, holy men held inviolate by the Britons. Soon after his arrival a violent storm had arisen which the inhabitants told him signified the passing of the mightier ones.[1] Plutarch also informs us that in that part of the world – 'five days off from Britain' – there is one island in which Cronus is confined, guarded in his sleep by Briareus; for his sleep has been devised as a control for him, and around him are many demigods as his attendants and servants.[2] The identity of Demetrius is uncertain, but he is believed to have been a native of Tarsus, a literary man sent by the Emperor Domitian on some mission to Britain – probably the Demetrius who dedicated two bronze tablets with Greek inscriptions, now in York Museum.[3]

As late as the sixth century AD the Byzantine writer Procopius has left us a remarkable echo of the Western World as the last home of the traditions of the Celtic lands of the Continent. He tells us that the people of Armorica had the task of conducting the souls of the dead to Britain. In the middle of the night they heard a knocking on the door, and a low voice called them. Then they went to the sea-shore without knowing what force drew them there. There they found boats which seemed empty, but which were so laden with the souls of the dead that their gunwales scarcely rose above the waves. In less than an hour they reached the end of their voyage, and there in the island of Britain they saw no-one, but they heard a voice which numbered the passengers, calling each by his own name. Breton folk-lore has located the place of departure as the Baie des Dépassés on the south-western tip of Brittany.[4]

The basic facts of the religion of the continental Celts have already been stated in chapter 1, and need not be repeated here. Here we shall confine ourselves to a brief summary of the corresponding features of Celtic religion in Britain, and to a somewhat fuller picture of one or two Gaulish cults which Classical authors have recorded in some detail in their native setting. It is hoped that in this way the essential unity of Gaulish and British religion will be made clear, and a background established for the development of the Celtic mythological literature recorded from the western Celts, especially from Ireland.

We have seen in chapter 1 that one of the most fundamental features of Gaulish religion is the wide prevalence of sanctuaries connected with natural features, especially springs, rivers, lakes and forests. The Gauls were not city dwellers, and their native sanctuaries are those of a nature religion. Strabo (IV.i.13) tells us – again on the authority of Posidonius

---

[1] Plutarch, *Moralia De Defectu Oraculorum*, cap. 18.
[2] *Moralia* XII, *De Facie quae in orbe lunae apparet*, cap. 26.
[3] On Demetrius see Rhys Roberts, *Demetrius* (London, 1927), 273.
[4] Procopius, *Gothic War* VIII xx, 45–49.

– of a vast votive treasure of the tribe of the Volcae Tectosages which had been stored away in sacred enclosures (ἐν σηκοῖς ἀποκείμενα) and part in sacred lakes (ἐν λίμναις ἱεραῖς). He adds that there were many places where treasures of gold were stored in *Celtica*, and that heavy masses of gold and silver were submerged in lakes because there the treasure was most inviolable. In the neighbourhood of Toulouse there was a temple containing very great treasures, for many had dedicated them and no-one dared to lay hands on them. One recalls the hoard from Llyn-Cerrig-Bach in Anglesey recovered in 1943. The site had been part of a lake into which had been thrown a large number of weapons, chariot furniture, tools, slave-chains [Plate 22], portions of trumpets, cauldrons, and fragments of bronze decorated with La Tène designs. The whole is believed to have been the site of sacrificial offerings made between the mid-second century BC and the second century AD.[1]

An important sanctuary of the goddess Sequana existed from Gaulish times near the source of the Šeine, and here in the marshlands numerous pieces of wooden sculpture have recently come to light, including a number of statues dating from the second century AD. The sanctuary will be discussed more fully in chapter 12 below, but here we may compare the sanctuary at the spring of the native British goddess Coventina at the Roman fort (Fort VII) of Brocolitia (Carrawburgh)[2] on the south side of Hadrian's Wall. The spring, which still bubbles up, was originally covered by a temple of Celtic type which contained a well or basin, and into this had been thrown a great number of money offerings, and, even in the fifth century, altars and sculptured tablets from the temple – perhaps by Christians.[3] Among these are a marble slab with an inscription 'to the goddess Coventina', and a bas-relief depicting Coventina herself reclining on a water-borne leaf [Plate 42], holding a water-plant in her right hand, and a flowing goblet in her left. One of the sculptured bas-reliefs represents three water-nymphs, each holding a vase from which an abundant stream is flowing [Plate 43].

The most impressive passages about the Gaulish forest sanctuaries occur in Lucan's *Pharsalia*. In l. 452 f. he refers to the Gaulish druids 'who dwell in deep groves (*nemora alta*) and sequestered uninhabited woods', and who 'practise barbarous rites and a sinister mode of worship', to which the scholiast adds:

'They worship the gods in woods without making use of temples.'[4]

[1] Cyril Fox, *F.E.I.A.*
[2] I. A. Richmond, *R.B.* 196. For a fuller account of the site see J. C. Bruce, *The Hand-Book to the Roman Wall* (7th edition, Newcastle-upon-Tyne, 1914) pp. 119 f.; 126 ff. See further n. 3 below.
[3] For an inventory of the inscribed stones on this site see Collingwood and Wright, *R.I.B.* pp. 485–98 (nrs. 1520–62).
[4] H. Usener, *Scholia in Lucanum* (Leipzig, 1869), p. 33. The manuscript of the *Scholia* is tenth century.

This reference in the *Pharsalia* to sacred woods recalls another passage in the same poem (l. 399 ff.) where Lucan relates how Caesar felled a sacred wood near Marseilles in which trunks of trees are crudely sculptured to represent gods (*simulacra maesta deorum*). Here, says Lucan, barbarous rites are practised in honour of the gods, and the altars are heaped with hideous offerings, and every tree is sprinkled with human blood; and he tells of the water which fell in abundance from dark springs and of the coverts where wild beasts would not lie down in this motionless thicket. A priest (*sacerdos*) officiates for the spirit of the place (*dominus loci*).

It is an eerie spot:

> The people never frequented the place to worship very near it, but left it to the gods ... The priest himself dreads the approach and fears to come upon the lord of the grove.

Even after making due allowance for Lucan's fine rhetoric in this passage we cannot doubt the existence of the sacred wood near Marseilles felled by Caesar, and the superstitious dread of the natives who were called upon to cut down the trees 'untouched by men's hands from ancient times'.

In Britain our evidence for woodland sanctuaries is less ample, but Dio Cassius states that the Britons have sanctuaries (ἱερά) under Boudicca, and offer human sacrifices to the goddess of victory *Andraste* or *Andate* in a sacred wood (ἄλσος).[1] We may refer also to the groves on the island of Anglesey which Tacitus tells us[2] had been devoted to barbarous superstitions, and which were destroyed by Suetonius Paulinus shortly before AD 61 (cf. p. 25 above). The occurrence of the element *nemet* in British place-names again links up these British sanctuaries with those of Gaul (cf. p. 2). One of the most interesting of the links is a late name in the eleventh-century Breton cartulary of Quimperlé, where a forest in Finisterre is referred to thus: 'Quam vocant nemet'.[3]

We do not know when native temple structures first made their appearance in Gaul, though the new technique of the excavation of wooden remains[4] may throw light on this. A single wooden prototype of pre-Roman Iron Age temples of typical form has come to light, not in Gaul, but at Heathrow in Middlesex in Britain.[5] Caesar never mentions temples in Gaul, although Suetonius accuses him in vague terms of having robbed Gaulish *fana* and *templa*.[6] Greek and Roman writers do not use the words ναός, *aedes* to denote Celtic temples, and we have no

---

[1] LXII, vi, 7. On the form of the name see Dottin, *Manuel*, 313.
[2] *Annals*, XIV, 30.　　　　　　　　　　　　　　　　　　　[3] Loth, *Chrestomathie* 222.
[4] Reference may be made to Woodhenge, Sutton Hoo, Yeavering, and now Dunbar—all in Britain; and to sites in Gaul referred to in ch. XII below.
[5] I. A. Richmond, *R.B.*, 192; Powell, *Celts*, 145 f.　　　　　　[6] Suetonius, *Caesar*, 54.

description of Gaulish altars, for which Latin writers use the terms *arae*, *altaria*. During the Gallo-Roman period, however, structural sanctuaries become widespread in both Gaul and Britain, and in both countries, in Britain especially, local wayside shrines have left many traces. Certain Celtic temples in the estuary of the Rhône have been excavated. These temples will be described more fully in chapter 12 below. Here we will only mention that the porticos of the larger temples are of monumental structure, 'veritable *propylaea* of Hellenic conception', and the ambitious architecture, combined with native Celtic features, notably the cult of the human head, suggests an adaptation of Classical architectural building tradition to a Celto-Ligurian religious cult.

The structural plan of the many native Celtic stone-built temples from the Roman period in both Gaul and Britain remains constant, though there is some variety in shape. The normal form was a square box-like building consisting of a *cella* or sanctuary, sometimes raised and surrounded by a portico or verandah, which might be closed or with low walls designed to carry columns. The *cella* was small, entered by a door, and lighted by small windows above the portico, and the public were evidently excluded from the *cella*. The whole was sometimes contained in a square enclosure. Both in Gaul and Britain, however, both round and polygonal temples existed while retaining the same scheme of *cella* surrounded by a peristyle.[1]

Many of the wayside shrines in Britain, which are common in the neighbourhood of Roman roads, are associated with Roman gods; but dedications to native gods are also common, especially in the north. In several cases later Roman structures have been superimposed on earlier Celtic sanctuaries. A famous example in Britain of the persistence of a native dedication is that at Gosbecks Farm near Colchester, where a Roman temple of Celtic pattern had been substituted for an original large ditch surrounding the same rectangular plot, and contained pre-Roman rubbish. Here a bronze statue of Mercury gives us the clue to the later dedication.[2] At Frilford, north-east of Abingdon, two Romanized shrines have been superimposed on an earlier wooden building which had consisted of a circular ditched enclosure containing an open wooden shed. This had been razed to the ground in the Roman period and replaced by a circular enclosure, while a new temple of the common Celtic box-like design was built beside it.[3] The sanctuary continued in use into the fifth century.

The most important native dedication of a Romano-British temple in Britain is that of Lydney on the precipitous west bank of the River Severn in Gloucestershire. It is in origin a forest sanctuary, being situated in the Forest of Dean. The god of this temple is *Nodons* or

---

[1] I. A. Richmond, *R.B.*, 192 ff. [2] *Ibid.*, 136 f., 194. [3] *Ibid.*, 142 f.

Nodens, who is undoubtedly Nuadu or Nuada *Argetlám*, 'Nuadu of the Silver Hand'.[1] Lydney was a therapeutic temple of Aesculapian type and a pilgrim sanctuary, and its most important period is later than 364. It is a large complex of buildings of the type of Classical sanctuaries of healing, and included a long portico like a cloister divided into compartments to accommodate the patients; a courtyard building with further apartments and a reception hall; and ample baths. It is interesting to reflect that Irish mythological tradition explains the epithet of Nodens by his having an artificial hand made of silver. The association with the Lydney therapeutic temple is clear; but Lydney was a wealthy temple and it is possible that the 'silver hand' owed its origin to the rich offerings made to the god. The name *Nuadu Argetlám* is also known to Welsh tradition as *Lludd Llaw Ereint* ('Lludd of the Silver Hand') in *Culhwch and Olwen* (p. 274,) where the form Lludd is probably due to assimilation,[2] and the name *Gwynn fab Nudd* in the same story contains the Welsh for *Nuadu*.[3]

The local nature of most British sanctuaries and the distribution of dedications show that the religion of pre-Roman Britain, like that of pre-Roman Gaul, was essentially a nature religion.

The wide distribution of statuary, both in the round and in relief, makes it clear that the Gauls sometimes pictured their gods in human form, though this is perhaps a relatively late development. Among statues of Gaulish gods a number occur in groups of three, and traces of supernatural triads are also found occasionally in Britain, e.g. at Brocolitia (cf. p. 131 above). Caesar gives the names of five Roman gods whom he equates with Celtic gods, without, however, giving us any Celtic names (p. 13); Lucan on the other hand names three Celtic gods. These lists suggest that the gods in question were imagined in human form; but neither in Gaul nor in Britain have we any evidence for the notion of a supreme god, or on the other hand anything like the Greek pantheon. In Gaul, however, certain cults have a wide distribution, and of two of the gods, Belenus and Ogmios, Roman writers have left us notices which suggest that a rich literature of the gods must have been current in Gallo-Roman circles. It may even have left its impress on native art, such as frescoes and coins.

The Greek writer Lucian, who was born at Samosata on the Euphrates in the second century AD, relates that as he was travelling in Gaul, apparently in the neighbourhood of the Atlantic, he came upon a picture of an old man, clad in a lion's skin, leading a group of followers whose ears are attached to his own tongue by little gold and amber

---

[1] See R. E. M. Wheeler, *Lydney*; see especially Appendix I, pp. 132 ff. by J. R. R. Tolkien.
[2] See J. Vendryes, ÉC 6 (1954), 362.
[3] There is some confusion of names, for Gwynn son of Nudd is made to be the lover of Ludd's daughter, Creiddylad.

chains of great beauty and delicacy. The men are not being forced along, but follow him eagerly and heap praises on him, and it is clear that they would regret their liberty. A Greek-speaking Gaul who was standing near explained to him that the old man represents eloquence and is pictured as Heracles, clad in his lion's skin, because the Celts believe that eloquence is of greater power than physical strength, and also that eloquence attains its climax in old age. His name is Ogmios.[1] A temple to Hercules and the Muses was erected in the Circus Flaminius by M. Fulvius Nobilior after his capture of Ambracia in 189 BC because he had learned in Greece that Heracles was a musagetes.[2] Traces of this pictorial conception of eloquence still linger in Irish mythology and saga. Reference may be made to the entry of the 'cauldron of covetousness' in *Cormac's Glossary*, s.v. *bóige*,[3] and a passage in *Táin Bó Cualnge*[4] describing a dark man, apparently supernatural, who is carrying seven chains round his neck, to the end of which seven heads are attached. It would be interesting to know the relationship between these traditions and the designs on certain Gaulish gold coins which show human heads attached to a cord surrounding the large head in the main field of the coins [Plate 11, ii and iii].

We have a valuable reference to another purely native Gaulish god, Belenus, from the Gallo-Roman poet Ausonius of Bordeaux in the latter part of the fourth century. Ausonius tells us that a certain Phoebicius, grand-father of his own contemporary Delphidius, himself a famous teacher of the University of Bordeaux, had been *aedituus* or 'temple priest' of the god Belenus. Belenus is attested as the chief god of Noricum, and as highly venerated at Aquileia, where he was equated with Apollo.[5] The name is found on inscriptions in the Eastern Alps, in northern Italy and southern Gaul, and among the Ligurians. It has been suggested – quite gratuitously as it would seem – that Ausonius has here introduced an exotic name without local foundation. Against this we would urge the wide southern distribution of the name in areas subject to considerable Greek influence; the equation of Belenus with Apollo at Aquileia; and the Greek associations of the names of his own son Attius Patera and his grandson Delphidius, both famous for their eloquence. The family claimed to be descended from the druids of Armorica, and it will be remembered that Caesar records that although the druids transmitted their learning exclusively in oral form, yet they made use of the Greek alphabet for almost all the rest of their corres-

---

[1] Lucian, *Heracles* 1 ff. See F. Benoit, Ogam V (1953), 33 ff.
[2] See S. B. Platner, *Topographical Dictionary of Ancient Rome* (Oxford, 1929), s.v. Hercules Musarum, 255.
[3] Kuno Meyer, S.C., no. 141.   [4] Ed. E. Windisch (Leipzig, 1905), p. 797, l. 5524.
[5] Herodian VIII, 3, 8. (Zwicker, *Fontes* I, p. 91.)

pondence. The entire picture of a Gaulish god Belenus, equated with Apollo, and his temple-priest and two succeeding generations of the priest's family all bearing names of Delphic associations, all famous for their eloquence and claiming descent from a backward druidical stock of remote western Gaul, is as convincing as it is picturesque, a welcome glimpse of a Gaulish god and his attendant priest in the twilight of Gaulish heathendom. Both the cult of Belenus and Lucian's vignette of Ogmios are among our more interesting and less common traces of Greek influence among the gods known in southern Gaul.

Beyond Roman Gaul, however, the ancient Celtic culture of the Iron Age remained untouched by Roman influence in Ireland, the only Celtic country which has preserved a great wealth of ancient mythological stories.

Even in Ireland, however, we have only the vestiges of a lost mythology. Two considerable sagas survive, *The Battle of Moytura* and *The Wooing of Étaín*, and Thurneysen well said that if we had more like these, we should be freed from some rather airy speculation about Celtic gods.[1] There are shorter tales about the Dagda and his son Oengus mac Óc, Elcmar of the Bruig, Manannán mac Lir, and other divine beings; and there are fragments of tradition scattered through the *Dindshenchas*, the 'historical' poems, *Cóir Anmann*, *Acallam na Senórach* and the sagas of the Ulster Cycle.

O'Rahilly discerned behind the sagas the pseudo-history of the Book of Invasions, and in early genealogies the tradition of an Otherworld god, who was lord of a heavenly feast, ancestor of men, and upholder of the cosmic order. This god, in one of his forms, was the Dagda, and Conn, Cú Roí, Fergus, Mac Cécht and other legendary figures are identified with him. He was adored under several aspects, as god of the sun (Aed, Balor, Goll), of thunder and lightning, of wind and clouds (Nuadu), of weather and agriculture, of war, of healing (Dian Cécht), and of crafts (Goibniu). His weapon was the thunderbolt, sometimes imagined as a spear, a sword, a hammer, or some other instrument. The several aspects of one god would be in accord with Vedic tradition as presented by Macdonell.[2]

To this god is opposed a 'more human-like deity', the Hero, who slays the great god with his own weapon.[3] O'Rahilly identifies him with Lug, and also with Cú Chulainn, Cormac and Finn.

The Otherworld god was the Traveller of the Heavens, god of the sky, and had a spouse, Grian or Áine,[4] and they were sometimes

[1] *Z.C.P.*, xxii, 3.
[2] *Vedic Mythology*, 16.
[3] *E.I.H.M.*, 60
[4] *Ibid.*, 290.

imagined as horse and mare like Poseidon and Demeter. This Irish god would thus resemble Zeus, with the added feature of the Dying God.

It was apparently O'Rahilly's intention to present his argument in more detail later, but unhappily he did not live to do so. It is not convincing as he stated it.

Irish mythology is a great contrast to Greek mythology because the gods were not organized in early times by the poets into a great heavenly community like the gods of Olympus. They do not live in the sky or on the mountain-tops. They live individually either underground or on distant islands across the sea.

The ancient mythological stories of Ireland may be divided into four chief groups. We do not include here stories of local cults of springs and rivers and lakes, such as are prominent in Gaulish religion. These are not prominent as independent cults in Ireland, and occur chiefly – and not even very commonly – in connexion with important gods, such as the Dagda, whose home was Bruig na Bóinne, close to the Boyne.[1]

Group 1 is about the older Celtic gods, who are known from early times in Gaul, and also, perhaps later, from Britain.

Group 2 presents the native Irish gods whose homes are in the *síd*-mounds, the great barrows of the dead. These are the gods of whom the majority of our most picturesque stories are told.

Group 3 is about the gods, also known from sources outside Ireland, who dwell beyond the sea.

Group 4. Stories of the Otherworld – *Tír Tairngiri*, 'the land of Promise'; *Tír na nÓc*, 'the land of the Young'; *Mag Mell*, 'The Delightful Plain'; and of mortals who visit it. These are commonly referred to as *echtrai*, 'adventures, and *baili*, 'visions, ecstasies'.

The great god of the Celts was probably Lug, as the name appears in Irish, and there is a trace in Irish tradition of his supremacy, for he is called *lámfota* 'long-armed', and this epithet corresponds to the epithet and to the description of Savitar in some hymns of the Rigveda.

Savitar in the Rigveda is imagined as stretching out his arms to command day and night. Apparently the sun, rising and setting with its beams of light, was likened to a great hand. Savitar is called *pṛthupāṇi* ('having a large hand') in one hymn, and is the god who orders all things, whom all obey: 'the god with the great hand stretches up his arms so that all obey' *RV* 2, 38.2. It seems that the Celtic Lugus (Irish *Lug*) is to be identified with this Hindu god of the sky, although we have no early account in Irish how Lug acquired the epithet *lámfota*.[2]

The god with the large hand is known from rock-carvings in Sweden

---

[1] *EIHM* 516.
[2] For modern accounts see *Math.* 67, 71. In Wales he appears as Lleu Llaw Gyffes in the story of *Math fab Mathonwy*, but the epithet is unexplained.

that date from the early Bronze Age. He appears too in images from south Russia and the Caucasus; and Güntert suggests that he may be an aspect, a 'person', of the mighty sky-god Varuṇa, and draws the conclusion that in prehistoric times Indo-European tribes who still shared a common culture occupied a territory stretching from Sweden to the Punjab.[1] This area may then be extended to include Ireland, for Lug is apparently the Irish Savitar. He survives vestigially on the Continent in the widely scattered place-name *Lugudunum, Lugdunum*,[2] and in the two dedications to the *Lugoues*, and one in the singular, *Luguei* at Peñalba.[3] One of these, at Asma, Tarragona, was made by a guild of shoemakers (*collegio satorum*), and it is astonishing to find that one effigy of the God with the Large Hand, from Backa near Brastad in Sweden is popularly known as 'The Shoemaker'. This is a very strange example of folk-memory, but it tends to confirm the identification of Lug with this divinity.[4]

In Irish tradition the legend of Perseus has been attached to Lug, and he slays Balor whose daughter Ethne was his mother. The tale is told of both Lug and Finn, and must be an old tradition. Finn's mother, Muirne, was the daughter of Tadg mac Nuadat, lord of Almu, whom Finn overcame and deposed. O'Rahilly rightly sees here the trace of a primitive myth in which Finn slew his maternal grandfather Nuadu.[5] But he regards Lug (Finn) as a hero who slays the god, whereas we suggest that Lug was himself the greatest of the gods.

The triad of ancient Gaulish divinities, the *matronae* (L. *matres*) (cf. pp. 13–14 above) has also survived in the three goddesses of war in Ireland – the Mórrígan ('great queen')[6] and Macha and Bodb.

Another goddess attested by inscriptions both in Gaul and Britain is the goddess Brigit (cf. the name of the *Brigantes* in N. England). The Book of Invasions represents her as the daughter of the Dagda, greatest of the Irish native gods. According to the story in *Cormac's Glossary* she is the patron of poets while her two sisters are goddesses of smiths and of laws. She appears to have been Christianized as St Brigit, whose shrine is at Kildare, where her sacred fire was kept burning.[7]

The earliest native Irish gods, those included in Group 2 above, live underground, occasionally in caves, more often in the prehistoric tombs of the ancient dead chieftains. The most famous of these is *Bruig na Bóinne* [Plates 44, 46], one of three great beehive-shaped tombs, like the

---

[1] H. Güntert, *Der arische Weltkönig und Heiland*, 45, 58–165.

[2] Whatmough's objection that the name is attested in Gaulish only in the plural (*Lugoues*) is not persuasive. He suggests a comparison with *lougeon* 'marsh, swamp', *Ogam*, vii 354. We now have a dedication in the singular.   [3] See D. Ellis Evans, *Gaulish Personal Names*, p. 221.

[4] See J. Gricourt, *Ogam*, vii 65 f.   [5] *E.I.H.M.*, 279.

[6] O'Rahilly prefers this form *EIHM* 314, but Thurneysen gives *Morrígain* as the earlier form, which he explains as 'queen of phantoms' ('Maren-königin'), *Heldensage* 63.

[7] Giraldus Cambrensis, *Top. Hib.* II xxxiv-xxxvi.

so-called 'Treasury of Atreus' in Greece. It is now called New Grange and is lit by electric light, so that it is possible to see from inside the impressive corbelled dome [Plate 45]. These gods of the underworld are called *aes síde* (sing. *síd*), and their homes, the burial-mounds, are *síde*. One of them is *Brí Léith*, near Ardagh in Co. Longford, the home of the god Midir (cf. p. 143 below), who had been the fosterer of the god Oengus mac Óc, son of the Dagda and Boann.

The Dagda is the most prominent of the older chthonic gods. His name means literally 'the good god'; but the epithet does not imply that he is 'good' in the moral sense. When the Dagda's turn comes to state his qualifications in the council of war before the battle of Moytura he declares: 'All that you promise to do I will do, myself alone.' 'It is you who are the good god,' they say. And from this day he is called the Dagda, i.e. 'good for everything' – magician, warrior, artisan, all-powerful, omniscient. He is *Ruad Ro-fhessa*, 'Lord of Great Knowledge'.[1]

One of our earliest Irish prose stories tells of the Dagda and his son Oengus, whose mother Boann was the goddess of the Boyne. By her union with the Dagda, Boann became the mother of Oengus of the Bruig. The common source of both the Boyne and the Shannon is traditionally in the well of Segais, the supernatural source of all knowledge, situated in the Land of Promise. It was surrounded by hazel trees, the nuts of which fell into the well producing bubbles of inspiration, or, according to an alternative tradition, were eaten by the salmon of knowledge which dwelt in the well. Both versions occur in Irish literature in stories about the source of wisdom.[2]

Oengus mac Óc lives in the great *síd* Bruig na Bóinne, where at night he is visited by visions of a beautiful maiden in his sleep, and he falls into a wasting sickness for love of her. His parents are sent for, and after much enquiry they find that the girl is Caer from *Síd Uamain* in Connacht, the province ruled in the Heroic Age by Ailill and Medb. Hither comes the Mac Óc and finds Caer and her maidens in the form of white swans wearing silver chains, on Loch Bél Dracon at Crotta Cliach in Mag Femin. He calls her to him, and they go to his home in the Bruig. The text of this story is thought to date probably from the eighth century.[3]

One of the most fascinating of the stories of the Underworld is another Connacht tale, *Echtra Nerai* ('*The Adventure of Nera*'). Here the Underworld is entered through a 'cave' (*uaim*) in the rock near the court of Ailill and Medb at Cruachain in Connacht. As the court are celebrating the feast of *Samain* (cf. p. 103 above), Nera goes outside and cuts down

[1] *EIHM* 318
[2] *Ib.* 322. So too the Ganges has its source in a lake in heaven; see Lüders, *Varuna*, 25 f.
[3] F. Shaw, *The Dream of Oengus* (Dublin, 1936).

a corpse from the gallows who complains of thirst, and after giving him a drink Nera replaces him on the gallows.[1] On returning to the court he finds that the *síd*-hosts have come and burnt it, and left a heap of the severed heads of his people.

Nera at once sets off in pursuit, and follows the retreating procession of the *aes síde*, who are clearly dead men, for each remarks to his neighbour that there must be a living man in the procession because it has become heavier. When they enter the *síd* of Cruachain the severed heads are displayed as trophies to the king; and the king finds a home and a wife for Nera, and his daily task is to supply the king with firewood.

Then in a vision his wife warns him that at the next *Samain* the *aes síde* will again destroy the court unless he goes and warns the king. He takes wild garlic and primroses and fern to prove that he comes from the Underworld, and he goes to the court of Ailill and Medb and warns them. They destroy the *síd*, but Nera was left 'inside and has not come out until now, nor will he come till Doom'. From the time that he joined the procession of the *síde* and entered the Underworld he had become one of the dead.[2]

The storytellers of ancient Ireland by whom these tales were handed down spoke of the gods and people of the spirit world as *aes síde*, or *sluag síde*, 'the host of the *síde*'. But by the time the stories came to be recorded they had long ago ceased to have any religious or cult significance. The gods are no longer thought of as spirits living unseen in our midst, but as beings of the far past. The scribes who wrote down the stories were Christian monks. To one version of the text of the *Táin Bó Cualnge* the following colophon is added by a monk or clerk: 'I who have written out this history, or more properly fiction, do not accept as matter of belief certain things in this history, or rather fiction; for some things are diabolical impositions, some are poetical inventions, some have a semblance of truth, some have not, and some are meant to be the entertainment of fools.' Although the clerks have lovingly preserved these traditions of an age long past, they have humanized the gods, even sophisticated them. They have deprived them of their original prestige as objects of cult, and relegated them to an artificial setting fitting them to a scheme of pseudo-history which was quite foreign to their origin. We may compare the way in which our Teutonic god *Othinn* (*Woden*) is made the ancestor of the earliest Anglo-Saxon kings in our own early records.

The writers of the later legends in Ireland made no distinction between the native Irish gods, the ancient Celtic gods of Gaul who also

[1] The motif of the corpse recalls a similar episode in the *Vetālapañcaviṃśati;* see H. Zimmer, *The King and the Corpse* (N.Y. 1956).
[2] *Heldensage* 311.

survived in Irish mythology, and the gods from beyond the sea. They call all the gods alike by the common name of Tuatha Dé Danann, 'Tribes of the goddess *Danann*', or simply the *Tuatha Dé*, 'The Tribes of the goddess'. The name implies a goddess *Danu* or *Danann*,[1] but little is known of her from Irish mythology beyond her name. In some texts she is referred to as the mother of the three mythical brothers Brian, Iucharba and Iuchar. She doubtless corresponds to *Dôn*, in the Welsh story of *Math, son of Mathonwy* (cf. pp. 272 f. below). Math's sister is Dôn, the mother of Math's nephews Gilfaethwy and Gwydion. In Welsh tradition Math and his nephews are human beings, not gods; but they are great magicians, and their expertise in magic seems like a late echo of their divinity. Indeed in Wales the Tuatha Dé Danann have been transformed into heroes in the medieval stories of the Mabinogion, while the learned and sophisticated treatment which in medieval times has adapted the gods to a chronological scheme is found in Wales in the early chapters of the *Historia Brittonum* of Nennius already by the early ninth century.[2]

The later Irish writers had a good idea that in prehistoric times Ireland had been populated by a series of immigrations and invasions; and they believed that the Goidels were the ruling population of Ireland at the beginning of the historical period. The gods must therefore be earlier. They pictured them as entering Ireland from overseas, just like the later human conquerors of Ireland. The account of the immigration in the Book of Invasions (p. 5) refers to them all as Tuatha Dé Danann. The inhabitants of Ireland whom they found in possession of the land were the Fir Bolg, who are pictured as agriculturalists, in contrast to the Tuatha Dé Danann who possessed magic and handicrafts. The earliest form of the story is that in the *Historia Brittonum*, cap. 3.

The traditional Irish account of the invasion of Ireland by the conquering gods represents them as coming from overseas by way of Norway and northern Scotland, led by their druids in a magic mist. Their king was Nuada and they conquered the Fir Bolg, the older inhabitants, by their magic skill and arts, in the first Battle of Moytura, fought near Lough Arrow, Co. Sligo, but Nuada lost an arm in the battle. The Fir Bolg took refuge among the Fomoiri (literally 'under (-sea) phantoms')[3] in the Hebrides and Isle of Man. The Tuatha Dé Danann now settled in Ireland as the conquering gods, and made an alliance with the Fomoiri from overseas. The Fomoiri are represented as half human, half monster, with one hand, one leg and three rows of teeth. Their leader Balor had one eye in the middle of his forehead and was grandfather to Lug. Their king, Bres, was related to the

---

[1] *EIHM* 308–15.   [2] See *Heldensage* 63; *EIHM* 475 f.   [3] *Heldensage* 64.

Tuatha Dé, and he ruled Ireland as regent after Nuada had lost his arm in the Battle of Moytura. However the exactions of the Fomoiri were intolerable to the people of Ireland. Moreover they were stingy of their victuals, and when the chiefs of the Tuatha Dé went to the feasts of Bres, 'their knives were not greased by them' and however often they visited him 'their breath did not smell of ale', and he did not patronize their poets or their hornblowers.

Bres was deposed, and departed to the land of the Fomorians. Nuadu was given a silver arm, made for him by Dian Cécht the leech and Creidne the smith, and he again became king.

Then Balor, king of the Isles and Indech, king of the Fomorians, raised an army and made a bridge of ships from Inse Gall (The Hebrides) to Ireland. There never came to Ireland a host more terrible than the Fomorians.

In describing the council of war of the Tuatha Dé before the battle, the storyteller has left us a picture of the assembled gods. Nuadu gave a feast at Tara to Tuatha Dé Danann, and when all were assembled a stranger in splendid attire came to the gate and asked admittance. The porter asked who was there, and his servants said that he was Lug son of Cian son of Dian Cécht, and of Eithne daughter of Balor.[1] The porter asked him: 'What craft do you practise, for no one enters Tara without a craft?' For every craft that Lug claimed to possess, the porter named one of the gods who was supreme in this same skill. Lug said: 'I am a carpenter'. 'We do not want one: we have a carpenter'. Lug said: 'I am a smith'. 'We do not want one: we have a smith.' Lug said: 'I am a champion'. 'We do not want one: we have a champion'. Lug claimed to be harper, hero, poet, historian, sorcerer, leech, cupbearer and brazier, and bade the porter ask the king whether he had a man who possessed all these gifts. Nuadu ordered that he be tested in the game of chess, and the stranger won the game. 'Let him come in', said Nuadu, 'for never before has such a man come into this fort'. And Nuadu decided to entrust Lug with the defence of Ireland.

The other gods are assembled and Lug asks them what magic powers they have. Goibniu the smith will make spear-points; Luchta the wright will make spear-shafts and shields; Creidne the metal-worker will make rivets for the spears, hilts for the swords, bosses and rims for the shields.[2] Dian Cécht the leech will heal the wounded. Ogma the champion, the Mórrígan goddess of the battlefield, the sorcerers, cup-bearers and druids, even the Dagda himself, all say what they will do against the enemy.

During the battle Lug was exhorting the Men of Ireland to fight

[1] See p. 138 above.
[2] These are the Three Gods of Craftsmanship (trí dé dána), E.I.H.M., 314 f.

bravely so that they might be in bondage no longer. The Mórrígan came and was heartening them to fight fiercely and fervently. Many were slain, but the Tuatha Dé Danann had a magic well into which dead and wounded were thrown and were restored to life and health. The Fomorians discovered it and covered it with a heap of stones.

Nuadu was killed by the champion Balor, king of the Isles. Balor had an evil eye which was never opened, save on a battlefield. Five men used then to lift up the lid of the eye with a handle.[1] Lug and Balor met in the battle, and Lug challenged Balor in a boastful speech. (The passage is obscure).[2] 'Lift up my eye-lid, lad', said Balor, 'so that I may see this prattler who addresses me!' When the lid of Balor's eye was raised, Lug cast a stone from his sling and drove the eye through the back of Balor's head so that it gazed upon the army of the Fomorians, and many of them were killed.

Finally the Fomorians fled to their ships. The slain were as many as the stars of heaven, the sand of the sea, the flakes of snow, the drops of dew on the grass, the crested waves in a storm. After the battle, the Mórrígan proclaimed the victory to the royal hills and fairy hosts of Ireland, and to the chief lakes, rivers and estuaries, and prophesied the degeneration of future years.

The story of the god Midir of Brí Léith really links the gods of the síd-mounds with a different group, the gods from overseas. The home of Midir is in the Land of Promise and is localized in the síd-mound of Brí Léith, west of Ardagh in Co. Longford. He claims that Étaín in her former existence was his wife, but that she has been separated from him by the magic of a jealous rival. When Étaín in her later existence becomes the wife of Eochaid, king of Tara, Midir comes to reclaim her. Midir and Eochaid play at chess for high stakes. At first Midir allows Eochaid to win, and Eochaid lays the forfeit on Midir that he and his supernatural host are to build a great causeway across the bog of central Meath. When it is finished Midir again comes to play, and this time he wins, and demands a kiss from Étaín as his prize. A month later he returns to claim it. While the king and his court are feasting, and all the entrances are barred, Midir appears in their midst in all his supernatural beauty and splendour, and carries off Étaín through the smoke-hole in the roof, and they are seen as two birds circling in the sky above the hall.

In this story, or rather cycle of stories, Étaín lives in at least three generations, perhaps more, re-born each time, not just living on to old age. In each rebirth she keeps her own name, though her husband's name differs in every case. First she is Étaín wife of the god Midir in the

---

[1] Cf. the giant Ysbaddaden in *Culhwch and Olwen*, p. 275 below.
[2] *Z.C.P.*, XII 403.

síd-mound. Then she is Étaín wife of Eochaid, king of Tara. Then she is reborn as Étaín, her own daughter, indistinguishable from herself.

The Irish mythological traditions which are distinct in origin from those of the gods of the Underworld, are those of Lug and Manannán, both of whom are associated with rebirth. We have seen traces of the ancient Celtic cult of Lug on the Continent, but not of Manannán. In Irish mythology Manannán is king of the Land of Promise, or Mag Mell. According to Irish tradition he had fostered Lug in the Land of Promise and bestowed on him his famous armour – his helmet of invisibility, and his shield, which Finn mac Umaill had later. The Welsh tradition (the *Mabinogi* of *Manawydan*) has preserved his family connexions better than the Irish. Here he is Manawydan, son of Llŷr, and brother of Bran the Blessed. One of the earliest Irish stories, *The Voyage of Bran* pictures them meeting in mid-ocean while Manannán is on his way to Ireland from the Land of Promise; and by his magic he transforms the sea and fish into the flowery plain with its flocks from the Land of Promise. The lyrics in which Manannán sings of the Land of Promise contain some of the loveliest imagery in Irish mythological tradition.

One story of rebirth in which Manannán appears is that of Mongán, king of Dál nAraidi († 615). The story relates that the king, Fiachna Lurgan, goes to Alba (Scotland) to help his ally, Aedán mac Gabráin (St Columba's king) against the Saxons. He leaves his wife in the royal rath at Moylinny, where a noble-looking man appears to her and tells her that her husband will be killed in battle next day unless she will consent to bear a son by himself, who will be the famous Mongán. To save her husband's life the woman consents, and next day this noble-looking man appears before the armies of Aedán and Fiachna and vanquishes Fiachna's opponent. When Fiachna returns home and his wife tells him all that has occurred, Fiachna thanks her for what she has done for him, and the story concludes:

> So this Mongán is a son of Manannán mac Lir, though he is called Mongán son of Fiachna. For when he [i.e. Manannán] went from her in the morning he left a quatrain with Mongán's mother, saying:
> 'I go home,
> The pale pure morning draws near:
> Manannán son of Lir
> Is the name of him who has come to you.'[1]

Mongán inherited some of the qualities of Manannán. When he was three nights old Manannán came for him and took him away and fostered him in the Land of Promise till he was twelve or perhaps

[1] *V.B.*, I 42 f.

sixteen years old. Another story says that Mongán was Finn mac Cumaill reborn, but that he would not let it be known. It was, however, announced in the rath of Moylinny by Caílte, Finn's foster-son, who came to the rath from the land of the dead. As Mongán was commonly regarded as the son of Fiachna Finn ('the Fair'), it is just conceivable that the notion that he was a rebirth of Finn may be secondary.

The strangest thing about these stories of Mongán is that he lived in the Christian period. A poem attributed to the poet Mael Muru of Fahan in Donegal claims that Mongán came from 'the flock-abounding Land of Promise' to converse with Colum Cille; and that he managed to get into heaven by having his head under Colum Cille's cowl. Is it possible that there had been a heathen reaction among the Cruithni under Fiachna, and that they were re-converted under Mongán, possibly under the influence of Colum Cille? Good relations between Fiachna, king of the Cruithni, and Aedán mac Gabráin, Columba's king in Irish Dál Riata, which are clearly implied in the story of the conception of Mongán, give some colour to such a suggestion.

It would be hazardous to assume that the cult of Manannán mac Lir has always been confined to the Irish Sea or even that it originated in this area. Early Icelandic and Norse literature has recorded traditions which have close affinities with those of Manannán and the Land of Promise. Mythological traditions relate to a certain Guthmundr of Glasisvellir who ruled a supernatural region resembling Tír Tairngire and whose subjects are said not to die, but to live from generation to generation, and his realm is called *Ódainsakr*, 'the field of the not dead', and *Land lifanda manna*, 'the land of living men'. The stories imply that it was a land of rebirth, a land of youth and of immortality. The Hebrides are a possible centre of distribution in the northern seas. The early Norse poem *Rígsthula* certainly originated in an Irish milieu, and here the Norse hero *Rígr* (Irish *rí*, 'king') is a begetter of human offspring, and perhaps associated with the sea.[1] In Norse sagas also, and in the Norse Helgi poems of the Older Edda, the rebirth of the dead is effected by the visit of a mortal to the land of the dead and to the barrows in which the dead are buried.[2]

History and tradition alike echo the high prestige of women of Celtic mythology. Roman history has recorded no male enemies in Celtic Britain of the stature of Boudicca and Cartimandua. In the Heroic Age of Ireland Medb, Queen of Connacht, is the reigning sovereign. Ailill, her husband, is never more than her consort, and Medb is the greatest personality of any royal line of the Heroic Age.

In Irish and Welsh stories of Celtic Britain the great heroes are even

[1] See *GL* I 420.
[2] For a study of Marannán see Vendryes, ÉC VI (1953), 239 ff.

taught feats of arms by women. In the Irish saga known as 'The Wooing of Emer' Cú Chulainn is trained as a warrior by two warlike queens – Scáthach, who is also a *fáith*, i.e. 'a prophetess', an expert in supernatural wisdom – and Aífe. In the Welsh story of *Peredur* (later Percival) the hero is trained by the nine *gwiddonod* of Gloucester, who seem to be women of a similar profession. They wear helmets and armour, and they instruct Peredur in chivalry and feats of arms, and supply him with horse and armour. These women also train other young men, and they live their with parents in a settled home, a 'llys' or court.

This high prestige of women is something very old in the British Isles. Among the ancient Picts succession was through the female line. Bede tells us that even in his own day whenever the royal succession among the Picts came in question their ruler was chosen by succession from the female line. Prowess in arms at least seems not to have been lacking among Gaulish women. Ammianus Marcellinus, who wrote during the fourth century AD, has left us (XV, xii) an unforgettable picture of the Gaulish women warriors:

> Nearly all the Gauls are of a lofty stature, fair, and of ruddy complexion; terrible from the sternness of their eyes, very quarrelsome, and of great pride and insolence. A whole troop of foreigners would not be able to withstand a single Gaul if he called his wife to his assistance, who is usually very strong, and with blue eyes; especially when, swelling her neck, gnashing her teeth, and brandishing her sallow arms of enormous size, she begins to strike blows mingled with kicks, as if they were so many missiles sent from the string of a catapult. (Yonge's transl.)

It has been suggested above that the Irish gods fall naturally into three main groups, of whom the first, who are also found in Gaul, are possibly the oldest. The second are associated with the prehistoric grave-mounds, and would seem to be chthonic. The third are gods of 're-birth'. There is a tendency among leading modern scholars to recognize a fourth class, consisting of certain men and women, heroes and heroines, who appear in Irish literary and historical traditions as human, but who are now generally believed to have been originally gods and goddesses. This relatively recent habit of thought is not confined to Irish scholars. It began among German students of folklore and mythology early last century and has affected mythological studies widely, both ancient Greek and modern Slavonic no less than Teutonic and Celtic. The subject cannot be discussed here, but a few instances may be mentioned of this new category of Irish 'gods'. This recent tendency forms an interesting contrast to the euhemerizing activities of the early medieval historians who represented the Irish gods as human invaders taking possession of Ireland by force of arms (cf. p. 141 above).

It has been thought that Cú Roí mac Dáiri, the ruler of Munster in the *Táin Bó Cualnge*, was a god because of certain magical attributes which he is said to have possessed, and certain ritual functions which he fulfilled in his own person. Yet in the heroic stories he is always represented as a human hero. O'Rahilly declared that Cormac mac Airt (cf. p. 34 above) was in reality, not a king but a god. Most Irish scholars now believe that Medb, Queen of Connacht in, *Táin Bó Cualnge*, was a goddess. The evidence is partly philological – her name denoting 'intoxication' – partly the long list of husbands attributed to her, partly her ritual marriage (p. 87). In Irish tradition, however, as in Greek, characters of the Heroic Age are never represented as gods, and literary traditions consistently represent them as human. The tradition may be accepted as it stands.

In an illuminating article Binchy has recently set in a wider context the ceremonial with which Medb is traditionally associated, demonstrating its archaic character and its relationship to royal investiture of other Irish kings, and to kings in other parts of the world which imbued them with divine powers.[1] The consecration of a human ruler with a ceremonial which endowed him with divine powers may be compared to certain ceremonies of 'rebirth' on the island of Bali in Indonesia, by which those who perform it become *dvija*, 'twice born', like the upper castes of India, and like them become 'gods'. Reference may also be made to a custom formerly practised in Travancore in south-west India, where the rulers are drawn from the *kṣatriya* caste, and the descent is through the female line. Here nevertheless before the rajah can mount the throne he is subjected to a ritual by which he exchanges his *kṣatriya* caste for that of a Brahmin, a 'god', one of the 'god-people'. The ceremonial symbolizes the double birth of the *dvija*, as man and god. The *kṣatriya* is, in fact, reborn.

The Irish gods are always pictured as beautiful in appearance and gloriously dressed. Lug has a golden helmet and golden armour and his shield is famous. An early poem uses the figure 'Lug of the shield, a fair *scál*', i.e. a fair phantom, or spirit (p. 218), and the late saga of the 'Fate of the Children of Tuireann' represents him as wearing the magical armour of his fosterer Manannán from the Land of Promise. Manannán himself is thus described at his first meeting with Fiachna Finn:

> He wore a green cloak of one colour, and a brooch of white silver in the cloak over his breast, and a satin shirt next his white skin. A circlet of gold around his hair, and two sandals of gold under his feet.

[1] See *Ériu* xviii 134 f.

And again we recall the Gauls as described by Ammianus Marcellinus (XV, xii):

> They are all exceedingly careful of cleanliness and neatness, nor in all the country ... could any man or woman, however poor, be seen either ragged or dirty.

On no occasion are we ever privileged to see the gods assembled as a community in Tír Tairngire or Tír na nÓc; but on more than one occasion we are privileged visitors with a king of Tara who is conducted there on a temporary visit, a kind of mystery. One of the early Irish tales with the title *Baile in Scáil* tells how the prehistoric king Conn Cétchathach was suddenly enveloped in a magical mist as he was on the royal ramparts of Tara with his three druids and his three poets. A horseman came riding through the mist who took them with him to his house in a rath with a golden tree beside the door. In the house was the god Lug, of great stature and beauty, and there beside a silver kieve full of ale sat a beautiful maiden, the 'Sovereignty of Ireland'. From a golden vessel she ladled out many drinks for Conn; and with every drink Lug, standing by, named one of Conn's descendants who would succeed him in the sovereignty, and Conn wrote down their names in *ogam* on a piece of wood. Finally the mist dispersed and Conn and his companions found themselves back in Tara.[1] A similar adventure – a mystery we may call it – befell Conn's grandson, Cormac mac Airt, but here instead of Lug, the god presiding over the rath in the Land of Promise is Manannán mac Lir. On this occasion Manannán has stolen Cormac's wife and son and daughter and taken them to his home in the Land of Promise.

This story of Cormac's Adventure in the Land of Promise (*Echtrae Cormaic i Tír Tairngiri*) is one of the clearest examples in Irish literature of the magic power of Truth, the *satyakriyá* of the Hindus (p. 88). Cormac went in search of his wife and son and daughter, and his companions were cut off from him by a magic mist, so that he found himself alone on a great plain. There was a fortress in the plain, surrounded by a wall of bronze, and a house of bright silver within, half-thatched with birds' wings. He came to another grander fortress where he found a splendid palace with wattling of silver and thatch of birds' wings; and in the palace he found a handsome warrior and a beautiful girl wearing a helmet of gold awaiting him. His feet were washed by invisible hands, and his bath was heated by hot stones which came and went of themselves. A pig was brought in to provide for the noble guest, but the cook said that it could be cooked only by the telling of a true story for each quarter. Four true stories were told,

---

[1] *EIHM* 283.

the last by Cormac himself, who related how his wife and son and daughter were carried off and that he had come in search of them .And the pig was found to be cooked. Then his wife and son and daughter were brought in, and a gold cup was brought which had the quality that if three falsehoods were told over it, it fell into three parts, and if three true statements were then made, it was joined together again. Three falsehoods were told and the cup broke. Then the warrior told Cormac that neither his wife nor his daughter had looked upon a man nor his son upon a woman since they had left Tara; and the cup was mended at once. 'Take your family now, said the warrior, 'and take the cup so that you may have it to distinguish truth from falsehood. I am Manannán mac Lir, king of the Land of Promise, and it was to visit the Land of Promise that I brought you here'.

Irish mythology demonstrates as clearly as Greek mythology the wide gulf which separates mythology from religion. In both Greek and Irish religions, cults must at some remote period have given rise to the mythology; but the mythologies have travelled far in time, and sometimes in place from their original cult centres. They have reached us, not as religion, but as literary themes. There is neither awe nor reverence for the oldest gods, and gradually, as the gulf widens and religion and belief wanes, a spirit of light humour, even crude horse-play, colours the pictures of these gods. In the second Battle of Moytura, the Dagda, once regarded as *Ruad Ro-fhessa*, the 'lord of great knowledge' (p. 139), has become a grotesque and cumbersome old man, 'so fat and unwieldy that men laughed when he attempted to move about'. He has a cauldron which holds eighty gallons of milk, and as much meat and fat – whole goats and sheep and swine. All this goes to the making of the Dagda's porridge. His ladle is big enough to hold a man and woman. Yet strangely enough this deterioration does not touch Lug or Manannán. They are in a class apart. Their beauty and their dignity never tarnish, nor the splendour of their appearance. In the great battle which establishes the independence of the gods against the *Fomoiri* it is Lug, the stranger from across the sea, Lug of all the arts (*Samildánach*), who leads the gods to victory; even though the Dagda, representative of the older native gods, who had also possessed all the arts and all knowledge, is present.

Perhaps the wide gulf which separates Irish mythology from religious cult is one reason why the Christian monks have felt no inhibition in recording the mythological stories in their books. On the other hand no scruples prevented them from recording the magical practices implied in the mythological stories. The use of the mysterious practice of imposing magical prohibitions known as *gessa* is constantly referred to, and it was the violation of the personal *gessa* imposed on Conaire

Mór, the prehistoric king of Ireland, that brought about his destruction in the story of the Destruction of Da Derga's Hostel. Clairvoyance is widely recognized and its incidence is usually preceded by the verb *adciu* 'I see' – i.e. with my eye of inner vision: 'I see red, I see very red.'[1] Charms and incantations are freely used. The technique for obtaining a supernatural vision is recorded verbatim in one Irish text, and is known as *Imbas forosnai*, 'Inspiration which enlightens', and the names of other charms are recorded with their appropriate poetical formulae.

Irish mythology is a strange world of the imagination. Well might the ancient people of Mediterranean lands speak of the Celtic peoples, even those of Gaul, as 'beyond the setting sun, remote from our world'. Yet they are even more remote from the world of the Middle Ages. The Irish gods are neither 'little people' nor 'fairies', but tall and beautiful and fair; in all their physical strength and power and fairness of countenance, and even dress, they are superior to human men and women. They recall rather the descriptions of the Gauls which we find in Classical writers. The supernatural and the marvellous are invested with restraint and dignity. No question of guilt, or punishment or judgment in an after life ever disturbs the serenity of what Gerard Murphy has called the 'strange loveliness' of Celtic mythology. It is this 'strange loveliness' of 'the otherworld atmosphere which gives its special beauty to the Irish mythological cycle.'

[1] C. O'Rahilly (ed.), *Táin Bó Cúalnge*, p. 143.

CHAPTER 8

CELTIC CHRISTIANITY AND ITS LITERATURE

THE introduction of Christianity into Gaul was a slow and gradual process. Of the beginning of the conversion we have no information whatever, but from the second century we have contemporary records of Christians in Lyons and Vienne. The community of Lyons was presided over by Bishop Pothinus, and the priest Irenaeus, who ultimately succeeded him in the see. In 177 a persecution of incredible severity descended upon the little community, and a number were subjected to imprisonment, followed by hideous tortures and death. Among the martyrs was the bishop Pothinus. As he was ninety years of age at the time, his original appointment to the see is hardly likely to have been very recent, and we are therefore perhaps justified in surmising that the Christian community of Lyons was not new at this time, despite the reference by Eusebius (*Ecclesiastical History* V.13) to 'those through whom our affairs had been established', and the statement by Sulpicius Severus that the Gospel had been slow to cross the Alps into Gaul.

Our information about this persecution and its sufferings is derived from an Epistle sent from the Gallican Churches to the Churches of Asia and Phrygia and extracted by Eusebius, bishop of Caesarea (*c.* 260–*c.* 340), from a number of accounts of Gallican martyrdoms. The Epistle is 'the first piece of the archives of the Church of Gaul, and is essentially reliable'.[1] It was incorporated by Eusebius in his Collection of Martyrdoms. This is now lost, but he has included portions of it in his *Ecclesiastical History* (V.1–3),[2] which is our fullest and most reliable source of information about the situation in Lyons and about the individual martyrs and their sufferings. Additional information is recorded by Gregory, bishop of Tours (*c.* 540–94), who had access to some sources of information, perhaps at Lyons, now no longer available, and who has recorded it chiefly in his work, *De Gloria Martyrum*, cap. 48.

The epistle itself claims to be written by the 'servants of Christ at Vienne and Lyons to the brethren throughout Asia and Phrygia', as

[1] *G.C.* 13.
[2] Migne, *P.G.* XX, col. 407 ff.; English translation by T. H. Bindley, *The Epistle of the Gallican Churches* (London, 1900).

well as to Eleutherius, the bishop of Rome. Eusebius, who seems to have had their letter before him, tells us (V.3,4) that it was taken to Rome by the priest Irenaeus: 'We have charged Irenaeus, our brother and our companion, to deliver this letter to you,' they wrote to the Pope, 'and we beg you to hold him in esteem as a zealot of Christ's testament.' (V.4) According to the testimony of St Jerome[1] Irenaeus fulfilled his mission, and we have no reason to doubt it. His absence from Lyons would best account for his not being involved in the persecutions. Later testimony speaks of his own martyrdom, but this is uncertain, and the date and manner of his death are unknown.

According to Gregory of Tours[2] Pothinus was probably the first bishop of Lyons. Of the personal history of Irenaeus himself (*c.* 130– *c.* 200) little is known. Gregory of Tours states that he had been 'directed' (*directus*) to Lyons by St Polycarp, who was bishop of Smyrna. Eusebius quotes from a letter purporting to have been written by Irenaeus to a friend, in which Irenaeus claims to have listened as a boy in Smyrna to St Polycarp (*c.* 69–*c.* 155), the martyred bishop of Smyrna, and to have heard him tell of his intercourse with St John and the other disciples who had seen the Lord.[3] Irenaeus was very possibly in Rome when St Polycarp came there to discuss with Anicetus the Easter controversy, and Eusebius refers to the friendly terms of the two bishops.[4]

We have no reason to doubt these early experiences of Irenaeus with the Greek teachers of Asia Minor and Rome, and indeed his own distinguished reputation as a scholar is fully consistent with such a preparation. He evidently wrote much, and though much of his writing has perished, enough has survived in translations into Latin, Syriac, and Armenian to demonstrate that he must have done much to establish the Church of Lyons as an important link between the Churches of the East and West. He was in fact the first great Catholic theologian, and apart from a recently discovered Armenian translation of 'The Demonstration of the Apostolic Teaching', his theological works are concerned with Christian apologetics in defence of orthodoxy. His principal work was the *Adversus Omnes Haereses* which was a direct attack on Gnosticism, and though written and partly preserved in Greek, it survives as a whole in an early Latin translation. Greek was still the principal language of the Church, but Lyons was a Latin city, and Irenaeus apologizes for what he regards as the deficiencies of his Greek style, on the ground that he is resident among the Keltae and for the most using 'a barbarous dialect'.[5]

[1] *De Viris Illustribus*, XXXV; P.L. XXIII, col. 649.
[2] *Historia Francorum* V, I. 29.
[3] *H.E.* V, 20; cf. Irenaeus, *Adversus omnes Haereses*, III. 3. 4.
[4] *H.E.* V, 24.   [5] *Adversus omnes Haereses*, Preface.

The most interesting fact known of his actual function in his office as bishop is his intervention *c.* 190 in the famous Easter controversy, which figures so prominently in the following centuries. A divergence between the various European churches and those of Asia had been in existence since apostolic times regarding both the date and the manner of celebrating Easter. The Asiatics, relying on an ancient local tradition, regarded Easter as the anniversary of the Saviour's death, and treated it as a fast, on whatever day of the week it fell, even if it fell on a Sunday; and even in Rome they continued to follow their traditional practice, declaring that they could not renounce the custom derived from the great luminaries of the Church who had died in Asia, in particular the apostle John. In 189 Pope Victor was inclined to cut off and excommunicate the Asiatics; but the bishops urged peace, and among them Irenaeus wrote in the name of the brethren whom he governed in Gaul, emphasizing that the point at issue was not only the question of date, but also the manner of fasting, and that their differences had arisen gradually over a long period of time; and he reminded Victor of the more conciliatory attitude of his predecessor Anicetus and his successors. Victor had the good sense to accept his counsels of conciliation.

Irenaeus mentions churches in Germania[1] and also in Celtic countries, and it seems that Christianity had already spread to some extent in Gaul, possibly with Lyons as a kind of mother-church, a radiating centre.[2] No other bishopric is named in the second century. After the death of Irenaeus the first Gaulish bishop mentioned in the documents is Saturninus of Toulouse, whose *Passio* fixes the beginning of his episcopate in 250; and contemporary documents show that by this time Gaul had a recognized episcopal organization, especially in the south, in the urban areas. Progress in the Christianization of northern Gaul was slower, however, for here the ancient Gaulish agricultural estates, in contrast to the Rhône valley, offered fewer natural opportunities for the development of the organization of the new religion.

The fourth century brought a new era to Christianity in Gaul and in the West generally with the reign of Constantine the Great (274–337), who became senior Augustus in 313, and who, the same year, together with his brother-in-law Licinius, issued the famous Edict of Milan which granted regulations in favour of the Christians. In 323 he became sole Emperor of East and West and although he did not become a professing Christian till officially baptized on his death-bed, he gave both legal and political help and encouragement to the Church. The persecutions were a thing of the past. Full liberty of conscience was established throughout the Empire.

---

[1] *Adv. Haeres.* I. X. 2. Tertullian. *Adv. Judaeos* VII.
[2] Cf. Duchesne, *E.H.C.* I, 185.

By substituting Christianity for the official cult of the emperor as a state religion, Constantine created a unifying principle of government guided by the religious sanctions of a popular religion. In the hope of promoting unity within the Church he devoted special care to the suppression of schism and heresy. The Donatist schism, especially fierce in the Christian Church in Africa, called for his early attention, and in 314 he called a council of the bishops of the western provinces to meet at Arles, attended by the bishops of Spain, Italy, Africa and even Great Britain,[1] to discuss various questions touching Church discipline, among them the Easter question.

The Donatist schism had been a local matter within the Western Church. Far more momentous was the Arian question which divided the whole Christian world. The conflict had begun in Alexandria early in the fourth century, occasioned immediately by the priest Arius, who, following the teaching of Lucian of Antioch, denied the true divinity of Christ. The point at issue was, of course, a fundamental one, and aroused a fierce and widespread controversy. In the hope of promoting unity between the two halves of his Empire, and the Churches of East and West, Constantine called the Council of Nicaea in 325. More than three hundred bishops attended the Council, the majority from the Churches associated with Alexandria and Antioch; Britain was not represented, and Gaul by only one modest signature.

In Gaul itself the most outstanding force in the Church, and the protagonist in the Arian controversy, was St Hilary, who became bishop of Poitiers shortly after 350. His brilliant writings were the chief contribution of Gaul to the questions which rent the Church in his day, and together with the writings of St Athanasius, laid the foundations of the Catholicism of the Western Church. During Hilary's exile in Phrygia from c. 356–c. 360, as a result of his unbending opposition to Arianism, he became the strongest pillar of the Western Church, all the more influential for the intimate knowledge of the Eastern Church which his exile had forced upon him. As a result of the leisure which his freedom from episcopal duties granted him, he had been enabled to compose his greatest work, the De Trinitate. Meanwhile shortly after Hilary's return to Gaul in 360 the Gaulish bishops sent a letter in which they paid homage to Hilary and reiterated their adherence to the formula of Nicaea. The letter marks the end of the Arian crisis in the Church of Gaul, and Sulpicius Severus claims that Hilary was universally recognized to have effected the return of the Church to its former state.[2] Both his eloquence and his learning were greatly appreciated by his contemporaries.[3] He died c. 367. In the history of the Church of

---

[1] Eusebius, *Hist. Eccles.* X, v.   [2] *Chronica*, II, 45.
[3] St Jerome, *Commentarius ad Galatas* II, Preface; Sulpicius Severus, *Chronica* II. 42.

Gaul his is the first great name which we meet among the masters of thought since Irenaeus. His principal achievement had been the consolidation of Western Catholicism. On the foundations laid during the fourth century Christianity gradually established itself as the national Church of Gaul, and created the system of ecclesiastical organization naturally forming an integral part of the Roman civil administration within which it had arisen, and by which it had been made financially stable.

During the reign of Constantine many churches had received wide powers to establish themselves within the city walls. The bishop, now an official, was naturally installed within the city itself, and the ecclesiastical organization everywhere modelled itself on that of the civil service of the Empire. Towards the close of the fourth century almost every city had its bishop. On the death of Theodosius in 395 the Church of Gaul was already organized into its framework of dioceses and its episcopal hierarchy. During this period Christianity was spreading widely in Gaul. The nobility were joining the Church, not only in the cities, but also in the suburbs, the *vici*, which came to form the nucleus of the 'parish' endowed with a church and a priest, such as the church alluded to by St Paulinus of Nola in the neighbourhood of Bordeaux.[1] Such urban parishes were visited by the bishop on his episcopal visitations, and are pictured for us by Sulpicius Severus in his *Life of St Martin*, cap. 11 ff. With the spread of the Faith among the Christian landed gentry, privately owned Churches sprang up, built at the expense of the landowners on their own estates. One of the most charming subjects in the personal correspondence between Sulpicius Severus and St Paulinus of Nola is the recurrent theme of their pride and pleasure in the building and adornment of their own churches.

The term, the 'Church of Gaul', is a loose one, and more exactly denotes the Churches of the Gaulish provinces. There was no authoritative ecclesiastical centre, no primacy of Gaul. The Church was organized within the civil provinces which exercised authority superior to that of the bishops for important affairs, such as the ordination of bishops and the creation of new churches. Gradually the provincial council arose, presided over by the bishop of the civil metropolis. In 392 St Ambrose refers to the numerous councils of the Gaulish bishops. As late as 404 Pope Innocent I, in a letter to Victricius, bishop of Rouen, forbade the bishops to submit their differences to the bishops of other provinces, urging them to settle their own affairs save only by recourse to the Apostolic Seat.[2]

The traditional Roman political framework in which the Church developed could hardly fail to have some influence on the nature of

---

[1] *Epistolae* XII; cf. XX, 3.   [2] Letter *Etsi tibi*, *P.L.* XX, col. 472, cap. III.

Christian worship. The poet Ausonius of Bordeaux, himself a professing and practising Christian, evidently regarded his attendance at early morning prayers in his private church as obligatory; but they took their assigned place in his 'daily round', and when he deems, as he naïvely tells us, that 'God has been prayed to enough' he turns as a matter of course to give the routine orders to his cook Sosias. Even during the late fifth century the letters and poems of Sidonius Apollinaris, bishop of Auvergne, charming and personal and intimate as they are, convey rather the impression of an official ecclesiastic than of a man with a deep inner religious life and vision. Yet we must not allow ourselves to be swayed by Salvian into the belief that the Gaulish bishops were without due care for their flocks. During the corn-famine the bishops gave generously of their own personal stores, transporting their stocks at their own expense to the districts which were most in need, going far beyond their official routine duties. Indeed all our evidence testifies to the care with which they discharged the responsibilities of their calling.

In this period of official Christian organization and personal security and conformity a new light broke into Gaul from the Eastern Mediterranean, suffusing the new religion with a more intense spiritual life. From the third century AD asceticism had spread among Christian communities from Egypt to Syria and far Mesopotamian lands, inducing them to abandon all worldly cares and responsibilities, and to retreat into the desert where they could devote themselves to a life of solitude and spiritual contemplation. In Egypt from the third century two areas were distinguished by a difference in religious practice. In the deserts of Nitria, Skete and Climax to the west of the Nile Delta lived numbers of Christian ascetics, some in almost total solitude and simplicity and austerity of life, following their own individual rules, with no common discipline, and assembling for the eucharist only on Saturdays and Sundays. In Upper Egypt community life was developed early in the fourth century under Pachomius, whose military training in early life was probably in part responsible for the success of his organization of the cenobitic life and common rule in his monastery of Tabennesi.

Both these forms of asceticism spread to Western Europe in the fourth century and may be said to have transformed the official religion. Tidings of the intense religious life of the Desert Fathers may have first reached Gaul through St Athanasius, who was in exile in Trier from his bishopric in Alexandria during the year 336. Between 356 and 362 he wrote the *Life of St Antony* who had lived for thirty-five years in solitude in a ruinous Roman fort in the mountain of Pispir between the Nile and the Dead Sea, and this brilliantly written biography could not fail to have its effect on the more spiritual of the Christians of the West. Gradually the ideal of eremitism spread from the solitaries of Lower

Egypt and reached Gaul, partly by the accounts of travellers who had visited them, as we learn from the *Dialogues* of Sulpicius Severus; partly by knowledge of small communities such as those on the islands fringing the Italian coast, of whom we read in the poem, *De Reditu Suo*, by Rutilius Namatianus, which relates his return voyage from Italy to Gaul, and refers incidentally to small communities on the islands of Gorgon and Capraria.

Early in the fifth century the eremitical ideal inspired St Honoratus, whose education had been in Greece, to found a monastic community on the island of Lérins off the coast of Provence. The learning and devotion of its monks rapidly gained for the little community a prestige almost equivalent to that of a western university. Shortly after the foundation of this island community cenobitic monasteries arose in southern Provence, the most famous being that of St Victor near Marseilles. The influence of both these monasteries was widespread and permanent, largely due to their intellectual activity. Among the future bishops nursed in Lérins Honoratus himself, Eucherius of Lyons, Faustus of Riez, Caesarius of Arles, are among the most impressive ecclesiastical names of the fifth century in Gaul, while the *Institutes* and the *Conferences*, the writings of John Cassian, abbot of the neighbouring cenobitic monastery of St Victor near Marseilles, are the most important writings on monastic discipline in the Western Church before the Rule of St Benedict.

Simultaneously with these famous monastic foundations a humbler and less formal monastic habit was gaining ground in Gaul, perhaps as a natural corollary to the privately owned and endowed Churches. St Jerome refers to a domestic monastery, 'a Choir of the blessed'[1] at Aquileia, in which he used to meet Rufinius. St Augustine tells of a community outside the walls of Milan, with St Ambrose at its head, and of another at Trier in which there was a book containing a *Life of St Antony*,[2] and we may perhaps compare the community described by St Victricius, Bishop of Rouen, in his *De Laude Sanctorum*.[3] We have seen how Sulpicius Severus in Gaul, and his life-long friend and correspondent St Paulinus at Nola in Italy, vied with one another in building and beautifying each his own church for the use of the community. Sulpicius Severus speaks of himself as surrounded by a *turba monachorum*, and in his *Dialogues* he represents his friend Posthumianus, recently returned from his sojourn with a solitary ascetic in the North African desert, as narrating his experiences to an eager listening audience. To St Paulinus the new vision of Christianity, born of the mysticism and asceticism of the East, had come as a revelation of blinding glory, an imperative call to renounce the world and devote his wealth and his vast estates – his

---

[1] *Chron.* s.a. 379.   [2] *Confessions* VIII. 6.   [3] Migne, *P.L.* XX, col. 445.

regna, as Ausonius calls them – to Christ, founding a private monastery where he lived at Nola in the Campania with his Spanish wife Therasia, henceforth in the relationship of brother and sister. He refers to their establishment as a *monasterium*,[1] and its few select occupants as a *fraternitas monacha*.[2] His correspondence with his old friend and teacher Ausonius is our most eloquent testimony to the irresistible force with which this new ascetic ideal flooded the quiet officialism of Gaulish Christianity.

The great pioneer of the monastic movement in the West was St Martin, bishop of Tours.[3] He was probably born in 316, and died in 397. In early life he had been a soldier in the Roman army in Pannonia – now Hungary – near the Danube, but having been converted to Christianity he sought and obtained his release from the military authorities while the army was at Worms; but the exact date is uncertain. He spent a brief period as a solitary in a cell at Milan; but it was during the period when the Arian controversy was at its height, and Martin had evidently already developed a profound admiration for Hilary of Poitiers, whose intellectual life, like his own, had been largely formed in the atmosphere of the Greek Church. On Hilary's return from exile Martin sought him out, and after an unsuccessful attempt to find him in Rome, followed him to Gaul. Here he settled under Hilary's auspices, first living ascetically with a few monks in caves and wooden cells at Ligugé, and later founding his *magnum monasterium*, his 'great monastery', Marmoutier, in the neighbourhood of Tours. *C.* 370 he was consecrated bishop of Tours. Ligugé was the first monastery in Gaul, and Martin the earliest of the monastic bishops, who became a special characteristic of the 'Celtic Church' for several centuries.

In his career and personality Martin combined the practical organizer and the mystic, and these gifts, and the episcopal patronage of the great bishop Hilary, combined to make him the traditional founder of Western monasticism. Hilary was the chief influence in his life, and there can be no doubt that Martin's work was inspired and guided by Hilary personally. How far Martin's early prestige, first in Gaul and later in Britain, is due to his disciple, Sulpicius Severus, who devoted much of his life and literary career to the creation of our picture of the saint, it is difficult to say. Martin has left us no writings of his own, but the charm of the writings of Severus, and the intimate picture which he has bequeathed to us, are inseparable from the saint who has inspired them.

It is a remarkable thing that western monasticism, inspired and supported by Hilary, the pillar of Western Catholicism, should have

---

[1] *Ep.* 5, 15.   [2] *Ep.* 23, 8.
[3] For an account of St Martin see É. Griffe, *G.C.*, Ch. VI.

been a subject of active disapproval by the Gaulish bishops. Their dislike of it is constantly referred to in the correspondence between Sulpicius Severus and St Paulinus of Nola. The democratic system which prevailed, and has always prevailed, in the monastic communities, was quite alien to the ecclesiastical hierarchy based on the Roman civil administrative system. This growing hostility between the episcopal and the monastic elements in Gaul became more pronounced in the early years of the fifth century, and episcopal disapproval was especially directed against monastic appointments to vacant bishoprics. This disapproval was expressed unequivocally from the papal chair, and is voiced emphatically in a famous letter, the *Cuperemus quidem*, addressed in 428 by Celestine, bishop of Rome, to the bishops of Vienne and Narbonne on the occasion of the election of a bishop to the vacant see of Arles. The pope protests against the election of 'wanderers and strangers' (*peregrini et extranei*) to episcopal seats over the heads of the local clergy, who were known to their flocks and had a right to preferment in the districts in which they had laboured. He expresses his dislike of monastic bishops in no equivocal terms.

> They who have not grown up in the Church act contrary to the Church's usages, ... coming from other customs they have brought their traditional ways with them ... clad in a cloak and with a girdle round their loins ... Such a practice may perhaps be followed ... by those who dwell in remote places and pass their lives far from their fellow men. But why should they dress in this way in the churches of God, changing the usage of so many years, of such great prelates, for another habit?[1]

We have dwelt on the early Christianity of Gaul because contemporary records are comparatively full and authentic. For the history of the early Church in Britain[2] we have no contemporary local records apart from a few stone inscriptions in the West. Local literary records in Britain do not begin before the sixth century, and in Ireland, where writing was introduced in all probability in the fifth century, in the time of St Patrick, his own writings are our only genuine documents of so early a date. We are therefore chiefly dependent on contemporary continental writers for our knowledge of the earliest Christianity in Britain, and for this purpose our fullest sources of information come from Gaul.

Our earliest direct references to Christianity in Britain, however, come from two north African sources. Tertullian, writing *c.* 200, states that the Gospel had already reached parts of Britain beyond the Romanized areas (*Britannorum inaccessa Romanis loca Christo vero subdita*);[3]

---

[1] *Ep.* 4, Mansi. III, p. 264; Migne, *P.L.* I, col. 430.
[2] See J. M. C. Toynbee, 'Christianity in Roman Britain', JBAA XVI (1953), 3 ff.; Hugh Williams, *C.R.B.*
[3] *Carmen apologeticum adversus Judaeos* vii.

and Origen, writing *c.* 240, refers to Christianity as a force which was unifying the Britons (*quando enim terra Britanniae ante adventum Christi in unius dei consensit religionem?*).[1] Well-attested traditions relate three early martyrdoms in Britain – that of St Alban at Verulamium[2] and of Aaron and Julius at Carlisle or Chester, or possibly at Caerleon. An acrostic scratched on red wall-plaster from a Roman house at Cirencester has been credibly interpreted as a cross composed of the words *Pater noster*, together with the *alpha* and *omega*, the whole forming a Christian cryptogram, suggesting that it was used as a Christian symbol in Britain already before the Peace of the Church under Constantine in 312.

We have no records of the conversion of Britain, or of the source from which Christianity was first introduced; but it was evidently already well established comparatively early in Roman times, and the attendance of three British bishops at the Councils of Arles in 314[3] and Rimini[4] in 359 imply that it was already an organized institution.[5] It was evidently in full communication and sympathy with the Church of Gaul throughout the fourth century, for St Athanasius refers to the Church in Britain as having accepted the definitions established at the Council of Nicaea in 325,[6] and both Hilary of Poitiers[7] and Athanasius[8] mention the British bishops as well as those of Gaul as among their supporters. In Constantine's circular letter to all parts of the Empire inculcating unity in the observance of Easter the Britons are included among the countries to whom it is addressed.[9] The letters of St Jerome habitually specify Britain as among the nations who worship Christ.

In recent years archaeology has added to our knowledge of Christianity in Britain during the Roman period. A small building excavated at Silchester has been generally accepted since 1893 as a Christian church on account of its plan, but though it has been recently re-excavated the results have not yet been published and the Christian purpose of the building is not certainly proved. In the Roman city of Caerwent a small building was inserted in the ruins of the Roman public baths, with a plan and orientation strongly suggestive of a Christian Church[10] which might suggest a survival of Romano-British Christianity into post-Roman times; but again proof is lacking. Bede speaks of a church at Verulamium on the scene of St Alban's martyrdom as still surviving in

---

[1] *Homily iv in Ezek. Hieron. interpr.*
[2] See the late fifth century *Life of St Germanus* by Constantius; the reference by the sixth-century poet Venantius Fortunatus (*M.G.H.* XI; *Poet.* IV, i); and Bede, *Hist. Eccles.* I, 7. Cf. W. Levison, *Antiquity* XV (1941), 337 ff.
[3] Eusebius, *Hist. Eccles.* X. 5, 21 f.   [4] Sulpicius Severus, *Chronica* II, 41.
[5] See I. Richmond, *A.J.* CIII (1947), 64.   [6] Athanasius, *Ad Jovianum imp.*
[7] *De Synodis*; Migne, *P.L.*, *Hilarii Op.* ii, col. 479.
[8] *Apol. Cont. Arian.*; *Hist. Arian ad Monach.* Prol. cap. 28.
[9] Eusebius, *Vita Const.* III. 17.
[10] V. E. Nash-Williams, *Archaeologia* LXXX (1930), p. 235, fig. 1; B.B.C.S. XV, ii (1953), p. 165 ff.

his own day, and of others at Canterbury restored by the Saxon king Ethelbert of Kent, of which one, just outside the city, was assigned to his queen Bertha and her Frankish chaplain Liudhard, and others were also used by Augustine and his monks and their converts.

The most important excavation of a Roman Christian site in Britain is that of the villa of Lullingstone in Kent in 1949.[1] Between the years 364 and 370 the owner of the villa and his family became Christians. At least two of its upper rooms seem to have been transformed for use as a Christian chapel, and on one of the walls fragments of painted wall-plaster have been reconstructed and represent six human figures with arms extended laterally, in the *orans* attitude of prayer; and in addition a large *Chi-Rho* monogram in a floral wreath was painted beside the praying figures. Another *Chi-Rho* monogram encircled by a wreath was painted on the wall of the ante-chamber. Evidently the occupants of the villa were Christians during the second half of the fourth century, and it is probable, though again not proved, that they had arranged this part of the house as a domestic oratory or a multi-cellular house-church, such as preceded the independent basilicas, and Christian worship evidently continued into the fifth century. Already before the close of the Roman Occupation, as a result of the peace of the Church under Constantine, Christianity had become the official religion in Britain.

Even after the withdrawal of the Romans, communication between the British and the continental Churches continued. The barbarian pirates, already rendering the North Sea and the English Channel difficult and dangerous, were no absolute deterrent to the voyages of ecclesiastics and even private travellers to and from the Continent. Strangely enough it was at precisely this period that Rome is first recorded to have taken an active interest in affairs in Britain. At this time a certain Pelagius, a monk of Celtic birth, probably a Briton, was prominent in the spread of certain views on the Continent which were regarded as heretical, and we learn from Prosper of Aquitaine, whose authority in this matter is entirely trustworthy, that Britain was regarded as a stronghold of the heresy.[2]

The views of Pelagius[3] are nowhere set forth by himself *in extenso*, and we are chiefly dependent on the reports of his opponents. The heresy attributed to him was the denial of original sin, and the claim that man is able to avoid sin by his own efforts without divine grace. Whether Pelagius developed the views attributed to him before he left Britain for the Continent is unknown, but the long and bitter controversy which

[1] G. W. Meates, *L.R.V.*; *ibid.*, Ministry of Works Guide-book (London, 1962).
[2] *Prosperi Tironis Epitoma Chronicon*, s.a. 429 ed. Mommsen, *Chronica Minora* I (Berlin, 1892), p. 341 ff.
[3] For recent works on Pelagius see G. de Plinval, *Pélage* (1943); J. Ferguson, *Pelagius* (1950).

ensued, commonly referred to as 'Grace and Free Will', probably had the effect of bringing Britain into closer touch with the continental Church than she had been before.

Accordingly in 429 Pope Celestine sent Germanus, bishop of Auxerre, as his own representative (*vice sua*) to Britain to uproot the evil.[1] We have a detailed account of this visit from Constantius,[2] apparently a presbyter of Lyons, who wrote before the close of the century, probably at the request of the bishop of Lyons. Constantius also records a second visit by St Germanus, probably *c.* 445, but for this second visit we have no supporting evidence. The nature of the narrative of Constantius indicates that it was composed primarily for edification, rather than as a historical document, and the author himself is at pains to disclaim complete responsibility for the authenticity of his facts. His literary conscience still adheres to the critical standards of the Roman high-schools of Gaul.[3]

Even Britain was still benefiting from the education of the schools founded by the Romans in this country, still taking an active part in continental thought, and Britishers were still able to travel freely to and from the Continent. This we learn from a collection of anonymous letters,[4] perhaps Pelagian in tone and certainly liberal, even democratic, in outlook, which are believed to date from this period. One delightfully personal letter in the series purports to have been written by a Briton travelling abroad to his father, probably a bishop, as his son addresses him as '*honorificentia tua*' and '*parens delectissime*'. The writer of this particular letter is taking his little daughter with him for training as a religious devotee in Sicily, and begs his father not to grieve on her account, but to think of her as he would if she were a boy 'who for his education must be separated for the time being from those who love him'.[5]

In all probability Christianity had an unbroken history in Britain. In eastern Britain the invasions of the heathen Saxons made communication with the Continental Church increasingly difficult, and from the fifth century onwards our continental sources cease, and we are dependent on British records, archaeological, epigraphical and literary, supplemented from Irish (Latin) sources in all these disciplines. The picture which they present is of the continuous spread of Christianity westwards in our islands beyond the borders of the Roman Empire.

---

[1] Prosper, *Epitoma Chronicon*, s.a. 429.
[2] A critical discussion of the person of Constantius and his account of St Germanus is given by N. K. Chadwick, *P.L.E.C.G.*, ch. IX, and references, especially those to the works of the late W. Levison.
[3] For an account of these see Haarhoff, *The Schools of Gaul* (Oxford, 1920).
[4] See C. P. Caspari, *Briefe* (Christiania, 1890).
[5] *Briefe*, p. 15.

In the British kingdom of Strathclyde remains of two early Christian cemeteries have been traced by the inscriptions on the famous Catstone at Kirkliston some six miles west of Edinburgh,[1] standing *in situ* in the midst of the graves; and by the even more famous tombstone of Yarrowkirk near Selkirk, which also once stood in a large Christian cemetery.[2] In the south-western peninsula of Galloway is an extensive concentration of early inscribed stones.[3] The oldest is believed to be the *Latinus* stone at Whithorn of fifth or early sixth century date. The most interesting of the Kirkmadrine stones, a memorial to three priests, also probably dates from the fifth century.[4] Three of the Kirkmadrine stones, and two at Whithorn commemorate Christians, and must have stood on ancient church sites. Excavations are bringing to light early churches in the neighbourhood, notably those at the traditional site of St Ninian's chapel on the Isle of Whithorn, at Whithorn itself,[5] and on Ardwell Island.[6] An eighth century tradition recorded by Bede (*H.E.* III. 4) states that St Ninian[7] converted the Southern Picts 'long before' St Columba converted the Northern Picts. St Columba died in 597. Bede adds that Ninian's *locus* (monastic site) was known as *Candida Casa* ('the white house') 'because he there built a church of stone which was unusual among the British'.[8]

We have no records of the conversion of the Isle of Man, Wales, or Cornwall, but in Wales continuity from Roman time is indicated, though not actually proved. One stone from Pentrefoelas in Denbighshire, of the fifth or early sixth century, is very possibly connected with an early Christian cemetery on the site where the stone was found.[9] Perhaps the most cogent evidence for the early date of the Christian Church in Wales is the existence in Irish of a series of Christian Latin loan-words which would appear to have been introduced into Ireland by British missionaries before the date of the coming of Palladius to

---

[1] J. Anderson, *S.E.C.T.*, 247 f.

[2] *Ibid.*, 351; K. Jackson, *Antiquity* XXIX (1955).

[3] For a brief official note on the subject see C. A. Radford & G. Donaldson, *Whithorn and Kirkmadrine*; also S. Cruden, *E.C.P.M.S.*, and the short bibliography *ad fin* (both Ministry of Works illustrated guides, published at Edinburgh, 1957). See especially C. A. Ralegh Radford, *Antiquity* XVI (1942), p. 1 ff.

[4] *Whithorn and Kirkmadrine*, p. 46, and plate opposite p. 40.

[5] *Ibid.*, loc. cit.

[6] Charles Thomas, *Excavations on Ardwell Island*, etc. 1964. Preliminary Reports, Edinburgh 1964, 1965.

[7] For a valuable study of the documents relating to Ninian see W. Levison, *Antiquity* XIV (1940), p. 280. For some recent studies see N. K. Chadwick, TDGS XXVII (1959), 9; John MacQueen, *St Nynia*.

[8] The name undoubtedly refers to the exceptional building technique of dressed stone, in contrast to the wooden buildings which were usual in Britain at that period. Cf. Belgrade (*Beograd*, 'The white city'). The word is common in Yugoslavia with this significance. See A. B. Lord, *The Singer of Tales* (Harvard, 1960), p. 35. Russian oral epics habitually speak of *bélokammenaya Moskra*, 'Moscow of the white stone walls', with reference to the rusticated masonry of the Kremlin.

[9] V. E. Nash-Williams, *E.C.M.W.*, no. 183.

Ireland in 431 (cf. p. 166 below). This religious vocabulary, with some Irish additions, was just enough to provide a skeleton service of Christian terminology for a community with an organization still elementary.[1] The earliest Welsh saint of native tradition is St Dubricius (Welsh *Dyfrig*), but the earliest *Life* of a Welsh saint is probably that of St Samson of Dol in Brittany, which is not earlier than the seventh century.

It is probable that in the days of the early Church the countries on the shores of the Solway Firth, Morecambe Bay, and the Irish Sea, were in close touch, and in this, as in other matters, shared a common culture. Manx Christianity[2] may have been introduced at an early period from the flourishing Christian Church of Galloway. However that may be, tradition and archaeology alike suggest that the conversion of the Isle of Man probably goes back to the fifth century, the period of the saint to whom the Cathedral of St Germans on Peel Island is dedicated. Dedications to St Patrick are likely to be later, and the early pre-Norse crosses do not reveal special Irish affinities. Of the six ogam stones one from Knock y Doonee in Andreas, inscribed in both ogams and Latin letters, is ascribed to the fifth century. Of the three most interesting inscribed monuments, the oldest is the so-called 'marigold' pillar with the inscription recording Bishop Inreit, which is ascribed to the seventh century.

Early records are entirely wanting, but the archaeological remains suggest that the Manx church corresponded closely to the early institutions of the Celtic Church everywhere in the British Isles, being monastic in organization, and consisting of a principal monastic foundation corresponding to the Welsh *clas* churches and a number of subordinate churches, known in Wales as *llan*. The only pre-Norse monastic foundation in Man, corresponding to the *clas* churches in Wales, is at Maughold, where a rich collection of crosses has survived, and where the important stele of Inreit suggests that Maughold was the seat of early bishops. Here, as elsewhere in Ireland and Scotland, we find in solitary places small hermitages, whether single, or grouped in an enclosure and containing a small oratory, such as at *Cronk na Irree Laa* a few miles south of Peel. A special feature of Man is the number of small oratories enclosed in an earthen bank, often enclosing early graves. These are widespread throughout the island, the remains of four being enclosed within the churchyard of Maughold alone. Within the enclosure small stone-built sanctuaries, more or less rectangular, are generally found, known as *keills*. Precise dating is at present impossible, but this grouping in relation to the church at Maughold is comparable with the numerous

[1] Binchy, S.H., no. 2, p. 166.
[2] For a brief account of Manx Christianity see Anne Ashley, *C.I.M.*

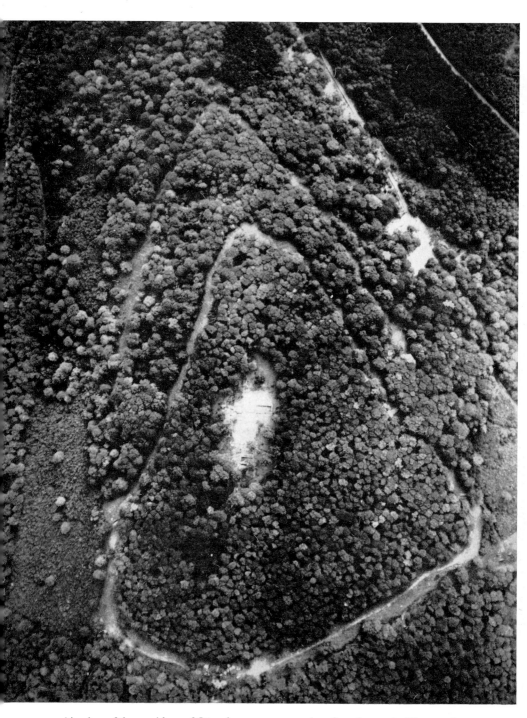

1 Air-view of the oppidum of Otzenhausen, commonly referred to as the Hunnenrings, near Trier. The ramparts are clearly marked, though now covered with forest. This was presumably the stronghold of the Gaulish tribe of the Treveri, and dates from the late second century B.C.

2 Pre-Roman road between Saignon and Sivergues, on the high plateau of Claparedes (Vaucluse). The road is stone-paved and the kerb on the left is clearly preserved.

3 Outer wall of the Celto-Ligurian oppidum of Entremont, with slightly rounded fortified tower of a great bastion. It probably dates from the third century B.C. Entremont was a great sanctuary of the Gaulish tribe of the Salyes near Aix-en-Provence. It was destroyed by the Romans in 124 B.C.

4 The 'Gundestrup Bowl'. This magnificent silver cauldron is 42 cm. high and 69
cm. across, and weighs nearly 9 kg. It was discovered in a peat-bog in Denmark but
is believed to be of Celtic manufacture, and to date from the second or first century
B.C. Left, three exterior panels; above, two interior panels.

7 (below) Black earthenware vase with grooved decoration. It comes from St Etienne au Temple (Marne).

5 (above) Black earthenware 'carinated' or ridged bowl. This type of pottery is known as 'Marne' ware. This specimen was found in the Gaulish cemetery of the Croncs, in the Commune of Bergères-les-Vertus (Marne).
6 (below) Vase composed of sheet bronze, its cover surmounted by a cock. It comes from Piémont, Commune of Bussy-le-Château (Marne).

10 (bottom right) Small bronze cult chariot from Merida, Spain. A mounted Iberian and his dog are pursuing a wild boar. The group is depicted on a wheeled vehicle or platform, and a curious feature is the series of little bells suspended from the rear. The modelling and proportions of the figures are of a high quality.

8 (above) This spectacular early La Tène type of helmet, was found at Amfreville (Eure). It is made of bronze, with two iron hoops. The whole was covered with gold foil, and enamel studs were mounted around the lower edge. The large ornaments have been lost from the sides. The height is 6¼ inches.

9 (right) This beautiful bronze flagon is one of the chief treasures of Gaulish art. The handle is in the form of a predatory animal, while two smaller animals surmount the lid, and all are stalking the unsuspecting little duck on the spout.

11 Coins of the independent Gaulish tribes. (i) Lemovices Stater, reverse. This
design depicts a two-horse chariot and driver. (ii) Namnetes, Gold stater. Obverse.
Note the 'pearled' cord surrounding the main design to which a tiny human head
is attached. (iii) Venetes Obverse. Head surrounded by a 'pearled' cord to each
end of which tiny human heads are attached. Above head is a hippocamp.
(iv) Coriosolitae. Stater, alloy. Obverse. (v) Coriosolitae. Stater, alloy. Reverse.
(vi) Redones. Stater, alloy. Reverse. (vii) Arverni. Vercingetorix. Obverse.

12 (right) Head of the famous Roman marble effigy of 'The Dying Gaul'. The original was in bronze, and was erected by Attalos I of Pergamon in Mysia (Asia Minor). The nobility of the head is very striking, and the characteristic Gaulish flowing hair, moustache and torc.

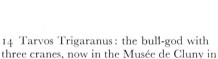

13 (below) A Gaulish warrior, characteristically depicted leaning on his long shield of La Tène type. We may compare the Battersea shield (plate 23).
This is a Roman statue of the Augustan Age from Mondragon (Vaucluse).

14 Tarvos Trigaranus: the bull-god with three cranes, now in the Musée de Cluny in Paris.

15 The 'Bartlow Hills', East Anglia. This is an air view of four of the eastern rows of barrows of Roman origin, commonly known as the Bartlow Hills, on the Cambridge-Essex border. They evidently formed a cemetery laid out in two parallel rows running nearly north and south. These barrows were probably the family graves of Romano-British chiefs. Excavations, conducted at various times, have produced interesting objects of the heathen period.

16 This is an air view of a number of earthworks on the Hill of Tara, Co. Meath. The two ring-forts in the foreground are enclosed in the earthwork known as Ráth na Ríogh.

17 (above) Navan Fort, Co.
Armagh. This is Emain Macha,
the most renowned site of any
royal dwelling in Irish literature.
It is about two miles from Armagh,
and survives today as a low mound.

18 (left) Entrance to Grianán
Ailech, Co. Donegal, a strong
stone hill-fort on a hill some 800
feet high a few miles west of
Londonderry. This stronghold of
the Northern Uí Néill is the chief
fortress of early northern Ireland.

19 (above) Dùn Oengusa, Aran Islands, Co. Galway. This magnificent prehistoric fortress stands precariously on the edge of the cliff facing the Atlantic on Aranmore.

20 (left) Grianán Ailech (see pl. 18). This plate represents a flash-light photograph of the interior of the intramural corridor of the fort, to which the entrance is shown in pl. 18. The building technique is of special interest.

21 Head of a man in British limestone, eight inches high, found in Northgate Street, Gloucester. The date is first century A.D., but the treatment is characteristically and conventionally Celtic – the heavy grooved locks of the hair, the stylized ears, the wedge-shaped nose, and the slit-like mouth, and large protruding eyes. A Celtic characteristic also is the shape of the face, tapering to a narrow chin – or, as the Irish sagas describe it, 'a face broad above, narrow below'.

22 (right) Iron slave-chain to secure a gang of captives, from Llyn Cerrig Bach in Anglesey. It is identical with others found in the territory of the Catuvellauni and elsewhere.

23 (below) This beautiful work of art, now in the British Museum, is generally known as the 'Battersea shield', because it was found in the River Thames at Battersea. It dates from *c.* 75 B.C., and is a late example of the Gallo-British tradition of Celtic art.

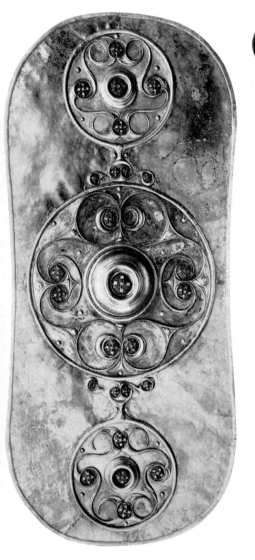

24 Conventional bronze horse mask found in the excavations of the great tribal capital of the Brigantes at Stanwick in Yorkshire. It may have formed an element in a chariot decoration.

25 Massive collar of cast bronze
from Stitchell, Roxburghshire.
It was found in digging a well
in 1747. The collar is jointed,
hinged in the centre and
fastening in front by a pin. It
is a very heavy object, varying
from $1\frac{3}{4}$ to $1\frac{1}{4}$ inches in thick-
ness. The ornament is cast in
solid relief except for the two
repoussé panels on either side
of the spring, and the spirals
are characteristic of later
Celtic art.

26 This is the famous
Birdlip bronze mirror from
Birdlip in Gloucestershire.
It is one of the finest
examples of a series of bronze
mirrors of late La Tène
Celtic design, with its riot
of curvilinear patterns
emphasized by 'hatched' or
'basket' ground-work.

27 Iron fire-dog from Lord's Bridge, Cambridgeshire. This is the most beautiful specimen of a rare class of La Tène III (late Iron Age) Celtic iron fire-dogs, found in both inhumation and cremation burials.

28 (below left) Iron fire-dog from Capel Garmon, Denbigh. It dates from the first century A.D. and is probably an adaptation of the simpler forms characteristic of Belgic settlements in southern Britain. An interesting addition in the Capel Garmon fire-dog is the loops attached to the upright shafts for holding spits.

29 (below right) Iron fire-dog from Welwyn, Hertfordshire. This specimen, like that from Lord's Bridge (cf. 27 above) is of La Tène III type. It is of mid first century date, and was a part of the elaborate furnishings contained in one of two burial vaults at Welwyn, which also contained a number of bronze utensils, two silver cups (see no. 33) fine large wine amphorae and three pairs of iron fire-dogs. The whole represented a Belgic cremation interment.

30 Bronze plaque from Tal y Llyn, Merionethshire. This is one of three trapezoid plaques, identical in size, slightly more than six inches long, made of thin sheet metal, which had evidently been riveted to some object. The embossed pattern on each of the plaques is a pair of opposed human masks, joined by a single neck, and the details of features and hair are characteristic of continental early and middle La Tène art.

31 The Aylesford bucket was part of an elaborate interment in a circle of pit burials at Aylesford, Kent, constituting a Belgic cemetery of about the period of Caesar's invasion.

32 Gold torc from Snettisham, Norfolk. This is one of a series of torcs found during ploughing operations at Ken Hill, Snettisham, in 1948–50. The find included over fifty torcs and rings of gold alloy.

33 (below) Silver wine-cup from Welwyn, Hertfordshire. This delicately incised cup of Italian manufacture is one of two discovered in 1906 in a Belgic cremation cemetery, which included two vaults, elaborately furnished with Mediterranean imports and typical late Celtic objects. (See no. 29.)

34 The Turoe Stone, Co. Galway. This stone is ornamented with incised design of the early Iron Age or La Tène Style. It is believed to be a cult object, but its true purpose is unknown.

35 Ogam inscriptions from Drumloban, Co. Waterford. (See p. 210.)

conhu ʒᴀ ib⁊ Ꝺ iɴꝺ ꝁ ꞇ ᴇɴ ɪo ᴇ ɪ ᴀ ᴘꝺ⁊ ꞅ ꞃ ᴍ ᴜɴꝺᴀ
ᴘᴀ nc ᴀ ᴄᴀ ꞁ Ꞁ ɪ ꞃ ᴏ ꜧᴀ̅ ꞃ ᴏ ꞃ ꞇ ɪᴜ ᴀ ꞃ ᴄᴜ nꞁ ᴀ
ꞃᴊᴊ. ᴘᴀ nᴇ ꞃ ꝺ ᴄ ᴏꝺᴜ ꞇ ᴄᴀ ᴀ ʒ ᴄᴀ ꞁ ᴀ nᵹᴇ ꞁ . ⊦ ᴘᴀ nᴄ ᴏᴜ h
ᴄ ᴀ ᴅ ᴄ ᴀᴜ ᴘ ꜧꞁ ᴀ ꝺ ᴏ ᴄ ᴀ ᴄ ᴊ . ᴄᴏ ꜧꞁ ɪn ꝼ ᴏ ᵹᴄ ᴀ nᵹᴇ ꞁ . ⊦ ᴀ ᴄᴀꞁ
ꞁ ᴍ ᴀ ᴄᴀꞁꞁ ᴀ ᴍ ꞅ ꞃ ᴘᴀ nᴄ ᴇ ꞃ ꝺ ᴏ ꞇ ꞇ Ꞁ ꞃ ꞁ ᴏ ꞁ ꜧ ꞃ ᴄ ⁊ ᴍ ᴀ ᴄᴀꞁꞁ ᴀ ᴛ
ꞃ ᴏꞇ ꜧ ꞁꝼ ⁊ ᴀ ꞃ ᴀ ꞃ ᴘ ꞇ . ꞅ ᴄ ꞃ ꞃ ᴇ ꞅ ꞃ ᴏꞃ ᴏ ꞃ ꞇ ᴏꞃ ꞃ ᴀ ᴘ ᴀ ᴏ ᴄ ꜧ .
ꝺ ɪ ᴄ ꞅ ꞃ ᴄ ꞇ . ⊦ ᴀ ꞃ ᴀꞁ ᴜ ᴊ . ᴜ ᴄ ᴄ ᴀ ⁊ ꞃ ᴏꞁᴜ ⁊ ᴄ ᴏ̅ ᴘ ᴏꞃ ꞇ ᴀ ꞇ ꞃ ᴏ ᴄ

37 (above) Dunadd, Argyll. This is the rock-fortress of the Cenél Gabráin, one of the branches of the Irish settlers from the kingdom of Dál Riata in Co. Antrim, in the fifth century. It stands on the little river Add and although archaeological remains prove some early defensive works on the summit, its chief defence must always have been Crinan Moss which here surrounds it, but which has recently been drained and cultivated.

36 (left) The *Liber Hymnorum*. Folio 31 *verso* (enlarged) of the manuscript of the 'Book of Hymns', which has been in the Library of Trinity College, Dublin, since the seventeenth century. The codex is of eleventh century date and is beautifully written with illuminated capitals.

38 Original door-frame of the Celto-Ligurian sanctuary of Roquepertuse (Bouches-du-Rhône). Three vertical pillars are furnished with niches for human skulls. Above the door-frame is a gigantic bird. The pillars retain traces of paintings of fish and foliage. The height is $2\frac{1}{2}$ metres, and the date third century B.C.

39 (right) A vertical pillar carved with twelve heads from the Celto-Ligurian sanctuary of Entremont (see 3).
It was later used to form the threshold of the 'Hall of the Heads' at the shrine. The carving is assigned to the third century B.C. at latest. The height of the whole stone is 1 m. 60 cm. The carved heads on the lower part of the stone are arranged in groups of two and three.

40 (below) Stone reliefs of 'têtes coupées', or severed heads, on a limestone block from the Celto-Ligurian sanctuary of Entremont, Aix-en-Provence (Bouches-du-Rhône). The block is 40 cm. high, 40 cm. long, and probably formed a portion of a pillar. It is assigned to the third or second century B.C.

41 (left) The monster of Noves (Bouches-du-Rhône). A seated anthropophagous monster rests its fore-paws on two bearded human severed heads, their eyes closed in death. A human arm with bracelet protrudes from the monster's mouth, and its back is covered with scales. The group is of native stone and is 1 m. 12 cm. high. The date is pre-Roman, probably La Tène II.

42 (right) The water-goddess Coventina. This is a recessed and gabled dedication tablet, found in the well sacred to the goddess Coventina at Carrawburgh (Brocolitia) on Hadrian's Wall, Northumberland.

43 (below) Three water-nymphs from Carrawburgh (Brocolitia) on Hadrian's Wall, Northumberland. This triptych was found in Coventina's Well (see 42 above). It represents a native carving in relief of three partially-draped figures reclining under niches of Classical style. Each nymph holds an urn from which water flows. The stone is native and the date second or third century A.D.

44 Brug na Bóinne, or 'New Grange', Co. Meath, a heathen sanctuary, is a superb megalithic tumulus of uncertain date, perhaps as early as 3000 B.C.

45 Brug na Bóinne, 'New Grange', Co. Meath. This photograph shows the interior of the corbelled dome, some twenty feet high.

46 Brug na Bôinne, 'New Grange', Co. Meath. View from the central chamber
looking towards the entrance passage.

47 Rathcroghan, Co. Roscommon. This is an entry to the 'Underworld' of Irish mythology, known as 'The Cave of Croghan'. A small amount of artificial stone structure at the left-hand supports the capstone, and is more easily discerned on the spot, but does not extend more than a yard or two into the interior.

48 Rathcroghan, Co. Roscommon. This flash-light photograph shows the interior of the 'cave'. (See above.)

49 The Skelligs, Co. Kerry. The view in the foreground is of the famous early Christian monastic settlement on Skellig Michael, eight miles out in the Atlantic from the Kerry coast. In the middle distance is the uninhabited rock known as the Little Skellig, a haunt of gannets. In the background are the hills and mountains of Kerry.

50 Inishmurray, Co. Sligo. This is the most fully preserved cashel wall of the early Christian island sanctuaries. Internal steps lead up to the summit and the cashel wall itself has an interior chamber entered from the doorway on the right. The sanctuary is on the edge of the sea, which is visible in the background, and the Sligo coast lies beyond. The remains of the plan of the monastery are largely preserved.

51 Tempall Benén (Church of St Benignus), Aranmore (Co. Galway). This tiny but impressive little church consists of a single chamber, oblong in plan, measuring internally only 10½ by 7 feet, with no division between nave and chancel, and about 15 feet high. Its orientation, almost exactly north and south, is unique. The side-walls contain some very large stones. The site is splendidly chosen, for despite its small size, this hill-top church is a land-mark visible far out in Galway Bay.

52 (above) Clochán na Carraige, Aranmore (Co. Galway). A rare but not unique, survival of the little bee-hive shaped monastic cells, known as Clochán, 'little house of stone' which may be as early as the sixth century.

53 (below) The famous Gallarus Oratory near Kilmalkedar (Co. Kerry). (Sixth or seventh century.)

54 (above) 'St Columcille's House', Kells (Co. Meath). It is generally believed to be the church completed according to the Annals of Ulster in 813 (recte 814), ten years after the establishment of the monks from Iona in Kells. Their first church at Kells had been destroyed and rebuilt in 807. The building is a single cell, measuring 19 feet by 15 feet 6 inches.

55 (above right) The Seven Churches of Aranmore, Co. Galway. In the early Celtic Church important ecclesiastical sites were characterized by a number of small churches before the development of large structures was introduced under later foreign influence.

56 (below right) The Round Tower, Ardmore, Co. Waterford. One of the finest of these towers. The site is early, and has three ogam stones and an ancient oratory, as well as the ruins of a late romanesque cathedral.

57 Carved head, Cashel, Co.
Tipperary. This is one of a large
number of carved masks or human
heads, which decorate arches, capitals
and other features of Cormac's
Chapel, the most remarkable being a
continuous row on the external
corbel-table supporting the roof.

58 Carved head, Mellifont Abbey
(Co. Louth). Mellifont was the earliest
Cistercian House in Ireland, dating
from 1142, and founded by Donough
O'Carroll, King of Oriel, under the
influence of St Malachy, archbishop
of Armagh, a friend of St Bernard of
Clairvaux.

59 (bottom left) The Rock of Cashel, Co. Tipperary. This magnificent site was the
fortress and ancient capital of Munster. In the foreground are the ruins of the
cathedral, founded in 1169; a perfect round tower, over 90 feet high, probably of
tenth century date; and St Patrick's Cross, 7½ feet high, richly covered on both faces
with figures in high relief. In the background is a plain rectangular castle of three
storeys; and beyond the rock on low ground Hoare Abbey, built soon after 1272,
occupied by monks from Mellifont.

60 (above) Boyle Abbey, Co. Roscommon. Cistercian abbey church of the
Transition Period, settled from Mellifont in 1161. The church is one of the largest of
the Order in Ireland and of impressive height. Our photograph shows ne east end
of the church with three lancet windows.

61 Jerpoint Abbey, Co. Kilkenny. Cistercian abbey of regular plan, a grand-daughter of Mellifont. It belongs to the Transitional Period (*c.* 1160–1200) or early Romanesque.

62 Jerpoint Abbey: details of the cloister (fifteenth century) partly restored.

63 This is the famous stone pyramid carved in relief from Pfalzfeld, found at St Goar in the Hunsrück. It is one of the earliest and most typically Celtic of our carved monuments. 148 cm. high.

64 (above) Celtic mythical beast
carved in granite, now in the
Museum of Cluny.

65 (right) Bronze stag from Neuvy-
en-Sullias (Loiret), a part of the
famous hoard to which belong also
66, 69 and 70.

66 Bronze boar from Neuvy-en-Sullias (Loiret). This is one of the best specimens of
Gaulish animal sculpture. It is 68 cm. in height.

67 Head of a hero or chieftain from Mšecké Žehrovice, Bohemia, carved in local
limestone. This regarded as one of the finest examples of the stylization of the
human face produced by Celtic art. The hair and features are essentially Celtic. The
prominent eyes, unformed ears, the triangular nose and slit-like mouth, the backward
swept ridged fringe and the torc are all characteristic, as are also the flourishes of the
moustache and eyebrows. Height 24 cm. *Circa* 100 B.C.

68 This head forms part of a squatting figure of a god from Bouray (Seine-et-Oise). Date uncertain, between third century B.C. and the Roman period.

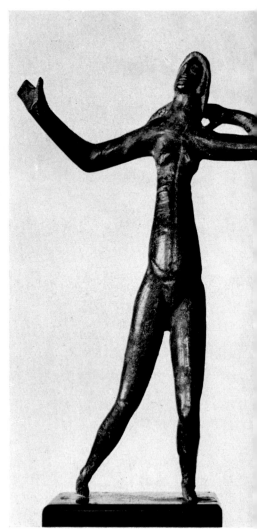

70 Gallo-Roman cast bronze statuette of a dancing girl, from Neuvy-en-Sullias (Loiret). The height is 14 cm. The hair is covered by a net or shawl that hangs down behind.

69 Gallo-Roman cast bronze statuette of a man from Neuvy-en-Sullias (Loiret); cf. 73. He is perhaps dancing, or perhaps originally walking and carrying an object now lost. The hair and beard are indicated in the Celtic conventional style. On the right thigh is stamped the word *Sovto* or *Scuto*. The height is 20 cm.

71 This striking mask of bronze is from Garancières-en-Beauce (Eure-et-Loir). The features are in the archaic purely Celtic style (hair in parallel ridges back to front, triangular nose, conventional high-set ears, narrow mouth, chin not naturalistically moulded, heavy neck). The eye-sockets are cut out and were probably filled with some material such as enamel or coloured stone. The mask is open at the back. The height is 9.8 cm.

73 Gallo-Roman wooden sculpture from the same sanctuary as 72. This is one of several series of heads carved one above another on one piece of wood. The shallow incisions left by the chisel between the heads suggests that it was perhaps intended to separate them at a later stage. The heads are not identical in features. The purpose of these staves is quite unknown, and the resemblance to the stone pillar with carved super-imposed heads from Entremont (pl. 39) is very striking.

72 Gallo-Roman wooden sculpture from the sanctuary, doubtless thera-peutic, at the source of the Seine, some 35 km. to the north-west of Dijon.

74 Wooden figure sculpture from the same sanctuary as 72. The figure is graceful, and faintly reminiscent of a Roman statue of a woman.

75 (right) Carved wooden head from the same sanctuary as 72.

76 (bottom left) Wooden sculpture from the same sanctuary as 72. This woman's head is a further advance in sculpture from the male heads. It is delicately and realistically modelled.

77 (bottom right) Carved wooden head from the same sanctuary as 72, showing far more art than 75.

78 (above) Silver Brooch from Hunterston, Ayrshire. Perhaps early eighth century, and may be of Hebridean origin. On the back a runic inscription records the names of two former owners.

79 (left) Welsh silver penannular brooch from Pant-Y-Saer, Anglesey. Probably sixth century A.D.

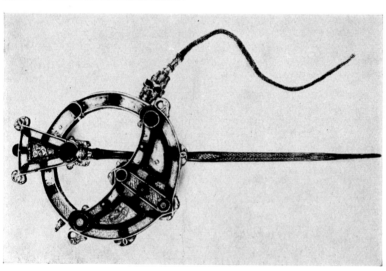

80 The 'Tara brooch' (eighth century, National museum of Ireland) was found in a wooden box with a number of viking objects at Bettystown (Co. Meath) near the mouth of the River Boyne, and is the finest of the Irish penannular brooches. It is made of bronze, penannular in form, and the chain attached indicates that it was one of a pair which probably fastened a cloak. It is richly decorated with gold thread, amber and enamel.

81 The Ardagh Chalice (eighth century, National Museum of Ireland). This supreme treasure of Irish ecclesiastical art and technique is a large silver two-handled cup decorated with gold, gilt bronze and enamel. The decoration has much in common with the Tara brooch, notably in the interlacing filigree beasts of gold wire in the upper band of ornament and in the blue and red enamel and gold in the studs.

82 The Ardagh Chalice (see 81). Details of the convex underside of the base. The pattern consists of concentric panels of fine silver interlace, cable pattern and running spirals, and again the intertwined mythical beasts with snake-like head.

83 The Cross of Cong, from Cong (Co. Galway), is a large processional cross 2 feet 6 inches high, which was also a reliquary, made about 1123 by order of the King of Connacht. It is formed of riveted sheets of bronze. The entire surface is covered with small gilt bronze panels filled with inter-twined designs of combined ribbon-work, bodies of stylized animals, and wiry serpents. As in the design on the foot of the Ardagh Chalice (82) this richly patterned ground sets in high relief the quiet simple setting of the large rock crystal at the centre.

84 The Athlone Plaque. It was probably attached to the binding of a book, and is of mid-eighth century date.

85 (below right) St Patrick's Bell-Shrine, probably made in the north of Armagh between 1094 and 1105. It is made of bronze and ornamented with gold, silver and enamels, and elaborate filigree work covers all the panels.

86 The Lismore Crozier. This is the most elaborate of a series of croziers produced in the early twelfth century. An inscription gives its date as 1100.

87 The Book of Durrow. This superb Irish illuminated manuscript dates from the seventh century. It is a small volume of the Gospels $(9\frac{1}{2}$ by $6\frac{1}{2}$ inches), and is known to have been in the possession of the Columban monastery of Durrow, near Tullamore (Co. Offaly).

88 The Book of Durrow. This is the symbol of the evangelist St Matthew on folio 21 verso. Here as elsewhere the symbol of the evangelist is surrounded by a border of interlacing. The full-length figure is deliberately stylized. The dress is of chequer-board geometrical design, and four colours only are used: black-brown, red, yellow, and green. The art is mature, and the impressive little figure is boldly set against a reserved background to which it chiefly owes its effect.

89 The Book of Kells, folio 7 verso. This large manuscript of the Gospels (13 by 9½ inches) is written in a beautiful round half-uncial hand on thick glazed vellum. The Annals of Ulster relate how in 1007 'the great Gospel of Columcille, the chief relic of the western world, on account of its ornamental cover, was stolen out of the Stone Church of Kells', and how it was found after some months under a sod, stripped of its gold cover. The manuscript is the most elaborately decorated of all the early Gospel Books, and the most varied and brilliant in its effects.

90 The Book of Kells, folio 34 recto. This is known as the great monogram page, and illustrates the text of St Matthew 1.18: '*Christi Autem generatio*'. The wealth of traditional Celtic ornament defies brief analysis. The page has been described as perhaps 'the most elaborate specimen of calligraphy that was ever executed'.

91 Cross Slab, Aberlemno (Angus). The front of the slab has a tall wheel cross carved in high relief, decorated with Celtic conventional designs. Our photograph is a narrative scene on the back of the slab representing horsemen and warriors, probably in battle. A panel above contains Pictish symbols, notably the Z-rod.

92 Pictish symbol stone, Dunnichen (Angus). This great decorated boulder stands a few miles from Forfar in the heart of the Southern Picts, known as Dunnichen, 'The fort of Nechtan'. The decoration belongs to the earliest class of Pictish symbols. The origin and significance of the symbols are unknown.

93 Glamis Cross, in the garden of the manse, Glamis (Angus). The crucifixion is never represented on the Pictish stones, but the cross occurs frequently. Here it is carved in high relief, the surface entirely covered with conventional Celtic design, chiefly knotwork. The background panels depict Pictish motifs of human figures, and symbols.

94 The Carew Cross. This tall wheel-headed cross, 13 feet 6 inches high, stands in a commanding position by the road-side near Carew Castle. It is decorated throughout with conventional carved designs in low relief, both in front and in the rear, chiefly knot-work and plait-work, but also other motifs such as the swastika, key-patterns etc.

95 (below) Anglian Cross, Whithorn, Wigtownshire (tenth century). This cross, with its carved conventional decoration of interlace throughout the whole shaft, belongs to the western border group (see 94 above). The head is circular with a central boss and the cross has expanding arms separated at the terminals by a shallow groove, with deep circular sinkings between the arms. This is a distinctive example of the Whithorn school of stone sepulchral sculpture.

96 Crucifixion slab from the Calf of Man (Isle of Man). This is a broken slab of unique design, and probably of eighth or ninth century date. It is the most delicate piece of Manx carving that has survived.

97 and 98 Stele from Fahan Mura (Co. Donegal). This is an imposing cross almost 9 feet high, belonging to an early northern group characteristic of the Inishowen Peninsula.

99 (left) Cross of Moone (Co. Kildare). This stately wheel-headed cross, carved in low flat relief in granite, belongs to an early group of Irish ninth and tenth century crosses in the valley of the River Barrow. It has many original features in its carved panels, the most striking being the uniform figures of the twelve disciples, rising in three tiers on the narrow pyramidal base immediately below the crucifixion scene in the tapering panel below the shaft.

100 (right) South Cross of Clonmacnois (Co. Offaly), east face. This is another (cf. 99 above) of the ninth-tenth century Irish high crosses. It belongs to a transitional group of the midland area and has retained the short shaft and heavy proportions characteristic of the group. The heavy mouldings and bosses of this beautiful cross form a striking contrast to the delicate carving in low relief of the conventional interlace of the ground-work.

101 (above left) The 'Cross of the Scriptures', west side, Clonmacnois (Co. Offaly).
It bears an inscription requesting a prayer for Flann, King of Munster, who died in
904. This is one of the finest of the high crosses, with an advanced scriptural
iconography.

102 (above right) The Cross of Muiredach, west side, Monasterboice (Co. Louth).
This is one of the most famous of the wheel-headed Irish crosses, comparable in design
with the 'Cross of the Scriptures' at Clonmacnois (101 above) but the relief carving
is much bolder, and its modelling is more expert.

103 (above left) St Martin's Cross, Iona (tenth century). Front or west side. This wheeled high cross is closely related to the Irish high crosses, and is a type not found in Scotland except in the west, remote from the Pictish areas.

104 (above right) The Cross of Patrick and Columba, west face, Kells (Co. Meath), an early example of the figured cross.

105 The Ruthwell Cross now stands in the church at Ruthwell (Dumfriesshire). Though on Scottish soil, this stately cross, 17 feet high, is a purely Anglian monument, the supreme achievement of Anglo-Saxon sculpture dating from the seventh century.

chapels associated with important Irish monasteries such as Glenda-lough and Aran, where they are still to be seen.

The Christianity of Cornwall probably shared with Wales a con-tinuous history from Roman times, for although we have no actual record so early, there were no land barriers, and it has been shown (p. 50 above) that the Severn Sea united South Wales and Cornwall in a common culture. We have nine memorial stones which can be dated by their Roman lettering to the fifth or sixth century, and two bearing an early form of the *Chi-Rho* monogram.[1]

It was the Romans who first taught the British to cut stone, and it is no doubt ultimately to this Roman technique that the Britons owe their wealth of early stone inscriptions. The Britons moreover had Roman stone inscriptions constantly before their eyes in all parts of the country. On the other hand all the British (Latin) inscriptions are funeral monuments, whereas most of the Roman monuments are official and military. Moreover the British inscriptions of the fifth century are almost entirely personal and Christian, for which we lack precedent among the early Christians of Roman Britain, who do not seem to have erected tombstones. The British inscriptions from the fifth to the seventh cen-turies are closely comparable to those of Christian Gaul, not only in the institution of commemorating the dead in this way, but also in the formulae used and in the type of lettering. Although in general there is a slight time-lag in Britain in the phraseology and epigraphy, the conclu-sion is unavoidable that the epigraphy of the earliest British memorial stones is derived from Gaul in the first half of the fifth century. This important Christian Gaulish influence evidently reached the western shores of Britain by sea.[2]

One important inscription in Anglesey is of special interest in this respect. We have already referred to the inscribed memorial tablet in the church of Llangadwaladr commemorating the 'renowned king Catamanus', i.e. king Cadfan of North Wales, who died in 625. The lettering of the inscription is in almost pure manuscript half-uncials, and represents the latest fashion in the continental manuscript lettering of the time. Two other Anglesey inscriptions (CIIC nos. 968, 971) have similar lettering. The son of Cadfan was the great Cadwallon, who slew King Edwin of Northumbria, and the church was evidently founded by his grandson Cadwaladr who died in 664. The dynasty had just cause to commemorate its founder in the laudatory terms reminiscent of bardic panegyric, and under their auspices the court of Anglesey and North

---

[1] *A.C.S.*, 121 ff.
[2] On the origin and nature of these inscriptions see K. Jackson, *L.H.E.B.*, 157 ff.; and for a detailed critical inventory see Nash-Williams, *E.C.I.W. passim*.

Wales may well have opened cultural communications with some Gaulish court of which we find later echoes in the early ninth century.

The Saxon raids on eastern and south-eastern Britain did not cut off the British Isles from communication with the Continent, and though these raids must have been a serious hindrance to ecclesiastical communication they certainly did not preclude it. It is on record that St Victricius,[1] bishop of Rouen from c. 380 to c. 408, with whom both St Martin and St Paulinus of Nola were acquainted, visited Britain c. 395; and the history of Pelagianism, the anonymous letters referred to above, and the visit of St Germanus to Britain in 429 suggest uninterrupted relations with Britain throughout the fifth century. The history of the colonization of Brittany confirms this, and in the sixth century a regular sea-route must have united the countries surrounding the Irish Sea with Gaul. This was, in fact, the period in which Christianity was established in Ireland from overseas.

The conversion of Ireland is generally believed to have begun in the fifth century, probably early in the century, and perhaps from two directions. Our earliest reliable notice is contained in Prosper's *Chronicle* s.a. 431, according to which a certain Palladius was ordained by Celestine, and sent as first bishop to the Irish 'believing in Christ'. The reliability of Prosper's testimony is beyond doubt, and implies that already before 431 there were communities of Christians in Ireland already sufficiently organized to justify Rome in sending a bishop to minister to their needs and to include them in the Roman obedience. So far our direct continental evidence gives us no hint as to the source of the initial conversion, but makes it clear that the earliest Christian organization was from Rome.

From now onwards we must rely on Latin records made in Ireland. Early and continuous Irish tradition (in Latin works) claims that Christianity was introduced into Ireland by St Patrick[2] about the same time as the mission of Palladius, or shortly after. The *Annals of Ulster* (s.a. 431), doubtless relying on Prosper, record Palladius as having been sent by the bishop of Rome, Celestine, as first bishop of the Scots (Irish). In the following year the same annals record s.a. 432 the arrival of Patrick in Ireland. We really know nothing further about the mission of Palladius. The *Annals of Ulster* have a number of further entries recording the death of Patrick at various dates, e.g. 457 where he is referred to as *senex Patricius* (*Quies senis Patricii ut alii libri dicunt*); 461 (*Hic alii quietem Patrici dicunt*), and again in 492. These discrepancies

[1] See Kenney, *Sources*, p. 159, n. 7.
[2] For St Patrick see D. A. Binchy, 'Patrick and his Biographers', S.H. no. 2, p. 7 ff.

have been very variously explained,[1] and are possibly in part due to the composite nature of the annals; but for our purpose the important fact is that the earliest Irish historical tradition believed that Christianity was effectively introduced into Ireland in the fifth century.

Our earliest and indeed our only reliable historical documents for the mission of Patrick and the foundation of his Church are two Latin letters believed on internal evidence to date from this period, and claiming categorically to have been written by the saint himself. These are the *Confession* and the *Letter to the Soldiers of Coroticus*. Both are brief, but both are of great importance. The former claims that Patrick was a member of a Romanized British family, that he had been carried off to Ireland as a slave at the age of sixteen, that he had spent six years there, and then escaped, and that in response to a vision he returned to Ireland and founded a Church, 'in the ends of the earth', '*ad exteras partes ubi nemo ultra erat*' (*Confessio*, 51), '*in ultimis terrae*' (ibid. 58). These expressions have no geographical significance, but are an ancient traditional form of reference to the British Isles, still current, but no longer intended to be interpreted literally. It is thus that St Columbanus, as late as the early seventh century, refers to Ireland in his letter to Pope Boniface IV: (AD 612–13) 'We, all the Irish, dwellers at the ends of the earth'.[2]

No *acta* of the saint have survived; and no early *vitae* and few early traditions of his disciples. Almost all the early documents claiming to be from his hand or those of his disciples have been shown to be spurious.[3] The biographical narratives of Muirchu and Tirechán, composed in the late seventh century, claim, probably with justice, to have incorporated traditions of at least a generation earlier, and are consistent with other surviving traditions incorporated in later works. These early documents present us with a consistent picture of a Church founded by Patrick in the fifth century, completely Roman in origin, tradition, character, and episcopal organization. In this respect they are consistent with the *Confession*, in which he leaves us in no doubt that he regards both himself and his fellow-countrymen in Britain as Roman citizens.

We may leave aside the difficult and controversial question of the authenticity and bias of the Patrician documents as a whole, for his own writings give us a clear indication of his mission and of a Church which he claimed to have founded, and these fifth-century writings are certainly our earliest evidence for Christianity in our islands from the time that direct Continental evidence ceases. It is a fact generally accepted that all

---

[1] For some discussion see D. A. Binchy, S.H., no. 2, p. 111 ff.; T. F. O'Rahilly, *T.P.* Cf. also for the chronological question James Carney, *S.I.L.H.* ch. ix.

[2] *Toti Iberi, ultimi habitatores mundi* (G. S. M. Walker, *Sancti Columbani Opera* (Dublin, 1957), 38.23).

[3] D. A. Binchy, S.H. no. 2, p. 42 ff.

these early documents imply the existence of a Church in Ireland from the fifth century, organized in all essential respects on lines comparable with that of the contemporary episcopal church in Gaul. This Gaulish Church we have already seen to have been essentially an urban Church, reflecting the official legal and administrative system of the Roman civil service. This was probably the organization of the early Church in Britain also, and the one with which Patrick would be familiar. The later traditions of his sojourn in Lérins and his contact with St Martin of Tours, indeed with any Continental Church, are entirely without foundation.

Yet in admitting the establishment of an Irish episcopal Church by Patrick we are confronted by a serious problem. In our traditional picture of the Irish Church in the sixth century the Patrician Church plays relatively little part. The organization is partly episcopal but largely monastic. Nothing authentic is known of Patrick's immediate successors, and the great ecclesiastical establishments which are traditionally reported to have sprung up throughout Ireland at this period never claim to have been established by him, or by Palladius, or by any of their disciples. This Irish Church in the sixth century comes before us as organized and governed increasingly on monastic lines. There is, however, no central organization with authority over all the monasteries. Each large monastery is independent and governed by an abbot with full rights and responsibilities over its lands and finances, though often in more or less close relationship with great secular authorities, on whose patronage they seem to have been in some measure dependent for their establishment and survival.

Each of these large independent monasteries was entirely self-governing. They each had their own rules, and their own ascetic discipline. They correspond in form and prestige to the Welsh *clas* churches, the 'mother' churches of Wales, sometimes forming centres of subordinate ecclesiastical establishments, and from time to time even founding or giving their protection and blessing, and extending their benefits and their discipline to anchorite retreats (cf. p. 171 below). Among the great Irish monastic establishments claiming their foundation from saints traditionally ascribed to the sixth century were Clonmacnoise in the west from St Kieran, which developed as an important religious and educational establishment; Bangor in Co. Down in the north-east from St Comgall, which became a great centre of historical studies; Clonard in the east from St Finnian, proverbial for the number of saints traditionally fostered there; Lismore in the south, founded by Mo-Chuta, which developed interesting intellectual contacts with the Continent. Other important early foundations are Ardmore in Co. Waterford, traditionally founded by St Declan, the chief saint of the Dési, and still today a quiet retreat which has hardly undergone any change since the erection of its round tower; and Imblech Ibair (Emly), the chief church of the Eóganacht of ancient Munster, about fifty miles inland from Ardmore, founded by St Ailbe. These Munster churches claimed by tradition to have been founded before the coming of St Patrick, and in this they may indeed be right.

We do not know precisely how or when the monastic system entered Ireland. It is in some respects comparable with that introduced by St Martin into Gaul, and it spread rapidly throughout the country, and with it the new spirit of mysticism, a new and stricter way of life, a more intense devotion and ascetic discipline. This movement had its origin, as we have seen, in the ascetics of the eastern deserts, Egypt, Syria and Mesopotamia. In accordance with their retirement from the world these ascetics also renounced worldly rank and abandoned their relatives and even their personal names. Eugippius tells us in his *Life of St Severinus*, the apostle to the Danube tribes in Noricum (in modern Austria), that to the end of his life the saint never revealed his name. This practical democracy, which has always been, and still is, a fundamental principle of monasticism, was doubtless one of the principal elements in its rapid success in the West. We have also seen that it is one of the features in the new monastic movement in Gaul which gave serious offence to Pope Celestine (cf. p. 159 above).

In fact this new movement in Gaul had had a harder battle to fight where the episcopal system of Church government was deeply rooted in the system of Roman local government. In Ireland no initial difficulty of organization existed. It was a pastoral country, with no towns, and had never been under Roman administration. The monasteries served as an admirable centre for the religious needs and the civilizing amenities of the surrounding tribes. There was therefore no clash between the episcopal and monastic rights, such as occurred in Gaul. Independent of one another as the great monastic organizations were, the chief clash was one which occasionally arose between one monastery and another. The annals record several instances in which such hostilities even amounted to armed conflicts in later times. In general, however, the Ireland of the seventh century presents us with a map of great monastic foundations, independent, deeply religious, eagerly cultivating education and scholarship, and the arts of civilization.

It is important to emphasize that here, as in Gaul, the difference between the diocesan and the monastic churches is simply one of Church government and ecclesiastical practice, not of doctrine. The monastic church was never heretical or schismatic. It adhered in all respects to the established hierarchy of the Catholic Church with the bishop at the head, and the presbyter, deacon and subordinate clergy below him. The bishop was responsible for the consecration of churches and of other bishops. He often lived within the monastery, and sometimes bishop and abbot were the same person. There was no cleavage, and although this monastic development has come to be habitually designated 'The Celtic Church' the term is not strictly accurate, for the Church was in all essentials Catholic. Nevertheless during the period when the barbarian invasions made travel difficult, and the Church in the Celtic countries was relatively debarred from close regular participation in the developments of the continental Church as these took place from time to time, the Church in Ireland grew conservative and in some respects out of date in its practices, and the term 'Celtic Church' has come to denote this conservative form of Church practice. In Ireland the monasteries were so powerful and numerous that the 'Celtic' and the 'Irish Church' have come to be practically interchangeable terms.

We do not know by what route the monastic movements entered the British Isles. Various indications suggest the south of Ireland, possibly by way of Ardmore; but whether from Gaul direct, by way of Aquitaine, or from northern Spain, or direct from the Eastern Mediterranean is unknown. All three have been suggested. Moreover in close relationship with the monastic development there appeared in all the Western Celtic churches a movement of greater asceticism, commonly referred to as the 'anchorite reform'; but the term is perhaps misleading, for the 'anchorites' not rarely formed a body within an actual monastery, or within its obedience, while at other times the more ascetic anchorites lived as solitaries, or in very small groups in remote islands in the sea, or in solitary places. The Scottish place-name *Dysert*, Irish *dísert* (L. *desertum*) still recalls these early retreats, and the ruins of their beehive-shaped buildings (*clochán*) [Plate 52] still survive on the island of Inishmurray off the coast of Sligo (cf. Plate 50) and the little settlement like an eagle's eyrie at the top of some 600 steps on the rock of Skellig Michael eight miles out in the Atlantic off the Kerry coast (cf. Plate 49); in islands in the Inner Hebrides of Scotland, and on North Rona[1] with its oratory and graveyard sixty miles north of the Butt of Lewis, and Sula-Sker[2] ten miles out from Rona, with chapel and bee-hive huts. It was in search of just such a solitary place in the Ocean that Cormac úa Liatháin, abbot of Durrow and also a bishop and an anchorite, found himself astray in the Arctic regions, and eventually arrived in Iona.[3] The most interesting of these voyages is the historical voyage of St

---

[1] See SECT, I, 116; Stewart, *Ronay* (Oxford, 1937); Nisbet and Gaile, A.J., CXVI (1961), 88.

[2] AJ, SECT, 114.

[3] Adamnán, *Vita Columbae*, V, 6; II, 40. Cormac's three voyages perhaps formed the subject of a saga cycle. We may compare the voyage of Brendan and other *immrama* discussed on p. 189 below.

Colman who is related by Bede (H.E. IV, 4) to have retired with his followers after the Synod of Whitby in 663 to the island of Inishbofin off the west coast of Mayo.

The isolation of the anchorites' retreats has ensured their preservation, whether wholly or partially intact, and the simplicity of their architecture may easily mislead us in regard to the building technique of the early Irish Church. In the remoter islands only the local stone could be used, and such as could be easily flaked, since available tools precluded elaborate quarrying. The technique is in general surprisingly competent, the rude stone slabs or flakes being carefully corbelled to form a vault and so laid as to slope slightly outwards to carry off the rain. The *clochán* excavated by F. Henry on Inishkea North[1] off the west coast of Co. Mayo are elaborate little structures, and those of Skellig Michael reveal by the prominent stones which protrude at easy stages cork-screw fashion up the external face of the *clochán* the native substitute for scaffolding in construction.[2] All the *clocháin* are bone-dry inside, and the largest could comfortably accommodate more than a dozen persons.

On the other hand, O'Kelly has shown[3] that in the more easily accessible Church Island close inshore on the Kerry coast near Valencia, where the local co-operation of a congregation could be counted on for transport and labour, suitable building stone was brought by sea, and a more advanced building erected. Few of the early churches on the mainland have survived destruction, but among a few survivals partially preserved, the little Church of Kilmalkedar, and the so-called Gallerus oratory – the latter still perfect (cf. Plate 53) – illustrate the builders' skill in a more ambitious form of construction.[4] These churches are not round but quadrilateral, with rounded angles only. The walls of Gallerus are so constructed by their internal batter as to reduce the span required by the corbelled roof. The inclination of the jambs of the door and the internal splay of the tiny windows also serve a structural purpose. Again the stones are so laid as to carry off the rain externally, and leave the structure bone-dry inside.

The technique of all early Irish church buildings precluded the possibility of large structures. These Irish churches, all small, whether single or in groups, thus conform naturally to the tradition of the early Armenian churches as a number of small buildings. In Ireland this grouping can be traced in the monastic settlement of Inishmurray

[1] J.R.S.A.I. (1945), 127 ff.
[2] We are indebted to Dr Harold Taylor who demonstrated the structural necessity and competence of these protruding stones for indicating the ascent of a *clochán* on Skellig by their means.
[3] 'Church Island', *P.R.I.A.*, LIX (1957–9) Section C, p. 57 ff.
[4] For a general account and plans of all these early *clocháin* and oratories, see H. G. Leask, *Irish Churches and Monastic Buildings*, Vol. I (Dundalk, 1955), p. 25 ff.

off the Sligo coast, in the settlement of Skellig Michael, in the group of later buildings known as the 'Seven Churches' on Aranmore in Galway Bay [Plate 55], and survived in the monastic settlements of Ardmore (cf. Plate 56) and Clonmacnoise. With the Norman Conquest and the introduction of the Cistercian Order into Ireland (cf. p. 196 below) all this was changed. The archaic building conception of Irish tradition passed almost in a night, transformed into the impressive Norman church of Cashel and the lovely abbeys of Mellifont, Jerpoint and Boyle (cf. Plates 59–62).

The Anchorites[1] are often identified with the Culdees, with whom they had much in common; but the exact nature of the Culdees is still obscure. The name seems to mean 'companion of God' (cf. Latin *comes*) and comes to be used in the sense of 'client', 'dependent', perhaps on the analogy of the legal relationship.[2] Such organization as the term implies is vague and seems to have varied locally, and in Scotland at least it suggests a comparatively late development. The early Rule of the Anchorites, which is commonly known as the *Rule of Columcille*, enjoins them to be alone in a desert place in the neighbourhood of a chief monastery; but the so-called 'Anchorite reform' has no technical significance beyond that certain documents, such as the *Rule of Tallaght*,[3] give evidence that from time to time certain monasteries formulated their rule under an abbot of a strict persuasion.[4]

An Irish document known as the *Catalogus Sanctorum*, claiming to be contemporary with our ascetics, but in reality of the ninth or even the tenth century,[5] divides the saints of Ireland into three orders, placing St Patrick in the first order, the great monastic founding saints in the second, and the third order, we are informed, are 'those who dwell in desert places and live on herbs, and water, and alms, and have nothing of their own'. In reality there is no chronological order. These ascetics and anchorites are contemporary with the great saints of the sixth century,[6] and the term 'anchorite reform' is somewhat misleading. They represent a widespread influence from Eastern asceticism, which is found in Gaul where solitaries in the forest of La Perche and elsewhere were known to Gregory of Tours; and in Brittany in the little archipelago off the Paimpol Peninsula in the north[7] and even in the province

---

[1] A valuable study of the anchorites and culdees was contributed by R. Flower, 'The Two Eyes of Ireland', to the *Church of Ireland Conference, A.D.* 432–1932 (Dublin, 1932), p. 66 ff.
[2] We are indebted to Professor D. A. Binchy for this suggestion.
[3] Ed. E. Gwynn, *Hermathena* XLIV, 2nd suppl. vol. (Dublin, 1927), p. 31.
[4] Some discussion of the interesting views of the late Robin Flower on this question is given by N. K. Chadwick in *A.S.*, 88 f.
[5] The text is printed by Haddan & Stubbs, *Councils* II. ii, p. 292 f. See the important study by Paul Grosjean, S.J., Bollandist, A.B. LXXIII (1955), 197 ff.
[6] See Father John Ryan, *I.M.*, 260.
[7] Pierre Barbier, 'Les Vestiges monastiques des Iles de l'embouchure du Trieux: l'île

of Galicia in northern Spain; but it is above all in the Celtic Church of the west that the life of silent contemplation is most deeply rooted, and eventually inspired a class of hermit poetry unique in the purity and simplicity of its personal devotion and its love of all the little things of nature (p. 225).

It was inevitable that a struggle for supremacy should arise between the diocesan church system of the Patrician tradition[1] and the 'federation of monastic communities',[2] the monastic system of the so-called 'Celtic Church' – the former based on long-established usage and the highest prestige in the Continental Church, the latter an innovation, but in Ireland firmly established. Of the early phase of the struggle we know little, largely owing to the fact that no external authority makes any reference to St Patrick. Neither Gildas nor Bede mention him. Adamnán has no word of Patrick or his Church, nor yet has Columbanus. Yet in the seventh century we have the Life of Patrick by Muirchu emphasizing the rise of Armagh as the church founded by him; and the *Memoir* by Tírechán defining the extent of his *paruchia* and virtually claiming it as coterminous with Ireland itself. A struggle for supremacy in the Church in Ireland was already under way, and by the ninth century the prestige of Patrick and the Church of Armagh was supreme. The Age of the Saints was a memory. It was long cherished and of infinite value in the spiritual history of the Irish people at home and in their intellectual influence abroad. But it was no longer paramount in official circles.

The outcome of the struggle turned on the principle of unity. The absence of any form of central organization in the Celtic Church, as in the early Irish political system, rendered it vulnerable, and certain to be superseded by any strong centralized authority. This occurred with the conquest of Ulster, the most powerful kingdom of Ireland at this period, by the dynasties of the Uí Néill (cf. p. 57 f. above), all owing a nominal allegiance[3] to their over-king at Tara. Hitherto there had been no central paramount dynasty in Ireland. It appears from the Irish Laws that the highest type of kingship in Ireland in the early period is the king of a province.[4] The so-called 'high-king' (the *ard-rí*) of Ireland is a pure fiction, created later as propaganda in support of the Tara dynasty. The task was not a difficult one, for with the conquest of the Ulaid the Uí Néill had also possessed themselves of Emain Macha, the

---

Saint-Maudez et l'île-verte', *S.E.C.* (LXXX, 1951), 5 ff.; cf. *ibid.*, *Le Trégor Historique et Monumental* (Saint-Brieuc, 1960), pp. 48 f.; 104; 247 f., and figures 19, 20.
[1] See Binchy, SH, no. 2, 169.
[2] *Ibid.*, loc. cit.
[3] As Binchy has emphasized, S.H. no. 2, p. 149 ff.
[4] *Ibid.*, p. 63.

ancient Ulidian capital two miles from Armagh. The inherited oral culture of Emain and the new Latin culture, including the art of writing, sedulously cultivated at Armagh, were henceforth wholly at the service of the Uí Néill. The cult of St Patrick and the earliest written documents became their chief strength, creating an ancient fictitious high-kingship of Ireland and supporting it with all the strength of a powerful church.

Meanwhile the Northern branch of the Uí Néill dynasty, situated in the north-west of Ireland, in their advance eastwards, had conquered Oriel and threatened the little northern kingdom of Dál Riata (p. 58) In the fifth century a branch of the Dalriadic dynasty expanded across the sea and founded a dynasty in south-western Scotland, and a Scottish kingdom of Dál Riata, later known as the kingdom of Argyll. The territory must have been hitherto under Pictish rule, but tradition records no opposition, and for all we know to the contrary the new kingdom may have been the result of a peaceful penetration with Pictish acquiescence. The kings of the Northern Uí Néill continued to alternate succession to the kingship of Tara until the end of the tenth century,[1] but the Northern dynasty seems also to have gained suzerainty over Dál Riata, perhaps by the Battle of Moira (637),[2] and so established a special relationship to the Scottish kingdom.

The prince of the Northern Uí Néill who represented the dynasty in Argyll was St Columba. As a son, a potential heir to the kingship of Tara, his personal prestige was high. He adopted the surest way to establish the power of the new kingdom by uniting his political prestige with that of Dál Riata, and by establishing a new centre for the Celtic form of the Irish Church at Iona, which should be, like Armagh itself, under royal prerogative. It was here that he inaugurated Aedán as king of the new kingdom of Dál Riata in Scotland. It was from here that he negotiated a peaceful settlement with Brude mac Maelchon, king of the Northern Picts, the *rex potentissimus*, of Bede, and with this double royal support established his powerful monastic sanctuary on Iona to be henceforth the head of the Celtic Church. The constructive statesmanship and the spiritual and intellectual integrity of Columba resulted in the peaceful creation of what was to become politically the kingdom of Scotland, and ecclesiastically the head of the Celtic Church in Ireland, Scotland and England.

The spiritual life of Columba has come down to us chiefly through the work of the panegyric poets of his native land, and the prose biography of Adamnán. Of the poems and literary works attributed to him and his contemporaries all are of later date, with the possible exception of the *Amra Choluim Chille* (cf. Plate 36), a composition of highly artificial

[1] *C.I.*, 129.   [2] *Phases*, 200.

alliterative verse,[1] attributed to the Irish bard Dallán Forgaill, which is now believed to be a genuine sixth century document. This *amra* ('Eulogy') is an encomium on the saint by the bard Dallán, prompted traditionally by gratitude for Columba's support of the poets of Ireland, who were threatened with banishment on account of their extravagant claims in payment for their works.

The institutions of the monastery of Iona were typical of the monastic Celtic Church. Columba was a priest and an abbot, but never a bishop, and he always deferred to a bishop in the celebration of the Mass. Bede (H.E. III, 4) mentions it as a peculiarity of the Columban Church that its head was always a priest. The successors of Columba in the abbacy followed the traditional Irish pattern of the coarbship, that is to say, the abbot was commonly a member (a *com-orba*, 'co-heir') of the family of the original founder. The Columban Church was essentially Irish. Its greatest abbot, the saint's biographer Adamnán, was a great-grandson of the first cousin of Columba, and himself a member of the *Cenél Conaill* of the Northern Uí Néill. It is striking testimony to the early prestige of Iona that it rapidly became the head of the 'Columban' communities in Ireland, and almost achieved for them the unity which might have established them as a permanent institution. The Viking raids sapped the strength of Iona. It was pillaged in 795, 802, and 806, and in 825 the community were massacred. The relics and the jurisdiction of the Columban churches seem to have been divided about this time between Dunkeld in the safer inland region on the Upper Tay, and Kells in Ireland, and Kells henceforward became the centre of the Columban Church.

There were other and more fundamental reasons for the decline of the prestige of the Columban Church, as we shall see. By the end of the seventh century the cult of St Patrick and the importance of Armagh as his principal sanctuary had become paramount in Ireland with the expansion and consolidation of the power of the kings of Tara. The biography of the saint by Muirchu, and the Memoir by Tírechán, both written in the interests of Armagh, did much to support the cult of Patrick, while Muirchu's emphasis on the saint's observance of the Easter festival at Tara had underlined the importance of Catholic unity in conformity with Roman usage. Numerous writings, now regarded as post-Patrician forgeries, but purporting to be contemporary documents, attest the tradition of a strong movement, sponsored by the Irish monastic scriptoria, towards furthering the saint who had come to Ireland, not as a monastic founder, but as a direct emissary from the

---

[1] For an account of the manuscripts and subject matter, together with an English translation, see Whitley Stokes, R.C. XX (1899), p. 30 ff. For a discussion of the metre see Calvert Watkins, *Celtica* VI, 219, 228, 237, 243.

episcopal Church sponsored by Rome and Gaul, and already established in Britain.

The difference of organization and of the principle of government which we have traced in the early Church in Gaul and in Ireland was not confined to these countries. It prevailed throughout the Celtic countries, insular and continental. This difference gave rise during the seventh century to a controversy commonly referred to as the 'Easter Controversy' because the dating of Easter formed the terms of reference on which the dispute turned. The Catholic Church had officially adopted the practice of the dating of Easter as fixed in 457 by Victorius of Aquitaine. The Celtic Church, on the other hand, justly proud of its long and honourable record, preferred to adhere to the traditions handed down by its *seniores*. In reality, however, the long and hard-fought controversy which ensued was not one of superficial details. The issue lay much deeper, and was nothing less than the struggle of the Church of Rome on the one hand to establish unity and supremacy which alone would safeguard the survival of Catholic Christianity in the West; the struggle of the Celtic Church, on the other hand, to maintain its spiritual independence and right to adhere to its own ancient and honourable traditional usages.

In our islands the issue was disputed separately in the different countries. It is highly significant that the south of Ireland, always in direct touch with continental developments, was the first to accept the Roman Order. A letter from Cummian, who was probably abbot of Durrow, to Segéne, bishop of Iona (623–52), suggests that already by 629 most of the south-east of Ireland had celebrated Easter according to Roman practice. The letter is still extant,[1] though the text is much corrupted, and this is the only surviving controversial document written in Ireland on the paschal controversy. To defeat opponents the pro-Roman party sent to Rome for guidance – note again the apparently easy communication – and in 636 the south of Ireland joined the 'new Order which had lately come from Rome'. It is interesting to observe that in this they were ahead of the Celtic Church in Britain. Moreover it was nearly sixty years before the north of Ireland conformed.

The church in Northumbria had had a chequered career. Edwin, the Anglian king of united Bernicia and Deira, had been converted by St Paulinus from Canterbury in 627. On his death he was succeeded by Oswald who had spent his exile during Edwin's reign in Scotland, and on his accession had introduced the saintly Aidan from Iona and established the Columban Church in Northumbria. Oswald was succeeded by his brother Oswiu who had shared his northern exile; but Oswiu had married a daughter of Edwin, who naturally adhered to the

---

[1] The text is translated by Kenney, *Sources*, p. 220 f.

Roman form of Christianity in which she had been instructed by Paulinus. The co-existence of the two usages at the Northumbrian court created an impossible situation, and was resolved at the Synod of Whitby in 663 by King Oswiu giving the prerogative to the Roman Order.

St Paulinus had been sent to Canterbury direct from Rome, and after the Synod of Whitby it was only to be expected that the Northumbrian Church would make efforts to bring the whole of the Columban churches into the Roman obedience. It is probable that the revival, towards the close of the seventh century, of the bishopric of Whithorn in Galloway, which now lay in Anglian territory, was intended to form a centre for pressure on Ireland to this end. Its first bishop was Pecthelm, a pupil of Aldhelm of Malmesbury and correspondent of Bede. During 686 and the two following years Adamnán, the abbot of Iona, had been at the court of his *amicus*, his royal *alumnus*, King Aldfrith, now ruling in Northumbria, and had now transferred his adherence to the Roman rule. As a result he went to Ireland to teach the new discipline, and as Bede tells us, 'he brought almost all that were not under the domination of Iona into Catholic unity'. The victory of the Roman party in Ireland was probably ratified at the Synod of Birr, *c.* 697, at which Adamnán himself presided. Adamnán then returned to Iona where he died shortly afterwards (704). Twelve years later, Egbert, who had spent many years in Ireland, converted Ireland to the new observance and in 716 Iona celebrated Easter by the Roman dating. In the following year the king of the southern Picts expelled the Columban clergy from his kingdom. The supremacy of Iona as head of the Irish Church now came to an end. The victory of the Church of St Patrick and of the see of Armagh was complete.

In Wales and the continental Celtic Churches conformity came later. Bede has told us nothing of the conversion of Wales to Christianity, but he devotes a long narrative to the efforts of St Augustine of Canterbury to win their obedience. Bede pictures Augustine making two journeys to the west to interview a number of the British bishops, and to adjure them to preserve Catholic unity and jointly with him to preach the Gospel to the heathen (*gentibus*), i.e. doubtless the Saxons. On their refusal he leaves them with a prophecy, tantamount to a curse, that they will suffer vengeance from the hands of their enemy – a prophecy which Bede evidently regards as fulfilled in the Battle of Chester in 616. Bede is our only authority for this story, which he relates in the style of a saga in three episodes, and he has evidently derived the whole narrative from oral tradition. In fact the Welsh did not submit to the Archbishop of Canterbury till more than a generation after Bede's death, and in Cornwall not till the tenth century. The Continent naturally accepted the reformed Easter earlier than Britain – Spanish

Galicia as early as 633, and in the Celtic monastic foundations of central Europe the reform had largely been accepted by the eighth century; but the changes were very gradual and ancient usages died hard. In 818 the great abbey of Landévennec in Brittany under its abbot Matmonoc accepted the behest of Louis the Pious to abandon Celtic practices and adopt the Roman tonsure and the Rule of St Benedict, and the other Breton monasteries followed in due course.

It is one of the most impressive facts of the Celtic Church that there were no martyrs. Even the Easter controversy had been a worthy and dignified one on both sides. It had, moreover, given birth to a corpus of literature by the adherents of both parties which is our principal basis for the spiritual history of the period. In the documents which had their origin in the so-called 'Roman' party we detect the first influences of contemporary continental literary discipline – the beginning of chronology and of historical records in local annalistic chronicles, and of a sense of the importance of precision in documentation. The most important Irish compilation of records of councils and of canon law was the *Collectio Canonum Hibernensis* which had appeared in Gaul in the eighth century, and which was known and copied early in Brittany. In Ireland a compendium was made, and copies and versions were multiplied early in the eighth century by members of the 'Roman' party.[1] The documents of the Irish party were undoubtedly inspired by a desire to formulate the traditions, the rules, the ideals which had been handed down to them by their *seniores*, and to which they still clung. Theirs is not a literature of trained theologians or of speculative thought; but in the Rules, such as that of Tallaght, the so-called *Regula Monachorum* or 'Monks' Rule' by Columbanus of Bobbio, and in the Penitentials, there breathes the spirit of unworldliness of the early Celtic Church, which earnestly inculcates and formulates the austere form of its discipline.

The most influential development in the literature of the controversy was the recording of the *vitae* of the Celtic saints, their *acta*, the manner of their birth and death, their miracles – without which in this uncritical age no cult could be established, no saint or sanctuary gain popularity. The *vita* had a history on the Continent as old as Christianity itself. The earliest form is perhaps the *Acta* of the Apostles in the New Testament. A later development is the funeral sermon, a natural transference to Christian purposes of the heroic panegyric and elegiac orations of heathen Classical times. Famous Christian examples are the funeral oration of the Christian rhetor, Pacatus, for St Paulinus of Nola († 431), and in the West the commemorative sermon of St Hilary of Arles for St

[1] See Kenney, *Sources*, p. 247 ff.

Honoratus, founder of the monastery of Lérins early in the fifth century.[1] Already between 356 and 362 St Athanasius had adopted the narrative form made popular by late Greek romances, and adapted it with brilliant success to his *Life of St Antony*, and the permanent place of the *vita* in hagiography in the West had been ensured by Sulpicius Severus in his *Life of St Martin.*

Our earliest extant *vita* of St Patrick was written by Muirchu (cf. p. 175 above), who claims in his Preface to be composing in a new form, such as had been introduced by his 'father' Cogitosus. This is probably a reference to the *Life of St Brigit* composed by Cogitosus earlier in the seventh century.[2] In view of the narrative form of Muirchu's *Life of St Patrick*, the author's reference to the 'new style' suggests that the narrative style had already reached Ireland and superseded the older form of *acta*. The School of Armagh to which Muirchu adhered was already *en rapport* with the latest literary fashions.

The Classic *vita* of the 'Celtic' party is the *Life of St Columba*[3] by Adamnán, his collateral descendant and coarb in the abbacy. This is not, strictly speaking, a biography, and is not composed in a unified narrative form. It is divided into three parts, of which the first consists of the saint's prophecies, the second of his miracles, the third of his visions. By the time it was written, probably between 685 and 689,[4] this form of literary framework was already old-fashioned, having been superseded by the narrative models made popular by Athanasius and Sulpicius Severus. But Adamnán was not unaware of the later narrative form of hagiography, for the *Life of St Germanus* by Constantius was already known in Ireland, and is actually cited by Adamnán himself in the *Vita* (ii, 34). Indeed Adamnán was both well informed and intellectually advanced by the standards of his time. He was well read in the literature current on the Continent.[5] In another work by him, *De Locis Sanctis*,[6] he relates what he had learned from a Gaulish bishop Arculf, who had come to land in Iona while forced out of his course during a voyage from the eastern Mediterranean, where he had visited Jerusalem and many other 'holy places'. Bede knew the work, which Adamnán presented to King Aldfrith of Northumbria, and evidently esteemed it highly, for he relates the circumstances of its composition (H.E. v 15), and gives some details of its contents, adding that the king had the work circulated, and the writer was sent back to his own land enriched with

---

[1] English translation by F. R. Hoare, *W.F.*, 247 ff.   [2] Kenney, *Sources*, p. 432.
[3] The edition by Bishop William Reeves (Dublin, 1857) is still the classic work on the subject. The best modern edition and translation is by A. O. and M. O. Anderson (Edinburgh and London, 1961).
[4] Kenney, *Sources*, p. 432.
[5] For the literary works used by Adamnán see the study by Gertrud Brüning, ZCP XI (1917), 217 ff.; D. A. Bullough, SHR xliv (1965), 23 ff.
[6] Edited and translated by Denis Meehan (Dublin, 1958).

many gifts. The whole incident and its record are significant of the newly awakening interest felt in Celtic lands regarding the geography of the modern world to which the travels of the *peregrini* must have greatly contributed, as the narratives of Arculf by Adamnán and of Fidelis by Dícuill (cf. p. 182 below) prove.

Adamnán's *Life of St Columba* is a historical work of high value. Like all hagiographers of the period he wrote primarily for edification, rather than for historical purposes. Yet his references to historical persons and events have a precision and actuality rare for his time, and despite much that is vague and inadmissible, he gives us on the whole our most illuminating picture of the life of the early Church in Britain before the work of Bede.[1] It is, in fact, the most distinguished record that we possess of the old Celtic monastic Church of Ireland.

The most illustrious and influential of the adherents to the Celtic Order was St Columbanus. He was the first to carry the controversy beyond the borders of the Insular Celts and to plead the cause of the Celtic Order before the Holy See in a series of letters to Popes Gregory I and Boniface IV,[2] which are a unique source for the Irish attitude in the Easter controversy. He is also the most famous of the early *peregrini*, men who, like St Colman of Lindisfarne, left their country with a group of adherents for the sake of a religious ideal, and founded religious communities of the stricter discipline in distant regions. He was a Leinsterman by birth, a member of the community of St Comgall of Bangor in Co. Down, but *c.* 590 he set out with twelve disciples as a *peregrinus* to the Continent, passing through Western Gaul to Burgundy. Here he settled in a retreat in the forest of Annegray, and later established two other religious foundations at Luxeuil and Fontaine, the former of which became a famous school of learning; but his attitude in the Easter controversy, and his outspoken views on the necessity for the stricter discipline, rendered him unpopular with the court and bishops of Burgundy, and he was forced to leave the country, passing to the courts of Neustria and Austrasia and thence to Switzerland.

In the neighbourhood of Bregenz he made a stay of some duration in the company of his Irish friend and disciple, St Gall, who had followed him throughout his wanderings from the monastery at Bangor. Eventually St Gall decided to settle permanently in Switzerland, and at his tomb a monastery developed into the famous school of learning which still bears his name, and houses one of the most precious libraries in Europe.[3] Columbanus himself, however, passed over the Alps into Lombardy, where he was welcomed by the king and queen, who granted

[1] See D. Binchy, S.H. no. 2, 57.
[2] For the letters see G. S. M. Walker, *Sancti Columbani Opera* (Dublin, 1957), p. 36 ff.
[3] See J. M. Clark, *A.St.G.*, *passim*; and more recently Hans Reinhardt, *Der St Galler Klosterplan* (St Gallen, 1952).

him a valley in the Appennines in which to settle. Here his long saintly Odyssey found its final consummation in his foundation of the monastery of Bobbio, no less famous as a school of learning than St Gall. Both monasteries became important gathering places for Irish *peregrini* travelling to Rome. A valuable *Life of St Columbanus* was written by the monk Jonas who had entered Bobbio in 618 and who must have known many of the saint's companions.[1]

The influence of Columbanus on the civilization of Western Europe has been held comparable with that of St Columba.[2] In particular his influence through his continental monastic foundations has been a major factor in the development of the intellectual life of the early Middle Ages. Moreover, the impetus which his foundations gave to learning and to books, and to the realization of the potential revolution in the intellectual life inherent in the art of writing, extends far beyond his personal literary achievement. He was the last and greatest founder of Celtic monasticism in its most rigorous form, including the insistence on the abbatial control of monastic administration.

Columbanus was not an original thinker or a profound scholar, and his influence, like that of his great namesake Columba, is to be measured rather by his immediate permanent practical achievement than by his literary work. Yet he was not deficient by the standard of Latin education of his day, and his style still retains its power to impress us by its vigorous and direct rhetoric. The *Regula Monachorum*[3] is undoubtedly in the main the work of his hand and is the earliest surviving rule of Irish origin. Although written on the Continent it is completely representative of the Irish Church, and probably reproduces the Rule of St Comgall's famous monastery at Bangor in which Columbanus had been trained. It is intended especially for the guidance of the spiritual life of cenobitic communities, inculcating absolute obedience, constant toil, and ceaseless austerities and devotional exercises. The *Penitential* which passes under his name is also based in the main on earlier Irish penitential tradition,[4] but lays special emphasis on the importance of the frequent practice of private confession.

The ancient and much traversed route to Rome over the Alps, the old Roman road known later as the *via barbaresca*, became the chief pilgrims' route in the Age of the Saints; and on the way there were special inns for the pilgrims.[5] The Abbey of St Gall was close to this route, and the *Life of St Gall* and other documents have preserved for us details of the distinctive pilgrims' habit and behaviour. As in all caravan journeys,

[1] Kenney, *Sources*, p. 203 f.   [2] *Ibid.*, p. 187.
[3] *Ibid.*, p. 197 f.; Walker, *op. cit.* 122.
[4] Kenney, pp. 200, 240 ff.; Walker, *op. cit.* 168.
[5] For the following information and references to these Irishmen on the Continent see J. M. Clark, *A.St.G.*, p. 26 ff.

ancient and modern, the travellers moved in large parties, and Walafrid Strabo, writing in the early ninth century, tells us that the habit of wandering had become almost a second nature to the Scots (i.e. the Irish). They could not presumably carry books with them in any quantity, but it is significant that writing-tablets were known in Germany as '*pugilares Scotorum*' ('the writing tablets of the Irish').

The devotion of Irish monks to learning was already well known outside Ireland in the eighth century. In one of his most remarkable passages Bede tells us (H.E. iii 27) of the devotion of the Irish monasteries to learning, and of their generosity to English students, 'nobles and others', who came to them either to pursue religious studies or to live a life of stricter discipline. Some of these embraced the monastic life, while others preferred to pursue their studies, visiting the cells of various teachers. The Irish welcomed them, dispensing free hospitality and supplying them with books for their reading and instruction free of charge. Even on the Continent we gather from Notker Balbulus (*c.* 840–912)[1] that two Irishmen arrived in Gaul incomparably well versed in sacred and profane learning, which they offered for sale as vociferously as others do their wares. They were honourably received by Charlemagne from whom they asked no payment for their teaching save a habitation and their food and clothing. For one of them he established a school in Gaul for noble and humble alike, while the other was established as a teacher on equally liberal lines in Pavia.[2]

One of the earliest of these Irish scholars who frequented the Carolingian court and became a teacher in the palace school was Dícuill,[3] whose learning and literary work are of great interest, and remarkable for their time. He was probably a monk of Iona perhaps taught by Suibne, the abbot who died in 772. In Iona he had been present during the visit of a *peregrinus* to the Holy Land before 767, and he had known Irish anchorites in the Northern Isles, apparently the *papar* (Irish anchorites) in *Thile* (Iceland) and the Faroe Islands, who had been obliged to abandon their settlements by the Vikings (cf. p. 117 above). It seems probable that he himself had also visited the Faroes, and it has been conjectured that his settlement on the Continent may have been the result of the sack of Iona in 806. His chief literary works are a treatise on astronomy and computistical matter, written in a mixture of prose and rhythmical verse, and *De Mensura Orbis Terrae*. The latter is

[1] *Gesta Caroli Magni: Mon. Germ. Hist., Script.* (ed. Pertz) II, 731.
[2] This aspect of Irish intellectual activity has been brilliantly demonstrated by Nigra, Traube, Manitius, and in more recent work, by Gougaud, J. M. Clark, Derolez and others. Cf. further *S.E.B.C.* by Chadwick, Hughes, Brooke and Jackson, 101 ff. For a valuable recent study see K. Hughes, 'Irish Monks and Learning', in *Los Monjes y los Estudios* (Abadia de Poblet, 1963).
[3] For Dícuill see Kenney, *Sources*, p. 545 ff.: J. J. Tierney (ed.), *Dicuili Liber de Mensura Orbis Terrae* (Dublin, 1966).

the earliest geographical survey of its kind compiled in the Frankish Empire, and although based in the main on Roman geography, especially the work of Pliny, the author has too lively a mind to resist inserting some delightful reminiscences of his own – the elephant sent by Harun al Rashid to Charlemagne in 804; the account which he had himself heard of the pilgrimage of the monk Fidelis to the Holy Land; and an account of Iceland and the Faroes. His geographical work anticipates King Alfred's translation of Orosius by inserting contemporary matter significant of the expanding interest in geography in the West in the ninth century.

By the middle of the ninth century, at a time when the barbarian invasions were threatening the traditional Classical learning on the Continent, new life was breathed into both scholarship and independent speculative thought in Western Europe from the British Isles by both Anglo-Saxon and Celtic, especially Irish scholars. The Irish in particular have left a deep and abiding influence on the European culture of the ninth and following centuries. Of remarkable interest are the circles of learned Irishmen centred at Laon, north east of Paris, and Liège, east of Brussels, who about the middle of the ninth century, settled for at least a decade in these continental centres. About this time we have record of a number of individual Irishmen who had come on a mission to the court of King Charles the Bald at Liège from Mael Sechlainn, the Irish king, announcing a victory over the Norsemen, and begging a free passage as *peregrini*, that is to say as pilgrims, to Rome. About the same time, and perhaps as a member of the same mission we also find at Liège Sedulius Scottus, or Scottigena, poet, scholar, scribe, theologian, and courtier, one of the most learned men of his time. He is closely associated with a little group of scholars who, like himself, have probably sojourned on their way to Liège at the court of Merfyn Frych, king of North Wales, which seems to have had a claim to some culture (cf. pp. 109–10 above). The evidence indeed suggests that the court of Merfyn in North Wales was at this time a recognized halt and centre of culture on the regular route of *peregrini* from Ireland to the court of Charles the Bald at Liège, and that Irish, and perhaps Welsh scholars also were honoured at Liège for their learning and courtly polish.

Of the Irish scholars attached to the court at Liège the central figure was undoubtedly Sedulius Scottus.[1] The precise place of his origin and education are unknown, though indications in his writings suggest that some at least of his literary sources were of Irish provenance. In the words of Laistner, 'Like some uncharted comet the Irishman Sedulius

---

[1] For Sedulius and his circle see Kenney, *Sources*, p. 563 ff.; M. L. W. Laistner, *T.L.*, 251; cf. a study by N. K. Chadwick, *S.E.B.C.*, 93 ff., and the references there cited.

appeared at Liège about the middle of the ninth century (845–58) to vanish again as mysteriously as he had come.'[1] His work is no less remarkable for its wide range than for the precision and facility of his Latin scholarship, especially his command of an extensive variety of Latin metres. His good taste in Latin prose style is shown by the value that he set on Cicero. In his collection of extracts from Latin authors which he assembled in the *Collectaneum*[2] he refers to no less than seven of the works of Cicero, while the majority of his contemporaries are limited to one or two. That he possessed some knowledge of Greek, probably not very profound, is generally acknowledged. A colophon in Greek characters to a manuscript of the Greek Psalter, now in Paris, runs: 'Sidulios Skottos ego egrapsa' ('I, Sedulius Scottus wrote it').[3]

The writings of Sedulius reveal him as in the full current of the literary fashions of his time. In the *Collectaneum*, which has been called his commonplace book, he assembled extracts of outstanding merit from Classical authors, and at a time when books and libraries were comparatively rare such collections had a practical value. The form reached its classic development in the *Adages* of Erasmus. His *Liber de Rectoribus Christianis*,[4] written in prose interspersed with verse, which chiefly summarizes the preceding prose passages, is an early example of the series of studies in political theory, and more especially in regard to the duties of rulers, which gained such wide currency throughout Europe from Russia to Iceland, in the Middle Ages, and which are commonly referred to as 'Mirrors of Princes'. It is significant that Sedulius was evidently influenced in this work by the chapter on the Unjust King in an anonymous Irish treatise *De Duodecim abusivis saeculi*, written early in the preceding century. He shared the lively interest of his time in grammatical treatises, and wrote commentaries on Eutyches, Priscian, and Donatus, and he made contributions to the current literature of Biblical exegesis with a *Collectaneum in Matthaeum* and a *Collectaneum in omnes beati Pauli Epistolas*. The latter has a special interest for us in that it forms one of a group of Pauline commentaries almost all of which are of direct Irish origin. This, as Kenney points out,[5] makes it probable that Sedulius either wrote his Collectaneum in Ireland, or used books brought from Ireland.

Today we remember Sedulius with most pleasure for his poems,[6] eighty-three in number; for he carried his learning with the ease and grace of his countrymen, and while he is unique in his period for the

---

[1] *T.L.*, 251.
[2] Edited by S. Hellmann, *Sedulius Scottus*, 92 ff.
[3] Manitius, *G.L.L.M.* I, p. 318. See however, Hellmann, *op. cit.* p. 95, n. 2.
[4] Edited by Hellmann, *Sedulius Scottus*, 1 ff.
[5] *Sources*, p. 565, n. 2.
[6] Edited by Traube, *M.G.H. Poet. Lat. Aevi Carol.* III (1886), pp. 151–237.

variety and correctness of his lyric metres, he possessed the lightness of touch which characterizes the well educated mind. It is in this brightness of spirit that he composed poems to Hartgar, bishop of Liège (840–54), begging to be admitted into his school, and begging, both seriously and humorously, for benefits for himself and his fellow scholars – for wine, and meat, and honey, and for better lodgings. The same facility and tact which enabled him to beg from Hartgar without giving offence, enabled him also to greet his successor, Bishop Franco. Indeed like a modern poet laureate Sedulius was a master of occasional verse, and a large proportion of his poems deal in a dignified style with contemporary public events, such as the death of Bishop Hartgar (no. XVII), and the accession of his successor Franco (XVIII, XIX, LXVI). Many are addressed to royalty – to King Charles the Bald himself, to the Emperor Lothair, his Empress Ermengarde, and their sons Louis and Charles (XII–XXVII *et alia*). Three of his poems on contemporary events (XLV–XLVII) link him again in all probability with the court of North Wales. One of these, which bears the title *De Strage Normannorum* (XLV) is virtually a hymn of thanksgiving for a victory over the Danes – that '*gens inimica*', '*homines viles*' – and was probably inspired by the battle in which their leader Gormr was killed (p. 112). Another poem (XLVII) appears to refer to an 'altar' set up by King Roricus, doubtless Rhodri Mawr of North Wales. It is not impossible that these three poems were composed before Sedulius came to the Continent; but Charles was so seriously harassed by the Norsemen at this time that the death of their leader would certainly be an occasion for rejoicing at Liège, and it would be natural for Sedulius to celebrate this great event.

It is perhaps in his gayer occasional trifles that the humour of Sedulius marks him off from the more sombre cast of thought of the Middle Ages. It is thus that he addresses his friend Robert by the grammatical declension of his name (LVIII).

> Bonus vir est Robertus,
> Laudes gliscunt Roberti.
> Christe, fave Roberto,
> Longaevum fac Robertum. ...

His gift of light humour is seen in its most engaging form in a mock heroic poem of 140 lines on the death of a ram torn to pieces by a dog (XLI). The poem is complete with a formal epitaph. The ram at bay cows the attacking dogs – all but one – by a heroic ten-line speech in the grand manner, and after this heroic death Sedulius, with daring levity, pronounces a formal eulogy in the exalted manner of Classical epic:

> Without blemish was he, and spake not empty words, Báá or Béé were the mystic sounds he used to utter. As a lamb enthroned on high to redeem

sinners the Son of God Himself tasted bitter death. Going the road of death, torn by cruel hounds, thus good bell-wether thou dost perish for the unrepentant thief. As a ram was made a sacrificial offering for Isaac, so thou art a pleasing victim for a poor wretch.[1]

The poetical quality of the art of Sedulius expresses itself most fully in his treatment of serious themes – religious festivals, national disasters, of the gentler aspects of nature symbolized in Spring. In a passage of the *Liber de Rectoribus* he passes by a natural transition from the horrors of war to a vigorous passage on a storm in the natural universe:

> When the east wind's gusty gale rages boisterously, thundering down from the high mountains, the white hail falls in clouds, and straightway forests totter, and the ocean tide is upheaved, and the wind hurls threats at the stars as the lightning crackles, then fear strikes the heart of trembling mortals, lest heaven-sent wrath lay low the race of earthly men.[2]

In contrast to the vigour of this threat of nature in tumult he reflects her gentler mood in Spring in the little verses on Easter, when

> The earth makes flower-bearing bulbs to swell with blossom and rejoices to have a painted robe of flowers. Now bright-plumed birds soothe the air with song, from their young beaks they pour a song of lofty triumph. The skies exult, the earth is glad, and now re-echoes an hundredfold its notes of Halleluia. Now the church choir, singing in chant of Sion, lifts up its hosanna to the sky's poles above.[3]

Among the most charming of the lighter poems of Sedulius is the little eclogue *De Rosae Liliúque Certamine* (LXXXI), an idyllic dialogue in which the lily and the rose each claims superiority – the rose for her bright colour as the sister of the dawn, beloved of Phoebus; the lily with her pallor as symbol of virginity, beloved of Apollo. The dispute is brought to a conclusion by Spring, who is pictured as a youth reclining on the grass, who reminds them that they are both twin sisters, daughters of the earth, their mother.

Contemporary with the little group of scholars and poets gathered around Sedulius at Liège is the most outstanding intellectual Irishman on the continent in the ninth century, Johannes Scottus Eriugena, 'John the Irishman',[4] of whom it has been justly said that, with the exception of Columbanus, he was the most important individual whom Ireland gave to the Continent in the Middle Ages.[5] The two men are however immeasurably different. Columbanus was essentially a practical partici-

---

[1] Hellmann, *Sedulius*, 204; *M.G.H., Poet.* III, p. 219; Laistner's translation, *T.L.*, 394.
[2] Hellmann, *Sedulius*, p. 71; *M.G.H., Poet.* III, p. 612. Laistner's translation, *T.L.*, 394.
[3] *M.G.H., Poet.* III, p. 219, *De Pascha* III; Laistner's translation, *T.L.*, p. 394.
[4] A valuable account of John Scottus is that of Laistner, *T.L.*, see especially 244 ff.; 323 ff.; Kenney, *Sources*, p. 569 ff.   [5] Kenney, *Sources*, p. 571.

pator in the struggle for the survival of the Irish Church of his native tradition, an upholder of its ideals and a practical guide to those who were its members. John was above all a scholar and a thinker, partly theologian, partly philosopher; but his independence and originality of thought defies facile classification. His origin and early life are unknown; but he appears *c.* 850 as the outstanding personality of another group of Irish scholars in the sphere of Charles the Bald centred at Laon and Rheims. He seems to have been a member of the palace school, at least from 845 to 870, and though his knowledge of both Latin and Greek are outstanding we have no evidence that he was an ecclesiastic, and little knowledge of his personal life.

From the point of view of Irish scholarship the greatest interest of the Irish scholars in these centres west of the Rhine is the study of Greek. Indeed all knowledge of Greek under the Franks at this time seems to have been an Irish monopoly, shared in very varying degrees by a number of their members, among them Martin of Laon and Sedulius himself. We have a Greek Psalter at the close of which is a Greek colophon: 'I, Sedulius Scottus, wrote it.' But the Greek knowledge of John was unique among his contemporary continental scholars, and was on a level of scholarship which enabled him to interpret correctly even difficult Greek texts, and was justly valued by Charles the Bald, who commissioned him to undertake the translation of the Pseudo-Dionysius, a particularly difficult author, and of the *Ambigua* by Maximus Confessor († 662). He also translated other texts from the Greek fathers. His great work, however, is a highly original treatise incorporating his philosophical and theological views on the Creator and the Universe, written in Latin between 862 and 866 with a Greek title, and a Latin sub-title, *On the Division of the Universe.* But John was centuries ahead of his time, and his original work carries us beyond the Celtic world into the Europe of the Middle Ages.

The learning of the Irish ecclesiastics had made astonishing strides in our period. We have seen, however, that it is no new development. We have Bede's frank acknowledgment of the devotion of Ireland to learning which was no new thing in his day. Moreover it is hardly sufficiently realized even yet how independent this intellectual development was from the art of writing. Writing was merely incidental to the long history of Irish, as of all Celtic, learning. The history of the Celtic literature preserved from pagan Ireland, and only at a comparatively late date incorporated in written texts, proves beyond any doubt that the literature of the Christian Church and Latin learning among Irish scholars was only the final flowering of centuries of the high cultivation, first in Gaul and later in the Western Celtic countries, of oral tradition, which had been made possible by the high and honourable status accorded to the *filid,* the class of intellectual men responsible for its formulation and faithful transmission.

The idealism and asceticism of the Age of the Saints, which found its most remarkable expression in the voyages of the *peregrini* to seek a life of solitude in the ocean, has inspired a special group of Irish stories, which are among the most delightful in the literature, known as *Immrama* (sing. *immram*), which will be discussed more fully in ch. 10 (p. 256). They are not in origin fictitious. They are in part a reflection of voyages such as those of Cormac ua Liatháin seeking a solitude in the ocean, as related to us by Adamnán (cf. p. 170 above), and of the three Irishmen who are related in the Anglo-Saxon Chronicle to have visited King Alfred in 891. But we have seen (pp. 129 f. and 137) that stories of such voyages were already fully developed in the Irish literary traditions of the heathen period, and are closely related to the *echtrai* ('adventures'). The two stories of St Brendan's voyages to be considered later are in fact a direct reflection of the *peregrinatio,* the voluntary exile which was one of the characteristic ascetic practices of the Age of the Saints. Perhaps the chief difference between the *echtrai* and the *immrama* lies in the fact that in the *echtrae* the interest is concentrated on the scene in the Otherworld, while the journey, which may be over the sea in a coracle or underground, is merely a subordinate framework. In the *immrama,* the Otherworld is definitely located on islands in the western ocean, and the story is the narrative of the voyage and the adventures which befall the travellers in their search for this 'promised land' from the time of their setting out till their return.

Of the Christian *immrama* the oldest is *Immram Curaig Maíle Dúin,* 'The Voyage of Mael Dúin's Boat', which in its present form dates from the tenth century, but is probably based on an eighth century original,[1] and which will be discussed on p. 256 below. It may be said here briefly that the story of Mael Dúin and his foster-brothers relates their voyage over an endless ocean, visiting fantastically magical islands, and monsters reminiscent of medieval bestiaries and late Classical wonder tales. Two other Christian *immrama* listed in the Book of Leinster are also preserved. One of these is *Immram Snédgosa ocus Maic Riagla,* 'The Voyage of Snédgus and Mac Riagla', a saga of the ninth or tenth century, of which the original version is a poem of seventy-six stanzas.[2] An interesting reference in the poem to the Norse raids, introduced as a cautionary element, suggests the tenth century as its most probable date. The story is of two *peregrini* from Iona who voyage in the Western

---

[1] See M. Dillon, *E.I.L.,* 125 ff. and the references there cited; Kenney, *Sources,* p. 410, n. 140; translation by P. W. Joyce, *O.C.R.,* 112 ff. Ed. and transl. H. P. A. Oskamp, *The Voyage of Mael Dúin* (Groningen, 1970).

[2] Dillon, *E.I.L.,* 130; Kenney, *Sources,* p. 447 f.; edited and translated by Whitley Stokes, R.C. IX, 14 ff.

Ocean, visiting eight islands. The incidents are partly borrowed from *Immram Maele Dúin, Curaig Maele Dúin* and from the vision literature discussed below, and contain much Biblical matter. The third *immram* referred to in the *Book of Leinster* list is the *Immram Curaig Úa Corra* ('The Voyage of the Boat of the Uí Chorra') preserved in late manuscripts. The text as we have it is also late, but it contains older material already found in the Voyage of Mael Dúin and the Voyage of Brendan (see below), and the tale is possibly based on an early, even eighth century original.[1]

By *c.* 800 tales of the pilgrimages of the Irish saints across the sea were already current in Irish monastic circles. Of these the most famous were the stories of the voyages of St Brendan of Clonfert,[2] both the account contained in the *Vita Brendani* – of which there are two distinct versions and many variants – and the more famous account in the *Navigatio Brendani*. The evidence suggests that the ocean voyage, which figures so prominently in the *Vita* as we have it, was not a part of the original *Vita*, which may have included only the saint's journey to Britain. On the other hand the ocean voyage forms the subject of the far more famous and developed form of the Brendan story, the *Navigatio Brendani*, which would seem to be a composition of at latest the tenth century, very probably of the first half of the century.[3] Allusions to the Brendan story in the earliest *Lives* of St Malo suggest that if they were part of the original texts the Brendan legend might date from the early ninth century.[4]

The relationship of the various Brendan legends to one another are, in fact, somewhat confusing, and it is very possible that the great voyage of Brendan of Clonfert may have been originally attached to his older contemporary, Saint Brendan of Birr. The *Martyrology of Tallaght*, perhaps of ninth century date, commemorates on 22 March the 'going forth of the family of Brendan',[5] where the reference is to Brendan of Birr. The Voyage of Mael Dúin, which is believed to be older than the *Navigatio* legend, speaks of a solitary survivor of fifteen disciples of Brendan of Birr who had founded a hermitage in the Western Ocean,[6] and in the *Martyrology of Oengus the Culdee* (at 29 November) which is believed to be earlier than AD 800, there appears to be an obscure allusion to the sea in connexion with his name. The *Litany of the Pilgrim Saints*,[7] contained in the *Book of Leinster*, alludes to the pilgrimage of Brendan, but without further specification.

---

[1] Kenney, *Sources*, p. 741; edited and translated by Whitley Stokes, R.C. XIV (1893), 22 ff.; also translated by P. W. Joyce, *O.C.R.*, 130.
[2] Kenney, *Sources*, pp. 406 ff.; Plummer, *L.I.S.*, Vol. I, Introduction, p. xvi ff.; Text of the Irish *Vita*, Vol. I, p. 44 ff.; Translation Vol. II, p. 44 ff.
[3] Kenney, *Sources*, p. 414 ff.   [4] *Ibid.*, p. 410.
[5] *Ibid.*, p. 410, n. 140.   [6] *Ibid.*, loc. cit.
[7] *Ibid.*, p. 728.

During the late ninth or early tenth century the *Navigatio Brendani* was composed on the model of such works as the Voyage of Mael Dúin. It is a Latin prose work and has been preserved practically intact, and the manuscript evidence shows that it cannot be later than the first half of the tenth century, and is derived from an earlier copy. The hero is St Brendan the Navigator who is said in the *Annals of Ulster*, s.a. 557 (*recte* 558) or 563 (*recte* 564) to have founded the monastery of Clonfert in Co. Galway, and to have died in 564 (*recte* 565). The earliest reference to the saint, however, is in Adamnán's *Life of St Columba* (I, 26; III, 19), and Adamnán's reference and the *Vita* suggest that his origin was in Kerry. The *Navigatio*, as its name would suggest, relates, not to the life of the saint, but to his voyage only, which within its supernatural framework presents us with a veiled picture of the ideal monastic life. Great emphasis is laid on Brendan's precepts and on the observances of the monastic routine, and the author was undoubtedly a monk.

The *Navigatio*[1] opens with a visit to Brendan one evening by a certain father Barinthus who had just returned from a visit to Mernoc. Mernoc had once been a member of his own community, but had fled away to embrace a solitary life, and now had many monks in his charge on the Island of Delights. Mernoc's community is pictured much like the Desert communities of Egypt, each monk living in his own cell and meeting in church for divine office, their food being of the simplest vegetables and fruits. Barinthus relates that he and Mernoc had entered a small boat together and sailed westward to the island called the 'Land of Promise of the Saints', where they landed and spent fifteen days, experiencing all the delights of the flowers and fruits of this supernatural realm, but were not allowed to penetrate into more than half the island, after which they returned to Mernoc's community in the Island of Delights, and forty days later Barinthus left to return to his own cell, spending the night with St Brendan and his brethren on his way.

After a fast of forty days, however, Brendan and fourteen monks set out to the west in a curragh to seek the Land of Promise of the Saints, of which Barinthus had spoken, and the narrative relates with much picturesque detail their visits to many islands and their supernatural adventures. They first visited St Enda's monastery on Aranmore, after which the narrative relates their supernatural adventures in many islands of the Western Ocean. On one island were many flocks of sheep larger than oxen; on another was a 'Paradise of birds'. The island of St

[1] For the *Navigatio*, see Kenney, *Sources*, more especially pp. 411 ff.; 414 ff.; C. Selmer, *Navigatio Sancti Brendani Abbatis* (Notre Dame, 1959). Oskamp maintains that the Voyage of Mael Dúin and the *Navigatio* derive from a common source; *op. cit.* 86.

Ailbe offers a detailed picture of the routine of a silent community of Christian monks, and the voyage thereafter offers marvels such as we find in the post-Classical *Liber monstrorum*. Brendan and his brethren are supernaturally nourished and safely guided and protected throughout by a supernatural youth who directs their course and their religious observances as a kind of spiritual mentor. The monks celebrate each Easter by camping on what they take to be a large island, but which is in reality a whale Jasconius (Irish *iasc*, 'fish'). They are nourished by supernatural fish and fruits, and escape the perils of a volcanic island. They visit Judas Iscariot sitting on a rock in brief respite from the torments of Hell. They also visit the cave in which dwells the hermit Paul; and finally they reach the Land of Promise of the Saints. They are not allowed to penetrate to the interior, however, and after receiving the blessing of their angelic guide they travel to the Island of Delights, and after three days there they return to Brendan's own monastery.

The *Navigatio* is the most charming of all the *immrama*, and even today has lost nothing of its appeal, partly on account of the simplicity and intimacy of its gifted narrative, even more for the gentle and affectionate relations between Brendan and his monks. The structure also is interesting and unusual, for we have here, in fact, three *immrama* in one – the brief opening account of the initial voyage of Barinthus to visit the monastery of his former monk, Mernoc, on the 'Island of Delights'; the more fully related but still summary account of the joint subsequent voyage of Barinthus and Mernoc to the island 'Land of Promise of the Saints', and the final voyage of St Brendan and his followers to the island 'Land of Promise', and their final return to Brendan's own monastery, which is related *in extenso*, and to which the two former brief voyages serve as *remscéla*, 'preliminary stories'. It is a fine literary work, and it became deservedly popular throughout Europe in the Middle Ages, and was translated into many languages.[1]

Throughout the narrative great emphasis is laid on Brendan's precepts to his monks and on the careful observance of the monastic routine, and the author was undoubtedly a monk. Nevertheless the tale is not written from the point of view of Brendan's community, or even exclusively from the point of view of the Irish Church. 'Its tone is more cosmopolitan than that of any other Irish hagiographical document.'[2] The objective of Brendan's voyage in the *Navigatio* is not an island retreat in which to live as an anchorite, but *Tír Tairngiri*, the 'Land of Promise' in the full Christian interpretation of the term, the spiritual 'promised land' of the saints in that early conception of Paradise –

[1] For a discussion of the possible routes by which the Brendan legend reached the Continent, see C. Selmer, 'The Beginnings of the Brendan Legend', *The Catholic Historical Review* XXIX (1943), 169.
[2] Kenney, *Sources*, p. 411.

peaceful, genial, care-free, abundant, reached after many perils and temptations, but without any Purgatory or emphasis on the medieval conception of Hell. The *Navigatio* has been justly described as an epic, indeed the 'Odyssey of the Old Irish Church'.[1]

The *Vita Brendani* has perhaps been influenced by the *Navigatio* which is believed to have left traces in the manuscripts. The briefer account of Brendan's voyage is included in the *Vita*, from whatever source, and we thus possess two apparently independent accounts of the saint's *immram*. Unlike the *Navigatio*, however, the *Vita* has been very imperfectly transmitted, and we possess only a number of mixed versions. Two Latin *vitae* are extant, both published by Plummer,[2] in a number of variant texts, the *Vita Sancti Abbatis de Cluainferta* i, and the *Vita Brendani Secunda*, the latter in a single manuscript dating from the end of the twelfth century. This *Vita* ii is described by Plummer as a peculiar recension of the *Navigatio* and need not detain us. There are also three Irish versions[3] of the *Vita*, of which the one contained in the *Book of Lismore*,[4] a manuscript of the latter half of the fifteenth century,[5] is probably based on a Latin version, though some elements which it contains are not found in any of our extant Latin versions, and this Irish version is not taken directly from any of them.[6] In both the Latin and the Irish versions of the *Vita* two voyages are ascribed to Brendan, the first unsuccessful, the second successful. He is said to have been born in Munster, the son of a certain Finnlug, in the time of Oengus mac Nadfroích, and to have been taken by Bishop Eirc to St Ita who fostered him for five years. After he had received Holy Orders, an angel from Heaven brought him this message:

> Arise, Brendan, for God has given you what you sought, even the Land of Promise.

Accordingly Brendan and his followers, ninety in all, set sail over the western seas in three curraghs, passing many marvellous islands for a space of years, variously given as five and seven, and every year they landed to celebrate Easter on the back of a whale. After many adventures and encounters with the devil, and a vision of Hell, they reached a certain beautiful island with a church and men's voices praising the

---

[1] *Ibid.* p. 415.
[2] The Latin texts of the *Vitae* are edited by C. Plummer, *V.S.H.*, *Vita Prima*, Vol. I, p. 98; *Vita Secunda*, Vol. II, Appendix I, p. 270. For an account of the texts see Vol. I, Introduction, p. xxxvi ff. The Irish Life is edited by C. Plummer, *L.I.S.*, Vol. I, p. 44 ff.; translation, Vol. II, p. 44 ff. See also Vol. I, Introduction, xvi ff. Texts of the Latin *Vita* and the *Navigatio* were published in a useful form by Bishop Moran, *Acta Sancti Brendani* (Dublin, 1872); and an English translation by D. O'Donoghue, *Brendaniana* (Dublin, 1893).
[3] Cf. note 2, p. 191.
[4] Edited andtrans lated by Whitley Stokes in *Lives of Saints from the Book of Lismore* (Oxford, 1890).
[5] *Ibid.*, p. v.   [6] Plummer, *V.S.H.* I, p. xxxix.

Lord, and here they received a divine message on a wood tablet bidding them return home:

> You will find the island which you seek, and this is not it.

On his return home Brendan consulted St Ita as to his voyaging, and she ascribed his failure to his having sailed in curraghs covered with skins of dead animals, whereupon he and his *familia* had a large wooden vessel built in Connacht, and having first visited Aranmore they sailed westward into the Ocean. Many and various were the enchanted islands that they found, including an island of mice as big as 'sea-cats', another where dwelt a monstrous sea-cat, and here also dwelt an ancient hermit who directed them to the island they were seeking. The Irish version breaks off with their reception there by a holy old man, clad only in white feathers like a dove, and a voice like an angel, from whom they received spiritual instruction. At this point the Irish *Life* breaks off, but the Latin versions tell of Brendan's return; of a subsequent voyage to Britain and of his visit to Gildas; of the many monasteries which he founded in Ireland, including the most famous of them all, Clonfert, and finally his death – believed to be in 577 – and his burial in Clonfert.

The emphasis in the *Vita* is perhaps rather on the saint's adventure (*echtrae*) than on his voyage (*immram*). He had set out on pilgrimage in response to a heavenly vision to seek a retreat in the Ocean, the spiritual goal of his vision; but he was not permitted to remain and returned to teach the way of salvation to the Irish. The account of his death in the arms of his sister Briga is beautifully described:

> On the Lord's day, after offering the Holy Sacrifice of the altar, St Brendan said to those about him:
> 'Commend to God in your prayers my departure from this life.'
> Whereupon his sister Briga said to him:
> 'Dear Father, what have you to fear?'
> 'I fear,' said he, 'as I pass away all alone and as the journey is darksome; I fear the unknown region, the presence of the King, the sentence of the Judge.'[1]

But the compiler of the *Martyrology of Oengus the Culdee* entertained no misgivings for Brendan. He enters his festival on 16 May with the words:

> The summons of Brendan of Cluain (i.e. Clonfert)
> Into the victorious eternal life.

An extensive literature related to that of the *echtrai* and the *immrama* is that of the Vision. The three together may be regarded as constituting

---

[1] The text is that of the *Codex Salmanticensis*, ed. W. Heist, *Vitae Sanctorum Hiberniae* (Brussels, 1965). See D. O'Donoghue, *Brendaniana*, p. 263; translation by O'Donoghue, loc. cit.

a kind of spiritual trilogy. The vision, like the *echtra* and the *immram*, had its precursor already in heathen literature, where it was known as a *baile* (cf. p. 137 above). In its Christian development it was known in Latin as a *visio*, in Irish by its derivative, *fís*, or more commonly *aislinge*; but the terms *baile* and *aislinge* are not always rigidly distinguished. The *aislinge* was a literary form widespread in the international literature of the Middle Ages, and is one of the commonest conventions in the Lives of saints. In the seventh century the Visions of St Columba form one of the three divisions into which Adamnán divides his Life of the saint (cf. p. 179 above). This literary genre is introduced incidentally with the vision of Drythelm related in Bede's *Ecclesiastical History* (V. 12). The culmination of this noble and dignified theme is Dante's *Divine Comedy*.

The Irish visions tell us much of what was read and studied in the early centuries of Christianity in the Irish world. The earliest account is that of Fursa.[1] The Irish version is preserved in a manuscript of the seventeenth century, but the text may be of thirteenth or fourteenth century date, and is a fairly close version of Bede's account (*H.E.*, III, 19). Two Latin versions of Fursa's *Life* exist, the first of which, the *Vita Prima*, which probably dates from the seventh century, is very close to Bede's own narrative and is probably derived from the 'little book' which Bede refers to three times as his own source.[2]

According to Bede's account Fursa was an Irish monk who desired to spend his life as a pilgrim for love of God, and accordingly crossed to Britain and settled in the territory of King Sigebert of East Anglia where he founded a monastery in Cnobheresburg, identified with Burgh Castle.[3] Apparently he had already, before leaving Ireland, had an illness in which, during a state of trance, he had seen a heavenly vision and received divine admonition to persist in the holy life.[4] In his Anglian monastery he fell sick, and one night in a trance his soul left his body and was granted a blessed vision of choirs of angels singing in Heaven. At cock-crow his soul returned to his body but three days later his soul again left his body, and was granted a vision of the blessed. Though evil spirits strenuously sought by their accusations to prevent his heavenly journey they were defeated by his angel guardians; but the contest is here represented as a spiritual one, unlike the fantastic horrors of the ordeals in Tundale's vision about to be considered. Moreover

[1] For particulars of manuscripts and editions see Kenney, *Sources*, p. 501 f.; Plummer, *Bede* II, 169 f.
[2] Kenney, *Sources*, p. 502. For a summary and brief account see Boswell, *I.P.D.*, 166 ff.
[3] See Plummer, *Bede* II, p. 440.
[4] The order of events in Bede's narrative is confused and Plummer appears to regard the first illness, trance and vision as taking place in Ireland in early life, the second as occurring in East Anglia (see *Bede*, II, p. 169 f.). It is to be suspected, however, that some form of duplication has taken place.

when Fursa reached a great height he saw the world below as a dark valley between great fires; but again the ordeal is a moral and spiritual one, and he was saved from the fire and the accusations of the devils by the angelic hosts. He then saw holy men of his own nation from whom he heard salutory things. Eventually his soul was returned to his body.

Bede goes on to inform us that Fursa subsequently made over the care of the monastery to others, and resolved to adopt the life of an anchorite; but finally under the threat of the heathen (i.e. Saxon) invasions he sailed to France, where he was well received at the court of the Frankish king Clovis, 'or by the patrician Erconwald', and, after founding a monastery near Paris, died and was interred at Péronne. The accounts of the life of Fursa are of exceptional interest in view of the validity of much of the historical milieu.

One of the earliest and best of the visions is composed in the vernacular, and is known as the *Fís Adamnán* ('The Vision of Adamnán').[1] The work will be discussed more fully below (p. 251 f.). Here it will be enough to mention that the work belongs to the literary genre which we are here discussing and purports to be a vision of the great abbot of Iona, but is probably a work of the tenth century as it stands. The theme of the narrative, like most of the Latin vision literature with which we are here more directly concerned, is a vision which appears to the saint in which his soul was parted from his body and made a journey, under the guidance of its guardian angel, to Heaven and to Hell.[2]

The *Vision of Tundale*[3] is a Latin work on a theme similar to that of the Irish *Fís Adamnán* and the Latin *Vision of Fursa*. The hero, however, is not an ecclesiastic but a sinner and a layman, a knight of Cashel, one who had been a formidable enemy of the Church until in a trance his soul suddenly left his body and was unable to make its return, being welcomed by a horde of tormenting demons. On Tundale's calling upon God now for the first time, his guardian angel banished the demons, and promised him mercy, but only after he should have first suffered trial. The scenes through which Tundale passes in succession, especially those of purgatory and Hell, are of the crudest material characteristic of the cosmopolitan teaching of the time, redeemed only by a genuine sympathy for the poor and respect for the Church, especially the ascetic devotees and saints whose 'countenance was like the sun at midday'. The charitable and devout dwell in the outer Heaven, surrounded by a

---

[1] Kenney, *Sources*, p. 444 f.; Irish text in Dottin, *Manuel d'Irlandais Moyen* (Paris, 1913), II, p. 101 ff.

[2] *Fís Adamnán* is translated by Boswell, *I.P.D.*, 28 f.

[3] See Kenney, *Sources*, p. 741 f. The Irish text is edited under the title *Aisling Tundail* (with a brief introduction by Kuno Meyer) in V.-H. Friedel and Kuno Meyer, *La Vision de Tondale* (Tnudgal) (Paris, 1907), p. 89 ff.; M. Dillon, *E.I.L.*, 132. The story is discussed and summarized by C. S. Boswell, *I.P.D.*, 212 ff.

wall of silver, the saints, the angels and God himself within the circuit of a wall of gold, and in a setting reminiscent of the 'Land of Promise'.

The author was a monk named Marcus, probably of the Irish monastery of Ratisbon in southern Germany. The allusions in the narrative suggest that the vision has its setting in 1148, and that it was written in 1149. The author was evidently a Munster man and an upholder of the reform of St Malachy, abbot of Bangor in Co. Down († 1148), who introduced the Cistercian Order into Ireland, and whom Tundale pictures in his vision of Heaven alongside St Patrick. With them are several bishops, four of whom Tundale had known in person. Indeed throughout the whole fantastic setting the author, like Dante, achieves some sense of actuality by relating Tundale's encounters in his vision with many well-known historical contemporaries.

The setting and the milieu are Irish and local, and the eschatology resembles that of the earlier Irish visionary literature; but there are also many traces of the apocryphal literature still circulating in Ireland in the twelfth century. The gentle humanity and the spirituality of the Irish vision literature in the native tradition, whether vernacular or Latin, has disappeared, and the crude symbolism of the medieval horrors of Hell and Purgatory have taken their place, redeemed only by the music and radiant light of the vision of Heaven. The images throughout are concrete, the experiences physical, and the Vision would seem to reflect eastern ecclesiastical art but without its dignity and its exaltation. The change in the spiritual climate from the Age of the Saints to the medieval Church is perhaps reflected in the fact that, with the exception of the *Navigatio Brendani*, the *Vision of Tundale* became the most widely popular of all stories of medieval Ireland, and was translated throughout Europe.

CHAPTER 9

THE CELTIC LANGUAGES AND
THE BEGINNINGS OF LITERATURE

(i)

IN discovering the Celts and tracing their early movements, we are guided by the names of settlements they founded, of men who led them, of the gods they honoured, that is to say, by features of language. The Celtic languages deserve a place in any discussion of the Celtic past, because they are one of the less known groups of the Indo-European family and in some respects one of the most interesting. Surviving in the historic period only on the north-western fringes of Europe, they show the archaic character that the study of linguistic geography has taught us to expect. In grammar and syntax, in the subordination of the word to the sentence as a unit, and even in some details of vocabulary, Old Irish resembles Sanskrit.

Something has been said already (p. 2 f.) about the documents in Gaulish that remain to us, place-names, personal names and inscriptions. These ancient sources tell us little about the grammar of Gaulish, but they do give us the characteristics of the Celtic sound-system as distinguished from that of Latin or Greek or Gothic or Sanskrit. We know from them that where Latin or Sanskrit has p, a Celtic language will have none; where Latin or Greek has $\bar{e}$, a Celtic language will have $\bar{\imath}$; where Latin or Greek has $\bar{o}$, Celtic will have $\bar{a}$. Thus *uer-* in Gaulish *Uercingetorix* is cognate with Latin *super*, Greek ὕπερ, and *-rix* is cognate with Latin *rex*; in the name *Eposognātus*, which means 'familiar with horses', the Gaulish equivalent of ἱππόδαμος, *-gnātus* is cognate with Latin *gnōtus*, Greek γνωτός.

The later forms of Celtic have a long history and are rich in literary sources, so that we can study their development for an unbroken period of more than twelve centuries. They fall into two groups, Brythonic and Goidelic, sometimes called P-Celtic and Q-Celtic because in Brythonic an original q^u- appears as p, whereas in Goidelic it remains as q in the earliest period and later becomes k (written 'c').[1] Familiar examples are the numeral 'four' (Latin *quattuor*) and the pronoun 'who' (Latin *quī*)[2] which appear in Welsh as *pedwar* and *pwy*, in Irish as *cethir* and *cia* respectively.[3]

---

[1] Gaulish here agrees with Brythonic, and is P-Celtic.
[2] In Latin this form serves as relative, in Welsh and Irish as interrogative.
[3] In the earlier Irish of the Ogam inscriptions, however, q is distinguished from c, as in MAQI, the genitive singular of the word for 'son', which occurs in most of the inscriptions.

OGAM

i
e
u
o
a
r
z
ng
g
m
q
c
t
d
h
n
s
f
l
b

The earliest Irish documents we have are inscriptions in a curious alphabet called *Ogam*, the key to which is given in a tract in the Book of Ballymote.[1] The older form of Ogam consists of fifteen consonants, in three groups of five, and five vowels, the consonants written as strokes to the right or left of a stem-line or diagonally across the line, the vowels as notches in the line; and the line is usually the corner, or arris, of a pillar-stone. The alphabet is based on the Latin alphabet, and each letter is named from a tree or a plant having it as initial. Thus B is called *beith* 'birch', C is *coll* 'hazel', D is *daur* 'oak', and so on. This nomenclature and the division into groups prompted the idea of an old connexion with the runic alphabet; but it seems more probable that Ogam was invented in Ireland when knowledge of writing first spread from Britain, but perhaps before Christianity was widely known. A curious fact is that the Middle Irish name for Q, *quert* agrees with Old English *cweorð*. The borrowing could be either way. The origin of Ogam is thus unknown, and the name itself is obscure. It can hardly be separated from Gaulish *Ogmios* (p. 135 f.), Irish *Ogma*, but the connexion is not clear. It was evidently a ceremonial script, for we find it only on memorial stones, and in the sagas it is associated either with funeral rites or with cryptic messages.[2]

Some of these inscriptions are perhaps pre-Christian, that is to say, as early as the fourth century. There is no means of dating them more exactly, but some are Christian, so that we have an approximate date; and they are in a form of language still close to Latin, and quite different from the earliest manuscript form in which the original final syllables have been lost or reduced. As this manuscript form goes back to the sixth century, a lapse of time prior to the sixth century must be allowed. There are about three hundred inscriptions known, most of them in west Munster, Érainn territory, and forty in Wales. A few have been found in Scotland and in the Isle of Man.

[1] Ed. Calder, *Auraicept na nÉces* 272 ff. There is an unpublished text of it in B.M. Additional 4783.

[2] For various opinions about the origin and name of Ogam, see MacNeill, PRIA xxvii (1909) C 329 ff.; Macalister, *The Secret Languages of Ireland* 20 ff.; Marstrander, NTS i 180 ff. (RC xlv 412); Thurneysen, *Beiträge zur Geschichte der deutschen Sprache u. Literatur*, lxi 188 ff.; Vendryes, *ÉC* iv 83 ff.; J. Kuryłowicz, BSL lvi 1 ff.; Richardson, *Hermathena* lxii (1943); O'Rahilly, EIHM 495; Jackson, LHEB 156; D. A. Binchy, *Studia Hibernica* 1, 8. O'Rahilly appears to think that Ogam was brought into Ireland from Gaul. Richardson stresses the importance of the special sign for *ng* (agma).

A notion of the form of the Irish language of this period is given by these three examples here presented in transcription: CUNAGUSOS MAQI MUCOI VIRAGNI '[The stone of] Cunagussus descendant of Viragnos', CIIC no. 70; DALAGNI MAQI DALI '[The stone of] Dalagnos son of Dalos' *ib*. no. 119; DUMELI MAQI GLASICONAS NIOTTA COBRANOR[IGAS] '[The stone of] Dumelos son of Glasicu sister's son of Cobranorix' *ib*. no. 252.

In normal Old Irish of the eighth century the last would be: *Dumil maicc Glaschon niad Cobarnríg*.

The Goidelic dialects are Irish, Scottish Gaelic and Manx. But the last two have a separate history only since the sixteenth century. The Brythonic dialects are Welsh, Cornish and Breton. Cornish and Breton can already be distinguished from Welsh in the very few documents that remain from early times (from the eighth to the eleventh century);[1] but it is only much later that Breton and Cornish are represented in texts of any extent, and for our immediate purpose Irish may be equated with Goidelic and Welsh with Brythonic. Moreover, the Welsh language, even in the earliest texts, presents a more advanced stage of development in both grammar and syntax than Old Irish, so that Old Irish is our earliest extant source for the characteristics of the Celtic languages.

In both Ireland and Wales, literature was in the hands of a professional class of poets who used a conventional form of language, and in the early period there is no evidence of dialect. In Ireland we have short poems in praise of famous men from as early as the sixth century, and one longer poem, the famous eulogy of St Columba, which is believed to have been written at the time of his death (AD 597).[2] The oldest passages of the law-tracts, composed in an archaic form of verse, are probably as old as the sixth century. Those ancient tracts are the earliest surviving evidence of any extent for any Celtic language, for the inscriptions consist almost entirely of proper names. They were probably preserved for centuries by oral tradition before they were first written, and they represent a very old inheritance of learning. The content of the law-tracts is in great part old Indo-European tradition, and the jurists who composed them were heirs to those learned men reported among the Celts of Gaul by Posidonius and Julius Caesar. A comparison with the Hindu *Mānavadharmaśāstra* suggests itself, and in fact there are notable points of resemblance (pp. 11 f., 95 f.).[3]

In Old Irish, as in Sanskrit, the verbs commonly form the various temporal and modal stems independently of each other, so that they cannot be arranged in 'conjugations', as they are in Latin. In this respect Irish has preserved the Indo-European system more faithfully

---

[1] A complete account of the sources is given by Jackson, LHEB 42 ff.　[2] See pp. 174–5
[3] See Binchy, 'The Linguistic and historical Value of the Irish Law Tracts' 23, 27, 30 (PBA xxix, 1943); R. Thurneysen and others, *Studies in Early Irish Law*, pp. vi, 183, 223.

than any other Western dialect. There are, however, two classes of 'weak' verbs, in -ā and -ī respectively, which correspond to the Latin first and fourth conjugations (*amāre, finīre*), and in the later language they gain ground, so that by the Modern Irish period (thirteenth century) the old 'strong' verbs have disappeared save for a few survivals which are classed as 'irregular'.

Another archaic feature of the verb is that when compounded with prepositions, it may have two, three or even four prepositions, of which the first is separable and may have a pronoun attached to it, as in Latin *ob vos sacro*. In the earliest period the first preverb, with or without a pronoun attached, may even stand at the head of the sentence with the verb at the end, as in Vedic; or the whole compound may be at the end without an infixed pronoun, the other normal Vedic type. Thus:

(a) Vedic: *prá tám mahyā raśanáyā nayanti*, 'they lead him with the great bridle'.

Irish: *ath márchathae fri crícha comnámat cuiretar*, 'great battalions are driven back towards the enemies' territories' (*ad-cuirethar*); *for-don itge Brigte bet*, 'May Brigit's prayers protect us!' (*for-bet*).

(b) Vedic: *mā no yajñād antargāta*, 'Do not exclude us from the sacrifice'.

Irish: *oen-chairde fón Eilg n-áragar*, 'one peace is established throughout Ireland' (*ad-regar*).[1]

In the classical Old Irish period (eighth and ninth centuries), the verb has become fixed in initial position, and this has been explained as a development from type (a), the main verb being attracted to initial position by the first preverb in compounds, and carrying the simple verb with it. In Early Welsh too the initial position of the verb is frequent, and in Modern Welsh it is the general rule. There is little doubt that originally the Welsh verbal system was like the Irish, and that initial position in Welsh is susceptible of the same explanation; but by the time that Welsh texts are plentiful, the language has reached the stage of Modern Irish, and the earlier system can be traced only in occasional forms that have survived.[2]

From an early time the professional poets were aware of language as something to be cultivated and preserved. In the monasteries this sentiment prompted the study of Priscian's grammar, and one of our principal collections of Old Irish glosses is from a manuscript of Priscian. In the lay-schools it led to the formation of a whole doctrine of grammar quite independent of the Latin tradition, such as is nowhere

---

[1] See Watkins, *Celtica* vi 32-37.

[2] See Henry Lewis, 'The Sentence in Welsh' pp. 11 f. (PBA xxviii, 1942) where the divergent word-order of Middle Welsh is discussed. Wagner contests the opinion that Irish is a lateral archaic dialect, and that the final position of the verb was normal in the earliest period; see TPS, 1970, 221 ff.; Pokorny Festschrift, 302 f.

else to be found in Europe. The earliest form of this native tradition is embodied in *Auraicept na nÉces*, 'The Scholars' Primer', which, while partly based on Donatus and Isidore, contains much that is purely Irish in origin.[1] But centuries later, perhaps in the fifteenth or sixteenth century, one or other of the bardic schools compiled grammatical tracts for the instruction of apprentice poets, which prescribed a literary standard for Modern Irish verse and prose.[2] These tracts are Modern Irish, and are beyond the limits that we have set ourselves, but they deserve mention for their originality and for the linguistic sense that directs the unknown authors. They have not yet received from linguists the attention they deserve.

Within the Indo-European family of languages, Celtic is most closely akin to Italic, and, as we might expect from the geographic position of the Celts when they first appear, there are details of grammar and vocabulary connecting Celtic and Germanic. These three indeed form a group of west European languages to the exclusion of Greek and Slavonic.

Features common to the three western languages are first a number of words that are peculiar to them, and second the merging of the perfect and aorist of the verb in a simple preterite tense.

Latin *uerus*, 'true' appears in German as *wâr*, Irish *fír*, Welsh *gwir*. Latin *caecus* 'blind' is Gothic *haihs* and Irish *caech*. There are names of trees and animals[3] and of tools,[4] besides a few more important words such as Irish *treb* (W. *tref*) 'home, dwelling' which appears as *-thorp* in English place-names and in Oscan (the dialect of the Samnites) as *tríibúm* 'a building', and a word for the 'community', preserved not in Latin but again in Oscan *touto* and in Irish *tuath* (W. *tud*) and Gothic Þ*iuda*. The Latin word for an inspired poet, *uates*, occurs in Irish as *fáith* (W. *gwawd* 'poem') and in Germanic as Gothic *wods* 'mad, possessed'.

In these three languages, too, the old difference between aorist and perfect disappeared early, and the preterite formations which emerged in each of them present a mixture of aorist and perfect forms. The perfect disappeared as a distinct tense later on in Greek and in Sanskrit, but the mixed preterite of the western languages is characteristic. And the same may be said of the loss of the optative as a distinct mood, which leaves only the subjunctive as a potential in opposition to the indicative.

[1] G. Calder, *Auraicept na nÉces* (rev. Thurneysen, ZCP xvii 277; xix 128).

[2] For the bardic schools, see O. Bergin, *Irish Bardic Poems*, Introd. Bergin edited the tracts in *Ériu*, viii–xiv. For the tracts see B. Ó Cuív, 'Linguistic Terminology in the Mediaeval Irish Bardic Tracts', TPS 1965 141 ff.

[3] Lat. *corulus* 'hazel', Ir. *coll*; Lat. *salix* 'willow' (OHG *salaha*), Ir. *sail*; Lat. *flos*, 'bloom', Ir. *bláth*; Lat. *piscis* 'fish', Ir. *iasc* are examples.

[4] *ueru* 'spit' (Goth. *qairu* 'post'), Ir. *bir*; *cribrum* 'sieve' (O.E. *hrídder*), Ir. *criathar*.

There are some words that Celtic shares only with Germanic, which point to a special relationship. Some of them can be shown to be loan-words from Celtic into Germanic, as having suffered a Celtic sound-change. For others there is a possibility that they belong to this group although no demonstration is possible. The rest are simply a common inheritance.

A clear example of borrowing is the word for 'kingdom'. We know that for Latin $\bar{e}$ and Celtic $\bar{\imath}$, Germanic regularly has $\bar{a}$. The Gothic word for kingdom is *reiki*, corresponding exactly to Old Irish *ríge*, and clearly a loan-word.

There are other words common to the two dialects that have legal or ritual values: Ir. *giall* 'hostage', OHG *gisal*; Ir. *rún* 'secret', Goth. *runa*; Ir. *dún* 'fort', 'enclosed dwelling', O.E. *tún*; Ir. *dligid* 'he owes', Goth. *dulgs* 'debt'; I-E *leiqᵘ-* in the sense 'to lend' (Germ. *leihen*, Ir. *airliciud*). And it has been suggested that these are also loans from Celtic and are evidence of a period of Celtic domination over German neighbours; but this opinion remains merely an opinion and seems incapable of proof. The Celts were in the early Iron Age doubtless culturally more advanced through contact with Mediterranean civilizations, and must have enjoyed a prestige sufficient to explain the borrowing; but these words may belong to the same category as the words for 'axe' (Ir. *biáil*, OHG *bīhal*), 'club' (Ir. *lorg*, O.N. *lurkr*); 'lead' (Ir. *luaide*, MHG *lot*); 'wood' (Ir. *fid*, OHG *witu*); 'herb' (Ir. *luib*, Goth. *lubja-*); 'trousers' (Gaul. *braca*,[1] OE *broc*); 'horse' (Ir. *marc*, OHG *marah*). They are words which occur only in Germanic and Celtic and which may belong to some northern European language of pre-Indo-European age.

The kinship between Celtic and Italic is much closer. Many features of sound and form and vocabulary bear witness to a close association of the Celts with the Italic tribes in prehistoric times, perhaps early in the second millennium BC. Both groups have preserved the three-vowel system, *e, o, a*, whereas *e > i* in Germanic. In both groups I-E *qᵘ* remains in one area and becomes *p* in another; and in both there is an assimilation of original *p* to a following *qᵘ*: Lat. *quinque*, Ir. *cóic* < **qᵘonqᵘe*; Osc. *pempe*, Welsh *pump*. Sanskrit *pañca* and Greek πέντε prove that **penqᵘe* was the original Indo-European form. So also to Lat. *coquo* 'I cook' (Gk. πέσσω) there corresponds Welsh *pobaf*. The long vowel in Latin *grānum*, Ir. *grán*; Lat. *nātus*, Gaul. *gnātos*; Lat. *plānus*, Ir. *lán* shows agreement in the treatment of *ī̥, n̥, l̥*.

But it is in the forms, the morphology of nouns and verbs, that the most impressive points of agreement are found. Just as Latin has a genitive singular of the second declension *domini*, so Gaulish has gen. *Segomari, Dannotali, Equi* (name of a month in the Coligny Calendar); and

---

[1] This word seems to be a borrowing from Germanic, for the English *-c* implies original *-g*.

in Irish the Ogam inscriptions still show MAQI. But Germanic, Greek, and Sanskrit have quite different endings for the genitive of *o*-stems.

For the superlative degree of adjectives Italic and Celtic present a suffix -*sṃmo*- which has borrowed the -*s*- of such comparatives as *plus*, *magis*, in contrast to *optimus, summus*, which have the older form. Thus to Latin *maximus, facillimus* (< **faklisṃmos*) correspond Irish *nessam* 'nearest', Welsh *nesaf* (Osc. n.pl.f. *nessimas*), and similarly Irish *messam* 'worst', Osc. a.pl.f. *messimas*.

One striking feature of the verbal system is the formation of the subjunctive stem. Here Irish is more archaic than Latin, which has developed regular 'conjugations'. In Irish there are two possible ways of forming the subjunctive, by adding *ā* to the root, or by adding -*s*-: *berid* 'he carries', subj. stem *berā*- (Lat. *ferat*); *rethid* 'runs', subj. stem *ress*- (< *ret-s*-), (cf. W. *gwares* 'that he may help'). While the *ā*-subjunctive appears in three of the four Latin conjugations, it is formed from the present stem, not from the root, and only a few isolated examples, e.g. *advenat* (*advenio*), *tagat* (*tango*), preserve the older system. The *s*-subjunctive appears in *dixo, dixim, aspexo, aspexim, faxo, faxim*, and similar forms. It is clear that Irish and Latin here share a common past.

The most interesting correspondence is the formation of passive and deponent in *r*. Umbrian *ferar* and Irish *berir* 'is carried', Latin *sequitur* and Irish *sechithir* 'follows', Latin *loquitur*, Irish -*tluchethar*, are impressive examples, although the deponent forms are not exactly equatable. These *r*-forms appear in Welsh and Breton too, and they appear at the opposite extreme of the Indo-European area, in Tokharian,[1] and also in Hittite. They are therefore a very old feature and their survival in Celtic and Italic is a strong link between the two groups.[2] Moreover, as the *r*-passive was a present tense, the preterite passive had to be managed otherwise, and in both groups the form is supplied by means of the participle in -*to*-: *actus* (*est*) in Latin, *ro acht* in Irish.

There is also a group of words that Celtic shares only with Italic, and which show no evidence of having been borrowed by either from the other: Ir. *fota* 'long', Lat. *uastus*; Ir. *moeth* 'soft', Lat. *mitis*; Ir. *bras* 'strong, vigorous', Lat. *grossus*. The word for 'earth, land'; Ir. *tír*, which is a neuter *s*-stem (< *tersros?*) is cognate with *tírim* 'dry', and both Oscan *teerum* and Latin *terra* are from the same root. There are also some words for parts of the body: Ir. *cúl* 'back of the head', Lat. *culus*; Ir. *druim* 'back', Lat. *dorsum*; Ir. *sál* 'heel', Lat. *talus*; Ir. *ucht* 'breast', Lat. *pectus*. And other examples are *culpa*, Ir. *col*; *saeculum*, Welsh *hoedl*; *scūtum*, Ir. *sciath*, W. *ysgwyd*, though in the last instance the Italic and Celtic forms

---

[1] The *ā*- subjunctive is also a feature of Tokharian.
[2] In terms of linguistic geography they appear as a common archaism. They are, however, historically a very early common innovation, as Pedersen has shown, *Groupement* pp. 14 ff.

have different vowel grades. The prepositions *cum* and *de*, Ir. *con-* and *di*, are found only in Italic and Celtic.

Venrdyes has observed too that both Italic and Celtic have lost the Indo-European words for 'son' and 'daughter', and while the innovations do not correspond,[1] the agreement of change points to some common change in the family system.

In recent years the tendency has been to deny that there was ever a period of Italo-Celtic unity, or to use the term Italo-Celtic simply as referring to common features of sound and form without implying anything more. Obviously the archaisms common to Irish and Sanskrit cannot mean close affinity, because the areas are at opposite extremes; but if two or three dialects in one continuous area show common survivals, a measure of affinity is implied. In this case the common innovations are impressive. In phonology there is the assimilation of *p* to a following *qᵘ* as in *quinque*; in morphology the genitive sg. m. in *-ī*, the superlative suffix of adjectives, the formation of the subjunctive, and of the preterite tense (shared with Germanic) and the preterite passive. In vocabulary only the new words for 'son' and 'daughter' are properly innovations, and they do not agree. The common words are presumably a shared inheritance from some neighbouring language. Added to all this, the survival of the passive and deponent in *-r* may fairly be allowed to count in the reckoning,[2] and we suggest that Pedersen was right when he insisted that a period of Italo-Celtic unity should be admitted, and that it should be dated much earlier, perhaps by a thousand years, than the Indo-Iranian period (*Groupement* 8; *Linguistic Science* 313, 318).

Some linguists will prefer to say merely that Italic and Celtic are closely akin. Those who hold that Oscan-Umbrian and British have their common features ($p < qᵘ$, $ī < ū$) by common inheritance rather than by chance, will think in terms of an original 'common' period. Linguistic geography has taught us to think always of groups of dialects in which isoglosses cross each other in great variety. Italo-Celtic, if the name is allowed, will have been a group of dialects spoken north of the Alps *c.* 2000 BC, having enough common features distinguishing them from Greek, on the one hand, and Germanic on the other, to mark them as one group. But it is a matter in which no certainty is attainable, and to some extent it is a matter of mere terminology. Watkins has recently argued strongly against the notion that there was ever a period of Italo-Celtic unity, while conceding that Italic and Celtic are closely akin.[3] Pedersen insisted that Italo-Celtic as one language was a fact of prehistory, and more recently Kuryłowicz discusses the 'Italo-Celtic'

[1] *filius*, Ir. *mac*, W. *mab*; *filia*, Ir. *ingen*, W. *merch*.
[2] For the importance of common survivals see J. Puhvel (ed.), *Ancient Indo-European Dialects* (Berkeley, 1966). [3] 'Italo-Celtic Re-visited' in J. Puhvel *op. cit.*

r-endings of the verb, and the 'Italo-Celtic' superlative adjective in -*is-amo-*.[1] Italic and Celtic are both archaic dialects of Indo-European, showing some common innovations and some interesting archaisms, geographically neighbours when their history begins. In our opinion the term Italo-Celtic is valid and corresponds to a reality, not that there was ever an Italo-Celtic nation, but that there was a group of dialects sufficiently akin to be so called.

If we suppose that the Celts emerge as a separate people about 2000 BC, Goidelic may be a very early form of Celtic, and Gaulish (with British) a later form;[2] and the first Celtic settlements of the British Isles may be dated to the early Bronze Age (*c.* 1800 BC), and even identified with the coming of the Beaker-Folk in the first half of the second millennium. This was suggested by Abercromby long ago (*Bronze Age Pottery* ii 99) and more recently by Crawford, Loth and Hubert. It would mean a lapse of time, more than a thousand years, between the first settlements and the Belgic invasions that Caesar mentions, quite long enough to explain the absence of any trace of Goidelic in Britain outside the areas of later Irish settlement. It would accord well with the archaic character of Irish tradition, and the survival in Ireland of Indo-European features of language and culture that recur only in India and Persia, and, for language, in Hittite or in the Tokharian dialects of Central Asia.

The discovery that fragments of manuscripts found in East Turkestan were in an Indo-European language was published by Sieg and Siegling in 1908. This was astonishing, but even more remarkable was the discovery that this Tokharian language was most closely akin to Celtic and Italic.[3] Then came the demonstration by Hrozny in 1915 that clay tablets in cuneiform script found at Boghazkoi in Asia Minor preserved the language of the Hittites, and that this language too is Indo-European. Again a special affinity with Celtic and Italic appeared. The connexion with Irish has since been shown to be of special interest.[4]

If the earliest Celtic settlements date from the Bronze Age, the question whether the invaders were Goidels or Brythons does not arise. Linguistic features that distinguish the Brythons may be much later, some of them innovations ($\bar{u} > \bar{\imath}$; $q^u > p$) which spread from a centre on the Continent and never reached the 'lateral' areas of Ireland and Spain. Rhys suggested this long ago.[5]

---

[1] *The Inflectional Categories of Indo-European* 64 ff., 238.

[2] But the distinction must not be exaggerated. The isogloss separating *p* and *q* is the main one, and this was no great obstacle, as the *Uoteporigis* inscription shows. For its relative unimportance, see E. Hamp, *Lochlann* i 211.

[3] H. Pedersen, *Tocharisch* pp. 2, 145, 152, 155.   [4] C. Watkins, *Celtica* vi 13 f.

[5] *EIHM* 436 n. 2. It could be true even if the change $q^u > p$ be of 'Italo-Celtic' date (p. 9 sup.), but Thurneysen pointed out that this may have happened in each language independently, ZCP xvi 287 n. 2.

(ii)

Whenever the Celts came, they brought with them ancient Indo-European institutions, and notably a tradition of bardic poetry which seems to correspond to the verse, lyric in form and heroic in content, celebrating famous men (κλέα ἀνδρῶν) which has been supposed for the Indo-European period.[1]

The learned class included priests, prophets and poets, if we adopt Caesar's classification, but there must have been jurists, historians and leeches as well. For by the time that Irish and Welsh documents become available, these three kinds of learning are prominent, and the pagan priests and prophets are only a memory. The traditional learning was handed down orally in law-tracts and genealogies, and the literature in poems and sagas which preserve very archaic literary forms.

In Wales the Four Ancient Books[2] contain a large collection of lyric verse on heroic themes, praise-poetry such as is described by Posidonius and Diodorus for the Gauls; but the earliest of these poems are perhaps not earlier than the ninth century. They deal mainly with the Men of the North, *Gwŷr y Gogledd*. Urbgen (Urien) of Rheged, Riderch (Rhydd-erch) of Strathclyde, Guallauc, and Morcant are four northern kings of the sixth century whose praises are sung, two of them in poems attributed to Taliesin who is supposed to have lived at that time.

The most moving of the early Welsh poems is the *Gododdin*; and it is also the most interesting in various ways. Indeed there is a problem of identity, for what is known as 'the *Gododdin*' appears to be a collection of short poems of uncertain date. It is preserved in the Book of Aneirin (thirteenth cent.) and has for its main theme a battle between Mynydd-awg, king of Manaw Gododdin, and the king of Deira. Gododdin was the territory between the Forth and the Tyne, west of Bernicia, and Catraeth is the Welsh form of Catterick in Yorkshire.[3] In the manuscript the title reads: *Hwn yw e Gododin. Aneirin ae cant.* 'This is the *Gododdin*. Aneirin composed it.' The poem is thus named from the tribe. It consists of one hundred and three stanzas (*awdlau*)[4] of varying length: the shortest has only three lines, the longest twenty-eight. The whole text makes more than 1200 lines, and a poem of this length would be unique of its kind; but the *Gododdin* seems to be a compilation of heroic poetry about the Men of the North. Sometimes several *awdlau* begin

---

[1] See Theodor Bergk, *Opusc. Phil.* ii 392–3, cited by Watkins, *Celtica* vi 199–200.
[2] Skene, *Four Ancient Books of Wales*, published the contents of the Black Book of Carmarthen, the Red Book of Hergest, the Book of Taliesin and the Book of Aneirin, now commonly known as the Four Ancient Books.
[3] See I. Ll Foster and G. E. Daniel, *Prehistoric and Early Wales* 234.
[4] The *awdl* is a stanza of verses bound together by end-rhyme, the verses having a varying number of syllables (see p. 210). When the end-rhyme changes, a new *awdl* begins.

each with the same words, as is so common in Welsh gnomic verse, and these must belong together. Sometimes the theme is praise of a single hero or of a group of heroes, who are not identified. One part of the text, about a fifth according to Sir Ifor Williams, shows traces of ninth century spelling, which point to an exemplar of that date. There may have been a ninth century nucleus around which the collection of poems has gathered. One is reminded of the Irish *Bórama*, in which the long struggle between Leinster and the North is related, with many incidental poems. But there is no convincing reason for any earlier date. Sir Ifor Williams, indeed, proposed that some of the *Gododdin* poems were composed in the sixth century, and some of the poems attributed to Taliesin as well. Apart from poems attributed to Taliesin and Aneirin, we have no Welsh texts of the sixth century, and we can only judge the state of the language at that time from the evidence of British names in Latin inscriptions. Jackson has examined this evidence in great detail, and has come to the conclusion that 'the Welsh language, in the form of Primitive Welsh, had come into existence not by the first but at any rate by the second half of the sixth century, and that the poems of Taliesin and Aneirin could have been composed in Welsh, not British, towards the end of that century' (*LHEB* p. 693). But his conclusion is partly based upon acceptance of the arguments of Morris Jones and Sir Ifor Williams (*ibid.* p. 651), and these arguments are incomplete.

An important study of the *Gododdin* has recently been made by Jackson.[1] Advancing from the position reached by Sir Ifor Williams in his *Canu Aneirin*, Jackson has successfully translated the greater part of the text and supplied a commentary on the whole text, with a close comparison of the two recensions. The metrical system is not exactly known. It is syllabic, not rhythmical, and the use of rhyme is established. A long line of nine or ten syllables is common, and a short line of five syllables also occurs. Alliteration is frequent but not required. We are faced with a very corrupt text and a tradition that has broken down. Jackson's conclusion is that both recensions derive from manuscripts that had centuries of oral tradition behind them. Language, metre, even the order of the stanzas, have suffered in transmission, and several passages are obviously interpolations. But Jackson defends the claim that the poem was composed by Aneirin *c.* 600 AD. This claim has since been re-examined by David Greene on linguistic grounds, phonology, morphology and syntax, and he rejects it. His conclusion is that there is no passage in the *Gododdin* or in the Taliesin poems where a ninth century date is excluded by the archaism of the language.[2]

---

[1] K. H. Jackson, *The Gododdin* (Edinburgh, 1969); rev. Mac Cana. *Celtica*, IX (1971) pp. 316 f.

[2] *Studia Celtica*, VI (1971) pp. 1 ff.

The more probable opinion is that the early songs of the *Gododdin* collection were composed in the ninth century on themes that were traditional, and attributed to Aneirin, just as so many poems were attributed to Taliesin that cannot, from the language, be as early as his time.

This early heroic poetry of Wales is court-poetry, lament for brave men fallen in battle, praise of famous princes, not the narrative of events. There is more warfare in the early Welsh poems than in the Irish, for the British were at war with the Anglo-Saxons already in the fifth century, whereas Ireland was free of foreign invasion until the Vikings came. And what remains to us, obscure and apparently often corrupt as it is, is nobler perhaps and better sustained than the earliest surviving fragments of Irish heroic verse. We find it hard to believe that it is not also later in date.

The *Gododdin*, which is believed to be the oldest of all, begins with a lament for a young warrior whose name is not even mentioned:

> A man in courage but a boy in years
> Brave in the din of battle
> Swift horses with long manes
> Under the graceful youth
> A light broad shield
> On the crupper of a swift horse.
> Clean blue swords,
> Fringes of fine gold.
> Before his wedding-feast
> His blood streamed to the ground.
> Before we could bury him
> He was food for ravens.

Several groups of stanzas (*awdlau*) begin with a formula: 'Men went to Catraeth'; 'He went down to battle'; 'Never hall was made'; 'It is a duty to sing'. For some stanzas two texts occur in the manuscript, and they vary so widely that one must suppose a long period of oral tradition. Sometimes three hundred are praised, of whom only one returned from the fight. More often the theme is praise of a single warrior, and it is not always clear that the battle of Catraeth is referred to.

Gwŷr a aeth Gatraeth oedd ffraeth eu llu; Glasfedd eu hancwyn, a gwenwyn fu.

Men went to Catraeth; they were ready for battle. Fresh mead was their feast, but it was poison.

Trichant trwy beiriant yn catau –	Three hundred by command in order of battle,
A gwedi elwch tawelwch fu.	And after the shouting there was silence.
Cyd elwynt i lannau i benydu,	Though they went to churches to do penance,
Dadl diau angau i eu treiddu.	True is the tale, death came to meet them.

.　　.　　.　　　　　　　　　.　　.　　.

Tri chan eurdorch a grysiasant	Three hundred wearing gold torques set out
Yn amwyn breithell, bu edrywant	To defend their land, sad was their fate.
Cyd ry lladded wy wy laddasant,	Though they were slain, they slew.
A hyd orffen byd edmyg fyddant.	They shall be honoured till the end of the world.
Ac o'r sawl a aethom o gydgarant	Of those of us kinsmen that set out,
Tru namyn un gwr nid enghysant.	Alas! only one returned.

In the manuscript as we have seen, the Gododdin poems are headed: *Hwn yw e Gododin. Aneirin ae cant* 'This is the *Gododdin*. Aneirin composed it.' The heading seems to cover the twelve hundred and fifty-seven lines that follow, for we then have a new title: *Eman a dechreu Gorchan Tutvwlch* 'Here begins the Song of Tudfwlch.' But the attribution to Aneirin is probably a fiction. T. Gwynn Jones said long ago: 'The Gododdin, as known to us, at least, is not a connected poem. It is rather a series of detached lays or stanzas' (*Cymmrodor* xxxii 4).[1]

Another famous poet of the seventh century was Taliesin. Morris Jones in his great study of the Book of Taliesin[2] stated the case for accepting some of the poems as genuine, and attempted translations of seven of them. Sir Ifor Williams came to the conclusion that twelve historical poems may fairly be attributed to Taliesin, and he edited them in his *Canu Taliesin*. Nine of them had already been accepted by Morris Jones, and the argument for admitting the language of the poems to be as early as the sixth century was stated by him with great care. But it is not convincing. He cites Rhys, who said that the language is 'not much older, if at all, than the manuscript on which it is written';[3] and the manuscript was written late in the thirteenth century. Scholars are now agreed that British had been transformed into Welsh by the end of the sixth century,[4] but it is hard to believe that the language of

---

[1] 'The Gododdin appears as a string of stanzas, evidently recovered from oral tradition, in which the sequence and relation of the parts had been lost', Morris Jones, *Cymmrodor* xxviii (1918), p. 7.

[2] *Cymmrodor* xxviii.　　　[3] Rhys, *Welsh Philology* pp. 138-9.　　　[4] Jackson, *LHEB* 693.

these poems is so old. The fragments of Old Welsh that survive are too meagre to provide a satisfactory criterion.[1]

The heroes celebrated in these poems are still heroes of the northern Britons. Urien, lord of Rheged, is the chief name, and Owein was his son. Rheged has been identified with the country around Carlisle. The poems are mostly in the *awdl* form, twenty-five to fifty lines in length, the basic line having nine syllables (*cyhydedd naw ban*); but lines of ten syllables, and a short line of five, six or seven syllables, also occur. Rhyme is required throughout. The 'Lament for Owein' is an *awdl* of heptasyllabic lines with the rhyme-scheme of Irish *rannaigecht*, final rhyme between the even lines and internal rhyme between the final of the odd lines and a word in the middle of the even (Irish *aicill*). It seems most unlikely that this fully developed system of rhymes should be as early as the sixth century.[2]

Here are two of the poems which Morris Jones and Sir Ifor Williams have claimed to be by Taliesin himself. Both of them have been translated by the two scholars,[3] and we rely upon them.

The Battle of Argoed Llwyfain

Bore duw Sadwrn cad fawr a fu	On Saturday morning there was a great battle
O'r pan ddwyre haul hyd pan gynnu.	From sunrise till sunset.
Dygryswys Fflamddwyn yn bedwar llu;	Fflamddwyn advanced with four companies;
Goddau a Rheged i ymddullu,	While the army of Goddau and Rheged was gathering.
Dyfyn o Argoed hyd Arfynydd.	Summoned from Argoed and as far as Arfynydd.
Ni cheffynt eirios hyd yr un dydd.	They shall not delay even for a day.
Atorelwis Fflamddwyn fawr drebystawd,	Fflamddwyn shouted with great boasting:
'A ddodynt yng ngwystlon? A ŷnt parawd?'	'Will they give me hostages? Are they ready?'
Ys atebwys Owain, dwyrain ffosawd,	Owein answered, the ravager of the east;
Nis dodynt, nid oeddynt, nid ŷnt parawd;	'They will not give them. They were not, they are not ready;

---

[1] The earliest manuscript evidence is the *Surexit Memorandum* in the book of St Chad, which probably dates from the eighth century, see *LHEB* 42 f. The earliest inscription in Welsh, as distinct from British, is the Cingen Stone, which was carved in the seventh century, see BBCS xi 92; *LHEB* 668.

[2] See Parry, *Oxford Book of Welsh Verse*, p. 538. Morris Jones analysed the metres of the poems he edited (*op. cit.*).

[3] *Cymmrodor*, xxviii 156; *Lectures on Early Welsh Poetry*, 63.

A chenau Coel byddai cymwyawg

Lew, cyn as talai o wystl nebawd.'
Atorelwis Urien, udd Erechwydd,
'O bydd ymgyfarfod am gerennydd,
Dyrchafwn eidoedd odd uch myn-
ydd,
Ac amborthwn wyneb odd uch ymyl,
A dyrchafwn beleidr odd uch pen
wŷr,
A chyrchwn Fflamddwyn yn ei luydd,

A lladdwn ac ef a'i gyweithydd.'
Rhag Argoed Llwyfain bu llawer
celain,
Rhuddai frain rhag rhyfelwyr,
A gwerin a gryswys gan hynefydd.

Armaaf flwyddyn nad wy cynnydd.

And a brave whelp of Coel's breed
would be sore afflicted
Before he gave a single hostage.'
Urien, lord of Yr Echwydd, shouted:
'If there be talk of peace,
Let us raise a rampart on the moun-
tain.
Let us raise our faces over the top.
Let us raise our spears over our heads,
men,
And charge Fflamddwyn in the midst
of his host
And slay him and his companions.'
By the Elm Wood there were many
corpses.
Ravens were blooded by the warriors
And men rushed forward with their
chief.
For a year I will sing a song to their
victory!

A Lament for Owein

Enaid Owain ab Urien
  Gobwyllid Rheen o'i raid.

Rheged udd ae cudd tromlas,

  Nid oedd fas i gywyddaid.
Isgell gŵr cerddglyd clodfawr,

  Esgyll gwawr gwaywawr llifaid,
Cany cheffir cystedlydd
  I udd Llwyfenydd llathraid.
Medel galon, gefeilad,
  Eisylud ei dad a'i daid.
Pan laddawdd Owain Fflamddwyn
  Nid oedd fwy nogyd cysgaid.
Cysgid Lloegr llydan nifer
  Â lleufer yn eu llygaid;
A rhai ni ffoynt haeach
  A oeddynt hyach no rhaid.
Owain a'u cosbes yn ddrud,
  Mal cnud yn dylud defaid.
Gŵr gwiw uch ei amliw seirch

  A roddai feirch i eirchiaid.

The soul of Owein ab Urien,
May the Lord have regard to his
need!
The Prince of Rheged who lies under
the heavy earth,
It was no shallow task to praise him!
The grave of a famous man renowned
in song,
His sharp spears like the rays of dawn,
For the equal will not be found
Of the glorious prince of Llwyfenydd.
Reaper of enemies, captor,
Like his father and grandfather.
When Owein slew Fflamddwyn,
It was no more than to fall asleep.
The wide host of Lloegr sleeps
With the light in their eyes.
And those that were loth to flee
Were bolder than was needed.
Owein punished them fiercely,
Like a pack of wolves chasing sheep.
A fine warrior in his many-coloured
harness,
Who gave horses to suppliants.

Cyd as cronnai mal caled,
    Rhy ranned rhag ei enaid.

Though he would gather like a miser,
It was given away for his soul's sake.

As for Llywarch Hen, none of the poetry formerly attributed to him is now believed to be his. It appears rather that there was a saga, or a cycle of sagas, about Llywarch Hen and his twenty-four sons, of which only the verse speeches have been preserved, and these may belong to the ninth century. This theory, put forward by Sir Ifor Williams, is all the more attractive because it brings Welsh literary tradition into accord with Irish. The characteristic form of Irish saga is a prose narrative with dialogue in verse, and it has been shown that this is also the ancient Indian form, and probably therefore the earliest Indo-European form.[1] Now it has been discovered in Wales. But the Welsh record corresponds to the *saṃvāda* or dialogue hymns of the Rigveda, the verse dialogue without its framework of prose; and we may suppose that the prose narrative was left to the oral tradition of the *cyfarwydd*. The verse, being bound by metrical rules, was, so to speak, canonical, and was written down when the monks began to record native, as opposed to Latin, documents.

Llywarch Hen was a chieftain of the northern Britons in the sixth century, and a cousin of Urien, prince of Rheged. His sons were all killed in battle during his lifetime, and legend presents him as a desolate old man, alone with his memories. The attribution of poems to him is on a par with the attribution of Fenian ballads to Oisín, son of Finn, except that Llywarch is an historical figure. The fragments of verse that survive, without the prose context, even where the text is clear, do not make a coherent whole. The most quotable are the *englynion* in lament of old age. As so often in early Welsh and Irish poetry, there are initial formulae which link the stanzas in groups.

Cyn bum cein faglawg, bum hy,

Before my back was bent, I was brave.

Am cynwysid yng nghyfrdy
Powys, paradwys Gymru.

I was welcomed in the drinking hall
Of Powys, the paradise of Wales.

Cyn bum cein faglawg, bum eirian;

Before my back was bent, I was comely.

Oedd cynwaew fy mhâr, oedd cyn-wan,
Wyf cefngrwm, wyf trwm, wyf truan.

My spear was the first, the foremost thrust.
My back is bowed. I am weighed down and sad.

---

[1] 'The Archaism of Irish Tradition', PBA xxxiii (1947), pp. 9-11.

Baglan brenn, neud cynhaeaf. — Little crutch of wood, it is Autumn.
Rhudd rhedyn; melyn calaf. — The bracken is brown, the stubble yellow.

Neur digereis a garaf. — I despised what now I love.

Baglan brenn, neud gaeaf hyn. — Little crutch of wood, it is Winter.
Yd fydd llafar gwŷr ar llynn. — Men talk much over their drink.
Neud diannerch fy erchwyn. — No one comes near my bedside.

Baglan brenn, neud gwaeannwyn. — Little crutch of wood, it is Spring-time.
Rhudd cogeu; goleu i gwyn. — Cuckoos are brown. There is light at a feast.
Wyf digarad gan forwyn. — No maiden loves me.

The lament goes on: what most he loved is now hateful, a woman, a stranger, a young horse; what most he hated is now come upon him, coughing, old age, sickness and sorrow. At the end of this rather dismal complaint, he even longs for death.

Another group of *englynion* formerly associated with the name of Llywarch Hen has been shown by Sir Ifor Williams to belong to the lost saga of Cynddylan, lord of Pengwern near Shrewsbury, who lived early in the seventh century, and died fighting against the English. In fact there is no mention of Llywarch in these poems. They are speeches put into the mouth of Heledd, sister of Cynddylan, who laments her brother's death. One passage is famous, and worth quoting. It begins with a lament for the hall of Cynddylan:

Stafell Cynddylan

Stafell Gynddylan ys tywyll heno, — The hall of Cynddylan is dark tonight,
Heb dân, heb wely; — Without fire, without bed.
Wylaf wers, tawaf wedy. — I shall weep a while and then be silent.

Stafell Gynddylan ys tywyll heno, — The hall of Cynddylan is dark tonight,
Heb dân, heb gannwyll; — Without fire, without candle.
Namyn Duw pwy a'm dyry pwyll? — Who but God keeps me sane?

Stafell Gynddylan, neud athwyd heb wedd, — Hall of Cynddylan, thou hast lost thy beauty.
Mae ym medd dy ysgwyd; — Thy shield is in the grave;
Hyd tra fu ni bu dollglwyd. — While he lived, there was here no hurdle in a gap.

213

Stafell Gynddylan ys tywyll heno,	The hall of Cynddylan is dark tonight,
Heb dân, heb gerddau;	Without fire, without musicians;
Dygystudd deurudd dagrau.	Tears furrow my cheeks.
Stafell Gynddylan, a'm gwân ei gweled	The hall of Cynddylan, it wounds me to see it,
Heb doed, heb dân;	Without roof, without fire;
Marw fy nglyw, byw fy hunan.	my lord is dead, and I live on.
Stafell Gynddylan, a'm erwan pob awr	The hall of Cynddylan grieves me always,
Gwedi mawr ymgyfrdan	after so many friendly meetings
A welais ar dy bentan.	that I saw around thy hearth.

Then Heledd describes the eagles as they scream over the bodies of the fallen:

Eryr Eli ban ei lef heno,	The eagle of Eli is screaming tonight.
Llewsai ef gwyar llyn,	He has feasted on blood,
Crau calon Cynddylan Wyn.	the heart's blood of Cynddylan the Fair.
Eryr Eli a glywaf heno,	The eagle of Eli, I hear him tonight.
Creulyd yw; nis beiddiaf.	Bloodstained is he. I dare not go near him.
Ef yng nghoed; trwm hoed arnaf.	He is in the forest. Heavy is my sorrow.
Eryr Pengwern pengarn llwyd, heno	The tufted grey eagle of Pengwern, tonight
Aruchel ei adlais,	His cry is loud,
Eiddig am gig a gerais.	greedy for the flesh of one I loved.
Eryr Pengwern pengarn llwyd, heno	The tufted grey eagle of Pengwern, tonight
Aruchel ei eban,	His clamour is loud,
Eiddig am gig Cynddylan.	greedy for the flesh of Cynddylan.
Eryr Pengwern pengarn llwyd, heno	The tufted grey eagle of Pengwern, tonight
Aruchel ei adaf,	His claw is raised,
Eiddig am gig a garaf.	greedy for the flesh of one I love.
Eryr Pengwern, pell galwawd heno,	The eagle of Pengwern will call afar tonight,
Ar waed gwŷr gwylawd;	He will feast(?) on the blood of men.
Rhy elwir Tren tref ddiffawd,	Tren shall be called an unlucky town.

Eryr Pengwern, pell gelwid heno	The eagle of Pengwern calls afar tonight
Ar waed gwŷr gwylid;	He feasts(?) on the blood of men.
Rhy elwir Tren tref lethrid.	Tren will be called a famous town.

There is another remarkable poem which introduces the fashion of prophecy so much practised in the later verse, *Armes Prydein* 'The Presage of Britain'. It was composed in the first half of the tenth century, and is a summons to the Britons to rise up and drive the Saxons from their country. Cynan and Cadwaladr, the last sovereign prince of Britain, who died in 682, will arise again to lead the victorious army, and the foreigners will be driven headlong into the sea, where they will wander with no place to land. The Men of Dublin and the Gaels of Ireland, together with Cornwall and Strathclyde, will join the Britons under the banner of Saint David in driving out the invader.

The poem is preserved in the Book of Taliesin (thirteenth century), and contains nine *awdlau*, 199 lines in all. It is the oldest and perhaps the best of the prophetic poems. Sir Ifor Williams, in the preface to his edition, argued successfully that *Armes Prydein* must be earlier than the Norman Invasion, since the enemy is still the Saxon, and earlier than the Battle of Brunanburh (937) in which Athelstan extinguished the hope here expressed by the poet. On the other hand, the Men of Dublin are mentioned as a separate kingdom, which he thinks unlikely before the second half of the ninth century. Athelstan must be the English king referred to, and he came to the throne in 925. A date *c.* 930 seems probable, perhaps after the humiliation of the council at Hereford, when Athelstan compelled the Welsh princes to submit, and to promise a yearly tribute, for the tribute is mentioned several times.[1]

Here is a passage to illustrate the form and content of the poem. The metre is syllabic, a line of nine syllables (sometimes ten) with end-rhyme throughout the *awdl*. Alliteration and internal rhyme are freely used, but end-rhyme is the only required ornament.

Ll. 127–146:

Dygorfu Cymry i beri cad,	The Cymry have been forced to battle
a llwyth lliaws gwlad a gynnullant,	and they will muster the kingdom's host
A lluman glan Dewi a ddrychafant	and raise aloft the gleaming banner of David
i dywyssaw Gwyddyl trwy lieingant.	to lead the Irish under its linen border,
A gynhon Dulyn genhyn y safant.	and the heathens of Dublin will stand beside us.

[1] See also *Lectures on Early Welsh Poetry* 53 f.

Pan ddyffont i'r gad nid ymwadant.	When they come to the battle they will not fail:
Gofynnant i'r Saeson py geisysant,	they will ask the Saxons what they wanted,
pwy meint eu dylyed o'r wlad a ddaliant,	what right they have to the land they hold,
cw mae eu herwi pan seiliasant,	where are the lands from which they set out,
cw mae eu cenedloedd, py fro pan ddoethant.	where are their kinsfolk, from what country are they come.
Yr amser Gwrtheyrn genhyn y sathrant.	Since the time of Gwrtheyrn they trample among us!
Ni cheffir o wir rantir an carant.	Not rightly is the patrimony of our kinsmen thus held.
Neu freint an seint pyr y sanghysant?	Why have they trod upon the sanctuaries of our saints?
Neu reitheu Dewi pyr y torrasant?	Why have they broken the laws of David?
Ymgedwynt Gymry pan ymwelant	The Cymry will take care when they meet
nid ahont allmyn o'r nen y safant,	that the foreigners shall not go from where they stand
hyd pan talhont seithweith gwerth digonsant	till they pay sevenfold for what they have done,
ac angau dihau yng ngwerth eu cam.	even to the doom of death for their crime.
Ef talhawr o anawr Garmawn garant	By the strength of the kinsmen of Garmon
y pedair blynedd a'r pedwar cant!	they shall pay for the four and four hundred years!

The tradition of the return of Cadwaladr to deliver the Cymry from their oppressors recurs in Geoffrey of Monmouth's *Historia Regum Britanniae*, and is a commonplace of the prophetic poems. Here it is foretold:

Yng nghoet ym maes [ym mro] ym mryn, cannwyll yn nhywyll a gerdd genhyn Cynan yn rhagwan ym mhob discyn. Saeson rhag Brython gwae a genyn. Cadwaladyr yn baladyr gan ei unbyn, trwy synnwyr yn llwyr yn eu dichlyn.	In wood and plain and hill and dale, like a torch in the darkness, Cynan will march with us in the van of every battle. The English will cry woe as they flee before the Britons. Cadwaladr with his chieftains will be a pillar of strength, hunting them down with cunning and persistence.
Pan syrthwynt eu clas dros eu herchwyn,	When their troops fall upon their beds, those foreigners will be in pain,

yng nghustudd a chrau rhudd ar rudd allmyn.
Yng ngorffen pob angraith anrhaith dengyn.
Seis ar hynt hyt Gaer Wynt kynt pwy kynt techyn.
Gwyn eu byd wy Gymry pan adroddynt
ry'n gwarawd y Drindawt o'n trallawd gynt.

with red blood on their cheeks.
    After each challenge, there will be great plunder. The English will flee headlong to Winchester as fast as they can.
    The Britons will rejoice when they announce that the Trinity has delivered us from our woe.

We have heard nothing of Arthurian tradition in the poems that have been mentioned, and in fact the King Arthur of Romance literature is a much more famous person than his Welsh original. There are a few early poems in which Arthur is mentioned, and two of them give him prominence.[1] One is a dialogue between him and his gatekeeper, in which Arthur names his companions and recounts their exploits. It is no. xxxi in the Black Book of Carmarthen, and breaks off unfinished. There are many references to episodes which must have been told in a heroic literature that is lost, and we are made to realize that what survives is merely the shadow of a vanished tradition. The other poem is *Preideu Annwfn* or 'The Spoils of Annwfn', no. xxx in the Book of Taliesin, which is an account of a journey to the Otherworld in quest of the magic cauldron. The poem is obscure and tells us very little about Arthur except that he led the expedition. Of three shiploads that set out, only seven men returned.

This early Welsh poetry is not widely known, on account of the difficulty of the language. It is of great interest, partly for this very reason, and also for the fragments of ancient tradition that it preserves.

The earliest Irish poetry that has been preserved dates from the sixth century. It is alliterative syllabic verse, lyric in form and heroic in content, in praise of famous men, or in lament for the death of a hero. The old prosody was syllabic and unrhymed. It was based upon a long line of seven syllables with trisyllabic cadence and caesura after the fourth, and a short line of five syllables. With a permitted extra syllable in initial position, and the possibility of acephaly and catalexis, there were lines of as many as eight syllables and as few as three. In the earliest period both quatrains and stanzas of irregular length occur, but later the quatrain is the normal form. Eighty-four metres are analysed in Murphy's *Early Irish Metrics*, and eighty of them are quatrains.

---

[1] See K. H. Jackson, *ALMA* 12–19. Loomis has stated the case for assuming a lost Arthurian cycle in Britain before Geoffrey of Monmouth, see 'The Arthurian Legend before 1139' in *Wales and the Arthurian Legend*, Cardiff, 1956. See also T. Jones, 'The Early Evolution of the Legend of Arthur', Nottingham Mediaeval Studies VIII (1964).

It has recently been shown successfully by Professor Calvert Watkins that this Irish heroic verse has a common origin with Greek and Vedic metres, and is an ancient Indo-European inheritance.[1] By the sixth century the use of end-rhyme appears. Later the number of syllables becomes more regular in each metre, and internal rhymes are introduced, so that the whole system is transformed. But the old heroic metre, based on a seven-syllable line with trisyllabic ending and no rhyme, survives as an epic form in the sagas into the early Modern Irish period.[2]

We have poems in praise of several kings of Leinster, Labraid Loingsech, Catháir Már, Énna Cennselach, and of other kings and warriors, legendary or historical, and the famous Eulogy of Saint Columba, in this ancient verse-form. In both form and content they answer well to the description of bardic poetry by Posidonius and Diodorus in their accounts of the Gaulish bards.

Luccreth mocu Iair (Chiara), Find Fili, Ferchertne Fili, Lugair Lánfili, Laidcenn mac Bairchedo, Torna Éces, Senchán Torpeist, and Dallán Forgaill are among the early poets whose names have come down to us. Colmán mac Léneéni, founder of the abbey of Cloyne, who died in 604, is another, and of his poetry several fragments survive. Only stray quatrains survive, as a rule, but the Eulogy of Saint Columba, attributed to Dallán, is a poem of some 150 lines; and four poems of the class called *fursundud* ('illumination') have 22, 54, 52, and 35 quatrains respectively. These latter are little more than lists of names, arranged in verse to aid the memory, and are hardly poetry. They are attributed to Luccreth mocu Chiara, Find Fili, and Laidcenn. Only the attribution of the *Amra* to Dallán Forgaill can be regarded as genuine; and the *Amra* is interesting more for its style and language than for its poetic quality.

Labraid Loingsech, a legendary king of Leinster, supposed to have reigned in the fourth century BC, is the hero of a saga, *The Destruction of Dinn Ríg*, which is the Origin-Tale of the Leinstermen (p. 241). Labraid seems to have been greatly cherished by the poets, for we have several fragments in praise of him:[3]

Lug of the shield, bright phantom,[4] there was none under Heaven so terrible as the son of Áine. A man higher than the gods, firm acorn, clean tree of many branches, grandson of Loegaire Lorc.

Here is another, attributed to Ferchertne Fili:

Dinn Ríg, strong Tuaim Tenbai – thirty nobles died there in anguish.

[1] 'Indo-European Metrics and Archaic Irish Verse', *Celtica* vi 194 ff.
[2] See G. Murphy, *Early Irish Metrics*, p. 19.
[3] The heroic verse which follows was edited and translated by Kuno Meyer in *ÄID* and *Bruchst.*   [4] See N. K. Chadwick, SGS iv 1.

Labraid, the fierce champion, crushed and burned them, the warrior of Ireland, grandson of Loegaire Lorc.

There are many more of these rhetorical praise-poems, or fragments of poems, which bring us back to the heroic age. Here is one dedicated to Mes Delmann, a legendary king of the Domnainn of Leinster, supposed to have lived in the first century:

Mál ad-rualaid iathu *m*arb	A prince has gone to the lands of the dead,
*m*ac *s*oer *S*étnai;	the noble son of Sétne;
*s*elaig *s*rathu Fomoire	he laid waste the valleys of the Fomoire,
for *d*oíne *d*omnaib.	overcoming worlds of men.
*D*i óchtur *A*linne	From the summit of Ailenn
oirt *t*riunu *t*alman;	he slew the strong ones of the earth,
*t*rebann *t*rén *t*uath *m*ár	strong tribune of great tribes,
*M*ess *D*elmann *D*omnann.	Mes Delmann of the Domnainn.

There is a problem with regard to these poems. It is agreed that they are not earlier than the seventh century, though some of them are attributed to poets supposed to be contemporaries of the kings whose praise is sung. Why should court-poets write in praise of kings of so remote a past? Was the ancestor-cult so strong, or these ancestors so famous, that the poets found them worthy subjects of repeated praise? Labraid Loingsech of Leinster does seem to have enjoyed great fame, as did Conn of the Hundred Battles and his brother Cathaír Már and his grandson Cormac mac Airt; and Niall of the Nine Hostages in the north and Conall Corc in the south. Maybe the few stories that survive about these early kings are mere fragments of a lost literature. But there is another possibility: these may be ritual praise-poems, composed for recitation at the inauguration of the king, like the Vedic *nārāśaṃsī* which was recited at the king's consecration in India.[1]

Here are two quatrains which have both rhyme and alliteration, with a varying number of syllables in the line. The style and temper are the same as before:

The Four Sons of Cú Chorbb, king of Leinster

Nia *C*orbb, *C*orbmacc, *C*airpre,	Nia Corbb, Corbmac, Cairpre,
caine *a*irt, *a*ra, oirt *a*irgtib,	a splendid warrior, charioteer who slew by hundreds,
ocus Messin *C*orbb, *c*oim eirr	and Messin Corbb, a handsome fighter
ara*ch*liched *c*airptib.	who fought from chariots.

[1] See P. Horsch, *Die vedische Gātha and Slokaliteratur* (Bern, 1968), p. 251.

Cethir *bráithir buirr bresta*,
  *f*ian, *f*orraigtis *f*orlond:

fri maccu ní gaibed
  Con Corbb *comlond*.

Four mighty warlike brothers,
a band who used to overcome a greater number;
no equal number could withstand the sons of Cú Chorbb.

And the following examples have rhyme, with a fixed number of syllables in the line:

Labraid Loingsech

Labraid luam na *lergge*,
  *f*aglaid fri *f*uam *f*airgge,
glass gluairgrinn fri *gente*,

  blass buainbinn na *bairddne*.

Labraid, pilot of the battlefield,
plunderer where the sea roars,
bright strong bolt against the heathens,
ever a sweet taste for bardic song.

Bran Berba (†795)

Bran *d*ond, *d*ín *s*luaig, *s*éol *ngairgge*,

*g*arg *r*ind, *r*echt *r*án, *r*uad n-*orbbai*,

*o*rb gaeth, grian laech, *l*án *f*airgge,

*f*ael *cr*ú, *c*ú *ch*uan nad *chorbbai*.

Bran the Brown, protection of the host, a fierce raider;
harsh spear, glorious one, strong by heredity;
heir to wisdom, sun of warriors, full tide;
a bloody wolf, dog of the pack, who does no wrong.

Fedlimid mac Crimthainn (†847)

Is hé Feidilmith in r*í*
  diarbo *o*pair *o*enlaith*i*

*a*ithrígad *C*onnacht cen *chath*
  ocus *M*ide do *m*annra*d*.

Fedlimid the king
for whom it was the work of a single day
to leave Connacht kingless without a battle, and to lay Meath in ruins.

Poetry of this kind has an appeal only by its heroic temper and for the ancient tradition it preserves. This was probably the earliest kind of poetry in the Indo-European tradition, mere sequences of terms of praise cast in lyric form. We do not know whether the quatrains that survive are mere fragments of longer poems. It is quite probable. If they are ritual poems as suggested above, they may have been quite short, as are the examples of *nārāśaṃsī* that have survived. The later bardic poems of the classical period are rarely less than twenty quatrains, and often more than twice as long. But these early verses preserve a tradition more ancient than anything that Greek or Latin literature has to show, and are comparable to the poetry in some of the Gupta inscriptions of India. Such poetry was still being composed in the eleventh century, with richer ornament of internal rhyme, for we have two fragments in praise of Mael Sechlainn, king of Ireland, who died in 1022.

Mael Sechlainn

A Maíl Sh*echlainn,*
nít *mess methchrainn*
airgfea R*echrainn*
  rebthruinn ruaid;
a *ch*liath *chorrga*
thromda thogda
d*orrga thogla*
  *T*emra *tuaid.*
	Mael Sechlainn, you are no fruit of a dead tree, you shall plunder Rechru, that sportive stalwart island.
	
	Phalanx of sharp spears, heavy and choice, angry javelin, destroyer from Tara in the north.

Mael Sechlaind mac *D*omnaill *dath-gil,* d*orn* i *Tailtin tulgatánaig;* daig ná daim *crannch*ur mo *ch*ara *anfad mara murbratánaig.*	Mael Sechlainn, son of fair Domnall, a strong hand over Tailtiu of the wattled breast-work. My friend is a fire-brand that will not suffer the casting of lots, a storm over the salmon-rich sea.

There was a tradition of satire in the early verse also, and here are some examples:

Ro cuala ní tabair eocha ar duana: dobeir aní as dúthaig dó bó.	I have heard that he gives no horses in reward for poems: he gives according to his nature – a cow!
Ní fuilet a maíne, nocho mó atá a maisse: nocho mór a gére, nocho déne acht braisse.	He has no wealth, nor has he beauty: his wit is feeble, prating is all he is good for.

Besides praise and satire, there are fragments of lament. A queen laments her dead husband, Aed mac Ainmirech († 598):

Batar inmuine in trí toíb frisná fresciu aithirrech, toibán Temro, toíb Taillten, toíb Aeda maicc Ainmirech.	Beloved were the three sides that I shall never see again, the dear side of Tara, the side of Tailtiu, and the side of Aed son of Ainmire.

By the eighth century the old metrical system inherited from prehistoric times had given place to this new form based upon rhyme, with the quatrain as the normal measure. The new ornament of rhyme was quickly elaborated, while the old ornament of alliteration was retained and improved. Rhyme appears first in Latin hymns of the third and fourth centuries. Commodian was probably the first to use it.[1] Augustine has it in his *Psalm against the Donatists*. 'But Sedulius, in the fifth century, is the first hymn-writer to make any considerable use of rhyme', says Raby.[2] The use of rhyme was taught by Virgilius Maro Grammaticus, whose work was well known in Ireland, and some of the earliest Irish Latin hymns are rhymed. The *Altus Prosator* of Saint Columba († 597) is in rhymed couplets, and Saint Columbanus († 615) uses disyllabic and even trisyllabic rhyme in his *Carmen de Mundi Transitu*. The Irish monks seized upon rhyme and made it a regular ornament of poetry long before it became customary elsewhere.

Murphy[3] points out an elaboration of rhyme such as never appears in continental hymns, in the Irish hymn to Saint Martin by Oengus mac Tipraiti († 745):

> Martinus mirus *more*
> *ore* laudavit Deum:
> pure corde *cantavit*
> atque *laudavit* eum.

Here beside end-rhyme between the even lines there is internal rhyme between the finals of the odd lines and a word in each following line. And the native Irish ornament of alliteration is also used with effect. This combination of end-rhyme, internal rhyme and alliteration, of which we have just seen early examples, constitutes the 'new form' (*nua-chruth*), recognized by the Irish metrical tracts. It was doubtless the invention of monks who were heirs to the old metrical tradition, and acquired the new ornament of rhyme with their Latin learning; and it is the basis of the Irish system of *Dán Dírech* and of the Welsh system of *Cynghanedd*. The Irish genius for poetry was later to develop this new craft in the use of consonance, assonance and alliteration with wonderful success.

In addition to the new form, however, the monks brought a new voice into poetry, and from the eighth century onwards we have lyric poems in which love of Nature, love of solitude and love of holiness, love of God, are the source of inspiration. The old theme, praise of famous men, is still cultivated by the professional poets. That was their duty and their means of livelihood. But the finest poetry of the succeeding ages, until the breakdown of the old Columban monasticism with the Cistercian reform in the twelfth century, was written in the monasteries by the *nua-litridi* ('new writers'), as they were called.

The new metres specially honoured as of equal status with the old were *dian* and *sétnad*. For these a price was allowed by the jurists, as for

[1] Rhyme occurs in metrical inscriptions, pagan and Christian, found in the Roman province of Africa, Raby, *Christian Latin Poetry*, p. 14.
[2] *ibid.* p. 25.   [3] Murphy, *Early Irish Metrics*, pp. 16–17.

the old metres;[1] and these two are based upon lines of seven or eight syllables. The Ambrosian hymns and hymns of Prudentius and Venantius Fortunatus, iambic or trochaic tetrameters, had the same syllabic count, and it is probable that the monks claimed special recognition for metres with such precious associations. But it is too much to say that the new metres derive from Latin models, as Murphy has done, following Thurneysen.[2] Watkins has shown that the seven syllable line was the basic long line of a native tradition of poetry going back to Indo-European times.[3]

Two famous hymns may be cited to illustrate the Ambrosian metre. The first is by St Ambrose himself:

> Splendor paternae gloriae,
> de luce lucem proferens,
> lux lucis et fons luminis,
> diem dies inluminans.

The second is still sung at the Office of Compline:

> Te lucis ante terminum
> rerum creator poscimus
> ut solita clementia
> sis praesul ad custodiam.

And here are verses from the *Vexilla Regis* by Venantius Fortunatus, in which rhyme is frequent:

> Confixa clavis viscera
> tendens manus, vestigia
> redemptionis gratia
> hic immolata est hostia ...

> Salve ara, salve victima,
> de passionis gloria,
> qua vita mortem pertulit
> et morte vitam reddidit.

These were some of the models which gave prestige to the Irish quatrain based on lines of seven or eight syllables. It was the rhymed form of these metres which actually gave a new form to Irish poetry.

In the monasteries, then, a new lyric poetry was born in which the theme is lyric as well as the form. 'These poems', says Kuno Meyer, 'occupy a unique position in the literature of the world. To seek out and watch and love Nature, in its tiniest phenomena as in its grandest, was given to no people so early and so fully as to the Celt.'[4]

---

[1] Murphy, *ibid.* p. 12.   [2] *ibid.* pp. 12, 25.   [3] *Celtica* vi, 218 ff.
[4] *Ancient Irish Poetry*, p. xii.

Here are two quatrains which appear on the margin of a ninth century manuscript of Priscian, preserved at Saint Gall in Switzerland. Alliteration and rhyme are indicated as before by *italics*:[1]

Dom-farcai *f*idbaide *f*ál
fom-chain *l*oíd *l*uin, *l*uad nad c*él.*
Huas mo *l*ebrán, ind *l*ínech
fomchain tr*írech* inna n-*én.*

A hedge of trees surrounds me, a blackbird's lay makes music for me – I shall tell it. Above my lined book the trilling of the birds makes music.

Fom-*ch*ain *c*oí *m*enn *m*edair *mass*
hi mbrott g*las* de *d*indgnaib *doss*
Dé bráth – nom *ch*oimmdiu *coíma*! – caín-scríbaimm fo *roída ross.*

The clear-voiced cuckoo sings me a lovely chant, in her grey cloak from bush to bush. God's Doom, may the Lord protect me! – happily I write under the greenwood.

Another stray quatrain is in the same mood, and here the rhymes are richer still:

Och, a luin is b*uide* duit.
Cáit sa m*uine* i fuil do n*et?*
A d*íthrebaig* nad *clind cloc,*
is *bind boc síthemail* t'*fet.*

Ah, blackbird, you are glad! Where is your nest in the thicket? Hermit that clinks no bell, sweet, soft, peaceful is your note.

The nimble bee:

Daith *b*ech *buide* a *h*uaim i n-*uaim*

ní s*uail* a *uide* la gr*éin:*
*f*ó for *f*uluth sa *mag már*
*d*ag a *d*agchomal 'na ch*éir.*

Nimble is the yellow bee from cup to cup,
he makes a great journey in the sun, boldly flitting into the great plain, then safely joins his brethren in the hive.

A rainstorm at night:

Uar ind adaig i *M*oín *M*óir
feraid *d*ertain, ní d*eróil:*
dorddán fris-tib in *g*aeth *g*lan
*g*éissid ós *ch*aille *cl*ith*ar.*

Cold is the night in Moín Mór. The rain pours down in flood: a deep roar, against which the wind laughs high, sounds over the sheltering wood.

Here there is no internal rhyme, but there is alliteration in each line. The end-rhymes are unrhythmical, and this fashion became most popular in later Irish and Welsh poetry. Watkins has shown that it may have begun in Irish when rhyme was introduced into the old metres, where the final syllable was anceps.[2]

---

[1] This is not all, for there is also a delicate correspondence called *uaithne* 'consonance', between the final of the first line and the rhyming finals of second and fourth: the vowel corresponds in quantity, and the final consonant in class and quality.
[2] *Celtica*, vi, 225.

Another example in the same metre and in the same mood may be given here. It cannot be earlier than the ninth century, for the warriors from Norway are mentioned:

Is acher in ga*í*th inn*ocht*,
fu-*f*uasna *f*airgge *f*ind-*f*olt:
n*í* *á*gor r*é*imm *m*ora *mind*
dond *l*aechraid *l*ainn *ó* L*o*thl*ainn*.[1]

This sudden awareness of nature comes as a delightful shock, and it is surely to be credited to the monks, who learned to love all created things as God's gifts to Man, and to seek happiness in the hermit's life. Robin Flower has explained the emergence of this personal poetry in Ireland as a result of the Culdee movement of the eighth century which flourished specially at Tallaght and Finglas, and gave a new impulse to religion and to literature. 'It was not only that these scribes and anchorites lived by the destiny of their dedication in an atmosphere of wood and sea; it was because they brought into that environment an eye washed miraculously clear by a continual spiritual exercise that they, first in Europe, had that strange vision of natural things in an almost unnatural purity.'[2]

Often, indeed, the note of holiness is clearly heard, and we are sure that the poet is a monk who is seeing Nature as a reflection of the divine beauty:

Dúthracar, a Maic Dé bí,
    a Rí suthain sen,
bothnat deirrit díthraba
    commad sí mo threb.

I wish, O Son of the living God, eternal ancient King, for a secret hut in the wilderness, that it might be my dwelling.

Uisce treglas tanaide
    do buith ina taíb,
linn glan do nigi pectha
    tría rath Spirta Naíb.

Shallow green water around it, a clear pool to wash away sins by the grace of the Holy Ghost.

Fidbaid álainn immocus
    impe do cech leith,
fri altram n-én n-ilgothach,
    fri clithar dia cleith.

A lovely wood nearby, around it on every side, to nurse the singing birds, for shelter to hide it.

Deisebar fri tesugud,
    sruthán dar a lainn,
talam togu co méit raith
    bad maith do cach clainn.

A southern aspect for warmth, a stream across its glebe, choice, prosperous land which would be good for every plant.

•   •   •   •   •   •

[1] Translated on p. 127.   [2] *The Irish Tradition* p. 42.

Eclais aíbinn anartach,
  aitreb Dé do nim,
sutrulla soillsi iar sain
  úas Scriptúir glain gil.

A pleasant church, with linen cloth, a dwelling for God from heaven, and shining candles above the pure white Scripture.

.   .   .

Mo lórtu bruit ocus bíd
  ónd Ríg as chaín clú,
mo bithse im śuidiu fri ré,
  guide Dé in nach dú.

Enough of food and clothing from the King of fair fame, and to be sitting for a while, praying to God in any place.[1]

Can it be that the first impulse came from the canticle *Benedicite opera Domini Dominum* which was sung as part of the Office of Lauds in Ireland and so appears in the Antiphonary of Bangor?[2]

One of the best of these longer poems is put into the mouth of Marbán the hermit, a brother of Guaire, king of Connacht. Guaire reigned in the seventh century, but the poem is much later, perhaps of the tenth century. Marbán had retired into a hermitage, living simply and alone, and the king went to persuade his brother to leave his cell and return to the life of a warrior. Here is Marbán's answer:

Atá úarboth dam i caill;
  nís fitir acht mo Fhíada:
uinnius di-śíu, coll an-all,
  bile rátha, nosn-íada.

I have a shieling in the wood. None knows it but my Lord: an ash-tree on this side, a hazel on that, a great tree by a rath encloses it.

.   .   .

Mét mo boithe bec nád bec,
  baile sétae sognath:
canaid sian mbinn dia beinn
  ben a lleinn co londath.

The size of my shieling is rather small, a homestead with familiar paths: from its gable a she-bird sings a sweet song in her thrush's cloak.

.   .   .

Aball ubull
(mára ratha)
  mbruidnech mbras;
barr dess dornach
collán cnóbec
  cróebach nglas.

A tree of apples as big as those of fairyland, great bounty; a pretty clustering crop from green-branched hazels with their tiny nuts.

---

[1] For text and translation, see Murphy, *Early Irish Lyrics* 28.
[2] Glyn Davies suggested long ago that the impulse may have come from some ancient book of devotions. *Cymmrodorion* 1912–13, p. 92. Professor MacEóin has shown that the *Canticum Trium Puerorum* is the source of the invocation of the elements in the Loricae, *Studia Hibernica* 2, 214.

Glére thiprat,
essa uisci
  (úais do dig);
bruinnit ilair
cáera ibair,
  fidait, fir.

An abundant well and falls of water, delicious drink; berries of yew, bird-cherry and privet break forth in plenty.

.   .   .   .   .   .

Tecat caínfinn,
corra, faílinn;
  fos-cain cúan;
ní céol ndogra
cerca odra
  a fráech rúad.

Fair white birds come, herons, sea-gulls – the sea sings to them, no mournful music; brown grouse from the russet heather.

.   .   .   .   .   .

Fogur gaíthe
fri fid flescach,
  forglas néol;
essa aba;
esnad ala:
  álainn céol.

The sound of the wind against a branching wood, grey cloud, river-falls, the cry of the swan: delightful music![1]

This song of praise is kept up for thirty-two quatrains, and Guaire replies that he would give his kingdom and all his inheritance to share such happiness.

The sensibility to form and colour and sound, the delight in detail, recur in songs of summer and winter which Kuno Meyer first made known.[2] His rendering of the Song of Summer, while not the most exact, is still the most successful, and some of it is borrowed here:

> May-Day, season supreme!
> Splendid is colour then.
> Blackbirds sing a full lay
> if there be a slender shaft of day.
>
> The hardy cuckoo calls aloud:
> Welcome, splendid summer!
> It calms the bitter storm
> which tears the branching wood.

.   .   .

[1] See Murphy, *Early Irish Lyrics* 10.
[2] *Four Old-Irish Songs of Summer and Winter*. London, 1903.

The corncrake, a strenuous bard, discourses;
the high, cold waterfall
sings joyfully from the warm pool,
rustling of rushes has come.

.   .   .

A timorous, tiny persistent little fellow
sings at the top of his voice,
the lark sings clear tidings:
'May-Day fair and peaceful!

That was written in the ninth century. It has seemed right to quote freely from this Irish nature poetry, because it is unique in European literature and not well known to the Common Reader.

In Wales too this new voice comes into poetry, but the early examples have not been even approximately dated, as grammatical criteria are lacking, and scholars have to depend on features of spelling and of rhyme. The Welsh nature poems seem to us to have their inspiration from the Irish, and the nature theme was then adapted to serve in gnomic poetry where it lost its savour and declined into mere formula. One passage from a poem in the Black Book of Carmarthen (thirteenth century) echoes the opening of the Irish poem on May-Day so closely that borrowing seems likely:

Cyntefin ceinaf amser,	May-Day, the fairest season,
Dyar adar, glas calledd,	loud are the birds, fresh the young grass,
Ereidr yn rhych, ych yng ngwedd,	ploughs in the furrow, oxen yoked,
Gwyrdd môr, brithotor tiredd.	the sea is green, the fields are speckled.
Ban ganont gogau ar flaen gwŷdd gwiw,	When the cuckoos sing in lovely trees,
Handid mwy fy llawfrydedd,	I grow more sorrowful;
Tost mwg, amlwg anhunedd,	smoke stings, my grief is plain,
Can ethynt fy ngheraint yn adwedd.	for my kinsfolk are departed.
Ym mryn, yn nhyno, yn ynysedd môr,	On hill and plain and islands of the sea,
Ymhob ffordd ydd eler	whatever road one travels,
Rhag Crist gwyn nid oes ynialedd.	there is no retreat from blessed Christ.

Another long sequence of *englynion* opens with lines describing winter:

228

Llym awel, llwm bryn, anodd caffael clyd,
    Llygrid rhyd, rhewid llyn,
    Rhy saif gŵr ar un conyn.

Keen is the wind, bare the hill, it is not easy to find shelter; foul is the ford, the lake is frozen; a man can stand on a single stalk.

Ton tra thon töid tu tir;
Goruchel gwaeddau rhag bron bannau bre;
    Braidd allan orsefir.

Wave over wave covers the shore; loud wails the wind against the mountain peaks; one can hardly stand outside.

Oer lle llwch rhag brythwch gaeaf;
    Crin cawn, calaf trwch,
    Cedig awel, coed ym mlwch.

The lake is a cold place in the winter storm, dry are the reeds, the stalks are broken, fierce is the wind, there are logs in the chest.

Oer gwely pysgawd yng nghysgawd iäen;
    Cul hydd, cawn barfawd;
    Byr diwedydd, gwŷdd gwyrawd.

The fish's bed is cold under the ice, the stag is lean, the reeds are bearded; the evening is short, trees bend.

But the verses that follow lapse into rather dreary gnomes, from which the quality of poetry is lacking. The making of these strings of *englynion* must have become a fashion, for several groups of them are linked by an initial formula: 'Snow falls', 'Mountain snow', and so on; and it marks a period of decline. The passage that we have quoted may be as early as the tenth century, and later poets may have added more and more *englynion* to make up the incoherent sequences as we find them in the manuscript. But Glyn Davies suggests, perhaps rightly, that these pages and others in the Black Book are a mere jumble of stanzas, a *débris* of poetry, recited to the scribe by one who could remember only fragments.[1]

By the time of the earliest extant Welsh poetry, the ornament of rhyme is well established, and we have nothing in Welsh to set beside the old unrhymed syllabic metres in Irish. But the origin of the *englyn* and of the later *cywydd* is probably to be found in the old Indo-European prosody, a line with a fixed number of syllables, subject to acephaly and catalexis, free as to quantity in the first part and with a fixed cadence after the caesura. This has been shown convincingly for the old Irish metres, and Ireland and Wales were heirs to a common Celtic heritage.

[1] *Cymmrodorion* 1912–13, p. 84.

CHAPTER 10

IRISH LITERATURE

WHEN we think of Irish or of Welsh literature, it is poetry and legend that claim our attention. Drama, rhetoric, philosophy, history suggest famous names in Greek and Roman tradition, and there were famous dramatists and philosophers in ancient India; but in Ireland and Wales, as in Anglo-Saxon England, literature of entertainment and antiquarian lore are all that have come down to us. Not indeed that history was neglected. Far from it. The Irish delighted in remembering the past. But learning was one of the duties of the *filid*, and it consisted largely of myth supplemented by deliberate invention, and the cataloguing, commonly in verse, of kings and their battles during the historic period, a record which is the more reliable as the events are less remote. The preserving of genealogies of the great families was a great part of the historian's duty, and this was prompted by zeal for the honour of the patron's family rather than for historical truth. These historians had not been to school to Herodotus; their chief aim was to sing the praise of their princes and to increase the fame of the tribe, not to discover the sequence of events and establish and explain the facts of history.[1]

Moreover, the legendary tales of Ireland and Wales have their origins in oral tradition, and are in fact anonymous. There is no known author of *Táin Bó Cualnge* or of *Culhwch and Olwen*. The poetry is largely anonymous too, as we have seen already, although here we have the work of individual unknown authors, sometimes ascribed to famous men of the past, Saint Columba or Find Mac Cumaill in Ireland, Aneirin or Taliesin in Wales. A remarkable feature of early Irish tradition is the total absence of narrative poetry, and the same may be said of Wales. The earliest Irish poetry is by court poets, praise, satire or lament, and the tales are told in prose.

The Irish stories, in their form and in their content, are fascinating and delightful, and at the same time disappointing and sometimes wearisome. What we have in the great manuscript collections that survive in the Book of the Dun Cow, Rawlinson B 502 or the Yellow Book of Lecan, to name three of the most famous, are very imperfect written records of oral tradition. We can be grateful to the scribes (the

[1] Cf. Winternitz's account of the Indian historians, *Geschichte der indischen Literatur*, iii, 81–82.

early ones were monks) for having written these texts at all, but, as Gerard Murphy has well said, when we imagine the oral tale as immeasurably better than the surviving monastic record, we are not indulging mere fantasy, but restoring a soul to the corpse that is buried in a manuscript.[1]

Irish literature in the period that concerns us, from the eighth to the twelfth century, presents heroic and mythological tradition that is free of Greek or Roman influence. The heroic tales describe a barbarian world in which some of the customs reported by classical authors of the Celts of Gaul are still observed. Loyalty, bravery, honour and hospitality are the virtues most admired. It is an aristocratic society. The gods sometimes interfere in the affairs of men, and in the mythological tales the notion of magic, of an unseen Otherworld, is commonplace.

One grand motif, which is the great Irish contribution to European literature, is the notion of love, sudden, overwhelming, lasting until death, love that brings sorrow to the lovers. It is best known in the story of Tristan and Isolde, which derives from Irish sources.[2]

The tales fall into cycles, mythology, the Ulster cycle, the Cycle of the Kings, and Fenian tales; and with the mythology may be grouped the tales of the Otherworld (*echtrai* 'adventures', and *immrama* 'voyages'), in which the hero sets out on a journey and finds himself in fairyland. These last are of special interest as possible sources of the Arthurian romances. There is an old list of tales in the Book of Leinster in which they are grouped not in cycles, but by types, as Destructions, Cattle-Raids, Courtships, Battles, Apparitions, Voyages, Tragedies, Adventures, Banquets, Sieges, Plunderings, Elopements, Eruptions, Visions, Love-Stories, Hostings and Invasions. Many of the titles given are of stories now lost, and not all that survive are included. We see, at least, what a mass of literature was there.

Of the mythological cycle only a few tales have survived, but there are references in the literature to many that have been lost. The finest is *The Wooing of Étaín*, of which we have a ninth-century text. There are three stories, which form a sequence. In the first Étaín becomes the wife of a fairy king, Midir of Brí Léith. Then, after a thousand years, she is re-born as a human, and becomes the wife of Eochaid Airem, king of Tara; and in the third story she returns with Midir to the Otherworld. There is a strange beauty here which is perhaps unequalled in any other Irish story, the temper of love, the power of magic, and a happy ending. And the form is unique, for it is one tale in three episodes, as it were a comedy in three acts (p. 143 f.).

The Battle of Moytura is our chief source for Irish, and indeed for Celtic mythology, for almost all the Irish gods appear there. The Irish

---

[1] *SM*, p. 11. [2] G. Schoepperle, *Tristan and Isolt* (London, 1913).

gods are called *Tuatha Dé Danann* 'Peoples of the goddess Danu' and they fight against a race of giants called *Fomoiri*. This is an account of the battle. Nuadu is here the king, and the Dagda ('Good God'), also called *Ollathair* ('Great Father'), Lug of the Long Arm, Goibniu the smith, Dian Cécht the leech, Credne the metal-worker, Luchta the wright, Ogma the champion and the Mórrígan are among those who take part. But the narrative is rambling and formless, and its value is rather mythological than literary (p. 141 f.)

The magic of the Otherworld is brought closer in the Adventures and Voyages. This Otherworld is thought of as in the western sea. It is called 'Land of the Living', 'Delightful Plain', 'Land of the Young' or 'Promised Land', the last a translation of *terra repromissionis*. It is a country where there is no sickness nor age nor death, where happiness lasts for ever and to wish for something is to possess it, where a hundred years are as one day. It is the Elysium of the Greeks, the *Jörd Lifanda Manna* of the Norse, and may represent ancient Indo-European tradition.

A beautiful girl approaches the hero and sings to him of this happy land. He follows her, and they sail away in a boat of glass and are seen no more. Or else he returns to find that all his companions are dead, for he has been away for hundreds of years. Sometimes the hero is on a journey, and a magic mist descends upon him. He finds himself before a fairy palace in which strange adventures befall him; and he returns having succeeded in his quest.

One of the oldest of the adventure-tales is the story of Bran son of Febal, who is lured away to the Land of Women, as it is called here, by a fairy visitor. She describes the beauty and pleasures of the Otherworld in a splendid poem of twenty-eight quatrains which sets the tone for many other such descriptions. There is an island supported by four pillars of gold. On a plain of silver games are held, with chariot-races and boat-races. Lovely colours shine on every side. Joy is constant. There is no sadness nor anger, neither sorrow nor sickness nor death. Music sounds always in the air. The sea washes the wave against the land, so that tresses of crystal fall on the shore. The chariots are of gold and silver and bronze, the horses golden chestnut, roan, even blue as the sky. The sun-god is described:

> A fair-haired man comes at sun-rise to light up the level lands. He rides over the white plain against which the ocean murmurs. He stirs the sea into blood.

Bran sets out upon the sea with twenty-seven companions. After two days and two nights he sees a man approaching, who drives his chariot over the water. It is the god Manannán, and he sings a lay in which the peculiar magic of these descriptions of the Otherworld again finds expression. Bran thinks that he is rowing upon the sea, but for Manannán it is a flowery plain. The waves that Bran sees are flowering shrubs. The leaping salmon are calves and frisking lambs. His boat is floating over an orchard of fruit-trees.

After some adventures Bran reaches the Island of Women, but he is afraid to land. The leader of the women throws him a ball of thread which sticks to his hand, and she draws his boat ashore.[1] They go into a great hall where there is a bed and a wife for every man. The food that they eat does not diminish. They thought they were there a year, but it was many years.

When Bran returned to Ireland, the people who had gathered on the shore asked him who he was, and he said: 'I am Bran son of Febal.' 'We know him not,' they said, 'but the Voyage of Bran is one of our ancient stories.' One man was put ashore, and he turned to ashes at once, as though he had been in the grave for hundreds of years. Bran told his adventures to the people and bade them farewell; and from that time forward his adventures are not known.

This tale is in the pagan tradition, and happiness is imagined as consisting of the pleasures of food and love as they are found in the Otherworld. The same is true of several other *echtrai*, and one must admire the fidelity with which Christian monks preserved them for us. *Echtrae Conli*, *Echtrae Loegairi*, *Echtrae Cormaic*, *Echtrae Airt meic Cuinn* and *Serglige Con Culainn* are other such tales, all of them infused with the same magic quality, which is echoed after four hundred years in the Arthurian romances.

In *The Adventure of Loegaire*, when the hero returns from his quest, the Connachtmen leap forward to welcome him home. 'Do not come near us,' said Loegaire, 'for we have come to say farewell.' His father, Crimthann Cass, king of Connacht, begs him to stay: 'Do not leave me! I will give you the kingdom of the Three Connachts, with their gold and silver, their steeds and bridles, and their fair women; but do not leave me!' Loegaire answers in a poem praising the joys of the Otherworld. They travel on the mist, leading a mighty army. There is delightful music, and the happiness of love:

> Delightful fairy music, travel from one kingdom to another, drinking mead from bright vessels, talking with one you love.
> We play with men of yellow gold on golden chessboards: we drink clear mead in the company of a proud armed warrior.
> Der Gréine, daughter of Fiachna, is my wife; and, to tell all, there is a wife for each of my fifty men.

After that he went from them into the fairy mound again, and he shares the kingdom of the fairy mound with Fiachna mac Rétach in the

[1] Cf. inf. p. 258.

fortress of Mag Mell, and Fiachna's daughter is with him, and he has not come out yet.

Here the Otherworld is identified with a fairy mound (*síd*). There are, indeed, two notions of the Otherworld. It can be reached either by a journey over the western sea, or by entering one of the mounds into which the *Tuatha Dé Danann* were believed to have fled when they were defeated by the sons of Míl. *Bruig na Bóinne*, now identified with the great Bronze Age burial-mound of New Grange in Co. Louth, was the dwelling of Oengus, who won it from the Dagda by a ruse. It was a wonderful place where fruit-trees were always in fruit. There was a roast pig and also a vat of fine liquor which never diminished when consumed. Brí Léith, a hill near Ardagh, Co. Longford, was the home of Midir; Bodb Derg, son of the Dagda, was the lord of Síd ar Femen, which is Slievenamon, Co. Tipperary; Síd Clettig on the Boyne was the home of Elcmar, and Síd Finnachaid that of Aillén mac Midgna, or of Lir. Nuadu dwelt in Síd Alman, the Hill of Allen, Co. Kildare. Siugmall, brother of Elcmar, was lord of Síd Nenta on Lough Ree. And the five (sometimes six) *bruidne* of Ireland, which had no local habitation, were also Otherworld dwellings. Each of them, we are told, had an inexhaustible cauldron, like the Dagda's cauldron, from which no company went away unsatisfied.

But there were also the islands of the Otherworld, and the gods associated with them seem to be distinguished from the *Tuatha Dé Danann*. Manannán mac Lir is the principal figure among them. He drives his chariot over the sea, and was said by Cormac mac Cuilennáin, the ninth century glossator, to have lived in the Isle of Man; but his true home was Emain Ablach, the Avalon of Arthurian tradition. With him are associated other deities who do not appear among the *Tuatha Dé Danann;* Labraid Swift-Hand-on-Sword and his wife Lí Ban; Eogan Inbir and his wife Bé Cuma; Eochaid Iuil and his wife Fand, who invites Cú Chulainn to be her lover, and several others. These 'nobles of the Land of Promise' may have belonged originally to a different cult, for there were several ethnic groups among the Celtic invaders of pre-history, Cruithin, Érainn, Goídil (Féni), and perhaps others as well (pp. 137–45).

The tales commonly known as the Ulster Cycle are so called because most of them are about warriors of the Ulaid, the dominant people in the province of Ulster (*Cóiced Ulad*) in pre-historic times. But Ailill and Medb, king and queen of Cruachain in Connacht, and some famous warriors of the Connacht-men are often in the story. Here the wonder and magic of the Otherworld are forgotten, and we are in an Heroic Age as Chadwick has defined it. These are not tales of mystery and imagination, but stories that are meant to be historical, and that have at least some history behind them. The weapons and war-chariots, the feasts and assemblies, the social order portrayed in the Ulster Cycle correspond closely to the accounts of the Celts of Gaul and Britain given us by ancient writers (pp. 8–9).

The central story of the cycle is the Cattle-Raid of Cooley, *Táin Bó Cualnge*; and the hero of the story, and of the whole cycle, is Cú Chulainn ('Culann's Hound'), brave, generous, handsome, beloved of women, who chose fame and an early death rather than a long life without honour. In the *Táin* Cú Chulainn stands alone defending Ulster against a whole army throughout the winter, while the Ulstermen lie stricken by a mysterious sickness. The climax of a series of single combats that he fights is his meeting with Fer Diad, his friend and fosterbrother, whom he slays after three days of fighting. The story ends with the coming of the Ulstermen and the rout of the Connacht army.

Many of the shorter sagas are linked to the *Táin* as prefatory tales (*rem-scéla*) which explain some episode in the great battle, and of these deservedly the most famous is the Exile of the Sons of Uisliu, *Longes Mac nUislenn*.[1] It explains why Fer Diad and others of the Ulster warriors were in the Connacht camp, fighting against Ulster; but that is not the real motif of the story. This saga is the earliest example in European literature of tragic love.

LONGES MAC N-UISLENN

The Exile of the Sons of Uisliu

The Ulaid were feasting one day in the house of Fedlimid, the story-teller of King Conchobar, and while they were there a girl-child was born to the wife of Fedlimid, and a druid prophesied about her future. The prophecy is in verse. The girl's name is to be Derdriu, and she will grow to be a woman of wonderful beauty and will cause enmity and trouble and will depart out of the kingdom. Many will die on account of her.

The Ulaid proposed to kill the child at once and so avoid the curse. But Conchobar ordered that she be spared and reared apart, hidden from men's eyes; and he said that he himself would take her for his wife. So Derdriu was entrusted to foster-parents and was reared in a dwelling apart. A wise woman, Leborcham, was the only other person allowed to see her.

Once the girl's foster-father was flaying a calf outside in the snow in winter to cook it for her; and she saw a raven drinking the blood in the

---

[1] Ed. with transl., V. Hull, New York, 1949.

snow. Then she said to Leborcham: 'Fair would be a man upon whom those three colours should be: his hair like the raven, and his cheek like the blood, and his body like the snow.' 'Grace and prosperity to you!' said Leborcham. 'He is not far from you, inside close by: Noísi the son of Usnech.'[1] 'I shall not be well,' said she, 'until I see him.'

Once that same Noísi was on the rampart of the fort sounding his cry. And sweet was the cry of the sons of Usnech. Every cow and every beast that would hear it used to give two-thirds excess of milk. For every man who heard it, it was enough of peace and entertainment. Good was their valour too. Though the whole province of the Ulaid should be around them in one place, if the three of them stood back to back, they would not overcome them, for the excellence of their defence. They were as swift as hounds at the hunt. They used to kill deer by their speed.

When Noísi was there outside, soon she went out to him, as though to go past him, and he did not recognize her. 'Fair is the heifer that goes past me,' said he. 'Heifers must grow big where there are no bulls,' said she. 'You have the bull of the province,' said he, 'the king of the Ulaid.' 'I would choose between you,' said she, 'and I would take a young bull like you.' 'No!' said he. Then she sprang towards him and caught his ears. 'Here are two ears of shame(?) and mockery,' said she, 'unless you take me with you.'

Noísi sounded his cry, and the Ulstermen sprang up as they heard it, and the sons of Usnech, his two brothers, went out to restrain and warn him. But his honour was challenged. 'We shall go into another country,' said he. 'There is not a king in Ireland that will not make us welcome.' That night they set out with one hundred and fifty warriors and one hundred and fifty women and one hundred and fifty hounds, and Derdriu was with them.

They fled to Scotland, and took service with the king. But Derdriu's beauty excited his envy, and the sons of Usnech had to flee and take refuge on an island in the sea.

Then Conchobar invited them back and sent Fergus, Dubthach and his son, Cormac, as sureties; but Noísi and his followers were killed when they came to Emain, and Derdriu was brought to Conchobar, and her hands were bound behind her back.

When the sureties heard of this treachery, they came and avenged the crime: three hundred of the Ulaid were killed, and women were killed, and Emain was burnt by Fergus. And Fergus, Dubthach and Cormac went to the court of Ailill and Medb, and for sixteen years the Ulaid had no peace.

Derdriu was for a year with Conchobar, and she never smiled or raised her head from her knee.

---

[1] Uisnech and Uisliu are alternative forms of the name.

And when the musicians came to her, she used to say:

'Though you think the eager warriors fair, who march proudly over Emain, more proudly used they to march to their house, the brave sons of Usnech. ...

Sweet to Conchobar, your king, are the pipers and horn-blowers, sweeter to me the cry of the sons of Uisliu. ...

Dear was the grey eye which women loved. It was fierce against an enemy. After a visit to the woods, noble course, delightful was his cry through the black forest.

I do not sleep; and I put no purple on my nails. Joy comes not into my mind, since the sons of Usnech do not come. ...

Joy is not for me in the assembly of Emain which nobles fill, nor peace nor happiness nor comfort, nor a big house nor fair ornament.'

And when Conchobar was comforting her she used to say:

'Conchobar, what are you doing? You have caused me sorrow and tears. As long as I live, I shall not love you.

What was dearest to me under heaven, and what was most beloved, you have taken him from me, – a great wrong – so that I shall not see him till I die. ...

Two bright cheeks, red lips, eyebrows black as a chafer, pearly teeth bright with the noble colour of snow. ...

Do not break my heart. Soon I shall die. Grief is stronger than the sea, if you could understand it, Conchobar.'

'What do you hate most of what you see?' said Conchobar. 'You,' she said, 'and Eogan son of Durthacht.' 'You shall be a year with Eogan,' said Conchobar. He gave her to Eogan. They went next day to the assembly of Macha. She was behind Eogan in the chariot. She had prophesied that she would not see two husbands on earth together. 'Well, Derdriu,' said Conchobar. 'You look like a sheep between two rams, between Eogan and me.' There was a big rock in front of her. She thrust her head against the rock, so that it shattered her head, and she died.
That is the exile of the Sons of Usnech, and the exile of Fergus and the Tragic Death of the sons of Usnech and of Derdriu.

This story is preserved in several manuscript versions and in modern folklore. The version presented here, from the Book of Leinster, is the oldest, and may be as early as the eighth century.

Next to *Táin Bó Cualnge* in length, and perhaps in importance too, is the story of Bricriu's Feast, *Fled Bricrenn*, in which the chief motif is the *curad-mír* or Hero's Portion, for which Cú Chulainn and two other warriors contend, just as Gaulish warriors did according to Posidonius.

A second theme is the Champion's Ordeal, when Cú Chulainn and his two rivals are challenged to cut off the head of a giant on condition that they allow him to cut off their heads on his return. It has been used again by the author of *Sir Gawayne and the Green Knight*.

The first of these themes is best presented in one of the liveliest and most entertaining of all the Irish sagas, *The Story of Mac Da Thó's Pig*. Here one warrior after another claims the right to carve the pig at a feast, and each in turn has to yield to a rival who establishes a better claim. The boasting of each claimant, and the scornful abuse that is then showered upon him, provide excellent dialogue. At last, when the Connacht champion, Cet mac Mágach, has put several Ulstermen to shame and is about to carve the pig, Conall Cernach enters the hall.

> The Ulstermen gave Conall a great welcome. Conchobar took off his hood and waved it about. 'We would like to get our supper,' said Conall. 'Who is carving for you?' 'It has been conceded to the man who is carving,' said Conchobar, 'Cet mac Mágach.' 'Is it true, Cet,' said Conall, 'that you are carving the pig?' Then Cet said:

> > Welcome to Conall
> > heart of stone
> > fierce energy of the lynx
> > glitter of ice
> > red strength of anger
> > in a warrior's breast
> > a wounder, a conqueror!
> > Son of Findchoem, you are a match for me!

> And Conall said:

> > Welcome to Cet
> > Cet son of Mágu
> > warrior's dwelling
> > heart of ice
> > plumage (?) of a swan
> > chariot-fighter strong in combat
> > angry sea
> > handsome fierce bull
> > Cet son of Mágu!

'Go away from the pig!' said Conall. 'What should bring you to it?' said Cet. 'Truly,' said Conall, 'that is to challenge me to a contest! I will contest with you for once, Cet,' said Conall. 'I swear the oath of my tribe, since first I took a spear in my hand I have not passed a single day without killing a Connachtman, nor a night without setting fire, and I have never slept without a Connachtman's head under my knee.' 'It is true,' said Cet, 'you are a better warrior than I. If it were Ánluan who were in the house, he would contest with you. It is bad for us that he is not in the house.'

'But he is!' said Conall, taking Ánluan's head from his belt. And he hurled it at Cet's chest so that blood flowed from his mouth. He went away from the pig, and Conall sat down by it.

Conall proceeds to take the best part for himself, and to the Connachtmen he gives only the fore-legs of the pig. Enraged by this, they rise from their places and the Ulstermen rise to oppose them, so that soon corpses are heaped upon the floor and blood is flowing through the doorways.

This admirable tale from the ninth century describes the very scene that Posidonius must have witnessed, or heard described, in Gaul a thousand years before. One could not have better evidence for the archaism of Irish tradition.

When Cú Chulainn was in the east, learning feats of arms from Scáthach so that he might win the hand of Emer, he fought against another woman-warrior, Aífe, an enemy of Scáthach; and he overcame her and had a son by her. All this is told in a long saga called 'The Wooing of Emer'. The boy is to come to Ireland when he grows to manhood, and he is not to tell his name on the demand of a single warrior. 'The Tragic Death of Aífe's Only Son' tells of the boy's coming to Ireland and of his death by the hand of his own father. It is the story of Sohrab and Rustum, the theme also of the Hildebrandslied, evidently an ancient Indo-European motif. It is of the ninth century in the form in which we have it. The simplicity and the restrained emotion of the story make it memorable.

AIDED OENFIR AÍFE

The Tragic Death of Aífe's Only Son

The men of Ulster were assembled at Trácht Éisi, when they saw a boy coming on the sea in a boat of bronze with gilded oars. He was performing strange feats, bringing down birds alive with his sling, and then releasing them. He would scatter them out of sight by a trick of his hands, and then sing to them so that they flew back to him. The Ulstermen were alarmed and sent a champion to meet him and prevent his landing, or discover his name. Condere goes first, but the boy defies him. Then the mighty Conall Cernach goes down. The boy hurls a stone from his sling, and Conall falls. The boy binds his arms with the strap of his own shield. 'Let someone else oppose him!' says Conall Cernach.

Cú Chulainn was practising his feats as he approached the youth, and the arm of Emer daughter of Forgall was around his neck. 'Do not go down!' said she. 'It is a son of yours that is down there. Do not kill your

239

only son! Refrain, O eager son of Soailte. It is not brave or wise to oppose your valiant son. ... Turn towards me. Listen. My advice is good. Let Cú Chulainn hear! I know what name he will tell, if the boy down there is Conla, Aífe's only son.'

Then Cú Chulainn said: 'Forbear, woman! I heed not a woman's advice. ... Make not your womanish talk of gentle conduct. ... The good spear drinks good liquor. Though it were he, indeed, woman,' said he, 'I would kill him for the honour of Ulster.'

Then he went down himself. 'You play well, boy,' said he. 'But your play is cruel,' said the little boy, 'that two of you do not come, so that I might tell my name to them.' 'Should I then have taken a child along with me?' said Cú Chulainn. 'You shall die, if you do not tell your name.' 'Be it so,' said the lad.

The boy came towards him. They smote each other. The boy shaved his head with his sword by a measured stroke. 'This is enough of insolence,' said Cú Chulainn. 'Let us wrestle then!' 'I shall not be able to reach up to your belt,' said the boy. The boy got upon two stones, and he thrust Cú Chulainn between the stones three times. And the boy did not move either of his feet from the stones, and his feet went into the stones up to his ankles. The mark of his feet is there still. Hence is named the Strand of the Track in Ulster.

Then they went into the sea to drown each other, and the boy put him under twice. He went against the boy in the shallow water and played him false with the *gae bolga*. For Scáthach had taught the use of that weapon to none but Cú Chulainn alone. He cast it at the boy through the water so that his entrails were about his feet. 'That is what Scáthach did not teach me!' said he. 'Woe to you who have wounded me!'

'It is true,' said Cú Chulainn. He took the boy in his arms and bore him away, and he carried him up and cast him before the Ulstermen. 'Here is my son for you, men of Ulster!' said he.

Another saga tells why the hero, Froech son of Fidach, took part in the Táin. It is a love-story, the wooing of Findabair, daughter of Medb and Ailill, by Froech. One passage shows well the sensitivity to form and colour that so often delights us in both verse and prose. Froech has been sent across a river to fetch a branch from a rowan tree:

Froech went then and broke off a branch from the tree, and brought it back over the water. Findabair used afterwards to say of anything beautiful she saw, that she thought it more beautiful to see Froech coming across a dark pool, the white body, the lovely hair, the shapely face, the grey eye, the gentle youth without fault or blemish, his face narrow below and broad above, his body straight and perfect, the branch with the red berries between his throat and his fair face. Findabair used to say that she had never seen anything half or a third as beautiful as he.

Something of the same incandescent quality shines out in the description of Étaín as she bathes at a spring. This Étaín was a daughter's daughter of Étaín, the wife of Midir (p. 231), and was a mortal. At the beginning of a saga, 'The Destruction of Ua Derga's Hostel', the king discovers her:

> He saw a woman at the edge of a well, and she had a silver comb with gold ornament. She was washing in a silver basin on which were four birds of gold, and bright little gems of purple carbuncle on the chasing of the basin. She wore a purple cloak of good fleece, held with silver brooches chased with gold, and a smock of green silk with gold embroidery. There were wonderful ornaments of animal design in gold and silver on her breast and shoulders. The sun shone upon her, so that the men saw the gold gleaming in the sunshine against the green silk. There were two golden tresses on her head, plaited in four, with a ball at the end of every lock. The colour of her hair was like the flower of the iris in summer or like pure gold after it has been polished. She was undoing her hair to wash it, so that her arms were out from beneath her dress. White as the snow of one night were her hands, and her lovely cheeks were soft and even, red as the mountain foxglove. Her eyebrows were as black as a beetle's back. Her teeth were like a shower of pearls. Her eyes were as blue as the hyacinth, her lips as red as Parthian leather. High, smooth, soft, and white were her shoulders, clear white her long fingers. Her hands were long. White as the foam of a wave was her side, long and slender, yielding, smooth, soft as wool. Her thighs were warm and smooth and white; her knees small and round and hard and bright. Her shins were short and bright and straight. Her heels were even and lovely. If a rule had been laid upon her feet it would hardly have shown any imperfections in them, unless it should crease the flesh or the skin. The blushing light of the moon was in her noble face, a lofty pride in her smooth brow. The radiance of love was in her eyes; the flush of pleasure on her cheeks, now red as a calf's blood and changing again to snowy whiteness. There was gentle dignity in her voice. Her step was firm and graceful. She had the walk of a queen. She was the fairest, loveliest, finest that men's eyes had seen of all the women of the world. They thought she was of the fairies. Of her it was said: 'All are lovely till compared with Étaín. All are fair till compared with Étaín.'

The Cycle of the Kings begins with a group of Origin-Tales which represent very old tradition. They are of the same *genre* as the Roman story of Romulus and Remus, or the Greek story of Athene and Poseidon at the founding of Athens. One of them specially deserves mention because it contains the motif of the Iron House, which, as we shall see, was borrowed into the Welsh story of Branwen (pp. 269–70). It is called 'The Destruction of Dinn Ríg', and tells the story of Labraid Loingsech, ancestor-god of the Lagin, or Leinstermen. It is a tale of vengeance, and dates from the ninth century in its present form.

Cobthach Coel, king of Brega, killed his brother, Loegaire Lorc, king of Ireland and his brother's son, Ailill Áine, who was king of Leinster.

Ailill's son, Labraid, was sent into exile. Later he returned with an army of Munstermen, captured Dinn Ríg, and became king of Leinster in his turn.

Labraid was at peace with Cobthach. He invited Cobthach to visit him, and a house was built for his entertainment. That house was strong, for it was made of iron, walls and floor and doors. The Leinstermen were a full year building it, and father spoke not to son, nor mother to daughter, as the proverb says: 'Every Leinsterman has his secret.' Cobthach came with thirty kings in his train, and all were burned in the iron house.

Many of the sagas are about kings of the historical period, and one of the best of them is 'The Tragic Death of Mael Fothartaig son of Rónán'. The text as we have it dates perhaps from the tenth century. It is the story of Phaedra and Hippolytus in an Irish setting, and is well told. In the first dialogue the tragic theme is brought in, and it is repeated at once when the boy meets the queen. The tension is never relaxed.

Rónán was king of Leinster in the seventh century, and died c. AD 624. In the saga his son Mael Fothartaig is the most famous boy in Leinster. It was around him that men gathered at assemblies and games. He was the darling of the girls and the lover of the young women. His mother died, and his father was for a long time without a wife.

'Why do you not marry?' said his son. 'You would be better off with a wife.' 'I am told,' said Rónán, 'that Echaid has a handsome daughter.' 'You are no husband for a girl,' said the lad. 'Will you not marry a settled woman? I would rather that for you than a skittish girl.'

But the old man married the girl, and she at once fell in love with his son, and sent her maid to persuade him. As the boy refused her love, she accused him falsely. 'A curse on your lips, wicked woman!' said Rónán. 'You lie!'

Mael Fothartaig came in, and was drying his legs at the fire. He spoke two lines of verse, and the girl was able to match them. 'It is true then,' said Rónán. And he told one of his men to kill the boy with a spear-thrust. When Mael Fothartaig was dying, he told his father the truth. There is a fine lament by the old king over his son's body towards the end. He praises Mael Fothartaig and his companions, and bids the servants feed the two dogs who mourn for their master:

> 'Doíléne has served me well:
> her head is in the lap of everyone in turn
> seeking one whom she will not find.

.   .   .   .

My son Mael Fothartaig
was the leader of the pack:
the tall, fair champion who shone abroad
has found a cold dwelling-place.'

Another important saga of the Cycle is 'The Story of Cano son of Gartnán'. It is more attractive for its matter than for its form in the only manuscript that preserves it, The Yellow Book of Lecan, for it is somewhat incoherent, and there are some obscure passages. The story is pure invention, for though the characters are historical, they are not contemporaries, and moreover it is plainly woven from several old motifs. One of these is the motif of Tristan, so that this tale ranks with the story of Deirdre as one of the early Celtic sources of the Tristan legend. The parallel here rests upon the love-theme, the fact that Créd is the young wife of an old king, whose name is Marcán (diminutive of Marc), and the final episode in which Cano approaches the coast in a ship, Créd dies before he reaches land, and he dies soon afterwards.[1] Another motif that occurs is the love of the unseen one, *adṛṣṭakāma* in Sanskrit tradition, which in Irish is called *grád écmaise* 'love of one known only by repute'; and there is also the motif of the external soul.

Cano was the son of a Scottish king. His death is recorded in the Annals in 688. In the story he comes to Ireland as an exile, and is received with honour by king Diarmait, whose daughter was already in love with him before she had seen him. She saves him from danger, and he goes away to visit Guaire, king of Connacht. He comes first to the house of Marcán, whose wife Créd was a daughter of Guaire. She too was already in love with him. Marcán had a son, Colcu, apparently a stepson of Créd. Later, when Cano was with Guaire, Créd and Marcán came to a feast, and also Colcu. Créd asked that she be allowed to pour the wine that night, and she gave a sleep-potion to all save herself and Cano. Then she entreated him, but he refused to be her lover while he was a mere adventurer, and promised to make her his queen when he should be king of Scotland. He gave her as a pledge a stone which contained his life.

Cano was recalled to Scotland and became king, and every year he used to make a tryst with Créd at Inber Colptha (the mouth of the Boyne), but Colcu was always there with a hundred men to prevent their meeting. At last they made a tryst at Loch Créde in the north. Créd came, bringing with her the magic stone. Cano approached from the east, so that they were within sight of each other, when Colcu appeared again and drove him off. Créd dashed her head against a

---

[1] Professor Binchy, who has edited this tale, finds little resemblance to the Tristan story, see *Scéla Cano meic Gartnáin* p. xvii.

rock, and the stone broke as she fell. Cano died three days after he had gone back to Scotland.

Even this bald summary shows the peculiar interest of the story, an historical figure being presented as the hero of a Tristan romance, with the extra distinction of an external soul. The manuscript text has not much style about it, but we have seen that a finer oral form is to be imagined (pp. 230–1).

The Fenian Cycle was the latest to take shape as a separate tradition in the literature. Recent research by Gerard Murphy and by O'Rahilly has shown that Finn, the central figure of the Fenian Cycle, is identical in origin with the great god of the Celts, Lug of the Long Arm. Finn is a warrior-hunter god, who slays a one-eyed god of fire, a burner. There are early references to Finn, but they are fragmentary; and the old list of sagas (p. 231) contains only a few Fenian titles. It is clear that even by the twelfth century, Finn and the *fiana* were only on the way to becoming famous in literature. It may be said that one of the titles in the list is *Aithed Gráinne re Diarmait*, 'The Elopement of Gráinne with Diarmait', and we know from other evidence that the famous love-story of Diarmaid and Gráinne was known in the tenth century, although the only surviving text of it is of the Modern Irish period (15th century?).[1] It is a variant of the Deirdre story (p. 235), and Gertrude Schoepperle showed long ago that these two stories represent the Celtic source of the romance of Tristan and Isolde.

The twelfth century was a period of recovery and reform in Ireland as elsewhere in Europe, and there was a great revival of literature and of learning. The Book of the Dun Cow, the so-called Book of Leinster, and the famous Rawlinson manuscript were all written at that time; and it was then too that the great classical themes of the Siege of Troy, the Aeneid, and the Destruction of Thebes were introduced into Irish. It was in this time of transition that there came the sudden flowering of the Fenian Cycle. It coincided with the first appearance in Ireland of ballad poetry, and the Fenian ballad appears as a new literary form.

One of the earliest of these Fenian ballads is the Sleep-Song for Diarmaid, supposed to be sung by Gráinne, as she watches over her lover asleep:

Codail beagán, beagán beag,	Sleep a little, just a little, for there is
óir ní heagail duit a bheag,	no danger in a little sleep, boy to
a ghiolla dia dtardus seirc,	whom I have given my love, Diar-
a mheic Í Dhuibhne, a Dhiarmaid.	maid, son of Ó Duibhne.

[1] Ed. with transl. by Neassa Ní Shéaghdha, *Tóraigheacht Dhiarmada agus Ghráinne* (Dublin, 1967).

Codail-se sunn go sáimh,
a Í Dhuibhne, a Dhiarmaid áin;
do-ghéan-sa t'fhoraire dhe,
a mheic Í dhealbhdha Dhuibhne

Sleep soundly here, noble Diarmaid
Ó Duibhne; I shall watch over you,
handsome son of Ó Duibhne.

She thinks of other lovers who eloped and slept in safety, and then she thinks of danger, and of the animals of the forest who seem to be afraid:

The stag in the east does not sleep; he does not cease to call:
even though he is in the forest, he has no thought of sleep.

The lively music does not cease in the curved branches of the trees;
they are noisy there, even the thrush is not asleep.

Tonight the grouse does not sleep in the deep rough heather;
shrill is the note of his clear voice; among the streams he does not sleep.

Fenian ballads became very popular, and the big collection known as *Duanaire Finn* has been made the subject of a special study by Gerard Murphy.[1] Many of them are in the form of a dialogue between Oisín, son of Finn (MacPherson's 'Ossian'), and Saint Patrick, in which Oisín tells the saint stories about the adventures of the *fiana*, or Fenians. Most of these ballads are of the Modern Irish period, but the dialogue tradition goes back to a famous prose text which ushers in the Fenian Cycle in the twelfth century, *Acallam na Senórach*, 'The Colloquy of the Ancient Men'. It is a frame-story which tells how Saint Patrick meets the Fenian warriors Oisín and Caílte, and journeys through Ireland with one or other of them. The warriors tell the saint more than two hundred anecdotes, many of them attached to the places they visit on their way. One conversation between Saint Patrick and Caílte begins well:

'Was he a good lord with whom you were, Finn mac Cumaill that is to say?' Upon which Caílte uttered this little tribute of praise:

'Were but the brown leaf which the wood sheds from it gold, were but the white wave silver, Finn would have given it all away.'

'Who or what was it that maintained you so in your life?' Patrick asked. And Caílte answered: 'Truth that was in our hearts, and strength in our arms, and fulfilment in our tongues.'

As they wander through Munster, they come to a place from which the Fenians had formerly set out to fight the battle of Ventry. Caílte tells the story of Cael who had seen a beautiful girl named Créd in a

[1] *DF* II and III, Dublin, 1933, 1953.

245

dream, and who wooed and won her on the way to the battle. Cael was drowned at Ventry, and his body was washed up from the sea; and Créd lay beside his body and lamented his death:

> The haven roars over the angry surf of Rinn Dá Bárc: the wave against the shore laments the drowning of the warrior of Loch Dá Chonn.

> Plaintful is the crane from the marsh of Druim Dá Thrén: she cannot protect her loved ones, the fox of Dá Lí pursues her nestlings.

> Sad is the note of the thrush in Dromkeen, and sad the music of the blackbird in Letterlee.

> Sad is the cry of the stag in Druim Dá Léis: the doe of Druim Síleann is dead, and the stag of Díleann laments her ...

The *Acallam* is one of the most successful works of Middle Irish literature, and could serve as a happy introduction to Modern Irish. Gerard Murphy has suggested that it may be a deliberate literary composition by an individual author, the scribe of the original manuscript, unlike the heroic sagas which clearly derive from oral tradition.[1] It would then present an interesting comparison with the Welsh *Mabinogion*.

In tracing the beginnings of Irish literature we saw the 'new forms' of poetry which the monks evolved, and the nature poetry and hermit poetry which was their special contribution. These new forms soon spread to the secular poetry, and from the ninth to the twelfth century there is a rich tradition. The hermit's voice is still heard, but there is humour and passion as well.

One famous manuscript, written perhaps at the Irish abbey of Reichenau on Lake Constance, has found its way to the Austrian abbey of Sankt Paul in Carinthia, where it is known as *das irische Schulheft*, 'the Irish Copybook'. It is, indeed, a student's note-book, notes on Virgil and on the Greek declensions, quotations from Horace, Saint Jerome and Saint Augustine; and among them are four Irish poems. One is a heroic poem in praise of Aed son of Diarmaid, and it is in the new form, showing the adoption by the professional poets of the rhymed quatrain for their panegyrics:

---

[1] *The Ossianic Lore and Romantic Tales of Medieval Ireland* (Dublin, 1961), p. 25.

*A*ed *oll* fri *a*ndud n-*á*ne,
Aed who is great in kindling brilliance,

Aed *fonn* fri *f*uilted *fé*le,
Aed who is a support in dispensing hospitality,

in *d*eil *d*elgnaide as ch*ó*emem
conspicuous pillar, dearest of the chieftains

di dindgnaib *Roerenn ré*de
of level Roeriu.

Mac *Diarmata d*il *d*amsa,
Son of Diarmaid, dear to me,

cid *iarfachta* ní *insa*;
if it be asked, it is not difficult to tell;

a *m*olad *m*aissiu *má*enib
his praise more precious than wealth

*l*úaidfidir *lá*edib limmsa
will be sung in lays by me.

There are eight quatrains, and end-rhyme and internal rhyme are freely used, as well as the old ornament of alliteration.

The other three poems are monastic, and in one of them the poet with delicate humour compares the zeal of his cat in catching mice with his own efforts in learning:

Messe ocus Pangur bán
cechtar nathar fria ṡaindán:
bíth a menmasam fri seilgg,
mu menma céin im ṡaincheirdd.

Pangur Bán and I, each of us at his special art: his mind is set upon hunting, and mine upon my proper craft.

Caraimse fos, ferr cach clú,
oc mu lebrán, léir ingnu;
ní foirmtech frimm Pangur bán:
caraid cesin a maccdán.

I love to stay – it is better than fame – at my book, eagerly pursuing knowledge. Pangur Bán does not envy me: he loves his childish art.

Ó ru biam, scél cen scís,
innar tegdais, ar n-oendís,
táithiunn, díchríchide clius,
ní fris tarddam ar n-áthius.

When we are alone together, content in our house, we have something to which we can apply our skill, an endless sport.

Gnáth, huaraib, ar gressaib gal
glenaid luch inna línsam;
os mé, du-fuit im lín chéin
dliged ndoraid cu ndronchéill.

Often at times with feats of valour, he catches a mouse in his net; and I, there falls into my net a difficult rule of hard meaning.

Fuachaidsem fri frega fál
a rosc, a nglése comlán;
fuachimm chéin fri fégi fis
mu rosc réil, cesu imdis.

He directs his full bright eye towards the wall; I direct my clear though feeble eye towards keenness of knowledge.

Faelidsem cu ndéne dul
hi nglen luch inna gérchrub;
hi tucu cheist ndoraid ndil
os mé chene am faelid.

He rejoices with swift action when a mouse is caught in his sharp claw; when I grasp a difficult matter, I too am joyful.

Cia beimmi amin nach ré
ní derban cách a chéle:
maith la cechtar nár a dán;
subaigthius a oenurán.

Though we be thus any time, neither disturbs the other; each of us likes his own art, alone in his pleasure.

Hé fesin as choimsid dáu
in muid du-ngní cach oenláu;
du thabairt doraid du glé
for mu mud céin am messe.

He is his own master at the task he follows every day; I ply my separate task, bringing what is dark into the light.

That poem was written early in the ninth century. From the same early time comes another which tells the sorrow of old age, and memories of youth, beauty and love. It is the 'Lament of the Old Woman of Beare':

Ebb-tide has come to me, as to the sea; old age makes me yellow; though I may grieve thereat, it comes happily to feed on me.

I am Buí, the hag of Beare. I used to wear a new smock always: today I am so forlorn that I do not even wear an old one.

It is wealth that you love, not people; in our day it was people that we loved.

Beloved were those over whose lands we rode: we fared well among them, and they made little of it.

Today you ask for plenty, and give little away: and although you bestow little, you make a great boast.

Swift chariots, and horses that won the prize, there was once a flood of them. Blessed be the King who gave them!

When my arms are seen, long and thin – pleasant was the art they practised: they used to be about glorious kings.

When my arms are seen, long and thin, they are not fit, I declare, to put around comely youths.

The girls are glad when May-Day comes: grief suits me better, for I am a wretched old woman.

I speak no honied words; no sheep are killed for my wedding; my hair is scant and grey; a mean veil is no shame to it.

I care not that a white veil be on my head: many a bright scarf was on my head when I drank good ale.

The wave of the great sea is noisy: winter has aroused it. I expect neither noble nor slave's son to visit me today.

I enjoyed the summer of youth while it lasted, and even the autumn; the winter of age, which overwhelms everyone, has begun to overtake me.

I had my day with kings, drinking mead and wine: today I drink whey and water with shrivelled hags.

The flood-wave and the swift ebb-wave: what the flood-wave brings you, the ebb-wave takes out of your hand.

The flood-wave and the ebb in turn have both come upon me so that I know them.

It is well for the islands of the wide sea: flood comes to them after ebb. I have no hope that flood after ebb will come to me.

There is an old story which tells of a sorrowful love, and recalls the tragic history of Abélard and Héloïse. This too belongs to the ninth century. Liadan and Cuirithir were lovers, and Liadan entered a convent. Her lover pursued her, and they placed themselves under the guidance of Saint Cummine the Tall. At first he allowed them to converse, but not to look upon each other. Later he permitted them to sleep together, with a child between them lest they should do wrong. It is an instance of *mulieris consortium,* which was a recognized form of asceticism in early Ireland and elsewhere. They failed in this test, and Cuirithir was sent to a monastery and later went into exile across the sea. Here is the lament of Liadan:

Cen áinius
in gním í dorigénus
an ro carus ro cráidius

Joyless what I have done! I have grieved the man I loved.

Ba mire
nád dernad a airer-som
mainbed omun ríg nime

It was madness not to do his will, but for the fear of heaven's King.

Níbu amlos
dosom an dál dúthracair
ascnam sech phéin i Pardos.

No misfortune was the lot that he desired, to seek Paradise without punishment.

Bec mbríge
ro chráidi friumm Cuirithir;
frissium ba mór mo míne.

It was a small thing that turned Cuirithir against me; I was gentle towards him.

Mé Liadan;
ro carussa Cuirithir;
is fírithir adfiadar.

I am Liadan; I loved Cuirithir; it is as true a word as ever spoken.

Gair bása
i comaitecht Chuirithir;
frissium ba maith mo gnássa.

Only a short time I was with Cuirithir; my companionship was good for him.

Céol caille fom-chanad la Cuirithir, la fogur fairge flainne.	The music of the forest sang to Cuiri- thir and me, and the sound of the raging sea.
Do-ménainn ní cráidfed frimm Cuirithir do dálaib cacha dénainn.	I should have thought that nothing I would do would turn Cuirithir against me.
Ní chela ba hésium mo chride-šerc, cia no carainn cách chena.	Conceal it not, he was my heart's love, whoever else I may have loved.
Deilm ndega ro thethainn mo chridese; ro fes nicon bía cena.[1]	A roaring flame has dissolved this heart of mine; without him for certain it cannot live.

One more example of personal poetry may be quoted for its humorous and moving comment on the human predicament. Here it is a monk who complains of distractions at prayer:

It is a shame how my thoughts wander! I fear great danger on the Day of Judgement.

During the psalms they stray on to a wrong path: they run, they distract me, they are sinful in the presence of the great God.

Through lively meetings, through crowds of foolish women, through woods and cities, they are swifter than the wind,

Now through pleasant paths, and again through unseemly wilderness.

Without a boat they can travel on the sea; with one swift leap they go from earth to heaven.

They run their foolish course, and after naughty roaming come back home again.

Though one try to bind or fetter them, they have no constancy, no mind for rest.

Neither knife nor scourge restrains them; they slip from my grasp like an eel's tail.

Neither lock nor vaulted prison nor any bond, fortress or sea or bare fastness, can stop their course.

O chaste Christ beloved, to whom every verdict is clear, may the grace of the sevenfold Spirit come to keep and check them!

O powerful God, Creator, rule this heart of mine, that Thou mayst be my love, that I may do Thy will!

[1] Murphy, *Early Irish Lyrics* 82.

O Christ, may I be united to Thee: may we be together! Thou art not fickle and inconstant: Thou art not as I am.

Latin was, of course, the first literary language of the monks, and the earliest writings we have are in Latin, beginning with the writings of Saint Patrick himself, the works of Saint Columbanus and Adamnán's *Vita Columbae*, which have been discussed already (pp. 167, 180 f.). Gradually the vernacular came to be used in prose as well as verse, at first perhaps merely to write glosses on a Latin text, as in the famous glossed codices of Würzburg, Milan and St Gall; but from the beginning of the eighth century there are prose tracts written in Irish.[1] The earliest is a homily on the Mass, preserved in a manuscript at Cambrai, which was written at the end of the seventh century. The Book of Armagh contains long notes in Irish of the early eighth century, and the author apologizes for using Irish on this occasion: 'Finiunt haec pauca per scotticam inperfecté scripta non quod ego non potuissem romana condere lingua sed quod uix in sua scotica hae fabulae agnosci possunt. Sin autem alias per latinam degestaé fuissent non tam incertus fuisset aliquis in eis quam imperitus quid legisset aut quam linguam sonasset pro habundantia scotaicorum nominum non habentium qualitatem.' In the Tripartite Life of Saint Patrick (*c.* 900) we have a sustained narrative in Irish prose.

A fine example of vernacular prose in the monastic tradition is *Fís Adamnán*, 'The Vision of Adamnán'. It belongs to a group of texts which derive from Jewish and Christian sources and describe visions of Heaven and Hell experienced by holy men. These visions provide interesting evidence of what was read and studied in Ireland in the eighth and ninth centuries, and it appears that apocryphal writings, condemned elsewhere, continued in favour among the Irish.

Saint Adamnán, author of the *Vita Columbae*, a beautiful Latin life of Saint Colmcille, was abbot of Iona (679–704), tenth in succession to Colmcille, its founder. He is credited with a vision of Heaven and Hell, the account of which is as early as the tenth century in its extant form. C. H. Boswell goes so far as to say that the unknown author excels all other precursors of Dante, and Seymour is of a like opinion.[2] The Vision of Adamnán is eloquent and simple: in style and structure it is probably the best that we have in Irish prose down to the twelfth century.

The soul of Adamnán went forth from his body, and was brought by his guardian angel to Heaven and to Hell. The host of Heaven is described: the apostles and the Blessed Virgin are around Christ. On Mary's right hand are holy virgins 'and no great space between them'.

---

[1] The language of the oldest law-tracts is earlier, but it is not certain when they were first ommitted to writing (p. 199).

[2] *IPD*; St John D. Seymour, *Irish Visions of the Otherworld*, 98 f.

Though the brightness and light in the land of the saints are great and wonderful, as we have said, more wonderful a thousand times is the brilliance in the plain of the heavenly host around the throne of the Lord himself. That throne is a well-wrought chair, supported by four pillars of precious stone. Though one should hear no other music but the fair harmony of those four pillars, it would be enough of happiness. Three stately birds are perched on the chair in the King's presence, and their task is to keep their minds ever intent upon their Creator. They sing the eight Hours, praising and glorifying the Lord, and a choir of archangels accompanies them. The birds and angels begin the music, and the whole host of Heaven responds, both saints and holy virgins.

Above the Glorious One seated on His throne, there is a mighty arch like a wrought helmet or a royal diadem. If human eyes should see it, they would melt away at once. There are three Zones around it, and what they are cannot be told. Six thousand thousands in the form of horses and of birds surround the fiery chair which blazes eternally.

To describe the mighty Lord who is on that throne is not possible for anyone save Him alone, unless He should tell it to the heavenly orders; for none shall tell His ardour and energy, His glow and gleam, His dignity and beauty, His constancy and firmness, the number of angels and arch-angels that sing their chant before Him ... Though one should gaze around, east and west and north and south, he will find on every side the noble face seven times as bright as the sun. He will see no human form, neither head nor feet, but a mass of fire blazing throughout the world, and all in fear and trembling in its presence.

After the description of the citadel, we are told of those who are outside the gate, awaiting the last judgment. A curtain of fire and a curtain of ice hang in the gateway and strike against each other with a sound terrible to the ears of sinners. To the host of Heaven within it is heard as sweet faint music.

There are seven heavens and six gates through which the souls must pass. When Adamnán has seen all this, he is brought to Hell over a bridge which leads across a valley of fire into the Land of Torment. The various torments suffered by those guilty of particular sins are described, as in the *Inferno*. After they have been shown to Adamnán, his soul is brought back to Heaven in the twinkling of an eye; but when it thinks to stay there, the voice of his guardian angel bids it return into the body it has left, and tell in assemblies and congregations, lay and cleric, the rewards of Heaven and the pains of Hell, as the angel has revealed them.

The Otherworld motif and the Christian Vision literature are parodied in an excellent satire called The Vision of Mac Con Glinne[1] which was composed in the twelfth century by some disillusioned scholar, whose

[1] ed. K. Meyer, London, Nutt, 1892.

wit and vigour invite comparison with Brian Merriman's 'Midnight Court'. The genealogical lore of the *filid*, the poetical descriptions of *Mag Mell*, visits to mortal heroes by fairy maidens, even the Bible itself is mocked by this nameless satirist who seems to be following the fashion of the troubadours.

Cathal, king of Munster, was possessed by a demon of gluttony, so that he ate immense quantities of food. There was at the time a scholar named Ainiér Mac Con Glinne who was famous for his gifts of satire and eulogy. One Saturday evening, as he was pursuing his reading at Roscommon, a longing came upon him to give up learning for poetry. He decided to go as a poet to the court of Cathal, in the hope of getting plenty to eat there, for he loved good food. On the morrow he set out for Cork, and by nightfall he arrived at the guesthouse of the monastery. He found the door open, in spite of wind and rain, and no one in attendance. The blanket was full of lice and fleas. The bath had not been emptied since the previous night, nor even the heating-stones taken out.

Since no one came to wash his feet, the scholar washed them himself in the dirty bath and lay down to sleep. But the lice and fleas were as many as the sands of the sea or as sparks of fire or the dewdrops on a May morning or the stars of heaven, and he could not rest. He took out his psalter and began to sing the psalms, 'and the learned and the books of Cork relate that the sound of the scholar's voice was heard a thousand paces beyond the city, singing his psalms, through spiritual mysteries, in dia-psalms and syn-psalms and decades, with *paters* and canticles and hymns at the end of each fifty'.

The abbot, Manchín, sends a servant with the guest's ration, which consists of a cup of whey-water. Mac Con Glinne satirizes this meagre fare and declines it. His conduct is reported to the abbot, who orders him to be stripped, beaten, and thrown into the river Lee, and left to sleep naked in the guesthouse. In the morning he shall be judged by the abbot and monks of Cork and shall be crucified for the honour of the abbot himself, of St Finnbarr, and of the church. The first part of this sentence is carried out, and next morning the monks assemble in the guesthouse. The abbot will have him crucified at once, but he asks for a trial; and, though they plead against him with much wisdom and learning, they cannot find anything in his sayings for which he deserves crucifixion. He is led out to his doom without the sanction of law, but he asks leave to eat his viaticum before he dies, and binds the abbot with sureties and pledges.

His satchel is brought to him, and he takes out two wheaten loaves and a piece of bacon. He takes tithes of the bread and meat and considers paying them to the clergy or bestowing them in alms, but he decides that none has greater need than himself, and, as for the monks of Cork, they are curs, thieves, and dung-hounds, and he will not have the devil accuse him, when he crosses the line, of paying tithes to them. So the first morsel he eats is the tithe. He finishes eating and is led away, but he continues to delay his execution by insisting on drinking water drop by drop from the pin of his brooch. At last he agrees to go in humility. An axe is given him, and he is made to cut his passion-tree and bear it on his back to the green of Cork.

As the monks are about to crucify him, Mac Con Glinne asks a boon of Manchín, namely, that he may have a last feast and fine raiment before going to his death. Manchín denies him this and says that, as the evening is far advanced, he shall be stripped of the scant clothing he wears and tied to a pillar, as a first punishment before the great punishment of the morrow. The monks bind him to the pillar and retire to supper, leaving him to fast. At midnight an angel appears to him and reveals a vision.

In the morning, when Manchín and his monks arrive, Mac Con Glinne begs leave to relate the vision. Manchín refuses, but the monks will hear it, and he proceeds to relate it. The prelude is a rhymed genealogy of Manchín in terms of food:

'Bless us, O cleric, famous pillar of learning,
Son of mead, son of juice, son of lard,
Son of stirabout, son of pottage, son of fair radiant fruit,
Son of smooth, clustering cream, son of buttermilk, son of curds,
Son of beer, glory of liquors, son of pleasant bragget,
Son of twisted leek, son of bacon, son of butter,
Son of full-fat sausage,' and so forth.

The vision which follows is a verse parody upon the Voyage-Tales. He sets out in a boat of lard on a lake of new milk.

The fort we reached was fair, with earthworks of thick custard, beyond the lake. Its bridge was of butter, its wall of wheat, the palisade was of bacon.

. . . .

Smooth pillars of old cheese, beams of juicy bacon, in due order, fine rafters of thick cream, with laths of curds supported the house.

. . . .

Behind was a spring of wine, rivers of beer and bragget, every full pool had a flavour. A flood of smooth malt over a bubbling spring spreads over the floor.

. . . .

I saw the chieftain in a mantle of beef-fat with his fair noble wife. I saw the server at the cauldron's mouth, his flesh-fork on his shoulder.

We are told that there was much more in the vision than the text relates; and when Mac Con Glinne had finished, Manchín announced that it had been revealed to him that this vision would cure the king of his disease, and that the scholar must go to king Cathal at once. Mac Con Glinne claims a reward. 'Are not thy body and soul reward enough?' says Manchín. And the scholar answers that he cares not for his life, for Heaven awaits him with its nine orders, the Cherubim and Seraphim, and all the faithful chanting in expectation of his soul. He must have as reward the abbot's cloak. Manchín refuses, but the monks insist, and the cloak is placed in the custody of the bishop of Cork, pending the successful cure of Cathal.

It would be too long to follow here the excellent humour of the story of the cure. Mac Con Glinne contrives to oblige the unhappy king to fast for two nights. He then orders a feast and has Cathal tied to the wall and brings in the luscious food. As he proceeds to eat it himself, the king roars and bellows and orders his death. Now Mac Con Glinne recites his vision in two poems which are fresh compositions on the same theme, new parodies of the *echtrae* motif. To these he adds a fable, again in parody, of the visits to mortals by persons of the Tuatha Dé Danann; but here, too, food is the theme. This fable is an excellent piece of humour and eloquence. In prose and verse the author mocks at the heroic and mythological sagas, the wonders of the Otherworld, and the fair maidens whose anatomy they describe in such detail. Even the scribes who recorded the tales are satirized, for the author solemnly retails conflicting versions of various episodes, the learned giving one, the books of Cork another, in mockery of the variants frequently given in the sagas. The satire is sustained at great length with unfailing merriment and with gluttonous descriptions of the food-paradise to which the scholar has journeyed. Meanwhile, we are left to imagine the distress of the hungry king.

'At the pleasure of the recital and the enumeration of the many and various delicious foods in the presence of the king, the lawless beast that lay in the entrails of Cathal son of Fínguine came up so that it was licking its lips outside his mouth.' The scholar was now bringing each tempting morsel to the lips of the king, and at last the demon of gluttony darted from his mouth, seized one of the morsels, and hid under the cooking-pot. The pot turned over and caught it. 'Thanks be to God and St Brigid!' said Mac Con Glinne, putting his right hand over his mouth and his left over the mouth of Cathal. Linen sheets were put around Cathal's head, and he was borne away. The house was then cleared and burnt to the ground, but the demon escaped and perched upon a neighbouring house. Mac Con Glinne called upon him to do reverence. The demon replied that he must, although he would not. If he had been suffered to remain three half-years longer in Cathal's mouth, he would have ruined all Ireland. If it were not for the wisdom of the monks of Cork and for the multitude of their bishops and confessors (this is a last thrust), if it had not been for the righteousness and honour of the king and the virtue, wisdom, and learning of Mac Con Glinne himself, he would have leaped into that scholar's throat, so that he would have been driven through Ireland with whips and scourges, until he was taken off by hunger. Mac Con Glinne made the Sign of the Cross against the demon with his gospel-book, and the demon flew into the air to join the host of Hell. Cathal rewarded Mac Con Glinne with cows and cloaks and rings and horses and sheep, and the abbot's cloak to boot.

The Otherworld motif which inspired the *echtrai* (p. 137) is also the matter of the *immrama* ('voyages'), and of these the most successful is the 'Voyage of Mael Dúin's Boat', which is supposed to be the source of the famous *Navigatio Brendani*. It is ascribed in one manuscript to Aed Finn, 'chief scholar of Ireland'; but he has not been identified. The tale is not later than the tenth century (188 f.).

Mael Dúin was a love-child and was fostered by the queen, who was a friend of his mother, and reared as one of her own children. Like Oengus in 'The Wooing of Étaín', he discovered from the taunt of a companion that he was not her son; and he then learned that his father, Ailill Ochair Ága, had been murdered by marauders from Leix. He asked the way to Leix, and wise men told him he must go by sea, so he went to Corcomroe (in the present County Clare) to consult a druid, who appointed the day on which he should begin to build his boat and the number of men he should take, namely, seventeen. However, after he had set sail, his three foster-brothers swam out after the boat and were taken aboard in violation of the druid's counsel.

They voyaged all day until midnight, when they reached two small islands from which there came a great noise of intoxication and boasting; and they heard one man cry out that he was the better warrior, for he had slain Ailill Ochair Ága, and none of Ailill's kindred had avenged the crime upon him. Mael Dúin's people rejoiced at having come straight to the house of the murderer; but, while they spoke together about it, a storm arose, and their boat was carried away to sea. When morning broke they saw no land. Mael Dúin reproached his foster-brothers for having brought this misfortune upon them by causing them to disobey the druid's instruction. They left their boat to sail wherever God might guide it, and so their wonderful voyage began.

The boat travels over the endless ocean and brings them to many marvellous islands, thirty-one in all. On the islands and in the open sea they encounter prodigies the account of which displays considerable power of imagination and a nice sense of humour.

On the first island they see a swarm of ants, each as big as a foal, which seek to devour them; so they flee. On another they find only great birds and take some of them for food; on another a wild beast like a horse with sharp nails on his hooves, and they flee in terror. The next island is occupied by demons who are having a horse-race. Sometimes they find food and drink made ready for them. A branch plucked by Mael Dúin bears three apples after three days, and they all eat of these apples for forty days and are satisfied.

They found another island surrounded by a stone wall. When they came near, a great beast arose and ran around the island. Mael Dúin thought it faster than the wind. It went to the summit of the island and stretched itself on the ground with its feet in the air. It would turn in its skin, the flesh and bones revolving and the skin unmoved; or at another time the skin turning like a mill, the bones and the flesh quite still.

They fled in haste, and the beast came down to the shore and hurled stones after them, one of which pierced Mael Dúin's shield and lodged in the boat's keel.

On one island there are apple-trees with golden apples. Red swine devour the apples by day and disappear underground at night. Then the sea-birds come and eat the apples. Mael Dúin says that it can fare no worse with them than with the birds, and they go ashore. The earth is hot so that they can hardly stay, for the swine are blazing hot. They fill the boat with apples and escape.

On the next island they find a feast prepared, and they eat and drink. There is a wealth of treasure guarded by a cat. One of the foster-brothers seizes a gold bracelet, and the cat jumps right through him and burns him to ashes. Later they come to an island inhabited by a hideous miller, who tells them that he grinds half the corn of Ireland in his mill, all that is ever begrudged. On another there are people whose bodies and clothes are black. They wail unceasingly. The lot falls on one of the two remaining foster-brothers who goes ashore; and at once he turns black and wails like the others. Two are sent to rescue him and suffer the same fate. Four more go and succeed in bringing back the last two, but not the foster-brother.

After other adventures they reach an island where they find an old man whose clothing is his hair. He tells them he is of the Men of Ireland. He is a pilgrim and has come out floating on a sod of earth which the Lord established in that place. The sod grew miraculously year by year to be an island, and the souls of his children and his kindred in the form of birds have settled in the trees there. All are fed by the ministry

257

of angels. He prophesies that Mael Dúin and his companions will return home safely, all save one man. After three days they depart.

At one time the sea is like green glass, transparent and beautiful; at another it is like a cloud, so that they fear it will not support them. Below them now is a wonderful country with great strongholds. A fearsome beast in a tree seizes an ox and devours it. In terror they sail over this region and escape. A stream of water flows through the air like a rainbow, and they pass below it and spear salmon from the water over their heads. From Sunday evening until Monday morning the stream subsides and does not flow. They fill their boat with salmon and go on their way. They behold a pillar of silver rising out of the sea to which a great silver net is attached. The boat passes through a mesh of the net. Diurán brings with him a piece of the net and vows to lay it on the altar at Armagh.

At last they reach an island, which is plainly the Land of Women of the *echtrai*. Seventeen girls are there preparing a bath for them. One of the girls comes to welcome them and announces that the queen invites them into the fort. A feast is served, and, when they have finished eating and drinking, each of Mael Dúin's men takes a wife, and Mael Dúin sleeps with the queen. In the morning she bids them abide there. Age will not come upon them, and they will live forever and enjoy the pleasures they have known there every night without any toil. One of Mael Dúin's companions grows weary and wishes to go home (as in *Echtrae Brain*), but Mael Dúin wishes to stay. The others prevail upon him, and one day, while the queen is away, they set sail. She rides down to the beach and throws a ball of thread to Mael Dúin. He catches it, and she draws the boat back to land (as in *Echtrae Brain*). Three times she treats them so, and at last Mael Dúin says that someone else must attend to the ball of thread. They set out again, and when the queen throws her ball of thread another man takes it and it clings to his hand, but Diurán cuts off his arm,[1] and they sail away.

Now comes an episode which Zimmer rightly held to be the occasion of the later attribution of a marvellous voyage to St Brendan of Clonfert.[2] They land on a large island, one half of which is wooded with yews and oaks, while the other is an open plain grazed by a great flock of sheep. They see a little church and a fort, and in the church they find an old monk. His hair covers him completely. He is one of the fifteen disciples of St Brendan of Birr who set out on a pilgrimage and landed there. All are dead save him alone. He bids them eat of the sheep, and they stay there for a while. (St Brendan of Birr died AD 565, St Brendan

---

[1] Meyer has pointed out that this motif is borrowed from the story of the Argonauts, ZCP x 360.
[2] ZfdA xxxiii 295 f.

of Clonfert, AD 576. And it is not here said that the former made the voyage himself, merely that fifteen of his monks did so. The latter, however, was known to have made other voyages and easily became the subject of a regular *immram*.)

On this same island they see a huge bird which eats the fruit of a branch which it carries in its claws. It is visited by two eagles, which pick the lice from its head and body and remove the old feathers. Then they pick some of the fruit and cast it into a lake, so that the foam of the water becomes red. The great bird descends into the lake and washes himself. Afterward his flight is swifter and stronger than before. They understand that he has undergone the renewal of youth according to the word of the prophet who says: *renovabitur ut aquilae iuventus tua* (Ps. ciii. 5). Diurán bathed in the lake, and he never lost a tooth or a hair of his head, nor did he suffer weakness or disease from that time forth.

On the next island the third of the foster-brothers meets his doom. It is inhabited by people who play and laugh unceasingly. The lot falls upon him to go ashore, and he at once begins to play and laugh like the others. His companions wait a long time, and then abandon him.

> Then they saw another island which was not large, with a wall of fire all around it; and that wall revolved about the island. There was an open doorway in the side of the wall, and each time the doorway came in front of them they saw the whole island and all that was on it with all its inhabitants, many handsome people in lovely garments with golden cups in their hands as they feasted. And they heard their ale-music. And they were for a long time watching the wonder which they saw, and they found it delightful.

Two more islands are visited, on one of which they meet a hermit who bids them return home and foretells that they will find the slayer of Mael Dúin's father but that they must spare him because God has saved them from many dangers. At last they see an Irish falcon flying to the south-east. They follow the course of its flight, and at nightfall they come to the first island, from which the wind had borne them out to sea. They are made welcome, and they relate all the wonders that God has shown them according to the word of the 'prophet' who says: *haec olim meminisse iuvabit*.

Mael Dúin returns to his own country. Diurán lays the silver on the altar of Armagh. They relate their adventures from beginning to end, and the dangers and perils which they had experienced on sea and land.

The Adventures and the Voyages have to do with the Otherworld, and so we are led back to where we started. The Fenian Cycle too has its origin in myth. The Ulster Cycle and the Cycle of the Kings are heroic in temper. If one were to attempt a history of early Irish literature, there would be nothing in it of the history of ideas, nor would there be an account of great writers, for the prose tales are anonymous, and of the poets whose names we know, none are outstanding. The best of the poetry is anonymous too. Indeed there would not be much history at all in the sense of development or progress, but merely a sequence of literary events in some degree of chronological order. The compass of Irish literature is not wide: the incandescent imagination that glows in the description of Étaín washing at a spring, or Froech swimming across a river, or of the sound and movement of the sea in several poems; the motif of the doomed lovers, the heroic figure of Cú Chulainn, the tragic fate of a son slain by his own father, the vivid account of feasting in a heroic society that we get in 'Bricriu's Feast' and 'The Story of Mac Da Thó's Pig', the wonderful nature poetry and hermit poetry; these are the elements that make up the claim of Irish literature to recognition. And then one must reckon in for credit the early time at which they appear.

Of the sagas it may be said that apart from their content, the literary form is of special interest. The oldest narrative form in Indo-European tradition seems to have been a prose narrative, with dialogue in verse. The verse was metrically fixed and unchanging, but the prose was left to the creative memory of the storyteller. This was the oldest Indian form, as found in the Buddhist Jātakas and in a few examples even in the ancient Brāhmaṇas of the Vedic period. It was also the Irish form; and it appears in some of the oral epics of Central Asia.[1] The Irish sagas are in prose, but when a champion claims his right to the Hero's Portion, he speaks in verse; when Deirdre says farewell to Scotland and when she laments the death of her lover, she speaks in verse. In India, and presumably in Greece, this ancient form developed into epic poetry, so that in the Mahābhārata and Rāmāyaṇa, and in Homer, we have long narrative poems. But in Ireland the old Indo-European form survived into the Middle Ages, providing another example of the great archaism of Irish tradition.

[1] For this form of 'prose narrative interspersed with speech poems' among the Kazaks and the Turkic peoples, see GL. III 48 ff. (= N. Chadwick and V. Zhirmunsky, *Oral Epics of Central Asia*, 55 ff.).

CHAPTER 11

WELSH LITERATURE

FROM what we have seen of the earliest Welsh poetry it is clear that only fragments have survived, half-remembered traditions of the Gododdin, poems attributed to Taliesin, among others the fine lament for Owein ab Urien, dialogue poems from lost sagas of Llywarch Hen and Cynddylan, and a few nature poems and gnomic verses. The great period of Welsh poetry was still to come, with the rise of the Court poets (*Gogynfeirdd*) in the twelfth century and the later glory of Dafydd ap Gwilym. In the meantime there is less evidence of poetic inspiration in Wales than in Ireland, although the contact between the two countries was close.

One legendary figure, Myrddin, is enshrined in traditions that link him with the Irish king Suibne Geilt, 'Sweeney the Mad'. Suibne, king of Dál nAraide, fought in the battle of Moira in 637, and is supposed to have lost his reason in the din of battle. *Buile Suibne*, 'The Frenzy of Sweeney', is the story of his life in the wilderness, with some fine poems in which the mad king laments his misery and describes the forest and the animals that roam there.

Myrddin was supposed to have lived in the sixth century, and to have fought on the losing side in the battle of Arfderydd (Arthuret, near Carlisle) in 573. He too went mad and fled into the forest of Celyddon (Caledonia). 'There he lived for half a century, with no company but the trees and the wild beasts, mourning for the slaying of Gwenddolau and afraid lest Rhydderch should come against him. In this frenzied condition Myrddin acquired the gift of prophecy.'[1]

In fact the name was invented by means of a false analysis of Caer-fyrddin (Carmarthen), of which the second element is derived from *moridūnon* 'sea-fort'. In one poem he is addressed as *Llallawc* and *Llallogan Vyrdin*, and his name is Laloicen in Joceline's Life of St Kentigern, and Lailoken in two other tales, forms plainly adapted from the Welsh epithet.[2] And the story of Myrddin and the Suibne story present a Celtic variant of the Wild Man theme.[3] The earliest reference to Myrddin is in the tenth century poem, *Armes Prydein*, and some verses attributed to him may be as old, for exact dating of anonymous Welsh

[1] *HWL* 27.   [2] Jarman, *The Legend of Merlin*, Cardiff 1960.
[3] Stith Thompson, *Motif Index* F 567.

poetry is difficult. *Buile Šuibne*, on the other hand, is hardly earlier than the twelfth century. Either side may have borrowed from the other, and the territory of Dál Riata, which lay partly in east Ulster and partly in Scotland, must have been a centre of exchange. It is geographically close to the scene in each case.

Like the Irish hermit, Marbán in *Tromdám Guaire*, Myrddin had a pet boar, and in one of the poems attributed to him he addresses it:

Afallen beren a phren melyn | A sweet yellow apple-tree
A dyf yn halar heb âr yn ei chylchyn; | grows on the bare headland.
A mi ddysgoganaf gad ym Mhrydyn | And I foretell a battle in Britain
Yn amwyn eu terfyn â gwŷr Dulyn. | in defence of its land against the men of Dublin.

Seithlong y deuant dros lydan lyn, | With seven ships they shall come over the wide water,

A saith cant dros fôr i oresgyn. | seven hundred men from across the sea for conquest.

O'r sawl y deuant nid ânt i gennyn | Of them who come, only seven shall escape from us,

Namyn saith lledwag gwedi eu lletgyn. | empty-handed after their defeat.

Afallen beren a dyf tra Rhun | A sweet apple-tree grows beyond the Rhun.

Cywaethlyswn yn ei bôn er bodd i fun, | I strove beneath it to please a girl,

A'm ysgwyd ar fy ysgwydd a'm cledd ar fy nghlun, | With my shield on my shoulder and my sword at my side,

Ac yng Nghoed Celyddon y cysgais fy hun. | and in Coed Celyddon I slept my sleep.

Oian a barchellan, pyr bwyllud hun? | Hark, little pig! Why did you think of sleep?

Andaw di adar dyfr yn ymeiddun. | Listen to the waterfowl at their mating!

Tëyrnedd dros fôr a ddaw ddyw Llun. | Lords from across the sea will come on a Monday.

Gwyn eu byd hwy Gymry o'r arofun. | The Welsh may rejoice at their plan![1]

This is vague stuff, partly recalling the saga of Myrddin, partly prophetic; and Professor Parry suggests that original poems about Myrddin may have been swamped by the prophecies. Prophecy was a literary fashion in Wales down to the fifteenth century, rather in the spirit of the Jacobite *aisling* in Ireland. It was prophecy born of defeat, foretelling a hero, Arthur, Cadwaladr, Owain, who would arise again to

[1] This may refer to the return of Rhys ap Tewdwr and Gruffudd ap Cynan, see Griffith, *Early Vaticination* 88.

deliver his people; and many of these prophetic poems were attributed to Taliesin or to the legendary Myrddin.[1] The address to his pet pig quoted above may have prompted a sequence of stanzas beginning: 'Hark, little pig', which would be later than the others, for one of them refers to the Norman invasion of Ireland:

Oian a barchellan, oedd rhaid gweddi	Hark little pig! We must pray
Rhag ofn pum pennaeth o Norddmandi;	for fear of the five chiefs from Normandy.
A'r pumed yn myned dros fôr heli	And one of the five will cross the salt sea
I oresgyn Iwerddon dirion drefi.	to conquer Ireland of the kindly homesteads.
Ef gwnahawd ryfel a dyfysgi	He shall make war and tumult
Ac arfau coch ac och ynddi.	and there shall be bloody weapons, and lamentation there.
Ac wyntwy yn ddiau a ddoant oheni	And they will come from there
Ac a wnânt enrhydedd ar fedd Dewi.	and do reverence at Saint David's tomb.
A mi ddysgoganaf fyd dyfysgi	And I foretell that there shall be tumult,
O ymladd mab a thad; gwlad a'i gwybi.	son fighting against father – the whole country shall know it.
A myned i Loegrwys ddiffwys drefi,	And they shall go into desert England.
Ac na bo gwared byth i Norddmandi.	May there be no help for Normandy for ever![2]

The prophecies of Myrddin have an antiquarian interest, as this sort of vaticination is characteristic; and the verse-form is important for the history of Welsh poetry. End-rhyme is still the only requirement.[3] It divides the poem into stanzas of eight or twelve lines. Alliteration and internal rhyme are frequent, but not required, so that we are still far from the *cynghanedd* system.

With the twelfth century the great period of Welsh poetry begins, and it may be significant that its beginning coincides with the rise of the bardic schools in Ireland, and follows upon the reign of Gruffudd ap Cynan, king of Gwynedd, whose mother was the daughter of a Norse king of Dublin. He spent his youth in Ireland, and it has been suggested that he brought back poets and musicians to Wales.[4] We know nothing of what occasioned the event in Ireland, but it is a fact that from the beginning of the twelfth century the craft of poetry was studied and

---

[1] *HWL* 26, 30.

[2] The reference is to Henry II, who visited St David's on his return from Ireland, and was later at war with his son, see *HWL* 32–33.

[3] Cf. sup. p. 216.

[4] See Arthur Jones, *The History of Gruffydd ap Cynan* 180 n. 4; HWL 45.

practised in a stricter form than before, and that there emerged the great families of hereditary bards, O'Daly, O'Higgins, O'Hussey, Macaward and others, who cultivated a classical form of language and diction which remained unchanged for five hundred years. It may have been a result of the revival of learning under Brian Boru. In Wales the rise of the *Gogynfeirdd* may have been due to the national recovery in the reign of Gruffudd. But it can hardly be doubted that there is a connexion between the appearance at about the same time in both countries of schools of poetry, and of the strict forms of *cynghanedd* in Wales and *dán direch* in Ireland.[1]

There had been native schools in Ireland from the remote past. The metrical tracts of the tenth century prescribe the metres and the heroic literature that were to be studied in each year of a twelve-year course of apprenticeship, and it is safe to assume that there was a long tradition behind them.[2] But these were apparently new schools, in the hands of new men who took over the discipline of poetry after the old order of *filid* had disappeared. Something similar must have happened in Wales.

Bardic poetry in Wales and in Ireland was a highly technical craft, bound by strict metrical rules, and conventions of form and diction. As Parry says, the sound is as important as the sense. Its normal theme, and its chief purpose, was praise of a patron. His courage in battle, his generosity and the glory of his ancestors are the subjects of praise; and with this convention established, the poetic achievement becomes one of craftsmanship.[3]

The earliest of the court poets whose work has survived is Meilyr (fl. 1100–37), who composed an elegy on Gruffudd ap Cynan. His son, Gwalchmai, praised Owain Gwynedd, son of Gruffudd, for his prowess against the Normans:

Ar gad gad greudde, ar gryd gryd graendde,	For battle a bloodier battle, for terror greater terror
Ac am Dâl Moelfre mil fanieri;	and a thousand banners around Tal Moelfre;
Ar lath lath lachar, ar bâr beri,	a flashing spear against each spear, lances to meet a lance,
Ar ffwyr ffwyr ffyrfgawdd, ar fawdd foddi;	fierce fury to meet fury, drowning those who sought to drown him.
A Menai heb drai o drallanw gwaedryar,	And the Menai without ebb from the flowing of blood,
A lliw gwyar gwŷr yn heli.	and the colour of men's blood was on the sea.

[1] The 'classical' period of bardic poetry is commonly said to begin *c.* 1250, but an historical poem which O'Brien dated *c.* 1120 shows conformity to strict rules for alliteration and rhyme, see *Ériu* xvi 157 ff. The full development of strict *cynghanedd* came in the fourteenth century.
[2] R. Thurneysen, Mittelirische Verslehren, *Irische Texte* ii.
[3] J. Vendryes, *La Poésie de Cour en Irlande et en Galles* (Paris, 1932).

Here already the torrent of alliteration and rhyme amounts to *cynghanedd* in its effect, although the strict rules of *cynghanedd* are not yet binding.

The princes themselves sometimes took to poetry, and there are poems by Hywel ab Owain Gwynedd, a grandson of Gruffudd ap Cynan, which are livelier verse, and have more magic in them, than the more formal work of the professional bards. In one of these, *Gorhoffedd Hywel ab Owain* ('Hywel ab Owain's Delight'), he praises Gwynedd, his father's kingdom:

Ton wen orewyn a orwlych bedd,	The foaming white wave washes over a grave,
Gwyddfa Rhufawn Befr, ben tëyrnedd.	the tomb of Rhufawn Pefr, prince of rulers
Caraf, drachas Lloegr, leudir gogledd heddiw,	I love today what the English hate, the bright land of the North,
Ac yn amgant Lliw lliaws calledd.	and the clustering reeds by the Lliw.
Caraf a'm rhoddes rybuched medd	I love those who gave me mead in plenty
Myn y dyhaedd mŷr, maith gyfrysedd.	where the seas reach in long contention.
Caraf ei theulu a'i thew annedd ynddi,	I love its household and its strong dwelling,
Ac wrth fodd ei rhi rhwyfaw dyhedd.	and to go to war at the king's pleasure
Caraf ei morfa a'i mynyddedd a'i chaer ger ei choed a'i chain diredd,	I love its fens and its mountains, its castle near the woods and its fair herds.
A dolydd ei dwfr a'i dyffrynnedd,	its river-meadows and its valleys,
A'i gwylain gwynion a'i gwymp wragedd.	its white seagulls and its lovely women.
Caraf ei milwyr a'i meirch hywedd,	I love its soldiers and its trained stallions,
A'i choed a'i chedyrn a'i chyfannedd.	its forest, its fastnesses and its farms.
Caraf ei meysydd a'i mân feillion arnaw	I love its fields with their little clover
Myn yd gafas ffaw ffyrf orfoledd.	Where fame won lasting glory.
Caraf ei brooedd, braint hyẅredd,	I love its lands, birthright of the brave,
A'i diffaith mawrfaith a'i marannedd ...	its wide wilderness and its wealth.

Another poem is about a girl:

Fy newis i, rhiain firain feindeg,	My choice, a slim, fair bright girl
Hirwen, yn ei llen lliw ehöeg.	tall, lovely in her heather-coloured gown;
A'm dewis synnwyr, synio ar wrei-giaidd,	My chosen joy to watch the maid
Pen ddywaid o fraidd weddaidd wofeg.	When she whispers gentle words.
A'm dewis gydran, cyhydreg â bun,	My chosen part to be with a girl,
A bod yn gyfrin am rin, am reg.	to be alone with her secret and her gift.
Dewis yw gennyf i, harddliw gwaneg,	My choice, foam-coloured one,
Y ddoeth i'th gyfoeth, dy goeth Gymraeg.	wise among women, is your fine Welsh.
Dewis gennyf di; beth yw gennyd di fi?	You are my choice. What am I to you?
Beth a dewi di, deg ei gosteg?	Why are you silent, sweet silence?
Dewisais i fun fal nad atreg gennyf;	I have chosen a girl and have no regret;
Iawn yw dewisaw dewisdyn teg.	it is right to choose a fair girl of choice.

There is joy and simplicity in these poems that sets them apart from the praise-poetry of the professional bards, who cultivated obscurity of diction and an archaic vocabulary. Metrically they are quite strict: nine syllables in the line, the first line of the couplet sometimes having ten or eleven; end-rhyme throughout, save in a few lines where there is compensation by internal rhyme in the next line. The metre is an *awdl* of *cyhydedd naw ban* (a couplet with nine syllables in each line), *cyhydedd hir* (a couplet of ten and nine), and *toddaid* (eleven and nine, with internal rhyme), with rich ornament of alliteration and internal rhyme, bringing us close to the fully developed *cynghanedd*.[1]

Another prince-poet is Owain Cyfeiliog, who was prince of Powys from 1149 to 1195, and of whose work only one poem survives. It is called *Hirlas Owain* 'Owain's Tall Blue Horn', and the theme is a banquet at the prince's court, where he calls on the cup-bearer to fill the horn for the warriors in turn.

Dywallaw, fenestr, na fynn angeu,	Fill, cup-bearer, if you would live,
Corn can anrhydedd yng nghyfe-ddeu,	the horn held in honour at the banquet,
Hirlas buelin uchel freinieu,	the long blue horn, high in renown,
Ariant a'i gortho, nid gortheneu;	ringed with rich silver,
A dyddwg Dudur, eryr aereu,	and bring to Tudur, eagle of battle,
Gwirawd gysefin o'r gwin gwineu;	the first draught of ruddy wine.

[1] Lloyd-Jones, *Court Poets* 26, PBA XXXIV (1949).

Oni ddaw i mewn o'r medd goreu	If there come not in a draught of the best mead
Gwirawd ran o ban, dy ben faddeu!	from the bowl, your head shall pay for it!
Ar llaw Foreiddig, llochiad cerddeu,	Bear to Moreiddig, protector of poets,
Cyrdd cenynt ei glod, cyn oer adneu.	whose praise the minstrels would sing, before the chilly grave.
Dierchyr frodyr, fryd uchel ddeu	Two fearless brothers they, lofty of mind,
Diarchar arial, a dan daleu,	of vigour that knows no fear and noble brows,
Cedwyr a'm gorug gwasanaetheu ...	warriors that did me service ...;
Moliant yw eu rhan, y rhei gynneu, –	Praise is their portion, these I spake of –
Marwnad bid, neud bu newid y ddeu!	nay, 'tis the death-song is their portion; they are dead both!
Och Grist! mor wyf drist o'r anaeleu	O Christ, how sad am I for the pain of his loss,
O goll Moreiddig, mawr ei eisieu!	Moreiddig, how great the need of him.[1]

Perhaps the grandest poem of this period of the *Gogynfeirdd* is that which marks its close, the famous lament for Llywelyn ap Gruffudd, the last of the Welsh princes, by Gruffudd ab yr Ynad Coch. Llywelyn was killed in an attack on the castle of Builth in 1282, and his death put an end to the hope of freedom in Wales. The same despair did not settle upon Ireland until the flight of the earls in 1607. In Wales, as in Ireland later, the poets realized the disaster that had befallen their country, and the traditions of courtly life on which they so much depended; and they proclaimed their sorrow. In this poem grief somehow lends the poet wings, and he soars beyond the bonds of professional praise-poetry. It says for Wales what was so finely said again for Ireland by Owen Roe Macaward in his lament for the Earls of Tyrone and Tyrconnell.

Oer calon dan fron o fraw – allwynin	My heart is cold within my breast from fear and pity
Am frenin, dderwin ddôr, Aberffraw.	For the king of Aberffraw, an oaken door.
Aur dilyfn a dalai o'i law,	He gave fine gold with a free hand;
Aur dalaith oedd deilwng iddaw. ...	the golden chaplet was his due. ...
Gwae fi am arglwydd, gwalch diwaradwydd;	Alas for my lord, the hawk unrivalled!
Gwae fi o'r aflwydd ei dramgwyddaw.	Alas for the sorrow of his fall!
Gwae fi o'r golled, gwae fi o'r dynged,	Alas for the loss, alas for the fate,
Gwae fi o'r clywed fod clwyf arnaw.	Alas for the news that he is stricken!

[1] transl. Bell.

The lament reaches its climax in lines that are famous among Welsh-men, and are indeed a grand expression of mourning. The music of the verse, with its elaborate ornament, is here no mere substitute for poetry. Here sound and sense combine in a flood of eloquence inspired by anger and sorrow:

Poni welwch-chwi hynt y gwynt a'r glaw?	See ye not the wind's rush and the rain?
Poni welwch-chwi'r deri'n ymdaraw?	See ye not how the oaks beat to-gether?
Poni welwch-chwi'r môr yn merwin-aw – 'r tir?	See ye not the sea, how it lashes the land?
Poni welwch-chwi'r gwir yn ymgy-weiriaw?	See ye not the truth in its travail?
Poni welwch-chwi'r haul yn hwylaw – 'r awyr?	See ye not the sun, how he hurries through heaven?
Poni welwch-chwi'r sŷr wedi r'syr-thiaw?	See ye not the stars, how they are fallen?
Poni chredwch-chwi i Dduw, ddy-niadon ynfyd?	Will ye not believe in God, fond menfolk?
Poni welwch-chwi'r byd wedi r'by-diaw.	See ye not the world in its peril?
Och hyd atat-ti, Dduw, na ddaw – môr dros dir!	Oh, that to Thee, O God, it might come, the sea flooding the land!
Pa beth y'n gedir i ohiriaw?	What thing is left us that we linger here?
Nid oes le y cyrcher rhag carchar braw;	There is no place to flee to from the prison of fear,
Nid oes le y triger; och o'r trigaw!	there is no place to abide in; alas, the abiding!
Nid oes na chyngor na chlo nac agor,	There is no counsel nor key nor open way
Unffordd i esgor brwyn gyngor braw.	to cast from our souls the sad conflict of fear.[1]

The rich patterns of alliteration and rhyme that are known as *cynghanedd* have not reached their full development, but the effect here is almost as though they had.[2] It would be worth the reader's while to hear this passage read in Welsh in order to have a right impression of the achievement.

The poems of the *gogynfeirdd* were recited in the hall by the *pencerdd* or the *bardd teulu*, and another entertainment was provided by the *cyfar-wydd*, the story-teller. Of the tales that were told only a few have been

---

[1] tr. Bell in *HWL*, p. 54.
[2] *Cynghanedd* was not fully developed till the fourteenth century, see *HWL* 122.

preserved, and they are commonly known as *Mabinogion*, since the famous translation by Lady Charlotte Guest became popular. But the title belongs properly to four tales, which in the manuscripts are described as 'branches of the *Mabinogion*', so that we speak commonly of 'the four branches'.

The Four Branches of the *Mabinogion* are a sort of miracle inasmuch as they came in the eleventh century, anonymous and unheralded by any earlier prose of their kind, yet written by a master of prose style, simple, eloquent and beautiful. The style is far above the content of the tales, for the narrative is not always coherent nor clearly motivated, nor is there a sequence of the four stories. The story of Manawydan is a sequel to that of Branwen, and Pryderi appears in all four; the marriage of Pwyll and Rhiannon is referred to in *Math*. But the four stories are independent. *Pwyll* and *Math* stand by themselves. Yet the Four Branches of the *Mabinogion* are clearly the work of one redactor, someone who had gathered together fragments of a vanishing tradition and possessed a gift for composition and a sense of style. The two that have most appeal are *Branwen* and *Math*.

Matthew Arnold first said of the *Mabinogion*: 'The mediaeval story-teller is pillaging an antiquity of which he does not fully possess the secret.' Gruffydd in his study of *Math fab Mathonwy* showed how much can be won from contemporary Irish and Scottish folklore to throw light on the composition of the *Mabinogion*, and incidentally he established the connexion in Irish tradition between the god Lug and the hero Finn mac Cumaill. His suggestion that the Four Branches were originally a sequence of tales with Pryderi as the central hero is, however, not convincing. Jackson in his Gregynog Lectures[1] has brought more light on the matter, and has shown convincingly that the stories were compiled by literary antiquarians after the tradition of the *cyfarwydd*, the professional storyteller, had been lost, and that they derive from various sources, international folk-lore motifs, old Celtic mythology, and borrowings from Irish sagas. The redaction that we have is the work of a single and singularly gifted author.

The tale of Branwen daughter of Llŷr has much to do with Ireland. Matholwch, king of Ireland comes to ask for Branwen, sister of Bran the Blessed, king of Britain. After she has been received as queen in Ireland, she is made to suffer cruel punishment in vengeance for an insult offered to Matholwch while he was in Britain. Bran hears of it and comes with an army to rescue her. The armies of both sides are destroyed in the ensuing battle. The seven Welsh survivors bring the head of Bran back with them, and finally they bury it in London.

Some episodes of the story introduce motifs that recur in Irish sagas.

[1] K. Jackson, *The International Popular Tale in Early Welsh Tradition*, Cardiff, 1961.

Mac Cana has made a careful and well balanced study of the tale in which he points to several episodes that seem to be simply borrowed.[1] One that has long been recognized as of Irish origin is that of the Iron House.[2]

In the story of Branwen, Bran the Blessed has given Matholwch a wonderful cauldron which restores the dead to life. Here is the passage describing how he came to possess it:

> One day I was hunting in Ireland, on the summit of a hill above a lake in Ireland called the Lake of the Cauldron; and I saw a tall fair-haired man coming from the lake with a cauldron on his back. And he was a huge, tall, evil-looking man; and there was a woman following him, and if he was tall, she was twice as tall. And they came towards me and greeted me. 'Well,' said I, 'what is your errand?' 'This is my errand, Lord,' said he. 'This woman will bear a child in six weeks, and the son that will be born of that pregnancy in six weeks will be a fully armed warrior.' I undertook to support them: they were with me for a year. For that year I kept them without hindrance: after that there was objection. And by the end of the fourth month they were making themselves hated and were wanton throughout the land, outraging and molesting and vexing both men and women. Thereupon my country rose up against me and demanded that I part with them, and gave me a choice between my country and them. I put it to the counsel of my people what should be done with them. They would not go willingly: they could not be made to go unwillingly by force of battle. And in this extremity, they caused a room to be built all of iron. And when the room was ready, they summoned all the smiths in Ireland, and all who possessed tongs and hammers, and they made them heap charcoal up to the height of the room. And food and drink in abundance were served to them, to the woman and the man and their children. And when it was known that they were drunk, fire was put to the coal all round the room, and the bellows that had been placed around the house were blown, a man to every two bellows; and they began to blow the bellows until the house was white-hot around them. Then they took counsel on the floor of the room; and he waited till the iron wall was white, and with the great heat he came against the wall with his shoulder and broke out through it, and his wife followed him. And none escaped from there save him and his wife. 'And then, I suppose, Lord,' said Matholwch to Bran the Blessed, 'he came over to you.' 'Then, indeed,' said he, 'he came here, and he gave me the cauldron.'

In several Irish sagas the τειχοσκοπία technique is employed to identify approaching strangers. A watcher describes what he sees, and from his description someone who knows them tells who they are. This is sometimes used to good effect as one group comes after another, more

---

[1] P. Mac Cana, *Branwen Daughter of Llŷr*, Cardiff, 1958.
[2] See C. O'Rahilly, *Ireland and Wales* 106 ff.

and more splendid, with a climax at the arrival of Cú Chulainn himself, as in 'Bricriu's Feast', or in Mac Roth's description of the approaching warriors to Fergus in *Táin Bó Cualnge*.[1] 'The Destruction of Da Derga's Hostel' introduces this motif to describe the company at the Hostel. Ingcél tells what he sees, and Fer Rogain recognizes the warriors from his description. In the course of this long account, there is one passage which closely resembles an episode in Branwen:

'I was almost overcome with terror as I beheld those three. There is nothing stranger than the two bald heads one on each side of a man with hair, two lakes one on each side of a mountain, two hides one on each side of an oak, two boats full of thorns on a round board, and a little stream of water, as it seemed, on which the sun shines as it flows down, and a hide arranged behind it, and the pillar of a palace like a great lance above it. The shaft would make a full load for a yoke of oxen. Find a likeness for that, Fer Rogain.' 'I can find it. That is Mac Cécht son of Snaide Teiched, champion of Conaire son of Eterscél. Mac Cécht is a good warrior. He was lying asleep on his couch when you saw him. The bald heads on each side of the man with hair that you saw are his knees on each side of his head. The lakes on each side of a mountain that you saw are his eyes on each side of his nose. The hides on each side of an oak that you saw are his ears on each side of his head. The two boats on a round board that you saw are his shoes upon his shield. The slender stream of water that you saw on which the sun shines as it flows down is the flickering of his sword. The hide arranged behind it is the scabbard of his sword. The pillar of a palace that you saw is his spear, and he brandishes that spear till the two ends come together. And he makes a cast of it as and when he likes. Mac Cécht is a good warrior.'[2]

In *Branwen* the Men of the Island of the Mighty are seen by the king's swineherds, coming to avenge the wrong done to the queen. The swineherds come to tell what they have seen:

'Hail to Your Lordship!' said they. 'We have seen a forest on the ocean, where we never before saw a single tree.' 'That is a strange thing,' said he. 'Do you see aught else?' 'Lord,' said they, 'we see a great mountain beside the forest, and it is moving; and a high ridge on the mountain with a lake on each side of the ridge; and the forest and the mountain and the rest are all in motion.' 'Well,' said he, 'there is no-one here who knows anything of that unless Branwen knows it. Ask her.'

Messengers went to Branwen. 'Lady,' said they, 'what do you think this is?' 'Though I am not a Lady,' said she, 'I know what this is. The men of the Island of the Mighty are coming over, for they have heard of my being punished and dishonoured.' 'What is the forest which they saw on the sea?' said they. 'The masts and spars of ships,' said she. 'And what was the mountain which they saw beside the ships?' 'That was my brother, Bran

[1] W. Faraday, *The Cattle-Raid of Cualnge* pp. 117 ff.
[2] E. Knott (ed.), *Togail Bruidne Da Derga* (Dublin, 1963), pp. 825-51.

the Blessed,' she said, 'wading through the shallows. There was no ship that could carry him.' 'What was the high ridge with a lake on each side?' 'That was he, looking upon this island,' said she, 'for he is angry. His eyes on each side of his nose are the two lakes on each side of the ridge.'

Mac Cana has shown convincingly that the author of *Branwen* has borrowed from the Irish saga, and from several other Irish stories; and that he has woven the old themes into a new texture which is not altogether coherent, but which succeeds all the same by virtue of its graceful style and the air of magic that pervades it.

These qualities appear again to good effect in the final episode of *Branwen*, when the survivors of the great battle in Ireland have returned to Wales with the severed head of Bran, and abide at Gwales[1] in Penfro. In origin it is an account of the happiness of the pagan Otherworld, but the monkish author seems not to realize this. The exuberant fancy of the Irish description of the Otherworld in 'The Voyage of Bran' and 'The Wasting Sickness of Cú Chulainn' are here exchanged for a tranquil simplicity. The heroes have been told that they shall enjoy this happiness for eighty years until they open the door looking out upon Aber Henvelen towards Cornwall:

> There they found a fair royal site above the sea. And there was a great hall, and to the hall they went. And they saw two open doors, but the third door, on the Cornwall side, was shut. 'Behold,' said Manawydan, 'the door that we are not to open.' And they spent that night there content and happy; and of all the sorrow that they had witnessed, or that they themselves had suffered, they remembered nothing, neither of that nor of any other grief.
>
> And there they spent the four score years, and knew that they had never passed a happier or more delightful time than that. It was no less agreeable than when they first came, nor could they tell from one another that they had been there so long. It was no less pleasant to have the head there with them than when Bran the Blessed had been alive among them. And from those four score years was named the Feasting of the Noble Head.

The grace and gladness of this prose is what charms the reader of the Mabinogion. *Branwen*, indeed, is fairly successful as a story, but *Math fab Mathonwy* is a medly of themes that are hard to disentangle, as Gruffydd has shown, and it is those qualities of form that outweigh the lack of purpose and construction.

Math is lord of Gwynedd. Gwydion son of Don tells him that Pryderi, a prince in the south, has wonderful swine, and promises to obtain them. He does so by magic, turning toadstools into horses, hounds and shields, which he barters for the precious swine. The enchantment lasts only for

---

[1] Probably the island of Grassholm in Pembrokeshire, see I. Williams, *Pedeir Keinc y Mabinogion*, pp. 214–15.

a day, and Gwydion escapes with his prize while the magic lasts. Pryderi comes in pursuit and is killed fighting against Math.

While Math is absent, Gwydion and his brother rape the maiden who has been Math's footholder.[1] In punishment Math turns them into deer, swine, wolves, in successive years till their crime is expiated.

Gwydion tells Math to take Arianrhod daughter of Don, his sister's daughter, as footholder, for the footholder must be a virgin. But she proves to be no maid. The child that she bears is adopted by Gwydion, and in four years he is as big as a boy of eight.

One day Gwydion brought the boy to visit his mother. She was angry at this reminder of her shame, and laid a curse on the child that he should have no name until she gave him one. Gwydion disguised himself and the boy as shoemakers, and Arianrhod was tricked into naming the boy Lleu Llawgyffes ('Bright One of the Dexterous Hand').[2] She then laid a curse on him that he should never take arms till she should give them to him. Gwydion created a hostile fleet by magic, and came with Lleu in disguise to defend Caer Arianrhod. Arianrhod gave them weapons to defend her, whereupon the ships vanished. Tricked again, she laid a curse on her son that he should never have a wife until she gave him one.

Math and Gwydion made a wife for Lleu out of flowers, and named her Blodeuwedd ('Flowerface'). One day, when Lleu was away at court, Gronw Pebyr came to Ardudwy on a hunting expedition. He and Blodeuwedd fell in love at once, and slept together for three nights. He told her to discover how Lleu could be killed.

Like Delilah in the Bible story, Blodeuwedd persuaded Lleu to tell her his secret. He had the gift of magic invulnerability: he could not be killed either in a house nor out of a house, neither on horse-back nor on foot. He said that he could be killed only by a spear that was worked on for a year only at Mass-time on Sundays. The only way in which he could be killed would be when standing with one foot on the back of a he-goat and the other on the edge of a bath-tub, and then only by the unique spear. Here three familiar folk-motifs are combined: the faithless wife discovering her husband's secret (ST. K 2213.4.1); the paradoxical tasks (ST. H 1050); unique invulnerability (ST. Z 310). Jackson observes that the combination of the two last seems to be archaic, and points to the parallel with Vritra in the *Mahābhārata*, who can be killed neither by day nor by night, neither by stone nor by wood and so on.[3]

---

[1] The king's footholder is an officer of the court according to Welsh law.

[2] Here there seems to be a survival of old tradition, for the dedication *Lugovibus* at Osma in Spain (*CIL* II 2818) is by shoemakers, so that the god Lugus would seem to have been their patron; and *Lleu* is the Welsh form of his name. See p. 13.

[3] W. J. Gruffydd, *Math* pp. 31, 301 ff.; Jackson, *The International Popular Tale and Early Welsh Tradition* 106 ff.

After a year Blodeuwedd contrived the required conditions, and Gronw Pebyr wounded Lleu with the venomous spear. He flew away in the form of an eagle.

Gwydion set out in search of Lleu, and found him by following a sow that fed on the maggots that fell from the dying eagle's flesh, as he roosted in a tree. Gwydion restored him to human form and healed him of his wound. Blodeuwedd was changed into an owl, and Gronw Pebyr was slain by Lleu.

Math is not successful as a story. There is no hero, unless it be Lleu Llawgyffes. His adventures are the main interest, but Gwydion is more of a champion than he. Lleu can be killed in a certain way, but the author seems to forget himself, for he is not killed, only changed into an eagle; and he later recovers and takes revenge. Yet Gwydion is at first a villain and suffers shameful punishment. Least of all is Pryderi the hero. He is merely cheated of his swine, and then killed in trying to recover them. The birth and youthful exploits of Lleu lead us to expect a heroic sequel, but all we are given is folk-lore. The name of the great god of the Celts is here a mere borrowing.

The story is, nevertheless, good entertainment, folk-tale and fairytale, in which men are changed into beasts, a fleet of ships or a wife can be made by magic, crimes are punished and virtue rewarded.

CULHWCH AND OLWEN

Culhwch and Olwen is in some respects the most interesting of the Welsh sagas. It contains a great amount of legendary material in which reference is made to persons and traditions that were once familiar to a Welsh audience, and some famous figures of Irish mythology and heroic legend are here included among Arthur's warriors, Cnychwr son of Nes, Cubert (= Cú Roí?) son of Daere and Fercos son of Roch. Manawydan son of Llŷr, who is the Irish Manannán, is also in the list of names. Moreover, Arthur and his court are here in the centre of the story, whereas they are not even mentioned in the Four Branches.

The story is more folk-tale than heroic saga, and indeed there is a general resemblance to modern Irish folktales about the King of Ireland's Son: the widowed king who marries again, the jealous stepmother who imposes on the king's son a quest to a giant's fortress, the helpers, the ordeals, the successful issue of the quest and a happy ending, with no exact geographical setting.

Goleuddydd, wife of Cilydd, bears a son at a place where a swineherd is keeping a herd of swine. Through terror of the swine, the child is born,[1] and he is put out to nurse.

The boy's mother soon died, and after seven years the king married again. When the queen discovered that the king had a son, she asked that he hide him no longer, and the lad was summoned to court. The queen swore a destiny upon him that he would never marry till he should win Olwen daughter of Ysbaddaden Chief Giant; and the king's son was at once filled with love for Olwen 'though he had never seen her'.[2] His father sent him to Arthur's court to ask for Olwen as a gift, for Arthur was his cousin.

Culhwch's arrival at the court of Arthur echoes the arrival of Lug of the Long Arm at the court of Nuadu in the Irish *Battle of Moytura*. At first he is refused admission, and then Arthur orders that he be admitted, and makes him welcome. Culhwch demands that Arthur get him Olwen, and invokes the names of Arthur's warriors. The list of more than two hundred and fifty names includes some, such as Manawydan son of Llyr, who cannot have been thought of as warriors at Arthur's court, and ends with the names of twenty women. It is plainly a mere catalogue of names, and to some of them brief notes of explanation are attached.

Then the great quest begins. When the warriors arrive at the fort of Ysbaddaden, a shepherd warns them that none who came on that quest before had come away alive. They force their way into the fort and salute the giant. His eyelids are raised up with forks, so that he may see them, and he hurls a poisoned spear at them.[3] Bedwyr catches the spear and hurls it back, wounding the giant in the knee.

After he has hurled three poisoned spears in vain, and himself received three wounds, the giant addresses Culhwch and imposes on him a series of impossible tasks which must be performed in order to win his daughter, Olwen. This list of tasks is again a collection of legendary motifs in which a great deal of lost tradition seems to be evoked. It makes tedious reading, but in delivery by a good storyteller, it might be entertaining. Forty tasks are recited, and to each Culhwch replies: 'It is easy for me to get that, though you think it is not easy.' The twenty-first task is to get the comb and scissors that are between the two ears of Twrch Trwyth son of Taredd Wledig, to dress the giant's hair; and nearly all the subsequent tasks are ancillary to this, a hound to hunt the boar, a leash for the hound, a collar for the leash, a huntsman to hold the leash, a horse for the huntsman, and so on.

[1] The famous Irish king Cormac was born in the forest during a thunderstorm, and was suckled by a wolf-bitch (see *CK* 24).
[2] Cf. the Irish *grád ecmaise*, p. 243.
[3] Balor, in the Irish *Battle of Moytura*, has the poison in his eye, the lid of which was raised by four men, when he wished to destroy an enemy (RC xii 100).

The earlier tasks include references to legendary or mythological figures, Amaethon son of Don, Mabon son of Modron, the birds of Rhiannon, the cauldron of Diwrnach the Irishman, pointing to a lost hoard of tradition.

Now the greater quest begins under the leadership of Arthur himself. In the sequel many of the tasks are performed and many are simply forgotten. The search for Mabon son of Modron is well told. The warriors go to consult the Ouzel of Cilgwri, who sends them to a stag, who sends them to an owl, who sends them to an eagle, who sends them to a salmon; and the salmon guides them to Caer Loyw (Gloucester) where Mabon is held captive. (Here the folk motif of The Oldest Animals is artlessly introduced.)

Some passages of the story are incoherent, as when Gwythyr saves an ant-hill from fire, and we are told that the grateful ants later brought flax seed for the performance of one of the tasks. The actual performance is never related. Later there is a digression about the rivalry of Gwythyr son of Greidawl and Gwynn son of Nudd for the hand of Creiddylad daughter of Lludd Llaw Ereint, and we are told that when they had been reconciled, Arthur obtained the steed and the leash that the giant had demanded.

After the performance of sundry tasks, Arthur gathered together the warriors of the Island of Britain and its three adjacent islands, and of France and Brittany and Normandy and the Summer Country; and he went to Ireland to hunt Twrch Trwyth. The rest of the saga is an account of the hunt. The magic boar crosses into Britain and is hunted across the Severn into Cornwall. The scissors and comb are captured, and the boar escapes into the sea.

One other task is performed, making rather an anti-climax to the story, and Culhwch returns in triumph with all his trophies to the giant's court. The giant was beheaded, 'and that night Culhwch slept with Olwen, and she was his only wife so long as he lived. And the hosts of Arthur dispersed, every one to his country.'

Of the five Welsh tales in which Arthur is prominent, *Culhwch and Olwen* is the most interesting. Here it is Arthur who receives the hero and who leads the hunt for Twrch Trwyth. The warriors who perform the other quests are men in his service. He appears not merely as king of Britain, but as ruler of France, Brittany and Normandy; and one of the principal passages in the story is the long and tedious list of his warriors. But he is not in the centre of the action. Culhwch and Ysbaddaden are the central figures, and we are not told much about Arthur himself. His sword, *Caledfwlch*, his shield and spear, and his ship, *Prydwen* (which is also mentioned in the old *Preideu Annwfn*) are already famous.

Another Arthurian tale is *Rhonabwy's Dream*, a strange and incoherent story in which Arthur cuts a rather poor figure. He is splashed with water by a horse crossing a ford, and one of his men strikes the horse. He then engages in a board-game with Owein, who denies his requests, and treats him as an equal. But even here he is the great emperor, and the armies of the Norsemen are in his service. When Rhonabwy asks whether the army will flee, he is told: 'The Emperor Arthur has never fled, and if you were heard saying that, you would be a lost man.' Moreover, all this happens in a dream, as Rhonabwy sleeps on a yellow ox-hide.

The other three Arthurian tales, *Gereint, Owein* and *Peredur* are strongly influenced by Norman-French literary convention. The relationship between them and the French romances, Erec, Yvain and Perceval, of Chrétien de Troyes has not been clearly established. They are not mere translations from the French, but they are believed to be adaptations of French romances which themselves derived from earlier Welsh sources.[1] A discussion of them is beyond our purpose.

These prose romances are the end of a tradition, and have no sequel in the literature. In Wales as in Ireland it was originally an oral tradition, and the tales were recited at the king's court, or the nobleman's house, by the *cyfarwydd*, and told in a ruder form no doubt by humbler storytellers beside the fire in the house of every man. In both countries Norman influence introduced new fashions in literature, and the future lay with translations, first from Latin and later from French. The Siege of Troy, the Aeneid, the Thebaid, and the Story of Alexander, Charlemagne, Marco Polo and Sir John Mandeville are the sort of entertainment that became fashionable among the great; and the native traditions survived mainly as folktales, told in the country cottages, as they are still told in parts of Ireland even now. It was poetry that flourished in Wales later on, and that has continued to flourish in a wonderful way.

[1] See Jones and Jones, *The Mabinogion* pp. xxviii ff.; Parry, *HWL* 87.

CHAPTER 12

CELTIC ART

THE preceding chapters will have made it clear that from the middle of the first millennium BC the Celts were the most powerful and the most impressive peoples in Europe beyond the frontiers of the Mediterranean lands. These Celtic tribes, originally widely dispersed throughout central Europe, gradually concentrated in the west into the more homogeneous political nation of the Gauls. While they have left only sparse records of themselves in written form, chiefly in inscriptions (pp. 2–3, 197 above), we have a considerable amount of information about their history and their institutions from the writings of the Classical peoples with whom they were in contact. In addition, we have an ever increasing source of information on their material culture and way of life from archaeology. We know something of how they lived and died; how they fought and what weapons they used; we know something of their religion and mythology, but owing to the absence of a fully literate society we have no written record from the Gauls themselves of their spiritual or their personal life.

We have, however, a direct contact with them through their art. From the earliest times, until its last fine flowering in the peripheral island countries of the West in the early Christian centuries, Celtic art is a rich and highly individual development, influenced and modified by Eastern and Southern influences, but never superseded, or even transformed by them. It is distinguished by a fundamental individuality which is essentially Celtic, and which remains constant throughout its history wherever the Celtic peoples are found. We can trace its early roots already in the period of Hallstatt culture in the first half of the first millennium BC; but the art which we would define as distinctively Celtic coincides with the Second Iron Age and is that of the La Tène period of about 500 BC to AD 100. This is the art of Gaul at the height of her power, before the Roman Conquest. The flowering of this art is in no way diminished in the insular Celtic countries during the early centuries of the Christian era. In the peripheral countries it survived the Roman Conquest, and in Ireland, where no Roman Conquest took place, this original Celtic art continued to flourish and develop until the Middle Ages, only partially modified by new motifs in the Viking Age.

Our leading authority on Continental Celtic art, the late Professor Jacobsthal, summarizes his impression at the close of his book on *Early Celtic Art* with the words: 'In my opinion the whole of Celtic art is a unit. It is the creation of one race, the Celts.'[1]

Celtic art has been justly called the first great contribution by the Barbarians to European Art (Jacobsthal, p. 163). Its origin is unknown, although it has been thought until recent times that it must have developed in the earliest phase from a single School; but where, when, how? What was the initial inspiration? The answer to these questions is hidden from us. Recent opinion[2] is less precise in this matter, interpreting it as a slow composite development under varying conditions and in varying localities. Yet it is a distinct national art. The salient features of Celtic art are quite different from those of other national arts, such as the art of the Phoenicians and the Iberians, the Etruscans, the Greeks. Yet Celtic art is no isolated development, and its history is eloquent of many foreign contacts. These have played a large part in its growth from different quarters and at different periods, and enable us to gain something of a chronology in its history over the centuries.

What, then, are the basic qualities which we recognize in Celtic art wherever it is found? Perhaps the most fundamental is its originality, the choice and combination of the motifs, chiefly from the world of nature, the animal and vegetable world, with only occasional and incidental human elements, the whole forming a fantastic creation of the imagination, remote from reality. An invariable element in these creations is the refinement of mind which inspires the compositions. There is a total absence of coarseness of conception or of treatment. This refinement expresses itself everywhere in delicacy of line, an unerring artistic taste in the use of flowing curves and their purpose in a given design.

The artistic result is the achievement of abstract perfection and grace. The Celtic artists had an instinctive realization of the value of the flowing line and sureness of touch in its delineation. They had a love of pattern. To them nature supplied the inspiration of an artistic motif, expressed at a remove from the sensory perceptions, not – we would insist – as a symbol, but as controlled by artistic instinct and technique. Celtic artists had a keen sense of the value of ornament and of its adaptation to a given material object, combined with an unerring sense of form, which is especially noticeable in their coins (cf. Plate 11; Varagnac, pp. 193–208). Their rich and even redundant wealth of design, amounting almost to a *horror vacui*, spent itself in a generous application of conscious artistic effort to make the most of its opportunities and of its material. This art is essentially imaginative rather

[1] Jacobsthal, *E.C.A.* (Oxford, 1944), I, p. 160.
[2] A. Varagnac, *A.G.*, *passim*.

than representational. It is rarely possible to distinguish the species of foliage in their designs. In both the plant and animal world the result is a stylization rather than a direct reproduction, and the blending of various species results in fantasies which remind us of the late Clasical bestiaries. This phase of Celtic art has given its stamp and characteristic features to its whole long history, and persists through the migrations and wars of the people and the period of the great Gaulish nation before the Roman conquest until we trace the lost grammar of native Celtic ornament in the beautiful curvilinear stylized floreate designs on the Marne pottery, preserved, for example, in the Museum of St Brieuc in Brittany, and in the art, many centuries later, of the ornamental marginal figures in Irish manuscripts, and perhaps – though here the intermediate stages are less certain – in the Pictish grave slabs.

This basic form of Celtic art reached its highest development in the period of the Empire. The Celtic art rooted in the Hallstatt phase in the first half of the first millennium BC had not been in any sense a national development, but was a part of the contemporary international art of Eurasia, and shared in the corresponding phase of the Greek 'geometrical period'. Its common features are the stylization of all natural representations into linear, and especially angular, geometrical forms and repetitions. Typical motifs are superimposed bands of identical wooden-looking horses in procession, and an endless repetition of rows of aquatic birds. It is a 'wholesale' art, such identical bands being easy to apply to metal-work and pottery, and cheap to reproduce.

By the eighth century a more advanced phase of art had developed in Greece and Italy, transformed by richer and more varied influences from the East, and known to Classical archaeologists as the Orientalizing period. Three centuries later a similar fashion developed in Gaul, involving a complete transformation from the older geometrical style to the richer, fuller, and freer play of the imagination in the artistic expression of the world of nature, a curvilinear, a more crowded, and essentially fantastic style, combined in such a way as to produce a totally new and very individual art. The cultural development of Gaul, in company with that of North Europe in general, lagged behind that of the Eastern Mediterranean countries, and in the Gaulish development of this new art the fresher and richer inspiration did not come directly from the East but tardily, by an indirect route, in part through Greece to Italy, and from Italy to Central Europe, perhaps also through the Caucasus; but the ultimate source was still the East.

This period of the art which we define as specifically Celtic, shows itself fully developed in fantastic combinations of animals and foliage, bizarre and unnatural images of natural objects, the flora and fauna of the East, lotuses, palms, lions, and the wild beasts of the desert, divorced from their realistic images and recombined in alien settings, sometimes wholly, sometimes only partially. The amazing thing about this new style of the La Tène period which succeeded to that of the Hallstatt is that it has no obvious beginnings, no gradual evolution. Like Pictish art in Scotland it is a mature and finished product when it first appears. Some new and powerful external stimulus could alone account for it, introducing foreign motifs into Celtic ateliers, such as the animals of the desert, the vegetation of the tropics. But how these Oriental elements came to the Northern Celts remains mysterious. Direct contacts are ruled out by the absence of evidence for direct political or trade relations, either across the Steppes or from Greece by sea. They would seem to have filtered through by intermediaries, especially and earliest through Etruria.

Many of the most fantastic motifs which characterize Celtic art are combined in the repoussé decoration of its greatest masterpiece, the large silver cauldron, commonly called the Gundestrup bowl (Plate 4). It was found in 1891 in separated sections in a peat-bog in Denmark, but it is of Celtic manufacture, and is generally thought to date from the first or second century BC. The presence of Oriental elements, such as the elephant, and other features in the design have suggested the middle Danube as its possible origin. The Scordisci of that region are reported by Athenaeus to value silver above gold,[1] and the remarkable size of the cauldron – 42 cm. high, 69 cm. across – and its weight of almost 9 kilogrammes are unique in silver objects among the Celts. Even more remarkable are the lively and spectacular scenes depicted on the surface inside and out – the horned god Cernunnos, and other divine beings; human masks; snakes; animals, natural and imaginary; birds; armed warriors in procession; and ritual scenes such as the drowning of a human being, held head downwards by the legs in a tub.[2]

Although we cannot establish the beginning of Celtic art as we have characterized it above, its native spiritual growth may be limited to the La Tène phase of culture in Europe. Its later developments were more splendid, but not, in general, different in kind. Celtic art has been called an art of ornament, of masks, of foliage, and beasts in a wholly imaginative combination, and these are certainly elements in which their art excels, and which separate it from the Greek world of natural man and his environment. It is the art of a people intensely aware of their environment in the world of nature before the first elements of scientific classification had begun. If it lacks the humanity of the Greek world it also lacks the arrogance which has dominated European art since Classical times – since the Greek red figure vases and the Greek

[1] *Celts*, p. 168. [2] J. Filip, *Celtic Civilisation* (Prague, 1962), p. 170.

masterpieces of sculpture first revealed to man his own dignity and supremacy in the world of creation.

The Gaulish artist crowded his canvas, aiming at effect by richness of fancy rather than by impressive economy. He never learnt the positive value of blank space to enhance the effect of a subject and form a major part of an artistic composition. This was the great discovery of Greeks of the period of the red figure vases which never reached the Gaulish artists, but we shall find it in the art of the insular Celts of Ireland. The affinities of the Gaulish artists remained with the Cycladic artists who loved to fill in the spaces around the main figures of their pottery with rosettes, shells, and little whorls faintly reminiscent of lower marine life. Characteristics of the earlier phases of Greek painters persisted in Celtic art, heavily sur-charged and enriched, especially in the Irish manuscripts. We can trace them especially in the illuminations of the Gospels in the *Book of Kells*. Here too the angular human figures, comparable to those of the early Slavonic ikons, are reminiscent of the human form on Greek black figure vases rather than of the natural human forms on the red figure.

One of the most striking, and perhaps the most revolutionary, features of La Tène art is the introduction of polychrome. This came into Gaul simultaneously with other Oriental fashions. In the early polychrome phase the element of colour was chiefly introduced by coral inlay; but in the second phase coral gives place largely to red enamel, which is much more richly and profusely used. Its origin is unknown, but it was probably in Central Asia – perhaps Persia. In Britain red enamel was used as a splendid ornament of jewelry, horse trappings, chariot mounts, and arms, among the most splendid examples being the Battersea shield of La Tène II [Plate 23]. With the height and proportions of this shield it is interesting to compare the stone sculpture of the Gaulish warrior of the Augustan era from Mondragon, now at Avignon [Plate 13]. This statue shows that the shield of La Tène II must have been still in use at the time of the Roman Conquest, and indeed most of the shield bosses found in the trenches at Alesia are of this type. Our plate helps us to picture 'the Aedui prince' Diviciacus, who had gone to Rome to beg help against the invasion of Ariovistus, and who is referred to in the anonymous Panegyric VIII (57) addressed to the Emperor Constantine in 310, as 'haranguing the senate, leaning on his shield'.

The developments in the technique of the period are chiefly seen in pottery and metalwork, because these are the objects which most commonly survive. The pottery of La Tène is well made and symmetrical, commonly of a beautifully polished black surface, and balanced on a small and delicate foot. The metalwork is mostly of bronze, often of perforated design, and worked with great expertise into articles of jewelry, horse-trappings and harness and chariot-mounts, as well as arms and weapons. Scabbards are beautifully worked, especially the chapes. These bronze objects are rendered vivid by a liberal use of champlevé and red enamel.

Celtic art culminated at the height of the power of the Gauls. In the peripheral countries, especially in insular Britain, which drew their inspiration from this great development of La Tène culture, the main features continued to develop and expand in beauty and technique. But the power of growth and creation, of apprehending a new vision in the art of representation, died in Gaul herself after the Roman Conquest. The great developments in naturalistic sculpture of the Greek Classical world surpassed and by-passed Celtic art of the great creative period. We shall see that the Gauls were influenced and stimulated indirectly by naturalistic Greek sculpture, but only at a later period, and as a secondary development.

Early Celtic art is a linear art, essentially frontal, a two-dimensional rather than a three-dimensional expression. It aims at conveying a visual rather than a tangible impression. Whether as a cause or as a result of this linear character, the art of their stone sculpture is relatively elementary in the early period, and also relatively rare. The linear tradition still survives in the indication of the features, especially the mouth, of the stone figure from Holzgerlingen, Würtemberg [Jacobsthal, *Imagery*, Pl. 1*b*], and even in the stone heads from Entremont. Native free-standing sculpture in stone is crude, and suggests that Celtic craftsmen did not realize or develop the technique of artistic work in stone as a native art until the influence of Mediterranean sculpture had reached the north. This is especially true of the early representation of the human form, which is suggestive of a stele when upright, and is lifeless when seated. Even the human heads, which are capable of evoking a strong emotional appeal, are the creation of a type, strongly and often beautifully expressed; but they are neither individualized nor refined in surface treatment.

In general, Celtic representation of living figures in metalwork is superior to that of stone sculpture, but is confined to miniature figures in bronze, chiefly attached as handles or other adjuncts to some larger, commonly utilitarian, object. Heads and busts are highly stylized, with features similar to those of the stone sculptures and characteristically Celtic. A typical example is the bronze relief from Waldalgesheim (Jacobsthal, pl. 8, fig. 156) with the characteristic Celtic head 'broad above, narrow below', the prominent eyes, triangular nose, the emphasized eyebrows, the narrow slit mouth, absence of clearly marked ears, a framework of two leaves pointing downwards, and an upturned curl at the tip which may well have developed as a stylized form of hair, although commonly regarded as typifying a Celtic god.

Celtic stone animal sculpture is extremely rare [Plate 64] and in bronze is also rare in naturalistic form. The most interesting examples are the bronze horse 12 cm. long from a Chariot-burial at Trier, which is a stiff and not competently anatomical model, and a boar from Budapest which would be a convincing animal if Celtic running spirals and half circles had not been substituted for bristles on the crest. A little bronze deer (10 cm. high) is pleasingly modelled but abstract in form (Jacobsthal, pl. 372). Its purpose is unknown, but certain details are reminiscent of Scythian technique. The use of birds as ornament, singly, in heraldic pairs, or in rows, is too widespread in the art of the Eurasian world from the Hallstatt period onwards to be regarded as purely Celtic, but was a prominent motif in Celtic art. The most effective example of the La Tène animal art is that of the conventionalized foxes (?) stalking the duck on the Lorraine flagon [Plate 9], a rare example of naturalistic grouping. The artist has caught to perfection the innocent unawareness of the duck and the eager predatory parent training her offspring to stalk. The details again show Oriental features and both coral and enamel are used, and conventional spirals indicate the leg joints, and line-hatchings, the natural hair; but this intimate little scene, on an object found, as is believed, on the Moselle, brings a rare homely touch into Gaulish art such as might well be used on an illuminated page for Ausonius's poem *Mosella*.

The convention of depicting an animal forming the handle is repeated in the Salzburg flagon (Jacobsthal pl. 382) and that from Borscher Aue near Geisa (Jacobsthal pls. 382, 383). In the latter the animal is standing on the shoulder of the jug and stretching up to the lip to drink. Despite the difference of motif it is impossible not to think of the dog, forming part of the handle of a spoon in the St Ninian's treasure from Shetland, and leaning forward to lick the contents greedily with protruding tongue[1].

It was the expertise of the Greeks in the working of stone – the natural medium of their country – which first developed in Europe the art of surface modelling, and of stone architecture for domestic and religious buildings. In the Celto-Ligurian *oppida* the original simple Celtic tradition of fortification developed into more urban plans with regular streets and temples; but since the discovery of native wooden sculpture in Gaul, to which we shall refer later, we may expect to find traces of more elaborate indigenous Gaulish wooden architecture than has been recognized. In both Gaul and Britain the skill in detecting

[1] Chadwick, *C.B.*, notes and references to Plate 54.

traces of early wooden remains is a relatively recent archaeological technique. We must be prepared for surprises.

The two regions where Celtic stone sculpture eventually developed are (1) Germany, where the art shows most originality, and where traces of foreign influence are relatively scarce; and (2) Provence, where foreign influence is traced through Marseilles, and where the earlier Ligurian culture has played a part. There can be no doubt that an important stimulus to the growth of stone statuary, especially in the south, was functional, and that it is closely bound up with the development of the great sanctuaries, as we shall see. In the north the architectural function of the stone figure from Holzgerlingen, Würtemberg (cf. *sup.*) is suggested by the tenon-joint at the bottom, which Jacobsthal believed to have been inserted into a wall.

Several examples of stone sculpture are known from the Rhineland and Würtemberg. The chief centre is Pfalzfeld in Hunsrück in the land of the Treveri, where Celtic Mounds are numerous. Here a famous limestone obelisk [Plate 63] is decorated on all its four sides with Celtic relief-motifs, and a human head, also in relief, is enclosed by great paired lobes or a bi-foliate leaf-shaped crown surmounted by scrolls. The pillar possibly terminated originally in a human head. The work is very archaic and may date from the fourth or third century BC (Filip, p. 161). The motif is peculiarly persistent, and may be compared with the design on the bronze plaque from Tal-y-Llyn, Merionethshire [Plate 30], of the early La Tène period.[1] The original Gaulish prototype is perhaps derived from fifth century Etruscan designs on jewelry.

The sculpture of the south again forms two groups. The first and least numerous and significant is all closely associated with Marseilles and is directly inspired by Greek statuary. The second group is the work of native artists in the tradition known as Celto-Ligurian, a combination of the oldest indigenous culture of the Mediterranean sea-board east of the lower Rhône, and a later, third century, Celtic superimposition. This group is very local and distinctive, differing widely from Greek and Roman statuary. Its products are all of local stone and the work of native artists. The most numerous and impressive have been found in the religious sanctuaries of Entremont and Roquepertuse north of Marseilles, of which the architectural features are discussed below. Other sanctuaries in the same area, such as that of Glanum (Greek *Glanon*), share a common chthonic feature as sanctuaries of the dead and the Underworld, which persisted in Glanum until the Augustan era. These ancient Celto-Ligurian sanctuaries have a history going back to Hallstatt times, and are of great architectural interest. Their lintels

[1] See H. N. Savory, 'A New hoard of La Tène metalwork from Wales', *Celticum* XII (1965) 163.

are deeply incised with geometrical figures and schematized horsemen. All have monumental porticos, *propylea*, decorated with painting and sculpture, and a primitive timber-work superstructure, characteristic of the domestic architecture of the region. The city-gate of Glanum is the oldest in Gaul, dating from the fourth century BC, with relief sculpture on the side-walls representing Gaulish captives.

At Roquepertuse the pillars are furnished with sculptured heads and still preserve remains of polychrome painting of geometrical designs, and designs of fish, birds, horses, and human beings, both painted and incised [Plate 38]. At Entremont, at the base of the wall of the sanctuary, fifteen skulls were exhumed which had been exposed there. A fragment of a lintel shows two skull-shaped cells with a sculptured model of a *tête coupée*, the features of typical Celtic style but here without mouth, while one of the pillars is decorated with 12 heads of the same fashion [Plate 39]. A later phase, still at Entremont, is represented by rounded pillars decorated on their sides with *têtes coupées* in relief, and, on their principal face, with a relief representing cavaliers armed with long rapiers of La Tène II type. The building is known as the 'Hall of the Skulls'. Lintels and pillars similarly furnished with cells occupied by sculptured and natural skulls are characteristic also of Glanum and of the great sanctuary of Roquepertuse.

Entremont dates from the third century, and was the religious capital of the Celto-Ligurian peoples who formed part of the confederation of the Salyens (Salluvii).[1] Indeed the situation of its *oppidum* and the quality of its statuary mark it out as the most important centre of the political and religious life of the Celto-Ligurian peoples, and demonstrate the close association of their native sculptures with religion and architecture.[2] The sanctuary of Roquepertuse belongs to the phase of La Tène II. The direct relationship with Gaulish civilization is emphasized by the prominence in both these sanctuaries of the human head, divorced from the human figure, and generally, to use the current French term, the *tête coupée*. These sanctuaries are sometimes furnished with actual human skulls fixed in the lintels or the pillars, or with substitutes in the form of sculptured models of masks of the dead, with closed eyes.

The numerous *têtes coupées* in the Celto-Ligurian sanctuaries suggest a cult of the skull, and illustrate what Diodorus and Strabo report on the authority of Posidonius of the early Gaulish custom of cutting off and preserving the heads of enemies. It is of special interest to note that *têtes coupées* are not found in all the sanctuaries, e.g. at Mouries, and that the pillars of Roquepertuse and the moulding of the lintel of Glanum had had their skull cells added after the building of the porticos, while

---

[1] F. Benoit, *A.M.V.R.*, p. 9. [2] Benoit, *A.M.V.R.*, p. 17.

at Entremont the 'Hall of the Skulls' belonged to the last phase of the *oppidum*, not long before its destruction in 123 BC. From this we might be tempted to conclude that the custom was not very ancient; but a considerable number of skulls bearing traces of suspension were found scattered on the surface of a road which had been metalled with the débris of great splendour from earlier buildings, perhaps indeed from an earlier occupation. Some of the heads, probably mummified, appear to have been cut off and pierced shortly after death. The cult of the head was widespread throughout the territory, and in the Celtic *oppidum* of Puig Castelar human skulls were found in which the nails from which they had hung were still present. The cult is associated with the period of La Tène II, and has possible wider affinities with the sculptured heads on the Cyclopean rampart at Tarragona, and in certain Spanish *oppida*, and also with the *têtes coupées* on the Etruscan gates of Perugia and Volterra. They are possibly not unconnected with the popularity of the mask as a motif in the Gaulish art of the same period.

The *têtes coupées* have been described as 'the first expression of naturalistic art which developed in the La Tène culture under the influence of Greco-Roman sculpture'.[1] It was in this Celto-Ligurian aera that the Celts of the later La Tène period learned the art of stone sculpture in the round. These monuments are by no means all naturalistic, and, in fact, the most impressive, the Monster of Noves [Plate 41], is a highly imaginative group, generally regarded as a symbol of death. The composition is an expert production, representing a monster with lion-like body and hideous head and gaping jaws from which protrudes a human limb, while its forelegs rest on two realistic stone models of *têtes coupées*. We are familiar with monsters from whose jaws human forms project in the art of Este and Watsch and other sites of the Hallstatt period, where it was a favourite motif, and we may look for a common centre of origin, – but where? The sculptor of the Monster of Noves was no amateur, and had nothing to learn about the technique of group sculpture. It can be viewed from all sides, and is as competent in its three-fold composition as the Greek statue group of the Laocoön.

It was believed in the past that it was from the wealth of statuary in these great southern sanctuaries of the mouth of the Rhône that the Gauls first learnt the art in the later La Tène period of naturalistic human stone sculpture in the round. Entremont, in particular, was rich not only in natural human heads (Benoit, pl. 35), but also in entire human figures. The heads show the typical Celtic traits with which we are familiar from the Irish sagas – the face 'broad above, narrow below' – and the typical prominent eyes, straight triangular nose, and

[1] Benoit, *A.M.V.R.*, p. 24.

wide slit-like mouth characteristic of Gaulish heads in all sculptures, and reproduced in the Celtic stone head from Gloucester [Plate 21]. At Entremont we have also natural life-size statues of the tribal heroes, chiefs, and queens, clad in contemporary costumes with armour and weapons denoting their rank, possibly actual portraits.

The temple site of Roquepertuse is rich in statues of the human form even more directly associated with its religious cult. Four or five human figures, squatting in the cross-legged 'Buddha posture', with which we are also familiar from the attitude of the God Cernunnos on the Gundestrup bowl [Plate 4], have been recovered from the actual interior of the sanctuary. Their arms and legs are bare, but the torso is clad in a short tunic, decorated with rectilinear geometrical patterns in light relief or incised and painted. The posture is erect and the figures are slim and well-proportioned, but stiff and lifeless, although the arm in at least two of the statues is separated freely from the torso. The stiff and hieratic posture may be partly accounted for functionally by their position in the sanctuary itself. Presumably they were not intended to be scrutinized at close range, but to impress the communal imagination of the worshippers.

In recent years discoveries have been coming to light which have revolutionized our ideas of Celtic figure sculpture and are forcing us to reconsider the problems of its origin and relationship. While it still remains true that the most important influences on stone free-standing figure sculpture of Gaul are from the great Celto-Ligurian sanctuaries at the mouth of the Rhône, it is now clear to us that central Gaul possessed indigenous wooden sculpture which by the first century BC reached a comparatively high standard of development, and which was localized in religious sanctuaries. This localization and religious association may be in part due to the accident of our record. The survival of wooden sculpture is so precarious that our specimens are naturally restricted to important sites which have demanded excavation in their own rights. The oldest wooden sculptures are often reminiscent of the statuary of Entremont and Roquepertuse[1]. A wooden head, the features crudely moulded and incised, has been found in a Gaulish sacred enclosure at Montbouy (Loiret); and in a sacred well on the same site a full-size wooden figure of equally elementary art. A hooded statue of oak more than three metres high, believed to be pre-Roman, has been excavated on the shore of Lake Geneva.[2] All the wooden full-length figures so far found, however, are reminiscent of tree-trunks, and recall perhaps the *simulacra* in the sacred wood referred to by Lucan.

The most important collection of Gaulish wooden sculpture so far

[1] Moreau, *W.K.*, pl. 77.
[2] F. Stahelin, *Die Schweiz in römischer Zeit* (Basle, 1948) p. 544, fig. 157.

unearthed is from the well-known Gallo-Roman sanctuary of Sequana at the source of the Seine, in which extensive excavations have been taking place since 1953, and are still in progress.[1] During the excavations of 1956-7, 190 pieces of wooden sculpture came to light in the marshy precincts, constituting, as Professor Martin assures us (p. 2), by their diversity, their originality, and the quality of their preservation, one of the most astonishing discoveries of Gallo-Roman archaeology [Plates 72-77]. This initial find produced 27 statues or statuettes of half a metre to 1.25 metres in height; 40 heads from life- to half life-size; 16 pieces with 2 or 3 heads carved in relief on a single stave; 14 torsos, naked, draped, or schematized; about 30 limbs and some representations of the human internal organs; 12 representations of animals, including a fine bull; etc. Men and women were both represented – men being in the majority – and travellers (perhaps pilgrims) recognizable by their cloaks and hoods [Plate 74]. The heads are the cream of the collection, ranging from blocks with only sparse and elementary modelling, with incised features and hair [Plate 75], to the realistic modelling governed by the bone structure of the face and massed hair in relief [Plate 76] which, in spite of the characteristically Celtic slit-like mouth, present a realistic human head. The head of a woman [Plate 77], in its modelling of structure, features, and the arrangement of the hair, has achieved complete mastery.

The locality and the nature of the sculptures, and especially the single human limbs and organs, leave no doubt that this School of sculpture belongs to a medical sanctuary, but as yet the precise function of the artist and his atelier have to be determined. Was his status an official one, associated with the sanctuary, or a commercial adjunct? Certain features, e.g. the rows of heads carved on a single stave [Plate 73], suggest comparison with Entremont, and the close association of realistic sculpture with religion established by all these Gaulish Schools of sculpture.

The importance of the indigenous wooden sculpture from Gaul demonstrates the independence of the artists, and the close relationship between art and the local material. The stone which had given permanence to the sculpture of the Mediterranean countries was naturally represented by wood in the more afforested countries of Central Europe. Our knowledge of Celtic sculpture and its history has accordingly been impoverished and even distorted by the perishable wood in which this sculpture is modelled.

---

[1] The following account of the wooden figures from Sequana, and the Plates, are from R. Martin, 'Sculptures en bois découvertes aux Sources de la Seine', *Revue archéologique de l'Est et du Centre-Est XIV* (Dijon, 1964). We are indebted to Dr Glyn Daniel for procuring this work for us. See also R. Martin, *Sanctuaire des sources de la Seine* (Dijon, Musée Archéologique, 1966).

In our endeavour to estimate the true significance of this Gaulish wooden sculpture it is important to bear in mind

(1) that as yet we are only on the verge of the subject. The excavations of Sequana are still in progress, and we are only in possession of the earliest results.

(2) That the specimens before us date from the Gallo-Roman Period, apparently from the first half of the first century AD. We do not know the date of the earliest development of this wooden sculpture.

(3) That the specimens before us give little indication of advanced treatment of the human form as a whole. The arms are not detached from the torso. The figure of Plate 74 is still not wholly free from the tree-trunk effect, although the cloak and position of the right arm is a common convention of Roman and Greek statues.

(4) This important school of Celtic wooden statuary which we know to have been flourishing in Gaul in the first century AD, whatever its origin, is not traceable in insular Celtic art, which is in general identical with that of the corresponding phase in Gaul. It would seem to strengthen the traditional view that Gaulish sculpture was profoundly modified in the late La Tène and Gallo-Roman Period by indirect Greek influences through Marseilles and the Celto-Ligurian sphere of the mouth of the Rhône. It was the early Celtic art of Gaul preceding that of the Gallo-Roman period which moulded the art of the insular Celtic countries and to which we must now turn.

During the period when early Celtic art was at its height in Gaul it penetrated to the Celtic people of Britain, where it flourished and developed an independent life of its own, always recognizable as fundamentally La Tène in origin and basic characteristics, but capable of taking original styles and local specialization in form. These local styles were the work of local schools which flourished in different parts of Britain in response to local demands, to the needs of different classes of the population, and to the nature of tribal relations with the Continent. We can distinguish the northern School working doubtless under the patronage of the Parisii and Brigantes, an eastern School in the territory of the Iceni, and a southern School under some more direct influence from the art centres of the Continent, especially the Belgae. This Celtic art, generally referred to as La Tène in its continental connexions, is commonly referred to as 'Late Celtic' in Britain, owing to the fact that it lingered here throughout the Roman period, and revived again to a new blossoming in the countries of northern and western Britain after the close of the Roman domination. Hallstatt art had already been introduced into Britain, chiefly by imports, throughout the Early Iron Age of the Hallstatt Period, but it was not till the later Iron Age in Gaul that the full wealth of Celtic art developed in the British Isles.

Continental La Tène art at its best is believed to have been introduced into Britain by imports during the third century BC but from the second century BC British Schools of Celtic art were producing independent works which, at least till the period of the Roman Conquest, were fully equal to the continental works. In Ireland, which the Romans never reached, the La Tène art had an unbroken and splendid development from its earliest beginnings till the Norman Conquest, even surviving and absorbing influences from the Vikings, to whose own art Celtic art had made heavy contributions. After the Norman Conquest of Ireland old traditional art forms continued to influence the new art forms introduced from the Continent by the Cistercian Order.

The La Tène art of Britain is identical with, and fully equal to that of Gaul at its best period. Emphasis has already been laid (p. 282 above) on the high quality of its metal work and its generous development of polychrome, particularly on the development in horse trappings and chariot mounts, in arms and armour, of which the shields from the Thames at Battersea and from the Witham near Lincoln are magnificent examples.[1] The Battersea shield [Plate 23] is believed to date from c. 75 BC. That from the Witham is perhaps earlier, and is even finer in its workmanship, and has been held to be superior in technique to any contemporary work of continental Celtic art. The shield boss from the Thames at Wandsworth, while less spectacular than the Battersea and Witham shields, is of even greater beauty and grace. The Celtic chieftains of the north shared this splendid panoply of the Celtic warrior chiefs of the south. One of the finests pieces of La Tène bronze armour in Britain is the bronze pony cap from Torrs, Kircudbrightshire, dating, as is believed, from the second half of the third century BC.[2] In or close by the Stanwick fortifications in the North Riding of Yorkshire, over ninety pieces of metalwork have been found, consisting largely of bronze horse trappings and chariot mounts, some retaining traces of enamel, and the presence of iron tyres suggests that they formed elements of chariot burial like the famous group in the East Riding.[3]

Somewhat later come the more elaborate moulded objects, such as the anthropoid hilted swords and daggers; and here we must remember the highly original naturalistic mannikin on the lost dagger – again from the Witham (Fox, *P. and P.* pl. 10, e); the most beautiful of all

[1] C. Fox, *P. and P.*, p. 26 ff. The Battersea shield, in colour, forms the frontispiece of the *British Museum Guide to the Antiquities of the Early Iron Age* (1925).
[2] See Fox, *op. cit.* p. 22 ff.; pl. 19; cf. fig. 16.
[3] *British Museum Guide to Early Iron Age Antiquities*, p. 138 ff., R. E. M. Wheeler, *Stanwick* p. 2 ff.

tankards – that from Trawsfynydd, Merioneth, with its elaborately moulded handle (Fox, pl. 64); the gold twisted torc with heavy moulded terminals from Needwood Forest, Staffordshire (Fox, pl. 25); the moulded gold bracelet and electrum torc from the Snettisham treasure, in north-west Norfolk (Fox, pl. 32, fig. 33). The territory of the Iceni, though yielding ample remains which testify to the survival of the traditional chariot warfare, is relatively poor in military weapons, but is extraordinarily rich in objects of personal adornment, and Snettisham has yielded the largest accumulation of precious metal hitherto recorded from Britain in the Iron Age [Plate 32]. Some of the material in this find is believed to have come from between south Suffolk and the Thames; but other torcs of gold alloyed with silver and copper, also found in north-west Norfolk, point to the use of such personal ornaments in the first century BC, and to the wealth of the ruling dynasty. Indeed this group of hoards contained over fifty torcs – more than from all the rest of Britain.[1]

More delicate in workmanship, and perhaps more closely linked with the earlier Classical tradition of the Continent, are the beautifully incised bronze mirrors which were made in the last quarter of the first century BC and were widely distributed in southern Britain. Their decoration has adapted to perfection the La Tène curvilinear technique with linked spirals and expanding ends, and is admirably suited to the shape of the circular groundwork of the mirror. The lobes and expanded leaf-like patterns are made to dominate the entire design by incised hatchings within the intervening spaces. The designs are sometimes regular, as in the mirrors from Birdlip, Gloucs. [Plate 26], and from Desborough, Northants (Fox, pl. 57, c); but more often an illusion of regularity is effected by a subtle assemblage of asymmetrical curves, as in the superb unprovenanced mirror in the Meyer museum at Liverpool (Fox, pl. 55). The harmony is maintained by an almost incredible sureness of taste and draughtsmanship. As Françoise Henry observes, we are familiar with this harmony achieved from irregularity of line in La Tène art, e.g. in the scabbard from Cernon-sur-Coole, Marne,[2] 'mais dans les Iles cette fantaisie semble s'ériger en loi'.[3] These bronze mirrors, and many other fine specimens decorated with La Tène type of ornament, are without parallel on the Continent, and have not been found among the Parisii and the Brigantes in the north. One naturally thinks of the Etruscan bronze mirrors of earlier times, but there appears to be no link.

From about the middle of the first century BC come the two most famous examples of bronze repoussé work in Britain, the so-called stave-buckets from Aylesford in Kent, and Marlborough in Wiltshire. The

[1] R. Rainbird Clarke, *East Anglia* (London, 1960), p. 104 f.
[2] See Déchelette, *Manuel* II, part iii, fig. 463, 2.　　　　　[3] *S.I.*, p. 35.

former is thought to be perhaps slightly the earlier of the two, and is certainly the more refined in workmanship [Plate 31]. It is only 10 inches in height, and is formed of wooden staves, held in position by three bronze hoops, the topmost of which is decorated with delicate 'leaf-comma' whorls, and delicious little fantastic horses, horned and beaked, with bi-furcated tails. A handle is attached by two human masks. The vessel was found in a grave in a Belgic cemetery and contained cinerary remains, and in the same grave were found a flagon of Classical proven-ance – Italo-Greek – and other grave-goods of both Classical and Belgic type, including cinerary urns – in fact a funerary group. The incomplete Marlborough 'bucket' belongs to the same type as that from Aylesford, and is believed to have been used, like the latter, to contain cremated bones. It is twice as tall as the Aylesford 'bucket', and was decorated with repoussé designs on all three metal bands, but less refined in detail than the Aylesford ornament. Here also we have stylized elongated animals, including sea-horses, and a naturalistic moustached head, together with several masks which have been compared with the head on the Gundestrup bowl. Details on both buckets recall designs on Armorican coinage, and the Marlborough bucket in particular is thought to have been probably an importation into this country from Armorica.

At this period Armorica shared in the art of the early Celtic styles of Gaul, and must have served in some degree as a link between the La Tène art of the Continent and that of Britain. In Brittany the curvilinear designs typical of this La Tène art, and of the pedestal vases characteris-tic of the Marne burials, are found also on the painted pottery,[1] and though the poverty of Armorica has left relatively few examples of the La Tène art on objects of outstanding value, the pottery shares both the design and the shapes characteristic of Gaulish La Tène, types II and III. The Celtic crannogs of Glastonbury and Meare in Somerset have left a wealth of pottery and wooden vessels incised with typical La Tène curvilinear designs (Fox, fig. 76) characteristic of that found in the cemeteries and *oppida* of Finistère, which are again characteristic of the pottery of Hunsbury in Northamptonshire,[2] and that found at Hengist-bury Head with Armorican coins of the Coriosolitae and the Andecavi.[3]

It is interesting to reflect that Armorica also shares with Ireland a rare type of monument decorated with ornament of a La Tène tradition similar to that on the bronze mirrors and to the designs on the pottery just discussed, but presumably of earlier date. This is the independent and free-standing incised stone sculpture, of which the two best known Irish examples are the Turoe stone, an almost hemispherical block,

[1] Déchelette, II, figs. 660–1, 663, 667, 668.   [2] Fox, fig. 77, c.
[3] H. Hubert, *The Rise of the Celts* (London, 1934), fig. 218 f.

referred to by Françoise Henry (*S.I.*, p. 35 f.) as the *doyenne* of stone sculptures [Plate 34], and the Castle Strange stone. With them we may compare the Kermaria stone from Pont l'Abbé, Finistère in Armorica, now in the museum of Saint-Germain.[1] The Turoe stone, like many later Celtic sculptures, is carved in only two planes – the depth of the ground-work and the external plane of the design, cut in very slight relief, the treatment closely reminiscent of that of Pfalzfeld[2] (cf. p. 285 above). The design is unmistakably that of the La Tène tradition, and the delicacy and perfection of technique is typical of Celtic work at its best, and betokens a high standard of achievement which – in regard to relief sculpture – does not necessarily imply a lengthy preceding local school of workmanship. The Castle Strange stone is in a different technique from that of the Turoe stone, being of the nature of a surface engraving with a design composed of related spirals, and it may also be later in date. Another much larger monument of the same class has been recently discovered at Killycluggin (Cavan). Its design, of great elegance, consists of finely engraved curves and spirals.

The earliest surviving monuments of Irish art are stone sculpture. Human figures are traced back to the Neolithic period, both as free-standing sculpture and as incised on wall-slabs. The earliest Irish Christian stone crosses, the thin incised slabs of Carndonagh and Fahan Mura in the neighbourhood of Inishowen in the north, dating probably from the second half of the seventh century, may perhaps represent an unbroken tradition from this Neolithic art. In general, however, there would seem to have been at least a partial break between the megalithic art and that of later times, which would naturally come about by the introduction of importations from both the Continent and Britain; but a break in art does not necessarily imply a total discontinuance of old motifs, and the technique of stone carving must certainly have had a continuous history, as is implied by the Turoe and other carved stones, bearing La Tène designs.

In the Rath of the Synods on Tara Hill remains have been found of habitations with traces of the work of smiths and enamellers, and of Roman importations from the first to the third century AD showing contacts with both Britain and Gaul. Only a few yards away the Mound of the Hostages was found on excavation to have been originally built over a megalithic tomb, which had been covered later with numerous Bronze Age burials, indicating for Tara an origin as a necropolis and a prehistoric sanctuary, adapted by the Celts later as a royal residence. Ireland is a museum of the life of the past, and continuity can never be ruled out.

The La Tène art of the Continental Celts of the second Iron Age is

---

[1] Figured in Déchelette, *Manuel* II, fig. 709.   [2] F. Henry, *A.I.*, p. 20; *I.A.*, 6.

believed to have been introduced into Ireland in the second century BC. Close contacts at this period were taking place with Britain, which exported a number of objects to Ireland; but the most important Irish contacts were with the Continent. Contacts with Britain came about naturally enough by trade and raiding; but the earliest Irish sculptured stones all have affinities with well-known Continental Celtic stone sculptures. The Turoe stone is very close in its technique to the stone from Pfalzfeld [Plates 34, 63], while the two crude yet impressive self-standing human figure sculptures from Boa Island, Fermanagh [*A.I.*, p. 50] and the screaming figure from Tanderagee, Armagh [*A.I.*, p. 51] with moustache and horned helmet, have more in common with the Continental Celtic statue from Holzgerlingen, or the fragment from Echterdingen than with the more advanced type of Celto-Ligurian statuary of the Mouth of Rhône. It has been suggested that these Irish sculptured stones and statues imply a cult introduced from Gaul by refugees fleeing before the Roman invasions (Henry, *A.I.*, p. 18). These early sculptured heads from Ireland are in striking contrast to the limestone head of a young Celtic man of the Roman period from Gloucester[1] [Plate 21], where the features and the treatment of the hair and the shape of the face are typically Celtic, but the plastic form has mastered the Classical Greco-Roman statuary presentation of the southern Gaulish sanctuaries at the mouth of the Rhône.

The chronology of the proto-historic phases of early Celtic art in Ireland is at present imprecise, and can only be determined by comparison with more or less parallel British and continental styles. The absence of Roman criteria and of Roman and continental coin evidence in Ireland is here a serious hiatus, and the long tradition of Celtic art in Ireland from the second century BC to the Norman Invasion, uninterrupted by any Roman conquest, makes questions of internal relative chronology within Ireland itself arbitrary and almost irrelevant. The masterly curvilinear art of the decorated bronze scabbards from the ruins of the Lisnacroghera *crannóg* (Co. Antrim) (Fox, *P. and P.*, pl. 73, b), and others closely related from the R. Bann at Toome and Coleraine, are all variations of the continental styles of La Tène II and III, and their close relationship with the style, incised on the Aylesford bucket [Plate 31] and the Glastonbury wooden bowl, both of the pre-Roman period in Britain, suggest an approximate date of *c.* 175 BC for the opening phase of La Tène art in Ireland on metal objects (Fox, *P. and P.*, fig. 26 and pl. 73, b). Though these objects are possibly later than their continental equivalents, owing to time-lag, they are not later than the beginning of our era. These Irish scabbards are perhaps the product of a single school, a later atelier, since they are not

[1] J. M. C. Toynbee, *Art in Roman Britain* (London, 1962), pl. 8, Fig. 7.

found anywhere else in Ireland, and they suggest that the early La Tène art of Ulster was particularly close to that of the Continent. The decoration on these Irish scabbards resembles closely that on the slightly later Bugthorpe scabbard from the East Riding of Yorkshire, which is the earliest example in Britain of the 'shaded' technique produced by hatching reserved areas of the pattern (cf. p. 292 above). It should be noted, however, that this technique is also a prominent feature on a shield-boss from Llyn-Cerrig-Bach in Anglesey (Fox, *P. and P.*, fig. 28).

We can only conjecture the manner in which the best La Tène art of this early period reached Ireland. Fox attributes the close relationship between the somewhat later Bugthorpe and Hunsbury scabbards and that of the Lisnacroghera style in part to cross-channel traffic, and 'a flourishing British settlement in Galloway, retaining early traditions for which the only known evidence is the Torrs pony-cap and horns' (*P and P.*, p. 43). Kuno Meyer had long ago suggested,[1] on literary evidence, that Gaulish mercenaries had entered Ireland in the service of Irish kings during the early centuries of our era, but his conclusions point rather to the south. Possibly both routes were used.

Among the earliest evidence of imports derived from Britain are the bronze pins and penannular brooches, the former perhaps slightly the earlier, the latter derived from Roman models. Both have a long life, and from at least as early as the beginning of our era were often elaborately decorated with enamel. The bronze pins are as frequent in Scotland as in England, and the penannular brooches are of wide distribution throughout the British Isles. From South Wales we have a bronze penannular brooch, and from a hut site at Pant-y-Saer, Anglesey, a silver example, complete with its long pin on a loose swivel[2] [Plate 79]. Its closest parallels are in the coastal districts of Scotland and date from the fourth to the sixth centuries.

Many of these pins and brooches, are richly enamelled. A particularly interesting enamelled pin comes from a hoard on Norrie's Law in Fife. It is decorated with enamel and Celtic and Pictish designs surmounted by a tiny cross, and it can be dated to the late seventh century by Byzantine coins within the hoard. A large silver penannular brooch comes from the same hoard.[3]

From the second century AD the Celtic revival, following upon Roman decline, had brought about a closer union between Ireland and Scotland, and a consequent common artistic development, and from the foundation of the Irish kingdom of Argyll in the fifth century this closer union may be said to have developed into a common culture. During

[1] *L.I.F.C.*, 8, n. 16.
[2] See N. K. Chadwick, *C.B.*, Plate 33; and references there cited.
[3] Joseph Anderson, *S.E.C.T.*, II, p. 314 ff.

this period, and especially during the following centuries under the stimulus and patronage of the Christian Church, ornamentation on metal work and jewelry was enriched with a great wealth of new resources. Not only was the use of red enamel greatly extended, but the surface was encrusted with semi-precious stones, garnets and even amber, and with coloured glass, and the technique of millefiori was introduced from Gallo-Roman jewelry. It was probably at this period that the Irish artists learnt to solder and to mount fine gold filigree, a technique admirably appropriate to the persistent traditional Celtic curvilinear decorative art.

Of this splendid development of native Celtic jewelry the two chief treasures are the Hunterston brooch in Scotland [Plate 78] and the Tara brooch in Ireland [Plate 80]. The former[1] is $4\frac{1}{2}$ × $4\frac{3}{4}$ inches in diameter, and what remains of its pin is $5\frac{1}{2}$ inches long. Its form is a flattened closed ring of silver, divided by ridges into panels, the larger ones filled with zoomorphic interlaced decoration and Celtic spirals and trumpet patterns, formed of filigree set on gold plates, and the corner spaces and the smaller panels are set with amber studs. The delicacy and tact and the sense of proportion with which the crowded ground is treated show the same unerring sense of composition which is characteristic of Celtic art everywhere, and which we shall find repeated in the manuscript illuminations. An interesting detail is the claim to private ownership made by two names scratched on the plain surface of the back of the brooch in runic letters of Scandinavian type peculiar to the Hebrides, and probably dating from about the tenth century. The inscriptions are in Old Norse, and may be translated 'Olfriti owns this brooch'; and 'Maelbritha owns this brooch'. The names, the former Norse and the latter Irish, carry us to the mixed Norse-Irish kingdom of the Hebrides.

The most outstanding of all the brooches, indeed the most precious gem of all the Irish jewelry, is the so-called Tara brooch. Like the Hunterston brooch, it is a closed-ring penannular brooch with a long pin working on a loose ring, and it is assigned to the early eighth century.[2] It is relatively small, indeed one of the smallest of the ornamental brooches, only $3\frac{1}{2}$ inches in diameter, and it originally formed one of a pair connected by a thick chain of wire, probably intended to be worn on the shoulders as fasteners of some garment. It is made of a ring of moulded bronze, and is decorated on front and back, its surface divided into compartments by relief mouldings, filled with decorative work of great refinement and elegance. The designs within the smaller panels are curvilinear conventional motifs formed by the application of fine

[1] See J. Anderson, *S.E.C.T.*, II, p. 1 ff.; figs. 1–3.
[2] Françoise Henry, *I.A.E.C.P.*, pp. 119; 150 f.

gold filigree wire interspersed with minute gold knobs, while the larger panels are filled by an intertwisted elongated bird form in a similar technique. Bird and beast heads project outward from the raised margin, the bird forms being unique on jewelry of this kind, and closely resembling many in the borders of the Lindisfarne Gospels. Red enamel and amber, small discs of blue and red glass, and tiny human heads carved in amethyst add polychrome splendour to the refinement and delicacy of this gem of art and craftsmanship.

It is impossible in our brief space to do more than hint at the splendour and wealth of the metal work of the Early Christian art of the eighth and ninth centuries in Ireland. In particular, the Church enriched its furnishings with objects which must have done worlds to arouse the imaginations of an illiterate congregation and to associate the Church with beauty and splendour lacking in their homely domestic dwellings. Everything shone and gleamed. On the altars chalices were adorned with gold and silver, and studded with jewels. The Gospels were bound in richly decorated covers, and encased in *cumdachs*, or shrines, studded with ornaments valuable enough to be ripped off and stolen. Reliquaries were valued as heirlooms, sometimes in the form of house-shrines, such as the one found in a Viking grave at Copenhagen, undoubtedly Irish loot (Henry, *I.A.E.C.P.*, pl. 27b), and the reliquary from Monymusk (Aberdeenshire), adorned with red and yellow enamel and elaborately decorated. This treasured heirloom is doubtless the *Brecbennach*, traditionally associated with St Columba, and had a function analogous to that of the *Cathach* in Ireland. Croziers were adorned with skilled bronze work [Plate 86]. The Kells crozier, now in the British Museum, is a particularly instructive example.[1] The close association of this industry in bronze and enamels with the Church is illustrated by the founders' hoards of crucibles, tongs, and other tools found in monastic precincts, e.g. in the monastery of Nendrum on Mahee Island in Strangford Lough. The small size of the objects, and the fragments of red enamel still remaining in the crucibles prove their purpose to have been for only such small objects as we have been discussing.

The Ardagh Chalice [Plates 81, 82] is deservedly the most famous piece of early Irish Christian metal-work, and must obviously have been a valued treasure of some church altar. It is a large two-handled cup of beaten silver on a silver stem, decorated with gold, gilt bronze and enamel (Henry, *A.I.*, pl. 120 f., pls. 107, 108). The design would be massive, were not one's eye directed to the symmetry and balance of the bowl and foot beautifully united by its golden collar, the polished simplicity of the silver surface, and the dazzling insistence of the red and blue enamel and gold filigree of its single band of decoration near the

[1] For details see M. and L. de Paor, *E.C.I.*, pp. 154, 166, and pl. 58-60.

top of the bowl, and of the surface and attachment of the handles. In subtle contrast with these bold effects are light and delicate engravings in double ribbon lines with intervening lightly punched dots, on the plain surface of the bowl outlining the attachment of the handles. Similar delicate engraving on the surface of the bowl records the names of the apostles and has added suggestive touches of animal ornament. The function of contrast and of the value of the reserved space in composition are blended with perfect artistic taste.

It is difficult for us to imagine the society in which such a masterpiece of ecclesiastical art as the Ardagh Chalice and the great illuminated manuscripts could be adequately appreciated and recompensed by an aristocracy governed by institutions as archaic as the Brehon Laws, and still upholding the heroic standards of society. The Ardagh Chalice belongs to the world of the hermit poetry. The introduction of Christianity had brought about a complete dichotomy in the ideals of early Christian Ireland. Yet both ideals are completely Irish, and the new and higher culture in the art and poetry of the Church alongside the heroic standards and oral literary forms of the ancient Celtic world are fused in the first millennium of our era in an individual form of idealism and culture which is the greatest gift of this remote Western Island to European society.

The art of the jewels and the bronze Church pieces constantly reminds us of its close association with the great illuminated manuscripts of the seventh to the ninth centuries. The correspondence between certain details of the art of the Tara brooch and the art represented by the Lindisfarne Gospels, the latter probably attributable to a date about AD 710-20, has already been emphasized. The similarity of the lettering of the inscription of the Ardagh Chalice to that of the big initial letters of the Lindisfarne Gospels not only constitutes a close link in date, but establishes the two objects as products of a single artistic phase. On the other hand, some objects, notably the belt-buckles in the Sutton Hoo ship-burial, now dated to approximately 625,[1] employ similar motifs, and it is becoming clearer that a common development is taking place in the artistic life of the whole of the British Isles from the middle of the seventh century.

To this same period and artistic phase we owe the rise of the great school of manuscript illumination in Ireland, the finest flower of Celtic art.[2] The vernacular Celtic style reached its highest development from the seventh to the end of the eighth or beginning of the ninth century,

---

[1] C. Hawkes, *Antiquity*, XXXVIII (1964), p. 252 ff.
[2] The great facsimile reproductions in colour of the *Book of Durrow* (published in two volumes, 1960) and the *Book of Kells* (published in three volumes in 1940) are done by the Urgraf Verlag of Bern.

that is to say until its first encounter with the Vikings. It is to this great period of the native Celtic art style that we owe the masterpieces of the Book of Durrow and the Book of Kells. From the end of the eighth century there is a gradual decline until about 850.

The Celtic manuscripts of the period are of two types, (1) the large Gospel books carefully written in uncial or half-uncial script, intended to lie on the altar; and (2) small portable books, in cursive hand for ready reference or private reading, 'pocket editions'. Almost all the decorated manuscripts are Gospels, and have striking decoration on the first page of each Gospel, composed chiefly of immense initial monograms covered with decoration. The left-hand page facing the beginning of the text is almost always covered entirely with decoration, which shows considerable variation and is known as a 'carpet page'. In addition to, or instead of, the carpet page, there is at the beginning of each Gospel the symbol of the Evangelist or his portrait. The carpet pages and the symbol pages are often framed in running patterns of interlaced ribbon designs of the traditional Coptic style (Henry, *A.I.*, pl. 31, 60), while the monograms make use exclusively of spirals and fine twists (*ibid.*, pl. 61).

The earliest of the fine illuminated manuscripts is the small Gospel book known as the Book of Durrow [Plates 87, 88], attributed to about 650 or only a little later.[1] In its reserve and complete mastery of composition and design it attains perhaps the high-water-mark of Irish illumination. These qualities of maturity in the Book of Durrow indicate the culmination of a tradition, whatever its origin. The art of the Book of Durrow employs the traditional linear spiral ornament in the great initials to the opening of the Gospels, but the decoration of the carpet pages, and the pages of the symbols of the Evangelists, are bordered with the interlacing early ribbon form comparable with the Carndonagh and Fahan Mura crosses, and betray the influence of enamel in some of the discs. The range of colours is limited to four – brown, red, yellow and green – and the total effect is of the mellow beauty of autumn leaves, in contrast with the brilliant polychrome of the later manuscripts, especially the jewelled effect of the Book of Kells with its liberal use of blue. Neither book employs gold leaf – that is for the future; but it is interesting to note that the Durrow colours are identical with those of Syrian manuscripts of a later date and probably of archaic tradition, and are similar in their use of these colours for broad ribbon meanders. The manuscript contains several pages devoted wholly to ornamentation, reminding one of the beautiful oriental carpets which may indeed have been one means of transmitting their designs, owing to the ready portability of fabrics.

The pages devoted to symbols of the Evangelists are perhaps the

[3] F. Henry, *S.I.*, p. 47; *ibid. I.A.E.C.P.*, p. 63.

most individual feature in the Book, both those devoted to the single figures and those divided into compartments containing the symbols. Here the Durrow manuscript shares with the Ardagh Chalice the relatively advanced sense of the value of the blank background to throw the principal design into higher relief. The human figures are particularly striking, deliberately avoiding naturalism and achieving an effect completely iconographical. The figure of St Matthew [Plate 88, cf. also Plate 89] without arms and with both feet parallel, and at right angles to the axis of his body, stiffly clad in a single chequered garment, is reminiscent of a mosaic rather than of a painting, but on its blank white vellum ground-work, surrounded by the frame of ribbon meanders, it is a work of mature art, not so much the beginning of a tradition as its culmination. These figure panels, as we might call them, and the Canons of Concordances of the Gospels framed in arcading, have their nearest analogies in the Syrian Gospels written by the monk Rabula in the sixth century,[1] and, like many features in the early Celtic Church, undoubtedly owe their inspiration to Eastern Mediterranean influences.

Of all Irish works of art the Book of Kells [Plates 89, 90] is by common consent the chief treasure, and among the great Gospel Books ranks with the Book of Durrow. Its precise origin is unknown, whether in the Irish Columban monastery of Iona, or in Ireland, and its date is uncertain, but the early ninth century is probable. Kells was heavily raided and pillaged from late in the ninth century and throughout the tenth, but when we have our first historical reference to the manuscript itself it is preserved in the church at Kells, for we read in the Annals of Ulster, s.a. 1006 'the great Gospel of Columcille was wickedly stolen in the night out of the western sacristy of the great stone church of Kells – the chief relic of the western world on account of its ornamental cover', and that it was found later, stripped of its gold, and buried under a sod. In 1661 the manuscript passed to Trinity College, Dublin, where it has remained ever since.

The codex[2] is of relatively large size, and consists of thick polished vellum on which the text is written in a beautiful round half-uncial hand characteristic of the best large Irish manuscripts. The contents are very varied. The first leaf contains some Hebrew words and their Latin equivalents, and the symbols of the Evangelists – the man or angel for St Matthew, the lion for St Mark, the calf for St Luke, the eagle for St John. The next eight illuminated pages are filled with the Eusebian Canons, written in narrow columns in an arcading of decorated pillars.

[1] See O. M. Dalton, *Byzantine Art and Archaeology* (Oxford, 1911), figs. 266 and 267.
[2] An inventory of the contents and 24 Plates of coloured reproductions in Sir Edward Sullivan, *The Book of Kells* (published by the Studio, 1914).

Folio 7v, contains a full-page illustration of the Virgin and Child with attendant angels and elaborately decorated border. The drawing of the figures, both here and in the portraits of the evangelists St Matthew and St Mark, while anatomically far in advance of those of Durrow, are deliberately stylized, and carefully avoid any suggestion of naturalism. We are again reminded of enamelled and metal ikons, or of mosaic work, and the art is as remote from the Classical ideal as are the serpents, fish and birds in the interlacing design of the border, from zoological reality. It is an art which suggests more than it shows, and is a creation of the Celtic mind.

This iconographical treatment of the larger human figures is, of course, a deliberate piece of advanced sophistication. Paradoxically enough many of the smaller angels and human figures introduced into the ornament are convincingly natural. The little human figure at the top of the splendid illumination of the opening words of St Matthew's Gospel, and the charming head which terminates the curl of the letter P. in the great monogram page [Plate 90], take their place without the slightest incongruity amid the rich and varied tapestry of these great pages of pure ornament. It is perhaps in this great monogram page more than any other that the artist shows his skill in harmonizing the most disparate elements into his design. In a small space at the foot of the great initial *Chi* is a quiet little miniature of two rats gnawing a Church wafer, watched by two cats, carefully distinguished by the artist as a tortoise-shell and a brindled, with two more rats perched on their backs. Is it a symbol of the peace by which the lion and the lamb shall lie down together? Is it merely an artistic whimsey like the marginalia of many of the scribes?

It is in these great ornamental pages that the Irish artists' combined resourcefulness and tact is seen in its highest perfection. Whether it be confined in a rigid frame-work, as in the great eight-circled cross (fo. 33v), or whether it twists and turns in tiny circles, filling with studded splendour and dazzling brilliance the great monogram page of St Matthew's Gospel (fo. 34r); or whether it be restrained within a more geometrical enclosure recalling the leaded lights of a stained glass window, as in the opening words of St Mark's Gospel, the rich scrolls, the trumpet patterns, and the ribbon meander interlock, and resolve themselves, flow, intertwine and concentrate, only to uncurl again in endless and effortless variety exquisitely controlled and subordinated to the main design and purpose of the page. The lines of the ornament constantly put us in mind of fine wire-work, and of the rich polychrome, of jewelry. We are far removed from the grave dignity, the mature restraint of the Durrow art, or its sombre autumnal colouring. The genius of Kells has the prodigal brilliance of easy mastery and unlimited resource. This profuse decoration, this prodigality of ornament, is scattered throughout the work, and is a perpetual delight as it appears, often with no apparent motive, in margins and inter-linear figures, bright, fantastic, graceful, throughout the text.

From the seventh and eighth centuries the great Irish convents, the source of our early Irish art treasures, were the objects of heavy Viking depredations, and the monks were often forced to move to safer centres, sometimes taking their books with them, and it becomes increasingly difficult to pin-point the home of a given manuscript. The monks from Lindisfarne, the prey of the Vikings in the ninth century, eventually settled at Durham, where the fragmentary Durham Gospels combines survivals of the Book of Durrow and the closely related Lindisfarne style of decoration. The famous Book of St Chad now at Lichfield (Moreau, pl. 103; Henry, *A.I.*, pl. 98), but known to have been in Wales probably before the end of the eighth century, has close affinities with these earliest Irish manuscripts.[1] The Rushworth or Mac Regol Gospels (Henry, *A.I.*, pls. 110, 287), which were in the north of England in the tenth century, probably came originally from the Abbey of Birr in County Offaly. The art of the splendid Echternach Gospels is so closely allied to that of the Book of Lindisfarne and the Durham Gospels that it is commonly thought that the Echternach Codex was written and decorated in Northumbria in the early eighth century, and carried to the Continent; but the details are equally close to the Irish art of the Book of Durrow. As F. Henry observes, the big lion, the symbol of St Mark 'which bounds, flame-like, shaking a cluster of golden curls, across a pavement of straight lines' behaves as 'one would expect the Durrow animal symbols to behave as soon as they had got bold enough to move' (*I.A.E.C.P.*, p. 129).

The influence of the art of this period was carried by Irish monks to continental monasteries, some of which kept in close touch with Ireland in the eighth and ninth centuries. Others, such as Luxeuil and Bobbio, were actually Irish foundations of the seventh century. It is commonly believed that the monks fleeing to the Continent to escape the Vikings carried their books with them, and no doubt this happened in some cases; but Irish influence in the continental books is more probably to be accounted for on the whole by the fact that under the monastic stimulus in Ireland in the preceding period art, learning, writing and the production of books had become a national accomplishment and trade. What the monks took to the Continent was their intellectual and

[1] On this MS. and the related style of decoration in the MSS of Durrow and Lindisfarne see the important study by F. Henry, 'The Lindisfarne Gospels', *Antiquity* XXXVII (1963), especially p. 104 ff.

artistic monopoly and means of livelihood, and all that appertained to the scholars' life, and to ecclesiastical art.

From the end of the eighth century the essential Celtic style, with its abundance of spiral and trumpet patterns and purely geometrical inter- lacings, began to decline, and was increasingly mingled with inter- lacing animals and birds which native Celtic art shared with the Teutonic art of the period. About 850 the art of the Vikings began to modify the Irish style of the period by the introduction of the so-called 'Jellinge style' from Norway, which had itself originated largely from imitation of Irish ornament. The resulting Hiberno-Viking style had a vigorous life in Ireland and the Isle of Man, and after the Irish victory of Clontarf in 1014 the revival of the Church stimulated zeal in restora- tion and in the creation of splendid new objects of Church use. Most of the *cumdachs*, or book-shrines, and the croziers were repaired and re- embellished during the period from about 1000 to 1125, and it is to the later part of the time that we owe the richest and most elaborate ornaments, the shrine of St Patrick's bell [Plate 85], the cross of Cong [Plate 83], the shrine of St Lachtin's arm, and the Lismore Crozier [Plate 86].

In fact, after the middle of the tenth century, the art of Ireland seems to have passed almost entirely into ecclesiastical channels, and when the Anglo-Norman conquest actually took place the introduction of foreign Orders and the part played by Canterbury in the 'Hiberno-Danish' bishoprics had already prepared the way for a new style of art and architecture derived from continental sources. Only rare traces of the ancient Celtic traditions may have modified the new Norman styles, possibly, for example, the stone heads on Cormac's Chapel at Cashel [Plate 57], where Celtic *têtes coupées* may have imposed themselves against the current of Norman and medieval types.

The vigour of Irish tradition, indeed the vigour of Celtic tradition throughout the British Isles, is most fully represented by the sculptured stone crosses. We have already seen that the art and technique of stone sculpture which developed in the La Tène period continues in close union with the art of the succeeding periods in an unbroken tradition until the Middle Ages. The great number of the crosses and the wealth of their decoration are a valuable supplement to our knowledge of the art of the rarer and more perishable objects in metal and on vellum. A few examples, like the crosses of Fahan Mura and the Muiredach Cross of Monasterboice, afford us some chronological guidance by their inscriptions. More often by their numbers and precise localities they can be classified into Schools and periods, and so help us by comparison to discern the affinities of smaller portable objects whose provenance is unknown.

The earliest type of Irish sculptured crosses are carved on the flat stone surfaces of upright slabs, suggesting comparison with a picture on a manuscript page. The background of the sculptures consists of upright independent slabs or steles on which are either incised or carved in shallow relief a simple cross or a crucifixion group and other figures, mostly human (Henry, *A.I.*, pls. 49–56). In view of the manifest influence of the Eastern Mediterranean Christian Church on early Irish Christianity it is natural to suspect an ultimate influence from Coptic steles on these early Irish monuments. In Ireland crosses of this type are not rare or confined to one period, and are sometimes found side by side with later types. The most interesting and elaborate are the crosses from Fahan Mura [Plates 97, 98] and Carndonagh, both from the neighbourhood of Inishowen in Donegal.

These form a coherent group, the relationship being clear from both the treatment of the figures and the wide interlacing ribbons which, bordered by a double line, occupy the whole of the interior of the cross of Fahan Mura on both the east and west faces. The eastern face is austere in treatment, and recalls Coptic steles in certain details; the western face is much freer, the ribbon interlace encroaching on the ribbed border, and the stem of the cross is flanked with two rigid little figures recalling by their stiff garments, and the absence of delineation of the arms, the figure of St Matthew in the *Book of Durrow*. The Fahan Cross is of unusual interest in that it bears an inscription in clear Greek letters, being the Greek version of a formula of the *Gloria Patri*: 'Glory and honour to the Father and to the Son and to the Holy Spirit'. The formula on the Fahan cross is the one mentioned in canons 13 and 15 of the fourth Council of Toledo, held in 633, which was perhaps replaced about that time by the more modern form 'Glory to the Father', but which continued in use in the Mozarabic liturgy, and was widely used in Greek liturgies until at least the ninth century. The formula was probably copied at Fahan from a page of a Greek manuscript, perhaps during the course of the seventh century, a date favoured by other evidence (Henry, *A.I.*, p. 162 f.).

Fahan was a very important monastery in the Columban tradition of the seventh century, and was under the direct patronage of the branch of the northern Uí Néill whose seat nearby was the fortress of Ailech [Plates 18, 20]. The Carndonagh Cross, on the other hand, only a few miles to the north, is a much cruder piece of work, both in execution and design, a provincial poor relation of the refined and carefully executed work of Fahan, yet it clearly belongs to the same School and period. It is a tall thin slab of sandstone, one side entirely covered with double contour ribbons, the other with sharply incised figures forming a continuous design, the whole centred upon an oval containing a head of

Christ in Glory. Other stylized figures, without indication of arms, are grouped on this same (eastern) face of the Cross, and the cross is associated with two little pillars (*A.I.*, pl. 59) bearing incised and lightly modelled figures of varying types – a warrior, an ecclesiastic, a harpist, and Jonah emerging from the whale. We are on the threshold of the narrative scenes of the later high crosses, and in the neighbouring cemetery is another cross of the same school. Meanwhile this Donegal school is not confined to Fahan and Carndonagh, but had left survivals on Inishkeel and on Caher and Tory islands.

With the high crosses we leave the slab crosses and find ourselves in a different world, a local Celtic milieu, for the high crosses are a specialized development of the British Isles. They have no parallels in contemporary continental sculpture, but they are found widespread from the eighth to the twelfth centuries throughout the British Isles, not only in Ireland, especially in the centre and south, but throughout England, in Cornwall, Wales, the Isle of Man, and Western Scotland. The art of the Cornish[1] and Welsh crosses[2] and of those of south-western Scotland [Plate 95] is largely geometrical interlacing ribbon and knot-work, and is artistically poor in comparison with the Irish and the highly original Pictish crosses; but the technique is generally faultless, which is all the more remarkable since these geometrical designs, especially of the angular variety (cf. the Carew Cross, Plate 94), are more exacting for the carver's skill than freer designs. A slip of the chisel can ruin an entire panel. This localization of art styles – we may refer to the unique slab from the Calf of Man [Plate 96] – and still more this perfection of technique in the high crosses of Britain, is the more remarkable since there are no indications of preliminary stages, or of gradual development and decline. Even if we postulate preliminary designs in metalwork, their faultless transference to stone is none the less puzzling. It is probable that the origins of the high cross, as of the stele, are to be sought in Mediterranean Christian lands, Armenia or elsewhere in the Byzantine empire, where political upheavals like the Arab conquest and the Iconoclastic Controversy must certainly have driven many expert artists into exile.

The Irish high crosses are heavy stone monuments, generally mounted on a solid, sometimes lofty stepped plinth. They fall into distinct groups. The first group is best represented by the two Ahenny Crosses in Tipperary, which date at latest from about 750 (Henry, *A.I.*, p. 170). The crosses of Lorrha and the two south crosses of Clonmacnoise

---

[1] Notably the Cardinham and the Sancreed Crosses (H. O'N. Hencken, *ACS*, figs. 50 and 51).

[2] Notably the Carew and Penmon Crosses, and one in Brecon Museum and the smaller Margam Cross. For the whole Series see V. E. Nash-Williams, *ECMW*, *passim*.

[Plates 100, 101] are from later in the century. The Moone Cross [Plate 99] has also been assigned to the eighth century from its similarity to the crosses of Group I. All the crosses of this group are closely related in style to the metal work of the early eighth century, and can occasionally be dated by their close relationship to metal work found in Viking graves of the early ninth century.[1] The entire surface of the stone tends to be covered with running ornament resembling embroidery, each ornament being contained in a bordered panel. The ornament frequently combines spirals with interlace and animal heads, and Greek key patterns. On the Ahenny and Kilkieran and the Lorrha crosses the entire surface is covered with spirals and interlaces, and it is only on the pedestals that scenes with human beings occur. On the North Ahenny cross horsemen and processions are found. Others, such as Kilrea and Killamery have scenes on the cross itself and even on the arms. The 'south cross' of Clonmacnoise has a crucifixion scene below the head of the cross. All these scenes, as well as the figures on the cross of Moone, are in very low relief, and with little moulding. The cross of Moone is of a remarkable style, a small head and slender shaft rising from a high though narrow pyramidal base. There is hardly any ornament, the surface being largely divided into panels containing geometrical figures and animals. In its economy of detail and bold and rigorously simple figures, it is one of the most original and impressive of the crosses.

To the second group belong the Clonmacnoise school. This school is assigned approximately to the end of the eighth century or the beginning of the ninth by an inscription on the Bealin Cross, which has been transferred from this original milieu to Bealin near Athlone.[2] This date receives support from the similarity of details in their decoration and animal designs to those of the Books of Kells and of Armagh. The mouldings and carvings are still in very low relief, and their abundant ornaments are of fine interlacing and complicated spirals, and interlacing animals. To these motifs are added 'narrative' hunting scenes, mostly in panels, of which the Cross of Banagher has fine examples. These striking cavalcades of horsemen and hunters are sometimes almost identical with the superimposed processions of warriors and huntsmen on the Pictish crosses which are almost unique in the Western art of the period. In the Pictish sculptures they are infinitely varied [Plates 91, 93]. Their immediate inspiration is obscure, but horsemen continue until the eleventh and twelfth centuries on the Irish crosses.

On the other hand, the crosses of Iona and the Irish kingdom of

[1] F. Henry, *I.H.C.*, p. 59.
[2] Henry, *A.I.* p. 172; pl. 88. For the 'north cross' of Clonmacnoise, *ibid.*, pl. 91; for one of the little pillars, pl. 95.

Argyll have developed the bolder form and design which is found already in the cross of Bealin, and which develops more fully later. In this style the crosses are enclosed in a circle, which may form a part of the solid head or may be perforated. The carving is in deeper relief and the great bosses standing out in high relief from the central disc and from the extremities of the arms are a striking development. These are clearly reminiscent of metal work, in which bosses formed of coral, or enamel were used to mask a metal stud, as can be seen in the Snettisham treasure from Norfolk, the great belt buckle from Sutton Hoo, and elsewhere.

Apart from the remarkable series of mounted horsemen and hunting scenes the great majority of figure and narrative scenes on the crosses are scriptural. The central theme is the Crucifixion, but apart from that, and doubtless leading up to it, the majority both in Ireland and Scotland illustrate scenes from the Old Testament. Especial favourites are the Fall, Daniel in the lions' den, Jonah and the whale, the three young men in the Fiery Furnace (from the Apocrypha), the sacrifice of Abel, David as harpist and warrior, and some episodes from the life of St Antony.

This general narrative repertoire, which Mlle. Henry aptly calls a 'theology in stone' (*S.I.*, p. 160), continues on the Irish crosses throughout the ninth and tenth centuries, after which it disappears without a trace. It is entirely absent from the crosses of the eleventh and twelfth centuries, and crosses like that of Dysert O'Dea revert to a covering of ornament – no longer spirals, but animal interlace – taking their place in the national revival which is reflected in the literature and scribal activity of the period, and looks back nostalgically to pre-Viking Ireland.

It is indeed a remarkable fact that in the first half of the ninth century the Viking invasions were at their height, and the destruction of the Irish monasteries was taking place on a great scale; yet, inexplicable as it seems to us, some seem to have been left immune, and an interlude of comparative peace in the late ninth and early tenth centuries has left us some of our finest crosses, notably those of Kells and Monasterboice. The crosses of this group seem to have formed a homogeneous Leinster tradition with a central School of sculpture at Monasterboice, and a continuous tradition until the twelfth century.

The treatment of the Crucifixion varies greatly in both time and place, but a constant feature in the Irish crosses is the presence on either side of the foot of the cross of two little figures, one lifting up the sponge, the other bearing a lance, as on the unfinished cross at Kells. We have seen them already on the steles from Fahan and Carndonagh (p. 305), and they occur on the eighth century Athlone gilded bronze plaque [Plate 84]. They serve once more to illustrate the close correspondence between the motifs on metal and stone. On the Irish crosses St John and the Virgin never appear in this position. In the early crosses the Crucifixion is generally represented in low relief on quite a small scale, and sometimes placed relatively low, and surmounted by a Christ in Glory, as on the Moone and Carndonagh crosses. In this and some other details, e.g. the meeting of St Paul and St Antony, and the flight into Egypt, the iconography of the Irish crosses have points in common with the Ruthwell Cross of Dumfriesshire [Plate 105].

They rarely make use of foliage, however, and we have nothing corresponding to the foliage panels of the great English and Scottish Border crosses – Ruthwell, Bewcastle, Jedburgh and Acca. Amid the scenes on the Irish crosses in direct transition from Carolingian and Byzantine iconography we find both on the Irish and Scottish sculptures realistic hunting scenes which may possibly have a symbolic significance, but are certainly elements of the traditional repertoire of the sculptor. What is the direct inspiration of the motifs in which monsters wage perpetual warfare against one another, against serpents, devour human heads, even human beings, recalling to our memories the old Celtic art of Watsch and Este, and the Celto-Iberian statue of the monster of Noves? [Plate 41]. How are we to interpret the juxtaposition of a panel on the Ahenny Cross depicting warriors on horseback and men in a chariot setting out with their dogs, apparently on a hunting expedition, with a neighbouring panel depicting a funeral procession, in which a headless corpse is carried on horseback, followed by a man bearing the head, and preceded by others carrying crosses?

The form of the cross and the presentation of the Crucifixion have undergone a complete transformation in the course of centuries. In our earliest examples, we have seen that the cross itself formed only a lightly incised symbol on a flat stone surface resembling a page of manuscript. Gradually the relief develops, the carving grows steadily bolder, and the page effect disappears, for example on the Pictish slab crosses of Glamis [Plate 93] and Aberlemno [Plate 91]. The architectural structure of the cross becomes fundamental. In Ireland the head of the high crosses is generally surrounded and strengthened by a circle or 'wheel'. This type of cross is confined in Scotland to the Irish districts – Argyll and the Hebrides, and assigned to the ninth and tenth centuries.[1] Heavy bosses protrude from the arms and head of the wheel crosses, e.g. on the Iona crosses of St Martin [Plate 103] and St John, and from the centre of the Kildalton cross on Islay. In most of these great wheel crosses the figure of Christ occupies the chief position, the central space of the intersection of the arms, even encroaching on the arms, e.g. at Castledermot (Henry, *I.H.C.*, pl. 23), and on the Kells market cross (*ib.*, pl. 31), the

[1] S. Cruden, *ECPMS*, p. 14 f.

cross of Muiredach at Monasterboice [Plate 102] and the 'Cross of the Scriptures' at Clonmacnoise [Plate 101]. In Ireland the cross becomes a crucifix on which the figure of Christ is sometimes sculptured in high relief, virtually an independent statue, as on the cross of Dysert O'Dea (*I.H.C.*, pl. 62), and the defaced cross on the Rock of Cashel (*ib.*, p. 64).

In our discussion of insular Celtic art we have dwelt most fully on the art of Ireland, for Celtic traditional art, like Celtic traditional literature, is there preserved in its richest and most conservative form. In Great Britain Celtic art and technique have a more strictly regional history. Wales has a wealth of stone crosses, both in relief and free-standing, dating from the seventh to the ninth centuries. Most of them are flat, but the most famous is the pillar-stone at Valle Crucis Abbey near Llangollen, which bears an inscription commemorating Elisedd who lived in the eighth century (p. 113). The high cross on a stepped base is found in both Wales and Cornwall, but figure scenes are not common, the sculptor's art being generally confined to geometrical designs covering the entire surface, and his artistic skill is revealed by the exact adaptation of his design to its framework, and the flawless execution of his work. The Whithorn and Kirkmadrine stones illustrate the unity of the Strathclyde School with this Western Border tradition. It is not until the great Northumbrian School of the early ninth century that we find a new stimulus from contemporary continental motifs, both the foliate tracery of Merovingian art, and the majestic dignity and serenity of the fully clothed Christ of the Crucifixion in the Ruthwell and Bewcastle crosses.

These carved tomb-stones of western Britain have a special value for us in that, unlike the Irish, they are rich in inscriptions, which tell us something of contemporary personnel. In Wales some of these records have specified the professions and the official status of the defunct, a doctor (*medicus*), a magistrate (*magistratus*), or, as on a memorial tablet with a tiny incised cross at Llangadwaladr in Anglesey, the early seventh century king Cadfan (*Catamanus*), *sapientis(s)imus opinatis(s)imus omnium regum* 'most learned and renowned of all kings'. Cornwall has nine stone inscriptions, mostly in Roman capitals, and a few in ogams. One near Fowey is of especial interest for it possibly commemorates the Trystan of early Cornish romantic legend. The Cornish wheel-headed crosses, sculptured in the round, date from the tenth century and are attributed to direct Irish influence; but the art in general is geometrical, like that of Wales.

The Isle of Man has more than ninety carved stones,[1] mostly un-decorated commemorative slabs with incised crosses. A particularly

[1] For details and plates see P. M. C. Kermode, *Manx Crosses* (London, 1907).

interesting one bearing five prominent bosses, commemorates a certain Guriat (p. 109), in all probability a member of the family from which descended Rhodri Mawr, king of North Wales (d. AD 878). A rare form of inscribed slab of probably the eighth century from Maughold, the earliest and most important Manx Church, is inscribed with two little archaic crosses, and above them a circle enclosing the marigold design of Mediterranean origin. The island has at all times been a focus of the cultures of the surrounding lands, and it has a wealth of stone sculptures illustrating heathen Scandinavian mythology and dating from Viking times. In contra-distinction to this heathen reper- toire is the unique little incised slab of the Crucifixion [Plate 96], assigned to the eighth or ninth century, found on the Calf of Man on the site of an early Celtic Chapel, doubtless a little Celtic monastery. The man holding the spear stands at the foot of the Cross, and the side which is broken away doubtless bore the man with the sponge. The detail of the iconography has no known parallel. It is a living Christ, with open eyes, carefully trimmed hair and forked beard, fully clad, not in a single vestment like a shroud, but in elaborate garments of many embroidered and otherwise varied patterns. The nails are emphasized in feet and hands, but the figure impresses one, not as a dead saviour but rather as a living king.

With southern and western Britain we leave the Celtic traditional art behind. Indeed with this Manx crucifixion we have already left it. Northern and eastern Scotland possess a richly furnished album in stone which knows no predecessors, no close affinities. This is the art of the Picts. Its earliest form is that of a series of symbols, chiefly geometrical, but partly of conventionalized animals and birds, incised with supreme art on the undressed surface of boulders. These symbols are widespread, but have never yet been interpreted. Over a hundred survive, believed to date from the sixth to the eighth centuries, and their range extends from the Shetlands and the Hebrides to the Firth of Forth. They also form incised tapestries on the walls of certain of the Fifeshire caves, and are found on small objects such as the bronze plate from the Laws, Angus;[1] and a silver leaf-shaped plate from Largo, Fife,[2] both now in the National Museum of Scotland.

The Pictish stone sculptures are never found free-standing, but a later class of Pictish carving, dating from the seventh to the ninth centuries, consists of upright dressed slabs bearing relief sculpture of a wider range and foreign influence – Celtic ornament, and the figure of the cross, though the Crucifixion never appears. Here the principal subjects are naturalistic animals and narrative scenes from the life of human beings, and though symbols still occur they are of a different range from those

[1] Chadwick, *C.B.*, fig. 28. [2] *Ib.*, fig. 29.

of our previous class. Indeed the stereotyped form of the symbols of class I, which is characteristic of the Northern Picts, has given place during the eighth century among the Southern Picts of the Tay Valley to a predominantly naturalistic art. The intrusion of interlace and scroll and knot-work is suggestive of the growing influence of Celtic political relations. Later in date are the similar sculptured slabs of greater size which have rejected the symbols but now combine with the naturalistic designs of class II stones features more especially characteristic of the art of Northumbria and Ireland. In fact the art of the Pictish people is a close parallel to their history, which we first meet at the height of their power in the sixth century under their great king, Brude mac Maelchon, the *rex potentissimus* of Bede's *Ecclesiastical History*. Only a powerful and highly organized realm could have been responsible for the unity, the wide range, and the high quality of early Pictish art. Only a high standard of refinement could have set the standard of its austere, possibly hieratic art. The origin of this art, like that of the pre-Celtic language of the earliest Picts, remains wholly unknown and almost beyond conjecture. The early Pictish sculptures carry us beyond the confines of the Celtic Realms.

EPILOGUE

We found the Celts in south central Europe in the Bronze Age, perhaps as early as 2000 BC, and saw them later spreading west to the Atlantic and into the British Isles, and east as far as Asia Minor. By the fourth century BC they were, in numbers and in the extent of Celtic territory, the greatest people in Europe. Then came a period of decline when the Gauls of north Italy were conquered by the Romans, and the tribes north of the Alps were subjugated or expelled by the Germans. Caesar's Gallic War ended with the heroic effort of Vercingetorix at Alesia. His defeat and capture in 52 BC marks the end of Gaulish independence. But the Gauls quickly took advantage of Roman citizenship and Roman education, so that by the close of the fourth century Gaul was the principal intellectual area of the western Empire. The Gauls became known for their eloquence in public speaking and their gift for poetry: the poet Ausonius, and Sidonius Apollinaris, bishop and writer, are well-known names, and St Jerome himself speaks of 'the richness and splendour of Gaulish oratory'.[1] This is in accord with the comment of Cato the Elder that the ancient Gauls specially wished to be able to speak well (p. 17).

The great contribution of the Celts in the prehistoric period was in the field of decorative art in stone and metal-work. The art-form called La Tène which is peculiar to them is abstract art, pure decoration, in contrast to the grander art of Greece and Rome where Man is at the centre. There is even a refusal of representation, for when animal forms are brought into the pattern, they are in fantastic shapes, mere elements in the scheme of curves and spirals and interlacements in which the artists took delight. La Tène art is usually considered to end soon after Roman influence became dominant in Celtic territory, c. AD 100, but the imaginative quality and decorative sense that mark it did not disappear without leaving a trace behind; and the tools and monuments of Roman Gaul owe much of their worth to the tradition.

In Ireland Roman influence was never established, and here the old style was preserved, and it put on more magnificence in the Middle Ages. The splendid metal-work of the Ardagh Chalice and the Tara

[1] See *PLECG* 26, 47 f., 296 f.

313

Brooch, the manuscript illumination of the Book of Durrow and the Book of Kells, the decorative panels of the Cross of Muiredach at Monasterboice, are in the tradition of La Tène.

The Celtic realms of the historic period are Ireland and Wales, with their respective outlying countries in Scotland and the Isle of Man, Cornwall and Brittany. And in the British Isles the Celtic genius found its fullest expression and realized its greatest achievement under the stimulus of Christianity. Ireland received Christianity from Britain, and 'by the sixth century Irish Christianity surpassed that of every other land in western Europe, not only in intensity and sanctity, but also in passionate devotion to learning and missionary enthusiasm ... The passionate enthusiasm with which the Irish devoted themselves to the study of sacred learning and the liberal arts from the seventh century is without parallel in the rest of Europe ... Before the eighth century there were at least fifty important centres where Irish influence was dominant, ranging from Brittany in the north-west to Würzburg and Salzburg in the east, and from the English Channel ... to Bobbio.'[1]

The sudden growth of learning and holiness in Ireland in the sixth century is an extraordinary fact which suggests some efficient cause, and it is possible that Ireland was a place of refuge for scholars fleeing from the barbarians in Gaul, even perhaps for refugees from Egypt fleeing from the Moors, who brought with them these monastic virtues.[2] In the sixth century St Columba converted the Picts of Scotland, and Columbanus was on his way towards establishing the tradition of the *Scotti peregrini*. From the founding of Clonmacnoise in 548 to the founding of the Irish monastery at Ratisbon in 1090, the Irish were a powerful influence in the western Church. Toynbee claims for them a degree of cultural superiority in western Europe during all this long time,[3] and, while that may be too bold a claim, the known facts prove a very high level of piety and of scholarship at home and abroad. Virgilius of Salzburg († 784), called The Geometer, was abbot of St Peter's, and governed the diocese of Salzburg for more than thirty years. He was apparently learned in cosmography, and was denounced by St Boniface for teaching the existence of the Antipodes. Clemens Scottus was head of the Palace School under Louis the Pious. His contemporary, Dícuill, was the author of the *Liber de Mensura Orbis Terrae*, said to be the best book on geography in the early Middle Ages.[4] Dúngal of St Denis wrote a treatise on an eclipse of the sun. Donatus, bishop of Fiesole from 826 to 877, was an accomplished poet. The two greatest names, Sedulius and

---

[1] S. J. Crawford, *Anglo-Saxon Influence on Western Christendom* 11, 17, 88.
[2] See Lynn White, *Latin Monasticism in Norman Sicily* (Cambridge, Mass., 1938) p. 21 n. 7, and pp. 16 f.
[3] *Study of History* (ed. Somervell) 155.
[4] L. Bieler, *Ireland, Harbinger of the Middle Ages* 125.

Eriugena, have been introduced earlier (pp. 183–7). And these are only some of the poets, scholars and saints whom Traube and his disciples have made known.[1] To the list of names must be added the witness of Bobbio and of St Gall. 'It is impossible for the classical scholar to exaggerate the significance of the part played by the Irish in the work of preserving classical literature.'[2]

During the ninth and tenth centuries Ireland was being ravaged by the Norsemen, and the monastic schools were plundered again and again, so that there must have been hundreds of refugees who now in turn sought the quiet of Irish monasteries in France and Germany, from Péronne, Laon and Rheims to Fulda and Würzburg. Their zeal for learning did not fail, and the scholarship of the Irish on the Continent was never at a higher level than in the ninth century, when most of those mentioned above were active.

Even at home, however, learning, literature and art survived, and even prospered, in spite of the Viking raids. It was during the Viking period that some of the grandest High Crosses were made, and fine metal-work was still being done. Indeed it is in some measure to this danger from the Norsemen that we owe the building of the handsome bell-towers which give dignity and grace to so many monastic sites. The early 'round towers', such as those of Clonmacnoise, Kells and Monasterboice, are thought to have been built in the tenth century, mainly as strongholds in which relics, treasures, and books could be housed, and in which the monks took refuge on occasion. The raised doorway, which can be approached only by a ladder, and the form and disposition of the windows, prove their defensive character. The annals record the burning of the tower of Slane in 948, when all the relics were destroyed and some of the monks were killed, and similar disasters are told repeatedly during the latter part of the tenth century. Some towers, those of Kildare, Timahoe and Devenish, show romanesque features, and are thus not earlier than the twelfth century. The round tower was now perhaps regarded as a necessary part of the monastic buildings, even when the monasteries were not in constant danger. The beautiful tower at Ardmore is an example from this period [Plate 56].[3]

In literature as in life, the Celtic peoples have given more to others than they managed to harvest for themselves. Two themes are prominent in early Irish literature, nature and tragic love. Kuno Meyer said well that the Irish were quick to take an artistic hint, and had a liking for the

[1] See also L. Weisgerber, 'Eine Irenwelle an Maas, Mosel und Rhein in Ottonischer Zeit', *Geschichte und Landeskunde* (Forschungen u. Darstellungen Franz Steinbach ... gewidmet), Bonn, 1960.
[2] E. Norden, *Die antike Kunstprosa* ii 667. There is no history of classical scholarship in Irish monasteries on the Continent.
[3] For an account of the Round Towers see F. Henry, *IA*, II 49–57.

half-said thing: the early nature poetry that we have presented is evidence of it. The motif of the Doomed Lovers was carried from Wales to Brittany and became one of the great matters of medieval and renaissance literature. Arthurian romance, *la matière de Bretagne* in its wider extension, is known to be another gift of Wales to Europe, although the Welsh sources are lost. After a splendid beginning, with heroic themes not unworthy of Homer, Irish literature perished in the manuscripts. The tales of battles, adventures and voyages were composed for recitation at the *Óenach* or in the houses of the great, and the written form is a poor record of the story.[1] In the peasants' cottages old stories were still recited but there, as folk tales, they became overlaid with international *märchen*-motifs, and the matter itself changed. Finn replaced Cú Chulainn, and the ballad appeared beside the folk-tale. The Fenian warriors are good-humoured giants.

Maybe society itself was somehow fossilized in Ireland and Wales even before the Normans came. The future lay with the Normans, and the native genius stood still. In the eleventh century there had been a revival of learning in Ireland, and a period of reform under Brian Boru. A Welshman, Sulien, came to Ireland to study *c.* 1045, and stayed there for several years before returning to Wales to teach at Llanbadarn Fawr.[2] The second great mission to Germany began at this time. In 1067 an Irish monk from Donegal, Muiredach mac Robartaig, went on pilgrimage to Rome with two companions. They stopped at Ratisbon on their journey and were asked to stay; and they established themselves at Weih-Sankt-Peter outside the city, living in separate huts in the Irish manner. Muiredach, or Marianus by his Latin name, stayed there till his death in 1080. Soon afterwards some of his monks made a new foundation, St James of Ratisbon, and adopted the Rule of St Benedict. This was the first of the Irish Benedictine abbeys on the Continent, the *Schottenklöster* as they were called. From Ratisbon foundations were made at Würzburg and Vienna, at Nürnberg, Bamberg and Eichstätt. There was even a monastery at Kiev for some time until the Mongol invasion in 1241. These abbeys kept in touch with Ireland, and drew their monks from the home country for three hundred years, a strange and almost accidental renewal of the great tradition of Columbanus. Then the supply of monks from Ireland failed, and the foundations passed, one by one, into other hands. St James is now the diocesan seminary of Ratisbon, Eichstätt is in the hands of German Capuchins; only the *Schottenkloster* of Vienna preserves its name, and there the Benedictines are still in possession, but they are no longer Irish.[3]

In Ireland the school of historical poets known as 'synthetic historians'

---

[1] See *GL*, III 180 ff.; *SM*, 7–13.   [2] See *HW* ii 460.
[3] See D. A. Binchy, 'Irish Benedictines in Medieval Germany', *Studies* xviii (1929), 194 ff.

appears at this time. Cinaed Ua Hartacáin († 975), Cúan Ua Lothcháin († 1024), Fland Mainistrech († 1056) and Gilla Coemáin († 1072) deserve mention, and if Fland were really the author of the great recension of *Táin Bó Cualnge* in the Book of Leinster, as Zimmer thought, he would have special honour.

The spirit of reform and the literary activity were most notable in the twelfth century, under the leadership of St Malachy, when diocesan rule was established in the Church, and the Cistercians came from Clairvaux and founded Mellifont. The literary men were now engaged in compiling old traditions and inventing new tales.[1] Down to the end of the twelfth century Irish literature is the greatest vernacular literature in Europe, and Welsh literature is next to it.

In Wales likewise there was a movement of recovery and reform. Here the Normans were already established in the south as conquerors, and everywhere along the Border there was the threat of foreign domination. The death of Henry I in 1135 was the occasion for a general effort to shake off the enemy. 'A new spirit of daring and independence seems to have seized the whole Welsh race.'[2] It was the age of Gruffydd ap Cynan, who had been building up the strength of Gwynedd and extending its territory. His son, Owain, became the most powerful of the Welsh princes, and added Ceredigion to the country under his control. The Normans suffered a disastrous defeat at Cardigan in 1136, and fled with heavy losses; and in the two following years Owain and his brother Cadwaladr again went south and completed their victory. Under Owain the Welsh nation attained the full measure of national consciousness,[3] and he lived to see the collapse of Henry II's expedition in 1165, after which the king abandoned hope of conquering Wales. The first Eisteddfod was held in 1176 in the new castle of Rhys ap Gruffydd at Aberteifi, and competitors were invited from Ireland and Scotland.

There may have been an impulse of response in both countries to the challenge of the Normans. A notable result of it was the increased activity of the bardic schools, an attempt to give new life to a very ancient custom; but no great writer appeared at that time anywhere in the Celtic countries in the native tradition. In Wales Meilyr, Cynddelw and Gruffudd ab yr Ynad Coch are well known poets of the time. One might add, for literature, the author of the Four Branches of the Mabinogion, if we could identify him.

Whatever the cause, the ancient practice of court poetry was the one literary *genre* that flourished in the later Middle Ages and down to modern times, in Scotland and Wales and Ireland, in forms more

---

[1] G. Murphy, *Ossianic Lore* 16–17; F. Henry, *op. cit.* iii 17.
[2] J. E. Lloyd, *History of Wales* ii 462, 523.   [3] *Ibid.* 487.

polished and more powerful than ever, *dán dírech* in Irish, *cynghanedd* in Welsh. This praise-poetry seems to have been all that the Welsh and Irish chieftains wanted to hear, and they were willing to pay for it. The poets were professional parasites, but they were more than that. They were custodians of a very old tradition, and the chief upholders of the honour and self-esteem of noblemen; and they were highly trained in the craft of poetry.

It has not been part of our plan to follow the fortunes of the Celtic peoples beyond the twelfth century. In Ireland old Celtic institutions lived on at least in the west and north until the end of the sixteenth century, Celt and Norman side by side, some of the Norman lords now Irish in speech and habit. In Wales the end of independence came in 1282 (p. 267), but there have been several periods of revival, and Wales is still strongly Celtic in speech and strongly separatist – or at least particularist – in feeling. In Scotland, where there never was a conquest, old Gaelic custom survived in the Highlands and Islands even longer than in Ireland. A bardic elegy in strict form was composed for James MacDonald who died in 1738.[1] Brittany was formally annexed to France only in 1532, and there, as in Wales, the people have clung to old tradition in language and culture with great loyalty. This recent history is beyond our competence, and outside the scope of our endeavour. Our endeavour has been to tell what is known of the Celts in prehistoric times, and of the Celtic peoples later in their separate realms, the founding of the Celtic kingdoms, their institutions, their languages and literatures, their art, and the part that they have played in the history of Europe.

[1] A. Cameron, *Reliquiae Celticae* ii 274.

ABBREVIATIONS

Periodicals

N.B. Abbreviations for periodicals are in roman type to distinguish them from abbreviations of book titles, which are in italics.

AA	Archaeologia Aeliana
AB	Analecta Bollandiana
AC	Archaeologia Cambrensis
AJ	The Antiquaries Journal
APAW	Abhandlungen der preussischen Akademie der Wissenschaften
Arch J	The Archaeological Journal
BBCS	The Bulletin of the Board of Celtic Studies
Beitr.	Beiträge zur Geschichte der deutschen Literatur
BSHAB	Bulletin de la Société d'Histoire et d'Archéologie de Bretagne
BSL	Bulletin de la Société de Linguistique de Paris
CHAJ	Cork Historical and Archaeological Journal
DR	The Dublin Review
ÉC	Études Celtiques
JA	Journal Asiatique
JBAA	Journal of the British Archaeological Association
JRIC	Journal of the Royal Institute of Cornwall, Second Series
JRS	Journal of Roman Studies
JRSAI	Journal of the Royal Society of Antiquaries of Ireland
MA	Medieval Archaeology
MSHAB	Mémoires de la Société d'Histoire et d'Archéologie de Bretagne
MSL	Mémoires de la Société de Linguistique
NA	Neues Archiv für Sächsische Geschichte
NTS	Norsk Tidsskrift for Sprogvidenskap
PBA	Proceedings of the British Academy
PRIA	Proceedings of the Royal Irish Academy
PSAS	Proceedings of the Society of Antiquaries of Scotland
RC	Revue Celtique
SÉC	Société d'Émulation des Côtes-du-Nord, Bulletins et Mémoires
SGS	Scottish Gaelic Studies
SH	Studia Hibernica
SHR	The Scottish Historical Review
SR	The Scottish Review
TCWS	Transactions of the Cumberland and Westmoreland Antiquarian Society
TDGS	Transactions of the Dumfriesshire and Galloway Natural History and Antiquarian Society
THSC	Transactions of the Honourable Society of Cymmrodorion
TLCAS	Transactions of the Lancashire and Cheshire Antiquarian Society
TPS	Transactions of the Philological Society
ZCP	Zeitschrift für Celtische Philologie
ZDMG	Zeitschrift der deutschen morgenlandischen Gesellschaft
ZfdA	Zeitschrift für deutsches Altertum

Books

N.B. Books referred to only once in the text are generally specified fully in the notes, and not entered in this list of abbreviations.

AB
Angles and Britons (O'Donnell Lectures, Cardiff, 1963).

ABR
J. M. C. Toynbee, *Art in Britain under the Romans* (Oxford, 1964).

ACS
H. O'Neill Hencken, *The Archaeology of Cornwall and Scilly* (London, 1932).

AG
A. Varagnac, *L'Art Gaulois* (Yonne, 2nd ed., 1964).

AI
F. Henry, *L'Art Irlandais*, 3 vols. (Yonne, 1963, 1964).

ÄID
K. Meyer, *Über die älteste irische Dichtung*, I–II (APAW Jahrgang 1931, Berlin 1913–14).

A. Inisfallen
The Annals of Inisfallen, edited and translated by Seán, Mac Airt (Dublin, 1951).

AIP
K. Meyer, *Selections from Ancient Irish Poetry* (2nd ed., London, 1913).

AL
Ancient Laws of Ireland, vol. 1–6, edited by W. M. Hennessy, W. N. Hancock, T. O'Mahony, A. G. Richey, R. Atkinson (Dublin, 1856–1901).

ALI
Ancient Laws and Institutes of Wales, edited by Aneurin Owen (London, 1841).

ALMA
Arthurian Literature in the Middle Ages, edited by R. S. Loomis (Oxford, 1959).

AMVR
F. Benoit, *L'Art Méditerranéen de la Vallée du Rhone* (Aix-en-Provence, 1955).

ARB
J. M. C. Toynbee, *Art in Roman Britain* (London, 1962).

AS
N. K. Chadwick, *The Age of the Saints in the Early Celtic Church* (O.U.P. 1961, reprinted 1963).

ASC
D. Whitelock, *The Anglo-Saxon Chronicle. A Revised Translation* (London, 1961).

ASE
F. M. Stenton, *Anglo-Saxon England* (2nd ed., Oxford, 1947).

ASG
J. M. Clark, *The Abbey of St. Gall* (Cambridge, 1926).

AT
The Annals of Tigernach, edited and translated by Whitley Stokes, R.C., vols. XVI, 1895, 170 ff.; XVII, 1896, 6 ff.

AU
The Annals of Ulster, in 4 vols. Vol. I edited and translated by W. M. Hennessy (Dublin, 1887); Vols. II–IV, B. MacCarthy (Dublin, 1893, 1895, 1901).

Bagendon
E. M. Clifford, *Bagendon* (Cambridge, 1961).

BB
Book of Ballymote, facsimile edition by R. Atkinson (Dublin, 1887).

Bede
C. Plummer, *Venerabilis Baedae Opera Historica*, 2 vols. (Oxford, 1896).

Bordeaux
C. Jullian, *Histoire de Bordeaux depuis les Origines jusqu'en 1895* (Bordeaux, 1895).

BRA
G. Simpson, *Britons and the Roman Army* (London, 1964).

Bruchst.
K. Meyer, *Bruchstücke der älteren Lyrik Irlands* (APAW, Berlin, 1919).

CA
Ifor Williams, *Canu Aneirin*, Cardiff, 1938.

Caspari
Caspari, *Briefe, Abhandlungen und Predigten* (Christiania, 1890). English translation by R. S. Haselhurst, under the title: *The Letters of Fastidius* (London, 1927). Our page references are to the English translation.

CB
N. K. Chadwick, *Celtic Britain* (London, 1964).

CB
John Rhŷs, *Celtic Britain* (3rd ed. London, 1904).

CC	Olivier Loyer, *Les Chrétientés Celtiques* (Paris, 1965).
CCH	Jan Filip, *Celtic Civilization and its Heritage* (Prague, 1960. English translation by R. F. Samsour, 1962).
CCL	Louis Gougaud, *Christianity in Celtic Lands*. Translated from the author's MS. by Maud Joynt (London, 1932).
CE	I. Ll. Foster and L. Alcock, *Culture and Environment* (London, 1963).
Celts	T. G. E. Powell, *The Celts* (London, 1958).
CG	D. A. Binchy, *Críth Gablach* (Dublin, 1941).
CGG	*Cogadh Gaedhel re Gallaibh*, edited and translated by J. H. Todd (London, 1867).
CGH	M. A. O'Brien, *Corpus Genealogiarum Hiberniae* (Dublin, 1962).
CI	E. MacNeill, *Celtic Ireland* (Dublin, 1921).
CIIC	R. A. S. Macalister, *Corpus Inscriptionum Insularum Celticarum*, 2 vols. (Dublin, 1945, 1949).
CIL	*Corpus Inscriptionum Latinarum.*
CK	Myles Dillon, *The Cycles of the Kings* (Oxford, 1946).
CM	K. H. Jackson, *A Celtic Miscellany* (London, 1951).
CPS	W. J. Watson, *History of the Celtic Place-Names of Scotland* (Edinburgh, 1926).
CRB	Hugh Williams, *Christianity in Roman Britain* (Oxford, 1912).
CS	W. F. Skene, *Celtic Scotland*, 3 vols. (Edinburgh, 1886–1890).
DF	*Duanaire Finn*, Irish text and translation by E. MacNeill and Gerard Murphy, 3 vols. (London, 1908, 1933, 1953).
DHC	M.–L. Sjoestedt, *Dieux et Héros des Celtes* (Paris, 1940). English translation with additional notes by Myles Dillon (London, 1949).
EA	Episcopal Acts and cognate documents relating to Welsh Dioceses 1066–1272, 2 vols., edited by James Conway Davies (Hist. Soc. Church in Wales, 1, 3, 4, 1946–48).
ÉB	J. Loth, *L'Émigration Bretonne en Armorique du Ve au VIIe Siècle de Notre Ère* (Paris, 1883).
EC	*The Early Cultures of North-West Europe*, edited by Sir C. Fox and B. Dickins (Cambridge, 1950).
ECA	P. Jacobsthal, *Early Celtic Art* (Oxford, 1944).
ECI	M. and L. de Paor, *Early Christian Ireland* (London, 1958).
ECMW	V. E. Nash-Williams, *The Early Christian Monuments of Wales* (Cardiff 1950).
ECPM	S. Cruden, *The Early Christian and Pictish Monuments of Scotland* (Edinburgh, 1957).
EGC	T. H. Bindley, *The Epistle of the Gallican Churches* (London, 1900).
EHC	L. Duchesne, *The Early History of the Church*. English translation of the first edition, reprinted (London, 1950).
EIHM	T. F. O'Rahilly, *Early Irish History and Mythology* (Dublin, 1946).
EIL	Myles Dillon, *Early Irish Literature* (Chicago, 1948).
EIS	*Early Irish Society*, edited by Myles Dillon (Dublin, 1954).
ES	H. M. Chadwick, *Early Scotland* (Cambridge, 1949).
ESEM	*Essays and Studies presented to Professor E. MacNeill*, edited by Rev. J. Ryan (Dublin, 1940).
ESSH	A. O. Anderson, *Early Sources of Scottish History*, 2 vols. (Edinburgh, 1922).
EWP	Ifor Williams, *Lectures on Early Welsh Poetry* (Dublin, 1944).
FABW	W. F. Skene, *The Four Ancient Books of Wales*, 2 vols. (Edinburgh, 1868). Vol. I Translation, Vol. II Welsh texts.

FCL	*The Fate of the Children of Lir*, edited and translated by R. J. O'Duffy (5th ed., Dublin, 1908).
FCT	*The Fate of the Children of Tuireann*, edited and translated by R. J. O'Duffy (Dublin, 1901).
FCU	*The Fate of the Children of Uisneach*, edited and translated by R. J. O'Duffy (Dublin, 1914).
FEIA	C. Fox, *A Find of the Early Iron Age from Llyn Cerrig Bach, Anglesey* (Cardiff, 1946).
Fontes	I. Zwicker, *Fontes Historiae Religionis Celticae*, 3 parts (Berlin, 1934–36).
FPRB	P. Salway, *The Frontier People of Roman Britain* (Cambridge, 1965).
FWS	*Festschrift für Whitley Stokes* (Leipzig, 1900).
GC	Élie Griffe, *La Gaule Chrétienne à l'Époque Romaine*, I (Paris and Toulouse, 1947).
GL	H. M. and N. K. Chadwick, *The Growth of Literature*, 3 vols. (Cambridge, 1932–1940).
GLL	M. Manitius, *Geschichte der lateinische Literatur des Mittelalters*, 3 vols. (Munich, 1911, 1923, 1931).
GPN	D. Ellis Evans, *Gaulish Personal Names* (London, 1967).
Groupement	H. Pedersen, *Le Groupement des Dialectes Indo-Européens* (København, 1925).
HB	H. Waquet, *Histoire de la Bretagne* (Paris, 1950).
HB	L. A. Le Moyne de la Borderie, *Histoire de Bretagne*, 6 vols. (Rennes and Paris, 1896–1914).
HB	E. Durtelle de Saint-Sauveur, *Histoire de Bretagne*, 2 vols. (4th ed., (Rennes, 1947).
HB	A. Rebillon, *Histoire de Bretagne* (Paris, 1957).
HD	Melville Richards, *The Laws of Hywel Dda* (Liverpool, 1954).
Heldensage	R. Thurneysen, *Die irische Helden- und Königsage* (Halle (Saale), 1921).
HG	C. Jullian, *Histoire de la Gaule*, 8 vols. (Paris, 1908–1926).
Hill-Forts	R. E. M. Wheeler and K. Richardson, *Hill-Forts of Northern France* (Oxford, 1957).
HIM	R. H. Kinvig, *A History of the Isle of Man* (2nd edition, Liverpool, 1950).
Hist. Brit.	*The Historia Brittonum* by Nennius. Ed. by T. Mommsen, Monumenta Germaniae Historica, auctores antiquissimi, t. XIII, (Berlin, 1898, reprinted 1961); also by F. Lot (Paris, 1934). Translated by A. W. Wade-Evans, *Nennius's History of the Britons* (London, 1938).
HW	J. E. Lloyd, *History of Wales*, 2 vols. (3rd ed., London, 1939).
HWL	T. Parry, *A History of Welsh Literature*. Translated by H. I. Bell (Oxford, 1955).
IA	F. Henry, *Irish Art in the Early Christian Period to A.D. 800* (London, 1965).
IAECP	F. Henry, *Irish Art in the Early Christian Period* (2nd ed., London, 1947).
ICCS	*Proceedings of the International Congress of Celtic Studies* (Dublin, 1962).
IDPP	T. F. O'Rahilly, *Irish Dialects Past and Present* (London, 1932).
IHC	F. Henry, *Irish High Crosses* (Dublin, 1964).
IM	J. Ryan, *Irish Monasticism* (Dublin and Cork, 1931).
Invasions	L. Musset, *Les Invasions: Les Vagues Germaniques* (Paris, 1965).
IPD	C. S. Boswell, *An Irish Precursor of Dante* (London, 1908).
IPG	E. MacNeill, *Early Irish Population Groups* (PRIA xxix C 1911).
Irland	L. Bieler, *Irland* (Lausanne and Freiburg, 1961). English edition, *Ireland* (London, 1963).

Ir. T	*Irische Texte*, ed. W. Stokes and E. Windisch (Leipzig, 1880–1905).
IT	R. Flower, *The Irish Tradition* (Oxford, 1947).
LB	*Leabhar Breac, the Speckled Book*, facsimile edition by S. Ferguson (Dublin, 1876).
LBS	S. Baring-Gould and J. Fisher, *The Lives of the British Saints*, 4 vols. (London, 1907–1913).
LC	*Lebor na Cert (The Book of Rights)*, edited and translated by Myles Dillon (Dublin, 1962).
Lec.	*The Book of Lecan*, facsimile edition by Kathleen Mulchrone (Dublin, 1937).
Légende	J. Marx, *La Légende Arthurienne et le Graal* (Paris, 1952).
LHEB	K. H. Jackson, *Language and History in Early Britain* (Edinburgh, 1953).
LIFC	K. Meyer, *Learning in Ireland in the Fifth Century and the Transmission of Letters* (Dublin, 1913).
LIS	C. Plummer, *Bethada Náem nÉrenn (Lives of Irish Saints)*. 2 vols. (Oxford, 1922).
LL	*The Book of Leinster*, facsimile edition by R. Atkinson (Dublin 1880).
LP	M. P. Charlesworth, *The Lost Province* (Cardiff, 1949).
LRB	A. Birley, *Life in Roman Britain* (London, 1964).
LRE	A. H. M. Jones, *The Later Roman Empire*, 3 vols., + one vol. maps (Oxford, 1964).
LRV	G. W. Meates, *Lullingstone Roman Villa* (London, 1955).
LS	D. A. White, *Litus Saxonicum* (Madison, Wisconsin, 1961).
LU	*Lebor na hUidre*, ed. R. Best and O. Bergin (Dublin 1929).
Lughnasa	Máire MacNeill, *The Festival of Lughnasa* (Oxford, 1962).
Manuel	J. Déchelette, *Manuel d'Archéologie Préhistorique Celtique et Gallo-Romaine*, II (Paris, 1914).
Manuel	G. Dottin, *Manuel pour servir à l'Étude de l'Antiquité Celtique* (2nd ed., Paris, 1915).
Math	W. J. Gruffydd, *Math vab Mathonwy* (Cardiff, 1928).
MD	*The Metrical Dindshenchas*. Edited and translated by E. Gwynn in 5 parts (Dublin, R.I.A., 1903–1935).
NB	C. Selmer, *Navigatio Sancti Brendani Abbatis* (Nôtre Dame, 1959).
ND	O. Seeck (editor), *Notitia Dignitatum* (Berlin, 1876).
OCR	P. W. Joyce, *Old Celtic Romances* (London, 1914).
OEN	H. M. Chadwick, *The Origin of the English Nation* (Cambridge, 1907).
OIT	K. H. Jackson, *The Oldest Irish Tradition: A Window on the Iron Age* (Cambridge, 1964).
ON	P. Hunter Blair, *The Origins of Northumbria* (Gateshead-on-Tyne, 1948).
Onomasticon	E. Hogan, *Onomasticon Goidelicum* (Dublin, 1910).
P and P	C. Fox, *Pattern and Purpose* (Cardiff, 1958).
P and S	W. F. Skene, *Chronicles of the Picts and Scots* (Edinburgh, 1867).
Pélage	G. de Plinval, *Pélage, Ses Écrits, Sa Vie, et sa Réforme* (Lausanne, 1943).
Pelagius	J. Ferguson, *Pelagius* (Cambridge, 1956).
PEW	I. Ll. Foster and G. E. Daniel (edd.), *Prehistoric and Early Wales* (London, 1965).
Phases	E. MacNeill, *Phases of Irish History* (Dublin, 1920).
PLECG	N. K. Chadwick, *Poetry and Letters in Early Christian Gaul* (London, 1955).
PP	*The Problem of the Picts*, edited by F. T. Wainwright (Edinburgh, 1965).
Rawl.	Rawlinson B 502, facsimile edition, ed. K. Meyer (Oxford, 1909).
RB	I. A. Richmond, *Roman Britain* (Harmondsworth, 1955; 2nd ed., 1963).

RBEE	P. Hunter Blair, *Roman Britain and Early England* (Edinburgh, 1963).
RBES	F. G. Collingwood and J. N. L. Myres, *Roman Britain and the English Settlements* (Oxford, 1936).
RC	I. A. Richmond and O. G. S. Crawford, *The British Section of the Ravenna Cosmography* (Oxford, 1949).
RCB	G. Webster and D. R. Dudley, *The Roman Conquest of Britain* (London, 1965).
RG	O. Brogan, *Roman Gaul* (London, 1953).
RIB	R. G. Collingwood and R. P. Wright, *The Roman Inscriptions of Britain* (Oxford, 1965).
RIN	C. G. Starr, *The Roman Imperial Navy* (Ithaca, N.Y., 1941).
RNNB	I. A. Richmond, *Roman and Native in North Britain* (Edinburgh, 1958).
ROB	F. Haverfield and G. Macdonald, *The Roman Occupation of Britain* (Oxford, 1924).
RRB	F. Haverfield, *The Romanization of Roman Britain*. (Revised by G. Macdonald, Oxford, 1923).
SC	*Sanas Cormaic, An Old-Irish Glossary*, edited by Kuno Meyer (Anecdota from Irish Manuscripts IV, Halle, 1912).
SCO	G. S. M. Walker, *Sancti Columbani Opera* (Dublin 1957).
SEBC	*Studies in the Early British Church*, by N. K. Chadwick, K. Hughes, Christopher Brooke, K. Jackson (Cambridge, 1958).
SEBH	*Studies in Early British History* by H. M. Chadwick and others (Cambridge, 1954, reprinted 1959).
SECT	J. Anderson, *Scotland in Early Christian Times* (Edinburgh, 1881).
SG	S. H. O'Grady, *Silva Gadelica* (London, 1892). Vol. I Irish Texts. Vol. II Translations.
SI	F. Henry, *La Sculpture Irlandaise* (Paris, 1933).
SILH	J. Carney, *Studies in Irish Literature and History* (Dublin, 1955).
SM	G. Murphy, *Saga and Myth in Ancient Ireland* (Dublin, 1961).
Sources	J. F. Kenney, *The Sources for the Early History of Ireland* (New York, 1929).
SS	S. Hellmann, *Sedulius Scottus* (Munich, 1906).
ST	Stith Thompson, *Motif-Index of Folk Literature*, 6 vols. (Copenhagen, 1955–58).
Stanwick	R. E. M. Wheeler, *The Stanwick Fortifications* (Oxford, 1954).
Táin	*Die altirische Heldensage Táin Bó Cúalnge*, edited and translated by E. Windisch (Leipzig, 1905). [New edition and translation by C. O'Rahilly, Dublin, 1967.]
TIG	*Three Irish Glossaries*, edited by Whitley Stokes (London, 1862).
TL	M. L. W. Laistner, *Thought and Letters in Western Europe A.D. 500–900* (2nd ed., London, 1957).
TP	T. F. O'Rahilly, *The Two Patricks* (Dublin, 1942).
Triads	*Trioedd Ynys Prydein. The Welsh Triads*, edited and translated by R. Bromwich (Cardiff, 1961).
Tripartite Life	*The Tripartite Life of Patrick with other Documents relating to that Saint*, 2 vols., edited by Whitley Stokes (London, 1887). I. Tripartite Life, Irish text and translation. II. Documents concerning S. Patrick, Irish text and translation.
TRS	O. G. S. Crawford, *Topography of Roman Scotland* (Cambridge, 1949).
TSC	J. Earle and C. Plummer, *Two Saxon Chronicles*, 2 vols. (Oxford, 1899).

TT	A. O. Curle, *The Treasure of Traprain: A Scottish Hoard of Roman Silver* (Glasgow, 1923).
VA	*Viking Antiquities in Great Britain and Ireland*, 6 parts (Oslo, 1940–54).
VB	K. Meyer, *The Voyage of Bran*, 2 vols. (Dublin: I, 1895, II, 1897).
VSBG	A. W. Wade-Evans, *Vitae Sanctorum Britanniae et Genealogiae* (Cardiff 1944).
VSH	C. Plummer, *Vitae Sanctorum Hiberniae*, 2 vols. (Oxford, 1910).
WF	F. R. Hoare, *The Western Fathers* (London, 1954).
WK	J. Moreau, *Die Welt der Kelten* (3rd ed., Stuttgart, 1961).
WP	J. Rhys and D. Brynmot-Jones, *The Welsh People* (London, 1900).
WTL	T. P. Ellis, *Welsh Tribal Law and Custom* (Oxford, 1926).
YBL	*The Yellow Book of Lecan.*

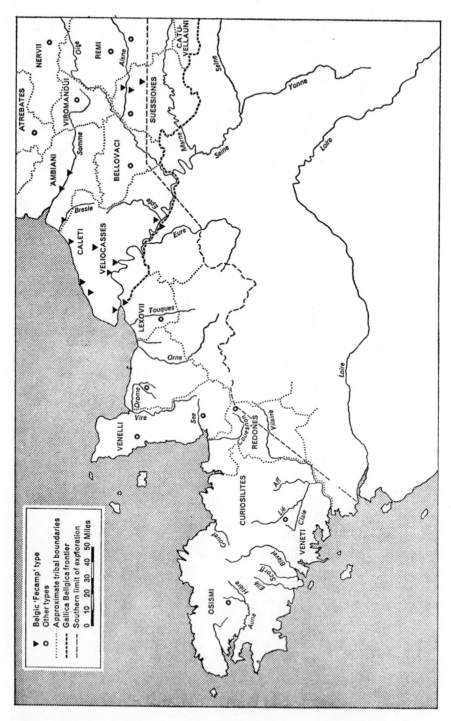

Map 1. Celtic Hill-Forts of North-Western France (after Wheeler and Richardson)

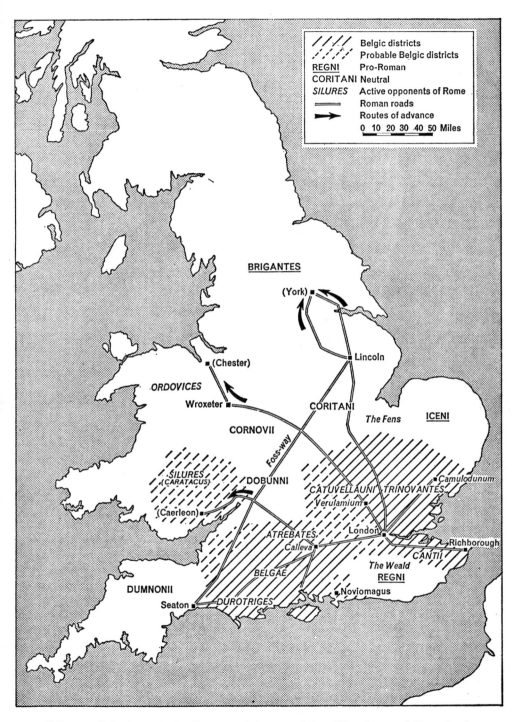

Map 2. Britain and the Roman Advance (after Hawkes and Dunning)

Map 3. Britain in 47 AD (after A. L. F. Rivet)

ORCADES Iae

CAIT

CORNAVII

AEBUDAE Iae

SCETIS

CALEDONII

CINÉL
BAETÁIN

ATHFÓTLA

CIRCENN

CINÉL
LOAIRN

FORTRENN

FIB

CINÉL COMGAILL
OR GABRÁIN

Antonine
Wall

MANAW
GODODDIN

LOTHIAN

DAMNONII

ILE

STRATHCLYDE
BRITONS

OTADINI

SELGOVAE

NOVANTAE

CUMBRI
(BRITONS)

Hadrian's Wall

Map 4. Early Scotland

MON
Din Lligwy
Penmon
Llansadwrn
Llangadwaladr
Aberffraw
Clynnogfawr
Caernarvon
▲ *Snowdon*

Deganwy
Abergele
Rhuddlan
St Asaph
RHOS
+ Bangor

■ Chester
■ Bangor

G
W
Y
N
E
D
D

AFLOGION
DUNODING

Offa's
Dyke
Wat's
Dyke

P
O
W
Y
S

Severn

• Chirbury

Llanbadarn ■
Arwystli ▲

GWERTHRYNION

CEREDIGION
Teifi

BUELLT
ELFAEL

Wye
Hereford
ANERCYNC
EUIAS
ERGING

S
E
L
S
Y
L
L
W
G

BRYCHEINIOG

DYFED
■ St Davids

Dinevor ■
Llanddowror ■
YSTRADTOWY
CETGUELI

Towy

G
W
E
N
T

Ynys Byr

GOWER
Loyngarth

GWYNLLWG EDLOGAN
GLYWYSING Caerleon
Caerwent

■ Margam
Llandaff
Llancarfan
Llantwit ■ Barry

0   10   20   30 Miles

Map 5. Wales in the Seventh and Eighth Centuries

Map 6. Ireland: the Five Fifths (after Mac Neill)

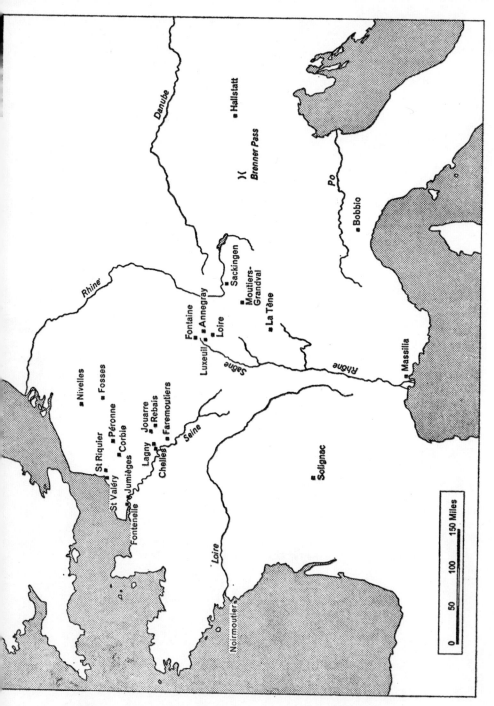

Map 7. Early Irish Monasteries in Western Europe

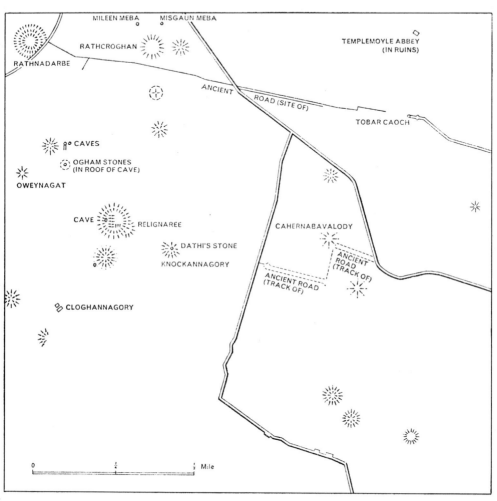

MILEEN MEBA
MISGAUN MEBA

RATHCROGHAN

TEMPLEMOYLE ABBEY
(IN RUINS)

RATHNADARBE

ANCIENT
ROAD (SITE OF)

TOBAR CAOCH

CAVES

OGHAM STONES
(IN ROOF OF CAVE)

OWEYNAGAT

CAHERNABAVALODY

CAVE
RELIGNAREE

DATHI'S STONE

KNOCKANNAGORY

ANCIENT
ROAD
(TRACK OF)

ANCIENT ROAD
(TRACK OF)

CLOGHANNAGORY

0   ¼   ½ Mile

Map 8. Plan of Cruachain

INDEX

rath, 90
Ravenna Cosmography, 19
Rebirth, Irish belief in, 145
Rechtaire, Irish officer of state, 92
Religion, pre-Christian, 10, 13, 134; *see also* Mythology
  local deities, 14
  mother-cult, 13–14
Repoussé work, Celtic bronze, 292–3
Rheged, Kingdom of, 74
Rhodri Mawr, King of North Wales, 77, 99, 108, 109, 110, 111, 112, 113, 114, 122
  ambition for united Celtic Britain, 114
  effect of his death, 115–16
  policy, 115–16
Rhonabwy's Dream, 276–7
Rhydderch Hen, King, 47, 76, 105
rí, 89
Rigveda
  relation to Irish metrical forms, 10
  syntax similar to Old Irish, 200
Riwal, legendary king of Dumnonia, 81, 82
Roman Britain
  barbarian raids, 30–2
  Celtic character, 43
  use of native tribes to aid defence, 43–45, 46, 47, 48
Rome, pilgrimages to, 110, 181–2
Roquepertuse, Celtic remains at, 285, 286, 288
ruiri, 89
Ruchworth Gospels, 303

Sacrifices, religious, 9, 15
St David's, Monastery of, 114
Samain, 103, 139, 140
Samson of Dol, St, 83, 164
Sanas Cormaic, see Cormac's Glossary
Sanctuaries, religious, 130–2, 288
Saturninus of Toulouse, 153
Saxons
  employed as Roman mercenaries, 44–5
  entry into Britain
    archaeological evidence, 44–5
    tradition, 43–4
  attacks on Gaul, 52
  attacks on Wales, 113
  factor in British emigration, 41
Saxon Shore, 31

Scabbards, Irish bronze, 295–6
Scholars, Irish, in Europe, 126–7, 180–7, 314–15, 316
Scone, 105, 108
Scordisci, 6, 281
Scotland, *see also* Dál Riata, Picts
  Anglian conquests, in, 76–7
  four nations distinguished, 72–4
  Irish settlement, in, 41–2, 65–6
  united kingdom, 106
  Viking settlements in islands of, 118–19
Scottish Gaelic, *see* Goidelic dialects
Sculpture, Celtic, 283
  stone, 285–8
    human, 287–8
    animal, 284
  wood, 288–9
Sedulius, 222
Sedulius Scottus, scholar, 112, 183–7
  poetry of, 184–6
Seisyllwg, Kingdom of, 111, 112, 114
Selgovae, 21
Septimius Severus, Emperor, 30
Sequana, Sanctuary of, 131, 289
  wooden sculpture at, 289
Severinus, Life of St, 169
Shrines, British Celtic, 133
Sickness, Irish law on maintenance in, 96–8
Síde (fairy-mounds), 137, 139
Sidonius Apollinaris, Bishop of Auvergne, 80, 156
Sigurðr the Stout, Norse leader, 95, 119, 122, 124
Sihtric, King of Dublin, 123, 124
Silchester, church at, 160
Silures, 21, 24
Slavery, Irish law on, 90
Snettisham treasure, 292
Social structure, Irish, 88–91
Sports, Irish, 103
Stave-buckets, Celtic, 292–3
Strabo, 7, 129, 130
  description of Gauls, 7–8
Strathclyde, Kingdom of, 73–4, 77
  dynasty, 47
Suetonius Paulinus, 25, 26, 132
Suibne (Swifneh), Irish scholar, 114, 127
Sulpicius Severus, 151, 154, 155, 157, 158, 159